Edward Bennett Williams for the Defense

Edward Bennett Williams for the Defense

Robert Pack

HARPER & ROW, PUBLISHERS, New York
Cambridge, Philadelphia, San Francisco,
London, Mexico City, São Paulo, Sydney

1817

FIRST EDITION

Designer: Charlotte Staub

Library of Congress Cataloging in Publication Data
Pack, Robert, 1942–
    Edward Bennett Williams for the defense.

    Bibliography: p.
    Includes index.
    1. Williams, Edward Bennett.   2. Lawyers—United
States—Biography.   I. Title.
KF373.W466P3   1983   345.73′0092′4 [B]   82–48129
ISBN 0–06–038035–7   347.30500924 [B]

---

83 84 85 86 87 10 9 8 7 6 5 4 3 2 1

Contents

Part Four: Crusaders' Alumni Association

Part Five: Jimmy Hoffa and the Teamsters

Part Six: The Superlawyer

A photo insert follows page 182.

Introduction

"If I ever committed a major crime and got caught, I'd want Edward Bennett Williams to defend me. If I had to pick the ten most interesting Americans, he'd be on my list, and I've never even met him." That is how Andy Rooney—commentator on "60 Minutes" and other CBS programs, syndicated columnist and best-selling author—describes the subject of this book.

Edward Bennett Williams. He is usually mentioned in the same breath with trial lawyers like F. Lee Bailey, Melvin Belli, and Louis Nizer, although, as will be seen, such comparisons seem unfair—to Williams.

Edward Bennett Williams. The three top stories in a New York tabloid on May 3, 1957, were: "MC CARTHY DEAD," "FRANK COSTELLO SHOT," and "DAVE BECK RECALLED BEFORE SENATE RACKETS COMMITTEE." Senator Joseph McCarthy, Mafia kingpin Frank Costello, and Teamster president Dave Beck were all clients of Williams, who was only thirty-six at the time. Such a hat trick, so far as is known, has never been matched. And those headlines didn't even include Jimmy Hoffa, arguably Williams's most famous client at that time.

It was in the 1950s that Williams began to be recognized as the nation's foremost trial lawyer. In 1959, *Life* magazine commented: "No trial lawyer in decades has burst so dramatically to prominence in the courtroom or set off such an astonished murmuring in the streets outside. . . . From coast to coast Williams is now considered the magic mouthpiece, the man who can get you out of bad trouble." Gay Talese, in a 1960 profile of Williams for the *New York Times* magazine, called him "the nation's hottest lawyer"; Eugene V. Rostow, then dean of Yale Law School, said in 1962 that Williams, "though still young, is already a legend in the line that includes Clarence Darrow"; and *Time* named Williams as "the country's top criminal lawyer" in 1967, adding, "In the courtroom he is in complete control. He has a computer memory for the remotest dates and details; his material is so well organized that documents flash into his hands like a magician's rabbits." And Federal Judge Richmond B. Keech, who presided over one of Williams's most important cases, said his conduct of the Aldo Icardi trial demonstrated the difference between "a brilliant lawyer and a brilliant working lawyer."

Edward Bennett Williams, however, is more than just a great lawyer. He is a heavyweight in both political and journalistic circles, whose pursuit of the Watergate scandal on behalf of the Democratic National Committee and the *Washington Post* placed him at the top of the White House enemies list and left President Nixon vowing to "fix the son of a bitch." A year or so later, when Nixon realized that only a miracle could keep him from losing his office, he approached Williams about taking his case—but Williams refused. Williams is also a prominent sports executive; he has owned stock in the Washington Redskins for twenty years and ran the club for most of that time until 1979, when he bought the Baltimore Orioles.

A strong argument can be made that someone who knew little or nothing about what has happened in America during the last thirty years could learn about the major developments of this era simply by studying the cases and causes that Williams has been associated with. In addition to McCarthy, Hoffa, Beck, and Costello, his clients have included Congressman Adam Clayton Powell, Jr.; Bernard Goldfine, whose gifts to President Eisenhower's top aide, Sherman Adams, resulted in Adams's ouster; LBJ protégé Bobby Baker; former Treasury secretary John Connally; and former CIA director Richard Helms. Williams won the only libel judgment ever awarded against columnist Drew Pearson, and, in another sensational case, he defended Aldo Icardi, who allegedly had murdered his commanding officer during a World War II espionage mission behind enemy lines in Italy.

He has also had dozens of other colorful clients, such as Frank Sinatra; Vito Genovese, Frank Costello's rival for Mafia leadership; Sam Giancana, a boss of the Mob in Chicago, and Gerardo Catena, who held a similar position in New Jersey; several people who were involved in some questionable ship deals with Aristotle Onassis; Joe DiMaggio; Hugh Hef-

ner; Burt Lancaster; Angie Dickinson; William F. Buckley, Jr.; Robert
Rossen and several other liberal Hollywood writers who had problems
during the McCarthy era; the Birdman of Alcatraz (Robert Stroud); Sug-
ar Ray Robinson; former senators Thomas Dodd and Daniel Brewster;
Confidential magazine; the *National Enquirer;* Igor Melekh, a Soviet
diplomat at the U.N. accused of espionage; financiers Louis Wolfson and
Robert Vesco; Hamilton Jordan, top aide to President Carter; Gerald
Ford; folk singer Peter Yarrow; cartoonist Al Capp; Dr. Armand Ham-
mer, head of Occidental Petroleum; Denver oilman Marvin Davis; and
New York Yankee owner George Steinbrenner.

Some of the people Williams has refused to represent have been equally
interesting. In addition to President Nixon, they have included Patty
Hearst, former Maryland governor Marvin Mandel, and antiwar activist
Dr. Benjamin Spock.

If anything, in view of Williams's multifaceted career, Andy Rooney's
description of him as one of the ten most interesting Americans seems
modest.

What follows is the story of Edward Bennett Williams's rise from an
impoverished childhood in Hartford during the Depression to the top in
the worlds of law, sports, politics, and the press. This book is the product
of two years' research. All of his important cases, congressional hearings
in which he has participated, and virtually everything that has been written by or about him have been studied. The research included numerous
sessions with Williams himself, as well as interviews with more than a
hundred others, including his friends and enemies, former clients, judges,
other lawyers, politicians, and associates from his involvement in football
and baseball. The goal all along has been to provide a complete and
objective biography of this complex, colorful, and fascinating individual.

Part
ONE

The Powerhouse

"I think we are going to fix the son of a bitch. Believe me. We are going to. We've got to, because he's a bad man." From the tapes of Richard Nixon.—This reference to Edward Bennett Williams is printed in large type and framed among the other trophies in Williams's office.

1

White House Enemy Number One

T he telephone awakened Joe Califano, Edward Bennett Williams's law partner, about 5:00 A.M. on Saturday, June 17, 1972. The news was urgent: A few hours earlier, five men had been arrested while copying files and bugging telephones inside the offices of the Democratic National Committee in the Watergate complex. Califano had been the DNC's attorney before he had joined Williams's law firm the previous year, and had brought the account with him. Upon hearing of the break-in, Califano instructed an aide at the DNC headquarters that a detailed list should be made of any evidence police confiscated. Next, Califano called a friend, Howard Simons, managing editor of the *Washington Post* (another client of the Williams firm), and told him the burglary might make a good story. Simons assigned a reporter to go to the Watergate. As reports poured in to Califano from various sources over the weekend, he became more and more convinced that there was "something fishy" about the intrusion. What especially aroused his suspicions was the police clamming up over even the most routine aspects of the case; he had to phone Washington Police Chief Jerry Wilson for any information.

On Monday, Califano discovered that one of the five men arrested at the Watergate, James W. McCord, Jr., was listed with the White House switchboard. By the next day, Califano had learned enough about the break-in to file a lawsuit on behalf of the DNC and its chairman, Lawrence F. O'Brien, against McCord and four Cuban refugees who had been captured along with McCord at the DNC. One of the Cubans was Bernard L. Barker, whom Edward Bennett Williams had once helped on a problem with his citizenship. Barker's lawyer during Watergate was Henry Rothblatt of New York, who, with Williams and F. Lee Bailey, had defended Colonel Robert B. Rheault, a Green Beret leader, and several of his troops, all of whom were accused of murdering a Vietnamese they suspected of being a double agent. McCord's lawyer in the Watergate case was Gerald Alch, from F. Lee Bailey's office.[1]

In the Watergate civil suit, which boiled down to Democrats against Republicans, Califano asked for a total of $1 million: $100,000 for compensatory damages, and $900,000 in punitive damages for the "willful and illegal violation" of the plaintiffs' "constitutional statutory and civil rights."[2] He charged that, among other sins, the defendants had "removed two ceiling panels from the rear of Plaintiff O'Brien's office for the purpose of installing a bugging device." McCord, chief of security for the Committee for the Re-election of the President and formerly a high-ranking official of the CIA,[3] and the four Cubans had "broke[n] into and entered the offices of Plaintiff Democratic National Committee for the purpose of copying Plaintiffs' files, installing telephonic and other bugging devices, obtaining confidential facts and information and otherwise disrupting the activities of Plaintiff Democratic National Committee and its member Democrat voters," according to Califano.[4] In just three days, Califano and his staff had put together an amazingly accurate account of the dirty tricks that had been employed.

Within a week, the suit was the subject of a hearing in front of U.S. District Judge Charles R. Richey. Kenneth Wells Parkinson, a lawyer for the Committee for the Re-election of the President, accused the lawyers for the plaintiffs of filing "this . . . highly-charged political case, the sole purpose of which is to destroy the Presidential chances of President Nixon." Edward Bennett Williams, in court on behalf of the DNC, objected that Parkinson was trying to "convert this into a political forum. . . . When counsel impugns the motivation of the suit, Your Honor, then I say he has transgressed the bounds of propriety and fair argument and decent advocacy." Richey overruled Williams's objection, and Parkinson went on to point out that the American Bar Association's canons of ethics made it improper for lawyers to discuss a pending case with reporters.[5] Parkinson added:

> And yet, may it please the court, I read in the newspapers that counsel for plaintiffs is reported having made certain statements from time to time to the press.
> I am concerned about that, and I also understand that there is some

relationship between Mr. Williams' firm and the Washington Post Newspaper Company.[6]

A decade later, Parkinson said he was especially displeased by one of Williams's tactics. He recalled that as the attorneys were leaving the courtroom, "Williams stated in a very loud voice, so that everyone could hear it, 'Until you made your argument, I thought your guys were innocent.'" Parkinson continued: "I was quite upset and outraged at what he had said for public consumption. It seemed to me he was motivated by the desire to get a catchy line in the press. It supported my belief that this case was nothing but a political maneuver." In fact, Williams's comment, along with a response from a defense attorney that "'[w]e don't have to take that [expletive deleted],'" was reported in a story that was played prominently in the next day's *Washington Post*.[7] The next time Parkinson was in court on the case, two months later, he complained to Judge Richey about what Williams had said.[8] There was nothing Richey could do by then, of course; the damage, if any, had already occurred.

Defense attorneys continued to maintain that the suit had been filed only to embarrass Nixon and help defeat him in November, and Williams just as steadfastly denied it. Recently, however, both Williams and Califano acknowledged that the case had not been filed without its news value in mind. Said Williams: "The purpose of the case was to win damages. But one of the most important side effects of it was that the activities of the [Nixon] Committee would have been exposed. If the country had known of all the facets of Watergate before the 1972 election, that certainly would have changed [the outcome]." Califano: "It was a very public lawsuit. It was designed as a very public act."

As the summer wore on, Califano was away from Washington much of the time. As a result, Williams participated extensively in the Democrats' civil case. Judge Richey ordered deposition-taking to proceed in August, but, to the chagrin of the plaintiffs and their lawyers, he directed that the testimony be kept secret.[9] Williams immediately used the depositions to interrogate a big fish: G. Gordon Liddy, one of the ringleaders. Liddy would later gloat that "Edward Bennett Williams took my deposition in the civil suit by the DNC but I gave him nothing,"[10] which was true. But Williams's questions showed that he was fully informed about the case; the Democrats had several investigators probing the break-in, led by Walter Sheridan, formerly Robert F. Kennedy's top sleuth. Liddy repeatedly invoked the Fifth Amendment and refused to answer Williams's inquiries on Watergate-related subjects. At last, however, Williams raised a question Liddy felt he could answer: "Was there a group over at the [Nixon] committee known as 'The Plumbers'?" After conferring with his lawyer, Liddy responded, "No. Not that I knew of, unless there were some plumbers in the basement working on the plumbing."[11]

Williams never gave any credence to Liddy's testimony, in particular his denying knowledge of the Plumbers. "He was perjuring himself," Williams says in reference to Liddy, who was convicted of conspiracy, burglary, and wiretapping, but not of lying under oath. (Williams no doubt would welcome a Liddy defamation suit against him even more than he would relish having other enemies, such as liberal attorney Joe Rauh, sue him.)

The next Watergate-connected visitor to Williams's office, on August 28, four days after Liddy, was Maurice Stans, who had served as secretary of commerce under Nixon and then as finance chairman of the president's reelection campaign. Stans answered all of Williams's questions, although once, after Williams asked him if campaign treasurer Hugh Sloan had "check[ed] with you" before destroying records of the campaign's finances, Stans replied, "I don't know the meaning of the word 'check.'"[12] Under examination by Williams, Stans testified that Liddy had once cashed a $25,000 donation in the form of a check from Minneapolis businessman Dwayne Andreas,* that the cash was part of $350,000 in currency that was kept in the office safe, and that he did not know the combination to the safe;[14] that he had "discharged" Liddy about ten days after McCord and the others were caught inside the Watergate, because Liddy "failed to cooperate with the FBI in its investigations,"[15] but that he had "not heard . . . until you [Williams] said it right now" that Liddy might have been at the Watergate on June 17;[16] that he did not know whether McCord reported to Liddy; and that he had never seen any reports "that were circulated by Mr. McCord concerning information that he had obtained which he believed would be interesting, informative or useful to . . .[Stans] or Mr. [John] Mitchell."[17]

The next day brought the arrival of one of the heavyweights in the developing case, E. Howard Hunt, in the company of his attorney, William O. Bittman, with whom Williams had clashed bitterly during the Bobby Baker case. As an official of the CIA from 1949 to 1970,[18] Hunt had been one of the main planners of the Bay of Pigs invasion in 1961, along with Bernard Barker. Since his retirement from the CIA in 1970, Hunt had worked in the private sector,[19] but had also been a White House consultant, operating out of the office of Charles Colson, special counsel to President Nixon.[20] Hunt was linked to the Watergate affair after his name and phone number, along with a notation that he worked at the White House, were found in Barker's address book following Barker's arrest.[21]

Before Williams could begin peppering him with questions, Hunt de-

---

*Two years later, Williams sucessfully defended Andreas against charges that he had illegally contributed $100,000 to the 1968 presidential campaign of Hubert Humphrey.[13]

clared in a prepared statement that because he faced possible criminal prosecution as a result of Watergate, "acting on the advice of counsel, I do not intend to respond to any questions which in any way relate to the alleged break-in at the Headquarters of the Democratic National Committee on June 17, 1972." Instead, Hunt said he would invoke the Fifth Amendment.[22] His lawyer, Bittman, still criticizes Williams for insisting that the deposition be taken even though he "was told before that Hunt would not testify." But Williams "wanted to go through with it anyway, for whatever reason. Either to make a record or to generate publicity."

The deposition proceeded, with Williams asking whether Hunt had slept at his home outside Washington on the nights of June 20, 21, and 22.[23] Williams explained that such questions were "highly relevant" because if Hunt "as a former CIA officer . . . went into hiding when the police and the FBI were seeking to interrogate him . . . I suggest to you quite strongly . . . that this may be an inference of guilty knowledge of a subject which is the predicate of this lawsuit."[24]

After nearly every one of William's questions, Hunt consulted with Bittman before replying, until Williams accused Bittman of "obstructing the examination with your frequent conferences."

"I take offense to that charge," retorted Bittman. "If you are going to make a charge on the record, then back it up or withdraw it, sir."

Williams claimed that nearly half the session had been "used in conferences that I think were really unnecessary."[25]

Bittman flared up again when Williams inquired if Hunt, while working for Colson, had investigated Senator Edward M. Kennedy and the Chappaquiddick incident. Bittman declared that "the interjecting of Senator Kennedy into this proceeding is outrageous," while Williams accused Bittman of trying "to impugn my motives . . . I do not enjoy your impugning my motives, and I do not want you to do it again in the course of these depositions or ever after." Bittman replied, "Mr. Williams, I will make whatever statements I believe are appropriate on this record, and I will not let you intimidate me."[26] Williams went on to raise questions about Hunt's methods of paying Bittman, who had received his fees largely in cash, to his later embarrassment. Hunt testified that he had paid Bittman out of his own pocket, that the money had not been advanced to him by the Nixon campaign, and that he did not know if he would be reimbursed.[27]

The circuslike atmosphere was maintained outside the hearing, as well. Hordes of reporters who had gathered to watch the Watergaters enter and leave Williams's office missed Hunt's arrival, leading Williams to speculate that the witness had gone inside several hours earlier and "'hidden in the men's room'" until he was called to testify. After the deposition was completed, reporters came across Hunt hiding on a partially vacant floor three levels below Williams's office, where he had been questioned. As soon as he was discovered, Hunt hopped aboard an elevator and left, his face covered with his hands, sunglasses, and a hat, in an attempt to frustrate photographers.[28]

The parade of witnesses to Williams's offices continued on August 30. Charles Colson showed up to complain that "every time I pick up a newspaper, I read where I am involved in the Watergate bugging case, which is not true, and it has been highly damaging to me personally."[29] He revealed what he thought of his interrogator after Williams inquired about the last time he had discussed Watergate with John Mitchell. Colson answered, "I probably last talked to him about it yesterday on the telephone when I told him I was going to be over here enjoying the pleasure of your company today."[30] Like the others, Colson could shed little light on the affair.

And finally, on September 1, 1972, it was Big Ed against the Big Enchilada. But not for long. John Mitchell, former attorney general and then Nixon campaign director until he resigned two weeks after Watergate, arrived at Williams's office with two lawyers. One of them, Kenneth Parkinson,* informed Williams that Mitchell would not answer questions pending a hearing before Judge Richey, "and I am instructing this witness to return to his office." Williams attempted to go on with his examination of Mitchell, but soon found himself engaging in a monologue. He stated for the record that "Mr. Mitchell and his lawyers . . . have just left the room where this deposition has been scheduled." Williams added: "I think that all counsel will agree that further interrogation of Mr. Mitchell would not be fruitful, and if that be the case, I will cease and desist asking questions of that vacant chair at the other end of this long table."

Henry Rothblatt, a defense attorney who was on cordial terms with Williams and had remained behind after Mitchell and his lawyers left, observed:

> Mr. Williams, I am impressed that you are a very great lawyer, but I would like to see you perform the miracle of getting answers out of a witness that is not present. That I would like to see you perform.
>
> Said Williams: I have a feeling, Mr. Rothblatt, that the deposition might be just as productive under these circumstances as some of the ones that we have already conducted. The deposition is terminated.[31]

At a hastily called hearing the next day, Saturday, September 2, Judge Richey ordered Mitchell to answer Williams's questions,[32] and Mitchell returned to Williams's office on September 5, the day after Labor Day. He was precisely as informative as Williams had expected. Was the job of finance chairman in the Nixon campaign "not an important position?"

---

* Mitchell would later hire Williams's sidekick, Bill Hundley, as his lawyer.

Mitchell: "You bet it was, an extremely important one." Well, then, surely Mitchell must have known who was finance chairman. Mitchell: "I have not the faintest idea. I am inclined to believe it was probably Mr. Stans . . . but I don't know that for a fact."[33] Had Mitchell known about the $350,000 in cash that was kept in the office safe? The former campaign chief: "No, sir."[34] How about surveillance of the DNC? Had Mitchell heard anything about that? Mitchell: "No, sir. I can't imagine a less productive activity than that."[35] And so forth.

Mitchell was the last of the major Watergate figures questioned by Williams. On September 21, Judge Richey ruled that the case could not possibly be resolved before the election, which was only six weeks away, and postponed any further action, including deposition-taking, until after Election Day.[36] By then, Williams had substantially phased out of the suit.

Williams professes to have been very upset by Richey's decision to call a halt to the proceedings. "I was within an eyelash of blowing Watergate open," he declares. "I would have gotten the whole story before I was through." Williams firmly believes that Richey's sympathies lay with the White House, perhaps because the judge hoped to curry favor there in order to advance himself on the bench. He regards Richey's decision to call a halt to the proceedings as outrageous. Richey, of course, insists that he was completely independent of Nixon and his aides.

Williams was not impressed by the quality of the testimony he did get to hear. "We were trapping one after another of the Nixon people in lies. They were all lying. I had a source of information* at the time that had them absolutely flabbergasted, because they didn't know where I was getting my information and they all suspected each other. So I was getting a lot more of the truth than I would have otherwise, for fear of perjury. That's why I think they were instrumental in bringing down the depositions and getting them sealed and stopped." He adds that "the smell of mendacity surrounding the depositions was beyond tolerance." The "mendacity" quote is one of his pet phrases. Williams has used it time and again in interviews about Watergate,[39] and he employed it at least once in court when he told the jury in the 1963 trial of former congressman Frank Boykin (see pp. 69, 369–370) that the prosecution had "'introduced an odor of mendacity into this hallowed place.'"[40]

---

*The source was Alfred C. Baldwin III, a former FBI agent who had been located by the Democrats' investigators. Baldwin, who worked for the Nixon reelection campaign, was watching the Watergate office building from the Howard Johnson hotel across the street the night of the ill-fated break-in. Although equipped with a walkie-talkie, he was unable to warn the burglars that the police were closing in, until too late.[37] Bob Woodward of the *Washington Post* regarded Baldwin as "the government's chief witness—the insider who was spilling the whole story. He seemed to have unimaginable secrets to tell."[38] Sam Ervin still refers to Baldwin as "the first person who had inside information who was willing to disclose it. Up to the time Baldwin talked, why, all of the people that had any knowledge of Watergate were silent in every language known to man."

According to Joe Califano, Williams "was never overwhelmed with the idea of representing the DNC. It took a tremendous amount of time," all of it *pro bono*. Califano estimates that he spent 100 percent of his time on DNC business from May until July 1972, as he was handling not only Watergate but many other suits for Democrats all over the country. He figures tha, altogether, he gave 40 percent of his work hours in 1972 to the DNC, and that, in sum, the firm of Williams, Connolly & Califano contributed $500,000 to the Democratic party in the form of time spent—a situation that Williams did not appreciate. Throughout the summer of 1972, Williams had been "bitching" about having to take the Watergate depositions in place of Califano. But after his interrogation of Mitchell, Williams turned enthusiastic, crowing to Califano, "'We've got something here. I don't know that much about politics, but I can tell when someone is lying.'"

The depositions were over, but Williams had succeeded in rattling the cage at a very exclusive address: 1600 Pennsylvania Avenue, NW. Ten days after Williams had questioned Mitchell, on September 15, 1972, President Nixon held a late-afternoon meeting with his chief of staff, H. R. Haldeman, and White House counsel John Dean, both of whom would later go to prison for their parts in the Watergate affair. Early on in the conversation, a mysterious "little red box" that might have been given to Williams was discussed:

> *Nixon:* What is the situation on your, uh, on the, on the little red box? Did they find what the hell that, that is? Have they found the box yet?
>
> *Dean:* [FBI Director L. Patrick] Gray has never had access to the box. He is now going to pursue the box. . . .
>
> *Haldeman:* The last public story was that she handed over to Edward Bennett Williams. . . .
>
> *Nixon:* Perhaps the Bureau ought to go over—
>
> *Haldeman:* The Bureau ought to go into Edward Bennett Williams and let's start questioning that son-of-a-bitch. Keep him tied up for a couple of weeks.
>
> *Nixon:* Yeah, I hope they do. They— The Bureau better get over pretty quick and get that red box. We want it cleared up.[41]

The session was interrupted for several minutes while the president accepted a phone call and said to his caller, "Did you put that last bug in? . . . And don't, don't bug anybody without asking me. Okay?"[42] Nixon then returned to his earlier thoughts and told Haldeman and Dean that the people who worked for him in the White House and in his reelection campaign should

> recognize this, this is, again this is war. . . . Don't worry. I wouldn't want to be on the other side right now. Would you? I wouldn't want to

be in Edward Bennett Williams', Williams' position after this election.

Dean: No. No.

Nixon: None of these bastards—

Dean: He, uh, he's done some rather unethical things that have come to light already, which in—again, Richey has brought to our attention.

Nixon: Yeah.

Dean: He went down—

Haldeman: Keep a log on all that.

Dean: Oh, we are, indeed. Yeah.

Nixon: Yeah.

Haldeman: Because afterwards that's the guy.

Nixon: We're going after him.

Haldeman: That's the guy we've got to ruin.

Dean: He had, he had an ex parte—

Nixon: You want to remember, too, he's an attorney for the *Washington Post*.

Dean: I'm well aware of that.

Nixon: I think we are going to fix the son-of-a-bitch. Believe me. We are going to. We've got to, because he's a bad man.

Dean: Absolutely.

Nixon: He misbehaved very badly in the Hoffa matter. Our—some pretty bad conduct, there, too, but go ahead.

Dean: Well, that's, uh, along that line, uh, one of the things I've tried to do, is just keep notes on a lot of the people who are emerging as,

Nixon: That's right.

Dean: as less than our friends.

Nixon: Great.

Dean: Because this is going to be over some day and they're—We shouldn't forget the way that some of them (unintelligible)—

Nixon: I want the most, I want the most comprehensive notes on all of those that have tried to do us in. . . . They are asking for it and they are going to get it. And this, this— We, we have not used the power in this first four years, as you know.

Dean: That's true.

Nixon: We have never used it. We haven't used the Bureau and we haven't used the Justice Department, but things are going to change now. . . .

Dean: That's an exciting prospect.

Nixon: It's got to be done. It's the only thing to do.

Haldeman: We've got to.[43]

Aside from Williams, the only other enemies singled out for special treatment were Speaker of the House Carl Albert, who was not mentioned with the same venom or at the same length as Williams,[44] and the *Washington Post,* which, Nixon forecast, was "going to have damnable, damnable problems" when the time came for the Post Company to renew the licenses for its television and radio stations.[45]*

The Watergate impresarios had made three specific charges against Williams: One, regarding the red box, is obscure; one, about his improper *ex parte* meeting with Judge Richey, is misleading; and the third, having to do with Williams's alleged misbehavior, is apparently incorrect. As to the red box, Williams has a vague memory that "someone came to me during the Watergate inquiry and had a red box which she believed to be an eavesdropping device that had been found in an office in a federal building. I think we found no validity to it. The story didn't hang together."

It is true that Williams, without any attorneys for the defendants present, met with Judge Richey over the DNC civil suit that was filed after the break-in. But the occasion was not nearly as sinister as Nixon and his aides wanted to believe. What had happened was that on August 31 defense lawyers had asked that McCord and the four Cubans who had been arrested at the Watergate be dismissed as defendants in the Democrats' suit. The plaintiffs would still have had the right to name other defendants. The plaintiffs' attorneys, led by Williams (Califano was still unavailable), had until September 8 to file a response to the defense motion. The plaintiffs asked for and were given until September 11 to answer, but they missed the September 11 deadline, and on September 12 Henry Rothblatt moved to have McCord and the other four dropped permanently because of the plaintiffs' failure to respond in time.[46] Although Williams and the other lawyers for the plaintiffs had committed nothing but a procedural blunder, it had a crucial effect: to release as civil defendants the five men who had been caught inside the DNC offices. The story was carried by major newspapers on the morning of September 13; and at lunchtime that day, Williams, along with Harold Ungar from his office, rushed to the courthouse to ask Richey to overlook his procedural mistake. Declaring that he had been occupied by another case, Williams told Richey:

> Because of the pillorying we took this morning for an oversight, I
> thought that I should come down here in the interests of our own pro-

---

*When Nixon first made public the September 15, 1972, transcript on April 30, 1974, the threats against Williams and the *Post* were omitted, according to a front-page story in the *Post* by Carl Bernstein and Bob Woodward on May 16, 1974. Bernstein and Woodward then obtained the complete transcript, which was compiled by the staff of the House Judiciary Committee.

fessional reputations and seek to resuscitate them, insofar as they can
be, because we have had nationwide damage this morning on the
ground that we made some mistake. It has, of course, embarrassed us
terribly professionally.[47]

Although no defense attorneys were present, making the hearing technically an *ex parte* one, Richey allowed Williams to give his argument for
fifteen minutes, without saying that Williams's tactic was improper, and a
court reporter transcribed the court session, providing a record for defense lawyers to study.[48] But then, according to Dean's statement to Nixon only two days later, Richey turned around and "brought to our attention . . . some rather unethical things" that Williams had done, such as
"an ex parte" meeting with the judge.[49]

Still, Richey had not cut Williams off at the time, and he asserts that
he felt all along that "there wasn't anything unethical on the part of Ed
Williams. Never. If there had been, I would have done something about
it." As for the statements on the September 15 tape, Richey declared, "I
don't know where John Dean got a lot of the things he said. Someday I
might endeavor to find out, but I'm too busy at this stage of my life,
trying to accomplish justice for millions of American people."

While the Williams-Richey maneuvers were taking place in September
1972, Larry O'Brien claimed he had "'unimpeachable evidence'" that his
phone at DNC headquarters had been tapped for several weeks before
June 17 and that he was the "'clear victim'" of a " 'Republican-sponsored
invasion.' "[50] Williams filed an amended complaint in the suit of O'Brien
and the DNC, increasing the amount of damages sought to $3.2 million,
and adding Stans, Hugh Sloan, Liddy, Hunt, and the Committee for the
Re-election of the President as defendants.[51] The Republicans responded
by filing a $2.5-million suit that accused the Democrats of abusing the
court process,[52] and Stans brought a $5-million libel suit against O'Brien
over the statements O'Brien had made about him.[53] John Dean said
during the September 15 meeting with Nixon and Haldeman that Richey
had suggested that "Maury [Stans] ought to file a libel action"[54]—which
Richey vehemently dismisses as "sheer poppycock" and as "absolutely
false."

When Nixon declared that Williams had "misbehaved very badly in the
Hoffa matter,"[55] he might have been expressing his opinion about Williams's conduct of the Hoffa bribery trial in 1957, but more than likely he
was referring to efforts by Hoffa, his supporters, and lawyers to persuade
Nixon to release Hoffa from prison (which Nixon finally did). If Nixon
was talking about the campaign to free Jimmy Hoffa, he was apparently
in error, for both Williams and Rufus King, Jr., the attorney who was in
charge of the move to win Hoffa's release, state categorically that Williams was not involved in any way.

As further evidence of the hatred for both Williams and the *Washington Post* that was felt by Nixon and his inner circle, John Mitchell told Carl Bernstein on the phone on the night of September 29, 1972, "'You fellows got a great ballgame going. As soon as you're through paying Ed Williams and the rest of those fellows, we're going to do a story on all of *you.*'" (During the same conversation, Mitchell also threatened that *Post* publisher "'Katie Graham's gonna get her tit caught in a big fat wringer'" if the *Post* printed a story saying that while Mitchell was attorney general he "personally controlled a secret Republican fund that was used to gather information about the Democrats." The *Post* did publish the article.)[56]

Dozens of people were placed on White House enemy lists, but Edward Bennett Williams and his client, the *Washington Post,* were the main foes specifically singled out by Nixon in talks with his aides. Williams, the onetime poor boy from Hartford, had come a long way. The experience was both flattering and frightening. "When it was disclosed that Nixon had targeted me that heavily, it was a badge of honor," Williams comments. "My kids were quite pleased about it." On the other hand, "It was not a very comfortable feeling to have the president of the United States obsessed with the idea of wreaking some kind of revenge against me." Laughing and snorting, Williams added, "To have all the forces of the United States government marshaled against you, as the president can do, puts you in a very unenviable position."

Even before Watergate, Williams had suffered what he thinks was a White House crusade against him. In 1971, he bought an office building at 1910 "K" Street NW, in downtown Washington. The U.S. Renegotiation Board, which had occupied the structure for about two decades, "immediately vacated the building. They left me with an empty, an absolutely empty, building and a big mortgage, which was very, very difficult for me." Williams then leased the building to the presidential campaign of his friend Edmund Muskie. When the "dirty tricks" of Nixon's men drove Muskie, the rival Nixon feared most, out of the race, the George McGovern campaign moved into Williams's building. Williams later discovered that James McCord rented space in the building next door, "under a facade to a third party," and "McCord and his gang went in there" and bugged the headquarters of first Muskie, then McGovern. Williams attributes the goings-on in and around his building to "that campaign Nixon was running against me" and other Democrats.

Now, with Williams having emerged after Watergate as lawyer for both the *Post* and the DNC, a full-fledged war was waged as part of Nixon's attempt to "fix the son-of-a-bitch." As one example, Nixon spoke to Charles Colson about trying to have Williams removed as the chief executive of the Washington Redskins. Watergate Special Prosecutor Leon Jaworski said that this was discussed on tapes that have never been made public. According to Jaworski, "What Nixon would do is, he would call Colson late at night. This was a practice of his. There was a period of time, about January of 1973, when he called Colson almost every evening. As a matter of fact, Colson told me one time that the calls came in so often that he knew the president would most likely call him at night and he would not even take a drink until after he had talked to Nixon. Sometimes they would talk several times during the night." Jaworski believes that "Nixon was by himself in the Executive Office Building and he would have some drinks, because it sounded very much to me like he had been drinking when these conversations went on. Not only did it sound a little different than the way he usually sounded, but it seemed to me he became a little more intense in what he was pursuing."

Jaworski informed Williams that Nixon had talked to Colson about ousting him as head of the Redskins, but as far as Jaworski and Williams knew, no tangible steps ever were taken. Nixon was not only an ardent Redskin fan, he was also a close friend of Redskin general manager and head coach George Allen. And Allen had long been close to Jack Kent Cooke, the principal stockholder in the Redskins. Williams says, however, that in 1972 and 1973, with the disposition of the estate of Redskin founder George Preston Marshall still unsettled (see chapter 4), Cooke was not yet in a position to ease Williams out of day-to-day control of the club.

In addition, Williams says that in the aftermath of Watergate, "I got probably the most intensive tax audit of anybody in America. They called them random audits. But they only single out a few people in the whole nation for the kind of audit they gave me. They came in, they examined every check of every business with which I have an association. They took months to do it. They even went to find out if my wife had deducted for withholding tax on our domestic help. She's probably one of the only women in America who does, because they won't work for you if you do. But she just did it because she happens to do everything that way." Williams adds that he had such an audit for three consecutive years. His belief that the audits were part of a vendetta against him was, he says, confirmed by Sheldon Cohen, onetime head of the IRS, who reported to Williams that the agency had been "out to zing me."

Furthermore, Williams's zeal in pursuing the Watergate case caused him to be removed as general counsel of the Teamsters Union. Teamster president Frank Fitzsimmons called Williams and warned that "if I didn't drop the [Watergate] case, they were going to take the account out of here. I told them to go to hell and take the goddamned account." Fitzsimmons transferred the union's legal business to a Washington law firm that Charles Colson had joined in March 1973 after he resigned from the White House staff.

Also, according to Leon Jaworski, Nixon aides instigated challenges to the Washington Post Company's broadcast licenses as a means of both punishing the *Post* and embarrassing Williams. Jaworski said that Nixon "thought, perhaps, that if the TV licenses were taken away it would reflect on Williams as their lawyer and he might lose the legal representation. In other words, he would do something to the *Post* and it would take care of Williams too."

Finally, while Williams was out watching his Redskins defeat the St. Louis Cardinals on October 21, 1973, his home in Potomac, Maryland, was burglarized. Williams initially thought the theft was related to Watergate, but he has his doubts now. The intruders not only stole jewelry and watches, however; they also rummaged through files in his briefcase that pertained to Watergate.

The pattern of proposed or implemented actions against Williams reached such proportions that Leon Jaworski became "very much disturbed over what Nixon might undertake to do to Edward Bennett Williams." Short of actual violence, Jaworski feared that "the more desperate Nixon got, the less I knew what the man might try to do and how he might try to involve innocent people." Jaworski conveyed his concerns to Williams early in 1974, after which both men kept a wary eye on the White House until Nixon's forced resignation that August.

Nixon and his accomplices were not alone in believing that Williams's role was crucial in unraveling Watergate. One expert on the subject, author Jim Hougan, even went so far as to speculate that Williams was Bob Woodward's mysterious "Deep Throat." Although Hougan no longer thinks Williams was Deep Throat, he wrote in 1978, "More than anyone else ... Ed Williams seems to have been in a position of near-omniscience so far as Watergate is concerned; as a candidate for 'Deep Throat' the Washington attorney has no rivals."[57] Another writer, Tom Dowling, also mentioned that Williams had once been "suspect number one in the ... Deep Throat sweepstakes."[58]

Asked directly if he was Deep Throat, Williams provides a rambling response without an explicit denial. He obviously gets a kick out of the notion. "I don't know if I was Deep Throat," he says. "I don't think I was Deep Throat. I mean, I don't know what they called me, Woodward and Bernstein. I don't know," he laughs. "I never gave them any confidential information. I gave them only information that I had which was permissible to give." He adds with a chuckle, "Oh, I'm sure I gave them information they didn't have previously, I'm sure I did that." Overall, he says, "It was a mutually beneficial relationship."

According to Ben Bradlee, Williams "far in a fucking way" got more from the *Post* than he gave in return. "Because I didn't get anything out of him. I thought, 'Holy God, we'll get everything. Ed is finally going to pay off.' And I couldn't get the time of day from him. He'd give me the shirt off his back, but he wouldn't give me that. We used to joke about it. When I thought my phone was being tapped, I used to say to him, 'Thanks for the grand jury minutes and all.' But it was just a joke."

When all is said and done, it seems extremely unlikely that Williams was Deep Throat, at least not as Throat was presented by Woodward and Bernstein. First of all, the idea of Williams meeting with Woodward late at night in parking garages is simply incredible. Why would Williams have stuck his neck out and inconvenienced himself to boot in order to help a reporter he hardly knew? Had he wanted to help the *Post,* he would have talked in confidence to Bradlee, with the sure knowledge that Bradlee would have gone to jail before he would have betrayed his source.

But suppose that much of the published version of Deep Throat is a red herring, as many followers of Watergate believe. Many in the know are convinced that Throat was a composite of several sources. One who will speak for the record, Leon Jaworski, had this to say: "I think Bob Woodward overplayed the importance of Deep Throat considerably. I think that some of the Deep Throat thing is a little bit of a fable. I think the man who acted as Deep Throat did not have near as much information [as Woodward has indicated]. He had a bunch of suspicions, but he didn't have much information." Jaworski added, "You could hardly mention anyone to me that would shock me more than to find that Williams was Deep Throat." He thought that if there was a Deep Throat, it was someone with "perhaps not too remote a White House connection."

Perhaps the best evidence that Williams was not Deep Throat was that the key source he had helped uncover, Alfred Baldwin, gave an exclusive interview about his involvement in Watergate to the *Los Angeles Times*— a colossal scoop.[59] Had Williams been Woodward's confidant, he hardly would have guided a story of that magnitude to another newspaper. In sum, Williams certainly was helpful to the *Post* in its coverage of Watergate, but if Deep Throat was a single person, Edward Bennett Williams was not the one.

Williams did come to the aid of Woodward, as well as Carl Bernstein, when the pair ran afoul of Judge "Maximum John" Sirica. In late 1972, Woodward and Bernstein contacted several members of the federal grand jury that was hearing evidence on Watergate—a questionable tactic. When the acts of the two reporters were revealed to Sirica, he hit the ceiling. Williams went to see him and tried to calm him down, which he was able to do by promising that Woodward and Bernstein would cease approaching the jurors.

"I really remonstrated with them over that," says Williams. "I told Bradlee they had to stop that. And I went down and apologized to Sirica for them and just pleaded their ignorance of their responsibilities and promised it wouldn't happen again. I know he would have punished them severely if there hadn't been an explanation and a commitment and an apology."

Sirica says that if the *Post* duo had actually obtained any leads from the jurors, he would have sent them to jail. As it was, on December 19, 1972, Sirica sternly told reporters who had gathered in his courtroom that "'a news media representative'" had improperly approached members of the grand jury, which he regarded as "'extremely serious.'" Without taking action against Woodward and Bernstein, or even mentioning them by name, Sirica warned the press that seeking out grand jurors would "'at least potentially'" place them in contempt of court.[60]

G. Gordon Liddy, for one, took a dim view. He stated that Sirica had "knuckled under to the *Post*'s powerful lawyer, Edward Bennett Williams." Noting that Sirica later said in his own book that he had given Woodward and Bernstein "a stiff lecture in open court,"[61] Liddy exclaimed, "Baloney. He never even identified Woodward and Bernstein. In the course of that 'stiff lecture in open court' he *never even mentioned their names.*"[62]

Williams acknowledges having had some misgivings about the two reporters calling the grand jurors. But he went to bat for them anyway, and his intercession with Judge Sirica helped keep them out of jail. Eugene McCarthy says that once while he was discussing Watergate with Williams "I sort of made a case against the *Post,* that they had done practically everything in the pursuit of the Watergate people that the Watergate people had done themselves. It was just a slightly different order. One broke and entered, the other got in under false pretenses."* According to McCarthy, Williams "sort of nodded." Even Ben Bradlee says, "If the truth will out, I think Ed thought that the *Post* was awful far out on a limb there for a while. Joe [Califano], I think, thought our case was better."

Williams was also unhappy with a passage in *All the President's Men.* Describing the decision to contact grand jurors, Woodward and Bernstein wrote: "Everyone in the room had private doubts about such a seedy venture. Bradlee, desperate for a story, and reassured by the lawyers, overcame his own."[64] After he saw the galleys of the book, Williams reportedly felt the alleged "reassurance" by attorneys to contact the jurors made him look "sleazy," and he insisted that Califano seek to have that part excised. Califano tried to persuade Richard Snyder of Simon & Schuster, the book's publisher, to take that portion out, telling him the book suggested that Bradlee had committed a crime and that Bradlee,

---

*Shortly after Sirica's lecture to the press against seeking out grand jurors, a potential witness in the case mistakenly understood Woodward to have identified himself as an FBI agent when he tried to question her. Williams again had to argue on behalf of Woodward and Bernstein to Sirica, who placed additional restrictions on the two eager reporters.[63]

Woodward, and Bernstein might all go to jail. Sensing that having his two authors and their boss imprisoned would be "magnificent publicity," Snyder instead ordered the book printed as quickly as possible. Not a word was changed, no one went to jail, and the only harm was that Williams was said to be "infuriated."[65]

By early 1973, Williams was for all intents and purposes out of the main part of the Watergate case. One year later, he turned up as the author of a *New York Times* Op-Ed piece defending the role of Nixon's attorney, James D. St. Clair. "As a lawyer, I have been at once saddened and dismayed to read and hear the criticisms that are being heaped upon James D. St. Clair for his defense of President Nixon," Williams wrote. "The President faces the strong possibility of being an 'accused,' in the formal sense of the term. . . . As such [he is] entitled to all the rights and safeguards forged for accused defendants through almost two centuries of constitutional history."[66]

Had Williams wanted to, he could have been defending Nixon himself, instead of defending Nixon's lawyer. He was contacted at least twice by Nixon sympathizer Rabbi Baruch Korff, and asked to be Nixon's attorney. Williams turned down the case, saying he had a conflict of interest as a lawyer for the opposite side. But if Williams had become Nixon's attorney, "I would have had him publicly destroy the tapes, instantly. They were not under subpoena initially. They would not have been destroying evidence being called for in any tribunal. I think that he could have said with some justification that he could not run the risk of having conversations he'd had with heads of state and with diplomats, ambassadors from other nations and his own aides be compromised." When he is reminded that neither the Senate Watergate Committee, the Special Prosecutor's Office, Judge Sirica, or anyone else wanted the recordings of Nixon's talks with foreign heads of state, Williams replies, "There was no time to sort those out." His answer begs the issue; the tapes that dealt with foreign policy could have been winnowed out and the ones that reflected on the president's guilt or innocence turned over to proper investigators, as they should have been.

Williams believes that Nixon's lawyers "should have told him to destroy the tapes. He was badly represented." Had Nixon destroyed the tapes, "he would have finished out his term," as Williams sees it. For that matter, Nixon might still be working in the Oval Office, as chief executive of the Second Constitutional Republic. In 1975, Williams made the same assertion, that Nixon should have burned the tapes "'on the White House lawn,'" during a PBS television interview with George Will on a program called "Edward Bennett Williams: Super-Lawyer." His after-the-fact advice to Nixon drew the wrath of *New York Post* columnist James A. Wechsler, who wrote:

Williams would have been the architect of the ultimate coverup in the worst political scandal in the country's history. . . . It apparently has not yet occurred to Williams that once he had heard the tapes documenting the Nixon cabal's conspiring to undermine free institutions and obstruct justice, a sense of national conscience might have impelled him to withdraw from the case. Nor is he seemingly distressed by any thought that his proposal for destructing the evidence would have made him an accomplice in the protection and perpetuation of a regime that he knew could not survive the light of disclosure. . . . The real question raised by Williams' strategic design for Nixon's salvation is whether there is no point at which an attorney's duty to an eminent client is transcended by any other consideration.[67]

Not only does Williams think the tapes should have been destroyed, he is also of the opinion that Gerald Ford was correct in pardoning Nixon. "I think we had had enough national damage resulting from Watergate," he says. "And I think the punishment inflicted upon him in history was great enough, to be removed as president of the United States, because he *was* removed as president."

And yet Nixon is the same man of whom Williams spoke with such venom during a "several martini" lunch in 1972 with George Stevens, head of the American Film Institute, that Stevens thought Williams's comments bordered on paranoia;[68] the same man of whom he had said, after White House speechwriter Patrick Buchanan asked him tauntingly in 1973, "'How about some of those crooks you defended?'" that the "'big difference'" between Nixon and his own clients was that "'I didn't run any of my clients for President'";[69] the same man of whom Williams still says that Watergate didn't change his opinion any, because it couldn't have gotten any worse.

As the Nixon presidency headed toward its ignoble end, Williams took on New York Yankee owner George Steinbrenner as a client. Steinbrenner was indicted in April of 1974 on fourteen felony counts that resulted from his allegedly diverting funds from the American Ship Building Company, of which he was chairman, into illegal contributions to several political campaigns, including Nixon's in 1972.[70] Williams worked out a plea bargain for Steinbrenner, who pleaded guilty to two counts and was fined $15,000, but not imprisoned.[71] According to Leon Jaworski, Williams "did his usual masterly job, and the sentence imposed was less than we had expected." Williams also pleaded Steinbrenner's case in front of baseball commissioner Bowie Kuhn, but Steinbrenner was still suspended from operating the Yankees for two years.[72] (Steinbrenner's guilty plea also gave rise to Billy Martin's classic comment in his three-sided feud with Reggie Jackson and Steinbrenner: "'The two of them deserve each other. One's a born liar, the other's convicted.'"[73]

Another Watergate-related client of Williams's was Dr. Armand Hammer, the immensely wealthy chairman of Occidental Petroleum. Like Steinbrenner, he had been accused of giving money illegally to the 1972 Nixon campaign. Louis Nizer, who had been Hammer's lawyer for many years, initially handled the case. Then, according to Nizer, "Dr. Hammer and I decided we would have to have Washington counsel, and who's better than Ed Williams?" (Henry Ruth, who supervised the case for the Watergate Special Prosecutor's Office, recalls conferring with Williams, Nizer and a third attorney for Hammer. Ruth refers to that session as "the world's most expensive meeting" of lawyers.) Hammer insisted that he was innocent and wanted to go to trial, but Nizer and Williams convinced him that because of his age, seventy-seven, and serious heart problem, the strain of a trial might jeopardize his life. The lawyers arranged for Hammer to plead guilty to three misdemeanors, in return for which the prosecution would not seek a prison sentence.

When Hammer appeared before Chief Judge William B. Jones of the U.S. District Court in Washington to enter his plea in late 1975, Jones started explaining to Hammer that he could send him to prison if he chose. Hammer became so upset that Jones called a recess so Hammer could talk with Williams and Nizer. Williams forcefully told Hammer that he would have to plead guilty without reservations, and, says Nizer, declared, "'This is my advice, if you want my advice, take it. If not, I ought to quit the case.'" According to Williams, Hammer insisted (without objections from Nizer) on writing a letter to Jones, the thrust of which "was that 'I didn't do anything.' When a judge gets a letter like that he can't accept the plea. I explained that to them. I knew the judge, Bill Jones, would vacate the plea. And all the work that had been done to get this very favorable disposition for Hammer would go up in smoke. It dismayed me that it could happen."

The discussion among Williams, Nizer, and Hammer was held in a conference room, and Nizer later wrote, "The argument grew so strident that a court attendant bade us to lower our voices, because they could be heard in the adjoining courtroom."[74] At last, Hammer agreed to return to court and plead guilty, and to act properly contrite to appease the judge. Jones accepted the plea and deferred sentencing pending completion of a probation report. While the report was being prepared, however, Hammer wrote a letter to the probation officer in which he said he was not really guilty. Jones revoked the plea bargain, and Williams made good his threat to withdraw from the case. The suit was then transferred to federal court in Los Angeles (Hammer's home), because of concern about his health, and he again pleaded guilty and was let off with a $3,000 fine.[75]

Williams returned to court one last time in connection with Watergate. On November 8, 1977, he argued in front of the Supreme Court on behalf of Warner Communications, which, along with the three television-radio networks and other broadcasters, had sued for the right to air twenty-two hours of Watergate tapes that had been used in court during trials. Williams told the High Court that Nixon did not have "a right not to be embarrassed by the sound of his own inculpatory words solely because he was President."[76] The court, in a 7–2 decision, held in favor of Nixon and prohibited the broadcasters from playing the tapes.[77]

I feel that if I get my ass in a sling, of whatever nature, I'd talk to [Edward Bennett Williams].

—Ben Bradlee

If I or my family needed legal help I would turn to Ed Williams. If anything happened to me, I would want my wife to go to Ed.

—Washington powerbroker and former secretary of defense Clark Clifford

2

The Insider's Insider

Starting in the late 1940s as an obscure young lawyer, Edward Bennett Williams emerged over the next three decades as a member of the most powerful and exclusive circles—politically, socially, and professionally. Deeply interested in politics since boyhood, he was, in his words, "surrounded by Republicans" at Hogan & Hartson, the Washington law firm he joined after graduation from law school in 1944. Williams gravitated to the GOP, and, like his father-in-law, Duke Guider, a partner in the Hogan firm, was a staunch supporter of Harold Stassen. Early law associates of Williams recall that a picture of Stassen hung in his office.

In 1948, Williams attended the GOP convention in Philadelphia as the guest of Senator Milton R. Young of North Dakota. In one of his first cases several years earlier, Williams had defended Young after a Washington cabdriver accused the senator of knocking him down during a dispute over a fare. "'I got a young lawyer who was just starting out in Washington,'" Young would say later. "'His name was Edward Bennett Williams.'" As it turned out, Williams had little to do in the case, because the hacker, John B. Edelkamp, Jr., dropped the suit soon after he filed it. Many years later, Edelkamp, by then an inmate in a California prison, wrote and apologized to Young, saying an overaggressive lawyer had talked him into suing. Edelkamp told Young:

> After reading the papers in the morning, I was beset by inordinate shame and embarrassment . . . [and] turned in my taxicab and left the city. . . . The essential purpose of this letter is to sincerely offer an apology (however late) from an old, tired failure who is trying to amend his past.[1]

From the start, Williams identified himself as a member of "the liberal, quote liberal, unquote, branch of the Republican Party," as opposed to the conservative wing that was dominated by his friend and client Senator Joseph McCarthy. Today Williams summarizes his position versus that of the right-wingers this way: "I felt that human rights were more important than property rights."

Williams supported the Eisenhower-Nixon ticket in both 1952 and 1956. He had nothing to do with Stassen's attempt to have Nixon dumped and himself substituted as Ike's running mate in 1956. In 1960, although Williams was backing Nixon for president, he was one of about 150 Catholic lay leaders (others included Eugene McCarthy and Clare Boothe Luce) who signed a petition urging that John F. Kennedy's Catholicism not be an issue in the campaign.[2] He did not have much influence in the Kennedy White House, however, because of his old feud with Kennedy and his brother Robert over Williams's advocacy of Jimmy Hoffa.

The treatment handed Williams's favorite, Nelson Rockefeller, at the 1964 Republican convention in San Francisco led to his switching parties. "They booed Nelson Rockefeller, for whom I had great admiration," says Williams. "They treated him shamefully. It seemed to me, at least, that Birchers were taking over the party. I had believed that there was room for liberals inside the Republican party. I thought there was room for liberals in both parties and that it was a good thing for the two-party system. At that time there were many liberals inside the Republican party. There were people like John Lindsay. There were people like Tom Kuchel [senator from California]. There were people like Earl Warren. And there were people like Ed Williams. I came to believe in 1964 that we were not welcome inside the Republican party. I tried to persuade John Lindsay and Mac Mathias [later a senator from Maryland] that we weren't welcome and had better exit. John Lindsay ultimately came to that conclusion. And I think sometimes Mac Mathias has wavered, but he has stayed." Even Williams's close friendship with Barry Goldwater, the GOP candidate in 1964, couldn't make the delegates' behavior toward Rockefeller acceptable to him. Besides, he and the ultraconservative Goldwater "just didn't agree on a lot of things." By November 1964, Williams was a member of a lawyers' committee for Lyndon Johnson and a donor to his campaign.

Williams visited Johnson in the White House about once a month during the five years LBJ was president. Meanwhile, Clark Clifford, the prototype Washington powerbroker and a friend of both Johnson and Williams, was talking up Williams to the president. "That's the type of fellow that I would like to see come into government," said Clifford of Williams. "Oftentimes, we don't get the best men into government. Ed Williams was one of the best. And I was boosting him from time to time."

One evening in the summer of 1967, Williams and his wife were invited to the White House for a private dinner in the Johnson family quarters. The rumor around Washington was that LBJ was going to offer Williams the post of ambassador to the United Nations. Johnson asked Williams if he could talk to him alone and led him into his bedroom. Agnes Williams followed along, "because she was so absolutely dedicated to the idea of my not taking any federal job. She wanted me to stay in the private sector. She just thought that I'd be happier doing what I was doing and that I'd be unhappy in the public sector because I wouldn't have the kind of authority I'd need." So Mrs. Williams was there, just in case her husband wavered under LBJ's legendary powers of persuasion.

To Williams's "relief," Johnson asked him to take the appointment of mayor of Washington, which was "so easy" for Williams to turn down. "I told him I couldn't be mayor, I couldn't let him make a mistake like that, it would be a terrible blunder, because he had to have a black mayor. I wouldn't have been able to resist, you know"—not that Williams had the slightest desire for that job—"if I hadn't had a good reason to give him. Then he began to perceive I was right. I said, 'The town's going to burn. It's heating up and it's going to surely burn and you have to have a black man to run the city when it burns.' Sure enough, I was right. It did burn," the following April after Martin Luther King, Jr., was assassinated. Johnson, meanwhile, had taken Williams's advice and appointed a black, Walter Washington, as mayor.

Several months later, Johnson offered Williams another post: head of the Criminal Division in the Justice Department, the number two job in the agency. "I thought I had passed beyond that professionally. I didn't want to be the second man in the department at that time. It might have been interesting to me when I was thirty-eight years old," about ten years earlier. What if Johnson had wanted to name Williams attorney general? "Different! I would have taken that."

Johnson was later to comment many times that he wished he had appointed Williams attorney general. LBJ expressed his regrets to his former aide Bobby Baker three months before the ex-president's death. Baker reported in his autobiography that he told Johnson:

> "Pound for pound, Edward Bennett Williams was the ablest lawyer
> in Washington and he definitely wanted to be a part of your team. He'd

have jumped at the chance to be your A. G." LBJ looked startled and said, "Then why in hell didn't he tell me? Why didn't *you* tell me? . . . I wish I'd known of Ed Williams's interest."[3]

Williams also says that Johnson might have been able to talk him into accepting an appointment to the Supreme Court, and he is glad such an offer was never extended. "I never had much interest to be a judge. I really, you know, have always felt that is like being an umpire. As long as you can play, you don't want to be an umpire, and I never wanted to be calling balls and strikes in a blue suit."

During his countless meetings with Johnson, Williams often discussed political issues with the president, particularly the status of J. Edgar Hoover and the progress of the Vietnam War. Williams says he was "constantly at loggerheads with Hoover over the fact that the Bureau was indiscriminately wiretapping in the face of a statute which made it a felony. Every time I would make a speech on that subject, he would go up and down like a Yo-Yo.* It drove him crazy when I said that they shouldn't do that, that they should obey the law." But when Williams talked about Hoover with Johnson and asked him why he let the old man stay in office, Johnson answered with a story about his uncle Hud, who "used to go on fishing trips on the Pedernales River with his friends. Uncle Hud always tented with a fellow who was a sleepwalker. They asked his uncle Hud why he always roomed with this fellow, and he said, 'Well, I'd rather have him inside my tent pissing out than outside my tent pissing in.' And that's why, he told me, he kept Hoover on."

Throughout most of the Vietnam War, Williams was of the opinion that "we should press vigorously to win, because I believed at that time that it was not just a civil war. I thought that it was a war in which the Soviet Union and China were seeking to spread their influence." For several years, he frequently discussed the war both with Johnson and with Clark Clifford, who held the same view. Then, in January 1968, LBJ appointed Clifford secretary of defense in place of Robert S. McNamara. At the time, as Williams puts it, "Bob McNamara's support and beliefs [on Vietnam] seemed to be shifting." Clifford spent his first few weeks at the Pentagon conducting what he calls "an exhaustive survey" of the war. He then turned out to be, to Johnson's discomfort, even more dovish than McNamara. Clifford told Williams of his change of heart and his reasons, and Williams came to feel the same way. "I think that Clark's judgment is nearly perfect when he has all the facts," says Williams. "And once he got to the point that he had all the facts, I was very much persuaded by his views."

Although Williams did not believe he should convey his new opinion to

---

* Williams delivered an attack on Hoover on April 30, 1967, on the CBS program "Face the Nation."

Johnson, his support helped Clifford mount his own arguments in favor of ending the war. "I welcomed all the help that I could get, and help from Ed Williams is obviously help indeed," comments Clifford. He adds that Johnson finally underwent "a remarkable change in his thinking" and reached the same conclusion. Johnson's switch, however, did not come in time to save his presidency, which Williams says with regret was "flawed by the tragedy of Vietnam. The fantastic things he did in the fields of education and civil rights will be overlooked" as a result.

Williams stayed in touch with Johnson after LBJ left the White House, and mentions with pride that he was the recipient of the last letter Johnson wrote before his death in 1973. The ex-president told Williams he was "thrilled" that Williams had agreed to speak at the Johnson Library in Austin and he invited Williams and his wife "to stay at the ranch for so long as we wished while we were down there." After Johnson's death, Williams found a place in his office for Chuck Robb, who had married Johnson's daughter Lynda Bird. Robb left William's firm to run for office; he was elected Virgina's lieutenant governor in 1977 and governor in 1981.

When Johnson bowed out of the 1968 race after faring poorly in the New Hampshire primary and the public-opinion polls, Williams stayed on the sidelines in the ensuing battle among Hubert Humphrey, Eugene McCarthy, and, until his assassination in June, Robert F. Kennedy. Williams regarded all three major candidates as friends—even RFK, with whom he had become reconciled as time had healed their breach over Jimmy Hoffa. In 1972, when McCarthy again sought the nomination, he gave the press a list of people he would appoint to cabinet-level positions, including Williams for FBI director (along with Golda Meir for secretary of defense and Indira Gandhi as secretary of offense).[4] McCarthy still recalls with delight and approval that Williams said "he'd take it for two weeks and burn all the files at the base of the Washington Monument."

Soon after Watergate, Larry O'Brien quit as chairman of the Democratic National Committee and Robert Strauss moved up from treasurer to succeed him. Strauss, who had gotten to know Williams well during Watergate, tapped him in 1974 to be the party's new treasurer. "I encouraged him to become treasurer, not because I thought he was a great fundraiser," says Strauss. "Ed can't raise money. He couldn't raise a quarter." Strauss regards Williams as "good for me to have in my political arsenal of assets, even though he doesn't know politics. He can pick up something quicker than almost anybody I know. He was helpful to me," as a sounding board and adviser, "when I needed him. Not as a fund-raiser. But that was the title that was open, treasurer." In other words, if the job of sergeant-at-arms had been vacant, Williams might just as well have wound up in that post. While Williams was treasurer, Strauss did most of the fund-raising himself, although at the 1976 Democratic convention, Williams, as treasurer, was allowed to announce proudly that the party's debt had been reduced from $9 million to $2.6 million during the previous four years.[5]

Ask Williams if he ever received any improper offers as DNC treasurer—the type that flowed into the Nixon campaign—and he scoffs, "I never could find anybody who wanted to make *any* donations," proper, improper, or otherwise. But, he quips, there were "many, many improper overtures. The creditors came to collect the bills that the Democrats owed them and I thought those overtures were improper. The creditors hounded me from the day I got in there. They were camping on the doorstep the whole time." He says he told the telephone company, one of the Democrats' major creditors and of course a monopoly in its field, "'I haven't got the money. If you'll just go away and leave me alone, I promise you that I'll continue to give you our business.'" Williams served three years as treasurer, resigning in 1977 after Jimmy Carter's election.

While Williams was party treasurer, Strauss urged him to consider running for the U.S. Senate from Maryland. He had been approached years earlier about running for senator from his native Connecticut, but had refused, in part because "it meant establishing a residence there and I had no interest in doing that." Williams, however, was genuinely intrigued with the idea of serving in the country's most exclusive club, and seriously considered making the race in Maryland in 1976. He even discussed the proposition at one of his periodic breakfast meetings in Annapolis with Governor Marvin Mandel, who advised Williams that because several Democrats in the state legislature were interested in the job, he should "'not be indecisive and should declare forthwith, and then maybe you'll preempt the field,'" as Williams remembers Mandel's words. Despite their friendship, Mandel did not promise support for Williams in the primary, indicating that he would have to stay neutral, at least publicly. Williams finally decided not to run, a wise choice, says his friend Gene McCarthy, who comments that, based on his own experience, "people much less energetic than Ed get pretty frustrated there."

As it turned out, if Williams had decided to run, a Mandel endorsement for another candidate might have been a big boost for a Williams campaign. The governor was indicted for racketeering and mail fraud, and both Mandel and Bill Hundley, who represented several of his codefendants, asked Williams to defend him. Williams refused the governor, telling him that "I was very busy at the time. I told him what was true," says Williams, "that I just couldn't go into a trial that promised to last for several months." What was even more true was that Williams doubted that Mandel "would be willing to give me the kind of control that I have to have." While Mandel's case was pending, "he was making public statements all the time which I thought were not consistent with his self-interest. He was constantly calling his own shots." Without Williams, Mandel went to trial in 1977, was found guilty, and received a three-year prison term.

At the time when Williams was DNC treasurer and was considering involvement in Maryland politics, President Gerald Ford made him an offer he found very hard to refuse: director of the CIA. Ford's invitation came in 1975, "at a time when [William] Colby was CIA director and Ford was telling the world that he had confidence in Colby." According to Williams, "He wanted to name me instantly, like the same day, unbelievably, but he did. I pondered it overnight and I was tempted. I must tell you, I was tempted. It was a really challenging thing." Williams reached the conclusion that he was simply too busy in his law practice. "I just wasn't prepared for it at a professional or personal level. I would have had to do too many disentangling things," and on notice that was much too sudden.

Several months later, in March 1976, however, Williams did accept an appointment from Ford to be one of seventeen members of the president's Foreign Intelligence Advisory Board, which oversees U.S. intelligence-gathering abroad. Others named by Ford included John Connally; former secretary of defense Melvin Laird; William J. Casey, whom President Reagan chose for CIA head in 1981; Clare Boothe Luce; Edwin Land, chairman of Polaroid; and Edward Teller, the nuclear scientist.[6]

Gerald Ford continued to call on Williams, long after he returned to private life. In 1982, California industrialist Justin Dart, a longtime Reagan insider, was quoted by the *Los Angeles Times* as saying that Ford was "'a dumb bastard'" who was "'pretty much of a nothing'" as president.[7] At Ford's request, Williams contacted a Dart aide to seek an apology and was told that Dart had already written Ford and expressed his regrets.

One of the most sensitive cases Williams ever handled was that of Richard Helms, William Colby's predecessor as director of the Central Intelligence Agency. Helms first found himself in need of a criminal lawyer in early 1976, three years after he resigned as CIA head in order to assume the post of ambassador to Iran. In January 1976, a month before the five-year statute of limitations would expire, Helms learned that the Justice Department was investigating whether he had violated the civil rights of the operators of a photographic studio in Fairfax, Virginia. Agents from the nearby headquarters of the CIA had staged a February 1971 break-in at the photo shop, which was run by Deborah Fitzgerald, who had worked in the CIA's records section, and Orlando Nuñez, once a Cuban official under Fidel Castro. CIA officials believed that Fitzgerald, who later married Nuñez, had searched the Agency's files to see what they contained on Nuñez.[8] Helms authorized agents to enter the studio secretly, because, as he explained in 1981, "We conceived this man

[Nuñez] to be a threat to us. We had every reason to believe that this photographic studio was nothing but a front for Cuban intelligence."

The CIA agents who broke into the shop apparently did not find what they were looking for,[9] but word of the potentially illegal entry leaked to the Justice Department, and Helms was notified in Tehran that he was under investigation. After consulting with such luminaries as Clark Clifford, Joe Califano, Averell Harriman, Lloyd Cutler, and Robert McNamara, Helms settled on the attorney who had received their virtually unanimous recommendation and the man he had been inclined toward all along—Edward Bennett Williams. Helms and Williams had been friendly for many years, and Helms had counseled Williams after the lawyer was named to President Ford's advisory panel. "In a case of the kind that was creeping up on me," says Helms, "I needed a fellow who had two attributes: One was that he be an absolutely topflight figure as a criminal trial lawyer, and secondly that he understand exactly what the problem was. I think Williams was ideally suited on both points."

The Justice Department had reportedly been prepared to prosecute Helms over the break-in, but had reconsidered after a series of meetings between Williams and DOJ officials. The decision against bringing Helms to trial was announced by Attorney General Edward H. Levi in a press release, an unusual measure, because the government rarely makes public cases in which someone is investigated and then not formally charged. Levi said the decision was based on the recommendations of Deputy Attorney General Harold R. Tyler, Jr., and Assistant Attorney General Stanley Pottinger, head of the department's Civil Rights Division, with whom Williams had met. Williams was quoted by Bob Woodward in the *Washington Post* as praising the Justice Department for "'an unusually smart decision,'" and as stating that "'If the government has a right to conduct electronic surveillance, then it has a right to make surreptitious entry,'"[10] a curious turnabout for someone who had been so unalterably opposed for so long to invasions of privacy by law-enforcement officials.

The issue of the break-in at the Fairfax photo studio had been settled in Helms's favor, but he still was faced with very serious accusations. On February 7 and March 6, 1973, he had testified in front of the Senate Foreign Relations Committee, which was weighing his confirmation as U.S. ambassador to Iran. Asked if the CIA, working with the International Telephone and Telegraph Corporation, had attempted to influence the 1970 Chilean presidential elections and prevent leftist candidate Salvador Allende from winning, Helms had answered in the negative.[11] His answers, as he acknowledges, were untrue, but he felt that the oath of office he had taken as director of the CIA took precedence over his vow to tell the truth to the Foreign Relations Committee, and that he could not reveal the Agency's secrets, regardless of the consequences. In short, Helms was caught between two conflicting pledges, and, at least theoretically, he might have faced prosecution for breaching his CIA oath if he had been frank in his Senate testimony.

"I have to say to you that as I look at it today," comments Helms, "I don't see how under the circumstances that existed at the time I could have handled the thing in any other way. I'm not being stubborn about this. I would just like somebody to point out to me how they would do it."

When Williams, who had the opportunity to hold the same job that led to Helms's difficulties, was asked what he would have done under the circumstances as CIA chief, he replied, "I would have refused to answer. I would just have said, 'I will not answer these questions. I believe that the answers to these questions would be so damaging to the security of the country and so perilous to the lives of people who are in other countries working for the United States that I refuse to answer, and you just do the best that you can with me,'" such as cite him for contempt.

That is the advice he would have offered Helms in 1973, but Helms went before the Foreign Relations Committee unaccompanied by counsel. Helms does not regard Williams's suggestion as a viable solution to his dilemma: "If I had declined to testify and risked contempt, I was in effect telling them that I had something to hide, which in effect gave them the information they wanted"—that the CIA had sought to prevent Allende from becoming president of Chile.

Following a lengthy internal investigation within the Agency, William Colby forwarded a report that outlined the potential perjury case against Helms to the Justice Department in December 1974. Colby's move, in violation of the first unwritten rule of espionage—Thou shalt not betray a spy on the same side—makes Helms bristle: "Colby, in turn, for reasons best known to himself, sent the findings down to the Department of Justice." Was Colby obliged to transmit the findings of a three-member CIA panel to the prosecutors? "Not that I'm aware of," says Helms wryly. Williams, who could have had Colby's job if he had wanted it, also understates his feelings by leaps and bounds: "To say that I'm not as impressed with Colby as I am with Helms is certainly true."

The Helms matter remained dormant within the Justice Department for two years. Then in January 1977, several days before the change of administration from Ford to Carter, Williams was officially notified that Helms's Senate testimony on Chile was receiving the most thorough scrutiny from a federal grand jury in Washington.[12] There have been numerous reports about Williams's threats—veiled and unveiled—to the Justice Department about the consequences of prosecuting Helms. One was that Williams told top Justice officials that Helms would seize the opportunity "to vindicate himself by laying it all out, and letting the facts . . . *all the facts* . . . speak for themselves."[13] A second was that Williams told Attorney General Griffin Bell in September 1977 "'that it would be unconscionable to indict the man and that *it would raise very serious national* *security problems.'*" [14] (Italics added.) Another was that one politician said that Williams had been "'threatening to subpoena every important person in the government,'" and, "'Any lawyer could have threatened, but Edward Bennett Williams was the only lawyer with the power to back it up.'" As a result, Williams was described as "'the most powerful lawyer in this town. . . . Let me amend that. Edward Bennett Williams may be the most powerful *person* in this town.'" [15] A fourth report said that Williams was "using pre-trial discovery as a sort of legal terror weapon" in defending indicted FBI man John J. Kearney, so the government knew exactly what to expect in the Helms dispute.[16]*

Williams's latest version of what happened is "I never threatened Griffin Bell with anything. I never at any time told him what I was going to do. At no time did I ever make any threats against the Department of Justice, the government of the United States, or anybody else. Contrary to what's been printed, that I engaged in graymail, that I scared 'em, that they ran for cover, that they thought I was going to take the house down, that's untrue." But, he adds with a laugh, "they knew I was going to defend it vigorously. I didn't have to tell them that. They could read my life story and know that I was going to defend it vigorously."

The gentle persuasion was neither instigated by Williams nor coming entirely from him. Fully appreciating Helms's delicate predicament, Williams made an exception in his case and bent his rule of demanding absolute control of the case. Helms—a nonpaying client at that—says Williams told him, "'Obviously, in your case I'm not going to ram this down your throat. I want to consult with you about what to do. Let's arrive at this decision together.'" And Helms says he was ready to go all out in defending himself, and let the chips fall where they might: "I had no reason to feel other than that I was being picked on here. Therefore, it would be desirable to go to trial and demonstrate this. Of course, I was aware that it would involve national security matters. The principal issue was what had happened in a foreign country. There was no way that this could be tried without dealing with foreign officials and foreign operations and a whole host of things. That I was sorry about. But it was the government that was coming after me, it wasn't me going after the government. They were the ones that were making the running here, as they say on the race course. So it seemed to me that it was their responsibility to worry about the national interest.

"Was I prepared to haul out everything and dump it on the table? Now I don't know whether I would have done that. It depends on the way the trial went. I'm not interested in hurting United States security. I spent a good part of my life trying to *de*fend it. So it doesn't make sense to turn

---

*Negotiations between Williams and Griffin Bell in 1977 led to the dismissal of charges that Kearney had conducted illegal surveillance of Weather Underground sympathizers.[17]

around and want to *of*fend it. But all I knew was that I wanted to clear myself and I was going to defend myself as actively as I could."

Other friends of Helms's, such as Clark Clifford, made the trek to the Justice Department to argue both that Helms should not be prosecuted and that, aside from considerations of right and wrong, a trial would probably unearth secrets that would best be left buried. Clifford says, "I went down [to the Justice Department] in my capacity as a former chairman of the Foreign Intelligence Advisory Board. I went down to discuss whether or not it might be exceedingly dangerous to have a public trial, in the course of which many of our intelligence practices or even some of our intelligence agents might come to public attention. Oh, yes, I thought it would be a very unfortunate business to have a trial"—especially since "I thought that Mr. Helms had conducted himself properly" as a Senate witness.

What is intriguing to contemplate is that Clifford apparently said pretty much the same thing that Williams did. But if Clark Clifford says something, it is regarded as kindly, grandfatherly advice, and if Edward Bennett Williams says substantially the same thing, a threat is inferred. The distinction is not simply one that is in the eyes of the beholder, but is due to the fact that over the years Williams has made clear to many people that the best way to treat him is very carefully and with respect, even fear.

Richard Helms was, as Thomas Powers so aptly says, "a man wrapped in the flag, with a derringer peeping out between the folds."[18] And Williams, in his inimitable style, made Helms's situation—that his back was against the wall—clear to the highest executives in the U.S. government. Again breaking with precedent, Attorney General Bell initiated plea-bargaining with Williams, instead of the other way around, following a strategy session in which President Carter, Vice President Mondale, National Security Adviser Zbigniew Brzezinski, Bell, and Assistant Attorney General Benjamin Civiletti, head of the Criminal Division within the Justice Department, had participated on July 25, 1977. At two meetings with prosecutors in September, Williams outlined the reasons against charging Helms, and Civiletti and his aides said that they were prepared to indict Helms on eight counts, relating to both his confirmation hearing in February 1973 and his testimony the following month before Senator Frank Church's Foreign Relations Subcommittee on Multinational Corporations. At the end of the second conference on September 20, Williams was invited to meet with Bell, who told him that if Helms would plead no contest to two misdemeanors, the government would recommend that he not be imprisoned or fined.[19]

Williams carried Bell's proposal to Helms, and, says Helms, advised him to accept it. "He went over with me in some detail what a trial would entail in terms of time, strain on the family, and strain on me, and what the chances were of a jury in the District of Columbia bringing in a verdict that would be an unhappy one." Williams's comment is that "it was better for him and the United States that the case be terminated in the way that it was." Helms's acceptance of Bell's offer "avoided months and months of testimony which would have gone into the most serious and sensitive problems of the United States government's relationships with other countries, that would have unearthed the most delicate secrets of the Central Intelligence Agency, that would have compromised agents all over the world. It was going to be a horrible thing if we had to try the case." Helms also feared a trial "that would have involved having associates of mine in the Agency called in by the prosecution to testify against me. I thought it would have had horrendous effects on our foreign policy and our foreign relations—the spectacle of a former director of Intelligence in the dock with all of those allegations flying around."

There was only one sticking point that had not been foreseen by Bell and the others who had hammered out the deal: A *nolo contendere* plea might have disqualified Helms from receiving his government pension. Gregory Craig, the young lawyer from Williams's office who assisted him in the Helms case, discovered the pension problem in his research. Helms was unwilling to risk his pension, and Williams explained the problem to Bell and Civiletti, who promised that the pension would not be affected by Helms's plea.

With all the details in the pact worked out, Helms was charged in a two-count criminal information that was signed by Civiletti. The accusation which Helms would not contest was that he "did refuse and fail to answer material questions" from the Senate about CIA efforts to prevent Allende from becoming president of Chile and about his knowledge of U.S. policy toward the 1970 election in Chile.[20] Nowhere in the charge was a word said about Helms having testified falsely. Due to Williams's hard-nosed bargaining, it was as if Helms had done exactly what Williams would have recommended in the first place: declined to answer and risked a contempt citation. The fact that Helms's answers had been untrue simply vanished into the Wonderland of legalese. Helms wound up being branded as unresponsive, not as a liar.

Williams still relishes the knowledge that "the charge we pleaded *nolo contendere* to isn't even a charge. It doesn't even ascend to the seriousness of a criminal charge. It just says that he refused to answer questions that were put to him. He *did* refuse to answer questions that were put to him. Not criminally. He refused to answer because he was under an obligation under his oath and under statutes not to answer." Williams even goes so far as to state that, because of an oversight, the information signed by Civiletti "did not state a criminal offense." His point is that the word *willfully* was not included in the charge, "and the language of the statute [2 U.S. Code, Section 192] requires that the word *willful* be in it. They didn't put that in. Therefore," claims Williams, "it didn't allege an offense. I could have knocked that over. I could still go down and knock that over on a posttrial motion, today, on the ground that he was never convicted of anything." Williams apparently is wrong on this last point; the word *willfully* is included in the statute, but not in reference to the part that was applied to Helms's case.*

Just when the Helms matter seemed to be settled to the satisfaction of all parties, a most unexpected and unwelcome obstacle popped up: The case was assigned, by a blind draw, to U.S. District Judge Barrington Parker, a strict jurist who refused to be bound by the terms of the plea bargain. Williams says that he, Bell, and Civiletti were all "dismayed that this judge would take that position when the government stated that it had a deep interest in having this done, and done expeditiously." The defendant, meanwhile, was aware only that "something had gone wrong. He [Parker] kept mouthing about not believing in plea bargains and all the rest of it."

Helms and Williams had come to court on October 31, 1977, all set for Helms to enter his *nolo* plea, have the bargain ratified by a judge, and be done in a matter of minutes. Thanks to Williams's machinations, the press had been kept in the dark (see chapter 3), and if events had gone according to Williams's plan, the media wouldn't even have learned what was afoot until Helms was long gone. But things started coming apart. When Parker refused to play along, Williams and Civiletti had three frantic meetings, during which Williams threatened to withdraw the plea bargain, and Civiletti warned him that Helms would be prosecuted on eight counts of perjury.[22] In the end, Williams recommended that Helms "gamble" that Parker would accept the plea bargain if Helms went ahead with his part of it. Helms entered his plea of *nolo contendere,* and tried to explain his dilemma to Judge Parker:

> Your Honor, I found myself in a position of conflict on this occasion. I had sworn my oath to preserve certain secrets from unauthorized disclosure.... I had put up my hand and sworn not to give up the secrets, and I was being asked questions that were directly on these issues. I didn't want to lie. I didn't want to mislead the Committee. I was simply trying to find my way through a very difficult situation in which I found myself.[23]

---

* The statute specifies that anyone properly summoned before either house of Congress or before a legitimately constituted congressional committee who "willfully makes default, or, who, having appeared, refuses to answer any question pertinent to the question under inquiry, shall be deemed guilty of a misdemeanor, punishable by a fine of not more that $1,000 nor less that $100 and imprisonment in a common jail for not less than one month nor more than twelve months."[21] The word *willfully,* then, appears to apply only to the clause, "makes default," and not to the clause "having appeared, refuses to answer any question pertinent to the question under inquiry."

To Williams's consternation, Parker not only failed to promise that he would honor the bargain, but declined to sentence Helms forthwith. He directed Williams to prepare a background report on Helms and scheduled sentencing for four days later, November 4, thereby ensuring that news reporters would be on hand en masse.

Inside a packed courtroom at the sentencing on November 4, Williams told Parker: "For Richard Helms to have made the requested disclosures at that time, Your Honor, he believed then and now would have cost lives. It would have compromised the nation's security. . . . It would have violated two oaths that he took." Noting that Helms had been a loyal public servant for thirty-five years, Williams declared, "I am very proud as a lawyer, Your Honor, to stand beside a man who has made these virtues (duty, respect for authority, obedience, honor and patriotism) the hallmarks of manhood and who has lived his whole life accordingly."[24]

Parker, however, took exception, lecturing Williams: "There have been a number of defendants before this Court within the last five years who have weighed this question as to what is in the best interests of the United States, and you have seen what has happened."

No, said Williams, there was "a sharp difference" between the Helms case and Watergate. "There were self-interests that were at work in those cases."[25]

Helms, according to Williams, "will bear the scar of a conviction for the rest of his days. His only consolation will be that it is a scar incurred in the service of his country for doing what he believed by his lights and his conscience was in the best interests of the United States." Therefore, said Williams—and Civiletti agreed with him—Helms should be given a light sentence.[26]

Parker continued to be a maverick right until the end. As Helms bristled (he said in 1981, "Would it have sat well with you? It was uncalled for"), the judge humiliated him publicly, addressing him as follows:

> You now stand before this Court in disgrace and shame. If public officials embark deliberately on a course to disobey and ignore the laws of our land because of some misguided and ill-conceived notion and belief that there are earlier commitments and considerations which they must first observe, the future of our country is in jeopardy.[27]

Finally, Parker handed Helms a two-year jail sentence, which he suspended, and fined him $2,000, the maximum, despite the fact that the prosecution had not asked for a fine. Helms's pension was not mentioned by Parker and was left unaffected.[28]

Outside the courtroom, Williams tried to take some of the sting out of Parker's relatively harsh action. Helms's plea, which Williams had characterized to Parker as a "scar" that he "will bear for the rest of his days," was, for press consumption, " 'a badge of honor. He will wear it like a banner.' "[29]

One journalist who followed the Helms case did not think much of Williams's sudden reversal. Jack Fuller of the *Chicago Tribune* wrote an editorial-page column titled "Words for Hire Add a Disturbing Note to the Helms Case." Fuller's lead was "What's the matter with lawyers?" Williams, he said, was "a masterful craftsman of trial law," but the contradiction between his in-court and outside rhetoric showed "what perplexes folks about men of the bar." Fuller continued:

> There was something upsetting about the performance of this lawyer who stands near the top of his profession and commands such respect in the national community. . . .
> [The contradictory statements] left the unsavory impression that to Williams, at least, words deserve no reverence. They are simply tools.
> Words for hire. Words not for expression but for manipulation. Words that do not emanate from some deep and honest center of a man but rather from a bag of tricks well learned.
> One can feel some sympathy for Richard Helms and his plight and still find his mouthpiece's conduct disturbing. . . .
> Neither the law nor the language is well served by crude displays like Williams'.[30]

Williams's explanation for his turnabout is that Parker's "tongue-lashing" was not a "fair deal" for Helms. "That's why I responded outside. I didn't have a chance to respond to the judge because the proceeding was over," so he decided to use the press as his forum.

As usual, Williams's performance throughout the case had satisfied the one to whom it meant the most: the client. Helms came away eternally grateful to Williams for winning him a relatively favorable disposition, and for not charging him a fee. Helm says that whenever he mentioned a fee, Williams "said not to worry about it. And every time I raised the subject, he said not to worry about it. Then, when the whole thing was over, I said, 'What do I owe you?' And he said, 'You don't owe me anything.' "

Helms was also left with the opinion that "it's really no wonder the firm has the reputation it does. They create a sense of reassurance just by the way they go at the job." He speaks with special praise of Gregory Craig, whose research disclosed the potential problem over Helms's pension. Otherwise, says Helms, he might have lost the pension before he even know he was risking it. And Helms marvels at how "keyed up" Williams was after the sentencing was over and they returned to his law office. "When he goes into court, he's all revved up and all the lights and signals are go, and it takes him quite a bit of time to unwind. He wanted to talk about it and talk about it, simply to give himself a chance to relax. He's all go."

If Williams ever needs a friend, all he has to do is look across Farragut Square to the building a block from his office, where Helms operates as a

lone-wolf consultant to businesses with interests abroad. The erstwhile
spymaster feels that he owes everything to the spymaster who could have
been.

Ed Williams was, in his words, "against Jimmy [Carter] always," as a
potential Democratic presidential nominee. That is significant, because
during Carter's first campaign in 1976, Williams was treasurer of the
Democratic party. Williams's favorite that year was his friend Senator
Henry ("Scoop") Jackson of Washington, who asked him to manage his
presidential campaign. But Williams had to turn Jackson down because
"he wanted me to drop everything and jump in and take over." Once
again, Williams had to decline bcause he couldn't leave his practice on
such short notice. That same year, Eugene McCarthy, who was running
for president as an independent candidate, solicited his support, but Williams was not interested. He remained within the Democratic framework,
a supporter, but not campaign official, of Scoop Jackson.

Williams did not need a personal slight to make him dislike Jimmy
Carter, but he got one anyway. During the 1976 convention in New York,
Bob Strauss threw a party for Carter. Strauss invited Williams, who insisted that Art Buchwald accompany him, even though Buchwald was, as
he says, "very seedy from a whole day covering the convention." But
Buchwald went along, and was in the reception line right behind Williams. As Williams stepped up, Strauss made the introductions: " 'Jimmy,
this is Ed Williams. He's the treasurer of the Democratic National Party,
and he's done a marvelous job.' " According to Buchwald, "Carter gave
him that fishy-eyed look of his, said, 'Nice to meet you, Mr. Williams,'
and shoved him on to Rosalynn." Next Buchwald was introduced to Carter, and "Jimmy gave me a big hello, and said to Rosalynn, 'Guess who's
here? Art Buchwald.' " Carter spent several minutes chatting with Buchwald, who soon found Williams "steaming. 'Goddamnit,' he says, 'I bring
you along, you look a mess, I've been working my ass off for the party six
months, you get the big hello and the big handshake, and all I get is the
fisheye.' "

Williams himself says he was "very unenthusiastic about the Carter
candidacy. I was so unenthusiastic about the Carter candidacy that I
thought that I should resign as treasurer," a suggestion that was also
coming from the Carter camp. "I was perfectly willing to step aside, but
Bob Strauss importuned me very vigorously not to do that, because he
thought it would be damaging to the party's campaign for the treasurer to
resign after the convention." Williams stayed on, but "I didn't function
very well as treasurer."

Three months after Carter took office, Williams received what he calls
"one of the great collector's items of the world": a form letter over Carter's mimeographed signature, announcing that the president had decided

to abolish the Foreign Intelligence Advisory Board. The letter, dated May 4, 1977, was bad enough, according to Williams: "We worked selflessly and without any money. It was absolutely outrageous that the members would be treated in that fashion, just in a perfunctory, cavalier way to be summarily discharged with a form letter which was not even signed" personally by Carter. But the letter wasn't the worst of it. Enclosed in the packet from the White House was an official form stating that the "nature of action" in connection with Williams's White House employment was "termination." And there was a "Notice to Federal Employee about Unemployment Compensation."

Comments Williams with disbelief, "He sent the unemployment form to me. He sent it to Clare Boothe Luce. To Dr. Edward Teller, John Connally, to General Lyman Lemnitzer, to Dr. Edwin Land, the head of Polaroid. He sent it to Dr. William Baker, the head of Bell Laboratories. He sent it to Bob Galvin, the chief executive of Motorola. We all got applications for unemployment compensation and we got fired." Williams was "tempted" to submit his form, even though he had never accepted the $100 a day that board members were entitled to. In the end, he simply kept the documents as a monument to Carter's incompetence.*

In early 1978, historian Allen Weinstein, in an Op-Ed article for the *New York Times,* proposed several people, including Edward Bennett Williams, for consideration as director of the FBI.[31] Unlike Eugene McCarthy's suggestion during his abortive 1972 presidential campaign, Weinstein's was completely serious. Needless to say, Jimmy Carter did not follow Weinstein's unsolicited advice.

Williams's enmity toward Carter increased in 1979 when Carter fired Joe Califano as secretary of Health, Education, and Welfare. Califano had not fitted in with the Georgians in Carter's inner circle. Williams had originally advised Califano against joining Carter's cabinet; to do so would require a 90-percent cut in Califano's income and would disrupt their "fantastic" partnership, says Califano. Williams speaks with scorn of Califano's dismissal: "I thought Joe Califano was one of the two or three ablest members of his cabinet. And then he was just summarily dismissed. It was just an outrage, I thought, just an outrage. Joe used to come to me and say that the rumors were flying that he was going to be fired. I said, 'It's impossible. I mean, he wrote a book called, *Why Not the Best?* And you're the best man he's got in the cabinet. He's not going to fire you.' I couldn't believe it when he fired Joe. But Carter had nothing

---

*In 1981 President Reagan revived the Foreign Intelligence Advisory Board and reappointed Williams, Connally, Luce, and several others. New members included Leon Jaworski; former astronaut Frank Borman, head of Eastern Airlines; Alfred Bloomingdale, department store magnate and member of Reagan's "kitchen cabinet"; and Anne Armstrong, a Republican leader and former ambassadress, who was named chairman.

but mediocre people, incompetent people, around him. And I think his administration was a failure as a result." Why didn't Carter select capable advisers? Because, says Williams, "he had a push-button line to the Deity and he didn't need us mortals."

That same trait of Carter's is mentioned by Clark Clifford, who had much more contact with Carter than did Williams, and who professes to like him. Clifford's observation is that Carter thought he had "in some manner become an instrument of Divine Providence" and could get advice "from some other place" than planet Earth.

Even Eugene McCarthy—who was never shy about disrupting the Democratic party when he belonged to it—regarded the 1980 attempt spearheaded by Williams to "open the Democratic convention" as "a desperate proposal" that never had a chance of succeeding. At a Washington press conference on July 31, 1980, Williams had been formally introduced as chairman of the Committee to Continue the Open Convention, an organization of Democrats who wanted delegates to be free to vote for the presidential candidate of their choice. Among the supporters of the open-convention movement were Senators Edward M. Kennedy, George McGovern, Daniel Moynihan, and Scoop Jackson; Governors Hugh Carey and Ella Grasso; Representatives Shirley Chisholm, Elizabeth Holtzman, Henry Reuss, Christopher Dodd—whose father, the late Senator Thomas Dodd, (D-Conn.) was a client of Williams's—and Patricia Schroeder; and former DNC chairman Larry O'Brien. Senate Majority Leader Robert Byrd signed on as the campaign picked up steam.[32] Under a rule backed by the supporters of President Carter, who had won more than enough delegates in the primaries to assure him of an easy first-ballot victory, delegates were bound to vote for the candidate to whom they had committed before the primaries. Any delegate who sought to change horses, without the permission of his or her candidate, could be yanked off the convention floor and replaced forthwith. The open-convention forces wanted the selection of a presidential nominee to be governed by the party's charter as revised in 1974, which read, "The Democratic Party shall not require a delegate to the party convention or caucus to cast a vote contrary to his or her expressed preference." They argued that the charter should supersede the Carter rule that bound the delegates.[33]

At his July 31 session with the media, Williams "waved his arms like a coach giving a locker-room pep talk and declared with great vigor that his purpose was 'to free the delegates . . . to eliminate the possibility of their being held hostage to an oppressive rule.'"[34] Later that day, Williams got phone calls from Carter's campaign manager, Bob Strauss, and from the president himself. Williams had tried to reach his chum Strauss before the press conference to let him know what was afoot, but Strauss had been on the West Coast and unavailable. Phoning in as soon as he could,

Strauss told Williams he was "'a damn fool.' We had a lot of laughs over the phone. I said, 'Williams, you've got no chance to win this damn thing. The most you're going to do is interrupt a vacation for me. I'm going to have to come back to Washington and spend three or four days smacking your little political ass.' I said, 'Can't you figure a way out of this damn foolishness, Ed? You've got to lose. When you don't have the votes, you're going to look bad, and you look good when you've got the votes. I've got the votes.'" Ironically, Strauss believed in the concept of an open convention, but the binding delegate rule had been "forced on me and on the party. I'm personally very comfortable in smoke-filled rooms."

Whether Williams would have liked to take Strauss's advice or not, it was too late. Several hours later, Williams was called by Carter, who, incredibly enough, did not seem to know at first to whom he was talking. Carter's first words were "'Hello, friend, I sure am glad to have your support.'" Williams quickly set him straight: "'You don't have my support. This is Edward Bennett Williams.'" Both Williams and Strauss, who heard about the incident from within the White House as well as from Williams, believe that Carter aides must have been dialing delegates around the country and then handing the phone to the president. Someone got Williams on the line without bothering to inform Carter who was on.

After Carter realized whom he had called, he and Williams chatted about the political situation and Williams tried to persuade him of the benefits of letting the delegates vote their own free wills. "I said, 'Why don't you get the nomination from a free convention? Why don't you let these people vote their consciences? Why are you afraid? At least it will be worth something if you get it from a convention that's not manacled.'" At that point, according to Williams, Carter declared, "'Let's cut the bullshit. I know you're for Scoop Jackson.'" At that moment, a "very surprised" Edward Bennett Williams liked Jimmy Carter "a little better" than he ever had before. For the first time, it seemed possible to him that beneath the grinning facade there might be an actual human being. "I thought there was some substance and reality there, if you pulled the veneer off. I kind of admired him for saying, 'Let's cut the bullshit.'"

Neither Williams nor Carter, of course, was going to make a sale to the other. Three days later, Williams was the guest on CBS's "Face the Nation," and he "pledged" his "positively absolute neutrality with respect to who the Democratic nominee may be. I have pledged to work for the Democratic nominee after he is named."[35]

Several months later, after all the campaign rhetoric had died down, Williams revealed that Carter had known what he was talking about: "I was for Jackson and Muskie, preferably as a combination, with either one" at the head of the ticket. "I believed with many others that Carter could not be elected president again. I believed that there was a very, very big chance of our losing the Congress if he ran. We thought that if we opened the convention we'd get a different candidate." So much for Williams's "positively absolute neutrality." As far as his "work for the Democratic nominee after he is named," that was nonexistent. Understandably so; Carter was probably better off not having his help, and there is strong reason to believe that Democratic heavyweight Williams did not vote for Carter either time he ran. Commenting on the first three presidential elections after he switched parties in 1964, Williams says he always supported the Democratic candidate—Johnson in 1964, Humphrey in 1968, and McGovern in 1972. But he declines to say for whom he voted in 1976 and 1980. The implication is clear: that Williams went with his friend Gerald Ford in 1976, and with either Ronald Reagan or John Anderson in 1980. Joe Califano is one Williams intimate who wouldn't be surprised if Williams had voted for Reagan.

The open-convention drive never really had a chance. The proponents did have logic on their side; as Williams said on "Face the Nation":

> I think that if they were not voting for delegates who were free to express their preference at the Convention there would be no need . . . to hold the Convention. They could have wired in the results of the primary and we'd save millions and millions of dollars and lots of rhetoric in New York on August 11th.[36]

But if the anyone-but-Carter faction had the most persuasive argument, the Carter forces, as Williams acknowledges, had the delegates locked up. "We were not able to compete with the power of the White House," he says. "Any delegate who wavered, they buttonholed. They had them to the White House; the president was spending an hour and a half to two hours a day calling delegates around the country; they just horse-shedded them."

Williams "found out early" that the Carter crew "played rough." How rough? On the opening night of the convention in New York, Williams and Governor Hugh Carey were allotted fifteen minutes to advocate opening the convention. Williams was to speak for eight minutes, Carey for seven. To begin with, Carter's people, who controlled the logistics of the convention, failed to send credentials so that Williams and Carey could gain access to Madison Square Garden, the convention site. "All afternoon they just kept telling us these fabrications. 'They're on the way, they're on the way, they're on the way!' So I finally said, 'Hugh, let's go. You're the governor of this state. Let's just go. We'll walk in.' So Hugh said, 'You're right. I'm going to get the bulls [Carey's bodyguards]. And the bulls will lead the caravan. And we're going to blaze the sirens and go to the Garden.' So we got in a car, I and he and [Carey's friend] Anne Ford Uzielli, and the cops blazed the sirens and we went down Seventh Avenue. And we just walked into the Garden, just walked in with an escort of policemen."

The credential problem had been surmounted, but the best was yet to come. Williams was slated to close the debate, and he planned to save about half of his eight minutes to give ad-lib rebuttals to what had been said before. "The first thing the Carter people said after we got to the Garden was 'We've changed it, you're opening.' So I rushed to a little anteroom, I had half an hour, and I scribbled out some notes to myself. It's very hard to make a speech if you have a clock on you. I can make a speech for an hour without notes, but it's very hard if you just have a time clock on you. So I scribbled out some notes in a notebook and then they told me I needed makeup. So I went into the makeup room. And while they had me covered with towels, somebody stole my notebook. So I had to get up and wing it for eight minutes on three networks, nationwide. And then afterwards we found the notebook in a garbage can in a back room of Madison Square Garden. They were not playing softball," says Williams with grudging admiration. "They were playing hardball. They treated us like dogs. Absolute dogs."

Williams had primed Scoop Jackson to be prepared to accept the nomination if the delegates were freed and Carter was rejected. He had also talked to Edmund Muskie, but Carter had appointed Muskie secretary of state several months earlier, and "they had a lock on him." Not that Williams believes Carter handed Muskie the job in order to remove him as a potential foe: "I think that's ascribing too much acumen to Carter." Muskie says he "totally discouraged" the dump-Carter side, as any interest on his part would have been "embarrassing" had it become public. There was no need, however, for Muskie to worry or for Jackson to be waiting in the wings. Carter won both the open-convention question and the nomination overwhelmingly, only to fulfill Williams's expectations and go down to a resounding defeat in November, taking Democratic control of the Senate, numerous members of Congress, and several governors with him. Ed Williams could only watch helplessly from the sidelines. He was no longer part of the game, nor did he want to be.

Seventy-two hours before Ronald Reagan had even been elected president, Williams had signed aboard his transition team. Reagan called Williams on the Saturday preceding the election and asked him to serve. Williams believes that Reagan, whom he had met only once, chose him at the suggestion of Gerald Ford, who was campaigning with Reagan in Michigan when the GOP candidate contacted Williams. Williams told Reagan he would be delighted to participate in his transition, but asked for and received Reagan's assurance that the appointment would not be announced publicly until after Election Day; lest it be "misconstrued as an endorsement." Reagan informed Williams that two other Democrats— Scoop Jackson and Senator Richard Stone of Florida—would also be on the transition team. Finding out from Jackson that he had not secured Reagan's promise to withhold news of the Washington senator's role in the transition until after the election, Williams advised Jackson to reach the agreement Williams had; Jackson did.

Williams's assignment in the changeover was foreign policy, and on November 21, 1980, he was part of a star-studded cast, including Gerald Ford; Henry Kissinger; Alexander Haig, Caspar Weinberger, and Jeane Kirkpatrick, whom Reagan named as secretary of state, secretary of defense and U.N. ambassador, respectively; Jackson; Stone; Senate Republican Leader Howard Baker, and others of similar stature, who met with Reagan and Vice President–elect George Bush to discuss foreign affairs.[37]

That Williams, the Republican turned Democrat party leader, should show up as an adviser to a conservative Republican who had just won the presidency was not so surprising. He has always been a relatively conservative Democrat, much more comfortable with Scoop Jackson and Edmund Muskie than with Ted Kennedy or George McGovern. True liberals who have known Williams well over the years, such as Joe Califano, and Michael Tigar (a young lawyer who worked for Williams), have no doubts that he is a conservative. And Williams's crony, Bob Strauss, says realistically, "I'm never surprised where Ed pops up." As for the Reagan transition team, "It looked good and he didn't have to do anything," adds Strauss.

Being tapped by Reagan a mere three months after Williams was playing an instrumental part in the Democratic presidential process underscored a fact of life in Washington: Presidents and political parties and politicians come and go, but Edward Bennett Williams stays. Even when he was on the outs with the occupant of the White House, as he was with Nixon and Carter, he was still very much a force to be reckoned with. Edward Bennett Williams is always in power.

It may be the most exclusive lunch club in the city of presidents. The members are Ed Williams, Ben Bradlee, and Art Buchwald. The three have enjoyed hundreds of lunches together over the years, and, as Buchwald explains, "People would say, 'Why do you guys meet for lunch? What do you talk about?' We'd say, 'We can't tell you because it's a club.'" A number of other prominent personalities sought membership, including several women, such as Katharine Graham. Applicants would be screened during luncheons with the full membership. Buchwald: "We'd say she was being interviewed to see if she was worthy of membership. We would indicate there was a possibility. And then each guy would call and say, 'I was for you, but the other two guys blackballed you.' The idea of the club was to cause trouble, which we did. Each guy was doing his own thing and nobody had anything to gain by each other's company, so we had a lot of fun. Except that every time Eddie said something about the Redskins, he'd receive a call an hour later from a *Post* reporter" who had been clued in by Bradlee. The reporter would say, "'I heard around town that . . .' and then he would repeat exactly what had been said at our table. I never got any stories out of it," laments Buchwald.

Buchwald did come up with one article, although it didn't stem directly from something Williams let slip. During an August 1972 lunch at the Sans Souci, a restaurant near the White House that was their favorite gathering spot for many years, Buchwald and Williams agreed that both ought to lose weight and that neither had the proper motivation. Then Williams suggested an incentive: "'Greed. Greed has been the motivating force in both our lives.' I couldn't argue with that," Buchwald later wrote. They decided to bet $100 a pound on who could lose the most weight by Thanksgiving, with the proceeds going to the winner's favorite charity, either Cardinal O'Boyle's Right to Life Committee if Williams won by losing, or the United Jewish Appeal if Buchwald emerged triumphant and thin.

As the months passed, the combatants taunted each other by sending cakes, pastries, and candies back and forth. Williams found that he couldn't stop eating, claiming he was "'under pressure,'" what with defending financier Louis Wolfson in New York and administering the Redskins (not to mention seeking to solve the Watergate puzzle). According to one of the contestants, Williams tried to call off the wager about halfway through. Buchwald, who had lost ten pounds while his foe had gained six, said nix. But then Buchwald made a fatal mistake: While introducing Williams to Israeli Ambassador Yitzhak Rabin, he revealed that "'Mr. Williams is going to buy Israel a new jet fighter plane.'" He suggested that Rabin should "'thank'" Williams "'personally.'" "'Now you've done it. You have humiliated me in front of the Israeli ambassador,'" said Williams. "'You have gotten me mad. I am going to get you if it's the last thing I do.'"

The big weigh-in was set for the day before Thanksgiving. Scores of people wanted to watch the ceremonies at the private Metropolitan Club, but only a select few were admitted. Buchwald, confident of victory, hired a violinist, who played "Hearts and Flowers" as Williams strode from the steam room to the scales, and "Let a Winner Lead the Way" as Buchwald made a dazzling entry. To Buchwald's horror, he had been overtaken in the stretch: Williams had shed twenty-one pounds (from 220 to 199), to Buchwald's sixteen (190 to 174). Making defeat even harder to bear, Buchwald's own violinist burst into a rendition of "Hail to the Redskins" to celebrate Williams's shocking triumph, which Buchwald termed "one of the great upsets in diet history." Buchwald claimed that Williams had lost about nineteen of his twenty-one pounds in fluid alone, and one friend said that if the weigh-in had been delayed fifteen minutes, Williams would have fainted.[38]

It was Buchwald, however, who had the last laugh. He sold an account of the battle, "An Absolutely Surefire Guaranteed Way to Lose Weight," to the *Saturday Evening Post,* which paid him $2,000. As soon as his check arrived, Buchwald recalls with great glee, he sent a copy of it over to Williams, along with a note: "'Thanks for the great idea for the magazine.'" Chortles Buchwald, "I netted $1,500. He was very pissed off." The $2,000 made up not only for his defeat, but for the staff of Cardinal O'Boyle's charity misspelling Buchwald's name when workers sent him a thank-you note for his $500 contribution.

Buchwald has other bones to pick with his chum. He holds Williams personally responsible for corrupting his children. "Our kids grew up sitting in Eddie's box" at Redskin games, says Buchwald. "They never knew what it was like to sit in the grandstand. It destroyed all our children, people bringing them hot dogs and hamburgers. It's a very bad start in life for any child. They never knew what it was like to be out in the grandstand with the common people."

The Buchwalds and Williamses also had a traditional Thanksgiving Day football game for many years, Hatfield vs. McCoy–style. One year Williams showed up with a ringer: Redskin quarterback Sonny Jurgensen. The way Buchwald remembers it, his side emerged the victor, because "Sonny and Eddie being on the same team, they canceled each other out. They both wanted to be quarterback." Buchwald adds, "It was the best Thanksgiving we ever had."

Ben Bradlee, the third member of the triumvirate, also speaks with great affection and humor about Williams. He remembers the time he was arrested in France in 1956 while working for *Newsweek,* and Williams, hearing the news, wired him, "'You needed me two days ago.'" Williams drew up Bradlee's will and represented him when Bradlee was accused of assaulting a fellow mourner at the funeral of a *Post* editor. Several years later, Williams bragged to Bradlee, "'I won that case for you.'" According to Bradlee, "He didn't do fuck-all for me. I think he made a call to the nut's lawyer" and nothing ever came of the case— which, of course, is often all Williams needs to do.

Very likely the ultimate proof of Williams's standing among the elite is Bradlee's comment, "I feel that if I get my ass in a sling, of whatever nature, I'd talk to him," echoed by Clark Clifford: "If I or my family needed legal help, I would turn to Ed Williams. If anything happened to me, I would want my wife to go to Ed." Also noteworthy is Henry Kissinger's attitude toward Williams, which he expressed to author Larry Leamer. Leamer included profiles of Williams, Kissinger, Bradlee, Katharine Graham, Ted Kennedy, Ralph Nader, Senate Democratic Leader Robert Byrd, and several others in a 1977 book, *Playing for Keeps in Washington.* Leamer recalls that while interviewing Kissinger, he mentioned some of the people who were subjects of his book, and Kissinger had a disparaging remark about every one but Williams. Williams himself enjoys describing how Kissinger used to call on him for advice when he was secretary of state. Kissinger would call Edward H. Levi, the attorney general in the Ford administration, and tell him, "'I'm sitting here with Edward Bennett Williams, and he says...' And Levi would say, 'You haven't committed murder, have you, Henry?' Nothing drove Levi more crazy. Henry always used to talk to me because he thought the lawyers at Justice were so bad."

Even Edward Bennett Williams's literary contacts qualify him as an insider's insider. In spite of his differences with her two husbands, Williams is friendly with Jacqueline Kennedy Onassis, currently a New York book editor. She has been after him for years to write his memoirs for her, and Williams has promised her that if he ever does produce his autobiography, she will have first crack at it.

During the 1975 trial of John Connally,* the following ex-change took place between U.S. District Judge George Hart, who presided over the case, and Edward Bennett Williams, at-torney for Connally, the Washington Post, *Warner Communications, and previously, for* Confidential *magazine.*

Williams: I wouldn't talk to these people [reporters], Judge. Tell you what I do. I found the best way not to have a problem is not to talk to them, not to take their calls.

Judge Hart: The one person I can't put any restriction on is Connally.

Williams: He hasn't talked to anybody. *I* put a restriction on him.

Judge Hart: These newspaper reporters . . . ever since *Sullivan versus New York Times*[†] . . . have got a license to lie.

Williams: That's right.[1]

3

The Champeen of the Free Press

Edward Bennett Williams's earliest in-depth dealings with the news media reflected a decidedly antipress position. During the early 1950s, he represented Senator Joseph McCarthy and a lawyer named Norman Littell in separate lawsuits against muckraking columnist Drew Pearson. Norman Littell was one of Williams's first prominent clients. He had been assistant attorney general from 1939 until 1944, when he opened his own Washington law practice. He had also been friendly with Pearson for several years, until on April 10, 1949, Pearson wrote: "The Justice Department is casting a quizzical eye on ex–Assistant Attorney General Norman Littell. They have reports that Littell is acting as a propagandist for the Dutch government, though he failed to register as a foreign agent."[2]

---

*Connally was charged with having illegally accepted a $10,000 gratuity for his role in helping raise milk price levels in 1971 when he was secretary of the Treasury. (See chapter 21.)

[†] In *New York Times Co.* v. *Sullivan,* 376 U.S. 254 (1964), the U.S. Supreme Court held that under the free-speech provision of the First Amendment, a public figure could not recover damages for libel unless malice was shown. *Malice* was defined as deliberate falsehood or reckless disregard for the truth.

Littell asserted that Pearson had made a "devastating statement" about him, that he had in effect said that Littell had committed a felony by not registering as a foreign agent. "If that statement was true, then I should have been in the penitentiary for up to ten years and subject to up to a $5,000 fine."[3] His response was to file a $300,000 libel suit against Pearson and the Bell Syndicate, which carried Pearson's column.[4]

Pearson claimed that he considered his item a "rather humorous" reference to "an old friend." According to Pearson, "I wrote it in that not unfriendly way. . . . If I had wanted to make it tough, I could have said truthfully that the FBI is investigating Mr. Norman Littell."[5] Williams, however, disputes Pearson's version of the flap: "He started the investigation by making a report, and then he wrote that Littell was being investigated. It was as though you went down to the local chief of police and said that I'd stolen your wallet and then wrote that I was being investigated for larceny. It was that simple." Littell brought suit against Pearson in July 1949.[6]

While the case was pending, Pearson added insult to injury. On May 21, 1950, he declared on his radio show and wrote in his column, both of which had national distribution, "There are some interesting pro-communist lobbies in Washington." Pearson called for "a full investigation of all subversives, all attorneys for communists, and of our national security, perhaps by a committee of prominent citizens." He suggested that his blue-ribbon panel should begin by taking a "look into the attorney for the communist Polish Embassy," who, according to Pearson, had helped thwart a probe into the escape of Gerhardt Eisler,[7] the "top Communist" in the U.S. Eisler had fled from New York aboard the Polish ship *Batory* two weeks earlier. He was said to be the head of a spy ring that was stealing atomic secrets and at the time of his flight was out of prison on $25,000 bail while appealing convictions for contempt of Congress and passport fraud.[8] In his May 21 broadcast, Pearson stated that, "unlike McCarthy [his archenemy], I believe in naming names." The "gentleman" who had helped Polish officials cover up Eisler's escape "is Norman Littell." Furthermore, Pearson linked "his [Littell's] activities" with a "government which does not believe in letting democracy live."[9]

On the strength of a recommendation by an "old friend," Nelson T. Hartson, Littell hired Williams as his lawyer at that point. Hartson was the senior partner in Hogan & Hartson, where Williams worked from 1944, when he graduated from Georgetown Law School, until 1949, when he went out on his own. Williams quickly filed a second suit against Pearson on behalf of Littell, who asked for another $300,000. Littell charged that Pearson had defamed him by publishing "false, scandalous . . . material" that "convey[ed] the impression to a wide audience that the plaintiff was and/or is a communist."[10]

Pearson was now the defendant in two defamation suits filed by Littell, each asking for $300,000. Six months passed without much action in either case. Then another attack, this time a physical one, was launched against Pearson by Joseph McCarthy. On December 12, 1950, Pearson and his wife attended a party at the Sulgrave Club in Washington. During the evening, McCarthy, who was also a guest, told Pearson that he was planning to deliver a speech on the Senate floor that would "put Pearson out of business." Pearson retorted, "'Joe, have you paid your income taxes yet?'" and McCarthy, a burly, much stronger man than Pearson, first challenged him to step outside,[11] and then, according to Pearson, approached the columnist from the rear while he was seated at the dinner table and "grasped . . . [Pearson's] neck in a painful and paralyzing manner." Later on, as Pearson was getting his coat at the end of the party, McCarthy, "without warning, without reason, cause or provocation . . . and with great violence" kneed Pearson in the groin, rendering him "immobile," and then started pummeling his head—according to the complaint in a suit Pearson filed.[12] The battle was broken up by Senator Richard M. Nixon, who later declared, "'I never saw a man slapped so hard. . . . If I hadn't pulled McCarthy away, he might have killed Pearson.'"[13]

About two dozen senators congratulated McCarthy,[14] and Arthur Watkins, the Republican senator from Utah who later presided over the censure hearing in which Williams defended McCarthy, said "he had heard two differing versions as to where Pearson was hit and was hoping both were accurate."[15] As *Time* magazine described the incident, "in their line, Pearson and McCarthy are the two biggest billygoats in the onion patch, and when they began butting, all present knew history was being made."[16] McCarthy himself was later quoted as saying he wasn't sure "'whether to kill Pearson or just maim him.'"[17]

The feud between Pearson and McCarthy dominated the Washington spotlight for the next few days. On December 13, the day after the fight, radio commentator Fulton Lewis, Jr., reported that McCarthy had hit Pearson so hard, he had lifted him "three feet off the ground."[18] The next day, Lewis told his audience that when Nixon had reached the scene, Pearson "was in a rather badly battered and most distraught condition, apparently on the verge of fainting, with his back against the wall, Senator McCarthy holding both of Pearson's hands against the wall."[19] On December 15, three days after the brawl, McCarthy fulfilled his promise to attack Pearson verbally. In his speech, a thirty-seven page mimeographed copy of which was distributed to the press, McCarthy called Pearson "'a smear columnist, a professional character assassin and the author of false and vile insinuations'"; "'a prostitute of the profession of journalism'"; "'this Moscow-directed character assassin'"; and "'an unprincipled, greedy, degenerate liar.'" McCarthy claimed that Pearson held an "'important place . . . in the Communist scheme of propaganda,'" and urged "'the American Public,'" as well as newspapers and advertisers, to boycott Pearson in order to "'see that this voice of international Communism is stilled.'"[20] McCarthy's speech was duly reported that night by Fulton Lewis,[21] and many other journalists.

Pearson, as could be expected, sued McCarthy. In his $5.1-million assault-defamation-antitrust-conspiracy case, Pearson also named as defendants Fulton Lewis; columnist Westbrook Pegler, who had written about the dispute; the *Washington Times Herald,* which had consistently sided with McCarthy in his feud with Pearson; McCarthy aide Don Surine; and several others. Pearson's theory was that after McCarthy had beaten him up, the senator and the others had conspired to destroy his reputation and put him out of business.[22]

McCarthy turned to John Sirica, a friend of his and of Williams, for help in selecting an attorney. As Sirica recalls it, McCarthy, forgetting that Sirica had introduced him to Williams at the 1948 Republican convention, asked, "'Did you ever hear of a kid lawyer* around town by the name of Edward Bennett Williams?'" Says Sirica, "I'll never forget that expression—'a kid lawyer.'" Sirica told the senator he knew Williams well, and "McCarthy said, 'What kind of lawyer is he?' I said, 'Fine lawyer. Works like hell. Very ambitious.' I told him everything nice I could think of. McCarthy said, 'I met him† and I'm kind of impressed with the guy. You say he's a good lawyer. I tell you what I'm going to do, I'm going to let him start on this case and see how he does.'"

The Pearson-McCarthy case was placed on a back burner while the two Littell suits against Pearson, which had been combined into one, proceeded. Although there is no evidence that Littell's suits and the McCarthy attack on Pearson were related, despite the fact that Williams represented both of Pearson's opponents, the columnist believed there was a connection. When Williams, taking Pearson's deposition in the Littell case, asked, "Did you know what Mr. Littell's general reputation was with respect to the subject of communism at the time you made this broadcast?" Pearson answered heatedly, "Well, I will tell you, Mr. Williams. Your other client has so muddied the water of this town it is very difficult to tell what the atmosphere regarding Communists and pro-Communists, and non-Communists is." Pearson added, "This town is, I regret to remind you, full of all sorts of rumors about people's connections, and you know why." On that note, Williams terminated the deposition.[24]

---

* Williams was then thirty, McCarthy forty-one.

† According to a version by William F. Buckley, Jr., who was fairly close to McCarthy, Williams, "a total stranger" to McCarthy, had "walked into" the senator's office one day and "volunteered to sue" Pearson "free of charge," as a means of winning "notoriety, which Williams clearly sought."[23] Buckley's account was wrong on virtually all major points: Williams did not seek out McCarthy as a client; Pearson sued McCarthy, not vice versa; and Williams charged McCarthy for his work on this case.

Pearson also swore in an affidavit in the Littell suit that he thought Williams had demanded a list of the newspapers in which his first column about Littell's Dutch activities appeared so that Williams could help McCarthy, not Littell. Pearson claimed that the list "would aid Senator McCarthy (and others) in his attempted boycott" of the newsman and would "enable McCarthy to continue his campaign of intimidation" against Pearson.[25] The columnist went so far as to assert that Williams had offered John Donovan, one of Pearson's lawyers, "a good job if he cooperated."[26] Williams says emphatically that there was no truth to Pearson's allegation.

Drew Pearson had been sued for libel many times, and had won every single case. As explained by Jack Anderson, who was Pearson's understudy and took over the "Washington Merry-Go-Round" column after his death, Pearson carried no libel insurance; if he had, he would have had to have his columns approved by his insurer. Instead, Pearson defended every libel suit all-out, and he was proud of his perfect record.

From the start of the Littell trial, however, Pearson was worried. He feared that U.S. District Judge Charles F. McLaughlin, who presided, was a "professional Catholic," and that Williams, a Catholic who taught at Georgetown Law School, "may have a sort of access to him."[27] (According to Jack Anderson, Pearson believed that he was the target of a "cabal" or "organized effort" of "the militant anti-Communist, right wing of the Catholic Church," mostly because Joseph McCarthy was also a Catholic.)

Pearson might have been more justified in fearing President Truman than Judge McLaughlin and a "Catholic cabal." HST disliked Pearson so much that he arranged for Littell to have access to the FBI file on the columnist. Littell inspected the FBI records and passed on their contents to Williams. The FBI reports helped Williams locate John Henshaw, a disgruntled former employee of Pearson's, who provided details of how Pearson had set up Littell.[28]

Henshaw was subpoenaed to testify for Littell at the trial, but he never showed up. Pearson's lawyers said they would stipulate to the testimony of the missing witness, but Williams declined their offer. Instead, he implied that Pearson was responsible for Henshaw's absence and asked Judge McLaughlin to issue a bench warrant for his arrest—in front of the jury. Outraged lawyers for Pearson objected to Williams's "highly prejudicial" behavior, but McLaughlin declined to grant a mistrial or to have Henshaw arrested.[29]

Williams was able to make use of the FBI report on Pearson; as Pearson's biographer, Oliver Pilat, wrote, "Littell had promised not to publicize the FBI file on Pearson, but Edward Bennett Williams considered it too precious to waste." Williams made a show of waving the FBI file in front of one of Pearson's key witnesses, "to jog the memory of the witness and discourage any attempt to conceal Pearson's trickery." (The file itself was not introduced as evidence.)[30]

After a two-week trial, the jury announced its verdict on May 15, 1953: Pearson had libeled Littell by writing that he was an unregistered agent for the Dutch government. Littell was awarded $50,000 compensatory damages and $1 punitive; he had sought $150,000 of each type.* In the case stemming from Pearson's comments about Littell's work for the Polish Embassy, the jury was unable to reach a verdict and a new trial was ordered.[32]

This was the first—and last—time that Drew Pearson lost a libel decision in court. And by Jack Anderson's count, he was sued hundreds of times for a total of more than $200 million in damages.[33] Williams's success drew acclaim from all sides. Norman Littell said thirty years later, "He had the elements of success in him. Hartson was right. And I was right in selecting him. He beat the pants off Drew Pearson." In addition, Pearson conceded that Williams had been "better" than his own attorneys,[34] and Warren Woods, one of Pearson's regular lawyers, who had opposed his choice of outside attorneys to try the case, said in 1981 that "Williams just destroyed them. He was so clearly better prepared, so much more capable of orchestrating jury response, that he just ran all over them."

The case also attracted interest from another direction: soon after the trial ended, two FBI agents called on Williams to ask how he had acquired the Bureau's files on Pearson. Williams says he told them the records had been provided by "'the president'"; the pair of G-men beat a hasty retreat, and "that was the end of the investigation."

Pearson appealed the verdict against him, but, meanwhile, attempts were made to reach a settlement. Pearson received incentive to settle after his lawyers learned from several jurors that the jury had been split 11–1 against him, so a retrial might result in a complete victory and a larger judgment for Littell.[35] At that point, Jiggs Donohue, a Washington political figure friendly with both Pearson and Williams, was dispatched by Pearson to negotiate with Williams. Donohue and Williams worked out the terms: Pearson would pay Littell $40,000 to settle the Dutch case; Littell would drop the Polish case; and Littell would stop sending threatening letters to newspapers that carried Pearson's column. Pearson was reluctant to pay Littell; he commented to Warren Woods, his lawyer, that "sometimes principle is damned important." To this Woods replied that "it was corny but true that principles were pretty expensive sometimes," and advised Pearson that appeals and a retrial would cost at least $40,000 even if Pearson prevailed.[36] The knowledge that any money he paid to

---

* The entire judgment was against Pearson; Littell had agreed to drop the Bell Syndicate as a defendant.[31]

Littell would be tax-deductible also helped convince Pearson to settle, according to Woods.[37] In the end, Pearson accepted the settlement (he had to mortgage his farm in Potomac, Maryland, in order to raise the $40,000),[38] and the cases were dropped.[39]

The ultimate irony of the victory that Williams won for Norman Littell was that the outcome would probably have been different if the dispute had occurred after the Supreme Court's 1964 decision in *New York Times Co.* v. *Sullivan.* Several jurors told one of Pearson's lawyers that they felt Pearson had shown no malice toward Littell,[40] and Warren Woods said shortly before his death in 1981, "In today's legal climate, summary judgment might have been obtained for Drew. After all, Littell was a public figure."

Nevertheless, Williams's abilities in the courtroom, combined with the law of the day, succeeded in placing the only blemish on Pearson's otherwise perfect record in defending libel suits.

Norman Littell's suits had been disposed of, but the case of Pearson against McCarthy was as yet unresolved. Pearson's lawyers were unfamiliar with Williams's methods when the case was filed in March of 1951, but they soon found out what they were up against. Warren Woods told Williams that he would make Pearson available for a deposition if Williams would agree to present McCarthy. Williams said he would talk to his client, "whom he referred to as 'Jumping Joe,'" and report back.[41] When Woods did not hear from Williams for several days, he decided to serve notice that he planned to take McCarthy's deposition. As a courtesy, he called Williams late one day to inform him that the notice was in the mail. The next morning, according to Pearson's lawyers, Williams "had a representative of his office . . . literally sit on the doorstep of the [Court] Clerk's office . . . waiting for the office to open in order to physically file his own notice before plaintiff's was filed."[42]

As Woods recalled, Williams attempted to have the depositions taken in private, but the court overruled him, and, to Williams's "discomfort," McCarthy was questioned in a "circus"-like atmosphere with the press present. During his interrogation, McCarthy called William A. Roberts, Woods's partner, who was questioning the senator, a "shyster." McCarthy also declared, "I am going to ask my counsel [Williams] . . . to get an order from the court ordering you to deport yourself like a lawyer, Mr. Roberts, or otherwise to find you in contempt."[43] Needless to say, no such order was granted, much less requested, but the McCarthy deposition was not very fruitful for the Pearson side, the senator having used the forum to claim that Pearson "is suing now because I had proven he had two men on his payroll who were members of the Communist party. Because I have exposed him as the mouthpiece of the Communist party."[44] However, the plaintiffs got in some licks of their own during the deposition of another

Williams client, McCarthy aide Donald Surine. One of Pearson's attorneys asked Surine, "Were the circumstances which resulted in your separation from the F.B.I. in any way connected with the alleged fact that you stayed with Doris Jo Perry at a hotel at Baltimore known as the Abbey Hotel?" Williams denounced that and similar questions to Surine as "designed simply to embarrass, humiliate and smear this witness."[45]

The case of *Pearson v. McCarthy et al* dragged on for several years, shedding more heat than light. Impetus to settle the suit was provided when the *Washington Post,* which published Pearson's column, purchased the *Times Herald,* one of the defendants, in March 1954. According to Woods, "In essence the *Post* told Drew, 'Let's get rid of this litigation, we own the *Times Herald* now,'" and, in 1955, Pearson and *Post* publisher Philip L. Graham signed a notice that the *Times Herald* was being dropped as a defendant.[46] About the same time, Pearson dismissed Westbrook Pegler from the suit;[47] Woods explained that "Drew and Pegler had about ten cases pending against each other around the country, and they agreed to drop them all." Finally, in early 1956, Pearson agreed to drop his case against McCarthy and all the other defendants.[48] By then, McCarthy had been censured by the Senate (see chapter 8), had faded from the national spotlight, and had but a year and a quarter to live.

Williams claims that resolution of the case was actually in favor of McCarthy. "There was no settlement," he declared. "No money was paid. Nothing was given to Pearson. I guess he decided it was an exercise in futility, he wasn't getting anywhere."

While it is true that no money changed hands between the parties to the suit, Pearson did receive some satisfaction. According to Woods, "McCarthy gave Drew a letter withdrawing his allegations before the Senate that Drew was a pipeline to Moscow and apologizing for having libeled him. However, Drew would never use that letter unless McCarthy returned to the attack against him."

That never happened, as McCarthy never repeated his allegations about Pearson. In fact, Pearson wrote in his diary on May 2, 1957, the day McCarthy died:

> Toward the end I couldn't help but feel sorry for him. He was a very lonesome guy. All the glamour that once surrounded him was gone. The newspaper men who had once hounded him wouldn't pay any attention to him any more. He used to carry press releases through the Capitol and try to hand them to newsmen. They were polite. They accepted the press releases but that was all.[49]

In his next media-related case, Williams turned up as attorney for *Confidential* magazine. *Confidential,* the *National Enquirer* of its day (the *Enquirer* itself retained Williams in 1981), was a bi-monthly that featured sex-oriented exposés of celebrities. With a circulation of 4 million per issue, by 1955, when Williams was hired to represent it, *Confidential* billed itself as having "the largest newsstand circulation of any magazine, anywhere and at any time."[50]

Confidential publisher Robert Harrison retained Williams after the post office issued an order on August 28, 1955, banning the November 1955 edition of the magazine from the mails. Williams, in turn, filed suit against Postmaster General Arthur J. Summerfield, seeking to nullify the Post Office ruling.[51] The case came on for a hearing on October 7, 1955, and Tom Wadden, Williams's law associate at the time, remembers vividly that Harrison had reservations about having hired Williams, who was thirty-five but looked much younger. Williams had told his client to meet him in the courtroom where the hearing was to be held. Harrison, who is said to have been somewhat eccentric, traveled from New York to Washington, found his way to the Federal Courthouse, and went to a courtroom. He waited a few minutes, but there was no sign of Williams. Wadden: "Harrison says, 'Goddammit, I hired this kid down here. And he's so young and wet behind the ears that he doesn't even know how to find the courtroom.' Of course, Harrison was in the wrong courtroom. That was typical of Bob's reaction to things."

Williams's argument was that the Post Office order was "radically unconstitutional," because it was issued after complaints from "anonymous informers," because the Post Office refused to state the nature of the complaints, and because no one from the Post Office had even seen the November issue before it was banned from the mails. In fact, he noted that the Post Office had actually lifted its prohibition on the November edition when it turned out that most copies of that issue had already been delivered before the August 28 edict was promulgated. Meanwhile, said Williams, the next edition, dated January 1956, was "rolling on the presses," and Harrison had already invested $300,000 in printing costs. "The threat of cancellation hovers like a specter over this plaintiff," who faced "corporate execution" and "complete financial destruction" if denied the use of the mails. "The First Amendment guarantees one thing minimally, and that is freedom from previous restraint, freedom from prior censorship."[52]

After hearing arguments from both sides, U.S. District Judge Luther W. Youngdahl handed down a ruling that was generally favorable to *Confidential*. It provided that the August 28 order of the Post Office be revoked; that *Confidential* furnish postal authorities with two copies of each edition within twenty-four hours after the first copies were printed and bound, and if the Post Office considered any issue nonmailable, an administrative hearing would be held before the magazine was denied access to the mails. The case was then dismissed.[53]

Harrison immediately submitted copies of the January 1956 issue to the Post Office, which approved it for mailing,[54] even though the cover promoted stories like "Gary Cooper's Lost Week-End With Anita Ekberg"; "The Lowdown On Kim Novak"; and "Surgery's *Newest* Bust Miracle."[55] Handling that issue must have been galling for some postal executives, because of an article titled "How 'Special' Is That Special Delivery Stamp?" which called special delivery "a $5 million-a-year flimflam," reported that "half of our special delivery letters are brought by the regular postmen," charged that "a private business that made these flat promises and took money for them would be in hot water with the law as fast as you could say, 'FBI,'" and suggested that "maybe the Post Office Department ought to investigate itself."[56]

Harrison had scarcely offered the March issue for perusal by the Post Office when William C. O'Brien, the Department's "Assistant Solicitor, Fraud and Mailability Division," swore out an affidavit to support a motion for an injunction declaring the latest edition of *Confidential* "nonmailable." O'Brien deemed the March issue "obscene, lewd, lascivious, indecent . . . [and] filthy." Among the items that O'Brien found particularly objectionable were:

—"'NUDE BODY FOUND in the Apartment of Will Rogers' Daughter! Will Rogers never met a man he didn't like, so it's a blessing he passed on before meeting some of his daughter's playmates, especially the one whose naked corpse was found in her apartment.'"

—"'s-H-H! Have you Heard the Latest About Sammy Davis Jr.? What is it Sammy's got that the girls go for? Ask that sexy redhead from "Phenix City"—or read it here!'"

—"'*Caught* . . . Guy Madison in Barbara Payton's Boudoir! . . . Guy Madison knew he shouldn't have been with Barbara Payton wearing only socks when Franchot Tone walked in. . . .'"

—"'Named . . . the Cutie Who Split Up the John Dereks!'"[57] (The "Cutie" was "19-year-old starlet Ursula Andress,"[58] who married Derek, but later was replaced by a continuing succession of Derek wives, including Bo.)

A banner headline on the March 1956 cover read, "DON'T BUY THOSE NEW ABORTION PILLS." According to the Post Office, that story also made the magazine unfit for mailing under a law that prohibited from the mails "every paper, writing, advertisement, or representation that any . . . drug, medicine, or thing may, or can, be used or applied for producing abortion."[59] The March issue became "Exhibit A" in a new attempt to ban *Confidential* from the mail.

When the two sides returned to court for a hearing on January 4, 1956, Williams was, as usual, prepared with a variety of well-planned tactics. Citing the landmark First Amendment case of *Near* v. *Minnesota*, 283 U.S. 697 (1931), as precedent for his proposition that "the appropriate remedial action is not injunction, but it is subsequent punishment," Williams offered to let the government take Harrison before a grand jury and indict him for publishing obscene material. "I will go with him to the grand jury room and I will testify from first-hand knowledge that a copy of such magazine has come into the District of Columbia," thereby giving prosecutors jurisdiction in the case, Williams declared.[60] His invitation, of course, was not accepted, but Williams recalled in 1981 that Harrison went "into a nervous prostration" over the prospect of indictment. "But I didn't think they had the courage to do that, because they couldn't have made a case."

As to the abortion issue, Williams pointed out that the story in question described the horrors of the new medication Aminopterin, which *Confidential* said, in Williams's words, "is a leukemic drug [that] will cause death to the mother and malformation and idiocy of the unborn child." The idea that such an article "will cause people to go out and buy Aminopterin to abort themselves . . . just is utterly fantastic," Williams told the court.[61]

Turning to the question of obscenity, Williams said the magazine was not obscene, although it might not conform with his tastes, or the judge's tastes, or the tastes of the government lawyers. *Confidential* might be "coarse" or "vulgar" or "racy." "Maybe this isn't the kind of diet that we live off intellectually. Maybe we don't use it or approve of it, but God forbid that [the government attorneys] or I become the censor of literature in the United States, because the day that comes, the First Amendment will be relegated into the graveyard of oblivion."[62] And if you think *Confidential* is obscene, said Williams, just wait until you see what "I have here." Whereupon he whipped out a bagful of "periodicals that went through the mails in the last 60 days that I think are obscene because they have undressed women and suggestive poses and that are calculated to arouse, maybe in youngsters, libidinous, lustful thoughts." For the benefit of Federal Judge Joseph C. McGarraghy, who had taken over the case, Williams added, "There is a whole bag of this, Your Honor, and I shall be glad to submit them for your consideration . . . to show you what goes through the mails, to which Mr. O'Brien is wholly insensitive."[63] (Williams now says he would refuse, if asked, to defend the right of magazines like *Hustler* to be published or to use the mails. "I really find that *Hustler* kind of stuff so offensive personally to me that I don't think I would . . . I mean, I would say to them, 'Look, you're right, you have a great constitutional point, you shouldn't be restrained, but please get somebody else.' There are more important things to do than to help pornography go through the mails," said Williams, adding that he feels he has "much more leeway" in rejecting clients in civil cases than he does in criminal proceedings; he insists on taking on any criminal defendant who will give him complete control of a case, who is truthful with him, and who can afford him.)

Williams's most telling point of all may have been the one that was related to the ineptitude of the government attorneys. As so often happened when lawyers on the public payroll went up against Williams, the government attorneys were overmatched. As Williams astutely told Judge McGarraghy, the Post Office, instead of filing a new suit, had tried to ban *Confidential* under a case that had been dismissed three months earlier by Judge Youngdahl! Williams told the court, "Your Honor, . . . I must call your attention to the fact that . . . it is basic hornbook law that one cannot use as a vehicle for obtaining injunctive relief a case that has been dismissed from the dockets of the Court."[64]

Faced with such arguments, there was little the government could do but give up as gracefully as possible. The suit was dropped, and *Confidential* used the mails without additional problems.[65]

[Epilogue: In 1958, two years after Williams had upheld *Confidential's* access to the mails, Robert Harrison approached a fellow scandalmonger with an idea for a new venture. Harrison, by then no longer *Confidential's* publisher, suggested to Williams's old antagonist, Drew Pearson, that they collaborate in producing a publication to be known as "'Drew Pearson's News Beat,'" which would be "devoted to cleaning up corruption, rather than cleaning up sex," as Pearson described it. Pearson said he was "sorely tempted" by the proposal, but he turned it down, because "it would ruin me to be associated with Harrison."[66]]

The ultimate tragedy of Phil Graham was that he seemed to have everything—all the elements for success and happiness: brains, charm, a devoted wife and four children, wealth and power. Graham's power was derived from his marriage to Katharine Meyer on June 5, 1940, six weeks before he turned twenty-five.[67] Almost seven years earlier to the day, on June 1, 1933, the bankrupt *Washington Post* had been sold in an auction held on the front steps of the newspaper to Eugene Meyer, the father of Katharine Meyer Graham. The price was $825,000; among those who were outbid was Evalyn Walsh McLean, whose husband, Ned McLean, had run the paper to ruin during the seventeen years since the death of his own father, John R. McLean. (Ironically, Ned McLean had obtained control of the paper by claiming that his father was not of sound mind when he drew up a will that left his estate in trust and froze out Ned.) Bidding for Mrs. McLean at the auction was her attorney, Nelson T. Hartson; she bowed out when the price went over $600,000.[68]

During the late 1930s and early 1940s, Phil Graham, his close friend Ed Prichard from Harvard Law School, and Joe Rauh were all law clerks to Supreme Court Justice Felix Frankfurter. Graham and Rauh went on to work together as bright young lawyers in FDR's Lend-Lease program, and Rauh remembers Graham and Prichard as "the two most promising men in Washington" of that era, "the two most brilliant, the two most likely to succeed." Contemplating the fact that, like Graham, Prichard fell so far—a ballot-box-stuffing scandal in his home state, Kentucky, destroyed his political career—Rauh comments, "It's so telling, how fragile life is."

In 1946, President Truman appointed Eugene Meyer first president of the new World Bank, and Meyer named Phil Graham to succeed him as publisher of the *Post*. Two years later, Meyer gave Phil Graham effective control of the paper by turning over all the voting stock to the Grahams—3,500 shares to Phil Graham, and only 1,500 shares to Meyer's own daughter, Katharine. Meyer's explanation: "'You never want a man working for his wife.'"[69]

During the next fifteen years, Philip Graham became a true power-broker. One of his best friends was Lyndon Johnson, and when Johnson was Senate majority leader and about to be nominated for vice president, Graham had his power of attorney. (Johnson had so much confidence in Graham that he let the publisher select and buy a new house for him.) Recognizing at the 1960 Democratic convention that LBJ could not win the presidential nomination, Graham switched to John F. Kennedy, then persuaded Kennedy and Johnson to share the same ticket, in spite of their mutual dislike. In the words of David Halberstam in *The Powers That Be,* Graham was "the kingmaker, he had helped broker the convention."[70]

Philip Graham and Edward Bennett Williams had become close friends in the late 1950s. They had much in common: Both were relatively young and on the rise in Washington. But about the time their friendship started, Graham began showing signs of severe mental illness. There would be periods when his behavior was entirely normal, and others when he took to his bed, or threw himself into bursts of manic activity, or gave bizarre orders to his aides.[71] During the six or seven years when he was ill, Graham came to rely on two people who were archenemies: Joe Rauh and Ed Williams. Rauh recalls that Graham would phone him and talk for hours, rambling on and on, and often making anti-Semitic remarks about the Meyer family (Graham at such times was apparently ashamed that his success was the result of his marrying the daughter of a Jew)—ignoring the fact that, as Graham knew, Rauh is Jewish. On other occasions, Williams would be the one whom Graham would call; the two would meet for endless lunches in out-of-the-way restaurants where no one would recognize them, and Graham would pour out his thoughts for hours on end.

Finally, in late December 1962, Phil Graham suffered "a severe nervous breakdown," leading to his being confined at Chestnut Lodge in Rockville, Maryland, from January 20 to 31, 1963.[72] Shortly before or after that episode, he went to Europe. While abroad, he visited the Paris office of *Newsweek,* which he had bought for the Post Company two years earlier. Robin Webb, a young Australian woman who worked for *Newsweek* in Paris, caught Graham's eye, and before long she was his mistress, globe-hopping with him and living with him in a Washington mansion he rented for $800 a month.

Graham took to telling almost anyone who would listen that he was going to divorce his wife, marry Robin Webb, and still retain control of the *Post* empire. He instructed Williams to handle his legal affairs, work out his divorce,* and draft a new will in place of his 1957 will, which left half of his estate to his wife—including enough Post Company voting stock to give her control—and the other half in trust for his children.[74] Instead of following Graham's orders, Williams tried to stall him, at least until he was lucid. "I told him not to make a will and urged him to make no changes until things settled down," says Williams. "I thought it was in his interest that I do everything I could during his period of aberration to influence him to go back to his family."

One day in February 1963, Graham barged into Williams's office looking for him, but Williams was out. Graham then insisted on seeing one of Williams's partners, Harold Ungar, and directed him to draw up a new will leaving a substantial part of his estate to Webb. "He came in and insisted on drawing a will—right then and there, and I yielded to his urgings," says Ungar, who had never met Graham until that moment and was not experienced in drafting wills. Ungar is still half-afraid that he was so inexperienced that any will he wrote might have resulted in the government taking most of the estate.

By now it was obvious to Williams that he could not put off Graham any longer, and on February 18, 1963, Williams drew up a will for Graham that revoked all previous wills, left two-thirds of his estate in trust for his children, and gave the other one-third to Robin Webb.[75] At the same time, Williams wrote a memorandum for his files in which he said that he had "grave questions about his [Graham's] competency to do the things that he was purporting to do, and that the reason why I was doing it was to retain his confidence as a friend so that I could continue to be with him and continue to exercise influence over his conduct." Williams says he considered refusing Graham's request and telling him that he was insane and could not make a new will in his condition. But, he adds, that "would have destroyed our relationship. And it would have destroyed him. What I was doing was trying to help him. It was clear to me that he was in the highest state of mania and that, therefore, following the state of mania, he would go into the deepest state of depression," and might commit suicide.

Scarcely a month after Williams drafted a will for him, Graham, in front of Williams and other lawyers from his firm, tore up that will and executed another one. The new will, dated March 22, 1963, reduced the

* If Williams had proceeded with a divorce, he would have been pitted against his friend Clark Clifford, who was Katharine Graham's attorney.[73]

amount he left in trust for his children to one-third of his estate, and left the rest to Robin Webb. Once again, as with the February will, Katharine Graham was not mentioned.[76] (Under District of Columbia law, she would have been entitled to claim one-third of her husband's estate, whether he left her anything or not.)

As the spring of 1963 wore on, Phil Graham grew worse and worse. During one telephone conversation with his old friend President Kennedy, he started talking high-handedly. When Kennedy objected, Graham asked imperiously, "'Do you know who you're talking to?'" The president answered, "'I know I'm not talking to the Phil Graham I have so much admiration for.'"[77] Williams finally decided that enough was enough. He knew better than to try to discourage Graham from his relationship with Webb. "It would have been an exercise in futility. He wouldn't have heeded it. He was in love with her. At least he thought he was in love with her." But Williams was able to persuade Graham that he should return to Chestnut Lodge. At Williams's suggestion, Graham reentered the Lodge on June 20, 1963.[78] At roughly the same time and also on the advice of Williams, the March 22 will was destroyed, in the presence of Williams and other witnesses.[79] "What I wanted to do," Williams explains, "was to get him back where he was, testamentary-wise. And do it during a period of lucidity. My position was that the new wills were nullities and the old will was still operative."

To Williams also fell the task of informing Robin Webb that the affair was "over. I told her to go home to Australia. She did. Incidentally, I'll tell you this about Robin Webb. Robin Webb, as far as I could observe, was never an instigator of those wills. She wasn't pushing him to do anything. The best proof of that is that she never once came in and made any claims. If you accept the fact that she was carrying on a meretricious relationship with a married man, then otherwise she comported herself in ladylike fashion."

Phil Graham was at Chestnut Lodge from June 20 until August 3, 1963.[80] On Saturday, August 3, he convinced his wife and the staff at the Lodge that he was better, and he was released to spend the weekend at the Graham country estate in Virginia. Graham told his wife he wanted to see Joe Rauh, and she called Rauh and arranged for him to visit Graham on August 6. "In retrospect, it shows how brilliant he was," comments Rauh. "He fooled the doctors, he fooled everyone." Soon after he arrived at his estate outside of Washington on August 3, Phil Graham took a gun and killed himself.[81]

He left an estate valued at $5.3 million, of which $3 million consisted of 7,889 shares (after stock splits) of voting stock in the Post Company—enough for controlling interest. He also left his business affairs in a tangled mess. By his will of September 18, 1957, and a codicil of June 5, 1961, he had left control of the Post Company to Katharine Graham and the rest of his estate to her and their four children, the eldest of whom was twenty when he died.[82] However, the wills of February and March 1963, under which Phil Graham expressed his wish to leave the bulk of his estate to Robin Webb, contained a standard clause revoking all previous wills. The two 1963 wills had been destroyed. But if either of them had ever taken effect before Graham tore them up, his previous will would have been revoked, and he would have died intestate, or with no will. And under the terms of a trust agreement dated August 3, 1948, at the time Eugene Meyer turned over control of the Post Company to Philip and Katharine Graham, Philip Graham's voting stock in the company would pass immediately to his children if he died without a will; Katharine Graham would receive none of the voting stock.[83] At best, Mrs. Graham would have had to share control of the company with the administrators of the trusts that had been set up for her children.

The immediate problem after Graham's death was the 1963 wills. An attorney named James F. Reilly was appointed guardian of the Graham children's interests. Speaking as "a close friend of the decedent, as well as his attorney," Williams reported to Reilly that "at the time of execution" of the 1963 wills "he had doubts as to the testator's mental capacity, but that he considered it therapeutically and psychologically beneficial to Mr. Graham that the instruments as prepared be formally executed."[84]

Based largely on the information provided by Williams, Reilly said there was "a serious question" about Graham's "mental capacity" to revoke his 1957 will in 1963 because of his "possible incompetence."[85] Reilly recommended to the probate court that a compromise be accepted between the interests of Katharine Graham and those of her children. The compromise specified that Reilly, as guardian for the children, would not raise the possible effect of the 1963 wills, leaving them as if they had never existed; Katharine Graham would renounce her claim to income for life from a trust that was established by the 1957 will; the 1957 will and 1961 codicil would dispose of Phil Graham's estate (except for the interest Katharine Graham gave up); and the value of the Graham children's trusts would be increased immediately from $500,000 to $1.4 million. The net effect was that in exchange for giving her children income she otherwise would have received, Katharine Graham acquired enough voting shares in the Post Company to give her immediate control of the company.[86]

Theodore Cogswell, registrar of wills for the District of Columbia, joined in Reilly's recommendation,[87] and on October 18, 1963, Judge Joseph C. McGarraghy of U.S. District Court approved the plan.[88] The *Washington Post, Newsweek,* and several television and radio stations were firmly in the hands of Katharine Meyer Graham.

[Epilogue: During the marital difficulties between Philip and Katharine Graham, their crowd was divided into two camps: "Phil People" and

"Kay People." In Mrs. Graham's mind, both Edward Bennett Williams and Ben Bradlee were "Phil People." In fact, as far as she was concerned, Williams was "a Mephistophelian figure, a member of the Red team, trying to steal the paper from her and her children." And Bradlee was "one of the worst offenders"; he had invited Phil Graham and Robin Webb to his house, thereby giving his approval to their relationship, and had supposedly said that "there was nothing wrong with Phil Graham that a quick divorce would not cure."[89] Williams says he thinks Kay Graham understood that "I was always on her side" after "I called and said, 'I have Phil back and I've sent Robin Webb back to Australia.'" He adds, "I was always on the side of the family. Because I thought that was Phil's side. I thought it was to Phil's interest *not* to cast aside his wife and children. I believed that he loved his wife and children and that he belonged with them." Soon after her husband's death, Mrs. Graham became a good friend of both Williams and Bradlee. Two years later, she named Bradlee editor of the *Post*. And then, in Bradlee's words, "I got him to be the *Post*'s lawyer." Bradlee says he recommended to Mrs. Graham, who had come to admire Williams, and to one of her advisers that the company retain Williams. "And it was done." As simple as that. Eventually, after Joe Califano joined Williams's firm in 1971, Williams took over most of the *Post*'s law business.]

The first time Ben Bradlee asked Ed Williams to give the *Post* legal advice turned out to be one of the most important. In 1971, the *New York Times* obtained a copy of the "Pentagon Papers"—containing revelations about the Vietnam War—and published excerpts. Subsequently, the Nixon administration won an injunction that prohibited the *Times* from printing additional stories, pending appeal. Then the *Post* acquired its own copy of the "Papers." Williams was not yet the newspaper's lawyer, and the *Post*'s attorneys seemed to Bradlee to be too cautious about approving publication. Bradlee, so committed to printing the story that he had decided to resign if he was overruled,[90] traced Williams to Chicago, where he was trying a case. When Williams got the message that Bradlee was trying to reach him, he was on his way to the airport in a limousine. He phoned Bradlee from the car, and, as Bradlee remembers, "He said, 'You gotta publish it.' And he wasn't up to his ass in legal precedents, either. It was his guts and his instincts, which is what I value more than anything about him." Williams's advice was all Bradlee needed to persuade others that his course was correct; the *Post* printed the story.

A couple of years later, Williams went to bat for *Post* columnist Maxine Cheshire, who was involved in a dispute with Frank Sinatra. Cheshire seemed to rub the folks in Sinatra's crowd a certain way. In May 1968, Sinatra, Washington fixer Irv Davidson, and several others gathered at the home of Drew Pearson to discuss ways of denying the Democratic presidential nomination to Robert F. Kennedy. Also on hand were Allen Dorfman, a reputed mobster who was attempting to get Kennedy's enemy, Jimmy Hoffa, out of prison; and Cheshire, who was looking for a story. When Cheshire asked Dorfman what he was up to on behalf of Hoffa, Dorfman retorted, "'Baby, I'm here to buy anyone who can be bought. Are you for sale?'"[91]

Five years later, at the second Nixon inaugural, Sinatra was one of the big-name entertainers, and he ran into Cheshire at a Republican celebration at the Jockey Club. Spotting Cheshire, Sinatra, without warning, started berating her: "'Get away from me. You scum, go home and take a bath. Print that, Miss Cheshire. . . . You're nothing but a $2 broad, you know that . . . you're a - - - -. That's spelled - - - -.'" (According to *Post* reporter Sally Quinn—who later married Bradlee—Sinatra "spelled out a four-letter expletive referring to a woman.") He continued attacking Cheshire: "'You do know what that means, don't you.'" Then Sinatra stuffed two one-dollar bills into Cheshire's empty glass and shouted, "'Here's $2, baby. That's what you're used to.'"

A number of people heard Sinatra,[92] and Cheshire seriously considered suing him for defamation. According to Cheshire, Williams (who had previously represented Sinatra on occasion) told Bradlee he'd sue Sinatra for free. "I gather that to know Sinatra is not necessarily to love him," Cheshire said in reference to Williams's offer. Shortly before she left the *Post* in 1981, she recalled that in her presence and Bradlee's, Williams phoned Mickey Rudin, Sinatra's lawyer, and said, "'Mickey, old boy, Little Boy Blue has blown his horn once too often.' I definitely got the feeling" that Williams disliked Sinatra and relished the idea of filing suit against him.* After further consideration, Cheshire decided not to take Sinatra to court. "I began to feel like a chorus girl suing for breach of promise; my virtue would be at issue." The suit never was filed, and Williams says that he and Sinatra are still on good terms.

On at least one occasion when *Post* executives failed to solicit Williams's opinion, disaster ensued. In 1980, the paper published "Jimmy's World," an account of an eight-year-old heroin addict. The sensational article, in which Janet Cooke of the *Post* reported that she had watched a twenty-seven-year-old addict inject heroin into "Jimmy's" veins, won a 1981 Pulitzer Prize for Cooke and the paper. A few days later, Cooke admitted that the story was false and resigned in disgrace; the *Post* declined the Pulitzer.

Immediately after the story appeared in September 1980, Washington officials questioned its validity, and Cooke's files were stored in a safe at Williams's firm to prevent them from being seized. Williams, however,

---

* According to Williams, neither Cheshire nor Bradlee was present when he called Rudin; the conversation did not take place as Cheshire reports it, and he would not have sued Sinatra for free. In the unlikely event the case had proceeded, the *Post* would have paid him.

was never asked for advice until the scandal broke. He understood why no one from the *Post* had talked to him earlier: Since "Jimmy" was a pseudonym and no real names were published, there was no potential libel problem. And *Post* executives have never asked his advice on matters that were strictly journalistic, as opposed to legal—whether it be to name Bradlee editor, or to give his opinion of the news merits of a particular story.

Still, Williams had his doubts from the first about "Jimmy's World." He spoke not only as someone who had defended hundreds of people accused of crimes, but as one who had served on drug task forces and created controversy by recommending that heroin addicts be given legal doses of the drug in order to deter them from crime. (At the same time, he has opposed the legalization of marijuana.) Commenting on the Cooke fiasco immediately after it made the front pages, Williams said, "I know the criminal mind. That story was so out of character and so bizarre that it had red flags all over it to me. Indeed, I assumed when I first saw that thing in print that they intended it to be received as a composite of reality. The adult . . . [wouldn't have shot up the child] in front of a reporter unless he was crazed." Having neglected to discuss the matter with Williams in advance of publication, the *Post* paid a heavy price.

In spite of his incomparable connections at the *Post*,* Williams has often been unhappy about the paper's coverage of some stories involving him. He blames the *Post* for reporting that he was seeking "special consideration" (which he says he wasn't) when he asked a local board to allow him to hook up to a public sewer line after he bought land for a home in Potomac, Maryland, in the early 1970s and found out the land was unsuitable for a septic tank. Several *Post* sports stories have upset Williams, particularly one after he purchased the Baltimore Orioles in 1979, in which the paper reported that he was telling the Baltimore public that he planned to keep the team there and telling people in Washington that he was going to move it to the nation's capital. Williams groused to his chum Bradlee that "we single-handedly deprived the capital of the free world of a baseball team." Adds Bradlee, "The story was absolutely true, but he didn't like it."

Bradlee does feel that the paper's coverage of Williams's handling of the estate of Washington Redskin founder George Preston Marshall (see chapter 4) has been "very tough, tougher than it should be," with *Post* reporters eager to see that "Bradlee's pal doesn't get a free ride." Bradlee: "I don't happen to think that he's a thief. And I think some of the reporters here go at it as if it was Watergate II." In general, Bradlee disqualifies himself from intervening in stories about Williams, realizing that "if I

---

* As another link between Williams and the paper, David Povich, the son of *Post* sports columnist Shirley Povich, has been a member of Williams's firm for about twenty years.

tried to do something for Williams, there'd be a revolt" in the newsroom. He did break up a "pissing match" between his sports editor, George Solomon, and Williams, who was yelling at Solomon, "'The *Washington Post* never gave me a break!'" Still, Bradlee and Williams have to treat each other with caution; Bradlee must regard Williams as a leading newsmaker in his paper's town, while Williams is always aware that at the *Post* "they print everything. If they know it, they print it. If I don't want to see something in print, I don't tell Ben, 'cause whatever I tell him, if I told him something in the most confidential way, I guarantee you it would be in print," says Williams.

The encounter between Williams and George Solomon was one of Williams's milder bouts with the media. One of his first flaps occurred about 1960, when the critic John Crosby appeared on "Mike Wallace Interviews" on a New York television station and suggested that Williams might be "immoral" because some of his clients were not to Crosby's liking. Williams, who later wrote that Crosby had "slandered me," [93] hired Theodore Kiendl, an attorney he befriended when they were on opposite sides of a case involving Joseph McCarthy, and demanded a retraction and damages from Wallace and his station.

According to Wallace, he mentioned the affair to Louis Nizer, who said, "'Mike, forget it. Ed's a good guy. I'll talk to him. You don't have to worry about it.'" But Nizer came back to Wallace and said that Williams was adamant and was going to sue. Morris Ernst volunteered to approach Williams on Wallace's behalf, but with the same results. Wallace learned that Williams would consider $1,000 enough to soothe his feelings and to "teach us a lesson," and Wallace, deciding that "discretion was the better part of valor," paid the sum to Williams in order to avoid a suit. Shortly afterward, Wallace ran into Williams at Toots Shor's. Williams reached out to shake hands, but Wallace just kept on walking. About fifteen years passed before Wallace could bring himself to speak to Williams, which he did after they met at a party in New York, but Wallace is still miffed that he paid Williams the $1,000.

Just about the time Williams and Wallace started speaking again, Williams got embroiled in a bitter dispute with Jack Anderson and his top reporter, Les Whitten. During the Watergate-related case of Armand Hammer, someone stole a report about the suit from the files of one of Hammer's lawyers and gave it to Whitten. Among Hammer's attorneys were Williams and Nizer. Whitten called Nizer for comment, and, says Whitten, Nizer was "very unhappy, he said he wished we wouldn't use it, that he thought it wasn't right. But he didn't lose his cool. *Nizer* believes in the First Amendment."

Whitten next phoned Williams, who was "very abusive. He was cursing and I lost my temper." Phrases like "chickenshit column" and "chickenshit lawyer" flew back and forth. Williams told Whitten that "if it was the last thing he did, he would have us kicked out of the *Washington Post*." The argument grew so loud that another reporter came in from the next office to listen to Whitten's end. Afterward, Whitten "often" thought that "maybe he got me to blow my stack so he could show malice. He's a pretty cool customer. Because if he had been tape-recording the things I said to him and had played it in front of a jury, he could sure as hell have shown malice on my part."

Whitten and Anderson discussed the situation and decided not to print the item. Whitten explains that the information in the report was not that interesting, and "we just would have been printing the thing to show what hotshots we were to have gotten the thing." Anderson insists that "I'm not afraid of Williams," and says that several lawyers offered to defend him and Whitten for free. But he says that he and Whitten agreed that the Hammer story was "marginal" and not worth the risk of a suit. The fact remains that Williams spoke very forcefully to Whitten—and the story was never printed. Williams himself says, "I told them that I would hold them accountable if they published a memorandum that they stole," but he denies threatening Anderson "or anybody else" that "I'd get 'em thrown out of the *Washington Post*. I couldn't get anybody thrown out of the *Washington Post*. So I wouldn't have told anyone I could get them thrown out of the *Washington Post*."

Williams and Anderson squared off again several years later, after Anderson sent out a column saying that fugitive financier Robert Vesco, Williams's onetime client, had offered to pay $10 million to a group of Georgians with links to White House Chief of Staff Hamilton Jordan in the hope of pressuring federal authorities to drop a variety of charges against Vesco. In spite of his dislike for Jordan's boss, Jimmy Carter, Williams agreed, at Robert Strauss's request, to take on Jordan as a client. Williams allegedly visited the *Post* to ask that changes be made in the column before it was printed (which Williams denies). At any rate, the column was amended before it was published. Williams says the Anderson story was "totally false" as it referred to Jordan, who seriously considered suing over the version that finally did appear in print, but decided a suit would be too time-consuming. According to a reliable source, Vesco was "miffed" that Williams called him and told him not to talk to Anderson; Vesco's opinion was that his own interests were hurt by Williams's representation of Jordan. He told at least one investigator, "'I'll give you Edward Bennett Williams,'" but nothing ever came of his offer to provide information that was allegedly damaging toward Williams. Whether because of this incident or not, Williams and Vesco are no longer attorney and client, nor are they on cordial terms. Nevertheless, Williams's intervention on behalf of Jordan paid off; in 1981, Anderson wrote several more columns about Vesco's overtures to the White House, and Hamilton Jordan was not mentioned in any of them.

Another journalist who attracted Williams's wrath was Laurence Leamer, whose 1977 book *Playing for Keeps in Washington,* contained a chapter on Williams. Leamer wrote that Williams "told his friends that he was leaving the [Catholic] Church."[94] Leamer's story enraged Williams, who belongs to the Knights of Malta, one of the highest honors a layman can attain in the Church. "I was so upset about that stuff that he wrote," says Williams, "that for fleeting moments I contemplated suing him for libel. Then I realized that all I'd do is increase his readership by tenfold, from two thousand reading it to maybe twenty thousand would read it." It was late one evening that Williams saw what Leamer had written. At eight o'clock the next morning, he phoned the writer at home and shouted at him, "'You little shit. You're not going to make one damned cent from this book.'" Leamer: "It was like Dr. Spock telling you you have V.D." Leamer was intent on at least making a good impression during the call from Williams. After Williams hung up, Leamer asked his wife, "'How did I sound?'" "'I don't know,'" she answered, "'you didn't say a word.'" Leamer had interviewed Williams several times, and Williams had even suggested that they collaborate on his memoirs. But during what Leamer terms Williams's "incredibly profane" tirade, he made a point of addressing Leamer (who pronounces his name "Lamer") as "Leemer."

Morton Mintz of the *Washington Post* had a similar experience. In 1963, Mintz covered the Baltimore trial of several men implicated in a savings-and-loan scandal, including two former congressmen—Frank W. Boykin (D-Ala. [Williams's client]) and Thomas F. Johnson (D-Md.). Previously, Mintz had tracked to Florida and interviewed a key witness in the case, a man named Louis Goldman. While Williams was examining Goldman in the courtroom, he kept asking the witness about comments attributed to him in Mintz's story and repeatedly referred to Mintz as "Meentz." Finally, during a recess, Mintz approached Williams and voiced his objections: "'I don't call you "Weeliams," so why do you pronounce my name as "Meentz"?'" Williams regarded Mintz with a look of "utter contempt and disdain" and said nothing. A year or so later, Mintz ran into Williams at a party at the British Embassy and tried to be cordial, but Williams ignored him.

Like Morton Mintz, Fred Graham had produced stories during his many years with the *New York Times* and CBS that Williams apparently had objected to. But Graham was still completely unprepared for the fury in Williams's attack on him. October 31, 1977, was John Sirica's last day as a regular U.S. district judge, before he retired to senior-judge status. Because of Sirica's prominence in Watergate, Graham was at the Federal Courthouse in Washington that day to interview Sirica for CBS. As Graham waited outside the building, he was "dumbfounded" to see former

CIA director Richard Helms and a lawyer from Williams's office enter the courthouse. Rumors had been flying that Helms and Williams were plea-bargaining with the Justice Department, but "never before" had a figure in such an important case appeared in court without the press being notified, at least not in Graham's experience. Obviously, reporters cannot check each of the two dozen or so courtrooms in the courthouse all day, each and every day, to see if anything important is transpiring. The press relies, as it must, on the courts and the lawyers for word of a story worth reporting.

Graham could not scrap the Sirica taping, so he called his office to send out another crew. Before any reporters could arrive on the scene, however, Helms entered his plea and departed. The entire Helms case would have been disposed of in virtual secrecy if Judge Barrington Parker had not upset Williams's applecart by deferring sentencing for four days. On November 1, Graham and Lesley Stahl said on the CBS "Morning News" that the Helms hearing had been secret. Williams was enraged, since the court session was technically open to the public.

Helms's sentencing took place on November 4. A large press contingent gathered outside afterward to interview Helms and Williams. The two emerged from the courthouse, and Williams made his famous "badge of honor" statement. Fred Graham asked the first question when Williams had finished speaking. Williams and Helms both fixed Graham with hostile stares, and the entire exchange that followed was recorded in a remarkable CBS film that was never aired.

Williams addressed Graham: "I want to say something to you too, Mr. Graham." In front of Graham's peers, Williams then went on to inform him angrily that the October 31 hearing had been held "in open in the court. . . . It was a wide-open procedure which you opted not to attend and you covered your own inertia and your own indolence by recklessly and irresponsibly attacking the system."

Even Williams's favorite newspaper, the *Washington Post,* had reported that the October 31 hearing was "conducted in near secrecy,"[95] but Graham was the one Williams chose to berate publicly. When Graham tried to explain about his appointment with Sirica, he was cut off. The next day, Graham called Williams, told him why he couldn't follow Helms into the courthouse on October 31, and received an apology. Graham then suggested to Williams that he would have a chance to voice his apologies in front of most of the same reporters who had heard the assault the day before: The same group would be assembling outside the Supreme Court a few days later when Williams was to argue a case there.

The day of Williams's Supreme Court appearance arrived. The press was on hand to interview him, and Fred Graham was hoping that Williams would retract his earlier slur. Instead, says Graham, Williams "walked past me like I was a cigar store Indian." The entire experience left Graham with the opinion that Williams "conned" Attorney General Griffin Bell, who was relatively new on the job, was unfamiliar with the custom of notifying the press, and, unlike Williams, had tried to behave like "a gentleman" in the Helms matter.

Not all of Williams's media battles were waged against journalists as well known as Mike Wallace, Jack Anderson, and Fred Graham. During the late 1970s, *Washingtonian* magazine commissioned reporter Paul Kaplan to write a long profile of Williams. Kaplan spent months researching and writing his story, but it never appeared in print. According to reliable sources, Williams called *Washingtonian* editor in chief Laughlin Phillips at home and told him, " 'You don't really need all the problems this is going to cause you.' " Phillips caved in and withheld the Kaplan article, although the same sources say Williams couldn't have done anything but bluff, since Kaplan's profile was 100 percent accurate.

Williams says he generally ignores all the "bullshit" that has been written about him, but he called Phillips "because he had somebody going around peddling venom, slanders against me. And I told him that he had to desist. I said to him, 'Look, you can print anything you want. But you're going to be accountable for what you print. I'm just going to tell you that right now.' And I meant it. People were calling me and telling me that he [Kaplan] was saying false and defamatory things about me, that he was slandering me through the city in an effort to elicit interviews. And I protested." Did he ever! Asked why he didn't sue Kaplan himself, Williams replied, "Because I don't engage in exercises in futility. He probably couldn't have put a deposit on a fried egg"—one of Williams's patented expressions of contempt. Once, at a 1974 meeting of National Football League owners who were weighing bids for a franchise, Williams told his fellow NFL executives that one candidate " 'does not have enough money to make a deposit on a fried egg.' " Before long, twenty dozen eggs were delivered anonymously to Williams's office, along with a newspaper clipping that contained his comment.[96]

To be sure, *Washingtonian* has never been Williams's favorite publication. About the time Kaplan was working on his story, saloonkeeper Duke Zeibert invited another writer for the magazine, Robert Shoffner, to join him and several dozen others in Williams's box at a Redskin game. Introducing Shoffner to Williams, Zeibert noted that " 'he works for *Washingtonian*.' " Williams said menacingly, " 'I'm just going to pretend I didn't hear that,' " stormed off and ignored Shoffner for the rest of the game. Not only did Williams insult the guest of his friend Zeibert, but it was an instance of massive overkill; Shoffner was *Washingtonian*'s restaurant and wine critic.

On occasion, Williams's hostility toward the press has backfired. In the aftermath of Watergate, investigative reporter Roy Meyers of the *Cleve-*

land Press was probing the involvement of George Steinbrenner in the scandal. As usual, Williams wanted his client to have as little to do with the news media as possible. Steinbrenner, however, allowed Meyers to tape-record a six-hour interview, provided Meyers would not quote him directly. Meyers later attempted to get help from the Watergate Special Prosecutor's Office, but Jim Doyle, spokesman for the Prosecutor's Office, told Meyers that the staff had a policy of refusing interviews. Meyers then called Williams and suggested that if the attorney would tell the prosecution that Steinbrenner had no objections, Doyle's people might cooperate. Meyers also informed Williams about the interview he had recorded with Steinbrenner's consent. "Steinbrenner did what?' " Williams shouted into the phone. He also wondered, in a very profane manner, just what " 'does George think he's doing?' "

An hour or so after his very brief conversation with Williams, Meyers received a call from Doyle, who had had a change of heart: " 'On second thought, we'll tell you anything you want to know' " And a half-hour after that, Steinbrenner's own publicist phoned to ask why Meyers was talking to Williams. The publicist told Meyers that the Watergate prosecutors " 'are not going to talk to you,' " to which Meyers had the satisfaction of replying, " 'That's where you're wrong.' "

Edward Bennett Williams has served as a director of the American Civil Liberties Union. He is the author of a book on civil liberties in which he vigorously defends freedom of the press. For many years he has accepted a hefty retainer as attorney for the *Washington Post,* and he advised the paper to be aggressive in its coverage of two of the most sensitive issues of this era, Watergate and the "Pentagon Papers." He has also represented other media enterprises, such as *Confidential* and Warner Communications. And, through Ben Bradlee, Katharine Graham and others, he has access and input at the highest levels of American journalism.

Nevertheless, when the chips are down and he or one of his clients is the subject of media scrutiny, it becomes obvious that asking Edward Bennett Williams to guard freedom of the press is much the same as asking the fox to guard the chicken coop.

"Listen, the guy's a Jekyll and Hyde. Anybody who deals with him knows that. One day he calls you up and he's ranting and raving. The next day he's as meek as a kitten. That's his training. He's an actor. . . . He's a cold-blooded fish. He uses people. . . . He doesn't care about people. He only cares what he can get out of them. . . . He's devious and deceitful. Another thing I don't appreciate is having somebody call me up at 11 o'clock at night, getting me out of bed, and telling me that if I didn't change quarterbacks I'm not going to get a new contract."—George Allen on Edward Bennett Williams, 1978.[1]

One thing I know and found out about Edward, he is extremely loyal to his friends. He has been very, very loyal to me and I know that I can always count on Edward if I need anything.— Marie Lombardi (Vince Lombardi's widow) on Edward Bennett Williams, 1981.

4

The Sportsman

George Preston Marshall was first and foremost a showman. Soon after he moved the Boston Redskins to Washington in 1937, he became the first owner of a professional football team to organize a marching band, complete with a theme song, "Hail to the Redskins," the words to which were written by actress Corinne Griffith, who was married to Marshall at the time.[2] Later in 1937, the Redskins' arrival in Manhattan for a game against the New York Giants prompted columnist Bill Corum to report, "'At the head of a one hundred and fifty piece brass band, and ten thousand fans, George Preston Marshall slipped unobtrusively into New York today.'"[3]

During the next quarter-century, Marshall established a huge radio and television network that blanketed most of the South and Southwest. Regarding the Redskins as a team for all of Dixie (the band played "Dixie" as well as "Hail to the Redskins" before all home games),* and afraid of

---

* Marshall jealously protected his territory against poachers such as Clint Murchison, the Texas millionaire, who tried for several years during the late 1950s to gain NFL approval for a franchise in Dallas. Bobby Baker, who was a Washington representative for Murchison, recalls that, at Murchison's direction and with Murchison's money, Baker bought the rights to "Hail to the Redskins" from bandleader Barnee Breeskin, who had coauthored the song with Corinne Griffith. The next time Marshall attempted to block Murchison's entry into

offending his southern following, Marshall steadfastly refused to hire black players. The sorry record of the Redskins following integration of the other National Football League teams in the late 1940s was mitigated for Marshall by the enormous profits his broadcast network earned.

Edward Bennett Williams had been interested in sports all his life, and in the late 1950s he and Marshall became friendly. By then, Marshall had sold a 25-percent interest in the team to broadcaster Harry Wismer and 6.2 percent to Milton King, Marshall's attorney and lifelong friend. Eventually, though, Marshall and Wismer fell out over how Marshall distributed the team's profits to stockholders—he didn't. Then, as now, the team's owners had the right of first refusal on any stock that one of them might want to sell, and Williams, aware of the dispute between Marshall and Wismer, received permission from the owners to bargain with Wismer.

Williams recalls very clearly that on George Washington's Birthday in 1961, at the Waldorf-Astoria Hotel, he met with Wismer (who was by then one of the principal owners of the New York Titans—later Jets—of the rival American Football League). The two finalized an agreement under which Williams would buy Wismer's 25-percent holding in the Redskins for $250,000. Williams returned to Washington and told Marshall that he had made a deal with Wismer, but that "I couldn't come into the company if he didn't break that racial barrier, because I thought it was an absolutely disastrous policy. I had strong moral reasons for my position, but I also had pragmatic ones. At that time, the NFL teams weren't pooling television money, you were selling your own television rights, and the two sponsors of the Redskins were Amoco and Marlboro. People were threatening to boycott Amoco and Marlboro if they continued to sponsor an all-white team." Furthermore, a federally financed stadium was being built in Washington, and Interior Secretary Stewart Udall, who had jurisdiction over the new ball park, had stated publicly that the Redskins would not be able to move there unless Marshall integrated the team. "It was just a terrible and ridiculous position for Marshall to have been in," says Williams. Marshall, however, did not see things Williams's way: "He not only became angry, he then told me that under no circumstances would he change, and I was not welcome in the ball club." Williams's agreement with Wismer fell through, and Wismer sold his stock to a world-class investor named Jack Kent Cooke. Cooke paid $350,000 for the stock, so Wismer netted an extra $100,000 because of the dispute between Williams and Marshall.)

---

the league, Murchison told Marshall bluntly that either the NFL awarded a team to Dallas or else Marshall could stop playing Murchison's song at Redskin games. Marshall relented, and Murchison's Dallas Cowboys entered the league in 1960. Three years later, Baker was implicated in a political corruption scandal and hired Williams (who had become a partner of Marshall in the interim) as his lawyer.

The close friendship between Williams and Marshall cooled for a few months, but Marshall saw the handwriting on the wall as the Redskins staggered through the 1961 season with one win, twelve losses, and one tie. (The victory came in the final game against Clint Murchison's expansion team, the Cowboys, who had also provided the tie; the Redskins were 0-12-0 against the rest of the league.) This abysmal record entitled the Redskins to the first choice in the college player draft, and Marshall decided initially to select Ernie Davis, a black who was a running back at Syracuse and was generally considered the outstanding college player of 1961. Fearing that Davis would refuse to be the Redskins' Jackie Robinson, Marshall called on Williams to enlist Adam Clayton Powell, whom Williams had recently defended in a tax-evasion trial, as an envoy to Davis.

Powell took on the job, and he and Williams went off to Syracuse to talk to Davis, who at first was very reluctant to join the Redskins, just as Marshall had anticipated. "But Adam was a great convincer," Williams comments, "and he convinced him to come to Washington." Meanwhile, "unbeknownst to us," Marshall made an "illegal" trade with the Cleveland Browns that involved Davis—illegal because it occurred before the 1961 season ended and while a league trading ban was still in effect. In exchange for the right to draft Davis, Marshall acquired all-pro Bobby Mitchell, backfield partner of Jim Brown, and the Cleveland team's first-round draft choice.

Except for the Redskins' obtaining Mitchell, both teams emerged from the trade empty-handed; Ernie Davis contracted leukemia and died several months later without ever playing a game in the NFL, and Marshall insisted on using the pick he got from the Browns to draft Leroy Jackson, a running back who, like Mitchell, was black. Jackson lasted two years, and then, as Williams has been saying ever since, "fumbled the bus ticket home when they cut him." Nevertheless, Williams's mission to Powell and then to Davis restored him to George Preston Marshall's good graces, and, with the approval of the other owners, he was invited by Marshall to buy into the team.

Williams's consequent involvement in professional sports plunged him into some of the most controversial and most widely publicized events of his life. The combination of high-powered attorney and the glamour world of sports proved irresistible to the press and generated far more media coverage than any of Williams's law cases, even the most important.* Whole forests would have to be felled to provide the newsprint that articles about him and the Washington Redskins and Baltimore Orioles

---

* As one indication of media fascination for Williams, Dave Burgin left the *San Francisco Examiner* to become sports editor of the *Washington Star* in 1971 largely because of his interest in Williams and his belief that Williams and George Allen would never get along. In one of his first moves at the *Star,* Burgin hired reporter Tom Dowling and assigned him virtually full-time to the Williams-Allen beat.

would consume. When Williams in effect fired George Allen as head coach and general manager of the Redskins in 1978, for instance, it was the lead item in the Washington news media (overshadowing President Carter's state of the union address, among other stories). The follow-up stories included one highly sympathetic to Williams that ran about 12,000 words in the *Washington Post* Sunday magazine—followed by a 5,000-word rebuttal in *Washingtonian* magazine.

The stock in Pro-Football, Incorporated, the corporate name of the Redskins, has had an interesting history. Williams bought 38 of the 1,000 existing shares, or 3.8 percent, from George Preston Marshall on March 28, 1962. The total price was $58,463, or $1,538 per share (which means that in theory the entire franchise was worth $1.5 million; however, that figure is misleadingly low, because minority shares in a closely held corporation are less valuable, per share, than those that make up the controlling interest). Williams paid Marshall $10,000 down, with the balance owed over three and a half years. Marshall insisted that the sale price be paid in installments, rather than all at once, presumably for tax purposes; in return, he agreed that Williams would pay no interest on the outstanding balance.[4] At about the same time, Williams purchased 12 more shares for a similar sum from Milton King. As of 1962, Marshall owned 52 percent of the Redskin stock; Jack Kent Cooke held the 25 percent he had acquired from Harry Wismer; Leo DeOrsey, another Washington lawyer, owned 13 percent (which he had purchased for $200,000 two months before Williams bought in, and on terms similar to Williams's deal with Marshall);[5] and Williams and King each owned 5 percent.[6]

Williams's association with the Redskins might have been a pleasant interlude from his law practice, but before long he was in the midst of a bitter Marshall family feud. Soon after Williams acquired his Redskin stock, the health of the sixty-five-year-old Marshall began to fail. By December 1963, he was found to have cerebral arteriosclerosis, a damaged heart, an aneurysm in his abdomen, diabetes, and emphysema, and his mental state left him "unable properly to care for his property and his interests."[7] By then, Marshall had been divorced from Corinne Griffith, and his immediate family consisted of two adult children from an earlier marriage—George Preston Marshall, Jr., of Fort Lauderdale and Catherine Marshall Price of New York City—and several grandchildren. Marshall Sr. had been estranged from his son and daughter from the 1930s, when his first marriage ended, until after he and Corinne Griffith were divorced in 1959.[8] On the motion of King, DeOrsey, and Williams, the three co-owners were appointed temporary conservators of Marshall's estate, which was mostly Redskin stock. (Cooke lived in California at the time.) The court also named John J. Carmody, another lawyer, as guardian of Marshall's interests.[9]

Almost immediately, the Marshall children objected to the arrangement and asked the court to make them the conservators.[10] When, however, Carmody interviewed Marshall Sr. in his hospital room, Marshall said he had consented to the temporary conservatorship by his partners and added that he did not want his affairs placed in the hands of his children.[11] Marshall repeated his preference for the Williams group in two other talks with Carmody several months later, and seemed to hold this position whenever he was lucid.[12] In August 1964, King, DeOrsey, and Williams became permanent conservators of Marshall's estate by court order—still against the wishes of the Marshall children.[13] But the legal cross fire that would tie up the courts for eight years had just begun; and, as the dispute was starting, Leo DeOrsey died in April 1965 and Williams replaced him as acting president of the Redskins.[14]

What followed was one of the more complicated cases in Washington legal annals. Carmody, the guardian, estimated at one point that fifteen different motions brought either by the conservators or by the Marshall children were pending in court; he also listed about fifty separate developments in the fight that had required his attention over a span of nearly five years.[15]

The arguments between the two sides shaped up as follows:

Marshall children: Williams, King, and DeOrsey had a conflict of interest as minority stockholders who had taken over control of the majority owner's stock. The conservators—particularly Williams and DeOrsey, who owed Marshall money for purchase of their stock—were in effect representing their own interests over Marshall's and could wind up "negotiating with themselves and making new arrangements."[16] The conservators were also using "their dual and conflicting roles to promote the perpetuation of their personal interests in permanent control over" the Redskins, "without reference to the best interests" of Marshall and his estate.[17] As a means of keeping themselves in power, the conservators were rejecting outside offers to buy the team.[18] Furthermore, Williams and King (after DeOrsey's death) were holding Marshall "a virtual prisoner" in his home in Georgetown,[19] and were doing everything they could to cut off contact between Marshall and his children.[20] Williams allegedly—"in pursuit of his own personal ambitions"—had once offered to put the Marshall children on the Redskin payroll as team scouts at a salary of $500 a month for each and had held out "other enticements" if the children would stop meddling in the conservators' management of the club.[21] Most of the allegations against the conservators were made in legal briefs filed by Francis X. McLaughlin, an attorney for Marshall's children. McLaughlin had once been a student of Williams's at Georgetown Law School and seemed to relish saying anything unflattering he could about Williams.

The conservators: Marshall had invited each of them to become a partner. All three were "close friends" of Marshall's, as well as "professional and confidential advisors of long standing." In fact, Marshall "really has no one else" who compared with King, DeOrsey, and Williams in experience in operating the team and interest in making it a success.[22] In addition, Williams and DeOrsey were "persons of considerable fortune" who were ready, willing, and able to pay the full price of their stock purchase at any time, and would have done so in the first place, except that Marshall had not wanted them to.[23] According to Stephen N. Jones, one of Marshall's doctors, visits from his children "impaired the well-being of the patient" and led to "a marked increase in the convulsive-type seizures to which the patient is subject."[24] Far from being held "a virtual prisoner," Marshall was well cared for and as comfortable as he could hope to be in view of the fact that he was virtually a vegetable who "is unable to manage his own bodily functions or to speak at will. He cannot communicate satisfactorily and is in a desperate physical condition. In fact, the Ward cannot voluntarily move his head from one side of the bed to the other."[25]

The battle between the friends and family of George Preston Marshall had been under way for about two years when it turned downright nasty. Before he fell ill, Marshall had executed a will in which he left the bulk of his estate, including his controlling interest in the Redskins, to set up a charity for the benefit of underprivileged children in the Washington area.[26]* Marshall's children learned what was in his will and set about persuading him to draw up a new one. Their first attempt was made in January 1966, when Marshall's daughter visited him and "continued her vain efforts until midnight," but was unable to talk him into changing his will.[28] Four months later, during a May 22, 1966, visit to Marshall's home, Marshall Jr. told nurse Juanita Belanger that if she would help him obtain a new will from his father, he would see to it that her three children received college educations. (The younger Marshall also told Belanger that day that "they," an apparent reference to Williams and King, were "'crooked.'")[29] Then, on June 9, Marshall Jr. arrived at his father's house late at night and, finding the front door locked and chained, forced his way into the house.[30] According to the younger Marshall, "My father was delighted to see me."[31]

By then, Marshall's children were telling the court that their father wanted to execute a new will that would leave his Redskin stock to "his only flesh and blood, and in this way he would try and make up to us the family life which had been denied to us in our youth,"[32] while Williams and King, the surviving conservators, were asking that the children be

---

* Marshall directed that the charity, to be known as the Redskin Foundation, "shall never use, contribute, or apply its money or property for any purpose which supports or employs the principle of racial integration in any form."[27]

blocked from "interfering with their father's estate . . . especially . . . from attempting to have him execute legal documents," as well as from "moving into quarters occupied by their father, either temporarily or permanently."[33]

Marshall Jr. replied that—on orders from Williams—he was "prevented . . . from being alone with my father to discuss family matters and his will." He charged that whenever he visited the house, two employees of the Redskins were present at all times to make sure that he could not see his father alone.[34] (One of the Redskin staffers mentioned by the younger Marshall, a man named Leroy Washington, who even slept at the house, allegedly to keep father and son apart, has been Williams's chauffeur and personal aide for much of the time since Marshall Sr.'s death in August 1969. Williams says Washington is not actually an employee of his but is on the payroll of the Redskins and the Baltimore Orioles—Williams's teams.) But the convervators' acts were endorsed by John J. Carmody, the impartial guardian of Marshall's estate, who reported to the court that Marshall still indicated he did not want his children staying at his house. Describing Marshall as "a very sick man," Carmody said the whole thing had become "macabre," with Marshall "subjected . . . to repeated importunities . . . to prepare a new will . . . at what very well may be his terminal illness."[35]

The whole affair finally came to a head on July 2, 1966. Ignoring an order by a federal judge that no documents be presented to Marshall Sr. for his signature until pending motions had been disposed of, Marshall's children, accompanied by two lawyers, arrived at his house. The group proceeded to Marshall's bedroom, where he lay "motionless in bed and indicated no understanding" of what was taking place. Catherine Marshall Price read from a piece of paper she held, in a tone so low that a nurse and a male attendant could not understand what she was saying. Price asked her father if Marshall Jr. could sign the father's name to the document from which she had read. "There was no reply to this request." And then Marshall Jr. and the two lawyers signed the piece of paper and the quartet departed.[36]

The document in question, of course, turned out to be a will by which Marshall purportedly left his entire estate "to my two children to share equally. I hereby emphasize that I want my property, including my Redskins stock, to go to my own flesh and blood and not to the Boys' Club or to any other person or group." The "will" also quoted Marshall as saying he understood what was in it, and that he "expressly" directed that his name be signed to it by someone else.[37]

Williams and King immediately demanded that Marshall's children be cited for contempt for failing to abide by the court order against their attempting to have their father sign anything.[38] They also asked that the court direct Marshall Jr. and Price to turn over to them the July 2 document.[39] Federal District Judge Alexander Holtzoff ordered that the document be given to the conservators; and after Marshall Jr. repeatedly refused to comply with that decree, Holtzoff cited him for contempt of court and ordered him jailed until he produced the document.[40]

The younger Marshall entered the District of Columbia jail on January 12, 1967, but not until he had held a press conference (accompanied by his lawyer, Francis X. McLaughlin) and declared that the document was in fact a will and that his father had entrusted it to him for safekeeping. Marshall Jr. said he had no intention of handing the will over to "'Williams . . . [who] wants to control the team, as he does now, and wants to maintain control after my father passes on.'"[41] He also accused Williams of having "'lied'" to the courts and the press and of "'stealing a football team for himself.'"[42]

The younger Marshall served three weeks in jail, and then was transferred to a hospital after he fainted in reaction to insulin he was taking for diabetes. After two weeks in the hospital's jail ward, he agreed to surrender the will pending appeal, and was released.[43]

As it turned out, the release of Marshall Jr. from jail did not untangle the web. A year or so later, he asked for money from his father and painted a bleak picture of his own situation. Marshall's son (then forty-three) was reportedly living in a rented room in Fort Lauderdale and working for $2.50 an hour in a shipyard, when his health permitted.[44] Meanwhile, Catherine Marshall Price (then forty-six) said that she needed financial aid from her father to care for her twenty-one-year-old son, who was "hopelessly" schizophrenic; he had been confined in two New York hospitals and then sent home to her after he was allegedly assaulted by other patients.[45]

To further complicate matters, Leo DeOrsey's widow publicly expressed displeasure with Williams's management of the Redskins. "'All they've been under Williams are losers,'" she declared. "'I'm for a new deal.'"[46] Her complaint was resolved when her fellow Redskin owners—Williams and King, acting for Marshall and themselves, and Cooke—agreed to buy DeOrsey's 130 shares from her and retire them. But that brought another twist: Francis McLaughlin, on behalf of Marshall's children, criticized the other three owners for paying Mrs. DeOrsey $1.3 million, which McLaughlin characterized as "a relatively low price" that tended to undervalue the entire team as being worth a total of $10 million.[47] Williams and King pointed out just how ludicrous McLaughlin's position was: Without confirming the accuracy of his figures, they said that if he was correct, they had bought the DeOrsey stock at a bargain price, possibly as much as 33 percent below its real value—a virtual steal for the remaining owners, including Marshall.[48]

While all this was going on, there were two more developments: The elder Marshall finally died, in 1969, and that same year Williams hired

Vince Lombardi as head coach and general manager. Lombardi joined the team only after being allowed to buy 50 shares; when he died of cancer eighteen months later, the club repurchased his stock from his widow. The latest maneuvers left 870 shares outstanding, with the Marshall estate owning 520, Cooke 250, and Williams and King 50 each.

While George Preston Marshall was still healthy, he had specified that his children's inheritance would be limited to $10,000 a year each.[49] The 1966 "will" that purportedly left control of the team to the Marshall children had been obtained by questionable means, but there was always the possibility that a court would find it valid. A settlement was finally reached between the two sides in January 1972. Under its terms, which the court approved, the 1966 document was declared invalid and the earlier will was admitted to probate. Pro-Football, Inc. (meaning Cooke, Williams, and King), purchased 260 of Marshall's 520 shares for $3 million and retired them. (The sale price was approximately the same as the fair market value set by an outside consultant who had been hired by the team and Marshall's estate.[50]) Each of Marshall's children received $750,000, tax-free; Williams, King, and Bernard Nordlinger, King's law partner, resigned as trustees of the estate; and law fees of $170,000 were awarded to Williams, King, et al, including $57,000 to Williams's firm.* In addition, the court approved and placed under seal a loan agreement by which the Redskins, King, Williams, and Cooke borrowed all or most of the $3 million for Marshall's 260 shares from American Security Bank in Washington.[51]

The Redskins' stock lineup now looked like this: Redskin Foundation, 260 shares; Cooke, 250; Williams, 50; and King, 50. What was of critical importance was that Cooke, Williams, and King, with 350 of the 610 outstanding shares, now held a majority interest in the team, the first time in its history that anyone other than Marshall or his estate had control. Two years later, the Redskin Foundation decided to sell its 260 shares,† and Cooke, King and Williams, exercising their right of first refusal, topped several other offers and bought the stock for an estimated $5–$6 million. Those 260 shares were retired;[53] Milton King died two years later and Cooke purchased his 50 shares. Since then, 350 shares remain outstanding, of which Cooke owns 300 and Williams 50.[54]

As of September 1980, the *Washington Post* estimated the value of the Redskin franchise as being at least $30 million.[55] If the *Post*'s figures are correct, Williams's 14.3-percent holding in the Redskins was worth over $4 million, and the approximately $80,000 he paid Marshall and King for

---

*The court also overturned the segregationist clause in Marshall's will, as part of the resolution of the case.

†For some unknown reason, George Preston Marshall, Jr., who no longer owned any interest in the club, apparently objected to this transaction, according to court records.[52]

a 5-percent interest in 1962 had bought stock that increased in value fifty-fold in eighteen years—not a bad rate of appreciation in anyone's league.

In spite of the startling increase in the value of his investment in the Redskins, Williams seized every opportunity to poormouth the club's finances. In 1973, he lamented that he was " 'gravely concerned about the economic aspect of our team,' " expressed anxiety about the " 'survival' " of the franchise, and told the press that " 'as investors, we'd be better off putting our money in municipal bonds . . . . None of the stockholders are making any money.' "[56] Two years later, it was the same old story: Williams claimed that the team had lost $500,000 in 1974, and " 'We aren't doing much better this year.' "[57] Never did he mention the interest payments he and his fellow owners were using to finance the retirement of Marshall's 520 shares—which amounted to $134,000 in 1973, $327,000 in 1974, and a whopping $841,000 in 1975, according to figures obtained by the *Post*.[58] Meanwhile, the ownership cited the team's alleged financial losses as justification for charging the highest ticket prices in the NFL.[59] Shortly before his death in 1976, however, Milton King acknowledged the real reason for the high cost of attending Redskin games: " 'We owe the banks a lot of money.' "[60]

Although most of the Washington media remained silent about the means whereby Williams and Cooke got control of the Redskins, Joseph Nocera took the two of them to task, especially Williams, in his 1978 *Washington Monthly* article "The Screwing of the Average Fan: Edward Bennett Williams and the Washington Redskins." Nocera, and others who later rehashed his story, outlined how the Redskin owners, primarily Williams, wrested control from the Marshall family, then raised ticket prices to finance the interest payments that were used to buy back the Marshall stock.[61] Nocera concluded that: "Edward Bennett Williams— vaunted man of integrity, one of the best trial lawyers in the country, respected if not loved by those who know him—fleeced the Redskin fans. He and Cooke and King took the Redskins rooters straight to the cleaners."[62]

Nocera's article was accurate. Yet, it reported only one side of the story. There is another side: Williams, King, Cooke, and company did not shaft Marshall's children; they merely carried out Marshall's wishes. Marshall *never* had much use for his children, and he *never* wanted them to own or operate the Redskins. Marshall distrusted his offspring, and placed his trust in his friends and business associates—King, Williams, and Cooke. Furthermore, it is completely inaccurate to say, as one published account did, that Williams had Marshall's son "jailed" for contempt of court.[63] Williams did not sneak into Marshall's house and have him "execute" a "will" while Marshall lay senseless in his bed; Marshall's children did that. Williams did not defy a court order to hand over the document thus procured; George Preston Marshall, Jr., did. And Williams did not cause anyone to be jailed; a federal judge sent Marshall Jr. to jail for refusing to obey his order.

Nor did Williams, King, and Cooke "screw" the "average fan." If any fan got "screwed," it was a self-administered act. There is a term for the process that resulted in increased ticket prices, and that term is *capitalism*. The laws of supply and demand were followed to the nth degree. Redskin fans have been willing to pay all the traffic would bear—even though every home game for nearly a decade has been available for viewing free of cost on network television. Not only is each seat sold for every game, there is a waiting list of more than 10,000 for season tickets, and that list would be much longer, except that team officials decided there was no need to add any more names to it. Why should Williams and his partners charge any less than what the customers will pay?

It is also important to bear in mind that, at all times, from 1963, when Marshall fell ill, until 1972, when the two sides settled their differences, his estate was under the supervision of a federal court. And virtually without exception, every impartial person connected with the case ruled in favor of the Williams side in each and every instance. John Carmody, the court-appointed guardian, praised Williams and the other conservators as "men of integrity."[64] One federal district judge, Alexander Holtzoff, found that the conservators had no conflict of interest and conducted themselves properly.[65] Another, George Hart, declared in reference to the conservators, "There was not the slightest wrongdoing on anybody's part."[66] A three-judge panel from the U.S. Court of Appeals held that the conservators "were uniquely qualified to run the Redskins," and added that the Marshall children and their lawyer, Francis McLaughlin, "have not presented, either in the District Court or in this court, any examples of wrongdoing by the conservators."[67]

As a matter of fact, the two federal district judges, Holtzoff and Hart, found fault with McLaughlin, rather than with the conservators. Holtzoff was angry that McLaughlin kept making allegations against Williams and the other conservators on "information and belief." When an attorney says he knows something on "information and belief," what he really means is, "I'm pretty sure this is true, but I can't prove it." Holtzoff lectured McLaughlin at some length:

> It seems to me that is a pretty serious matter, to make charges of improper conduct on information and belief. . . . I don't think that should be done. . . . I am suggesting to you that it is not proper for a member of the bar to file a motion or any other pleading or document under his signature containing serious charges of misconduct on information and belief without specifying the charges. I think that is highly questionable.[68]

And Judge Hart admonished McLaughlin that the lawyer and his clients were "just making a lot of allegations with nothing to back them up."[69] (McLaughlin apparently did not learn much from what Holtzoff and Hart told him; he now reports that he had "heard" that a court official, since dead, had accused Williams of conflict of interest in the Marshall case. The report in which the allegations against Williams were supposedly made had been placed under seal, according to McLaughlin, who not only could not produce a copy but admitted he had never even seen it himself.) However, because this dispute involved the Redskins, the interest of the public was whetted, and many people still accuse Williams of wrongdoing, without knowing all the facts. The most the published stories have shown is that his comments about the team losing money because of player salaries, George Allen's spending habits, the relatively small seating capacity of the stadium in Washington, and so forth, were misleading in the absence of any mention of the interest payments.

There was, however, one aspect of the Marshall controversy in which Williams's role was, to say the least, debatable. In October 1966, three months after Marshall's children procured what was allegedly a new will, Marshall's physician, Dr. Stephen N. Jones, had sworn out the affidavit already quoted in which he declared that he was advising the conservators (Williams and King) that "it is extremely undesirable, from the point of view of the patient's health, for either of the patient's children or any other person, except the usual staff, to live at [Marshall's] house" because visits by the children, "in my opinion, impaired the well-being of the patient."[70]

The problem presented by Jones's findings is Jones's relationship with one Edward Bennett Williams: Jones and Williams have been close friends since they were students together at Georgetown in the mid-1940s (in fact, Williams identifies Jones as one of his best friends, along with Ben Bradlee, Art Buchwald, and Bill Ragan, another contemporary of Williams and Jones at Georgetown), and Jones has been Williams's personal physician since 1948.* There is absolutely no indication that what Jones said about Marshall in his affidavit was anything less than the complete truth. Yet, the personal and professional relationship of Williams and Jones could only leave doubts in the mind of any objective observer about the propriety of Jones treating Marshall—much less suggesting that the less contact he had with his children, the better. If a doctor who was a close friend and the personal physician of either of the Marshall children had come in and said that visits from the children were

---

*In a letter to the federal district court in Washington dated December 3, 1956, Jones asked that the trial of Williams's client, Ian Woodner, be suspended for several weeks because Williams was suffering from "progressive hoarseness and discomfort in his throat." Jones stated that "Mr. Edward B. Williams has been under my professional care for the past eight years."[71]

beneficial to Marshall, Ed Williams would not have just hit the ceiling, he would have gone through the roof and exploded into orbit. Of all the doctors in the world, Stephen Jones—because of his close personal relationship with Williams—is the last one who should have been asked to minister to Marshall. And yet, that is exactly what happened; by Jones's own sworn statement to the court, "Since June, 1965, I have attended and treated Mr. George P. Marshall, *having been engaged for that purpose by the patient's court-appointed conservators.*"[72] (Italics added.)

Jones's link to Williams could only have fueled the court campaign of the Marshall children, had they been aware of it. Certainly, it would have been much more persuasive to the courts than many of the points McLaughlin did raise. Williams's introduction of Jones into the Marshall conflict ranks as one of the few unwise judgments of his entire career, which has been marked by his cleverness in depriving his enemies of any real substance for charges of impropriety. Again, there was nothing improper in the behavior of either Jones or Williams regarding Jones's treatment of Marshall; but as Ed Williams knows so well, appearance often is at least as important as reality.

On the field, in the stands, and overseeing the front office, Williams was having the time of his life with the Redskins. Three months after Leo DeOrsey's death left him in virtual control of the team's day-to-day affairs, Williams, the frustrated jock, showed up at his club's training camp in Carlisle, Pennsylvania, wearing shorts, a Redskin T-shirt, and athletic shoes. He proceeded to go through a workout with his players, running laps, doing calisthenics, and impressing squad members by demonstrating that at forty-five he could catch long passes and withstand the rigors of an entire workout.[73] That 1965 season got off to a disastrous start, however, with Williams's Redskins losing their first five games and fans displaying banners like "'We Want Louis Nizer.'"[74] After the fifth straight defeat, Williams, with the consent of Coach Bill McPeak, spoke to the players for two hours during a closed-door meeting that none of the coaches attended. Later, one of the athletes, Pat Richter, said that "'Mister Williams was the judge and jury. There were 40 of us on trial and we were all guilty.'" The rare intrusion into the locker room seemed to work, as the Redskins won their next three games and the players awarded Williams a coveted game ball in recognition of the boost he had given them.[75]

That season, for the last time, there were several thousand empty seats for each home game. Since then, all home games have been sold out. Near the end of 1965, however, Williams made the first of several bad decisions that hurt the Redskins' fortunes on the field. At a time when the club needed help at practically every position, Williams allowed Milton King to talk him into spending the Redskins' first draft choice on a place-kicker from King's alma mater, Princeton, instead of a player who could be used more often. To compound matters, the kicker, Charlie Gogolak, was a bust; he lasted three years and was released.

In the first year of the Williams regime, the Redskins were 6 and 8— their ninth consecutive losing season. Williams then made a move that he now concedes may have been a mistake: He fired Bill McPeak and replaced him with Otto Graham, the star quarterback of the Cleveland Browns in the 1940s and 1950s. Actually, Graham was Williams's fifth choice. According to Williams, he tried to hire Vince Lombardi and Paul Brown, the genius behind the Browns, each of whom turned him down because he could not offer them stock in the team; Bud Wilkinson, the former Oklahoma coach, who agreed to take the job but then learned that his employer, a sports foundation, wouldn't release him from his contract ("He could have walked out, but he wouldn't do that," says Williams); and Ara Parseghian, who preferred to stay at Notre Dame. So Williams reached further down on his list and succeeded in luring Graham away from his coaching job at the U.S. Coast Guard Academy. Graham said that the idea of working for Williams was in large part responsible for his decision to take over as coach of the Redskins: "'I'm here because of Ed Williams. Sure, he met my salary and other demands, but he understands competition . . . [because] he goes into court and gives it his best.'"[76]

There were signs from the start that Graham wouldn't work out. Before he coached the Redskins in a single game, he was quoted in a *Sports Illustrated* cover story as saying, "'I would rather lose two or three games and have every score 35–28 than win every ball game 3–0.'" The important thing, Graham added, was to be "'entertaining'"[77] The trouble was that with quarterback Sonny Jurgensen and his passing attack, the Redskins already were entertaining—in 1965, for instance, they had played one of their most thrilling games ever, overcoming a 21–0 deficit to beat the hated Cowboys, 34–31—but now Williams demanded a winner. The Redskins continued to be exciting under Graham, but winners they weren't. Williams endured three years with records of 7 and 7; 5 wins, 6 losses, and 3 ties; and 5 and 9. The next loss was Graham's job.

Looking back on Graham, whom he still considers a friend, Williams reflects: "I know it was a mistake to hire Otto Graham. Otto wasn't up to coaching a professional football team. He was a nice fellow and I'm very devoted to him, but I put him in a job which was over his head. He doesn't work hard enough to be a professional coach, he doesn't work the hours that they work. After three years, it was clear to me that we were going nowhere again."

In part, the Redskins were going "nowhere" because of more misguided player deals instigated by Williams. In 1966, he acquired the inimitable Joe Don Looney from the Detroit Lions, a decision that Williams says Graham "kind of agreed with, but all the assistants were opposed to." The assistant coaches might have been thinking about Looney's past record.

As a college player under Bud Wilkinson at Oklahoma, he had punched one of Wilkinson's aides. A first-round draft choice of the New York Giants in 1964, he quickly wore out his welcome despite his awesome abilities as a running back, and was traded to the Baltimore Colts, who, in turn, dispatched him to Detroit. With the Lions, Looney, ordered to carry plays to the quarterback, told Head Coach Harry Gilmer (once a Redskins quarterback), "'If you want a messenger-boy, call Western Union,'" and stalked off the field.

Looney spent less than two years with the Redskins and then drifted on, but not before becoming a disruptive influence on the squad. When last heard from, he was tending elephants for a guru in the Himalayas. Williams: "We were desperate for a running back. And there he was, and I thought we could handle him." They couldn't. The owner of the Lions, who dealt Looney to the Redskins, was a pal of Williams's, William Clay Ford of the Ford Fords. That same year, Williams bought a Lincoln Continental that operated about as well as Looney; Williams enjoyed telling Ford, "'I thought you were my friend, Bill, but you sold me two lemons in one year.'"[78]

Williams also initiated a trade of a first-round draft pick to Los Angeles for quarterback Gary Beban, who was a Redskin for parts of two seasons but got into games for so few plays that Williams describes him as probably the highest-paid Redskin of all time, on a per-play basis. That was another deal that Williams now considers "a terrible mistake." On the other hand, Williams vetoed Graham's wish to trade wide receiver Charley Taylor to the Rams, for what Williams calls "garbage." Taylor went on to catch more passes than any other player in pro-football history —and every single one of his receptions was as a Redskin. Williams also gave up a high draft choice in order to sign defensive back Pat Fischer, who had played out his option with the St. Louis Cardinals before the 1968 season. Fischer was a star with the Redskins for ten years, and Williams justifiably takes pride in that "great, great trade."

In spite of the team's failures on the field, invitations to sit with Williams and his celebrity friends in the owner's box soon became among the most sought-after badges of prestige in Washington. The regulars included Ben Bradlee, Art Buchwald, Joe DiMaggio, Ethel Kennedy, Edmund Muskie, and Earl Warren and his son-in-law, television moderator John Charles Daly. A procession of senators, cabinet members, and, on occasion, even a president of the United States enjoyed Williams's hospitality at D.C. (later, Robert F. Kennedy Memorial) Stadium.[79]

According to Bill Hundley, Williams, as Redskin representative to NFL councils in the mid-1960s, was one of the Young Turks who lobbied for merger with the rival American Football League and "tried to bring 'em [the older owners] into the twentieth century." Hundley was a friend whom Williams had guided into a job as head of NFL security when

Hundley left the Justice Department in 1966. He observed that NFL owners were divided into two groups, with Williams, Art Modell of the Cleveland Browns, and Jerry Wolman of the Philadelphia Eagles leading the progressive faction, and George Halas of the Chicago Bears and Dan Reeves of the Los Angeles Rams on the opposite side. The Williams group "felt the team didn't own the players," says Hundley. "They could see the handwriting on the wall. Some of those old owners used to talk about the players like they were chattels." The NFL-AFL merger was concluded in 1966, and players were treated more like human beings in the ensuing years—in stark contrast to the earlier days, when George Preston Marshall allegedly shipped an injured Redskin player home in a boxcar in order to save money.

Even though Williams was deeply involved with the Redskins and the entire structure of professional football, he realized that the game *was* a game and didn't take it all that seriously—except when the Redskins lost a tough one. During the late 1960s, Eugene McCarthy spoke at the annual awards banquet of the Washington Touchdown Club. As McCarthy remembers it, "I quoted the dean of my college, who said of the football coach when I was there, 'He's a good coach, and I'll tell you why: He's just smart enough to understand the game and not smart enough to lose interest.'" Adds McCarthy, "I think there were about three people in the whole crowd who laughed, and Williams was one." That, however, was the last time McCarthy addressed the Touchdown Club.

Near the end of the 1968 season, the Green Bay Packers visited Washington (and, of course, beat the Redskins, 27–7, to bring the 'Skins' record to 4 and 7, en route to 5 and 9). Vince Lombardi was with the Packers, although he had stepped down as coach the year before to be a full-time general manager. Lombardi was itching to be a coach again, and Williams, who had suffered long enough with Graham, spoke to him about taking over the Redskins. In addition to demanding the right to buy into the team, Lombardi had another condition: absolute control. That suited Williams perfectly: "I had been mucking in the machinery and holding coaches and general managers responsible, which was totally unfair. I didn't have the time to do it and I didn't have the qualifications to do it. So I got out of it."

The Lombardi Era got off to a promising start: a 7-5-2 record in 1969, his first year with the Redskins and the club's first winning season since 1955. To Williams, it was "the greatest coaching year that Vince Lombardi had in his whole career, and he's the greatest coach who ever lived, by my lights. He took a bunch of rinkydinks, just total rinkydinks [many of whom Williams himself had acquired], and took them to a winning season for the first time in many years. He did the most that could possibly have been done with that football team. So by my lights he had the greatest season ever."

Shortly after the season ended, Lombardi learned he had cancer, and just before the 1970 season opened, he was dead. Williams and Lombardi had been good friends for years, according to Marie Lombardi; she said her husband picked the Redskins over "many, many other offers" because of "his great respect for Williams." Williams spent hours every day at Lombardi's bedside, and when the coach died, so did some of Williams's interest in the Redskins. Several months later, he hired ex–Los Angeles Rams coach George Allen as Lombardi's replacement, a move that would cause Williams headaches for the next seven years.

In addition to promising entertaining football at the time he took over the Redskins, Otto Graham had declared, "'I want to win, I'm a great competitor, but I don't want to win at all costs. If I personally have to go out and do things that are morally wrong, dishonest, I wouldn't do it to be a winner.'"[80] Now Graham had been purged for losing, and his successor, Lombardi, had died. In the hope of making the Redskins consistent winners, Edward Bennett Williams turned to a man who was the complete antithesis of Otto Graham—George Allen.

Williams would have loved to hire his "good friend" Don Shula, but Shula was bound by an ironclad contract to the Miami Dolphins. Allen, on the other hand, was highly available, having just been fired by the Rams for the second time in two years. He had had a checkered past, including a stint as head coach at Whittier College, in the course of which he had befriended the school's most famous alumnus, Richard Nixon. (In later years, Allen would often be described as "Richard Nixon, with a football whistle.")

Allen first came to public attention as coach of the Chicago Bears' defensive unit, which carried the team to the 1963 world championship. After the title game, in which the Bears defeated the Giants as Allen's defense intercepted five passes, the players awarded Allen a game ball ("an unheard-of honor for an assistant coach," Allen said in his official biography). The Bear defense also gathered around Allen during the postgame celebration and, while CBS cameras and microphones carried the event to the whole nation, sang (affectionately), "To George, for he's a horse's ass." A couple of years later, the Rams tried to hire Allen as head coach. Normally, teams are delighted to see one of their assistant coaches move up to head coach, but "Papa Bear," George Halas, was not at all pleased. He filed suit to hold Allen to his contract with the Bears, and, having won his case, then and only then let Allen go to Los Angeles. In 1966, his first year with the Rams, Allen guided them to their first winning season in eight campaigns, and the next year he won numerous coach-of-the-year awards after leading his team to an 11-1-2 record and a division title. A year later, however, despite a 10-3-1 record, Rams owner Dan Reeves fired Allen, only to back down in the face of a revolt by the players.

At that time, Williams approached Allen about moving to Washington, and, according to Williams, Allen was all set to take the job until Reeves quickly rehired him. It was only then that Williams settled on Lombardi. But following the 1970 season, Reeves fired Allen a second time and made it stick, and this time Williams grabbed him for the Redskins. A stormy decade later, Williams commented that he was very much aware of Allen's past record, but it "didn't bother me. I didn't think there was anything alarming about George's relationship with Reeves [who has since died]. Reeves was not an easy man to get along with. Reeves was a total alcoholic."

And yet, some of what Williams—and most other people—knew about Allen when Williams hired him apparently wasn't true. For instance, Allen said at the time he was forty-eight,[81] having been born in 1922, as he has consistently maintained; several years later, the *Washington Post* reported that he may have been born in 1918.[82] Similarly, Allen claimed in his biographical material that he is six foot one,[83] but this is true only if one of his players is holding him about four inches above the ground.

In spite of his background, Allen was the coach Williams wanted—with some encouragement from Jack Kent Cooke, who owned the Los Angeles Lakers basketball team, the Los Angeles Kings hockey club, and the Forum where they played, and who had known Allen in L.A. sports circles. Final details of the deal were worked out at Cooke's ranch in the high Sierra; to commemorate the occasion, Allen gave Cooke two swans named Jack and George for the ranch pond. (The swans quickly fell prey to "mountain lions or whatever the hell they have up there that eats swans," according to Cooke.)

From Williams and Cooke, Allen got what was called at the time "the biggest deal ever given a football coach."[84] The seven-year pact provided for Allen to be paid $125,000 a year, plus performance bonuses; permitted him to buy 50 shares of Redskin stock at the price the team paid the Marshall estate ($11,141 a share); and gave him a $250,000 term life-insurance policy, moving expenses, and financing for the purchase of a house. The Redskins also paid Allen a $25,000 signing bonus.[85] Yet Williams felt sure the Redskins were getting their money's worth; he introduced Allen to the Washington press corps as "'the best football coach'" in the business, and vowed, "'Believe me, this is the last coach Edward Bennett Williams is going to hire or fire. . . . If we don't make it with George, they ought to fire the president.'"[86]

The signing of Allen quickly paid dividends. In his first season, 1971, the Redskins were one of the surprise teams of the year, compiling a 9-4-1 record for the club's best campaign and first playoff appearance since 1945. In 1972, the Redskins reached their postwar peak, winning the title in the NFC East with a log of 11-3; earning the NFC championship with two playoff victories, the second a 26-3 New Year's Eve rout of the archrival Cowboys; and making their first trip to the Super Bowl, which they lost to Don Shula's Miami Dolphins, 14–7.

Williams reveled in having transformed the Redskins into winners at last. He led a planeload of his friends to Los Angeles for the Super Bowl. Afterward, he was as down as he had been up. The next day, he and Bill Hundley had to fly to Las Vegas to appear in court on behalf of some casino owners they represented. They traveled in a small plane, and Hundley was nervous about flying in such a craft. Williams, on the other hand, "was in a state of acute depression because of the game," according to Hundley. His attitude was "'I don't care if the plane goes down.' It was one of the few times I've seen him preoccupied. All he wanted to do was go home and put his head under the covers and assume the fetal position."

Williams, of course, was the lead attorney, and he kept gathering the other lawyers around him in the courtroom. Hundley and the rest expected some major pronouncement on trial strategy, but, instead, all that was on Williams's mind was logistics: "'Fellas, I think if we get a plane from here to Atlanta and then change planes, we can get out of here and go home.'"

Still, nothing could detract from Williams's pride in the Redskins' having qualified for the Super Bowl, nor could anything short of a return trip and triumph satisfy him. But that was not to be. The Redskins followed up their Super Bowl season with records of 10–4, 10–4, 8–6, 10–4 and 9–5. They went to the playoffs in 1973, 1974, and 1976, but they failed to advance beyond the opening round.

Practically from the start, the relationship between Williams and Allen was strained. Early on, Williams took to quipping, "'I gave George Allen an unlimited budget, and he exceeded it.'" (To which Allen later retorted, "'It was Williams who signed the checks, not George Allen. . . . I'm not going to take the blame for the team losing money. He had the final authority, not me.'"[87] Furthermore, Allen declared, Williams and Cooke "'made millions and millions on stock'" during Allen's seven years in Washington.[88])

Allen had first run afoul of Williams several months after joining the Redskins. Just as Williams was attempting to convince the Marshall children that the club was in relatively poor financial shape and they should therefore accept less money than they wanted in settling their father's estate, Allen leaked a story that the team was about to build a $500,000 gym for the players and to add 2,500 seats at RFK Stadium, which would bring in about $250,000 a year in additional ticket revenues. Writer Tom Dowling was interviewing Allen when Williams called to rebuke the coach, and he started to leave Allen's office so the coach and the team president could talk in private. But Allen motioned Dowling to stay and said to Williams, "'I looked into that announcement. I didn't have anything to do with it.' He then went on blithely," reported Dowling, "to inform Williams that the story had been put out unilaterally by the one employee in the Redskin front office who never had been known to initiate a single story in the press."[89]

The next chink in the Williams-Allen relationship occurred in early 1972, after Allen in effect traded the same draft choice to two different teams. What Allen did was similar to writing a check without enough money in the bank and then rushing around to find money to cover the check before it bounced. Similarly, Allen intended to obtain a choice in the same round to send to the second team he had dealt with.

NFL commissioner Pete Rozelle says that what Allen did was "irresponsible," and he and many of the club owners were "very disturbed" about it. Reports circulated that Allen was "close to being thrown out of football,"[90] and Williams argued his case at two league hearings (which led to a classic headline in the *Washington Post,* "Allen Receives All-Pro Defense").[91] Dave Slattery, Williams's executive assistant, accompanied Williams and Allen to the NFL hearings on the trades. The three were walking to NFL headquarters in New York just before the second session, and, says Slattery, "George was kind of complaining that Rozelle had undressed him" at the first meeting. "George was sort of saying that Ed had not defended him hard enough. Ed stopped right in the square opposite the Plaza Hotel, turned around and looked at him and said, 'Goddamnit, George, you were guilty,' which never got through to Allen. Allen said he still wanted to get up and have his say, and Williams just looked at me and shook his head." Allen was not permitted to address the NFL moguls, but after Williams made what Art Modell called a "'most eloquent'" plea on Allen's behalf that "'captivated'" his audience, Allen was let off with a reprimand and the Redskins were fined $5,000.[92]

Williams believes Allen might have been suspended from the league but for his advocacy, and complains, "I spent more time defending George Allen for various infractions than I did anything else for those years. He was always breaking some rules, practicing guys he shouldn't have been practicing and making trades that he shouldn't have been making."

The Redskins' performance in the 1973 Super Bowl helped widen the rift between Williams and Allen. After Washington's loss, Williams was quoted in the press as saying, "'I don't think we were prepared mentally for the Super Bowl game,'" an obvious slap at Allen.[93] In Dave Slattery's opinion, "The beginning of the end of George Allen and the Redskins was the last three days before the Super Bowl. I think he went power-crazy." In one incident, Allen disciplined a popular member of the squad for breaking curfew, even though the player was injured and unable to participate in the game. Both Williams and Slattery believe Allen transmitted his tension to the players, who were too tight to do their best in the game.

Before the next season, Allen made one of his least successful moves, trading a first- and a second-draft choice to San Diego for Duane Thomas, a talented but moody runner who often refused to speak to his team-mates or coaches and who would be elected to team with Joe Don Looney in almost anyone's all-time, all-malcontent backfield. The Redskins paid an extremely high price for a player who was with the team for only two seasons and gained a total of 500 yards.[94] And if the Thomas trade was not the worst in the club's history, then Allen's 1975 signing of free agent Dave Butz—at a cost of two first-round picks and one in the second round—probably was. In return for Butz, a very large (six foot seven, 295-pound), very slow, and very mediocre defensive tackle, the Redskins paid his old team, the Cardinals, "the largest compensation in NFL histo-ry," by the Redskins' own reckoning.[95] Williams gave Allen a free hand on trades, but the Thomas and Butz deals helped sour Williams on Allen's "The Future Is Now" philosophy.

Another question about players—who should be the team's quarter-back—added to the conflict between Allen and Williams. Allen insisted on using Billy Kilmer, a journeyman he had picked up from the hapless New Orleans Saints, instead of first Sonny Jurgensen—whom many ex-perts, including Williams, consider one of the best passers of all time—and then Joe Theismann, whom Allen had obtained from Miami for yet another first-round draft pick.

Williams says he asked Allen "the hard questions: 'Why the hell do you have Kilmer in there?' There was no question about who was better. But he didn't like Jurgensen. And why didn't he play Theismann? I don't know why he didn't play Theismann. I would ask him. And Cooke would ask him. You know, Kilmer is like a .230 hitter. He might get three hits for you one night and everybody cheers for him, but he's a .230 hitter. They say Kilmer took us to the Super Bowl. The defense took us to the Super Bowl. We went despite Kilmer." Williams's point is substantiated by the team's performance in that game: Washington's only score came on a fluke play, the return for a touchdown of a botched Dolphin field-goal attempt.

Another bone of contention between Williams and Allen involved a prizefighter by the name of Mike Baker. Williams, a lifelong fight buff, undertook management of Baker, with Allen as his partner, in 1975. At the same time, Williams was attorney for the World Boxing Commission (WBC). Baker "built up a very respectable record . . . on a steady diet of stiffs, but couldn't beat a 'live' fighter," according to *Ring* magazine. He was given a junior middleweight title bout in 1976 "on the basis of what Muhammad Ali calls 'the right complexion and the right connection,' in this case Edward Bennett Williams, his manager and, not incidentally, the attorney for the WBC." Baker was knocked out by his opponent, Maurice Hope, in the seventh round.[96] Williams says that "management" of Baker by him and Allen amounted to their being responsible for paying Baker's bills. Williams is still waiting for Allen to pony up his share—waiting, but no longer hoping. Baker's earlier foes, as it turned out, were not the only "stiffs" connected with his boxing career.

In spite of the growing feud between the two men, it appeared in July 1977 that they had reached agreement on a new contract; Allen's first pact with the Redskins would expire the following February. At a press conference on July 14, Williams announced that Allen would coach the team for four more years (at an estimated $250,000 a season). "I think George Allen deserves one of the best contracts in coaching, and I think he has that,'" Williams declared.[97] Williams went ahead with the news session even though Allen had had to leave town to attend his mother's funeral, but one of the coach's sons was on hand to read a statement in which Allen said he was "'pleased'" to have a new contract so he could stay in Washington, where he had had "'the most gratifying years'" of his career. "'I appreciate the confidence Ed Williams has shown.'"[98] (Williams, looking "wan and pale," was only a week out of the hospital after abdominal surgery to remove a malignancy; Allen would later claim that he had wanted the press conference postponed because of his mother's death, but Williams insisted, ""'I haven't had a public appearance since I was in the hospital and I want to show people I'm all right, that I'm healthy,'"" so Allen "'went along.'"[99])

But Allen had merely agreed to terms; no new contract had been signed. Allen's lawyer, Ed Hookstratten of Los Angeles, received his first indication that there might be a problem when Williams sent him a copy of the new pact several weeks after Williams's news conference. Allen had let six and a half years pass without exercising his option to purchase 50 shares in the club at the 1971 price of $11,141 a share, or $557,050, but Hookstratten had understood from his contract talks with Jack Kent Cooke that the option would be extended for the four years of Allen's second contract. Hookstratten was "surprised" to discover that Williams's draft of a contract contained no option clause. The lawyer says he does not blame Williams for the omission, but he did believe he had "an agreement" with Cooke that never was put into effect. "They could call it a misunderstanding, I could call it something else," Hookstratten commented. Williams says he realized that "in the next contract it would be a mistake to give an option to him. He shouldn't be in ownership." Williams conveyed his feelings to Cooke, who agreed. Williams also wanted to regain more control over team finances from Allen, whom he had come to regard as "a profligate spender."

As the "agreement" between Williams and Allen on a new contract turned out not to be so firm, Williams started having more and more doubts about rehiring the coach. Much as he appreciated Allen's dedication to excel, he was reaching the conclusion that "it is possible to have it in excess. I thought there were times when George was a little bizarre in his behavior as a result of that commitment. He would be in such a high state of tension sometimes before games that were not of great significance. I began to believe at the end that if he were sure he could win a game, he would cut his arm off. He'd have this big knife and he'd go in the room where they did the laundry right off the dressing room, and no one else would be there and he would say, 'If I thought it would win the game for us, I'd cut off my arm.' It got me a little frightened when I saw that he had taken it to such extremes."

Allen also seemed to have forgotten that sports are merely a form of entertainment. Otto Graham had rejected the idea of 3–0 games, but by Allen's standards a perfect game might have been one in which his team scored a safety to win 2–0. Run, run, run and punt, then wait for the other team to make a mistake—that was Allen's game plan. If Williams wasn't entertained by that sort of football, how could the paying customers be?

As the 1977 season progressed, Williams started telling friends like Gene McCarthy that Allen was "being unreasonable in his demands: 'It's gone too far, we can't deal with him.'" Then, halfway through the season, the story broke in the press that Williams and Allen were having trouble ironing out details of the contract that had previously been considered a *fait accompli*.[100] At Thanksgiving, Dave Slattery visited Washington, ostensibly to see the Cowboys' game. (Slattery had resigned in 1976 after seventeen years with the team and had written in the *Washington Post* that working for the Redskins had become "intolerable" on account of Allen. "What had been an interesting, even fascinating, career had turned into a nightmare. . . . Hypocrisy, deception and deceit had become a way of life."[101]) According to an informed source, the real purpose of Slattery's being in Washington was to draft a new Redskin organizational plan, *sans* Allen. Williams was aware that the Los Angeles Rams might soon have a coaching vacancy and he had reached the conclusion that Allen wanted the Rams job.

A few weeks later, Williams dispatched Slattery to Chicago to feel out Jack Pardee about becoming coach of the Redskins; Pardee, a star with the Rams and Redskins (under Allen), was a favorite of Williams—and his contract as coach of the Bears was now expiring. Pardee's negotiations for a new contract with the Bears were being handled by his lawyer, Ed Hookstratten, who, to touch all bases, was also counsel for the Rams, as well as a personal attorney for Carroll Rosenbloom, the Rams' owner. Slattery, who had recommended to Williams that he replace Allen with Pardee, learned through an intermediary that Pardee was unhappy in Chicago and would welcome a move to Washington.

Finally, on Saturday, January 14, 1978, Williams invited Allen to his office and demanded an answer: "I said, 'George, are you gonna sign or are you not gonna sign? If you don't sign, I'm going to go out and I'm going to get another coach.' He said, 'Oh, I've gotta go home and talk to' whatever her name is [Etty, Allen's wife]. Well, I waited two days while he flew to California to cuckold me and get that Ram job. And I got another coach."

In a move that Cooke says he "very strongly" approved, Williams unilaterally ended talks with Allen. Williams also leaked word to the *Post* that Allen had reached the end of the road in Washington. The *Post* ran a copyrighted story by George Solomon on the front page of its January 19 editions. Both the headline and the lead of Solomon's scoop said that Allen had been "fired" after he repeatedly refused to sign his new contract.[102] Williams had gone to Ben Bradlee's home to await the first edition of the *Post,* and when it arrived late on the evening of January 18, Williams voiced strong objections to use of the word *fired*. "We had a big argument about whether or not he had fired him, which of course he had," says Bradlee. "I said, 'What the fuck do you think you did to him?' He still says sometimes that the *Post* fired Allen, he never did, he loves George. Which is a lot of shit, he hates him." Bradlee refused to order changes in the headline or the story.

Williams used Bradlee's home as a retreat from most of the media that night, although he did accept a call from Sonny Jurgensen, by then a television sportscaster, in time to confirm the demise of Allen for the eleven o'clock news. Wire services carried the story across the country; Ed Hookstratten says he first got word in Chicago, where he was discussing Pardee's future with Bear officials. The talks broke off and Pardee headed for Washington to sit down with Williams, as Hookstratten bowed out, believing that the Allen affair had muddied the waters between him and Redskin officials. Allen, meanwhile, complained that Williams had not had the courtesy to break the news to him directly, and said he had learned from his son, who heard it on the radio, that he was through with the Redskins. He said he had just returned from taking his wife out for her birthday dinner when his son informed them what had happened;[103] later, when it turned out that said dinner had taken place in Los Angeles, the Allens would deny that they had been there to speak to Ram executives.[104] Williams says he had let Allen know he was out by giving him an ultimatum Allen didn't meet, so he didn't tell the *Post* anything of which Allen wasn't already aware.

Media reaction was almost entirely favorable to Williams. The *Post* cited a *Sports Illustrated* poll branding Allen "the most disliked coach in the league."[105] *Washington Star* sports columnist Morris Siegel, who often played *Pravda* to Williams, praised the team president for taking "a bold, daring gamble" in the face of overwhelming fan support for Allen.[106] Another *Star* writer, Steve Guback, tracked Allen down and got his side of the story, which ran across the top of the front page.[107] But Guback's article was one of a handful that were at all sympathetic to Allen.

The biggest issue in the Allen ouster was Allen's true desire: Redskins or Rams. Allen, of course, declared, "'I haven't applied or approached anyone about another job since I've been here,'"[108] and maintained that he had been "'stabbed in the back'" by Williams.[109] But Morris Siegel quoted former Redskin official Joe Sullivan as saying that Allen "'was about to die sweating'" for a job with the Rams, and reported that Rams owner Carroll Rosenbloom said Allen had asked him for a job in 1973, right after the Redskins' loss in the Super Bowl. According to Rosenbloom, "'I quickly reminded George that he had five years left on his Washington contract.'"[110]

Allen's failure to exercise his option to buy stock in the Redskins may have signaled his intentions and may have been the biggest blunder of his life, outranking even his deals for Dave Butz and Duane Thomas and his machinations that left him a coach without a team. If he had bought the 50 shares he was offered, there would then have been 400 outstanding, with Cooke owning 300 and Williams and Allen 50 apiece. So Allen would have owned one-eighth of the team. Assuming the accuracy of estimates that the franchise was worth at least $30 million in 1980, Allen's 12½ percent of the team could have been worth as much as $3 million when he started negotiating for a new contract in 1977. Since he still had the right to buy at the 1971 price, he could theoretically have bought the 50 shares for $557,050, and then turned around and demanded that Cooke and Williams repurchase them at the going rate—about $3 million—or risk having an outsider buy into the team. In fact, Allen's contract with the Redskins still had six weeks to run when Williams broke off talks with him in mid-January 1978, and Allen could have invoked his option anytime in those six weeks. Had Allen done so, he would have scored a financial killing as well as a tremendous media coup, showing the public that he not only could outsmart Williams and Cooke but was sincere in his desire to stay with the Redskins.

As to the Rams, Allen may have understood that if he had owned stock in the Redskins, he never would have been able to divest himself of it in time for Rosenbloom to hire him, which Allen would have had to do in order to comply with NFL rules that prohibit a person associated with one franchise from owning stock in another. In order to be available for any opening with the Rams, Allen would have had to be clear of the Redskins immediately. Still, passing up the chance to buy stock worth $3 million for less than one-fifth its value is a decision that boggles the mind—unless the mind understands only X's and O's.

Before long, Allen got his wish: He was named coach of the Rams, in place of Chuck Knox, who did not get along with Rosenbloom and moved to the Buffalo Bills. Just six months later, midway through the 1978 exhibition season, Rosenbloom fired Allen, in one of the most abrupt sackings of a coach in NFL history. For the next four seasons, Allen was a football analyst for CBS, until he briefly became chief operating officer of the Montreal Alouettes of the Canadian Football League and then moved to the Chicago Blitz of the brand-new United States Football League. Neither league is held in great respect in the NFL, and Williams was amused by his antagonist's decline and exile after four fruitless years of seeking a head coaching job in the National Football League.*

Less than forty-eight hours after Williams in effect dismissed Allen (Williams still insists, "I didn't fire him. His contract expired"), the coach visited Redskin Park near Dulles Airport to collect his belongings. He carefully removed a near life-size picture of him and Richard Nixon, but gave a "scornful, mean look" to a handyman who asked him what to do with a picture of Williams and Allen.[112] Williams drove around outside, waiting for Allen to depart, and as soon as he did, Williams arrived and talked to remaining Redskin personnel. That night he had locks changed at the team's offices.[113] He had discovered that Allen had taken home "a lot of valuable film" showing Redskin practices and games as well as other teams in action. So Williams sent Redskin employees to "retrieve" the film "from Allen's house. We just sent our people out and took it from his garage. I told them to get it back. They went and got it back."

Several days later, Williams hired Pardee as coach and announced to the press, "'We've gone back to an open society.'"[114] He subsequently selected Bobby Beathard, an aide to Don Shula at Miami, as general manager, dividing Allen's old job into two, as Dave Slattery had suggested in his realignment of Redskin operations. George Allen, in the meantime, was given a farewell party at the Iranian Embassy; the shah's ex-son-in-law, Ambassador Ardeshir Zahedi, personally grilled chicken for Allen and his friends.[115]

The battle was over, with Williams a clear winner, but the war continued, largely in the media. The major salvo against Allen was fired in a monumentally long story in the *Post*'s Sunday magazine. It was written by two reporters and called "The Final Plays," as in Woodward and Bernstein's book on the end of the Nixon presidency, *The Final Days*. Allen was pictured as someone who was such a cheapskate that Williams's pal Duke Zeibert had to tip the waiters who served Allen when he visited Zeibert's eatery. Allen was also said to have charged the team for phone calls by him and his family; the rental of a private plane to fly him to a football game one of his sons played in; extra steaks when he went out to dinner; drinking glasses bearing Allen's likeness; and both employees and gardening equipment to maintain the coach's home in tip-top shape.[116]

---

*Allen was also offered an opportunity to buy all or part of the Montreal team. But the *Washington Post* expressed doubts that Allen would invest his own money, quoting "associates familiar with George's habits" as saying "he wouldn't make a nickel downpayment on a fried egg."[111]

In an attempt to balance the picture, the story quoted Etty Allen as declaring that "'a CIA man'" had found that the phone in the family home was tapped and implying that Williams was responsible. She also told how the team ordered two vehicles that had been loaned to Allen's sons repossessed; even worse, she asserted, team officials had "dumped the belongings [of one son] on the street" before reclaiming his pickup truck.[117] In general, though, the article gave Williams's side of Allen's ouster; Tom Dowling later wrote in his whimsical story "Saint Ed and the Dragon" that "the identity of Deep Throat" in "The Final Plays" "could not be more obvious. He is Edward Bennett Williams." Were "The Final Plays" to be footnoted, Dowling said, it would be "simple . . . Just E. B. Williams, followed by an unending string of *ibids*."[118]

Torn between two people who were not favorites of his, NFL commissioner Pete Rozelle sided with Williams. He fined Allen $3,000 for his public criticism of Williams and chastised him for his "'prior record of numerous violations of NFL rules by clubs under your direct administration and control. . . .Unfortunately, your performance away from the playing field fills us with dissatisfaction.'"[119] It was two months later that Rosenbloom fired Allen from the Rams.

Allen had remained friendly with Jack Kent Cooke. Several months after leaving Washington, he visited Cooke in Las Vegas and apologized for what he had said about Williams. Cooke: "I said, 'That's fine, George, you criticize, you defame Ed publicly, and then you come in here in the privacy of my home and apologize.'" Allen then called Williams and apologized to him personally, and also expressed his regrets to the media for his public comments about Williams. Three years later, however, Williams said he knew that Allen had apologized only because he'd hoped that would help him land another coaching job, perhaps even with the Redskins. In early 1981, after seasons of 8-8, 10-6, and 6-10 under Pardee and Beathard, Cooke decided that one or the other would have to go. Over Williams's objections, Cooke fired Pardee. Afterward, according to Williams, Allen was burning up the wires with phone calls to Cooke in pursuit of his old post. Cooke refused to give history a chance to repeat itself and hired Joe Gibbs, a San Diego Charger assistant coach, instead.

George Allen has little to say about his troubles with Williams. He does, however, make one telling point, suggesting that since coaches are often judged by their won-lost records, team owners should be, too. A look at Williams's record shows that he was in charge of the team for fourteen seasons, before Cooke moved to Washington and took over the operation. In seven of Williams's years at the helm (1971–77), Allen was the coach; the team had a record of 67-30-1 in those seasons, for a victory percentage of .691; had seven winning years; and qualified for the playoffs a total of five times. In Williams's seven seasons without Allen (1965–70 and 1978), the Redskins went 44-51-5, or .459; had one winning year; and went to the playoffs a total of zero times. Williams, to be sure, would be the last to criticize Allen's effectiveness as a coach, but he simply tired of everything else that went with having Allen around.

A year after Allen passed from the Redskin scene, Williams did, too, as Jack Kent Cooke relieved him of command and Williams turned to baseball and the Baltimore Orioles. In a way, Williams's leaving was much like his coming: In place of the WE WANT LOUIS NIZER banner that registered the fans's displeasure over the 1965 team's start, spectators displayed a streamer saying, "GO BACK HOME COOKE. WE WANT EBW," as the 1981 Redskins also lost their first five games. The following year, however, Beathard and Gibbs guided the Redskins to their first Super Bowl championship. Pardee, meanwhile, faded entirely from the football scene, and even Williams had to admit that he had been wrong and Cooke correct about who should be in charge of the team.

Owning a major-league baseball team had been a lifelong dream for Williams. When he was only eight, he had started working summers for his hometown minor-league team, the Hartford Senators, initially earning 50 cents or so a game, depending on how many sodas, ice-cream bars, hot dogs, or cushions he could sell. After several years, he graduated to bat boy and got to hang around such future major-leaguers as Birdie Tebbetts, Paul Richards, Van Lingle Mungo, and Hank Greenberg, whom he recalls most vividly. After coming to Hartford as a highly touted prospect for the parent Detroit Tigers, Greenberg "struck out about ninety times in a row and they gave him the air," according to Williams. "Boom! It was terrible. He was just a big gawky kid about eighteen or so. They sent him back [to the Tigers] and Detroit sent him somewhere else."

Greenberg, of course, became a big-league star, and in the 1950s both he and Williams were pals of Bill Veeck, then the owner of the Chicago White Sox. In 1960, Calvin Griffith, owner of the Washington Senators, decided he wanted to move his club to Minneapolis–St. Paul, and American League owners hatched a proposal to expand from eight to ten teams, placing new franchises in Los Angeles and Washington. Bill Veeck had a "modest little plan" of his own: He would vote approval of Griffith's transfer if Griffith in turn would vote for the people Veeck wanted to own the new teams—Greenberg in Los Angeles and a syndicate in Washington that included Williams. Baltimore beer baron Jerry Hoffberger was originally a leading member of the Williams group, but he bowed out when it seemed he might be able to increase his 27½-percent interest in the Orioles to majority ownership (which did come to pass). Williams and his remaining partners—including his longtime friend Joe DiMaggio, and Colman Stein from his law firm—quickly found enough financing to pledge $3.5 million for the new franchise, with another $1 million in reserve.

Veeck did indeed vote for Griffith's move, but A.L. owners were split over several competing bidders for the new Washington team, and on the eighth ballot Griffith double-crossed Veeck and Williams by casting the decisive vote for a rival syndicate. Williams had been confident that "'we could not lose,'" right up until the moment he was notified that the Washington team was not to be his, but he would say later that "'it may have been the best thing that ever happened to me.'" Veeck's plans fell through all around. Not only could he not join Williams as an owner of the new Washington team, as they had intended, but Hank Greenberg found the price of the Los Angeles franchise too steep and decided not to buy it.[120]

By 1968, Williams was disparaging the "'boredom'" in baseball and predicting that the game "'is really going to be up against it in five years'" because "'all those stadiums [are] in the bad part of town and they've turned baseball into a night game.'"[121] In 1971, however, after Bob Short, the new owner of the expansion Washington Senators, decided to move the club to Dallas-Fort Worth, D.C. mayor Walter Washington sent Williams as his representative to inquire about transferring the San Diego Padres of the National League to the nation's capital. Nothing came of that, but obviously Williams was still interested in acquiring a baseball team.

Finally, in 1978, former Treasury secretary William Simon invited Williams to join him in negotiating with Jerry Hoffberger, who had been trying to sell the Orioles for several years. Simon and Williams thought they had a deal with Hoffberger, but the Oriole owner continued talks with Baltimore investors who wanted to buy the club. "Bill thought Jerry was reneging on a commitment and he got angry and dropped out, leaving me alone." Williams made up his mind to go ahead on his own, and on August 2, 1979, Williams and Hoffberger announced that Williams was buying the Orioles. (The sale price was reported as $12 million at the time,[122] but Hoffberger later said in a statement to his shareholders that Williams paid $14.65 million.[123])

Williams says he was "worried" about buying 100 percent of the stock without partners, and he had to borrow a large part of the purchase price at an interest rate he admitted was about 20 percent. If he borrowed $10 million at 20 percent, the annual interest—without compounding and without any principal payments—would have been $2 million, a staggering amount for a relatively small business such as a baseball club. Word quickly circulated in the Baltimore-Washington area that Williams was hurting over his interest payments, and one friend of his, Bill Ragan, bought box seats for the season (and never went to a game) after Williams told him "how financially terrible" his deal was. Art Buchwald reported to Williams that he was telling people who asked him why Williams bought the team that the answer was "'Because you're a compulsive, stupid son of a bitch.'" Williams said to Buchwald, "'Yeah, stick with that one.'" Within two years, though, he paid off the entire loan.

Williams did not officially assume control of the Orioles until after the end of the 1979 season, in which the team won 102 games, more than any other club in the major leagues, and went to the seventh and final game of the World Series, only to lose the championship to the Pittsburgh Pirates. In one of his first moves after taking over, Williams appointed his friend and client Joe DiMaggio to the board of directors.*

Williams's acquisition of the Orioles put him on a collision course with Pete Rozelle, who was trying to enforce an NFL rule against an operator or majority owner of a professional football team also being in control of a franchise in another sport. Since Williams managed the Redskins and voted Cooke's 85.7 percent of Redskin stock, as well as his own 14.3 percent, buying the Orioles placed him in apparent violation of the NFL edict.

In earlier days, Rozelle and Williams had often been on the same side, with both testifying before Congress in 1973 that NFL home games should be blacked out from local television even if all seats in the stadium were sold,[125] and Williams carrying the league's ball in 1976 against a suit filed by a former Redskin charging that the college player draft violated antitrust laws.[126] But Williams's purchase of a baseball team presented a personal challenge to Rozelle, who was already sore at him because of a Williams speech at a recent NFL meeting. Subsequently, after the North American Soccer League filed an antitrust suit over the NFL rule barring cross-ownership, Williams would testify against league interests (according to Rozelle's way of thinking).

Rozelle was still smarting over the two incidents two years later. He recalled that at an NFL meeting in early June 1979, Williams had unexpectedly given a "very strong" speech in opposition to the cross-ownership rule without mentioning that he was working on a deal for the Orioles. To compound matters, stories about Williams's interest in buying the Orioles broke in the press just a few days later, and, Rozelle complains, "I read about it in the newspaper." Rozelle criticizes Williams for "decrying the rule without acknowledging that he was looking into buying the baseball team. I think he either shouldn't have made the speech, or he would have been better off if he was going ahead at that point, which he apparently was, in looking into the Orioles, to have been a little more candid. Because he was basing his opposition to the rule on general legal principles and then it turned out in the minds of many people that he might have had other motivation for it." Rozelle also says with some heat that because Williams had not given any advance notice that he planned to speak on

---

*Williams has negotiated DiMaggio's contracts for television commercials for many years, and threatened to sue *Sports Illustrated* when the magazine quoted the former Yankee star as saying baseball was "'just too dull'" and he didn't "'give a rap'" for the game.[124]

the rule, the league's lawyers were not present, and "I was forced to get them to come in in the afternoon and answer him." Williams says in response that he had been speaking out against the cross-ownership ban for many years, long before he started talks with Hoffberger about the Orioles.

Equally upsetting to Rozelle was Williams's position in the soccer suit, when he not only testified in court against the NFL rule but had the Redskins dropped as a defendant in the NASL case, on grounds that the club felt the same way the soccer league did. Rozelle stops just short of using the word *traitor* in describing how Williams "testified against his partners in the soccer suit." Williams retorts, "I didn't testify against the league. I testified to the facts. Maybe the facts were against his [Rozelle's] interests. But I answered the questions that they asked me," under subpoena by the NASL. He concedes that "I think the rule with respect to dual ownership is ridiculous" and "absurd. . . . All the ownership rules in football are archaic," such as directives that a corporation cannot control an NFL team, and that an individual person must own at least 51 percent of each club's stock.

The confrontation between Williams and Rozelle petered out when Cooke assumed control of the Redskins as Williams was buying the Orioles, but no love is lost between them. By Rozelle's reckoning, he hasn't seen or spoken to Williams since mid-1979.

In each of Williams's first three seasons as owner, the Orioles came close, but did not quite make the playoffs. Most frustrating of all was the 1982 pennant race, when the Orioles moved from far behind to draw even with the Milwaukee Brewers, only to lose the final game of the season and the flag to the Brewers. The pain of those first three years was mitigated for Williams by the knowledge that success then would have been attributed in large part to Jerry Hoffberger, whose administration assembled all the key players. In a sense, the more time that elapsed before the Orioles were back on top, the more Williams would be able to claim victory as his own.

Almost at once, and to his surprise, Williams found himself attending nearly every Orioles home game. He tended to get caught up in the action; neighboring spectators at one game in 1981 exchanged knowing glances when the owner registered disgust over manager Earl Weaver's choice for a relief pitcher by bringing his hand down with a loud smack on the counter in the owner's box. He shouted, "Stupid! Stupid!" at the unhearing Weaver—whom he and many others consider the best manager in the game. Williams suggested facetiously that Weaver was "trying to give me a heart attack" and proposed a straight one-for-one trade between two of his many enterprises: "Maybe I should manage the ball club and Earl should take over the law firm." Unlike owners of some sports franchises, however, Williams had the good grace not to use his telephone to discuss strategy with his manager during the game.

In his dealings with his players, Williams quickly established himself as one of baseball's most enlightened owners. He was much more willing than Hoffberger to pay competitive salaries to his stars and thus was able to sign most of them to new contracts. Comparing Williams to Hoffberger, pitcher Jim Palmer, an Oriole star since 1966, said Williams is "not as frugal," emphasizing every word.

Williams's willingness to view issues from the players' point of view had an immediate impact throughout baseball. He was one of the key figures in averting a player strike in May 1980. With owners and players at loggerheads over the question of whether a team that signed a free agent had to compensate his old club with another player, Williams worked out a last-minute compromise that postponed the strike.

Williams regards strikes as "suicide" and "like wars. Everybody loses. It's like a nuclear blast." So he was dismayed that the two sides failed to resolve their differences and the players did walk out in June 1981. From the strike's start, Williams moaned that "I could settle this strike in one hour if they'd let me," and wondered if he had "shot my wad" in 1980, which might render him ineffective in 1981. He was equally critical of the players, Baseball Commissioner Bowie Kuhn, and his fellow owners, and refused to be inhibited from expressing his views in public, even though the owners had imposed stiff sanctions on any of their number who violated their own gag order. After rumors circulated that he might be in line for a fine of $50,000 or more because of his outspoken opposition to the hard-line stance of a majority of owners, Williams said defiantly, "I wouldn't pay any fine. We would have had to have it out, that's all."

The strike finally ended after seven weeks (during which the Orioles lost an estimated $100,000 for each of twenty-five home dates that were canceled[127]). As in 1980, Williams was seen in the press as having been instrumental in persuading each side to accept a formula for compensating teams that had lost free agents to other clubs. The dispute was settled immediately after he led eight other American League owners in calling for the league to meet and try to find a position acceptable to both sides. "'I give him [Williams] credit. Calling the meeting forced a settlement to be made as early as it was,'" declared federal mediator Kenneth E. Moffett.[128]

In general, Williams, the consummate battler in other arenas, has emerged as the great compromiser in the treatment of professional athletes. His consistent efforts to see both sides of the issue in baseball's labor problems did not constitute an isolated example. He was also willing to accommodate Redskin fullback John Riggins, who walked out on the team in 1980 as a ploy to gain a guaranteed one-year extension of his contract. But Jack Kent Cooke, who was in charge of bargaining with

Riggins, insisted that he play under the terms that had been agreed upon four years earlier; Riggins declined, and the player sat out the season. His absence was very costly to the Redskins, who fell from 10-6 the previous year to 6-10 without him, but Cooke made a point that is scored all too infrequently these days: that athletes have some obligation to their teams.

Williams offers a possible explanation for the apparent contradiction between his sports and nonsports attitudes: "There's a very big difference between dealing with your own money and with someone else's money. In sports, I'm dealing with my own money. I'm not dealing for some client. So maybe I do feel more liberal in dealing with my own money. If I have the reputation of being hard-nosed in other dealings, other dealings would be not for me but for other people in my role as a lawyer."

In addition to offering moderate views on labor relations, Williams is trying to provide impetus toward changing the game of baseball in other ways, the most important of which is his advocacy of more revenue-sharing among the twenty-six teams. His proposal is twofold: Visiting teams would receive 40 percent of gate receipts, just as they do in the NFL, instead of the present 20 percent in the American League and 50 cents per ticket in the National League; and all broadcast income would be divided equally, which is the way NFL teams do it. He is especially concerned about the implications of pay television, which is clearly the wave of the future for baseball and all other sports. "When I go into New York and they get revenue for putting my game over the air, I want half the revenue," he remarks. "I'm half the attraction, I want half the revenue." Without revenue-sharing, he fears, baseball will wind up having just a handful of teams confined to a few giant television markets.

The overriding question about Williams's stewardship of the Orioles has been the same ever since he bought the team in 1979: Will he or won't he (move the club to Washington)? Williams's statement to the press when he announced he was buying the team did little to give a definitive answer: "'I did not buy the Baltimore Orioles to move them. I bought them to play in Baltimore and so long as the people of Baltimore support the Baltimore Orioles, they will stay here. That is my pledge to this city.'" What did he mean by "support"? "'I want the kind of support which will permit me to keep the Baltimore Orioles . . . a championship team.'"[129]

The Orioles' lease in Baltimore is year-to-year, and allows them to play up to thirteen games a season in Washington. But a few days after he bought the team, when the *Washington Post* quoted "sources close to Williams" as saying the new owner hoped to play thirteen games in Washington in 1980 and move all home games to RKF Stadium within three years,[130] Williams blasted the *Post* story as "'the nadir of irresponsible journalism . . . totally and absolutely without foundation.'"[131]

The issue was revived during the 1980 season when he told a *Post* reporter that unless the Orioles drew enough fans in Baltimore to let him compete with the Yankees and Red Sox, he would pursue "'all of my options. . . . This was to be a trial year for Baltimore attendance,'" he added, "'and the trial is just about to begin.'"[132] His remarks created a furor in Baltimore, with the *Sun* stating in its lead editorial (titled "'Williams Serves Notice'") that "'there would be better results without threats from Williams.'"[133] Following the 1980 season, in which the Orioles' total attendance was 1.8 million, the record high since the team moved to Baltimore in 1954, Williams attempted to put the matter to rest by vowing, "'The time may come when I leave baseball, but baseball will never leave Baltimore.'"[134]

All well and good. Nevertheless, Williams is the same man who pledged in reference to George Allen, "'Believe me, this is the last coach Edward Bennett Williams is going to hire or fire.'" Also, in the course of many interviews while this book was being prepared, Williams made clear that new conditions might cause him to change his mind about Baltimore, just as he did about George Allen. Before the 1982 season, in fact, he said he needed to sell 1.75 million tickets (at much higher prices than in the past) to break even, and that he could not afford to subsidize baseball in Baltimore. He found Oriole attendance in 1982—only 1.6 million, even though the team was in contention all year—extremely disappointing.

One of his most revealing comments on the subject was "Basically, what you have to look at is the television market." According to 1981 television-industry figures, Washington ranked eighth nationally, with 1.4 million households; Baltimore was nineteenth, with 800,000 homes; and the two cities combined would rank fifth, behind New York, Los Angeles, Chicago and Philadelphia.[135] "So, obviously, for television purposes, for marketing purposes, the ideal place for a stadium is in between" the two cities.

Whether a stadium ever will be constructed between Baltimore and Washington is uncertain. But Williams is very familiar with the deficiencies of Baltimore's Memorial Stadium compared to the empty stadium in Washington, which has adequate parking, good highway access and is located near a subway stop. Furthermore, the Washington metropolitan area is about 50 percent more populous than Baltimore and is much more affluent, with a whopping $40 billion in disposable personal income (three times as high as Baltimore's). Similarly, average household income in the Washington area in 1981 was more than twice that in Baltimore.[136]

As for Baltimore's support for the Orioles, even though the team has the best cumulative won-lost record in all of major-league baseball since 1957,[137] attendance in Baltimore has been dismal. Williams's estimate that the team must draw 1.75 million fans to break even should be weighed against the club's history, which reveals that in only three of its twenty-nine seasons in Baltimore has it attracted more than 1.2 million;

and in 1979 and 1980, the two best years, the team sold only 1.7 and 1.8 million tickets.[138] Teams with comparable won-lost records, like the Yankees and Dodgers, draw 2.5 to 3 million customers each year. Williams will continue to watch with a wary eye for the first sign of faltering in Baltimore's support for his team—as he has ever since the day he acquired the franchise.

In a pinch, Williams could no doubt unload the Orioles in a minute to his new friend, Denver oilman Marvin Davis. During the late 1970s, Williams reached agreement on Davis's behalf with Charles O. Finley, owner of the Oakland Athletics baseball team, for Finley to sell his franchise to Davis, but the deal fell through when the A's could not break their stadium lease so that Davis could move them to Denver. In 1980, Williams tried to help Davis buy the Denver Broncos of the NFL, but the owners, who disliked Davis, sold to an out-of-towner at a lower price than he had offered. As of 1981, Williams was trying—without success—to convince Robert Irsay, the eccentric owner of the Colts, to sell the club to Davis, with whom Williams would much prefer to share Baltimore's stadium. "Irsay will deny it, but it's true," says Williams of Davis's approaches to Irsay, which were instigated by Williams. It must be comforting for Williams to know that if he ever wants to get rid of the Orioles in a hurry, he has a close friend worth hundreds of millions of dollars who is only too eager to buy a sports team, preferably a baseball club.

But Williams did not buy the Orioles in order to sell them to Davis or anyone else. He bought them because he wanted to own a baseball club. And in the last analysis, there are two things worth remembering. First, Bill Veeck, who was Williams's initial tutor on the subject of baseball ownership, wrote twenty years ago, "Washington . . . happens to be an untapped gold mine. If I couldn't make a club go there I would turn in my shield."[139] That was before Washington turned into one of the biggest boom towns in the country, before the city had a subway system to carry fans to the new stadium.

Second, another American League team cannot go into Washington without Williams's approval, but he can't block a National League franchise from playing in the nation's capital. And Williams happens to feel that the Washington-Baltimore region is "like the [San Francisco] Bay Area. It will support only one team." As long as Williams owns that one team, he can play the two cities off against each other, sell tickets in both metropolitan areas, and treat the entire region as one huge television market. The day the National League takes over Washington, however, Edward Bennett Williams will be left in Baltimore—and left holding the bag. And if there is one lesson to be learned from studying the life of Edward Bennett Williams, it is that he is seldom—if ever—left holding the bag.

Part
TWO

Beginnings

5

From Hartford
to Georgetown

Gerald Chapman died suddenly on April 6, 1926. He was in his late thirties and had been in excellent health.

Chapman passed away on the gallows at the Connecticut State Prison in Wethersfield. He had been tried in Hartford a year earlier and convicted of murdering a police officer during a 1924 robbery in New Britain. In keeping with his image as America's "most desperate, resourceful bandit of the day," Chapman wore his patented "look of scorn for society" as executioners covered his head with a hood.

Thanks in part to what the press called his "native intelligence without integrity," Chapman had captured the public fancy with his escapades. He was best known for a 1921 mail-truck robbery in Manhattan that netted him and two others $2.4 million, and for several prison escapes, the most daring of which occurred in 1923, just a few days after he had been shot three times in another escape attempt. During his brief periods out of jail, Chapman's penchant for high living—fast cars, faster women, luxurious apartments, jewels, fur coats, and the New York nightclub circuit—led to his being called "the Count of Gramercy Park." Adding to Chapman's legend were his refusal to disclose who he was, where he was from, or when he was born (although there was speculation that he was the

111

black sheep of a well-to-do New York family), and his prison hobby: writing poetry. On account of his notoriety, hundreds of people turned out to watch him ride to the courthouse during his trial, and a crowd of about 1,500 gathered outside the prison the night of his execution.[1]

Among those who followed the Chapman saga with more than passing interest was young Eddie Williams of Hartford, who was four when Chapman killed the policeman; almost five when he was tried and convicted, and nearly six when the outlaw was put to death. More than half a century later, Williams would remember that he had been "riveted" by the Chapman case and that almost every day during the trial he had walked the two miles from his home to the courthouse to watch the lawyers enter and leave. The Chapman trial "was a very arresting kind of thing and it got me interested in the law," says Williams.

Wethersfield State Prison was also a familiar Williams haunt. It was next to a swimming hole known as the Cove, where he and his pals went skinny-dipping in the Connecticut River. Although Williams was too young to be at the prison gate the night Chapman died, he and his classmates toured the prison several years later. "I have a very vivid recollection of going there. The prisoners were watching a ball game in the yard and there was one fellow sitting all alone in the seats way out in right field. None of the other inmates would have anything to do with him." The outcast was Walter E. Shean, Chapman's partner in the robbery in which the cop was slain. Shean had turned state's evidence and been Chapman's chief accuser, in order to save his own neck.

So Walter Shean, who was not loyal to his friends, had none. That was one valuable lesson Eddie Williams would learn from the Chapman case. Another was an intense dislike for publicity that might hurt a client's case. Chapman had complained that extensive publicity had prejudiced the jurors who found him guilty: "'The newspapers have made me out a superbandit, an arch-criminal. They have not convicted the accused, but a man named Chapman.'"[2] As a lawyer, Williams would interpret very strictly the Sixth Amendment provision that "the accused shall enjoy the right to a speedy and public trial." The accused—and only the accused—is guaranteed a public trial; neither the prosecution nor the public is entitled to have a case tried in public. Williams also noticed that lawyers who defend notorious criminals receive more than the usual share of public attention. And he would be a lifelong opponent of capital punishment.

Hartford, where Edward Bennett Williams was born on May 31, 1920, was a city of 138,000. A center of the insurance industry then and now, Hartford was still a relatively small city with about 165,000 residents when he moved away in 1937.[3]

Williams was the only child of Joseph Barnard Williams and Mary Bennett Williams, who met when they worked at the Brown Thomson department store in downtown Hartford. Joseph Williams was born in 1884 in Middletown, about twenty miles south of Hartford, where his father, James Williams, a native of Wales, worked in an iron foundry. Mary Bennett Williams's parents were Peter and Margaret Reilly Bennett: Peter Bennett was born in Ireland and arrived in New York when he was about sixteen. Several years later, he moved to West Hartford, where he bought a small dairy farm that produced milk he carried to a market in town on a horsedrawn cart. Bennett died young, leaving his wife to raise a son and four daughters. The Bennett son also died early, and each of the daughters gave her sons the middle name of Bennett.[4]

As a department-store buyer and floorwalker, Joseph Williams never made much money. The family did not lack the essentials, but luxuries were few and far between. They lived in an apartment on the first floor of a two-story house in South Hartford. Although a bus stopped at the corner, Joseph Williams usually walked the two miles to work, both because he liked to walk and in order to save money. He is described as "a brilliant man" who read constantly and was never known to take a drink. He was also a strict father who expected his only child to make straight A's and thought it "terrible" on the rare occasions when the boy received a lesser grade. Unlike her husband, Mary Bennett Williams was "easygoing," had "a terrific sense of humor," and enjoyed playing bridge.[5] Nevertheless, she expected her son to be obedient; during neighborhood baseball games, Ed Williams's neighbor and closest friend, David Rosen, would often hear her blow her police whistle, the signal for her son to come home. And, no matter what he was doing, Ed Williams would rush home when his mother called.

Both Joseph and Mary Williams were devout Catholics who attended mass regularly and involved their son in church activities, including a summer camp. David Rosen, who is Jewish, was all set to join his chum at camp until Mrs. Williams advised Mrs. Rosen that the camp might not be quite right for David. Years later, when David Rosen was in the service during World War II, Mrs. Williams told Mrs. Rosen she was lighting candles for David "because she didn't want to take any chances."

Williams's childhood passion was baseball. He devised a baseball game that he and David Rosen could play with a deck of cards on rainy days. In good weather, they and other boys in the neighborhood formed a team they called the Barker Bulldogs. (Barker was the street next to the street where Williams lived, Adelaide.) Williams, who was one of the tallest players, was the first baseman, and a fairly good one, says Rosen. Williams, Rosen, and their friends also frequented the stadium of the minor-league Hartford Senators. Their standard operating procedure, according to Williams, was for "one guy to climb over the right-field fence, get the cop's attention, and then all the other kids would go over the left-field fence" to gain admission. The police, not totally unsympathetic to the situation of Depression Era boys who had no money to spend on ball games, often would look in the other direction and at times would literally lend a helping hand by boosting David Rosen, who was smaller than the others, over the fence. Rosen said the group had a similar ploy for getting into movies: One member would buy a ticket, wait until the picture started and the theater was dark, then open the door for his buddies.

Williams and Rosen tried a variety of plans for making money. Their first attempt met with little success: When they were about eight they learned about the practice of betting on what would be the last three digits of the Treasury balance, which appeared on the financial page each day. As Rosen recalls, "Ed said, 'Gee, why don't we work up our own pool?' We sold chances for five cents to all the kids in the neighborhood. Then for about three hours we sat there sweating, praying that nobody would hit, because we couldn't have paid them off, and imagining that we would wind up in jail. That lasted one day." Williams also held legitimate jobs, like working at the Hartford Senators' games, selling the *Saturday Evening Post, Ladies' Home Journal,* and other magazines door-to-door and pumping gas in a service station.

Williams entered the ninth grade at Bulkeley High School in September 1933. He quickly established himself as a leader in high school, where he accumulated a hoard of honors. He was president of the student council; coeditor of the student newspaper, the *Torch;* speaker of the Legislative Club; treasurer of the boys' Debating Club; a member of the Honor Society, based on character, service, scholarship, and leadership; and the winner of a coveted prize for excellence in English.

It was while he was in high school that Williams set his mind once and for all on becoming a lawyer. His girlfriend at Bulkeley, Muriel ("Jerry") Waterhouse, who met him the day they entered high school and went to the Bulkeley senior prom with Williams, says that from the time he was fifteen, "Ed always wanted to be a lawyer, there was never anything else in his mind." Several years before her death, Mary Bennett Williams told Gay Talese that her son "'used to stand up on a chair and imitate Franklin D. Roosevelt making radio speeches. . . . He used to study real hard in school. He'd go to his room at night and shut the door and not come out in an hour and a half. He wanted to *make* something of himself.'"[6] Williams had sent Roosevelt a congratulatory note after he was first elected president in 1932 and received back a letter thanking him and saying, "'I was glad to have your picture for it helps to know you better.'"[7] But shortly before Williams graduated from Bulkeley, he wrote a story in the *Dial,* the student literary magazine, criticizing FDR's attempt to pack the Supreme Court.[8]

During his high-school years, much of Williams's time outside of class was occupied by the school newspaper, the *Torch.* His first involvement with the *Torch* came during the spring of his sophomore year, when he was named to the sports staff.[9] (As a participant, his high-school sports activities were confined to a spell on the track team, where he ran the mile. By Williams's own admission, speed afoot was not one of his strong points as an athlete, and his times as a miler were better suited to an hourglass than to a stopwatch.)

In his junior year, Williams was named assistant editor of the *Torch*, sixth in line in the hierarchy, and he soon moved up to managing editor.[10] His specialty was writing a weekly column that was heavy on gossip and humor. The "Inside Stuff" column for December 4, 1936, over the byline "Repentant," reported that intramural basketball games were being closed to spectators because "some of the girl spectators were too ardent in their attention to the game." According to that same column,

> Any mention of the *Bridgeport Herald* suffices to make Ed Williams shudder. Can it be that an account of his unsullied past will be published in this cheap imitation of Inside Stuff? . . . The "Dial" room has instituted a system for paying for each issue and at the same time for restraining profanity. Anyone who swears in the room has to pay a penny for each swear word. Some get-rich quick artist suggested this scheme for the Torch room, but it wouldn't work, for who would pay up. See Ed Williams for detailed information.

Two weeks later, Williams signed "Inside Stuff" and said the column was being discontinued because, although "everything that was printed in this column was printed in the spirit of fun, . . . it was not always accepted that way, we are sad to say." He added:

> We apologize to those good teachers and students whose advice we scorned when they urged us for our own good to discontinue the printing of Inside Stuff. Above all, we apologize to those students whose feelings we hurt by some of our over-exuberant remarks. . . . And now, with crocodile tears blurring the letters on our good old Underwood, we wish to bid a sad farewell to our devoted readers.[11]

David Rosen, who preceded him as editor of the *Torch*, says he used to have to "bail out" Williams; the Bulkeley principal was not amused by everything that emerged from Williams's Underwood.

When Williams was named coeditor of the *Torch* in his final semester, one of his first acts was to change the motto that ran under the masthead from "A Journal for Publishing School News and Uniting the Student Body" to "New England's Snappiest Scholastic Weekly." And even though he was in charge of the paper, stories and anecdotes about Williams continued to appear. One said:

> Ed Williams considers himself a lady-killer, [but] the ladies seem unaware of it. He was walking with Jerry [Waterhouse] when they passed a pretty girl. At once he turned to her with a superior smile.

"Did you see that charming young lady smile at me?"

"Oh, that's nothing to worry about," replied Jerry consolingly. "The first time I saw you I laughed out loud." [12]

Today Williams is somewhat embarrassed by his high-school journalistic efforts, and feels they were not quite up to the standards of his close friend Ben Bradlee, executive editor of the *Washington Post*.

As early as his high-school days, Williams established a reputation as a perfectionist of sorts. David Rosen says that "if he didn't have lined paper, he would take white paper and a ruler and draw the lines"—unlike his contemporaries, who would "let the teacher worry about following our handwriting."

He also displayed an ability to learn rapidly, which would become one of his trademarks as an attorney. According to Jerry Waterhouse, who was also a leading student at Bulkeley, "Ed was very bright. He was not studious. He was just a quick study. If he hadn't done any Latin translation, I could walk down the corridor and read him the translation and he could pick it up just like that. I'd spend an hour and a half studying it, but in five minutes he could remember every word I'd said. It's just incredible. He's been like that ever since I've known him, and I've known him since he was thirteen years old."

Waterhouse, who got married shortly after she graduated from Smith College, has remained in touch with Williams over the years. She said that what she liked best about him, aside from the fact that he was "smart" and "just a very nice kid," was that, like her, he was "tall. He had reached full height, but not full weight. He was skinny." Williams is now a beefy 220 pounds or so, at least 60 pounds more than he carried on his six-foot-one-inch frame when he was dating Jerry Waterhouse.

Williams's main problem while he was in high school was finding a way to go to a college he wanted to attend. He was awarded a scholarship to Trinity College in Hartford, which would have been less expensive than going away to school, but he didn't want to go there. Fortunately for him, he had become a special favorite of Jane Dargan, Bulkeley's assistant principal, and she helped him win a scholarship to Holy Cross.

Williams graduated from Bulkeley in June 1937, just after his seventeenth birthday, making him the first member of his immediate family to go that far in school. He was voted the most popular boy in his class, and the senior-class prophecy was: "Ed Williams finally getting the scoop of the year." The yearbook described him as "known by everyone, principally for his leadership and scholarship. He always ruled with an iron hand and a dominating will . . . and for this reason accomplished much."

The following September, he enrolled at Holy Cross College in Worcester, Massachusetts, where he followed a liberal-arts course, heavy in literature, the classics, and philosophy. "Basically, I was thinking always about law school and was steeping myself in courses that would be conducive to legal training." As a recipient of an academic scholarship, he was placed in the honors track, where the professors, about half of whom were Jesuits, "drove us like hell, absolutely beyond anything I've ever been driven in my life. We *never* had any time off. We worked all the time, seven days a week, around the clock. It was just brutal." In those days, life was tightly controlled at "The Cross"; students had a dress code, attendance at mass was compulsory, and there were very strict curfews. He did find time to visit Jerry Waterhouse at her college; as his yearbook said, "When Ed decided to relax from studies . . . he didn't spare the horses . . . interests at Smith College."

He also participated in extracurricular activities, most of which revolved around debating. As a member of the Holy Cross debate team, he impressed a teammate, Robert Maheu, with the exacting preparation that others would notice when he was older. During the 1950s, before Maheu became top aide to Howard Hughes, he and Williams joined forces in several sensitive projects. (See Part Four.)

After receiving a grade of 97 in his oral examinations, Williams graduated first in his class in 1941. He was *summa cum laude* and was voted "most learned" by his classmates. Williams and his best friend and debate partner at Holy Cross, William Richardson, had discussed going to law school at Washington's Catholic University, where each had won a scholarship, and then practicing law together. But just before their graduation, Richardson decided to become a Jesuit priest, leaving Williams with a choice among three law schools: Catholic and Georgetown, each of which offered him a full scholarship, and Yale, which awarded him "the best they had to give at the time"—a partial scholarship that included a loan of $500 a year for three years, to be repaid in installments starting five years after his graduation.

Although Williams was seriously considering Yale, which had the best law school of the three, his father advised him to take one of the full scholarships. "He told me that I would never be able to repay the $1,500 loan to Yale. He had never had $1,500 in his whole life, and he was afraid I'd spend the rest of my life trying to repay the $1,500. I wasn't persuaded by that. But his worry and concern were enough to tip the balance, for me to come to Georgetown. I really wanted to come to Washington, and Catholic University didn't have quite as good a law school as Georgetown. Those were the Roosevelt years and Washington was the most exciting place in America to be at the time. I didn't want to go to New Haven. New Haven looked to me like another city like Hartford; it was just a replica of Hartford."

Williams entered Georgetown Law Center in September 1941, but soon left to join the army air force. The lure of "being a pilot, getting wings, all that stuff" seemed "romantic" to him until he had been in the service for about a year, when, while training in South Carolina to be a pilot, he cracked up a single-engine plane. Flying solo, he made a crash landing and spun upside down. Williams attributes the accident to "either a mechanical defect or a failure of the engine," not to pilot error. He suffered a severe concussion that left him with headaches for months, as well as a serious back injury, which has bothered him all his life. As a result of these injuries, he was discharged from the Army Air Force with the rank of lieutenant and returned to law school.

Back at Georgetown, Williams found the law school depleted by the war, with classes down to about one-tenth of their normal size. As Tom Rover, a classmate, put it, "Georgetown was a very quiet and lonely place at the time."

Williams's scholarship paid for everything—room, board, tuition, and books—but as part of his deal he had to work in the office of the undergraduate college and serve as a prefect, or dormitory counselor. Among his closest friends at Georgetown was William Ragan, who was about the same age but was an undergraduate. The two lived next door to each other and quickly discovered that they had much in common: Each was from Hartford; each was working his way through Georgetown (Ragan managed the school cafeteria); and each had dated Jerry Waterhouse. About thirty years later, after a few drinks at a cocktail party, Williams and Ragan shocked their old girlfriend (and her husband) by telephoning her.

As a scholarship student, Williams had to watch every penny. "There were times," says Ragan, when "we used to look between us and see how much money we had. If we had thirty-five or forty cents, it would be enough to buy a club sandwich, and we'd take it back to our rooms and split it." Their occasional snacks would entice a neighbor they came to call "The Animal" because he would "scratch on the door to try to come in and share our food." Tom Rover also noticed how frugally Williams lived, remembering that his dress wardrobe consisted of one suit with a pair of gray flannel slacks for variety.

Both Rover and Ragan say they expected big things of Williams from the time they befriended him at Georgetown. According to Rover, "Ed was kind of a hero" to the undergraduates on his corridor, one of whom nicknamed him "Flash" after Flash Gordon. "People had a sense of 'This guy really means business,' and that he was going to get somewhere. Even then."

Ragan would look in on his neighbor and find him "concentrating so hard that the words on those pages came right out to him, to his mind. You could almost see it. But if he wasn't studying, he was just as wild and happy as he could be. He could go from one extreme to another and do everything, work or play, so well."

Although Williams was too busy with his studies and his outside jobs to serve on the law review, he did write an article (signed "Edward B. Williams") about the Office of Price Administration. His conclusion was that the Emergency Price Control Act that had created the OPA was so onerous that it placed the small businessman "on the horns of the dilemma," forcing him to *"cease production or break the law."* And, Williams wrote, the law and its effects were "so patently repugnant" to the small manufacturer "that it is not at all anomalous to envision him as scorning the procedural remedies offered in the Act, and electing to meet the Attorney General in criminal court, if necessary."[13]

Georgetown's law school is near the U.S. Capitol and the Supreme Court, and Williams would often take walks to those buildings, which inspired him to continue with his studies, even though they filled him with "a certain boredom. Property rights, real property, wills, estates, and probates didn't interest me. I wasn't certain that I wanted to stay in the law. I was sort of unsettled at the time." He decided to stick it out, and graduated in 1944.

6
The
Young Lawyer

L ike Georgetown Law School, Hogan & Hartson, one of Washington's leading law firms, had lost many of its young attorneys, on whom the firm relied for the bulk of its trial work, to World War II military service. One day in the late spring of 1944, Howard Boyd, the head of Hogan & Hartson's trial department, encountered Al Philip Kane, a Georgetown law professor, on a street corner two doors from the building in downtown Washington that housed the Hogan firm's offices. Professor Kane, aware that Boyd's firm was looking for young talent, told Boyd "that there was a student at the law school whom he described as the brightest student he had ever encountered." According to Boyd, "Kane said this chap had been a flier and had crashed and bumped his head, which made him draft-proof.

"So, Professor Kane having said that to me, and since I had confidence in his ability to evaluate students, I asked him if he would send him up. In a short time, why, Ed came in. I chatted with Ed and I was so impressed with him that even though he had a couple of weeks yet left to finish in his school and he had not yet taken the bar, it was perfectly obvious what was going to be the outcome of those efforts. I made the determination that I wasn't going to let the guy get out of the building except that I had a commitment from him."

Williams had been planning all along to return to Hartford and practice law in a firm headed by Thomas Spellacy, whom he describes as "a political boss" of Hartford in that era. Like Frank J. Hogan,* the founder of Hogan & Hartson, Spellacy was a Georgetown Law graduate who liked to hire young attorneys from his alma mater.† Spellacy "had sort of a pattern of taking Georgetown lawyers and bringing them into his office, sponsoring them politically and moving them up the ladder," according to Williams. "The route was to come and run for the legislature first and then move up. And that was what I fully intended to do." More than twenty years after he graduated from law school, Williams was invited back to his hometown to address a meeting of the Connecticut Bar Association. He entertained the members by telling how

> I had a promise then from the late Tom Spellacy . . . that if I got through law school there would be a place in their office for me, and also that I could run for Alderman in the Seventh Ward. I came back when I finished law school, and they told me that I needed a little experience before I could be useful to them. So back I went to get a little experience. Now, I don't know how much experience that office requires, but it has occurred to me recently that I'm not going to make it.[1]

Williams could, of course, have returned to Hartford and joined Spellacy's firm from the time he received his Georgetown degree, "but all that changed when I got this offer to go to Hogan and Hartson. I thought it was super, I liked them, I decided I wanted to stay in Washington and I just didn't go back." Al Philip Kane, who was partly responsible for placing him at the Hogan firm, says Williams happened to be "in the right place at the right time." He added that he has often teased Williams that, but for the opportunity at Hogan & Hartson, he might have wound up as an assistant U.S. attorney in Connecticut.

Having decided to go to work at Hogan & Hartson, Williams spent several months as a law clerk there, doing research and waiting until the results of the District of Columbia bar examination were posted. He was admitted to the bar on October 10, 1944.

As the newest and youngest member of Hogan & Hartson, Williams, then twenty-four, was assigned to assist Howard Boyd in trying cases. Boyd, eleven years Williams's senior, had gone to college and law school at Georgetown, where, like his own father; Frank Hogan, and Williams, he also taught law. Early in the first administration of Franklin D. Roosevelt, Boyd served as secretary to Attorney General Homer S. Cummings before spending four years in the U.S. Attorney's Office and joining Hogan & Hartson in 1939.

---

* Not to be confused with the Frank Hogan who was New York's district attorney.

† When Williams joined Hogan & Hartson, more than half the firm's eighteen lawyers were graduates of Georgetown Law School.

During his early years with Hogan & Hartson, Williams helped Boyd try several dozen cases. Although Boyd had been a prosecutor for four years, Hogan & Hartson handled few, if any, criminal cases, and most of the suits he and Williams worked on were personal-injury actions. These were the cases in which Williams won his spurs, and from Boyd he learned that "the secret of great trial work is intense preparation. You know every facet of the case. Never ask a question for information. You know the answers when you ask a witness a question. You know more about the case than anybody else involved in the case—your opponent, the parties, anyone else."

Boyd, who left Hogan & Hartson in 1952 to take over as chief executive officer of the huge El Paso Gas Company in Houston, says of his former protégé, "It was perfectly apparent from his first identification with the Hogan office that he was going to be a leader in his field. And that, of course, he has proved to be. He is the most able trial lawyer in the United States today, and has been such for many years."

For Williams, learning how to be a trial attorney from Howard Boyd was not only rewarding but entertaining—entertaining for Williams, Boyd, and, often, for other people in court. Boyd recalled a case in which he and Williams were defending the streetcar company. Their best witness was killed in action at the end of World War II before the case came to trial, but Hogan & Hartson had an investigator named "Pop" Martin who had obtained a statement from the witness. Boyd and Williams decided that the only way to get the crucial evidence to the jury was to call Martin himself as a witness.

"I've forgotten whose idea it was, Ed's or mine," says Boyd, "but we thought it was damn clever at the time. After Pop had explained how he took the statement from the witness, I asked him, 'Can you tell us where the witness is?' We had prompted Pop to lower his head and say in a dramatic voice, 'He gave his life for his country.' Our adversary objected, and the judge, a very, very strict one, called the three of us to the bench. The judge looked at Ed and me and said, 'You know that was improper. You may proceed, gentlemen, but if you have the good fortune to win this case, Messrs. Boyd and Williams, I'll grant a new trial.'" Boyd and Williams won the case, but, for some reason neither one ever understood, the plaintiff never asked for a new trial and the verdict stood.

As Williams gained experience, he began trying cases himself, although Boyd would accompany him to court to keep an eye on him. In the first case Williams handled alone, he represented a bicyclist who had knocked down a pedestrian and was being sued. Williams filed a countersuit against the pedestrian for failing to get out of the biker's way and won a judgment of $500 for his client.

Williams's handling of two of his early cases especially pleased his mentor. In one, Boyd recalled, his client had been injured when the chair he sat in at a Washington hotel collapsed, and the man sued the hotel. "Somehow or other, Ed got hold of the chair and during the course of his argument to the jury he would pick it up a certain way and the thing would fall apart with a great clamor and then crash down on the floor in front of the jury. Ed, with pretended embarrassment, would pick it up and put it back together. I think it happened several times. That was Ed's style. He was just effective at capturing the attention of the jury."

While the jury was deliberating in that case, the counsel for the hotel offered to pay Williams's client $10,000 to settle the suit. Williams, with Boyd looking on, was in the midst of discussing the settlement with the opposing lawyer when the bailiff announced that the jury had reached a verdict. Faced with the need for an instant decision, Williams told Boyd he had "'a feeling'" that the jury was going to make a bigger award, and that they should not accept the $10,000 settlement. Boyd reminded Williams that that was a decision for the client to make, whereupon "Ed put it up to the client in a fashion that didn't really leave him much room to discuss or dissent," with the jurors "being pranced back into the courtroom. I thought it was quite courageous for a chap in what was really one of the first cases where he had the primary responsibility for conducting the trial." According to Boyd's recollection, the jurors awarded Williams's client a judgment of about $15,000, justifying Williams's reading of their mood. "It reflected a self-confidence and assurance and an ability to read the jury that has stood him in great stead in later years," said Boyd, adding, "I'm not sure I would have had that much courage."

The other of Williams's early cases that left Boyd with a lasting impression involved a woman who had entered the coffee shop of a downtown Washington department store. Part of the restaurant had been closed off and the tops of the stools had been removed to discourage people from sitting in the off-limits section. Nevertheless, the woman sat on the iron upright of one of the stools, claimed an injury, and sued the department store, which was represented by Williams. After a jury trial, the woman was awarded a few hundred dollars, but even though the amount of money was "inconsequential," Boyd said that "Ed was outraged! He said it was a miscarriage of justice, that he should appeal. I said, 'Some of these things, they're just miscarriages of justice and you make the most of them.' But Ed was most anxious to get that decision corrected. My recollection," said Boyd, "is that this was the first loss Ed had ever suffered. Frank Hogan used to say, 'Show me a lawyer who's never lost a case and I'll show you one who's never tried more than three.'" And Hogan was an expert, one of the best trial lawyers of the 1920s and 1930s, and a past president of the American Bar Association.

In this instance, Williams persuaded the department store's insurance company, which was willing to pay the small judgment, to let him appeal the case, lost it a second time—which made him "more outraged than he was the first time"—appealed again, and, finally, on his third try, won. Boyd's assessment: "It was a very revealing characteristic. It didn't make any difference how small it was, he was satisfied that he was on the right side of that, and that he should have won."

Once, Williams, as he often did, was defending Capital Transit in a suit filed by a woman named Ella Thomas, who claimed she had been injured when a city bus on which she was a passenger collided with another bus. Although doctors could find nothing wrong with Thomas, she did have a mysterious fever. Williams studied her charts thoroughly, and the same sequence of events kept leaping out at him: During her hospitalization, Thomas had requested a hot-water bottle about a half-hour before her temperature was to be taken. This pattern had been repeated about fifty times. The conclusion was obvious, and as he cross-examined Thomas, Williams began asking her about the hot-water bottle, the thermometer, and the relationship between the two. Finally, Thomas burst into tears. "'You think I put the thermometer on the hot water bottle, don't you?' she said. 'Well how else could I make them know how sick I was?'" Case dismissed.[2]

As time went by, word of the Howard and Ed show spread throughout the Washington legal community. Lawyers and law students began flocking to court to see them in action. One day Bill Ragan, Williams's friend and pupil, was in court when Williams got into an argument with U.S. District Judge Alexander Holtzoff. Williams made a point; Holtzoff said, "'I do not accept that'; and Ed said, 'You have to accept it.'" After this exchange was repeated two or three times, said Ragan, Holtzoff told Williams, "'I will see you in my chambers.' They went into chambers, and I was a little worried about what might happen to Ed, because Holtzoff was absolutely autocratic. When they came back into the courtroom, Holtzoff let Ed make his point, and the trial went on. I remember that very well."

Howard Boyd is given credit by Williams, and everyone else who saw them working together, for having played a dominant role in Williams's development as a lawyer. In later years, Williams would tell people like Tom Wadden, who practiced law with him, "'Well, Howard would do it this way, so that's how we'll do it.'" Williams and Boyd have remained close friends and mutual admirers for nearly forty years, and Boyd often referred El Paso Gas's law business to Williams.

Frank Hogan died just about the time Williams joined the firm Hogan had founded, and the two of them never met. But Hogan's partner, Nelson T. Hartson, was fond both of Williams and of Hogan's favorite granddaughter, Dorothy Adair Guider. Her father, John W. ("Duke") Guider—Hogan's son-in-law—was also a senior partner in the firm, and Nelson Hartson came to know well Guider's daughter Dorothy, who had been born with a deformed arm and was in frail health for most of her life.

One night in early 1946, after Williams had been with Hogan & Hartson for nearly two years, Hartson and his wife invited him to dinner. The way Williams tells it, he was asked to dinner because "when people have dinner parties, they like to have an equal number of men and women. At least they did then." When pressed, however, he admits that the "equal number of men and women" was two of each: Mr. and Mrs. Hartson, Williams and young Dorothy Guider. The purpose of the evening was obvious: to arrange a meeting between Williams and Frank Hogan's granddaughter. The outcome was a startling success: Within a few months, the young couple married.

Dorothy Adair Guider, known as D.A., came from a background almost totally opposite that of Williams. Born to wealth, she attended the exclusive Potomac and Madeira schools. Five years younger than Williams, she had graduated from Smith College and gone to work for the Book of the Month Club in New York just before she met Williams.

After dinner that first night at the Hartsons', Ed Williams and D.A. Guider went dancing at the Blue Room of the Shoreham Hotel, a popular Washington night spot. Their courtship can best be described as whirlwind, and on May 3, 1946, they were married at St. Thomas the Apostle Catholic Church in Washington.

To many people, marrying into a top law firm, as Williams had, might seem to be an ideal setup, especially for someone like Williams, who had been poor for most of his life. But instead of using his wife's family connections for advancement, Williams did exactly the opposite: "When I decided to get married, I decided simultaneously to get out of the law firm. I realized then that I had to leave because I didn't want to parade on that. I didn't want to have everybody else in the law firm explain whatever success I might have by saying, 'Well, he married the boss's granddaughter.' I didn't need that, I thought, to be successful."

Williams almost certainly would have left Hogan & Hartson whether he had married into the Hogan family or not. He was growing bored trying personal-injury cases that stemmed from streetcar accidents: "After five years, there was no conceivable factual situation I hadn't encountered. It was a tilled field. And I wasn't ready to quit practicing law at the age of thirty." Finally, remaining at Hogan & Hartson would have satisfied Williams's financial requirements but most likely would not have provided him with the glory and the power he also wanted. He says he always had it in mind to leave the firm after five years, and that's exactly what he did; in the spring of 1949, he resigned, with the full blessing of his wife and her family.

The decision by Williams to leave Hogan & Hartson turned out to have an effect on history: His exit created an opening that was filled by a struggling attorney named John J. Sirica. Sirica and Duke Guider were classmates at Georgetown Law, and in 1934 Sirica had turned down an offer from Guider to join the Hogan firm. He had cause to regret his decision; in 1949, when Williams left, Sirica, already forty-five, was practicing law in a two-room office that cost "about thirty dollars a month, and I paid a young lady about ten dollars a week to answer the phone. And it seemed like it never rang." Sirica was just barely eking out a living and was so "discouraged" that "I was all set to close up my little office" and look for work in another field "when my brother loaned me a thousand dollars to keep me going for a while." A short time later, Williams's move made room for Sirica, who, by chance, had tried to talk him out of leaving.

Sirica certainly would not have been appointed a judge if he had stopped practicing law. Furthermore, as Sirica concedes, "I don't think I would have been nominated to the court by President Eisenhower if I had still been in a little two-room office," in spite of the fact that Sirica had excellent connections with GOP leaders. "So I've always said to myself, 'Had it not been for Ed Williams leaving the firm, I may not have had the opportunity to go in there, and it may have resulted in my not ever being appointed to the bench.'" Instead, Sirica spent eight years at Hogan & Hartson, then was named a U.S. district judge in 1957. As a result of his close friendship with Williams (Williams and his wife were godparents of Sirica's daughter), Sirica has disqualified himself from hearing any of Williams's cases, except for routine motions.

Tom Wadden surveyed the men's grill of the exclusive Congressional Country Club in Potomac, Maryland, just around the corner from the suburban estate where Williams and his family now live. Both Wadden and Williams belong to Congressional, but Wadden wasn't searching for his onetime law partner. Wadden was looking to see whether another member, a retired attorney named Nicholas J. Chase, was present. Satisfied that Chase was not there, Wadden relaxed. "Let me tell you about Nick," he said. "Nick to this day is extremely bitter about Ed. The reason I looked around, Nick is a member out here. At the drop of a hat, Nick will start cutting Ed to ribbons. Just mention Ed's name, I don't care who's present."

Many people who have been associated in the law with Williams or known him well over the years say that anyone who would understand Edward Bennett Williams must first be informed about his brief and unhappy partnership with Nicholas Chase. Like Williams, Chase is from Connecticut (Windsor). Seven years older than Williams, he, too, graduated from Georgetown and taught law there. After several years as a government lawyer, Chase went to work for William Leahy, the outstanding trial lawyer of his time in Washington. Much, although not all, of

Leahy's practice was in criminal cases, and as a law student and novice attorney, Williams often took time off to visit the courthouse and observe Leahy in action.

Leahy, who was thirty-five years older than Williams, had much in common with him and came to be a hero figure to Williams. Like Williams, Leahy had graduated from Holy Cross and Georgetown Law School, and later taught at the law school. Like Williams, Leahy was poor and worked his way through school, in Leahy's case by teaching languages and public speaking.[3] Leahy was said to be

> a great trial lawyer who was a fighter and who had the gift of employing tact while pulling no punches. Before a jury, he could unleash the testimony of a witness or the arguments of opposing lawyers and at the same time, protect himself from counter-thrusts.
>
> Although he admitted getting angry at times, he never lost his temper. He knew that a judge or jury could easily be antagonized and he was ever vigilant against doing just that.[4]

Among Leahy's clients were Al Capone and Albert B. Fall, one of the accused in the Teapot Dome scandals. And he was once appointed by the judges of the U.S. District Court in Washington to prosecute the colorful gangster Jules ("Nicky") Arnstein.[5]

One of the cases Williams watched Leahy try, assisted by Chase, was for the legendary Boston politician James M. Curley. He was indicted in 1944 in Washington on charges of mail fraud in connection with a scheme to bilk investors of about $60,000 on the assurance that Curley and his business associates could obtain government contracts for them. After a two-month trial in 1945 and 1946, Curley was convicted on ten of fourteen counts and sent to federal prison.[6] President Truman commuted his sentence in 1947 after he had served five months of his term, and, in 1950, gave Curley a full and unconditional pardon.[7]

When Williams left Hogan & Hartson, it was Leahy's protégé, Nicholas Chase, with whom he opened an office. This choice of a partner was no accident, according to Chase, who says that Dorothy Williams was "very ambitious for Ed. She told my wife on more than one occasion that the city had been scoured and *they* had selected me to be Ed's partner." "They," said Chase, included Duke Guider and his family, Williams himself, "and others interested in getting Ed launched out of Hogan and Hartson," including presumably Howard Boyd, a close friend of Chase's.*

The two lawyers started practicing as partners in March 1949. They did have one advantage that resulted from Williams's marriage: The new firm set up shop in the Hill Building, a ten-story structure the Guider

---

*Chase's version of how they became partners, and of most other aspects of their relationship, is disputed by Williams.

family owned in downtown Washington. The firm was known as Chase & Williams, acknowledging that Chase was the senior partner, because he was established and Williams was not. In fact, Williams was such an unknown at the time that the opposition in one of the cases he handled during his brief partnership with Chase hired a detective agency to find out who he was. The probers stated that Williams had once lived and practiced law in Littleton, New Hampshire, which wasn't true. The Guiders owned a retreat in Littleton, where Duke Guider ultimately settled and operated a television station, but Williams merely visited Littleton on occasion; he never lived or worked there. The investigators did conclude that "Mr. Williams is reported to be a progressive type of young man, with good prospects for the future."

Almost from the start of their association, Chase and Williams had problems, problems that others had foreseen, if they had not. They had invited Bill Ragan, a fellow Connecticut Yankee, to go into partnership with them, but after "very briefly" considering the offer, Ragan refused. "I just couldn't see it," said Ragan. "That would be like sleeping with two kegs of dynamite. Chase was a great deal like Ed, very intense, and the two of them just weren't going to mix. I wasn't about to get involved in that."

One observer with firsthand knowledge of the partnership was Robert McChesney, who was a law student of Williams's at Georgetown. Unlike most members of the class, McChesney got to know Williams well because the two men's wives had been good friends since their high-school days. In early 1949, McChesney went to ask Williams whether he should join the law review or go to school at night and work at a law firm in the daytime. When Williams learned that McChesney had taught himself typing and shorthand, "he never answered my question. He said, 'Oh, you do that sort of thing? Nick Chase and I are getting ready to open up a shop and we only have a secretary in the morning.'

"This," said McChesney, "is the real beginning of Edward Bennett Williams. He could only afford one-half of a secretary, and I became the other half." The firm's offices were as small as the number of employees—three rooms, one for Chase, one for Williams, and one as a reception area.

McChesney quickly became aware that Chase and Williams "couldn't agree on anything, not even whether to close the door or not. They were always at odds. I think they were too much alike, they were both headliners." But he stayed on with the firm as a law clerk after he finished at Georgetown and was admitted to the bar. Chase, who had hardly known McChesney before he went to work at the firm, began to confide in him the problems he was having with Williams. That created even more tension between Chase and Williams, who had been McChesney's friend but did not want to talk to him about his differences with Chase. McChesney believes that Williams felt Chase "shouldn't be saying as much as he was to me. And I couldn't exactly blame him."

Although the partnership of Chase and Williams endured only a year or so, it lasted long enough to become peripherally involved in a political scandal. In addition to the two partners, the firm listed two men as associates: Harry M. Rubin, Jr., and Charles Shaver. Shaver was also general counsel for the Senate Select Committee on Small Business.[8]

In October 1951, it was revealed that the Reconstruction Finance Corporation had reversed itself and approved a $1.1-million loan for a proposed luxury hotel in Florida after Shaver and Mrs. Flo Bratten, secretary to Vice President Alben W. Barkley, had lobbied several RFC directors to grant the loan. Mrs. Bratten said she sought approval of the loan as a favor to a friend of hers, Sam Fleischer, head of a Minneapolis construction firm, who hoped to win a contract to build the Florida hotel. Shaver "admitted he knew at the time he went to the RFC that [his] law firm— Chase and Williams—was being retained by the Fleisher company and that he had probably discussed the loan with some member of the firm."

He immediately resigned from his Senate post, but the flap grew hotter as a freshman senator from California, Richard M. Nixon, announced that Senate investigators were studying " 'substantial deposits' " in Shaver's bank account. Nixon pressed for a full public hearing. Shaver explained that his winnings at racetracks and in poker games were the source of his bank deposits, which were described by investigators as " 'well in excess' " of his $8,300-a-year Senate salary.

Ultimately, Shaver was indicted for selling his influence and for conspiracy. He pleaded guilty to accepting $1,500 from firms seeking RFC loans and was fined $1,000 and placed on two years' probation.[9] By the time the Shaver case was disposed of, in 1951, the law firm of Chase and Williams had blown apart.

Nicholas Chase has the most to say about what happened between him and Williams: "*I* decided to dissolve the partnership. Williams tried to hold the partnership together. *I* know what happened. McChesney knows what happened. As a matter of fact, when I left the Hill Building, Williams wanted to go with me, even though his in-laws owned it. It was a unilateral determination by me. Period.

"Bill Leahy was the best trial lawyer in town, not the best criminal lawyer. That was very important to me, too—that I be identified as a trial lawyer and not as a criminal lawyer. It was very important to me, my wife, my children, my friends, my priest, my law professors, and everyone else. Very important to me. And still is."

Williams denies that he sought to go with Chase, and is adamant that their split was "mutual." Beyond that, all he had to say was "It just didn't work out. Partnerships are very sensitive relationships. We had personality differences. We both had the desire to be our own boss."

The crux of the matter seems to have been conflicting attitudes toward clients. Williams has three requirements that must be met before he will take a case: The prospective client must agree to surrender total control of the case to him; must be completely truthful with him; and must be able to pay whatever fee Williams sets. Otherwise, he does not judge his clients in terms of right or wrong, which he regards as moral, not legal, values, or even in terms of guilt or innocence, which he leaves to a judge and jury to decide. According to Bill Hundley, Williams is well aware of his clients' weak points. Hundley says that Williams can detach himself from his clients, even disparage them privately, and Williams himself is fond of pointing out that the Sixth Amendment guarantees every criminal defendant the right to counsel—not every criminal defendant except Jimmy Hoffa or Frank Costello. He often says, "Just because I defend a murderer doesn't mean I believe in murder," and, "All I do is defend my clients; I'm not running them for office." Nicholas Chase had a fourth criterion: that he be able to believe in his clients and their causes; if not, he refused to take them on.

Chase is proud of one thing: When he did leave Williams behind at the Hill Building, "there were several other people in the shop. Each was given freedom to choose as to whether he remained with Williams or went with me. All of the personnel went with me except Mr. Williams's secretary."

One of those who went with Chase was Robert McChesney. His departure was apparently an especially bitter pill for Williams, but McChesney says his decision "had nothing to do" with whether he liked or disliked Williams. "It was just that he was a bit of a workaholic. He was in the office seven days a week. I was quite the opposite. I didn't want to be a seven-day-a-week lawyer, or even a six-day one." But, says McChesney, "Apparently I didn't convince Williams that that was why I was leaving." Their friendship ended at the same time.

More than thirty years have passed since Nick Chase and Ed Williams chose, in Chase's words, to say "'You do it your way, I'll do it mine.'" Since then, they have said little more to each other than hello and good-bye, and have to some extent divided the Congressional Country Club into rival camps.

Nick Chase is rich. He lives in Kenwood, one of Washington's most prestigious suburbs, and owns a farm on Maryland's eastern shore and a vacation home at Rehoboth Beach, Delaware. Yet Williams has far surpassed his former partner in wealth, and his net worth on paper is at least $50 million. Among his holdings:

- The Hill Building, where he and Chase started out in 1949. Williams later inherited an interest in the building from his wife and then bought the remainder from the Guider family. During the 1970s, a station in Washington's new subway system was built beneath the building, which is just one block from the hub intersection in downtown Washington. Although the lot where the Hill Building is situated is quite small, its value per square foot is one of the highest in the entire Washington area.

- Several other buildings, including a site two blocks from the Hill Building where Williams would like to erect a new office tower for his law firm, which has long since outgrown the Hill Building.
- The Jefferson Hotel, a small but luxurious establishment six blocks up Sixteenth Street from the White House.
- His estate in Potomac.
- A summer home at Martha's Vineyard.
- The Baltimore Orioles, which may have appreciated in value by $10 million over the $14.65 million he paid for them in 1979, considering that the Philadelphia Phillies were sold for $30 million in 1981. Williams says he owns the Orioles outright, with no partners and no loan. He does, however, have a multimillion-dollar line of credit for the team.
- His 14.3-percent interest in the Washington Redskins, worth as much as $7 million in 1982.*
- A valuable, but indeterminate, interest in his law firm.

And, while Ed Williams is one of the most powerful and famous[†] people in the United States, Nick Chase is—by his own choice—relatively obscure.

The former partners have at least two traits in common, however: Each has lived his life according to his own rules, and neither expresses any regrets.

---

*Informed sources estimated the club's total value at about $50 million in March 1982, after the National Football League signed a five-year contract with the three television networks that will bring each team nearly $15 million per year for television rights alone.

[†]Williams is said to have accumulated enough press clippings to fill about forty scrapbooks.

Part
THREE

The
Rising Star

7
Hollywood Writers and HUAC

Among Edward Bennett Williams's first clients who were prominent in their own right were several Hollywood figures who sought his help during the Red-baiting era of the early 1950s. His involvement in these cases started in the summer of 1951, when he was approached by screenwriter Martin Berkeley. Berkeley had already been named as a member of the Communist party by Richard Collins, who had appeared before the infamous House Un-American Activities Committee (HUAC) the previous April.[1] Berkeley had responded to Collins's accusations by sending what he later described as a "very silly" telegram in which he told HUAC that Collins had lied and that he had never been a Communist.[2]

With Williams by his side, Berkeley, then forty-seven, testified at a HUAC hearing in Los Angeles on September 19, 1951, identifying himself as an actor turned writer who had had two plays produced on Broadway, moved to Hollywood in 1937, and then worked on several films, including *Green Grass of Wyoming*."[3]

Before Berkeley launched into the substance of his testimony, Williams informed the five-member HUAC subcommittee that the writer had received a call the previous night "threatening him and his family if he appeared here today and gave evidence disclosing names of members of the Communist Party which had not been known or disclosed prior to this session. That was the third of such phone calls that the witness has received in the course of the past week. The Federal Bureau of Investigation has been advised of these."[4]

Subcommittee Chairman John S. Wood (D-Ga.) assured Williams and Berkeley that "the full forces and power of the American Government will be utilized to protect this or any other witness who appears before this committee to give testimony in connection with its operations."

Berkeley, emphasizing that he was before the committee voluntarily and not under subpoena, then admitted that his telegram denying his membership in the Communist party and charging Collins with perjury was "not true." But, said Berkeley, "I was not at that time a member and have not been for many years. Why I sent the telegram—I did it in a moment of panic and was a damn fool."

Berkeley went on to assert that "since 1943 I have consistently fought the Communists in this town,"[5] and then, in one of the most astonishing performances of any witness before the committee, Berkeley named more than 100 people in the movie business who he said had been associated with the Communist party between 1936 and 1943, when he was a member.[6]

Among the people named by Martin Berkeley were some of the leading writers in the industry, including Dorothy Parker; Lillian Hellman; Dashiell Hammett; Ring Lardner, Jr.; Budd Schulberg; Waldo Salt; and Dalton Trumbo. Also on Berkeley's list were Robert Rossen and Sidney Buchman, both of whom subsequently hired Williams in connection with their own HUAC problems, and Carl Foreman,[7] whose attorney, Sidney Cohn, consulted Williams on his case. Berkeley singled out Foreman as the only Communist who at the time was still on the board of directors of the Screen Writers Guild, and said that Foreman—in contrast with Berkeley himself—had never taken the cure: "This man has never, to my knowledge, disavowed his communism."[8]

Berkeley concluded his testimony by playing up his own role as an anti-Communist and declaring that anyone who "joined the party since 1945 and who retains his membership today is a traitor."[9]

Berkeley's performance won for him the wholehearted praise of Subcommittee Chairman Wood: "It takes . . . a good deal of courage for a man who has once been identified with an organization of this sort, even though he has made a clean break and evidenced a desire and the zeal to combat the menace, to come out in the open and give testimony. For your cooperation in doing that the committee expresses to you not only our very deep and sincere appreciation, but the gratitude of every liberty-loving American citizen."[10]

Berkeley's testimony hit the film colony like a bomb. Williams himself wrote that Berkeley had "startled the entertainment world."[11] Others were more outspoken. Sidney Cohn—who has dozens of show-business figures as clients, has been associated with Williams in other cases, and says he regards Williams as a friend—to this day refers to Berkeley as "a liar and perjurer." Cohn says, "The big joke about Martin Berkeley was that he had copied his list" from the menu of a Hollywood hangout for celebrities. Adds Cohn: "I would never represent a stool pigeon. Everyone knew that."

Victor S. Navasky, who wrote the definitive book on the Red scandal in Hollywood, *Naming Names,* said Berkeley "named everyone he knew" and "corrupted the process by adding to the list some who didn't belong."[12] Navasky quoted Richard Collins, who had first named Berkeley, as saying that Berkeley had "panicked."[13] Most damaging to Williams, Navasky reported that HUAC investigator William Wheeler said, "'When Berkeley came down with his list of 154 people, I told him, I said, "Don't name that many. You're just going to get yourself in big, deep trouble." I said, "We don't need all this. Put the rest of it in executive committee."'"[14] But, in Wheeler's opinion, Berkeley ignored his advice because "'his ass-hole lawyer, Edward Bennett Williams, insisted.'"[15]

Williams finds Wheeler's version "an impossible tale" and "incredible" for a committee investigator, whose interest, he points out, would have been in having witnesses reveal as much information as the committee could get out of them. "I had no interest in us naming names," Williams adds. "I didn't have a feeling about whether they should or shouldn't. I was only representing them before the committee in a quasi-legal proceeding and they were there to answer the questions if they could. Almost all my clients answered the questions that were put to them." He also says he told his clients that they would have to answer the committee's questions "or they'd have to take a contempt citation." Although he regarded the HUAC hearings as "a Roman circus, a way for congressmen to get publicity and to expose for the sake of exposure," and a proceeding that "had no legislative purpose whatsoever," he noted that "the courts were very, very unwilling to find that the Congress didn't have a legislative purpose at hearings" until the precedent was established when he represented Aldo Icardi in 1956 (see chapter 10).

Six days after Berkeley had named him, Sidney Buchman appeared before the committee, accompanied by another lawyer. (Williams did not enter his case until it went to court.) Buchman, forty-nine, had won an Academy Award for writing the screenplay of *Here Comes Mr. Jordan* in 1941; his credits also included *Mr. Smith Goes to Washington, The Talk of the Town, A Song to Remember,* and *Jolson Sings Again.*[16] He was one of the most respected writers in Hollywood and had produced several movies as well. At the hearing, he readily admitted that he had been in the Communist party from 1938 until 1942 or 1943. But when asked about the activities of others, he not only refused to answer but, instead of invoking the Fifth Amendment privilege against self-incrimination, which would have gotten him off the hook, pleaded the First Amendment right against being forced to testify. "It is repugnant to an American to inform on his fellow citizens," Buchman declared. Professing that "I, myself, love America; that I will defend it with my life against any foe, Russia or otherwise," he added, "I realize my position [against testifying about others] may doom a career which has taken twenty years to build, but I have to take that risk."[17]

"Three days later," wrote Williams,

> Buchman left Hollywood and the movie industry. As he had predicted, his career was ruined. Because he had refused to "cooperate" with the committee by "naming names," he was no longer employable. But worse than that, he faced certain conviction for contempt. No conviction would have been possible had he declined, on the basis of the [Fifth Amendment] privilege, to give the committee any information at all. But Buchman took a position dictated by his conscience. He understood the problem. [But] he could not in conscience inform on others.[18]

Williams also praised Buchman's bravery, writing that what Martin Berkeley and others had done "is less courageous than the course followed by Buchman, but it has the virtue of being also less dangerous."[19]

In January 1952, Buchman was called twice by HUAC for follow-up testimony, but refused to appear, saying he had nothing to add to his previous answers. Indicted two months later on two counts of refusing to testify before a congressional committee, Buchman hired Williams to defend him. After a brief trial, he was found guilty on one count and was fined $150 and placed on probation for one year.[20] Twelve years would pass before he was again involved in a major film production.

On March 23, 1953, exactly one week after Buchman was sentenced, Williams was back before HUAC again, this time alongside producer Harold Hecht. Hecht, a forty-five-year-old former Hollywood agent turned producer, was one of those who had been named as a Communist by Martin Berkeley.[21] Hecht testified that he had associated in party activities with Berkeley and several others, most of whom—like Budd Schulberg, Frank Tuttle (a director), and Mel Levy—had already appeared before the committee.[22] Hecht acknowledged that he had been a party member from 1936 until 1939 or 1940, but said that since he had recognized "the sinister ways of the Communist Party," he had had nothing further to do with the party.[23]

One point that Hecht's day before the committee helped make clear was the depth of emotions surrounding the hearings. Hecht testified that during the lunch recess he was accosted in the hall outside and called "'a stool pigeon'" by George Willner, another Hollywood agent who had been identified by several other witnesses as a party member.[24] Ironically, Martin Berkeley had testified that Willner had once been his agent and had prevented Berkeley from obtaining writing assignments for a year and a half after Willner discovered that Berkeley had switched sides and become a militant anti-Communist.[25]

As a result of taking Harold Hecht's case, Williams became friendly both with him and with his partner in Hecht-Lancaster Productions, Burt Lancaster. Hecht and Lancaster offered Williams a 10-percent interest in their studio, which he made the mistake of turning down.* Very soon, Williams recalled, "they proceeded to have these smashing successes," including *Vera Cruz* (1954) and *Marty* (1955). He and Lancaster still have a standing joke "that he could never repay me for our fee arrangement" in the Harold Hecht case.†

The day after Hecht's HUAC appearance, Williams returned to the hearing room with Max Nathan Benoff, a thirty-seven-year-old writer of comedy. Benoff, feeling that he had little to lose, used the session to display his humor. He characterized his three-month membership in the party during 1944 as being so brief that he was "like a bathing beauty in a swimming pool, I dipped my toe, I dunked it and ran." Asked if he had studied any books an "dialectic materialism," Benoff replied, "I don't even study books on vegetarianism." And when Congressman Donald L. Jackson (R-Calif.) summed up Benoff's testimony by saying, "I think you and the Communist Party are about even. You got no laughs and they got no dues," Benoff came back with "That isn't fair. I don't like to leave with somebody topping me."[26]

Eight months later, in November 1953, Benoff, who had been having second thoughts about the impression he might have left after his March routine, asked to be allowed to testify before the committee again. Coming in this time without an attorney, he stated that he was now unemployed, and apologized for perhaps having been "too flippant" the previous March, declaring that communism is "a disease" and "a menace" that "has to be destroyed." Benoff emphasized that he was "deadly serious about this," praised the committee for the "wonderful" job it was doing, and went so far as to offer to work as a HUAC investigator.[27] So HUAC had at least one achievement: It stopped Max Benoff from cracking jokes in front of congressional committees, if nowhere else.

Williams's best-known Hollywood client in the HUAC era was Robert Rossen, one of the giants of the industry. After several years as a New

---

*Williams had soured on being financially involved in the motion-picture business after Robert Rossen, another client, gave him 10 percent of a film called *Alexander the Great*. That movie ran several million dollars over budget and never earned him a cent.

†Williams later represented Robert Stroud, the Birdman of Alcatraz, in an unsuccessful attempt to win his release from prison. It was Williams who arranged for Lancaster to play the lead in the film version of Stroud's life.

York playwright, Rossen moved to Hollywood in 1936, later formed his own production company, and won an Oscar for the 1949 film *All the King's Men,* which he adapted from Robert Penn Warren's novel based on the life of Huey Long. Rossen was producer and director of *All the King's Men,* as well as screenwriter.[28]

About a year later, Rossen was called before HUAC, and on June 25, 1951, accompanied by Sidney Cohn, he refused to answer most of the questions he was asked, although he did state that he was not then a party member.[29] Before long, Rossen found himself blacklisted. He was referred to two attorneys in Washington for help in regaining his right to work in Hollywood. Sue Rossen, his widow, later told Victor Navasky:

> One [lawyer] had plush offices and he was charging seventy-five dollars a minute and he was very formal and proper and distant. Then we went to see Ed Williams, who was in a cubbyhole, informal, sitting there in his shirtsleeves. He was impressive. I said, to use one of Bob's favorite expressions, "It's the difference between chicken shit and chicken salad." Ed thought he could get Bob up there without giving names—at least not in public, but that's not what happened.[30]

Williams finally found that the only way Rossen would be allowed to return to work was by cooperating with the committee. On May 5, 1953, Rossen testified again (this time without counsel), and named more than fifty show-business people he said he had known as Communist party members while he belonged from 1937 to 1947. Among those on his list were Ring Lardner, Jr.; Budd Schulberg; Sidney Buchman; Dalton Trumbo; Frank Tuttle; Waldo Salt; and Edward Dmytryk (one of the original Hollywood Ten who had been convicted of contempt for refusing to testify before HUAC in 1947).[31] Rossen stated that he had taken the Fifth Amendment in 1951 on the basis of "individual morality," but "I don't think, after two years of thinking, that any one individual can ... indulge himself in the luxury of individual morality or pit it against what I feel today very strongly is the security and safety of the Nation."[32]

Rossen's decision to name names caused him to be shunned by some members of the film community but got him removed from the blacklist.[33] He persuaded Williams to take a piece of his widely acclaimed 1961 movie *The Hustler,* which also turned out to be "useless" to Williams—"I think I made twenty-five hundred bucks on it."

During the HUAC era in Hollywood, Sidney Cohn consulted Williams about helping Carl Foreman, the screenwriter who had come in for special mention by Martin Berkeley. Foreman, who had written the script for *High Noon,* had moved to England amid the furor over Communists in the film industry. In the mid-1950s, he decided he would like to return to the U.S. and work in Hollywood again, but the State Department had asked him to surrender his passport and was refusing his reentry to this country because of his identification as a Communist.

Cohn approached Williams, who studied Foreman's case and said his fee would be $50,000 plus 10 percent of Foreman's next picture.* According to Cohn, Foreman was well established in Great Britain and was even friendly with Winston Churchill, who authorized him to make a film of the statesman's life. Because of his status in England, Foreman did not want to spend much money or effort to secure his right to return to the U.S., and he instructed Cohn not to pay Williams's price but to go ahead and see what he could do on his own.

Cohn proceeded without Williams and had Foreman's right to reenter the U.S. restored—thanks in part to the sloppy work of Secretary of State John Foster Dulles, who handled Foreman's case personally. Cohn says that Dulles drew up an affidavit that was "a travesty. It was one of the worst possible affidavits a litigant could draw. A kid in my office would have lost his job" for such work.

Williams was of more help to screenwriter Howard Koch, who, as one of the original Hollywood Ten, was asked to name names by HUAC even though he had never belonged to the Communist party. Koch, who had won an Academy Award as coauthor of *Casablanca,* found himself out of work after he declined to inform on his acquaintances. Unable to work in the American film industry, he spent several years abroad, returning to the U.S. in 1956. Although an approach to Williams had been made on Koch's behalf, Koch feared he was neither famous nor wealthy enough for Williams to take his case. To his surprise, Williams "took a genuine interest in my problem," and wrote a letter to be shown to anyone who might want to hire Koch, stating that he was "'eminently employable.'" When people in the movie business said they were still afraid to hire Koch for fear of having their films boycotted, Williams called the person primarily responsible for the screenwriter's problems and told him, "'My client, Howard Koch, is off your list or we sue you for a million dollars. Take your choice.'" According to Koch, "I was off the list the next day." [34]

In another case brought to him by Sidney Cohn, Williams helped entertainer Georgia Gibbs after a Syracuse grocery-chain owner refused to carry the products of companies that sponsored her broadcasts, on the ground that Gibbs was a subversive. Williams talked to the retailer and pointed out to him that "the only 'evidence' against her was that she had sung at a benefit for Henry Wallace in 1948 when Wallace, a former Vice President of the United States, was running for President on the Progressive Party ticket. The engagement had been arranged through her agent and she had been paid $500 for her appearance." [35] As soon as the truth about Gibbs was explained to the grocer by Williams, "the shameful

---

*Such a deal might have been very lucrative for Williams, because, it later turned out, Foreman was working on the script of *Bridge on the River Kwai* at the time.

boycott was ended by shamefaced men." But despite his success on Gibbs's behalf, Williams wrote that he found it "terrifying and disheartening to think that there are men in America who would act against a fellow citizen on evidence as thin as that on which the grocer acted."[36]

The witnesses whom Williams accompanied to HUAC hearings—such as Martin Berkeley, Harold Hecht, and Max Benoff, as well as Robert Rossen, to whom he gave advice—all named names, which has opened Williams to criticism in some quarters. But anyone who invoked the Fifth Amendment as grounds for refusing to disclose the names of associates was misusing the constitutional privilege, which is limited strictly to self-incrimination.

Because Williams was representing Senator Joseph McCarthy at the time he was counsel for the accused film people, he was also condemned as a "'McCarthyite'" and as a "'red,'"[37] as well as for being inconsistent. Sidney Cohn, for instance, says that he "could not in good conscience" have represented McCarthy, because he was deeply committed to the causes of his clients on the opposite side. As to allegations that Williams was on both sides of the Red issue, such charges miss a very important point: At the time Williams was representing Senator McCarthy, all his accused Hollywood clients had left the Communist party at least five to ten years earlier. Like McCarthy—and Williams—they were themselves vehement anti-Communists. There was no inconsistency if a lawyer who was generally sympathetic to McCarthy, if not to his methods, took on the case of a former Communist who had since switched sides. Furthermore, McCarthy himself was said to have had Communist support early in his political career.*

---

*In the 1946 Republican primary in Wisconsin, McCarthy scored an astonishing upset over Robert M. La Follette, Jr., who, like his father, the founder of the Progressive party, had spent more than twenty years in the U.S. Senate.[38] With more than 400,000 votes cast in the primary, McCarthy won by 5,400 votes, or slightly more than 1 percent. The *Madison Capitol-Times* quoted several Communists who were members of the state's Congress of Industrial Organizations as saying the CIO would oust La Follette from the Senate by supporting McCarthy, who then trounced the Democratic candidate in the general election.[39] In 1954, after McCarthy had burst into prominence with his attacks on Communists, CIO secretary-treasurer James B. Carey declared, "I do know the Communists supported him against Bob La Follette." McCarthy reportedly responded, "Communists have the same right to vote as anyone else, don't they?"[40]

8

Joe
McCarthy

O n February 9, 1950, after three years as an obscure freshman senator, Joseph R. McCarthy told a Lincoln's Day banquet audience
in Wheeling, West Virginia, that he had in his hand a list of
several dozen State Department employees who were known to Department officials as members of the Communist party, but who were still
allowed to hold their jobs. Eleven days later, McCarthy was called before
a specially created subcommittee of the Senate Foreign Relations committee and was asked to give proof of his charges. After several weeks and
more than 3 million words of testimony, McCarthy was unable to identify
positively a single State Department worker as a Communist. The Senate
subcommittee, chaired by Millard E. Tydings (D-Md.), voted to cite Mc-
Carthy as "irresponsible" for making "untruthful accusations" that
amounted to "a fraud and a hoax."[1]

That November, Tydings was defeated for reelection by an unknown
Republican, John Marshall Butler. Shortly before Election Day, Butler's
campaign forces had distributed several hundred thousand copies of a
leaflet that, by using a "composite" photograph, purported to show Tydings talking to Communist party leader Earl Browder. Orchestrating the
anti-Tydings barrage was the man he had lately chastised in the Senate,

Joseph R. McCarthy. Butler's upset of Tydings was the first indication of the power McCarthy was deriving from his war on communism. As the *New York Times* commented: "The Senate first began to suspect his influence, in some areas of the country at least, when the Republican John Marshall Butler came to the Senate in 1950 over the broken political career of the formidable Democratic Senator Millard E. Tydings of Maryland."[2]

The Senate launched an investigation into Tydings's allegations that unfair tactics had been used against him. McCarthy, an obvious target of the probe, consulted his pal John Sirica, just as he did in the same period when he faced the prospect of being sued by Drew Pearson. (McCarthy and Sirica had been bachelors around Washington until they were well into their forties, and had often double-dated and visited the racetrack together.) Sirica, by now getting established at Hogan & Hartson, was reluctant to abandon his secure position there in order to assist McCarthy. As he did in the Drew Pearson case, he suggested that McCarthy arrange to be represented by Edward Bennett Williams. In the Butler-Tydings dispute, that meant initially that Williams would be the attorney for Jon M. Jonkel, Butler's campaign manager, who was in for a grilling from the committee that would hold hearings on the election. McCarthy accepted Sirica's suggestion, and Williams was hired as Jonkel's attorney. One week later, on March 1, 1951, Jonkel began five days of testimony before the so-called Gillette Subcommittee, named after its chairman, Senator Guy M. Gillette (D-Iowa).[3]*

Jonkel's story was that he had been invited to head the Butler campaign by Ruth McCormick Miller, editor of the *Washington Times Herald* and a Butler supporter. As campaign manager, he was more concerned about winning the election than with keeping detailed financial records, and, as a result, he handled campaign contributions in a rather haphazard fashion. Instead of turning over about $27,000 to Butler's finance chairman, Jonkel himself endorsed checks from donors and used them to pay the campaign's bills.†

According to Jonkel, the Butler campaign had been helped by several people on McCarthy's staff, including Jean Kerr‡ and Don Surine.§ Jean Kerr, in fact, took a leave of absence from McCarthy's office and spent the last few weeks before the election working full-time for Butler. She

---

*The full name of the panel was the Subcommittee on Privileges and Elections of the Senate Committee on Rules and Administration.

†Of the $27,000, oilman Clint Murchison (future owner of the Dallas Cowboys) and his wife provided $10,000.[4]

‡Kerr, a onetime beauty queen, married McCarthy in 1953.

§Surine was also one of McCarthy's codefendants and was represented by Williams in the lawsuit filed by Drew Pearson.

seemed to be the person chiefly responsible for producing the four-page tabloid *From the Record,* which contained the composite picture of Tydings and Earl Browder. Although she and Jonkel had been the only people involved in what he termed the "creative conference stage" where *From the Record* was planned, Jonkel "had nothing to do" with the final copy. In fact, he claimed to have opposed distribution of the leaflet because he felt it might give Tydings cause for complaint if Butler won the race.[5]

McCarthy declined to appear as a witness before the Gillette Subcommittee, and this refusal to testify about the Maryland election later became the primary basis of his 1954 censure by the Senate. The Gillette Subcommittee, without McCarthy's version of what had happened, but giving weight to Jonkel's testimony, concluded that the Butler campaign had used "despicable" tactics against Tydings. However, the panel did not recommend that Butler be stripped of his seat.

Jonkel himself was charged with violating Maryland's election laws by mishandling campaign funds and failing to qualify as a designated political agent and resident of Maryland. He pleaded guilty and was fined $5,000[6]—the same amount he had earned in four months as Butler's campaign manager.[7] Immediately after Jonkel entered his guilty plea, Williams paid the $5,000 fine in cash, but Jonkel declined to reveal the source of the money.[8]*

In retrospect, there was little that Williams or any lawyer could have done for Jon Jonkel. He had broken the election laws and he had no choice but to admit it and take the consequences. Overall, he seems to have been the fall guy for McCarthy, Mrs. Miller, and the others responsible for Butler's victory. Even the money that Jonkel used improperly in the campaign was delivered by Jean Kerr and other McCarthy aides,[9] and it seems likely that McCarthy provided it. From Williams's perspective, all that mattered was that he handled himself well enough in the Jonkel matter to be called on by McCarthy, again and again.

As a lawyer and former Wisconsin judge, Joe McCarthy must have been aware of the old adage, "A lawyer who handles his own case has a fool for a client." Even so, he decided to represent himself when he brought a $2-million libel suit against fellow senator William Benton (D-Conn.) in 1952. And he had no sooner filed his complaint against Benton than he proved how apt the lawyers' saying was by referring to himself, the plaintiff, as "the defendant."[10]

The chain of events that led up to McCarthy's suit against Benton began immediately after the Gillette Subcommittee issued its finding that the Butler campaign had used "despicable" methods to topple Tydings.

*Williams says he no longer recalls who paid Jonkel's fine or his law fee.

Three days later, on August 6, 1951, Benton denounced McCarthy's activities in the campaign and urged that he either resign from the Senate or be removed.[11]

As portrayed by McCarthy, Benton, in a 30,000-word statement on September 28, 1951, "wilfully and maliciously sought the removal" of McCarthy from the Senate "by falsely charging that the plaintiff has a record of irresponsibility and lacks integrity of character . . .; by falsely charging . . . that the defendant [sic] is guilty of the crime of perjury"; and "falsely charged that [McCarthy] practiced fraud on the Senate," not to mention that Benton "made the false charge that the plaintiff is guilty of the crime of blackmail and the wrongful use of his influence."[12]

McCarthy presented himself, by contrast, as one who "for a long period of time in the past and at present is engaged in the public service of exposing Communists, fellow travelers and their collaborators inside and outside of the Government service."[13] He also alleged that Benton, as assistant secretary of state for public affairs from 1945 to 1947, had befriended some of the same (unnamed) people McCarthy was now attacking, so that Benton "bears ill will and malice against the plaintiff and has engaged in a campaign and scheme to injure . . . and to unseat" McCarthy from the Senate.[14]

Although members of Congress are, of course, immune to defamation suits that are based on their words on the floor or in front of a congressional committee, Benton had waived his senatorial immunity and allowed McCarthy to sue him.[15]

When McCarthy took Benton's deposition in the case, on June 4, 1952, Williams was sitting beside him, although he was not yet McCarthy's attorney in the suit, and Benton's lawyer, Theodore Kiendl, noted for the record that Williams was present. McCarthy responded, "Mr. Williams is my attorney in another law suit."[16]* Both McCarthy and Benton used the deposition as a forum for hurling insults back and forth:

> *McCarthy*: When I made the statement that there were 57 men in the State Department who were either Communists or doing the work of the Communist Party, I assume you considered that very irresponsible, right?
>
> *Benton*: I consider it irresponsible, Senator, if you don't have evidence that you are willing to take before a grand jury. . . . If you had the evidence, I think it is your duty as a Senator to name them. . . .
>
> *McCarthy*: You thought the number 57 was rather high, did you?
>
> *Benton*: You thought so yourself, because in the testimony before the Tydings committee—
>
> *McCarthy*: The question is did you think so, not what I thought. Try and stick to your own mind, will you? . . . You know you are not telling the truth here. . . .

* Pearson v. McCarthy, et al.

Benton: There is no doubt that Communists did infiltrate into the State Department. . . . [But] I took the lead in the State Department on tightening up the security regulations . . . long before February of 1950 and your speech at Wheeling, West Virginia.[17]

Williams could do little at the time but sit and squirm. One week later, however, he entered the case as McCarthy's attorney of record. Williams believes it was the Benton deposition that convinced McCarthy to hire him in that case: "He was terrible. He didn't know how to do it. He was no lawyer. And I think then he realized he needed lawyers."

Williams and Theodore Kiendl, Benton's attorney, spent several days traveling through West Virginia and taking depositions, during which time, Williams says, they became "very close and friendly. He was a great checker player. His greatest delight was to get out a checkerboard and a big box of candy and play checkers and eat candy. We finally sorted it out where I'd play with twelve men and he'd play with nine, and we would have a very good contest. He told me that the only good game he got in New York [where Kiendl's office was] was from a window washer who used to come through the window at lunchtime" and play him.

Back in Washington, Kiendl took the deposition of Paul G. Hoffman, first administrator of the Marshall Plan, who stated that McCarthy's allegations to the effect that General George C. Marshall and the Marshall Plan were somehow involved in a Communist conspiracy were "fantastically false." Williams boycotted the Hoffman deposition because Judge Burnita Shelton Matthews insisted it take place even though McCarthy was recovering from surgery and could not be present.[18]

Activity in the McCarthy-Benton case was recessed while Benton geared up to run for reelection from Connecticut in November 1952. That was when McCarthy scored his only real victory over Benton and once again showed his clout. He "intervened heavily" on behalf of Benton's opponent, William A. Purtell, and, like Millard Tydings two years before, Benton went down to defeat.[19]

After that, Williams and Kiendl were able to put a damper on the legal proceedings, and the case was finally dropped in March 1954. McCarthy announced that he had sent Williams around the country and the lawyer had been unable to find a single person who believed anything Benton said; consequently, Benton's remarks had not damaged the Wisconsin senator.[20]

According to Williams, McCarthy was "engaging in a little political poetic license," and in dropping the suit was finally following Williams's advice. "I did not file the suit. I undoubtedly advised him not to file the suit. I thought it was imprudent of him to file a suit against another senator. It never had much merit, never made much sense."

The pinnacle of Joe McCarthy's career was his investigation of subversives in the military, which came to be known as the Army-McCarthy hearings. These sessions ran for thirty-six days and were televised live to millions of Americans in the spring of 1954.

Before the start of the Army-McCarthy hearings, the senator asked Williams to be his counsel, but Williams refused. "It was quite clear that he just wanted me to carry his briefcase and that he wanted to run the hearings himself. I wasn't going to be a bag-carrier for him, or anyone else, then or now. So I wouldn't do it. I told him, 'You don't need me. If you want to run the case, you run the case. If I'm going to be in the case, I'm going to run it.'"

Roy Cohn, who became chief counsel after Williams turned down the job, said that Williams was in fact McCarthy's first choice, "but the invitation was not pressed, principally because of Jean's strong views. Mrs. McCarthy felt that when a man is fighting for his political life he should have someone alongside in sympathy and accord with his crusade."[21]

Much has been said about the feelings of McCarthy's inner circle, particularly his wife's, toward Williams. William F. Buckley, Jr., who, like Roy Cohn, was in tune philosophically with McCarthy, wrote that "Mrs. McCarthy recalls that she never believed, nor was led to believe, that Ed Williams believed in the mission of her husband, though the two were close friends."[22]

Williams has this to say: "I always had the friendliest and warmest relationship with Jean McCarthy, from the time she was Jean Kerr through the time she was Jean McCarthy," until her death in 1979. "Small wonder," however, "that she should have some doubts about my political purity by her lights, because I never concealed the fact that I had differences. . . . He and I had a basic philosophical difference about the purpose of a congressional committee. I believe that a congressional committee had for its *raison d'être* solely to inform Congress when it was going to legislate on a specific subject. He thought quite differently on that. He thought that the purpose of a congressional committee might be to inform the public on a subject, might be solely for exposure—exposure of evil, exposure of political ideology that was anathema to the public. I was strongly against that." In addition, Williams felt that McCarthy violated the rights of some of the witnesses who testified before his committee, and he disagreed on philosophical matters with the ultraconservative senator. Furthermore, Williams's wife took a dim view of his association with McCarthy, and reportedly said "she doesn't want Joe in her house."[23]

Even though he refused to serve as McCarthy's counsel in the Army-McCarthy hearings, Williams played a behind-the-scenes role, often meeting with McCarthy at night to give him advice. And when it became clear that Roy Cohn was going to be subjected to lengthy interrogation during the hearings and he considered hiring a lawyer, McCarthy's suggestion was "'Roy, run, don't walk to a lawyer! Get Eddie Williams.'" Williams, wrote Cohn, "still in his early thirties, was already earning a reputation as a brilliant trial counsel."[24] Cohn did talk to Williams, who prepared him to testify. But, says Williams, "I did not sit with him, did not appear with him. He preferred to be up there alone, which I thought was good judgment. I think it was in his interest to appear not to need counsel. He wasn't charged with anything. He was a lawyer, he was capable of taking care of himself."

Without Williams on hand at the Army-McCarthy hearings to exert at least a measure of control over the senator, McCarthy planted the seeds of his own destruction. The turning point, as Williams saw it, was when McCarthy attacked Fred Fisher, a young lawyer who assisted the army's chief counsel, Joseph Welch. The senator brought up Fisher's membership in the National Lawyers Guild, a group said to have Communist leanings. According to Williams, "Welch, a great courtroom lawyer, rose to the challenge" by making "a stirring plea on behalf of his young man" that "won the sympathy of millions of Americans. . . . The hearing went on, but Welch's plea . . . had changed its tone and direction." Williams also observed that he and Roy Cohn had "told McCarthy his case would be hurt by such a charge" against Fisher, and McCarthy had promised not to delve publicly into Fisher's background, which was irrelevant. "But McCarthy was a man who could never resist the temptation to touch a sign which said WET PAINT, and he had to touch this one."[25]

The stage was now set for the final act in the rise and fall of Joseph R. McCarthy, and Edward Bennett Williams was moving front and center.

The Senate had been probing the activities of Joe McCarthy since the Tydings-Butler election in 1950. Finally, on August 2, 1954, the upper house voted 75–12 to refer the question of disciplining him to a special six-member committee, which was to make recommendations to the entire Senate. Vice President Nixon was assigned the task of naming the committee members. He picked three Republicans—Arthur Watkins of Utah, who was appointed chairman; Francis Case of South Dakota; and Frank Carlson of Kansas—and three Democrats—Edwin Johnson of Colorado; John Stennis of Mississippi; and Sam Ervin of North Carolina, who had been appointed to the Senate just two months earlier after Senator Clyde Hoey died.

The McCarthy censure case was being billed in the press as "a national issue of the first importance,"[26] "a situation as strange as any in the Senate's history,"[27] and very possibly "one of the greatest controversies in Congressional history."[28]

After six weeks in Germany as a guest lecturer at the University of

Frankfurt Law School, Williams landed in New York on August 15 and read in the press that McCarthy had decided to have Williams defend him.[29] Initially reluctant to take the case or even to speak to the senator, Williams finally accepted a telephone call from McCarthy, who began by saying, "'Ed, I'm looking for a lawyer, thirty-four years old, with trial experience, who teaches at Georgetown University and has had some European teaching experience.'"[30] Williams found it hard to turn McCarthy down, even though "the Army-McCarthy fiasco [was] fresh in my mind [and] I was determined not to participate in a carnival of that character."[31]

This time, McCarthy agreed to give Williams complete control of the case, and "we shook hands on what I thought was a very carefully detailed understanding." Unfortunately, Williams "soon discovered I had been guilty of a tremendous oversight. I had not foreseen that under the terms of our agreement he would be free to make whatever comments he chose outside of the hearing room either about the hearing itself or about the committee members. He used that freedom to the fullest."[32] As Williams says now, "What was happening was the hearing would drag on and there would get to be a dull part and he would get up to leave. I had to stay there because I was running the hearing. I wouldn't know if he was going to the men's room or what he was going to do. But he'd go outside and he'd be on television while I was inside conducting the hearing. And the damage that was done in this case was done on television."

One expert, Senator Charles E. Potter (R-Mich.), who was reporting to President Eisenhower each night what went on at the censure hearings, commented that "Williams later said that he regretted not extending this agreement outside the hearing room. He might have known that Joe would bombard Watkins and the rest of the committee with mud and garbage gathered in the gutters he had known so long."[33]

While Williams had been in Germany, the Senate had approved McCarthy's request that it pay for his attorney and had set the lawyer's fee at the rate of $11,600 a year, the standard pay for a Senate committee counsel. Williams, however, thought it would have been wrong for him to be on the payroll of the body that was pressing charges against McCarthy at the time he was defending the senator. "Less altruistically," he was "concerned" that "I might be disqualified from cases against the government" during the hearings by virtue of a conflict of interest. And he was happy to represent McCarthy for free because "I thought it was an historic case. I wanted to participate in it. There were great issues involved." Therefore, although Williams charged McCarthy for his work in other matters, he refused to accept a fee in the censure case.

McCarthy faced censure on forty-six charges (many of them duplications). The Watkins Committee divided them into five categories:

1. McCarthy had failed to appear before or cooperate with the Gillette Sub-committee that investigated the 1950 Maryland election.
2. He had "incited" government employees to provide him with classified information.
3. The senator had illegally used and disseminated a secret FBI document, in possible violation of the Espionage Act.
4. McCarthy had abused fellow senators, particularly Senator Ralph E. Flanders (R-Vt.), whom he had said was "senile—I think they should get a man with a net and take him to a good quiet place," and Senator Robert C. Hendrickson (R-N.J.), whom McCarthy had called "a living miracle without brains or guts."
5. During the Army-McCarthy hearings, the senator had characterized General Ralph W. Zwicker—a hero of the Battle of the Bulge during World War II—as "unfit to wear the uniform." [34]

Arthur Watkins was "very much aware of what had happened at the recent Army-McCarthy hearings. . . . The shouting and name calling were beyond belief. Senator McCarthy, it seemed to me, was the principal actor." With McCarthy's "propensity to monopolize any proceedings" firmly in mind, Watkins was determined to "get off the front pages and back among the obituaries." Although nothing could have kept the censure case from being on page one, Watkins was able to work out with Williams a set of ground rules intended to tone down McCarthy:

- Williams would have "complete charge" on McCarthy's side.
- Williams *or* McCarthy—but not both— could speak on a subject or question a witness.
- The hearings would not be broadcast live. [35]

McCarthy was given permission to make a brief opening statement, which he did as the hearings began on August 31, 1954. He declared:

> Several years ago, Mr. Chairman, I became convinced that this country and its institutions were in imminent peril of destruction by international communism. . . . I conceived it my duty to expend every effort of mind and body to fight subversion, to help clean traitors and potential traitors out of the Government. . . . I believe that my accusers [may be] unwitting victims of powerful pressure groups in the country who are best characterized as opponents of a vigorous fight against communism. [36]

The committee then had a litany of McCarthy's transgressions read into the record. Among them:

- He had written letters to Senator Gillette stating, "'I am sure you realize that the Benton type of material can be found in the *Daily Worker* almost

any day of the week'"; "'Your Elections Subcommittee . . . is guilty of stealing just as clearly as though the members engaged in picking the pocket of
the taxpayers and turning the loot over to the Democratic National Committee'"; and "'Your Elections Subcommittee [is] even more dishonest than was
the Tydings committee.'" [37]

- McCarthy had said in another letter to Gillette and two other members of
  his subcommittee:

    "I have learned with regret that your public hearings are to open
    tomorrow without the presence of your star witness. You have my deep-
    est sympathy. . . .

    "If only you had set the hearings 10 days earlier before the judge
    committed your star witness to an institution for the criminally insane,
    you would not have been deprived of this important link in the chain of
    evidence against McCarthy. . . .

    "Certainly, you cannot be blamed for being unable to distinguish
    between his testimony and the testimony of the other witness, Benton. . . .

    "I ask you gentlemen not to be disturbed by those who point out that
    your committee is trying to do what the Communist Party has officially
    proclaimed as its No. 1 task [to destroy McCarthy]. You just keep
    right on in the same honest, painstaking way of developing the truth." [38]

- His slurs against Senators Flanders and Hendrickson. Williams was able to
  mitigate some of the sting in McCarthy's remarks about Flanders when he
  got an Associated Press reporter to acknowledge that McCarthy had attacked Flanders after the reporter showed McCarthy a copy of a speech in
  which Flanders had compared his fellow senator to Hitler. [39] But McCarthy
  probably nullified any points Williams had scored for him when he was
  sworn in as a witness and declared as to Flanders, "There is no doubt that I
  thought he was senile and referred to him as senile." [40]

Williams did help McCarthy's cause during his cross-examination of
columnist Walter Winchell, who was called as a witness against McCarthy on the charge of misuse of classified documents. Winchell testified
that four months earlier, during the Army-McCarthy hearings, he had
been handed a three-page summary of an FBI report signed by J. Edgar
Hoover pertaining to espionage at an army base, Fort Monmouth, New
Jersey; that he didn't know who had handed the report to him and
wouldn't reveal his source even if he did, but that he did not receive it
from McCarthy; that Hoover told him he would be arrested if he disclosed
the contents of the report; that McCarthy appeared to have a copy of the
same document, and that he (Winchell) later destroyed the copy he had
been given. [41] But Winchell then agreed with William's rhetorical statements: "You are unable to say here under oath . . . that you ever had in
your possession a true copy" of the document McCarthy had, and "The
fact of the matter is that even your so-called, what we will call the Winchell document did not have security information in it." [42] Williams also

objected to Winchell's repeating what Hoover had said to him and challenged the committee to subpoena Hoover himself as a witness.[43] The thought of the committee ordering J. Edgar Hoover to appear still amuses Williams: "He went to Congress when he chose to go, he didn't go when he didn't choose to go. I don't think they had the guts to call him."

Williams also produced a witness to refute the Zwicker charges against McCarthy. His witness, a salesman named William J. Harding, Jr., testified that he had been a spectator one day at the Army-McCarthy hearings and had overheard Zwicker, who was waiting to testify, call McCarthy an "'S.O.B.'"[44] Harding's testimony prompted Zwicker, who was present, to "smile broadly."[45]

Williams then got a crack at Zwicker himself. He says now that McCarthy's denunciation of Zwicker was "bad" and "I don't think it's ever proper to abuse a witness." He certainly did not attack Zwicker as McCarthy had, but he did go after the general with a vengeance. He accused Zwicker of "playing tweedledee and tweedledum";[46] asked sarcastically, "When did your recollection improve?"[47] and complained to Chairman Watkins that Zwicker "was not being truthful under oath."[48] At one point, Williams asked Zwicker if one of his answers was "fully candid"; the general, growing hot under the collar, replied, "I will permit you to interpret that, sir." Williams queried, "You have no comment on that?" and Zwicker's response was, "No comment."[49] William's handling of Zwicker prompted Watkins to admonish the lawyer: "There is no need to lecture the witness."[50] And when Zwicker testified that he could not recall having muttered that McCarthy was an "S.O.B.," Williams finally gave up, telling the committee, "I have no further questions,"[51] as a means of voicing his opinion of Zwicker's veracity.

In a move that was somewhat of a gamble, given McCarthy's outspoken hostility, Williams called the senator to testify in his own defense. McCarthy was in general "a model witness,"[52] although at one point he answered an order from Watkins that he "respond to the question" by declaring, "I will respond in my own fashion, Mr. Chairman."[53] McCarthy testified that Zwicker was "one of the most arrogant, one of the most evasive witnesses, that I have ever had before my committee, one of the most irritating," and repeated his charge that Zwicker "was not fit to wear the uniform of a general."[54] Under questioning by Williams, McCarthy also said it was his "practice" that "when somebody is identified as a Communist, we call them to the stand immediately, wherever possible, in order to permit them to admit it or deny it"[55]—which happened to be exactly what Williams objected to in McCarthy's investigations. Williams also led McCarthy through a series of questions that resulted in his client's explaining that during his investigations he was merely seeking information "with regard to illegal activities on the part of Federal employees. It did not include general classified material." Furthermore, McCarthy asserted,

"If I did not try to get that information, then I should be subject to censure."[56]

For the most part, the Watkins Committee hearings were frustrating to both Williams and McCarthy, as the chairman consistently ruled against positions raised by the defense. In one of the most dramatic moments, Williams attempted to show that other members of Congress (including Vice President Nixon when he was a congressman in 1948) had done many of the same things for which McCarthy was being charged,* but Watkins said that was irrelevant. Williams then asked for and was granted a brief recess to consider Watkins's ruling,[58] amid speculation "as to whether Senator McCarthy would return" or simply throw in the towel.

McCarthy did decide to continue, but Williams told the press during the recess that the Watkins ruling had destroyed 95 percent of the defense to the two charges of soliciting confidential information from federal employees and misusing classified data.[59]

When the hearing resumed, Williams tried to carry on his fight:

> *Williams*: Mr. Chairman, I am deeply sorry that the committee has taken this view of our evidence. I think candor dictates that I say to you, sir, that I am shocked at this ruling. I must also say that—
>
> *Watkins:* We have made the ruling. Of course, if you want to criticize the committee, why—
>
> *Williams*: I certainly have no desire in any way to criticize the members of this committee, but I do say again to you, sir, candor dictates that I say that I am shocked by the ruling.
>
> *Watkins:* The record will show your statement . . . In a courtroom . . . a defendant [would not be allowed to try to show] in a case in which he . . . is charged with stealing a pig that somebody else, one of his other neighbors, stole a cow or a horse.[60]

Similarly, Williams's suggestion that the money that had been appropriated to pay McCarthy's counsel be used to hire independent lawyers to help the committee evaluate the evidence made little impact on the senators. His point was that the committee's own attorneys were in effect prosecutors and could not be expected to view the case impartially. Watkins agreed to take Williams's motion under advisement,[61] but, of course, nothing ever came of it.

McCarthy could restrain himself no longer when Watkins refused to consider defense arguments that Senator Edwin Johnson might have a bias against him. The defense team had discovered that several months earlier the *Denver Post* had quoted Johnson in a copyrighted front-page

---

*As a member of the House Un-American Activities Committee, Nixon had apparently been given a summary of a secret FBI report, just as McCarthy had during the Army-McCarthy hearings.[57]

story as saying, "'In my opinion, there is not a man among the Democratic leaders of Congress who does not loathe Joe McCarthy. . . . I do not believe there are more than a half dozen Republicans who think McCarthy is all right. Most of them are thoroughly disgusted with him.'"[62]

Williams said he and McCarthy were not challenging Johnson's right to sit on the committee, but would like to study his comments further and decide what to do. Watkins directed Williams not to bother, noting that Johnson "was appointed by the Senate, and this committee has no authority to remove him or even to accept a resignation of his from the committee . . . We are not trying Senator Johnson."[63]*

At that point, McCarthy broke his pledge to Williams for the first time, grabbing the microphone from him[64] and shouting, "Mr. Chairman, I would like to ask one question. Are we entitled to know whether or not the quotations [attributed to Johnson] are correct or incorrect? I would like to know whether the *Denver Post*—"

Watkins cut McCarthy off once, twice, three times; ruled him "out of order"; suggested that if he and Williams wanted to discuss the matter with Johnson "you can go to the Senator and question and find out"— outside the hearing; and gaveled the day's session to a close.[65] The episode left McCarthy "shaking with rage" and sputtering to reporters, "'I think it's the most unheard of thing I ever heard of.'"[66] He also complained that the absence of radio and television inside the hearing room—at Williams's insistence, as well as Watkins's—made possible "'completely false reporting.'"[67]

The Watkins Committee deliberated for less than two weeks and then rejected virtually every argument raised by Williams in defense of McCarthy. The committee voted unanimously to recommend to the full Senate that McCarthy be censured for his actions toward the Gillette Subcommittee that studied the Tydings-Butler race, specifically his failure to appear and answer questions and his characterization of one of its members, Senator Hendrickson, as "a living miracle without brains or guts."[68] The Watkins Committee also found McCarthy censurable on a second count: his treatment of General Zwicker.[69]

The committee decided not to call for his censure on the other three counts, but criticized him in each instance:

- His implied invitation to federal employees to provide him with classified information "cannot be condoned and is deemed improper."[70]
- His offer to make public the summary of J. Edgar Hoover's report—which the senators found to be "legally classified"—was a "grave error" and showed "a high degree of irresponsibility."[71]
- His remark that Senator Flanders was "senile—I think they should get a

---

*Several years later, after Johnson had been elected governor of Colorado, he had a relative who needed a criminal attorney. At Johnson's request, Williams took on the case.

man with a net and take him to a good quiet place" was "highly improper,"
but not worthy of censure, because Flanders had provoked the attack by his
own conduct toward McCarthy.[72]

Hardly anyone was surprised by the findings of the Watkins Committee, least of all McCarthy and Williams, who says now that "I thought the
committee was going to decide adversely to him because he had so alien-
ated the members that it would have been a miracle if they had found in
his favor on anything."

The day the report was issued, Williams vowed "a vigorous and lengthy
fight" against censure before the full Senate.[73] His work was cut out for
him, because the unanimous recommendations of the six-member biparti-
san committee, made up of men with moderate political stances, was
viewed as carrying great weight with the other ninety senators.[74] McCarthy, meanwhile, said he didn't care whether he was censured or not, but
pledged to fight against establishing a precedent that would inhibit congressional investigations "and assist any Administration in power to cover
up its misdeeds."[75]

Ordinarily, the McCarthy censure would have been considered immediately by the full Senate, but 1954 was an election year, and Republicans,
who held a majority in the Senate, wanted to avoid having McCarthy
come up as a campaign issue. As a result, Majority Leader William
Knowland of California postponed floor debate until after the November
2 elections,[76] and set November 8 as the starting date.

Four days before the debate began, McCarthy offered a preview of
what lay ahead. At a Washington press conference, he branded the coming debate a "lynch party."[77]

Like McCarthy, Senator Watkins, who was chosen as floor manager
for the censure debate, had been elected in 1946. And because of that
twist of fate, the Senate seats of the two men, which are assigned on a
seniority basis, were next to each other. As the floor debate opened, "Senator Watkins stuck out his hand and Senator McCarthy took it in a brief
handshake."[78]

As the first order of business, McCarthy asked for and was granted
unanimous consent for Williams to sit next to him on the Senate floor.[79]
This time, however, Williams was not permitted to address the body that
was considering the charges, although he could talk to individual senators
on the floor.

The Senate had hardly moved into the substantive part of its debate
when McCarthy for all intents and purposes sealed his own fate. He again
went through the formality of obtaining unanimous consent, this time for
permission to insert into the *Congressional Record* his statement on the
proceedings against him.

In his speech—copies of which were distributed to the press, but which

McCarthy did not deliver on the Senate floor—he declared:

> The Communist Party—a relatively small group of deadly conspira-
> tors—has now extended its tentacles to . . . the United States Senate
> . . . [and] has made a committee of the Senate its unwitting handmaid-
> en. . . .
>
> [The Watkins committee] was the victim of a Communist campaign;
> and having been victimized, it became the Communist Party's involun-
> tary agent. . . .
>
> In the course of the Senate debate I shall demonstrate that the Wat-
> kins committee has done the work of the Communist Party, that it not
> only cooperated in the achievement of Communist goals, but that in
> writing the report it imitated Communist methods—that it distorted,
> misrepresented, and omitted in its effort to manufacture a plausible
> rationalization for advising the Senate to accede to the clamor for my
> scalp.[80]

The speech caused an immediate furor and later was used as additional
grounds for censuring him. Senator Watkins later said that if he had read
advance news accounts of McCarthy's statement, "I never would have
consented to printing that speech in the *Record* by unanimous consent."[81]

"I didn't write any of that bilge," Williams comments. "It was terrible.
I might have had a role in expunging things from it. But I wasn't one of
his writers." Williams "credits" Brent Bozell (brother-in-law of William
F. Buckley, Jr.), who assisted him during the Watkins Committee hearings, with writing McCarthy's speech, and Bozell acknowledges that "un-
witting handmaiden" was "my phrase."

Outrage at McCarthy's "handmaiden" declaration prompted Sam Ervin to deliver his first major speech in the Senate, in which he said that
McCarthy should be not only censured but expelled—because his "fantastic and foul accusations" against the Watkins Committee proved "moral
incapacity" if he didn't mean them and "mental incapacity" if he did
believe what he was saying.[82] In the same speech, Ervin made a remark
that would prove ironic in the light of events twenty years later, asserting,
"Other members of the Congress have fought communism with as much
devotion and with far more wisdom than has the junior Senator from
Wisconsin," and citing Vice President Nixon as his first example.[83]

Ervin declared that the situation for his colleagues to judge was: "Does
the Senate of the United States have enough manhood to stand up to
Senator McCarthy?"[84] The next day, Watkins himself echoed Ervin's
question: "How can the Senate hold up its head among the other free
deliberative bodies of the world unless it does something about this matter?" Watkins, describing both himself and the entire Senate as the victims of "abuse heaped upon abuse" by McCarthy, called for someone to
introduce a motion to censure McCarthy for his latest misconduct.[85] His
colleague from Utah, Wallace Bennett, announced his willingness to do

so,[86] and McCarthy's goose was virtually cooked—except for one last-ditch try at a compromise by Williams, Nixon, Barry Goldwater, Majority Leader William Knowland, Everett Dirksen, and Francis Case of the Watkins Committee, who had shocked many senators by reversing himself and announcing that he would not vote to censure.[87]

In the middle of the Senate discussion of his fate, on November 17, 1954, McCarthy was admitted to Bethesda Naval Hospital with a badly infected elbow, and the debate was recessed. During the break, Nixon, who, according to Williams, was "very friendly" to the beleaguered senator, called Williams to a meeting in his office. Nixon and his allies had worked out a compromise under which the Senate would adopt a resolution to the effect that it could not "condone" McCarthy's actions but would not censure him. Dirksen, "who was always sort of a pastor, a rabbi, if you will, to the other senators, had managed to get about half the Democrats to say they'd vote for it, and he had at least half the Republicans. So it was going to win," says Williams.

The Nixon group asked Williams what he thought of the deal, "and I said, 'Super.' I was young. I was thirty-four years old, it was the biggest case I had ever been in and I wanted to win it. That's all I cared about. It looked as though this would be a great opportunity to ring down the curtain and get the censure case over with. So I said, 'Super, I win. Man, I'm for this solution.'"

The senators asked Williams if he would present their proposal to McCarthy. He agreed, and Goldwater was assigned to accompany him to the hospital. "Barry and I went over there. He was up in the tower. We sat there and began a conversation with him. He had a water glass, as all hospital patients do, and a bottle of bourbon under the mattress, and he was just drinking bourbon out of the water glass. And the more bourbon he drank, the more bellicose he became and the more hostile he got to the idea of asking his friends to 'condone' him. It ended up in a raucous shouting match in which he said, 'Do you think that I could ask Herman Welker [R-Idaho] to condone me? That I could ask Bill Jenner [R-Ind.] to condone me?'" related Williams, raising his voice in imitation of McCarthy.

In the end, "he threw us out. So we left. This was in the dead of night, very, very late. We went back to my house, Barry and I, and we sat, just, you know, as two kindred spirits who had suffered a terrible defeat. I didn't even want to go back and tell this group the next day that he wouldn't take it. It was too humiliating. I told him, I said, 'You're going to lose, you're going to lose, you're going down in defeat.' But he would have preferred a defeat rather than this kind of resolution, because his judgment was so bad. He had an opportunity the next day and the next day and the next day to take it, and he wouldn't. He lost his judgment, whatever judgment he had was gone. And I'm not sure he ever had very good judgment."

The best McCarthy could do, upon his return to the Senate, was to back down on his choice of language, but not on what he had meant:

> Let me say that I am not wedded to any particular words; for example, when I referred to the Watkins committee as the "handmaidens of the Communist party," I should say now that "handmaidens" is not a proper word to use in that connection, because a handmaiden is a female servant, and certainly the members of the committee are not female servants.[88]

Insisting that such presumably conciliatory remarks were "not to be taken as any compromise on my part with the principles I have held and which I still hold," McCarthy said defiantly, "I have no apologies."[89]

His gesture was too little, too late. The final nail was driven into the coffin of his Senate standing by Senate Democratic Leader Lyndon B. Johnson (described by one newspaper as "one of the mildest-mannered" senators[90]), who announced that McCarthy's words in the "handmaiden" speech "do not belong in the pages of the *Congressional Record....* Such words would be much more fittingly inscribed on the wall of a men's room." Johnson said that if the Senate allowed McCarthy to go unpunished, "we might just as well turn over our jobs to a small group of men and go back home to plow the south 40 acres." He added, "I can conceive of no compromise on this question," and would therefore vote to censure McCarthy.[91] It was said that the position taken by the well-respected Johnson "more than any other caused the final condemnation."[92]

That night (December 1), with the handwriting on the wall, McCarthy, accompanied by Williams, went before an assemblage of television and newsreel cameramen to tell "the American people" that "they know I am being censured because I dared to do the dishonorable thing of exposing Communists in Government."[93] Williams, however, was with McCarthy only physically and not emotionally; he says he believed then and has ever since that McCarthy was censured for his behavior, not for his fight against communism.

McCarthy was finally censured by his colleagues on December 2, 1954. After Watkins decided to withdraw the charge relating to McCarthy's mistreatment of General Zwicker,[94] the Senate passed by a vote of 67 to 22* a resolution to "condemn"† McCarthy for his conduct toward the Gillette Subcommittee and his language in reference to the Watkins Committee during the Senate floor debate.[95]

---

*McCarthy voted "present."

†The word *censure* does not appear in the final text that was adopted by the Senate.

John F. Kennedy was one of only two senators who did not indicate where they stood on the most controversial issue decided by that body in many a year.* "I remember that very clearly," says Williams. "He was convalescing from back surgery† at Palm Beach. He was never at any of the debate sessions. He said that since he hadn't heard the debate, he wouldn't vote. But the fact of the matter is, nobody heard the debate. I'm the only person that heard the whole debate. The rest of them weren't there. There were never more than two or three of them on the floor. If Kennedy had chosen to vote, he could have read the *Congressional Record* and cast a vote. He didn't want to vote on that issue because it was a dynamite issue for him in Massachusetts, probably McCarthy's strongest state with the possible exception of Wisconsin" because of Massachusetts's huge Irish Catholic population. For Kennedy to have voted to censure McCarthy, Williams notes, would have antagonized many of his supporters, including his own father, who was a "very good friend" of McCarthy's; in fact, Robert F. Kennedy had been a lawyer on McCarthy's committee staff. On the other hand, "it would have been very, very damaging to his future political career" for Kennedy, who was planning to seek the vice-presidency two years later, to have voted against censure, especially since McCarthy had once called the Democratic party "the party of treason" and since every Democratic senator who cast a ballot on censure voted against McCarthy.

Granting that it was "a no-win situation, a hopeless situation" for JFK, Williams nevertheless is vastly amused that while Kennedy took advantage of his convalescence to duck the issue, he wrote *Profiles in Courage*—a book "about senators who voted on politically damaging issues."

McCarthy was but the fourth senator in U.S. history to be censured. Two members of the Senate were censured in 1902 for fighting on the floor of the chamber, and a third was censured in 1929 for bringing a lobbyist in the guise of one of his aides to a committee meeting that was closed to the public.[96]

Williams took the loss much harder than his client did. He said that McCarthy "regarded it [censure] as inevitable, and when it came he wore it as a badge of courage. He showed no disappointment and no regret. I think I had a monopoly on the disappointment over the case. I felt all the disappointment of a lawyer who has lost a big case which he could have settled in a way favorable to his client."[97]

One of the grounds on which McCarthy was condemned, his attacks on the Watkins Committee and the Senate during the floor debate, was beyond Williams's control; he never had a chance to argue it before the Watkins Committee or the full Senate. As to the only charge on which he

---

*The other was Alexander Wiley, McCarthy's fellow Wisconsin Republican.

†Kennedy was recorded as being "absent by leave of the Senate because of illness."

had defended McCarthy and on which the senator was finally punished—McCarthy's abuse of the Gillette Subcommittee and its members—Williams attempted to explain that away as a miscarriage of justice. Eight years later, in his book *One Man's Freedom*, Williams wrote:

> I feel sure the charge would not have been sustained if we had had the evidence which came to us only after the censure vote had been taken. Not till then did we learn that the Gillette Subcommittee had put a "mail cover" on McCarthy during the time it was investigating him. Had this fact been brought out before the Watkins Committee, it might well have changed the result at the committee level. . . . When the McCarthy mail cover came to light . . . the censure had already been voted. The hearing was over. The debate was over. There was no chance to reopen. The Senate had had its fill of the whole matter. History must show in one of its more ironical paragraphs that McCarthy was himself a casualty of a congressional investigation that flouted the rules of fair play.[98]

Actually, the existence of the mail cover was brought to the attention of the Watkins Committee—by Williams himself. Near the end of the committee's hearings, he informed the six senators of "reports that that committee had . . . a mail cover placed on Senator McCarthy."[99] In addition, in legal briefs he submitted to the Watkins Committee, he alluded to the fact that one member of the Gillette Subcommittee (Herman Welker, McCarthy's chief apologist within the senate) and two staff members of the Gillette panel had resigned because they "felt that the subcommittee was being prejudicially unfair to Senator McCarthy."[100] Furthermore, the Senate investigated the McCarthy mail cover at the same time the censure debate was taking place on the floor and found that although the senator's mail had been intercepted for a short time in 1952, he had suffered no real harm. Williams was told by McCarthy himself, "'There's nothing to be gained from pursuing this matter further,'"[101] just before the full Senate voted to censure him.

The wonder of it all is why Williams felt compelled to try to rationalize the defeat. No matter what sort of defense McCarthy had put up, he almost certainly would have been censured anyway by virtually the same vote, as he himself recognized. Nor did Williams need any excuses. By his conduct of the case, he covered himself with glory and drew almost unanimous praise except from true believers like Brent Bozell and Roy Cohn. Bozell says he was "discontented" with Williams because he did not sufficiently "identify himself with the anti-Communist cause" and "ought to have been tougher than he was on the Watkins Committee." Cohn later wrote that "McCarthy, I believe, made a serious mistake when he took on an attorney, albeit an able one, Edward Bennett Williams, to speak for him at the censure proceedings. He did not need counsel." Cohn felt that

McCarthy was "predestined to lose" and that if he had argued his own case "he would have gained in spirit" while he went "down fighting. . . . The Senate would have proceeded to censure Joe McCarthy, but the American people would have read his words and would have had a clearer idea of why it all happened the way it did." Cohn also said the muzzling of McCarthy during the Watkins Committee hearing frustrated the senator and caused him to give the "handmaiden" speech, and added that McCarthy himself later regretted having an attorney. He quoted McCarthy as saying:

> "Why couldn't I have gone down the way I was, being myself, instead of coming in with a new face and having to sit there and have a lawyer trying to talk to people in a kind of pleading way, trying to talk them out of the lynching party they were determined to have no matter what?" [102]

Williams's response to Cohn: "Roy Cohn obviously thought McCarthy was still capable of helping himself. I thought that the maximum service which I could render to him at that time was to keep him silent. I tried, but I was unsuccessful at keeping him silent. I really believe if I had kept him silent in the sense of not making any tirades outside the hearing room, but simply trying the case before the committee in an orderly fashion, we could have won the whole case."

The Senate vote to condemn McCarthy, coupled with the 1954 elections, which gave the Democrats control of the Senate and resulted in his ouster from the subcommittee chairmanship he had used as his main forum, effectively removed him from the national scene. After that, his decline was rapid. Ostracized by his fellow senators, he was no longer of interest to the press.

Williams believes the loss of notoriety was what destroyed McCarthy. "I thought at the time and I still think that he was much more interested in glory than he was in power. There are some people who break down the drives of ambitious men into money drives, power drives, and glory drives. If you had to do that for him, it would clearly have been a glory drive. He was addicted to publicity. There was nothing he enjoyed more than looking at himself on television and reading about himself in headlines. He was absolutely obsessed with the idea of coverage."

After the censure, McCarthy "no longer was regarded as a serious factor in American politics. The press no longer was chasing him for his every word. They were bored with him. They turned the lights out on him. And what broke him was when they turned the lights out."

Williams continued to represent McCarthy and remained friendly with him until his death in May 1957. Two cases were still pending after the censure debate was over: an income-tax audit by the Internal Revenue Service, and the suit that had been filed against the senator by Drew

Pearson, which was finally settled out of court in 1956. The audit of McCarthy's taxes for the years 1947 to 1952 finally resulted in the IRS admitting that McCarthy not only hadn't cheated on his taxes but had overpaid them by more than $1,000. When he announced the IRS ruling in his favor, McCarthy displayed for news photographers an income-tax refund check for $1,056.75, prompting the head of the Secret Service to accuse him of a possible violation of law. McCarthy also said he was considering a suit against the *Washington Star* on the advice of his attorney (Williams), who had told him that a 1954 *Star* article stating that McCarthy owed $25,000 in back taxes was libelous.[103] Nothing ever came of McCarthy's suggestion that he might sue, however.

The central irony of the McCarthy-Williams association was that Williams firmly established himself as a uniquely able attorney in a case in which there were five charges against his client and the client was in effect convicted on two and severely reprimanded on the other three. But the censure case riveted national attention on Williams, and for him it was a no-lose situation because McCarthy was perceived as never having had a chance from the start. In that respect, the McCarthy censure case was similar to the Jimmy Hoffa bribery trial in 1957, in which Williams earned the reputation of a legal miracle-worker.

The paths of Williams and McCarthy resembled a classic supply-and-demand chart: Williams's rocket was shooting up as fast as McCarthy's was plummeting. Within two and a half years of his censure, McCarthy was dead. But no opposing counsel would ever again have to commission a background report to find out who Edward Bennett Williams was.

Part
FOUR

Crusaders'
Alumni Association

9

The Onassis
Ship Deals

I f Aristotle Socrates Onassis had had his way, OPEC might have stood for Onassis Petroleum Exporting Corporation. Instead, the shipping billionaire's most grandiose scheme was foiled during the mid-1950s as a result of a wide-ranging campaign orchestrated by Stavros Niarchos, Onassis's shipping rival and brother-in-law. Niarchos's point man was Robert Maheu, formerly on the Holy Cross Crusaders' debate team with Edward Bennett Williams. Among those on Maheu's side were Vice President Richard M. Nixon; Warren Burger, then a high-ranking official of the Department of Justice; Williams; the CIA; the National Security Council; the U.S. State Department; and ARAMCO, the consortium of foreign oil companies that operated in Saudi Arabia.

Williams's involvement in Onassis's business started with the 1951 perjury indictment of a Washington lawyer named Robert Whittier Dudley. Earlier that year, a Senate committee headed by William Fulbright (D-Ark.) conducted an investigation into allegations that many loans awarded by the Reconstruction Finance Corporation were allocated on the basis of favoritism and influence-peddling. The findings of the Fulbright panel were turned over to a federal grand jury in Washington, which called

Dudley for testimony in June 1951. Dudley was alleged to have helped a client, the National Union Radio Corporation, obtain RFC loans totaling $1.5 million by arranging the delivery of two television sets provided by National Union to loan examiners at the RFC.[1] On June 12, 1951, during his fourth and final day in front of the grand jury, Dudley was asked by a prosecutor, "Do you know anything about any television sets which were purchased for people over at RFC? . . . Did you ever hear of that?" Dudley answered no to both questions.[2] Four months later, Dudley realized he had made a mistake, that the television sets had actually been turned over to RFC employees, although his understanding had been that they were to pay for them. He asked to be allowed to reappear before the grand jury and correct his testimony, but he was nevertheless indicted for perjury.[3]

During the 1940s, when Dudley worked for the Office of Price Administration, he had befriended another OPA employee, Richard M. Nixon. By the time he ran into problems with the RFC, he and Nixon lived near each other in the Spring Valley section of Washington. During one of Dudley's sessions with the grand jury, a government attorney asked if he hadn't discussed the case with then Senator Nixon. Dudley said he didn't recall any such conversation, causing the prosecutor to remark, "Mr. Dudley, you baffle me," implying that Dudley was lying. Dudley's first lawyer in the case, William H. Collins, sought unsuccessfully to have the perjury indictment dismissed, arguing that the prosecutor's comment on the purported Nixon-Dudley talk had prejudiced the grand jury.[4]

When the case went to trial in June 1953, Williams was called in to defend Dudley. During the brief trial, the defense presented Senator Estes Kefauver (D-Tenn.), renowned for his crusade against organized crime, and former congressman Joseph Casey (D-Mass.), Dudley's brother-in-law, as character witnesses.[5] At the end of the three-day trial, in his summation to the jury, Williams declared:

> I think it is a fair statement to say that Robert Dudley's whole life is on trial before you this afternoon. His whole future—professional, personal, family . . . all the aspirations that he has ever had in 40 years of living, all the dreams that he has had throughout his life, are riding on the outcome of this case.[6]

The effect was electrifying. The *Washington Post* reported that "one woman member of the panel began to cry [and] several others were on the verge of tears when Williams finished his speech,"[7] while the *Washington Star* said, "Tears flowed down the cheeks of several women jurors."[8]

In the words of Tom Wadden, a longtime law associate of Williams, "Ed and Bobby dripped sincerity in front of the jury and Bobby walked out of that one." Certainly, the jury took almost no time to find Dudley innocent; thirty years later, he said it seemed as though "the first juror was coming out of the jury room [to announce the verdict] as the last was going in."

That night (June 5, 1953), Dudley and his wife invited a dozen or so of their best friends to celebrate at their home. Among the guests was Richard Nixon. According to Williams, "It was a very gay evening. I will always remember that there was a lot of drinking and we sang songs and Nixon played the piano and it was one of those great nights that went on and on. I guess that was maybe the beginning of my friendship with Nixon," which lasted until Nixon left Washington for California in 1961, following his loss to John F. Kennedy. By the time Nixon returned to Washington as president in 1969, Williams had switched from Republican to Democrat and he and Nixon were no longer friendly.

Eight months after Dudley's acquittal, he again found himself in need of a criminal lawyer. This time, he and eight other men were charged with arranging illegally to give Aristotle Onassis control of surplus ships formerly owned by the U.S. government. The defendants, in addition to Onassis and Dudley, included Joseph Casey; Dudley's law partner, Joseph H. Rosenbaum; George Cokkinis, one of Onassis's top aides; and Robert L. Berenson, the Paris-based board chairman of Onassis's United States Petroleum Carriers, Inc. Also named as defendants were six corporations, most of them owned by Onassis.[9]

In a companion suit, similar charges were filed against Stavros Niarchos; Casey; Julius C. Holmes, a special assistant to Secretary of State John Foster Dulles; New York financier E. Stanley Klein; and several others.[10]

The indictments came at an exceptionally bad time for Onassis. Just a few weeks earlier, he had reached a secret agreement with the Saudi Arabian government to carry Saudi oil in his tankers. Onassis was attempting to work out the final details of the accord when he learned of the U.S charges against him. Any embarrassment to him just then might cause the Saudis to reconsider their deal.

The charges against Onassis, Niarchos, and their American associates were an outgrowth of hearings held in early 1952 by a star-studded Senate panel. Six senators had probed allegations that foreigners like Onassis had used American front men to obtain control of surplus U.S. vessels from World War II—contrary to U.S. law, which specified that Americans had to own the ships. Among the six who served on the Permanent Subcommittee on Investigations of the Senate Committee on Government Operations were Clyde Hoey (D-N.C.),* the chairman; Richard Nixon; Joseph McCarthy;† Hubert Humphrey; and John L. McClellan (D-Ark.).‡

When Dudley was called before the subcommittee on March 4, 1952,

---

*Hoey's death in 1954 created the vacancy that was filled by the appointment of Sam Ervin.

†After the Eisenhower landslide in November 1952 that gave the GOP control of the Senate, McCarthy, the senior Republican on the subcommittee, took over as chairman and used the subcommittee as the vehicle for his investigations into alleged subversion.

‡McClellan was later chairman of a Senate committee that investigated Jimmy Hoffa and the Teamsters Union, leading to the bribery case in which Williams defended Hoffa (see Part Five).

he was asked about his role in the transactions that involved Onassis. Senator Nixon did not let his friendship with Dudley inhibit him from asking several questions that presented the witness in a favorable light.[11] In the end, the subcommittee found that the shipping deals had netted stock worth $528,700 and law fees of $68,600 for Casey; stock worth $107,000 and $79,500 in fees for Dudley; and $327,500 in fees and another $156,000 in shipping stock for Dudley's law firm.[12] Altogether, the Americans associated with Onassis and Niarchos gained a profit of $3,250,000 on an investment of $101,000.[13]

Joseph Casey, who was identified as the principal figure in the U.S. group, offered the explanation that the profits were fair in view of the high-risk nature of the investment.[14] From what Onassis said, however, it was he who put up most of the money that was at risk. In addition to acknowledging that he owned 49 percent of the company that bought most of the surplus ships, he admitted that he "'lent'" his American partners most of the funds to buy the other 51 percent.[15]

Furthermore, Dudley testified that he and the other buyers of the ships were in an extremely favorable position because immediate charters by oil companies almost assured huge profits. According to Dudley:

> You had a situation which was very temporary in nature, caused by the backwash of the war, caused by a tremendous expansion in the petroleum industry, caused by perhaps miscalculation of tanker-transportation needs on the part of the principal oil companies, caused by a shortage of storage facilities in all transportation, plus a cold winter in 1947–48.[16]

As a result of the Hoey Subcommittee's investigation, Onassis, Dudley, Casey, Niarchos, et al, were indicted. Onassis's primary American lawyer, Edward J. Ross of New York, hired William Leahy, one of Williams's mentors from his early days as a lawyer, as Washington counsel for Onassis. At the same time, Williams was engaged as attorney for several other defendants, including Casey and Dudley.[17]

While attorneys for the Onassis group worked to have the charges dismissed, Niarchos's lawyers made a deal with Warren Burger (then assistant attorney general in charge of the Justice Department's Civil Division). Niarchos and his codefendants agreed to hand over nineteen ships and $4 million in cash. In return, the Justice Department dropped its proceedings.[18]

At a hearing in June 1954, Williams argued that the charges against several of Onassis's fellow defendants, including Casey, Dudley, Rosenbaum, and Nicolas Cokkinis (but not Onassis himself), should be dropped. Williams told U.S. District Judge Luther W. Youngdahl that the case ought to be dismissed because the defendants had obtained immunity from prosecution by giving self-incriminating testimony during their appearances before a grand jury two years earlier.

One of the remaining defendants, Julius Holmes, declined to join in Williams's motion, because Holmes, as a former State Department official, felt it would be beneath his dignity to be cleared on a technicality. Williams was riding to the courthouse with Joseph Casey "the day I was going to make the motion. And he told me that his sister, who lived in Clinton, Massachusetts, had gone to church and lit candles for him, Dudley, and Holmes. He said his sister had wired him that she had lit the candles because they had been indicted together and she hoped they would be successful in their efforts to get the case dismissed. Casey said he wired her back and said, 'Go back to church and blow out Julius's candle, he wants to be acquitted by the jury.'" Williams says that Holmes's lawyers were in court when he argued his motion, "and they were all hoping that I'd lose, because they were so embarrassed that they didn't make their client join in it."

Williams's move was successful, and Judge Youngdahl ordered the indictments against his clients dropped.[19] Two months later, the Justice Department decided to dismiss the charges against Holmes on the theory that it would be "impractical and improper" to try him after the cases against the others had been thrown out.[20] President Eisenhower then appointed Holmes ambassador to Iran.[21]

During the same period, Williams also represented Manuel Kulukundis, another Greek shipowner, who was indicted in three cases on charges similar to those against Onassis and Niarchos. Williams succeeded in having the cases against Kulukundis and several of his relatives dismissed, in return for payment of fines of several thousand dollars.[22] (As of 1981, Kulukundis, then eighty-one, was still said to be "the acknowledged head of the Greek shipping community" in New York.[23])

Williams rates his successes in the cases of Casey, Dudley, Rosenbaum, and the Kulukundis family among his top achievements in court. "They were tremendous legal victories," he says. "They didn't attract the kind of public attention [that some of his other cases, such as McCarthy, Jimmy Hoffa, and Frank Costello, did], but we had some spectacular results from very, very good theories and good concepts that had never been used before in shipping cases. Getting a number of people off on a theory of grand-jury immunity was quite an esoteric way out." Although the shipping cases were not heavily publicized, "they were very significant inside the profession. The biggest impact that I can make is within my own profession. When I have a tremendous victory inside my profession, it makes all the other lawyers say, 'Golly, we ought to get him.' The Hoffa thing may have had a tremendous impact across the nation publicly as far as getting my name known. But I don't get my law business from the public. I get it from lawyers. Ninety-eight percent of all my law business comes from other lawyers."

After November 18, 1954, when the indictment against Julius Holmes was dropped by the government, Onassis was the only person still in trouble. He continued to be under criminal indictment; and five days after Holmes was freed, the Department of Justice (in a suit signed by Warren Burger) filed a claim against him in federal district court in New York to recover $20 million Onassis had allegedly made from the onetime U.S. ships he had acquired.[24] To back up its claim, the government had seized about a dozen of Onassis's ships; they were among some forty foreign-owned vessels of which Washington had taken possession. Warren Burger, who technically became operator of the embargoed ships, was known as "'The Admiral'" within Justice Department circles.[25]

Now Onassis initiated serious negotiations with the Justice Department to obtain the release of his ships. A series of meetings was held, and Williams attended one in the office of Attorney General Herbert Brownell, along with Onassis, several of the shipper's London attorneys, and William Leahy. According to Williams, Leahy "was at the end of his career. He had a bad heart, and he asked me to come along because he didn't know if he could go through a long trial.* I went and sat in on the meeting with him, and I was going to try it for Onassis [if the case actually went to trial]."

Brownell, as a senior partner in the New York law firm of Lord, Day & Lord, had been one of a number of attorneys who had advised Onassis that his arrangement to buy the ships, with American citizens ostensibly owning a 51-percent interest, was legal. But in his new role as attorney general, Brownell was claiming that the deal he had approved when he was on the other side of the fence violated the law. Onassis, to say the least, was none too pleased.[26]

By the time of the conference in Brownell's office, Williams pointed out, "they had Aristotle Onassis's ships all tied up on the Eastern Seaboard. And they had him under indictment." Thus the meeting began under less than ideal circumstances from Onassis's perspective. As time went by and the lawyers engaged in complicated discussions about maritime law, Onassis grew more and more upset. Sitting next to him, Williams watched the "little fellow" wearing the "blue suede shoes and dark glasses.

"He hadn't said a word for forty-five minutes. And I looked at his feet. They were shuffling back and forth across the carpet because he was getting so nervous and restless and impatient. Finally he looked up" and addressed the attorney general of the United States of America as follows:

"'Ge-ne-ral!' Brownell looked up, and Onassis said, 'Let's cut the bullshit! What's the ransom for my ships?' Brownell jumped up and said the conference was over. So we left. About a year later, they told him what

---

*Leahy died in June 1956.

the ransom was and we paid it and they dismissed the indictment."

In return for paying $7 million in fines (spread over several years) and making other concessions, Onassis was allowed to retain his American vessels. The December 21, 1955, settlement was "'all dressed up to look like a government victory,'" according to Edward Ross, "'but even they knew we had won.'"[27]

The troubles of Aristotle Socrates Onassis, however, were far from over.

On January 20, 1954, Aristotle Onassis concluded an agreement with the Saudi Arabian government under which he ultimately could have gained a monopoly to transport Saudi Arabian oil. Robert Maheu calculated that via that contract with the Saudis—commonly referred to as the Jeddah Agreement—"Mr. Onassis in a period of several years would have been in a position to control more dead weight [shipping] tonnage than our government controlled!" Spyridon Catapodis, who asserted that Onassis had promised him huge sums of money to help negotiate the Jeddah Agreement, stated in an affidavit pertaining to the transaction that Onassis had told him the Jeddah Agreement would, in time, "'make him the richest and most powerful man in the world.'"[28] Catapodis's affidavit, which he executed on September 27, 1954, before the British consul at Nice, later figured in a $1.6-million libel suit filed by Williams against Onassis on behalf of Catapodis.

Also in the wake of the contract with the Saudis, the CIA speculated that once Onassis gained control of Saudi Arabian oil, he "'apparently has some mighty plans to monopolize the tanker industry by playing the same theme to Kuwait, Iran and Iraq.'"[29] There was even conjecture that "German industrial and financial interests bent on economic conquest of the Near and Middle East" were behind Onassis,[30] and visions of a Fourth Reich nurtured on Arab oil were strengthened by amendments to the Jeddah Agreement which specified that "'Jews [shall] have no direct or indirect interest in any of these companies'" and "'the company shall not deal with Israel.'"[31] In view of the wealth and power Onassis came to wield despite the subsequent cancellation of the Jeddah Agreement, one can only imagine the extent of his influence if his plans had not been thwarted by Maheu, Williams, and others.

In retrospect, the whole tale sounds like something straight out of the *Arabian Nights*. The only difference is that this story is true. In 1952, Spyridon Catapodis, a small-time Greek shipper known in casinos on the French Riviera as "'a legendary gambler, always in debt,'"[32] hatched a plan to arrange with the Iraqi government for Iraq's oil to be transported in ships provided by Catapodis. Catapodis realized that he could never obtain enough ships, but that Onassis, an acquaintance of his, could. He approached Onassis, who, according to Catapodis, expressed interest.

Meanwhile, a change in government took place in Iraq, the new regime nationalized the oil industry, and the attention of Catapodis and Onassis shifted to Saudi Arabia.[33] Catapodis later stated that Onassis promised him that if he could work out a deal with the Saudis, "'[h]e would give me a share of profits amounting to about a million dollars per year free of tax.'"[34]

Catapodis proceeded to negotiate with the Saudis, until he learned in the fall of 1953 that Hjalmar Schacht, the former Nazi minister of finance (referred to by one writer as "the German financial genius who sustained Hitler for so long"[35]), had also approached the Saudis on behalf of an "unnamed principal" and offered them terms "identical" to those broached by Catapodis as Onassis's agent.

Discovering what appeared to be a double cross by Onassis, Catapodis stormed from the Paris hotel where he had been bargaining with Saudi representatives to Onassis's Paris town house. There Onassis's wife told Catapodis, "'I'm sorry but you can't see my husband now, he's asleep.'" Catapodis informed Mrs. Onassis, "'I don't care if he's asleep or dead, I'm going to see him,'" whereupon she awakened her husband and he came downstairs in pajamas and robe. Catapodis then dragged Onassis to where the Saudis were waiting, and Onassis, admitting that Schacht had also been representing him, agreed to let Catapodis conduct the rest of the negotiations.

On November 11, 1953, Onassis signed two documents, one an official agreement for Saudi Arabian government records and the other a private contract granting £200,000 plus a minimum of £50,000 each year the Jeddah Agreement remained in effect to a Saudi named Mohammed Abdullah Alireza, for his "help" in putting the deal together. Alireza, the Saudi counterpart of Catapodis, was president of his country's chamber of commerce and a brother of the Saudi minister of state.[36] Catapodis would later state in his affidavit in Nice "'that bribe payments amounting to more than $1,000,000 had been paid to Saudi Arabian officials'" to bring about the Jeddah Agreement.[37]

Within a few weeks after Alireza received the two documents, he noticed "to his surprise" that "while the ink used by Onassis in signing the official contract, destined for government use, stood out indelibly, the product used on the companion agreement appeared to be vanishing like a ghost at dawn."[38] Alireza demanded that Onassis give him a substitute paper, which the shipping magnate did.[39]

The following January, Onassis, accompanied by his wife, his aide, Nicolas Cokkinis, and Catapodis, arrived in Jeddah. Four days later, on January 20, 1954, the final agreement was signed by Onassis and the Saudi minister of finance, Shiek Abdullah al-Suleiman al-Hamdan.[40]

The merrymaking over the formalizing of the final accord had scarcely subsided when Catapodis made the same unhappy discovery that Mohammed Alireza had made two months earlier: The ink was rapidly fading from Onassis's signature on his copy of a document that promised Catapodis £125,000 upon the signing of the Jeddah Agreement; £75,000 the day Onassis's first tanker sailed from Saudi Arabia; 5 percent of the shipping firm that would transport Saudi oil; and an interest in income from all future cargoes.

Catapodis, accompanied this time by an American named Leon Turrou, again paid an unscheduled call on Onassis in Paris.[41] Turrou, an ex–FBI agent and army intelligence officer reputed to be a secret agent of the CIA, was—at least on the surface—an employee of J. Paul Getty, a business associate of Onassis.[42] Catapodis complained to Onassis about the fading signature, and Onassis, showing friendly concern, deftly pocketed the document while Turrou frantically tried to call Catapodis's attention to his "partner's" maneuver. Catapodis finally left after Onassis promised to give him a new contract signed in more permanent ink. (Onassis asked, "'What did you think—I go around with disappearing ink in my pen?'")[43] But Onassis still had the original, and the replacement he had promised Catapodis never materialized.[44] *

Catapodis continued trying to persuade Onassis to uphold his end of their supposed bargain, but he never received a single cent—much less another copy of the contract. Three months later, on May 5, 1954, he was finally able to arrange an appointment with Onassis in Monte Carlo, but Onassis failed to show up. The enraged Catapodis learned that, instead of meeting him, Onassis was on his way to Nice Airport, where he was about to board a plane for London and New York. Catapodis, taking the Greek Consul with him, rushed to the airport, where he accosted Onassis (who

---

*The visit of Catapodis and Turrou to Onassis's home may have been the incident to which Maheu was referring when he testified under oath in 1975 that "after consulting with the [Central Intelligence] Agency, he arranged for a listening device to be placed in the room of the contract holder [Onassis]; and that he provided the impetus for the termination of the contract by publicizing its terms in a Rome newspaper which he said he had purchased with CIA funds."

Maheu's testimony—at least the version of it made semipublic by the Senate committee that called him as a witness—only served to further cloud the issue. In an interview in Washington in 1981, Maheu said that what he had actually told the senators was that the newspaper that originally published the details of the Jeddah Agreement was in Athens—not Rome—and that it was purchased with funds provided by Niarchos—not the CIA.

A summary of Maheu's testimony, complete with citations to dates and page numbers in the Senate transcript, was printed, then buried in the stacks at the Library of Congress—which is particularly curious in view of the fact that the testimony itself is classified, and is so secret that even Maheu is only permitted to examine it in a Capitol office, and cannot copy it or make notes from it.

Maheu testified about his role in undermining the "contract holder" when he was called as a witness before a Senate committee investigating alleged plots by U.S. intelligence agencies to assassinate foreign heads of state; he was asked about his part in attempting to "terminate with extreme prejudice" Fidel Castro during the early 1960s.[45]

was a much smaller man), grabbed his throat, called him "'not even a Greek . . . but a Goddamned Turk'" (the ultimate insult), and spat in his face. Onassis, forced practically to his knees by the burly, 220-pound Catapodis, cried out to the Greek consul, "'Do something! Stop him! Don't you see what this man is doing to me?'" The consul replied, "'I would have done exactly the same.'" In the end, Catapodis let Onassis catch his plane only after Onassis repeated his vow to make good on their deal.[46]

By now Catapodis was bragging at the gambling tables of the Riviera about the fantastic coup he and Onassis had scored, and about the money he was going to make. Garbled accounts began reaching Niarchos and the major oil companies who did business in Saudi Arabia. Officials of ARAMCO,* the major Western firm producing oil in Saudi Arabia, were deeply worried.[47] So was Niarchos, who hired Maheu to "scuttle the deal," as Maheu put it in 1981. Maheu found that Onassis's opponents had good cause for concern; the Jeddah Agreement contained a grandfather clause under which tankers not owned by Onassis would have been phased out of the transport of Saudi oil, leaving Onassis with a monopoly.[48]

After his investigators uncovered the grandfather clause in the Jeddah Agreement in the summer of 1954, Maheu reported their findings to Vice President Nixon, who headed the National Security Council under Eisenhower. Maheu recalled in 1981 that Nixon's reaction was "'Would you package all this for a presentation to the National Security Council?'"[†] Maheu did, and he says his information produced a dramatic effect: "That was the first time Washington officialdom became concerned" about the Jeddah Agreement. "It was the following day that our State Department denounced the agreement. And that following night two of the top officials of CIA went to Saudi Arabia."

Before long, Maheu flew to London and met with Stavros Niarchos, who suggested that he contact Catapodis. And one month later, Catapodis gave his affidavit to the British consul in Nice. Attached to it were "nu-

---

*Standard Oil of New Jersey, Standard Oil of California, and Texaco each owned 30 percent of ARAMCO, while Socony-Vacuum, or Mobil, owned the other 10 percent.

†Author Jim Hougan reported in *Spooks* that Maheu's Washington-based private investigative agency formed the basis of the "Mission Impossible" television series, and that John Gerrity, who accompanied Maheu to the meeting with Nixon, said that "'Nixon gave us the whole bit—you know, the "Your assignment, John, should you choose to accept it."'"[49] Maheu certainly was involved in some very sensitive assignments for the CIA during this period; in one, he produced a film "purporting to depict a foreign leader [in bed] with a woman in the Soviet Union. The CIA planned to circulate the film, representing it to have been produced by the Soviet Union," in order to get in the foreign leader's good graces. Maheu testified that "he had located an actor resembling the leader and had arranged for the production of the film," which, however, "was never used."[50]

merous" documents describing how he had negotiated the Jeddah Agreement and bribed Saudia officials on behalf of Onassis, who in turn had promised Catapodis "approximately $1,000,000 a year, free and clear of all taxes, which the plaintiff [Catapodis] stated . . . was to represent a portion of the anticipated annual profit to be realized by the defendant [Onassis]" from the contract.[51]

Still without satisfaction in the case, Catapodis filed a criminal fraud complaint against Onassis in a Paris court on November 19, 1954. As part of this action, Catapodis alleged that, as to his own contract with Onassis, the billionaire "had signed the letter with disappearing or fading ink so that his signature thereto began to fade and ultimately disappeared," and that Onassis subsequently persuaded Catapodis to return the original to him, but broke his promise to supply a substitute.[52]

Catapodis revealed to the press that he had brought suit against Onassis, and journalists immediately sought a comment from the defendant. Onassis denied that Catapodis had ever been his agent, said the signature on the purported Onassis-Catapodis agreement was not his, and termed the Catapodis allegations "'a palpable fraud.'"[53]

Catapodis's charges and Onassis's denials were duly reported in the news media, and at that point Maheu referred Catapodis to Williams, who filed a $1.6-million libel action against Onassis. The suit, brought by Catapodis in U.S. District Court in Washington on December 3, 1954, and signed by Williams, asked for $400,000 in civil damages for each of four stories that had been printed about the Catapodis-Onassis dispute— on the front page of the *New York Times* on November 20, 1954; in the *New York Herald Tribune* on the same date; in *Time*'s issue of November 22, 1954; and in *Newsweek* one week later.[54]

One of the most unexpected aspects of this libel suit was that Catapodis dared to present himself as the injured party. For it was he who had made the most damaging allegations in the whole affair, claiming that Onassis had defrauded him of millions of dollars, signed their agreement in disappearing ink, and then refused to give Catapodis a new document or to return the first. It was Catapodis who informed the press of the Paris suit even before Onassis or his attorneys had learned of it—possibly "in violation of the requirement of French law and legal procedure that the criminal complaint should remain secret and impounded for the purpose of protecting the name, character and reputation of the defendant," according to Onassis.[55]

No responsible journalist would have reported Catapodis's complaint against Onassis without obtaining Onassis's version; the reporters called Onassis for comment as a matter of routine, and Onassis, also routinely in this type of case, denied Catapodis's charges. Still, the headlines ("Onassis Accused of Defrauding His Agent on Arabian Oil Deal" on page one of the *New York Times*, and "Agent Accuses Onassis of Fraud in Tanker

Deal" in the *New York Herald Tribune*), as well as the stories, were generally favorable to Catapodis and correspondingly negative toward Onassis. Nonetheless, Catapodis—abetted by Williams—claimed that *he* was the victim in the mutual mudslinging between the two.

There was hardly any action in the libel suit of *Catapodis* v. *Onassis* for nearly eighteen months after Williams filed it. Matters were finally brought to a head on April 26, 1956, when Edward J. Ross, Onassis's attorney, formally notified the court that he wished to take depositions from two people: Spyridon Catapodis and Robert A. Maheu. Ross sought to question Maheu on a wide variety of subjects, including "the employment of Robert A. Maheu or Robert A. Maheu Associates by Stavros Niarchos . . . or by any domestic or foreign corporations in which Stavros Niarchos may have any interest, direct or indirect"; as well as about Maheu's dealings with Leon G. Turrou, Nicolas Cokkinis, Mohammed Alireza, Sheik Abdullah Suleiman al Hamdan, King Saud of Saudi Arabia, ARAMCO, and others.[56]

Maheu's responses to questions on these points would no doubt have been very interesting. But such was not to be; on May 14, 1956—the same day Maheu's deposition was to have been taken and exactly one week before Ross proposed to question Catapodis under oath—Williams filed notice with the court that Catapodis had decided to dismiss the case "with prejudice," meaning Catapodis could not change his mind and revive the suit at a later date.[57]

Spyridon Catapodis wound up as a loser on all counts and in all courts. A companion libel suit in New York was also withdrawn.[58] A $14-million suit for the commissions Catapodis felt Onassis owed him under the missing contract was also filed in New York but was dismissed for lack of jurisdiction, since both parties lived abroad.[59] Catapodis's criminal suit against Onassis was dismissed by a Paris judge who noted that Catapodis had somehow succeeded in making copies of every document except the only one that was important, the alleged contract between himself and Onassis.[60] Yet, Joachim Joesten, one of a very few writers who were granted extensive access to Onassis, and who produced a generally favorable biography of the tycoon, concluded: "I am fully satisfied that Catapodis, by and large, told the truth."[61] Joesten added,

> He was defeated, but not because his detailed account was proved false. It never was. . . . The photostats supported many of his contentions, for instance that Onassis offered or gave bribes to the venal Saudi officials. Catapodis, however, was unable to produce in court the one document he needed. . . : his contract with Onassis. That piece of evidence has been lacking because Onassis managed to spirit it away.
>   And so, in the end, Catapodis was left holding the bag.[62]

But Onassis also emerged from the Saudi Arabian episode a loser. As

Robert Maheu points out, not a single drop of Arabian oil was ever moved an inch in one of Onassis's ships, in part because Catapodis's suits against Onassis diminished Onassis's standing with Saudi officials. In the end, the Jeddah Agreement proved to be as valuable to Onassis as a contract without a signature. Onassis was left with the conviction that he had been the victim of a conspiracy (an assessment his biographer Joesten thought "accurate"). "'Never before in the history of business was so much power combined to fight and destroy an individual,'" said Onassis.[63] Lending credence to this theory was the fact that Niarchos refused to testify about the campaign against his rival without clearance "'by Washington,'"[64] and that during the caper Maheu was allowed to send coded messages to Niarchos via CIA channels.[65]

Reflecting recently on what little he could recall of the Catapodis-Onassis affair, Williams said he was certain he had never even met Catapodis and that at Maheu's behest he had acted as "a messenger, a mail drop" in filing suit against Onassis in Washington so that Onassis could be served with legal papers in the District of Columbia if need be. He said he had found the whole matter "very troublesome" because of a potential conflict of interest presented by his accompanying Onassis to the meeting with Brownell—with the prospect that Williams would become his lawyer—and yet suing him on behalf of Catapodis.

"The time is very troublesome to me on this lawsuit because obviously I wouldn't have filed a suit against Onassis if I were representing him at the time," said Williams. "Under any circumstances. So it had to be a different time. Leahy was representing him. But I was there with Leahy. Therefore, I would not have filed a suit against someone if I had served in any representative capacity. So it had to be at a different time." He could not provide records to show the date of the Onassis-Brownell meeting; nor could the Justice Department, and Warren Burger declined repeated requests for an interview. Williams was certain, however, that Brownell was attorney general;* that Onassis, Leahy, and several of Onassis's British lawyers were present; and that the topic under discussion was the surplus ships. He also said several times that "I would have been the lawyer [for Onassis] if Mr. Leahy had not been able to function."

It would seem logical that the meeting occurred late in 1954, about a year before Onassis and the government settled their differences and shortly after the government filed its $20-million damage suit against Onassis. That would also have been about the time Williams filed Catapodis's suit against Onassis, on December 3, 1954. In the opinion of Edward Ross, Onassis's New York lawyer, if Williams did represent both Onassis and Catapodis, "there's a conflict of interest there."

---

* Brownell served as attorney general from January 21, 1953, until November 8, 1957.

The Onassis venture was the first of many in which Williams and his friend from Holy Cross, Robert Maheu, worked together. From the time Maheu left the FBI in 1954 to set up his own investigative agency* until he moved away from Washington about five years later, he was the person to whom Williams "always" turned when he needed a detective—about a dozen times during that period.

As yet another link in the "old boy" network that revolved around the law firm founded by Frank Hogan, Maheu began doing jobs for Howard Hughes through Seymour Mintz, a senior partner at Hogan & Hartson. According to Maheu, Mintz hired him for "a very small assignment. I did not know for whom I worked. A few months later a second assignment came and at that time Mintz identified his client [Hughes] and told me it was the same client for whom I had worked earlier." Mintz was married to the former wife of Colman Stein, who succeeded Nicholas Chase as Williams's law partner in 1951.

Williams continued to influence Maheu's career long after Maheu left Washington. Maheu says Williams helped smooth his first trip to Las Vegas (about 1959) while he was in Los Angeles, trying to decide whether to go to work for Hughes full-time. A Los Angeles attorney asked Maheu if he would serve a subpoena in a divorce case on Beldon Katleman, owner of the El Rancho Vegas casino-hotel. Maheu agreed to take on the assignment, "just flat picked up the phone" and called El Rancho for a reservation, "and they laughed at me. I remembered Ed had told me once, 'If you ever have any trouble getting reservations in Las Vegas, call me.' So I called him. He says, 'Hang on right there. Hopefully, in a few minutes you'll be getting a phone call from someone.' A few minutes later, I got a phone call and a fella said, 'My name is Johnny. I just heard from Ed Williams. I hear you want some reservations.' I said, 'yes.' He said, 'Where?' I said, 'The El Rancho.' He said 'You got 'em.'"

Maheu and "Johnny" arranged to meet in Las Vegas and Maheu arrived to find a "very suave, well-dressed gentleman" waiting for him. His telephone acquaintance introduced himself as Johnny Roselli—a well-known Mob figure who was reputedly one of the Mafia's top operatives on the West Coast.[67] Roselli said to Maheu, "'I hope you know that as long as you're here you're a guest of Mr. Katleman. I think you ought to meet him. But I want to tell you in advance that he's playing it very cool these days because there are some people trying to lay a paper on him.' Before I knew it," said Maheu, "I'm in a little corner that you can't see from anywhere else, with Katleman and Zsa Zsa Gabor, who was appearing at the hotel at the time, and Roselli. And I have in my pocket the subpoena.

---

*While he was launching his own agency, Maheu was "initially paid a monthly retainer by the CIA of $500," according to Senate testimony by a high (and unnamed) CIA official. This was at the time that Maheu was working on the Onassis case, as well as the Aldo Icardi case (see chapter 10).[66]

It didn't take me long to decide that I'm not going to serve it. I figured this would have been an embarrassment to Ed and to Roselli."

Maheu later told Roselli the whole story and the two became fast friends. The friendship paid off when Roselli subsequently persuaded the owners of the Desert Inn to let Hughes remain as a guest at the hotel, even though they wanted him to leave. While Hughes was there, Roselli also helped arrange the sale of that hotel and the Sands Hotel to him.

Maheu and Roselli were in touch on another matter in 1960. That August, according to a Senate report, the CIA "took steps to enlist members of the criminal underworld with gambling syndicate contacts to aid in assassinating" Fidel Castro. The CIA "decided to rely on Robert A. Maheu to recruit someone 'tough enough' to handle the job." The CIA had previously called on Maheu "in several sensitive covert operations" in which the Agency "didn't want to have an Agency person or a government person get caught."

Maheu, who "was told to offer money, probably $150,000 for Castro's assassination," broached the idea to Roselli, who reluctantly agreed to participate because "he felt that he had an obligation to his government." In October 1960 in Miami, Roselli introduced Maheu to two "individuals" on whom he planned to rely: "'Sam Gold'" (later identified as Sam Giancana, a top Chicago Mafioso), and "'Joe'" (an alias for Santos Trafficante), who was "the Cosa Nostra chieftain in Cuba." According to Maheu, who said he "met almost daily with Giancana over a substantial period of time," it was "Giancana's job to locate someone in Castro's entourage who could accomplish the assassination." Several attempts on Castro's life failed. In February 1962, Richard Helms took charge of the mission and gave "'explicit orders'" to have Roselli "maintain his Cuban contacts, but not to deal with Maheu or Giancana . . . whom he had decided were 'untrustworthy' and 'surplus.'"[68] Despite all this, Castro stayed alive, and some assassination theorists suggest that he learned of the plots against him, blamed them on President Kennedy, and initiated the murder of JFK in revenge.

In 1965, Sam Giancana hired Williams and Tom Wadden after he was hailed before a federal grand jury in Chicago that was probing organized crime. Giancana was given immunity from prosecution and Williams advised him that he would have to testify or be held in contempt of court. Giancana originally agreed to answer questions in front of the jurors, but changed his mind and was imprisoned for contempt—to his astonishment. He had told Williams that "the government would not press to put him in jail for contempt because he had worked in close liaison with the government in a plot to assassinate Castro. I didn't believe it. It sounded like a fairy tale to me. And I found out it was true. Maheu gave me all the details."

In June 1975, just before he was to have testified before the Senate committee that questioned Maheu, Ginacana was murdered at his home in Chicago. The go-between from Maheu to Giancana, Johnny Roselli, did testify before the Senate panel. In August 1975, ten days after he disappeared from his home in Miami, his body was found "in a chain-wrapped 55-gallon drum floating in Biscayne Bay."[69] Roselli's attorney at the time was Tom Wadden.

And, to make the circle complete, the widow of the man who may have been the victim of a backfire in the Maheu-CIA-Mafia plot herself married the target of one of Maheu's earlier efforts at international intrigue. Like Robert Maheu, Sam Giancana, Johnny Roselli, Richard Helms, Aristotle Onassis and John F. Kennedy,* Jacqueline Kennedy Onassis had associated over the years with the individual who once turned down the CIA directorship: Edward Bennett Williams.

*See Hoffa section.

Right: Yearbook photograph, Holy Cross College, 1941.

Below: Edward Bennett Williams confers with his client, Senator Joseph McCarthy, during the 1954 Senate hearings that culminated in McCarthy's censure—the beginning of the end for McCarthy. (United Press)

Right: Williams and Robert Maheu (left) investigated the case of Aldo Icardi in 1956. They interviewed Vincenzo Moscatelli (center), a leading Communist politician in Italy, who admitted that his Red partisans had committed the World War II murder of which Icardi was accused. The three men are standing outside the Italian Chamber of Deputies, where Moscatelli served as a senator, and Maheu is carrying a tape recorder built into a briefcase—one of the first of its kind—with which he secretly taped Moscatelli's "confession."

Below: Williams was Dave Beck's attorney when the Teamster president appeared before the Senate Rackets Committee in 1957. (Wide World Photos)

Above: A bored Williams gets the word from Beck's successor, Jimmy Hoffa, during the Senate Rackets hearings in 1958. (Wide World Photos)

Below: Williams and Hoffa reach out for a document during the Senate probe. (Wide World Photos)

Right: During the late 1950s and early 1960s, Williams represented Mafia kingpin Frank Costello. Here Williams has just obtained Costello's release on bail in 1957. (Wide World Photos)

Below: Williams with his first wife, Dorothy, and their children, Joby (left), 4, and Ellen Adair, 2, in 1958. (Wide World Photos)

Above: Williams at work in 1958 with Vincent Fuller and Agnes Neill, two of his assistants. In 1959, Williams's first wife died, and a year later he married Neill. In 1982, Fuller successfully defended Ronald Reagan's assailant, John Hinckley. (Wide World Photos)

Below: Another of Williams's notorious clients was industrialist Bernard Goldfine, the central figure in the biggest scandal of the Eisenhower administration. At left is Goldfine's secretary, Mildred Paperman. (Wide World Photos)

Left: Williams defended Congressman Adam Clayton Powell, Jr., against income-tax-evasion charges in 1960. The case was dropped after a trial resulted in a hung jury. (United Press International)

Below: Williams displays a bug allegedly used to incriminate his client, LBJ protégé Bobby Baker, in 1964. Baker is at far left. (United Press International)

Above: Williams and Bobby Baker are the center of attention at 1964 Senate hearings on Baker's financial dealings. (Wide World Photos)

Left: Edward Bennett Williams arriving at the Federal Courthouse in Washington with his client, John Connally, on April 7, 1975. That day Williams cross-examined and destroyed Jake Jacobsen, who had accused Connally of illegally taking cash in exchange for his influence; Connally was acquitted. (Wide World Photos)

Top: Williams angrily lectures CBS reporter Fred Graham after the 1977 sentencing of former CIA director Richard Helms (*center*). (© CBS, Inc.)

Above: Williams as newly named chairman of Stop Jimmy Carter drive on eve of 1980 Democratic convention with Congressmen Don Edwards (left) and Michael Barnes. (Wide World Photos)

Below: Williams at a 1981 game between his baseball team, the Baltimore Orioles, and the New York Yankees. With him is Yankee owner George Steinbrenner, a friend and onetime client of Williams's. (Jerry Wachter)

10

Aldo Icardi:
Espionage and Murder

The airplane carrying the three Americans and their two allies from the Italian resistance had taken off from Algiers hours earlier. Then, it was broad daylight. Now, late in the night of September 26, 1944, after a flight across the Mediterranean, the five men had reached their destination: the mountainous countryside near Lake Maggiore and Lake Orta in northernmost Italy, north of Milan and Turin, hard by the Swiss border. The drop point was some 100 miles behind German lines, far away from help. The five soldiers—Major William V. Holohan of the Office of Strategic Services (the forerunner of the CIA); Lieutenant Aldo Icardi, a twenty-three-year-old Pittsburgh native who was fluent in Italian; Sergeant Carl LoDolce, twenty-one, of Rochester, a skilled radio operator; and the two Italians—leaped out into the cool night air. The Chrysler Mission was under way.

Slightly more than two months later, Holohan, the commander of the Chrysler Mission, disappeared. He vanished from a lakeside villa amid the clatter of gunfire and the thud of exploding grenades on December 6, 1944—exactly six months after Allied forces had landed at Normandy. He wasn't seen again until six years later, when his body was pulled from the icy waters of Lake Orta. Major Holohan had been shot twice in the head, zipped into his sleeping bag, and dumped into the lake. Aldo Icardi, who took command of the enterprise, was later charged with his murder. The case, which created a sensation on two continents, was "replete with wartime espionage, alleged murder, teachery, larceny and even lust,"[1] according to Edward Bennett Williams, who defended Icardi in the U.S.

The three Americans—at least one of whom, Aldo Icardi, was making his first jump in combat—parachuted into northern Italy expecting to be there only a few weeks.* Information relayed by OSS operatives indicated that the Germans would soon fall back from Italy and concentrate on trying to save the Fatherland. When that happened, the job of the Americans would be finished. Meanwhile, their assignment was to coordinate activities among several partisan groups—some of them Communist, some anti-Communist.

Holohan, Icardi, and LoDolce were an odd trio, having in common only the fact that each had volunteered for the dangerous mission. Holohan was a fortyish, Harvard Law–trained SEC attorney, originally from New York. Like General "Wild Bill" Donovan, head of the OSS, Holohan was Irish. He spoke no Italian and insisted on wearing his uniform at all times, in the hope that if he was captured he would be treated as a prisoner of war rather than executed as a spy. Icardi, whose looks and command of the language allowed him to blend in easily with the inhabitants, roamed at will, hardly ever in uniform. LoDolce, like Icardi, spoke Italian well, but had little opportunity to use it; he spent most of his time holed up in whatever served as the mission's constantly changing headquarters, maintaining radio contact with an OSS base in Switzerland. Fear was Lo-Dolce's principal emotion; he knew that at any moment the Germans and Italian fascists might zero in on his transmissions. Several months after Icardi succeeded Holohan, he decided that LoDolce had become "so goosey he couldn't function," and sent him to join the regular American forces.

In addition to giving direction to the various partisan factions, the Americans had hoped to use their radio to arrange for guns and other supplies to be airlifted to resistance fighters. Prior to Holohan's death, only one airdrop took place, chiefly because the major distrusted the Communists, who were by far the most numerous and powerful underground group in the Chrysler Mission's sector.

Following Holohan's December 6 "disappearance" ("I insist on that fiction. As far as I know, he disappeared," says Icardi), the new commander called for about fifty drops. One of them, about a month after Holohan had vanished, took place in broad daylight. Icardi said more

---

*This account of the Chrysler Mission is based on a 1981 interview with Aldo Icardi.

than a quarter-century later that "in retrospect, I'm not even sure why we did it. It was really a dangerous act, really arrogance to even try it." As it was, Allied planes hovered overhead for about two hours at midday, dropping five-foot-high canisters weighing about 200 pounds apiece. Not until the spring of 1945, with the war in Europe winding down, did Icardi rejoin the Allied armies, bringing Chrysler Mission to an end. He left behind a mystery that would never be unraveled to the satisfaction of everyone concerned.

Michael Stern, a Rome-based American correspondent, offered a radically different version of the Chrysler Mission and the men who participated in it. Stern, who wrote three articles about the operation in *True* magazine, as well as lengthy descriptions in two books, branded Icardi a "murderer" and "notorious criminal," comparable, in Stern's judgment, to Al Capone.[2] According to Stern:

Icardi and Holohan had been foes almost from first sight. They differed on virtually every subject, from who would jump out of the plane first to the purpose of the mission (unlike Holohan, Icardi would have given weapons to any effective partisan band—which essentially meant the Communists). Early on, Icardi endangered the mission by asking a courier to smuggle a letter to his uncle in Italy.[3]

Shortly before Holohan "disappeared" on December 6, Icardi allegedly told one of the partisan leaders, "'There'll be no more drops for anybody unless we get rid of the bastard. If we could send him to Switzerland without shoes [jargon for murdering him], there would be enough arms for everybody.'"[4]

In the end, Icardi decided that Holohan had to be "wasted." He had cyanide put in Holohan's soup, and when the major didn't die fast enough, Icardi ordered LoDolce to flip a coin with him, the loser (LoDolce, naturally) to have the task of shooting Holohan. LoDolce went to Holohan's bedroom, where the major was writhing in pain, and shot him twice in the head. The body was dumped in the lake and Icardi staged a phony firefight to make it look as if Holohan's disappearance were the result of enemy action.[5]

Although Stern had no doubt that Icardi was responsible for the murder, he seemed unable to decide whether the execution was "cold-bloodedly" directed by Vincenzo Moscatelli, the leader of the Communist partisans in the area[6] or carried out on orders from OSS headquarters in Switzerland because Holohan failed to achieve the goals of the mission as planned[7] or simply a "heinous crime" instigated by Icardi on his own.[8]

Stern charged that after Holohan "disappeared," Icardi willingly became an accomplice in Communist plans to take over postwar Italy by calling in fifty-one drops of guns and munitions, much of which was buried by the Communists in anticipation of "X day—the day the Western powers would be at war with Russia, [when] Red workers would seize control of the plants," which "would become self-sustaining fortresses inside the large cities. . . . All Italy would be rendered economically helpless."[9]

Shortly after the war ended, Major Holohan's brother, Joseph R. Holahan,* a New York stockbroker, was notified by the army that the major had been killed in action and that his body had never been found. From the start, Joseph Holahan disbelieved the army's account of what had happened to his brother, and he joined Michael Stern in seeking answers about the case.[10] About that same time, Icardi—not yet suspected of Major Holohan's murder—was discharged from the service and, by "more than coincidence," according to Stern, went off to Peru, which was "one of the hardest countries in the world from which to extradite a man charged with a crime."[11] Icardi, however, points out that he was studying law in Peru and had returned to the U.S. long before his alleged involvement was made public in 1951.

Michael Stern's first story appeared in the September 1951 edition of *True*. Several days before that issue hit the newsstands, the Department of Defense, having received an advance copy, distributed a press release with substantially the same facts—and the same mistakes—as those contained in Stern's article.[12] The release of the information by the Defense Department before the story in *True* was generally available would later prove a factor in Icardi's decision not to sue Stern or *True*. Thanks to the government's disclosure of Icardi's supposed role (the government is immune from liability in such cases), Stern could rightfully point out that it was not he who had first publicized the accusations.

The Pentagon press release had a more immediate effect: Carl LoDolce, who one year earlier had admitted to Rochester police and agents of the U.S. Army's Criminal Investigation Division that he had murdered Major Holohan on Icardi's orders,[13] recanted his confession two days after the accusations against Icardi were made public. Stern had admittedly accosted LoDolce in Rochester during his investigation and had led LoDolce to believe he was a military intelligence operative instead of a newsman.[14]

Because of Stern's article, Icardi "stood convicted in the court of public opinion and sentenced to infamy,"[15] Edward Bennett Williams wrote in 1962. Nevertheless, Icardi was, to all intents and purposes, immune from prosecution. The alleged crime could not be prosecuted in civilian courts in the United States because it had occurred while Icardi was in the service. And under the military law in effect in 1944, he could not be charged with any criminal act that might have taken place then, because by 1951 he was no longer in the service. It was a true Catch-22 situation, leaving Icardi the apparent winner.

---

*The brothers spelled their last names differently.

His triumph was short-lived. On March 26, 1953, he accepted the "invitation" of a House of Representatives subcommittee to appear "voluntarily" as a witness and tell his side of the story. Icardi testified under oath that he had nothing to do with Holohan's death. Subsequently, his testimony was used as the basis for an eight-count perjury indictment against him.

Also during 1953, an Italian court tried Icardi and LoDolce *in absentia* for the murder of Holohan. At the trial, held in October 1953 in the north Italian town of Novara, Stern abandoned all pretense of journalistic objectivity. By his own account, he volunteered to be a witness for the prosecution, and when it looked as if he would not be called, he insisted on being allowed to testify. Taking the witness stand near the end of the trial, he was asked his view "'as to the guilt or innocence of Icardi and LoDolce,'" and responded: "'Their guilt is a matter of mathematical certainty.'"

Stern also reported gleefully that a defense lawyer for one of the Italians charged in the case referred to Icardi as a "'pig,'" and added, "'And one has to apologize to the pig when he calls Icardi by that name.'" [16]

Icardi was found guilty on all counts (including aggravated homicide; conspiracy to commit homicide; aggravated robbery, for stealing mission funds; and criminal conspiracy, for seeking to dispose of Holohan's body in the lake), and was sentenced *in absentia* to life imprisonment. LoDolce, likewise absent from the Italian court, was convicted on all counts and sentenced to seventeen years in prison. Three of the Italian partisans were acquitted—two because the court found that they had been "forced" to take part in Holohan's murder "on pain of death"—and a fourth Italian was convicted of illegally possessing the weapon used to shoot Holohan and was fined $17. [17] Michael Stern had at last obtained a conviction against Icardi, but the alleged murderer was still free—as long as he stayed out of Italy.

In August 1955, Aldo Icardi learned that he was the target of a grand-jury investigation in Washington and that he would probably be indicted for perjury because of his 1953 testimony before the House panel. He met with two lawyers who were friends of his, Ruggero Aldisert (later a federal appeals court judge in Pittsburgh) and Samuel Rodgers (who became a local judge there). Among them, Icardi, Aldisert, and Rodgers decided Icardi would have to hire a Washington attorney to defend him, and Edward Bennett Williams was one of several they were considering.

Icardi wanted more than simply to be acquitted; he also sought the chance "to practice my chosen profession." Because of the serious charges against him, he had been denied admission to the Pennsylvania Bar and had been forced to work as a legal assistant. Icardi had had in mind the goal of gaining admission to the bar when he agreed to testify before the House subcommittee and had answered all questions instead of pleading the Fifth Amendment. He, Aldisert, and Rodgers had concluded that hiding behind the Fifth Amendment might have placed him beyond the reach of the criminal courts forever,* but would also have killed whatever chance he might have had of being allowed to practice law.

Icardi tracked Williams to the Guider family home in New Hampshire, where he was vacationing, and called him there. "He responded immediately," according to Icardi. "He said, 'I know who you are. I've been following your case with great interest.'" An appointment was made for the following Monday at Williams's office in Washington.

The initial meeting between Williams and Icardi, Aldisert, and Rodgers was "electric," Icardi recalled. "Ed Williams was the first lawyer we had met whose concept of the problem coincided exactly with ours, which was to maintain as public a profile as possible and to meet the challenges as they arose," but not to go looking for risks—which is why he had not been present at the Italian trial. "We had never encountered a lawyer" who shared their views. "Most of them said, 'You should demand.' 'You should sue for libel.' 'You should challenge.' 'You should go to Italy.' The libel issue always came up. Williams agreed with our whole philosophy. To us, that demonstrated that the man had the ability to perceive the human aspect of my case and not just the legal aspect.

"Williams also showed that not only had he been following my case as he had said in the telephone call, but somehow, some way, he had already been doing some preparation. He knew nearly every detail of the background. Of course, I'm not too surprised. In my short exposure to him, I observed that he had a photographic memory. To be blunt about it, lawyers don't normally throw bouquets at other lawyers. We're all egocentric individuals. You don't concede anything about another lawyer unless he's really good. Well, Williams impressed the three of us [all attorneys] in the very first interview we had with him." Furthermore, said Icardi, Williams recognized that Icardi was the victim of "an all-out war" being waged against him by "some powerful supporters of the Holohan family" who were involved in New York politics—the "foremost" of whom was Attorney General Brownell.

Icardi, Aldisert, and Rodgers discussed the interview with Williams overnight, decided to cancel an appointment with Paul Porter, senior partner in Arnold, Porter & Fortas, one of the city's top law firms, and returned to Williams's office the next morning. "We made the decision that we were going to ask Williams to represent me. Without any further ado. It wasn't a normal development of a client-attorney relationship. It was kind of like spontaneous combustion. He wanted us and we wanted him and there really wasn't much discussion."

Williams said he would need to go to Italy to investigate the case,

* LoDolce, by contrast, refused to testify at the congressional hearing without a subpoena and never faced any charges in the U.S. stemming from the Holohan matter.

would pay his own way, and would require $1,000 to pay Robert Maheu, whom he wanted to take with him. "He was almost apologetic," said Icardi. "He never made any request for any money except this money. It seemed as though he realized that I didn't have any substantial resources. He said, 'Can you do that?'" Icardi agreed to raise the thousand dollars somehow. Williams's modest request also proved to Icardi how committed he was to the case. If he had quoted a fee of $100,000 or so, "it would have been interpreted by me as an impossible demand, an indication that he wasn't really interested in taking the case."

About two weeks after the meeting in Williams's office, Aldo Icardi was indicted on eight counts of perjury, leaving him liable to as much as forty years in prison.[18] The indictment, handed down on August 29, 1955, was the culmination of an investigation that lasted several years, saw more than a dozen Italians transported to Washington at government expense to give testimony to the grand jurors, and cost an estimated half-million dollars.[19]

When the idea of conducting a counterinvestigation for Icardi was proposed to Robert Maheu, he agreed to take the assignment without payment other than his expenses because "I thought this would be an interesting assignment and I had faith and confidence in Ed. When Ed told me that he was convinced that Icardi was innocent, that was good enough for me."

Williams had warned Maheu that their trip would be made under "very adverse conditions because the Italian authorities would not look favorably toward anyone who was defending someone whom they had already tried and found guilty." Deciding that he and Williams would need all the help they could get, Maheu hired Giuseppe Dosi, former head of the Italian International Police and one of the founders of Interpol, the international police agency. Maheu had used Dosi in other cases, including the Onassis investigation.

Williams and Maheu left New York on March 9, 1956,[20] planning to fly to Paris and then on to Rome, from where they would drive with Dosi up to the Lake Orta region. "Anticipating that the Italian authorities would be waiting for us," Maheu had "sent Dosi ahead to check the Rome airport, and he had furnished me with the number of a phone booth there. His original assignment was to case the airport and particularly the car that had been designated for us to see if we were being surveilled or if preparations were being made to surveille us."

When Williams and Maheu landed in Paris, Maheu, without telling Williams, for fear of upsetting him needlessly, "made my phone call and in prearranged innocuous language Dosi informed me that they were expecting us." Maheu then advised Williams that they would have to change their plans, fly to Geneva, and then take a night train into Italy. "We never canceled anything," Maheu continued. "We just didn't show up in Rome." Agents from Italian and U.S. military intelligence caught up with the two Americans about two days later in the lake country, "but by then we were pretty much into the investigation."

The Williams-Maheu excursion continued, although not under the best of circumstances. Williams said several witnesses, under orders from Italian authorities, refused to talk to them. One of the Italian partisans, Giuseppe Manini—the man who had allegedly poisoned Major Holohan's soup[21]—did allow Williams, Maheu, and Dosi to interview him in his home, passing the time by playing with his switchblade knife while Dosi presented the Americans' questions to him. At last, when Manini was confronted with the accusation that he had signed conflicting statements about December 6, 1944, "he exploded in a burst of profanity," Williams said. "When he ordered us from his home, we left. The switchblade was very persuasive." (Subsequently, Williams and Maheu learned that Manini had been discharged from the Italian Army for psychiatric reasons.[22])

As the two-week investigation proceeded, the biggest liability of all turned out to be the other Giuseppe—Dosi—on whom Maheu and Williams were totally dependent. "I have never to this day seen a man who could eat such a big breakfast, then a few hours later eat such a big lunch, and in the meantime spend so much time resting," said Maheu. "I never could understand how a human could consume so much food. He was having three times as much food as Ed and I put together."

Williams was even less delighted. "We'd work in the morning. All the time that we were working, Dosi was thinking of what restaurant would be nearby. Then he'd eat this fantastic lunch, a couple of bottles of Chianti and some pasta, and then he had to sleep till four o'clock in the afternoon. We broke from twelve until four every day, the most important hours of the day, while he napped. That used to steam me, because the worst thing in life to me is wasting time and I saw big hunks of the day gone while he ate and napped. I regarded that as salt in the wound because we were paying him fifty dollars a day."

Dosi's quest for food and rest, however, paled into insignificance when he proved to be a fifth columnist. "The *real outrage* never came to me until later, when I found out that the U.S. government was paying him a hundred dollars a day to tell them everything that we were doing while we were there." Williams chuckled with the resignation that a quarter-century had brought. "We were taking great precautions, see, to go around Italy and make sure no one was following us. We would take trains through strange places, we went through some damn trail through the Alps into Switzerland, just so they wouldn't be following us, and the son of a bitch was with us and all the time he was writing down everything that we said. He was making a report every day to [Henry] Manfredi, who was the principal [U.S.] government agent in Italy. Dosi was telling him who we'd interviewed, exactly what they'd said, what I said to Maheu, what Maheu said to me as we talked about the case.

"Maheu, see, had assumed a false identification during World War Two and had worked, I guess, in counterespionage. For a long time during World War Two he was known [in Europe] as Robert Marchand. He was all over. He knew everybody. He knew Interpol people and he got this guy, Dosi." Williams said Maheu may have been embarrassed when the two of them discovered Dosi's deception, but "he wasn't as chagrined as I was."

Maheu had in fact become suspicious when he noticed that Italian agents had spotted Dosi with the two Americans. "He had to make a choice. He realized that we were a one-shot deal." But Maheu appreciated Dosi's predicament and later hired him again for assignments "where there was no conflict with the Italian government—and he was extremely effective."

The bizarre trip paid off, though, with the uncovering of two crucial bits of evidence:

- Williams, "in his usual persistence," according to Maheu, "had insisted on seeing the photographs of Holohan's body and found that one of his hands had been severed. Ed was familiar with the fact that that was one of the things that the Communists did when they found a traitor in their midst or someone that they wanted to dispose of."
- And most important of all, Vincenzo Moscatelli, the leader of the Communist partisans in the lake area during World War II, "confessed" that the Communists, not Icardi, were responsible for Holohan's murder.

Ending their investigation in Rome, Williams and Maheu made an appointment with Moscatelli, who had risen to leadership in Italy's Communist party and was a member of the Italian House of Deputies. They met Moscatelli at the legislature and the three retired to a small café nearby, the Ristorante de Pancrazia.

Moscatelli, then forty-eight and one of Italy's leading politicians, may well have underestimated his two companions: Robert Maheu, thirty-six, stocky, balding and nondescript-looking; and Edward Bennett Williams, whose boyish appearance and curly hair made it easy for him to be mistaken for a law student or a novice lawyer, not a man of thirty-four who shortly before had defended the most notorious American of his time, Joseph McCarthy.

During the war, Moscatelli had worked with at least two Americans: Major Holohan, who was uniquely unqualified for the task of espionage; and Aldo Icardi, a minor operative (even if he had entitled his book about his wartime endeavors *American Master Spy* [23]). It would thus be understandable if Moscatelli had little more than contempt for Americans. He could have had no way of knowing what he was up against at the Ristorante de Pancrazia: arguably the best one-two punch the United States had to offer in the true master spy and the man who could have been spymaster.

As the lunch continued for hours, the two unprepossessing Americans made sure that Moscatelli's wineglass was kept full. While he drank, he talked. And while he talked, the tape recorder built into Maheu's briefcase, one of the first of its kind, rolled round and round. Every word that Moscatelli uttered was preserved for posterity.*

Moscatelli readily acknowledged that he and his fellow partisans were responsible for the death of Major Holohan. He told Williams and Maheu—and their tape recorder—that Holohan "frankly had been a bad choice," as Maheu put it in 1981. "Because he refused to take off his uniform he threatened the whole mission, which not only involved our group but the Italians." Moscatelli said matter-of-factly that Holohan was a threat to the war effort and that he had had the major removed. And he did not implicate Icardi in Holohan's death.

Whether or not a recording obtained in that fashion would have been admissible in a U.S. court is debatable. Certainly, the prosecution would have objected to its use. But even if Williams had not been able to introduce it as evidence at Icardi's trial, the tape was still extremely valuable; if Moscatelli had been brought to the U.S. to testify and if he had any trouble recalling the details of his "confession" absolving Icardi of guilt, the message could have been brought home to him pointedly that while he was a "guest" of the court, he was subject to the same requirements of U.S. law as Icardi or anyone else, and that any discrepancy between his version at the Ristorante de Pancrazia and his testimony from the witness stand would make interesting fodder for U.S. authorities to ponder. In short, the tape could have been used to impress upon Moscatelli that his testimony had better help clear Icardi of perjury—or else Moscatelli might find himself in exactly the same fix. Best of all, Moscatelli, being unfamiliar with U.S. law, wouldn't have known all the nuances of his predicament and would have had little choice but to take the word of his erstwhile luncheon partners, whether their lesson on American law was in strict conformity with reality or not.

The return of Williams and Maheu to Washington was delayed by engine trouble in London, but the two former Crusader teammates arrived back home in late March, about three weeks before the trial was to begin, convinced that their two-week, 12,500-mile journey had provided them with the evidence that would exonerate Icardi.

---

*Both Williams and Maheu confirmed that Moscatelli's statement was tape-recorded secretly.

The trial of *U.S.* v. *Aldo Lorenzo Icardi* on six counts of perjury* started on Monday, April 16, 1956, before Federal District Judge Richmond B. Keech. Although Icardi was formally charged with lying to a subcommittee of the House Armed Services Committee, much more was at stake. Because Icardi was accused of having been untruthful when he denied involvement in the murder of Major Holohan, conviction on the perjury indictment would be tantamount to a finding that he was guilty of murder. And although Icardi was beyond the reach of the law on a murder charge, a verdict of guilty on the perjury charge would have left him facing imprisonment of up to thirty years.

Williams, who had become "absolutely obsessed with the case," had continued to immerse himself in it following his return from Europe. The more he studied it, the more captivated he was. "I thought it was one of the most fascinating cases I've ever been in, at the time and ever since," he said. "It had everything. It was a case of espionage, during wartime, men being dropped behind enemy lines, gold, women. It also had one of the most intriguing and fascinating legal issues, one that was vitally important at the time: just how far a congressional committee could go in investigating, and for what purpose. In addition to the factual situation, it had this overriding legal issue, which made it irresistible to me."

The public interest in the case was so great that *Life* commissioned an artist to sketch "a brilliant attorney in action." Text accompanying the drawings labeled Williams the "Star of the Trial," and reported that Williams's "brilliant record as a trial lawyer brought brother lawyers crowding into the courtroom just to see him in action." Williams was shown "in a dozen attitudes as he paces between the jury box and an array of war maps, delivers a two-hour opening talk with sweeping gestures."[24]

As the trial opened on April 16, Williams moved for a postponement of at least thirty days, a result of the "shocking contempt" he attributed to Michael Stern and *True,* which had teamed up for a final distraction. Over the previous weekend, *True* had distributed to the Washington press corps advance copies of Stern's latest broadside against Icardi, to be carried in the soon-to-be-released May 1956 issue.[25] The title of Stern's story was "The Case Against Aldo Icardi, MURDERER." Underneath the headline, in boldface print, was the message *"True* exposed Icardi as a murderer. Now he is on trial only for perjury. Here is new evidence to prove his guilt beyond all reasonable doubt."

In the body of the story, Stern wrote that Icardi was on trial "because *True* first disclosed his heinous crime, relentlessly pursued him, finally helped trap him." After comparing Icardi to Al Capone, Stern bragged that "I have been investigating the Holohan murder for more than five

---

*Two counts were dropped during pretrial maneuvering.

years now."[26] This was one of the most telling of all the statements Stern made about the Icardi case; by then, no one except Icardi had more at stake than Stern, who concluded his carefully timed attack on Icardi by declaring, "If he is found guilty, it will be as a perjurer, not as a murderer, which I know he is."[27] *True* billed itself on the cover as the largest-selling men's magazine, with circulation of 2.3 million. In addition, Stern's latest blast was picked up by wire services, newspapers, and broadcast media, effectively poisoning the well of public opinion. Nevertheless, Judge Keech denied Williams's motion for a one-month stay, ruling that prospective jurors could be questioned as to whether they had read *True*'s allegations, and, if so, whether they believe them. Keech ordered the trial to go forward.[28]

With the trial on, Williams made his opening argument the next day, telling the jury: "We will show you that the last time that Aldo Icardi saw Major William Holohan, Major William Holohan was alive, standing at the edge of the water at Lake Orta. . . .The disappearance of Major Holohan was a political move engineered by the Communist group headed by Moscatelli, a man of few scruples who was capable of weakening the opposite party in order to enrich his group." Williams told the jury that Holohan was "liquidated" four days after he had a confrontation with Moscatelli, "because Moscatelli believed that he constituted an obstruction to Moscatelli and his plans after the war and during the concluding aspects of the war." After tracing the Allied campaign in Italy up to the Chrysler Mission, Williams concluded by promising to show that Icardi was "not a murderer or a thief or a liar, but . . . one of the real heroes of World War II."[29]

Williams's speech lasted for two hours, much longer than Judge Keech and other jurists generally preferred. "But this opening statement was so informative that I didn't mind," said Keech twenty-five years later. He added that Williams's conduct of the trial was "magnificent" and showed the difference between "a brilliant lawyer and a brilliant working lawyer."

Following Williams's opening statement, the prosecution called as its first witness Congressman W. Sterling Cole (R-N.Y.),* chairman of the subcommittee that had questioned Icardi about Holohan's death. Cole testified that his panel was primarily interested in "making inquiry regarding the death of Major Holohan, [and] apprehension of the guilty person, if there was evidence of a crime having been committed." He added, "The particular hearing on March 26th [1953], at which Mr. Icardi appeared, was to afford him an opportunity of telling his story."[30]

Cole was then turned over to Williams for cross-examination. Williams

---

*The jurors were held outside the courtroom during Cole's testimony, because he was questioned on a matter of law (the legitimacy of the subcommittee's actions), not on the facts.

began by forcing Cole to admit again that "the primary purpose of the subcommittee's hearings was to see "whether a crime had been committed."[31] The defense attorney also had Cole repeat twice that the subcommittee had wanted "to be fair" with Icardi[32] and "give him the opportunity to tell his story."[33] None of Cole's reasons had anything to do with enacting legislation.

Early on, Williams was able to elicit from Cole the admission that, long before he invited Icardi to testify, the congressman had been aware that a law adopted in 1952 had closed the exact loophole through which Icardi had escaped. The new law allowed the military to prosecute members of the service after their discharge for crimes committed while they were in uniform.[34]

Williams also got Cole to acknowledge that Michael Stern had been called as a witness before the subcommittee "simply to get his hearsay version of what happened."[35]

Having scored points almost at will during his interrogation of Congressman Cole, Williams completed his cross-examination and turned the witness back to the prosecution for redirect. A few minutes later, Williams again faced Cole, this time on re-cross-examination. Violating one of his cardinal rules, which is never to ask a witness a question without knowing the answer, Williams struck "a bonanza which electrified the courtroom":[36]

> *Williams:* Did you talk to anyone, I say, anyone at all, sir, before Mr. Icardi was invited to testify with respect—did you talk to anyone with respect to setting up a perjury case against Mr. Icardi?
>
> *Cole:* I cannot quite subscribe to setting up a perjury case. I can, in response, say that the question of perjury was a subject of discussion.
>
> *Williams:* And that was a subject of discussion before he was called?
>
> *Cole:* Yes, sir, before and after and—
>
> *Williams:* Before?
>
> *Cole:* Yes, sir . . .
>
> *Williams:* You did talk in the committee about a perjury case on Icardi?
>
> *Cole:* The subject of perjury in connection with the hearings about to be held by the committee were [sic] discussed. . . .
>
> *Williams:* But you had discussed this possibility beforehand?
>
> *Cole:* Perjury, whenever we swear a witness before a committee of Congress it is for the purpose of eliciting the truth and the consequences of not telling the truth are perjury. So inevitably the subject of prosecution for perjury is discussed.
>
> *Williams:* But you had discussed a possible perjury prosecution of Icardi before he was invited to testify?

Cole: I would not say we had discussed a prosecution. The subject of perjury was discussed. ... It is my recollection that the question of prosecution for perjury was entered into in the discussion of the question of swearing him under oath.[37]

Saving his best for last, Williams finished off Congressman Cole with a technical knockout:

Williams: Didn't you have a conversation [with the other subcommittee member and staff] during which you discussed inviting Icardi to testify, during which you discussed that you would swear him if he accepted the invitation, and during which you discussed that a perjury case could be spelled out against him if he testified in accordance with the reports that you then had in your committee files obtained from the Army?

Cole: I cannot deny that that happened. On the other hand, I cannot swear that it did happen. I could very readily say that in all probability it did happen.

Williams: And your best recollection here today is that it did happen?

Cole: It could very well have happened.

Williams: And that is your best recollection here today?

Cole: I would not swear that it did, but it is my recollection.

Williams: It is your recollection that it did, is that your answer, sir?

Cole: Yes, sir.

Williams: I have no further questions.[38]

In a devastating cross-examination of Congressman Cole, Williams had hammered home time and again that the subcommittee had been trying to solve a crime and give Icardi a chance to tell his side of the story; that a law covering the Icardi situation was already on the books before Icardi was called; and that Cole and the rest of the subcommittee had worked out a plan in advance to set Icardi up for a perjury indictment. None of the subcommittee's lines of questioning had had anything to do with gathering information that would result in the enactment of legislation.

The next day, Williams argued forcefully to Judge Keech that the subcommittee had gone far beyond its rightful job—passing laws. The subcommittee, Williams explained to Keech,

conducted a trial, and I suppose that the record in this case, Your Honor, is the greatest argument that has ever been written against legislative trials, because they called two men—a writer for a pulp magazine, who gave them five hours of rumor and hearsay, and they called an investigator [Henry Manfredi] who had no firsthand knowledge but who gave them also all he had—rumor and hearsay. And they conducted a trial. ...

We can all reach the same conclusion regardless of what factual situation we accept, whether we look at them [the subcommittee members] as benevolent and generous with Icardi and honestly intending to give him a forum to clear his name or whether we look at them in a less benevolent way as conspiring and plotting to get him in and set up a perjury case—you come up with one and the same result. In neither case was he called in furtherance of any legislative purpose.[39]

Then, when one of the government attorneys tried to justify the subcommittee's actions, Judge Keech asked incredulously, "You say that if he had gone up there and pled guilty that that would have been pertinent to the inquiry?"[40]

Near the end of his statement to Keech in support of his motion to have the judge direct an acquittal, Williams was most eloquent:

> To what legislative purpose, Your Honor, was it whether Holohan in 1944, some ten years previously, had drunk poison? . . . To what legislative purpose did any of these questions pertain? And I think Your Honor asked that question several times throughout the day, and by my lights, you didn't get an answer to it throughout the day. . . . You didn't get an answer, Your Honor, because there isn't one.[41]

Williams also asked the judge to consider overnight the fact that the subcommittee had repeatedly referred to Icardi as "'the accused.'" The congressmen, said Williams, "say the accused—the accused. They even adopt the language of a grand jury when they filed their report in this case."[42]

Williams's motion was the sort that lawyers make routinely as many as six, eight, ten times during the course of a trial. For example, the defense in a criminal trial virtually always moves for an acquittal at the conclusion of the prosecution's case, arguing that the government's evidence is not strong enough to justify a finding of guilty.* And almost as often as the motion is made, it is dismissed, to the surprise of no one. As to the Icardi trial, the defendant himself said in 1981, "In retrospect, my guess is, having practiced myself,† it was a motion Ed probably didn't expect to have granted." This time, though, Judge Keech bought Williams's theory.

The first real indication Williams had that he had struck gold came the next morning, April 19, 1956, when he arrived at the courthouse and was told that Judge Keech was writing an opinion and was not ready to begin the day's session. "It was not likely that he'd be writing an opinion if he were going to summarily rule against me," said Williams. "He wouldn't

---

*Williams's motion in the Icardi trial, of course, came long before the prosecution had finished presenting its case. Had Judge Keech denied the motion, Williams almost certainly would have moved for a directed verdict at the end of the government case.

†About fifteen years after the trial, Icardi moved from Pennsylvania to a distant state, where he was admitted to the bar.

have to write an opinion" if his decision was to deny the motion. Although "it's almost unheard of" for a motion like this one to be granted, Williams thought "we had a good, solid legal argument and we might prevail. I had good feelings about the prospects of success after I argued it. The fact that Judge Keech moved all the testimony [on this point] up front, that he heard long, long argument on it . . . suggested that he was very disturbed by the point."

At last Judge Keech took the bench and started reading his opinion. Dealing first with expected testimony from Giuseppe Manini—the man with the poison and the switchblade—and two other Italians who were "alleged eye-witnesses to what occurred at the Villa Castelnuovo on the night of December 6, 1944," Judge Keech declared that "each of them could have had good reason to cast responsibility for a brutal murder on someone other than himself."[43]

Judge Keech then turned to the main thrust of Williams's motion and said the Cole Subcommittee was acting as "a committing magistrate" during its questioning of Icardi. "Neither affording an individual a forum in which to protest his innocence nor extracting testimony with a view to a perjury prosecution is a valid legislative purpose," said Keech. Furthermore, congressional powers "cannot be extended to sanction a legislative trial and conviction of the individual toward whom the evidence points the finger of suspicion."[44] The judge ended by stating, "I shall ask the Marshal to call in the jury and I shall direct a verdict of acquittal for the defendant."[45]

Pandemonium reigned in the courtroom, and Icardi broke down and wept, leaning on Williams.[46] The throngs who had come to watch an Edward Bennett Williams performance had gotten what they had bargained for, and more.

The dramatic victory drew many glowing reviews for Williams. Icardi's hometown newspaper, the *Pittsburgh Post Gazette*, commented that one result "will probably be the emergence of Edward Bennett Williams as one of the outstanding criminal defense lawyers in the United States."[47] In a profile of Williams titled "6th-Amendment Lawyer," the *New York Times* stated, "The only problem in hiring Mr. Williams these days may be the limits of his time. He has made a phenomenal success as a trial lawyer in Washington in eleven years of practice, and he is not likely to become less busy after today's events."[48]

As might be expected, one of the few sour notes was sounded by Michael Stern, who wrote later that Williams's theory that Vincenzo Moscatelli and the Communists were responsible for the death of Major Holohan—a version that Stern himself had once subscribed to[49]—was "arrant nonsense."[50] Stern also claimed that because Williams elaborated on the Moscatelli theme in *One Man's Freedom* as part of an "error-ridden account" that "airily disregards the body of fact already collected" (by

Stern, of course), Williams had shown himself to be "a particularly inept" reporter.[51]

Stern himself got his facts wrong in at least one demonstrable instance. Ridiculing Icardi's explanation for not suing *True* or Stern on the ground that he couldn't afford to, Stern pointed out that Icardi "was able to afford Edward Bennett Williams, one of the country's best-known attorneys."[52] In fact, according to Icardi, Williams refused to accept a fee. "I asked him, 'how much do I owe you? Whatever it is, I'll see that you get paid. It may not be right away. But I owe you.' He said, 'You don't owe me anything.' I felt totally obligated to the man." Aside from donating his own time and expenses, Williams also had other costs, such as $50 a day for Giuseppe Dosi (excluding his meals), or about $700 for the time Williams and Maheu were in Italy. But the only money that Williams accepted from Icardi was the $1,000 for Maheu's expenses.

The outcome of the trial did not settle the issue on the merits and left unanswered in the public mind the question of whether Aldo Icardi was to blame for the death of Major Holohan. However, as Robert Maheu said in 1981, "Why would Moscatelli tell us, 'We did it and the son of a bitch deserved it,' if he wasn't telling the truth? I can't think of a better source of information than Moscatelli." Moscatelli's declaration was what is known in the law as an admission against interest, which courts usually find more persuasive than many other forms of evidence.

Williams still ranks his cross-examination of Congressman Cole as his most effective for its immediate results: "I snapped Stubby Cole on the stand and got him to confess that he was going for perjury on Icardi. It undid his whole case. It had electric results. Immediate, electric results."

The Icardi case was also one of several in which Williams established an important legal precedent: that a congressional committee cannot exceed its constitutional powers. The decision helped swing the pendulum away from the abuses of Congress during the days when HUAC and Joe McCarthy were riding high.

One footnote to the surprise ending was that Bill Hundley, later Williams's close friend, was left holding the bag. At the time of the trial, Hundley was a Justice Department lawyer, responsible for providing housing for more than a dozen Italians who had been flown to Washington to testify against Icardi. "We had them stashed away all over town," says Hundley, "all these crazy Italian underground types. When the trial ended, they said, 'What do we do now?' And we had to tell them, 'Go home, it's all over.'"

In 1981, Aldo Icardi commented innocently that while he, Williams, and other members of the defense team were discussing the case in 1956, the name of Joe Louis (an acquaintance of Williams's) came up: "Of course, when we were selecting a jury, we talked about trying to get Joe

Louis on the jury. Kind of a humorous aside. Even in those days, there was a large number of blacks on the jury panel." Icardi had no idea how important that "humorous aside" would prove to be one year after his trial.

Part
FIVE

Jimmy Hoffa
and the Teamsters

11

The Teamsters' Men in Washington

E ddie Cheyfitz was a classic Washington fixer. Before a heart attack killed him in 1959, when he was only forty-five, Cheyfitz burned a bright path on the Washington scene. Charming, dapper, and energetic, he was well connected with both management and labor; he was, in his own words, a man who could "carry water on both shoulders."[1] Some observers, such as labor writer Clark Mollenhoff, felt that Edward Bennett Williams was in part a creation of the fertile brain of Eddie Cheyfitz.[2] At the very least, Cheyfitz must be credited with linking Williams to the International Brotherhood of Teamsters, Chauffeurs, Warehousemen and Helpers, and putting Williams into the case that would establish his reputation once and for all as a legal miracle-worker, the 1957 Jimmy Hoffa bribery trial.

Born in Montreal on September 13, 1913, Edward T. Cheyfitz grew up in Toledo and went on to the University of Michigan. Before he graduated from Michigan in 1934, Cheyfitz joined the Communist party; this led him to move to the Soviet Union and spend two years teaching chemistry and physics there. Returning to the U.S. about 1936, Cheyfitz became an official of the Communist-connected Mine, Mill and Smelter Workers

Union of the old CIO.[3] Disillusioned by the alliance of Hitler and Stalin in 1939, he quit the Communist party,[4] and turned into a "very vigorous anti-Communist and an informant for the FBI for years on communism in America," according to Williams, who added that Cheyfitz "overcompensated" and was "like a reformed alcoholic" on the subject of communism.

By 1946, Cheyfitz had evolved into an organizer and charter member of a civic committee to bring about harmony between labor and management in Toledo, where he was chairman of the Mine, Mill and Smelter Workers local. (On the eighteen-member board with Cheyfitz was Michael DiSalle, then vice-mayor of Toledo and later governor of Ohio.)[5]

Capping his surge to respectability, Cheyfitz was invited to lecture at Princeton.[6] He also wrote a book on the labor movement that drew heavily on his Communist past and yet was a virtual hymn to democracy. Among his observations:

> Without constructive collective bargaining there can be no strong, united, free America[7]. . . . This much is certain. There must be a full opportunity for free collective bargaining if capitalism is to survive. The realistic alternatives facing the democratic industrial society are to make collective bargaining work or to give way to the police state.[8]

In 1948, Cheyfitz, who had established himself in the nation's capital as a public-relations consultant for such clients as Libbey-Owens-Ford, Continental Can, and the American Merchant Marine Institute, enrolled in night classes at Georgetown Law School. He had little in common with his classmates: He was already a successful businessman, had a wife and two sons, and at thirty-five, was much older than most of the other students. (For that matter, he was also seven years older than Williams, who was one of his professors.) When Cheyfitz graduated in 1952,[9] Williams invited him to share office space in the Hill Building, which Nicholas Chase had vacated the year before.

Each had something to offer the other: Williams was emerging as a topnotch trial lawyer and could arrange cheap rent for Cheyfitz, who, in turn, had connections in business, labor, and—not least of all—the press. In the opinion of Clark Mollenhoff, Williams did not suffer as a result of his association with Cheyfitz:

> Ed Williams was just another bright young lawyer in 1952 when he went into a law association with one of the shrewdest public relations men in Washington, Edward T. Cheyfitz. In a few years he had parlayed a few big-name clients, a few victories and connections in a civil liberties group [the American Civil Liberties Union] into a big reputation. . . . Williams was a press agent's dream. He was a tall, curly-haired, and articulate charmer . . . the type the women jurors would love. "A great trial lawyer," Cheyfitz proclaimed in 1953 and 1954, spreading the word to his newspaper friends that Edward Bennett Williams was going to be one of the great names in law.[10]

Cheyfitz's law practice was unlike that of anyone else in Williams's office. He seldom, if ever, appeared in court. Williams says their relationship was "very loose-knit. I had some associates. I had some that I paid as lawyers. All he did, he had space in my suite. He rented an office from me. I carried him on my stationery. Sometimes we worked on cases together and shared fees."

During the late 1940s and early 1950s, Cheyfitz had been chief aide to Eric Johnston, head of the Motion Picture Association of America, and this connection accounted for some of the entertainment figures who became Williams's clients during the HUAC era. Cheyfitz's most important contribution, however, consisted of bringing Teamster Union business to his office associate. Back in 1949, when Cheyfitz still worked for the MPAA, Teamster leader Dave Beck had asked Eric Johnston, an old friend, to arrange for a European trip of Beck's to be filmed. Cheyfitz quickly leaked the story to one of his pals in the press, and the news story that resulted made Beck look bad. To smooth things over, Cheyfitz then got the same writer to publish an article favorable to Beck. Impressed by Cheyfitz's connections and clout, Beck hired him as his public-relations consultant.[11]

In 1956, through Cheyfitz, Williams was hired to defend several Teamster officials in Minneapolis. Sidney Brennan, an international vice-president of the union; Gerald Connelly, a former Teamster organizer in Minneapolis; Eugene Williams, a local Teamster business agent; and Jack Jorgensen, president of the Teamsters' joint council in Minneapolis, were charged with violating the Taft-Hartley Labor Act by accepting $5,000 to settle a 1953 strike against the Archer-Daniels-Midland Company in the Twin Cities.[12] After the defendants were found guilty on all counts, they appealed all the way to the U.S. Supreme Court, but the verdict stood.[13] All four were fined, and Connelly was also sentenced to two years in prison.[14] Connelly had compiled an enviable record: The previous day, he had been sentenced to a year in jail for bombing the car of another union leader,[15] and during the same period he was also charged with another bombing and with stealing money from the union.[16] *

After Jimmy Hoffa took control of the Teamsters Union in 1957, he ordered that union funds be used to pay the defendants' lawyers. The legal fees amounted to $54,000, of which Williams received half. This arrangement moved Senator John L. McClellan, chairman of a Senate committee that probed the Teamsters,† to complain that "[t]hey were robbing the union in the first place, and then the union pays to defend them."[17] the committee's chief counsel, Robert F. Kennedy, commented:

> Gerald Connelly, now in the penitentiary, was linked to an attempted

---

* Williams did not defend Connelly in the bombing and theft cases.

† The Senate Select Committee on Improper Activities in the Labor or Management Field, referred to hereafter as the McClellan Committee.

murder in Miami, Fla., fled to Minneapolis, and there was put in charge of a Teamster local. Within a short time, he was involved in two extortions and the dynamiting of the home and automobile of a Teamster official who did not support him. Were his activities condemned by the Teamster hierarchy? To the contrary, his legal bills for fighting [the various charges against him] were paid by Hoffa out of Teamster union funds.[18]

Williams's lack of success in defending the Minneapolis group did not keep him from being retained by Teamster president Dave Beck when he was called before the McClellan Committee in May 1957. By then, Beck's fortunes were in an irreversible decline. Although Eddie Cheyfitz referred Beck to Williams, Cheyfitz had recognized "the realities of the power struggle inside the Teamsters Union" between Beck and Hoffa,[19] had decided that as far as his work for Beck was concerned, "the advertising had outrun the product," and had dropped Beck as a client more than a year earlier.[20] Moreover, Cheyfitz had become "a constant source of information, furnishing data" on Beck, and was pressing for him to be replaced by Hoffa, whom Cheyfitz was touting as "a reformed and able leader," according to Robert Kennedy.[21] Beck, accompanied by other attorneys, had been grilled by the McClellan Committee in March 1957,[22] and on May 2 had been indicted by a federal grand jury in Washington State, where he was from, on charges of evading $56,000 in income taxes.[23] Also, his life had been threatened by anonymous callers, and the Washington, D.C., police had asked Robert Maheu to "spend some time with Beck in his apartment . . . as a favor to them. They did not feel that they could officially be there themselves."

Beck, this time with Williams by his side, returned to testify in front of the McClellan Committee on May 8, 1957. Several days earlier, Williams had picked up a copy of a New York tabloid at La Guardia Airport. There were only five words on the front page: MCCARTHY DEAD and FRANK COSTELLO SHOT. The number three story, inside, was "Dave Beck Recalled Before Senate Rackets Committee."[24] The three lead articles were about one former client of Williams's (McCarthy) and two current ones.

As Beck's lawyer at the McClellan Committee hearings, Williams was balked on virtually every point he raised, including his argument that a previous statement by McClellan that "the only reason" for interrogating Beck about his finances was "so that the country might know and so that teamsters might know what kind of a man headed the union" proved that the committee was not involved in a "valid legislative function." Williams insisted, "I do not conceive that the committee has the power of exposition or degradation or humiliation or castigation. I conceive that the committee—" At that point McClellan cut him off: "Just one moment. I am not going to go back and rehash the record. . . . The record is the record."[25]

Williams repeatedly asked that Beck be excused as a witness because he would plead the Fifth Amendment on account of his pending criminal tax case, but the chairman consistently overruled him.[26] Committee counsel Kennedy then asked Beck a number of questions about his alleged misuse of union funds, but Beck refused to answer any. Finally, Williams agreed to stipulate that all fifty-two charges on Kennedy's list—which RFK had thoughtfully mimeographed to achieve the widest possible distribution[27]—could be entered into the record without Kennedy's having to ask about them.[28] Included in the fifty-two allegations were the following:

- Beck had paid for construction work on his own property with union funds.
- Union money had been used to buy him a car.
- Two reporters, paid by the Teamsters, had been hired to write a biography of Beck.
- Beck's family owned substantial interests in a toy truck business and a beer distributorship, both of which had been aided by Teamster money and influence.[29]

Later in the hearings, McClellan asked Beck, "Are you in favor of union officials being honest in the administration of union funds?" and Williams interceded: "I don't think that question—" McClellan responded sharply, "I did not ask counsel what he thought. I wanted to ask the witness the question." Williams insisted, "May I be heard?" and McClellan fired back, "Briefly. . . . Let me say to you that I do not need a lecture on the law. I believe I know the rights of this committee and this witness."[30] And McClellan concluded:

> For the benefit of counsel, I may say to you, sir, in spite of his efforts not to be helpful, I think that your client has been very helpful to the Congress and it has shown them definite areas where they should legislate and must legislate if the honest working people of this country are to be protected from such rascality as has been going on in this union. . . . [Beck] has been very helpful, although not intentionally so, by his refusal to be cooperative.[31]

Three months later, McClellan compared the testimony of Beck and another Williams client, Jimmy Hoffa, pointing out that Beck had pleaded the Fifth Amendment 140 times in a single session, while Hoffa had given answers—although evasive ones—to 111 questions in one day. Each Teamster leader had been about as helpful a witness as the other, in McClellan's judgment.[32]

In part because of his performance in front of the McClellan Committee—refusing to answer many questions and leaving himself open to public lectures from McClellan, Kennedy, and others—Beck's time in the sun was over. Four days after he appeared with Williams before the committee, he was expelled as vice-president and member of the AFL-CIO executive council because of allegations that he had misused Teamster funds.[33] A few days later, he announced he would not seek reelection as Teamster president when his term expired on December 1.[34] In August, Beck was indicted a second time for tax evasion;[35] in October, he was forced to resign as union head six weeks early;[36] and in December, he was convicted of embezzling $1,900 from the sale of a Cadillac that belonged to the union.[37] In 1962, he went to federal prison on a five-year sentence for income-tax evasion; he was released in 1964 after serving half his term.[38]

Although Williams represented the two rivals for the Teamster presidency—Beck and Hoffa—at the same time, there is no evidence that he did anything less than his best for Beck. Nevertheless, with Beck out of the way, all that stood between Jimmy Hoffa and the Teamster presidency was a bribery trial in which Edward Bennett Williams would defend him.

As an experienced investigator, John Cye Cheasty (rhymes with hasty) always liked to know who was paying his fees. During a meeting on February 13, 1957, at the seedy Congressional Hotel near the U.S. Capitol, Cheasty asked Miami attorney Hyman Fischbach, who wanted Cheasty to work on a case, the name of his client.[39] Fischbach, after all, was reputed to have close ties to Mafia kingpin Meyer Lansky.[40] Fischbach, instead of uttering the client's name, whipped out his address book, opened it, and pointed to a name. Cheasty testified several months later that when Fischbach "showed me this name I whistled and I said, 'Well, Mr. Big himself.'" Fischbach responded, "'Nothing but the best.'" The name was Jimmy Hoffa.[41]

At the time, James Riddle Hoffa, forty-four, was president of Teamsters Local 299 in Detroit, head of the powerful Central Conference of Teamsters, and ninth vice-president of the international union. It was an open secret, however, that he had his sights set on moving up to the post then held by Dave Beck: the presidency of the entire 1.5-million-member Teamsters Union. However, one month earlier, the McClellan Committee had begun a probe of Hoffa's activities. Even as Hoffa's goals were well known, so were the plans of the McClellan Committee to remove both Hoffa and Beck from positions of influence within the union. The Teamster probe took on added significance because, with Senator John F. Kennedy a member of the McClellan Committee and Robert F. Kennedy its chief counsel, it was also assumed that the Kennedy brothers intended to use the investigation to help JFK become president in 1960.

The man Fischbach approached on behalf of Hoffa, John Cye Cheasty, was a forty-nine-year-old lawyer and sleuth known to his friends as Cye. Tall and burly, Cheasty lived in Brooklyn and operated out of an office on Wall Street. For nearly thirty years, he had been an investigator for the Secret Service, the Internal Revenue Service, Naval Intelligence, and the

New York State Crime Commission, and, more recently, a private eye.

In the course of their February 13 meeting, Fischbach, according to Cheasty, explained that the McClellan panel was after Hoffa, "and as far as he could see the only thing that could be done was to put a man on the inside of the Committee who could feed information out."

Cheasty told Fischbach, "It was very funny he should bring up this committee," because a friend of Cheasty's who was on the committee staff had recently invited him to apply for a job there. Told that if he accepted Fischbach's assignment, Hoffa would be "the paymaster," Cheasty insisted on talking directly to Hoffa.[42] That very night, he and Fischbach flew to Detroit and met with the boss of Local 299.[43] Making the introductions, Fischbach said to Hoffa, "'This is the man I told you about.'"[44] After chatting briefly with Cheasty, Hoffa informed the investigator that

> [h]e wanted somebody on this committee . . . to get him . . . information. . . . He wanted somebody on the inside who could pass out the information and tell him who was going to be subpoenaed, when they were going to be subpoenaed, what questions they were going to be asked, what material and information the committee had on them, and he wanted to know that in advance so that he could prepare these men, . . . get them ready for their testimony.[45]

Furthermore, said Cheasty, Hoffa mentioned "a man named Cheyfitz,"[46] whom Hoffa identified as an "'ex-Commie, publicity director for Beck, now with Ed Williams' law office.'" Hoffa said he had "'hired him [Cheyfitz] as a lawyer to tie him up.'"[47] (As a matter of fact, Hoffa at about this same time had made a big production of publicly handing Cheyfitz a one-dollar bill and telling him, "'From now on everything between us is privileged. You are now my lawyer.'"[48]) Hoffa also said that night in Detroit that Cheyfitz was "making about $60,000 a year" from the Teamsters "and he would like to get a check up on him and see what he is doing" to earn his pay. He also directed Cheasty "to find out what Bob Kennedy was doing visiting at Ed Williams' house twice a week. He said they are going out there and he wants to know what is going on."[49]*

During the hour-long conversation in Hoffa's office, neither he nor Fischbach asked Cheasty to perform legal duties of any kind. Instead, said Cheasty, Hoffa directed him "to get a job on the Committee and pass them the information. That was my job."[50] Hoffa also informed Cheasty

---

* Williams points out that at the time of the first Hoffa-Cheasty meeting, neither Hoffa nor Beck was a client of his, and Kennedy was not a frequent visitor to his home, although the two were close friends. "Knowing Hoffa," says Williams, "and knowing how suspicious he was of all people and paranoid even about some people, and knowing that Cheyfitz was associated with me, he probably was curious about my friendship with Bobby Kennedy."

that he "already had somebody" in Senator Joseph McCarthy's office who was acting as a spy for him,* as well as "a girl" on the staff of the McClellan Committee itself.[51]

Turning to the critical point, money, Hoffa agreed to pay Cheasty $2,000 a month, or $18,000 for the entire job, on the assumption, as Hoffa told Cheasty, that Cheasty would have the summer off because "'Bob Kennedy will go to Hyannis for the summer and there will be nothing to do.'" Hoffa then reached into a drawer of his desk, pulled out nine hundred-dollar bills and two fifties, for a $1,000 retainer, and tossed them across the desk to Cheasty.[52]

Leaving the meeting, Cheasty and Fischbach went to a nearby hotel, where Cheasty registered as "Daniel Smith" and Fischbach identified himself as "J. Thorpe Smythe." The next day, Cheasty flew home to New York, where he immediately called his friends on the McClellan Committee staff and was put through to Robert Kennedy.[53] Cheasty told Kennedy, "'I've got information that will make your hair curl,'"[54] and the two men agreed to meet the following day in Kennedy's Washington office.

Cheasty explained recently why he decided to offer himself as an undercover agent for the committee: "You have to realize that I was a naval officer. I don't want to wave the flag or anything like that," but what Hoffa was proposing "was goddamned near treason. I just decided, 'You s.o.b., what they hell are you trying to do?'"

On February 15, 1957, Cheasty repeated his story to Kennedy in person and turned over to Kennedy the $700 he had left from the $1,000 Hoffa had given him.[55] Kennedy was so impressed by Cheasty's tale that he arranged for him to tell it again that same day—this time under oath and in the presence of Committee Chairman McClellan and FBI agent Courtney Evans.[56] McClellan convened a secret meeting of his committee to hear Cheasty; in doing so, he violated Senate rules—as Williams would point out repeatedly at Hoffa's trial—by failing to notify Senator Irving Ives of New York, the senior Republican on the committee.[57] McClellan and Kennedy apparently felt that if Ives were notified, the other six senators on the committee would have had to be informed as well, and Cheasty's role was so sensitive that they wanted to keep it secret. In addition, according to a source familiar with the personalities involved, at least some of the four Democrats on the committee, along with Kennedy and his staff, mistrusted several of their GOP colleagues, believing they might try to protect the Teamsters.

In the dramatic closed session of the committee that evening, Cheasty once again reported how Hoffa had hired him to spy on the committee.[58] According to Senator McClellan, "within a matter of minutes," J. Edgar Hoover had been advised of Cheasty's statement, had been placed "in full

---

*McCarthy was a member of the committee until his death three months later.

charge of the case," and had suggested that the committee add Cheasty to its staff.[59] Cheasty's mission was such a closely held secret—with only McClellan, Kennedy, Hoover, and a few others privy to it—that another staffer, unaware of what Cheasty was doing, once "complained bitterly" to Kennedy that Cheasty was "loafing on his job."[60]

Cheasty, aided by more than two dozen FBI agents, then began functioning as a double agent. From February 15 until Hoffa was arrested on March 13 and charged with attempting to bribe Cheasty, Kennedy and Cheasty talked at least twice a week, and Kennedy told Cheasty exactly what information to feed Hoffa.[61]

Hyman Fischbach had told Cheasty that if he needed to contact Hoffa in a hurry, he should call Metropolitan 8-6565 in Washington—the law offices of Williams and Cheyfitz.[62] On February 19, using the alias "Eddie Smith," and with two FBI agents listening to his end of the conversation, Cheasty placed a call from a pay phone at the Capitol to Hoffa, who was indeed at that number. Armed with the material that Kennedy had fed to him, Cheasty told Hoffa that for the first time he was in a position to reveal confidential details about committee business. They arranged to meet thirty minutes later at the corner of Seventeenth and "I" streets, across the street from Williams's office. FBI agents drove Cheasty there, and, at six o'clock that snowy evening, Cheasty and Hoffa met on the street and Cheasty passed to Hoffa the names of four people who were going to be subpoenaed by the McClellan Committee.[63]

That same night, by chance, Eddie Cheyfitz had invited Hoffa and Kennedy to his home for dinner. For some time, Cheyfitz had been trying to introduce the two men, in the hope that Kennedy would recognize Hoffa as an honest labor leader who could serve the country's best interests by taking over the Teamster presidency. The dinner had been arranged before Cheasty approached Kennedy, and now Kennedy was on the horns of a dilemma: Should he go ahead with the dinner, which might appear improper to some, or should he break the date, "which might seem peculiar and arouse suspicion of Cheasty"? Kennedy opted to go ahead with the evening's plans, and so, at the same moment Cheasty was striding away from his appointment with Hoffa, Cheyfitz was driving up in his car to collect Hoffa and take him to his house for dinner with RFK. Kennedy, in fact, was late arriving at Cheyfitz's home because he had waited in his office until he received the phone call reporting that Cheasty had made the delivery to Hoffa.

Cheyfitz's dinner, the lone informal encounter between Kennedy and Hoffa, set the pattern for their future relationship. Kennedy was struck by how short Hoffa was (five foot five) and how tough he tried to appear. During the evening, Hoffa declared, "'I do to others what they do to me, only worse,'" prompting Kennedy to reply, "'Maybe I should have worn my bulletproof vest.'" Driving home later, Kennedy mused, "It is important to Jimmy Hoffa that he appear the tough guy to the world."[64]

Hoffa, for his part, was equally unimpressed. Five months later, he testified at his trial that "[n]aturally there was quite a conflict of opinion between Mr. Kennedy and myself since he happened to have a million dollars which we didn't have."[65] Hoffa, having been poor and having had to scratch and claw his way to the top, had only contempt for Kennedy's inherited wealth and position. He also observed that when Kennedy first arrived, he said to Cheyfitz, "'I'd like to talk to Hoffa alone . . . almost as if he was speaking to the butler.'"[66]

During the course of that encounter, according to Kennedy, Hoffa "volunteered" that Clyde Crosby—a Portland, Oregon, Teamster official whose name was on the list of future committee witnesses Kennedy had given Cheasty for transmission to Hoffa—"'was a fine fellow and . . . would make a good witness before the Committee.'"[67] "With some grimness," Kennedy gave "no indication that I knew where Hoffa had acquired this information."[68] The dinner broke up after several hours and Kennedy and Hoffa parted, enemies from first sight.

Kennedy has been widely criticized for going through with the dinner, knowing, as he did, that preparations were being made to charge Hoffa with a crime. Several weeks later, Williams commented at lunch with Drew Pearson (of all people) that "the ethics of decency should have required that Kennedy at least stay away from the dinner."[69] Oliver Gasch, who as U.S. attorney for the District of Columbia was in overall charge of the bribery case against Hoffa, questioned how a jury could believe Hoffa needed to hire an informant, since "he had little Bobby Kennedy." Edward Troxell, Hoffa's prosecutor, felt the case was "weakened" by Kennedy's meeting with Hoffa. He recalled that he had learned about the Cheyfitz dinner while he was preparing for the trial and had confronted Kennedy about it in Senator McClellan's office. Kennedy, said Troxell, "stood silent. He took the position he didn't have to answer these questions. And McClellan finally spoke up and said, 'Answer the man's questions, Bobby.'" After Kennedy admitted his imprudent act, Troxell admonished, "'I hope you don't do that again.'"

The day after the dinner, February 20, Cheasty was formally sworn in as an investigator for the McClellan Committee.[70] By thus adding him to the committee payroll, Kennedy set up the basis for implicating Hoffa in the crime of bribing a government official. During the next three weeks, Cheasty and Hoffa spoke on the phone several times, with Hoffa asking for more information from committee files and Cheasty finally suggesting that they meet again in Washington on March 12.[71]

As Williams would call to the jury's attention during the trial, Cheasty "panted so hard" to nail Hoffa that on the crucial date of March 12 he called Hoffa a total of seven times.[72] By now, practically everything was in place for the arrest of Jimmy Hoffa. Late that afternoon, Cheasty arrived by taxi outside the Dupont Plaza Hotel, where Hoffa was staying. Driving the cab was an FBI agent. Hoffa, by prearrangement with Cheasty, got into the cab. After they had ridden just a few feet, however, Hoffa suggested that they get out of the cab, depriving the FBI agent of the chance to overhear their conversation. Cheasty, "for the appearance of the thing," paid the agent a dollar. Then Cheasty handed Hoffa some committee papers selected by Kennedy, including reports on evidence that was being developed against his rival, Beck. Hoffa asked Cheasty to let him take the files to his hotel room and show them to his lawyer;* Cheasty agreed, and Hoffa said, "'I got a couple of thousand here for you. Do you want it now?'" Cheasty replied, "'Well, nobody ever said No to money,'" whereupon Hoffa shook hands with him and slipped him "a wad of bills in a rubber band," which turned out to be $2,000 in fifty-dollar bills.[73] While this transaction was taking place at Dupont Circle, FBI agents were shooting moving pictures, and other agents were walking through the plaza and watching the two men.[†]

At eleven o'clock that night, Cheasty again traveled to the Dupont Plaza Hotel, where he retrieved the committee papers from Hoffa, who remarked that "[i]t looked like Beck's goose was cooked if that is what they have on Beck, and at that same time [Hoffa] expressed the desire to receive more information of the same character."[75]

The trap that had been carefully prepared for Hoffa was now complete, with two exceptions, and they were attended to the next day, March 13, 1957. First, Kennedy had Cheasty pose some inconsequential questions to a minor witness at a McClellan Committee hearing.[76] This was necessary in order to establish publicly that Cheasty was working for the committee. And, finally, arrangements were made for Cheasty to hand over more documents to Hoffa, who was to be arrested immediately thereafter; to satisfy the requirements of law, Hoffa had to be taken into custody with committee documents in his possession.

Events went according to plan. Cheasty called Hoffa that day and said he had more committee files for him. They agreed to meet late that night at Hoffa's hotel. Cheasty arrived about eleven o'clock, turned over some more papers to Hoffa, and departed.[77] The Teamster leader was immediately arrested by FBI agents, hauled off to FBI headquarters, and then transferred to the Federal Courthouse for a preliminary hearing.[78]

Waiting for Hoffa at the courthouse was Robert F. Kennedy, along with his wife, Ethel. For Mrs. Kennedy, who had "'never been to an arraignment,'" the whole night was "'very exciting,'" according to a pro-

---

* Williams had not yet been hired as Hoffa's lawyer.

† During Hoffa's trial, the photographs, bearing such captions as "Hoffa taking paper with left hand;" "Hoffa looking at paper," and "Cheasty putting money in his pocket," were entered as evidence against the Teamster official.[74]

file of her on the front page of the *Washington Star*'s society section ten days later. Ethel Kennedy described how "'all evening I knew Bobby was restless. He said he was waiting for an important call. . . . Bobby wouldn't tell me what it was all about. Finally the call came. . . . Then Bobby told me the story, and said I could go along.'"[79] Kennedy also gave his wife a job in connection with the evening's activities: She was assigned to tip the press about the arrest of Hoffa,[80] and she did her task well, as fifty or more reporters showed up for the postmidnight booking.[81] Nor was Robert Kennedy disappointed by the stories that Hoffa's arrest generated. *Newsweek,* for instance, portrayed him as the Democrats' "bright new star," someone with "political ambition himself," and "the man who dug up the evidence and planned the strategy of the Teamsters' investigation."[82]

Williams, meanwhile, exhausted from working on the Frank Costello case in New York, was contemplating a trip to Florida for some rest and relaxation. "'I had just gone to bed when the phone rang,'" he said.[83] The caller was Eddie Cheyfitz, who had been at the hotel when Hoffa was taken into custody, had seen him led away by the FBI, and had rushed to the courthouse to confer with his client. "At my request," Hoffa later declared,[84] Cheyfitz called Williams, although of course it was Cheyfitz who initiated the contact. As Cheyfitz explained to Clark Mollenhoff, the Hoffa case was a no-lose situation for Williams: "'If Hoffa is convicted, it is what everyone expects. . . . If Hoffa is acquitted, then Williams is a hero. It will put him in a class with [Clarence] Darrow.'"[85]

Williams reached the courthouse about 1:00 A.M. on March 14, at least half an hour after Hoffa had been brought there.[86] Hoffa and Kennedy had found themselves together in a room at the courthouse, and initially, Kennedy reported, Hoffa "'stared at me for three minutes, with complete hatred in his eyes.'"[87] But soon both men relaxed somewhat, and they launched into a debate over who could do the most push-ups, with Hoffa claiming thirty-five, Kennedy more.[88] Just as they had "about exhausted this topic," Williams walked in and the two chums had what was most likely their first unpleasant exchange. According to Kennedy, Williams "demanded" to know, "'What's this all about?'" But Kennedy felt "it was not my place to enlighten him, and I told him so."[89]

Shortly after 1:00 A.M., Hoffa was given a preliminary hearing before a U.S. commissioner, who ruled that, in view of the bribery complaint against him, Hoffa's bail should be set at $25,000. The government then asked that the hearing be delayed for two weeks so that the case against Hoffa could be fully prepared. Williams said he thought the government's request was "reasonable," provided it was not simply a ploy to take the case to the grand jury and dispense with a preliminary hearing. (The prosecution must present evidence at a preliminary hearing to show that its case is strong enough to justify holding the accused over for trial. If a grand jury issues an indictment, however, the preliminary hearing is dispensed with and the government need not disclose much of its case to the defendant before trial.) Prosecutors branded Williams's remarks as "impertinent"—the first of many such exchanges during the Hoffa case—and the U.S. commissioner granted the government's motion to continue the hearing until March 28. Exactly thirteen and a half hours after the preliminary hearing was suspended, the prosecution started to "parade" its witnesses before a grand jury sitting in the same courthouse. Williams, who had predicted to the U.S. commissioner several hours earlier, "I don't believe we will ever have a [preliminary] hearing in this case,"[90] was outraged.

Several hours after Hoffa's arrest, just as the grand jury began weighing the case against him, Senate Rackets Committee chairman John L. McClellan declared to the press that Hoffa's attempts to bribe Cheasty were "'clearly indicative of the steps that the gangster elements are undertaking and will continue to undertake to hinder, hamper, obstruct and destroy this committee.'" Outlining Hoffa's power, McClellan told reporters that he "'practically controls all transportation except railroad between the Atlantic Ocean and the Rocky Mountains.'" Then committee member Karl Mundt asserted to the assembled media that Robert Kennedy and his staff and the FBI should be congratulated for "'demonstrating to the country that goon squad methods applied to the United States Senate will not work.'"[91] Again Williams was infuriated, this time claiming that the government had initiated Hoffa's "trial by newspaper."[92]

The grand jury sat for five days in closed session to hear the prosecution's case against Hoffa. On the next-to-last day, March 18, Congressman Clare E. Hoffman (R-Mich.) criticized Hoffa on the floor of the House of Representatives and had his statement inserted in the *Congressional Record*. Williams vilified that oration as "a ten-page excoriation, a ten-page castigation of the defendant Hoffa [that] went back over the years and . . . purported to trace this man's record, charging him with extortion, charging him with hurting the Korean war effort; it is one of the most villainous attacks made on another human being, in the *Congressional Record*, and it got wide publicity at the time."[93]

In view of the barrage of anti-Hoffa publicity, it was hardly a surprise that on March 19 the grand jury handed down a three-count indictment against Hoffa and Hyman Fischbach, charging them with conspiracy, bribing a government official—Cheasty—with intent to influence his actions, and corruptly impeding an investigation of a Senate committee. Conviction on all three counts would expose the defendants to as much as thirteen years in prison.[94]

The case against Hoffa appeared so strong that it was widely cited as presenting Williams with his toughest challenge.[95] All this left Robert Kennedy riding high, so high that several days after Hoffa's arrest, when several reporters asked Kennedy what he would do if Hoffa was acquitted,

Kennedy was shocked. "I had never considered that possibility," he wrote. "Hoffa would be convicted. There could be no doubt of it. I knew the evidence; I knew the chief witness; I knew the case." As a result, Kennedy, assuming his remark was off the record, joked, "'I'll jump off the Capitol.'"[96] In fact, his words were widely quoted.

Publicly, Cheasty was also looking good. The day after Hoffa's arrest, Senator McClellan told the press, "'We are grateful to Mr. Cheasty, a member of our staff, for his great courage and patriotic devotion, and for his loyalty to his country.'"[97]

Not all was roses, however, for Cheasty. Because of the threats he received after Hoffa's capture, he had to be provided with round-the-clock bodyguards[98]—standard procedure for those who offended the sensibilities of Jimmy Hoffa.* According to Cheasty, "The day that Hoffa was arrested I was taken into protective custody by the FBI. It was felt that there was a tremendous threat." He adds that there was "a general pervasive fear that we were up against the Mob," and says that an acquaintance who was connected with the Mafia "came to me while this was on and he said, 'Hoffa tried to put a contract out on you with Albert.' He just said, 'With Albert.' I knew that this guy knew Albert Anastasia [the head of Murder, Incorporated]. He said, 'I talked to Albert and it's okay, you've got nothing to worry about. Albert said, no, he wouldn't handle it.'" Nevertheless, Cheasty was armed "all the time except when I went into the courtroom," as a precaution over and above his bodyguards.†

The threats to his well-being were bad enough. But for John Cye Cheasty, the most grueling part of his ordeal lay ahead.

---

*William Bittman, who prosecuted Hoffa in Chicago in 1964 and won a conviction against him for misuse of Teamster funds (Williams did not defend Hoffa in that case), had a similar experience. Bittman says that "for the first and last time in my life" he was given bodyguards after threats were made against him during the trial. In 1967, Bittman secured the conviction of Bobby Baker, whom Williams defended (see chapter 20).

†Several months later, during his trial, Hoffa declared to Clark Mollenhoff that he would "'take care of Cheasty later.'"[99]

12

The Best Defense
Is a Good Offense

With Dave Beck on his way out as Teamster chieftain, only a conviction in the bribery case could keep Jimmy Hoffa from being elected president at the union meeting set for September 1957. Given Hoffa's situation, the strategy of his defense team—led by Edward Bennett Williams—was to delay in any way possible Hoffa's trial.*

From the start, Williams used every tactic he could invent to shift the government's case against Hoffa into neutral. A month after his client's arrest, Williams moved for either a continuance in the trial or a change of venue, asserting that virtually unprecedented volumes of publicity, "emanating from United States Senators and the F.B.I., could leave no room for doubt in the public mind" that Hoffa and his codefendant, Hyman Fischbach, were guilty.[1]

Williams also produced an affidavit from his longtime friend and collaborator Robert Maheu, who offered facts to back up the lawyer's claims that Hoffa could not receive a fair trial in the District of Columbia.

---

*Midway through the trial, Hyman Fischbach's lawyer fell ill, the cases were severed, and the trial continued as to Hoffa alone.

217

Maheu reported that his "international investigative organization" had conducted a random poll of more than 1,000 Washington residents during the two months following Hoffa's arrest, that slightly over half the people questioned had heard of Hoffa, and, among those who had formed an opinion of him, four out of five had an unfavorable impression.[2]

Maheu's poll was part of the record considered at a May 10 hearing held by U.S. District Judge Burnita Shelton Matthews, who had been assigned to the Hoffa trial. The court session was dominated by the hostility between Williams and Principal Assistant U.S. Attorney Edward P. Troxell that would mark the trial itself. Early on, Troxell noted that Williams had just been hired to represent Hoffa's Teamster rival, Dave Beck. Added Troxell: "I also point out the conflict of interests, Your Honor, and commend it to Your Honor's attention." Williams shot back, "Your Honor, I don't need any lecture from Mr. Troxell as to my obligations in representing clients. I would think that Mr. Troxell's performance in this case would recommend him least of anyone to stand up in court and talk to me about conflict of interest."* Judge Matthews, sounding like a schoolteacher separating two bad boys, replied, "Now, gentlemen, I would like to get on" with the hearing.[3] At the end of the hearing, she ruled against virtually all defense motions, denying Fischbach's move to sever his case from Hoffa's, Williams's request for a change of venue, and his attempt to delay the trial for six months. She did, however, agree to a postponement of a little more than a month, until June 17.[4]

On June 14, three days before the starting date set by Judge Matthews, she held another hearing on a defense motion for a postponement. Troxell read into the record an article from the previous day's *New York Daily News* alleging that Hoffa hoped to delay his trial beyond the Teamsters Union convention in September so that he could be elected president.[5] Williams was in New York on a case involving Frank Costello and he sent Agnes Neill—his law associate and future wife—to argue his motion before Judge Matthews. She explained that although she was not attorney of record for Hoffa, Williams "can't be in two places at once," and "Mr. Troxell has made rather serious allegations of bad faith on his [Williams's] part, and I wish that he were here to answer for himself, but in his absence I will do the best I can."[6]

Judge Matthews wasn't having any of Neill's argument. "Miss Neill, I think you are out of order. You came down here and you said you didn't represent Mr. Hoffa, and you have no standing here." When Neill attempted to speak anyway, Judge Matthews cut her off with "Will you be seated." The judge, angered by Williams's failure to show up, declared,

---

* Williams was still sore because Troxell had turned around and taken Hoffa's case to the grand jury hours after the prosecutor had asked for and been given a two-week continuance in the preliminary hearing on March 14.

"Mr. Williams has had his opportunity to be here today and he has not appeared, and he didn't notify the Court in advance."[7]

The very next day, a Saturday, Williams was in Judge Matthews's court, pleading that he was "physically exhausted" by three weeks in New York on the Costello case. He was not ready "to shift gears completely" and begin the Hoffa trial and he asked for a postponement of two weeks, or even one week: "I really need this, Your Honor." Judge Matthews had lost patience with Williams; she told him, "You should be prepared because you were given the extra time" after the hearing on May 10, and she ordered the trial to start in four days, on June 19.[8]

The Department of Justice was now faced with a dilemma. It wanted both the Costello and Hoffa cases to go forward as quickly as possible. Williams had obtained Costello's release from prison pending appeal of his convictions; the sooner that was resolved, the sooner the government could lock Costello up again. On the other hand, the Justice Department was no less eager to move ahead with the Hoffa trial, secure his conviction, and thus prevent his taking Beck's place as union president. One of the cases would have to be stayed, because both Hoffa and Costello had a constitutional right to counsel of choice, and each had selected Edward Bennett Williams.

What finally tipped the scales in favor of starting the Hoffa trial right away and allowing Costello to remain free a little longer was concern for the health of Hoffa's accuser, John Cye Cheasty.* Oliver Gasch, the U.S. attorney in overall charge of the Hoffa case, says that Cheasty's health "was very precarious. I used to get down on my knees and pray for that man because his health was so precarious and he was under such a tremendous strain." Gasch was not at all sure Cheasty would survive the trial, and this fear was shared by others who were involved. According to Clark Mollenhoff, both "Bob Kennedy and I were fearful the ordeal of cross-examination could kill Cheasty and wreck the case."[10]

The trial got under way on June 19, as Judge Matthews had directed. In one of his first ploys, Williams subpoenaed Cheasty's wife.† Both Gasch and Troxell objected that the subpoena of Mrs. Cheasty was nothing but "harassment";[12] Cheasty himself used the same word in 1981 to describe Williams's action. "I don't know what testimony she could have given," added Cheasty. In a letter to Judge Matthews dated June 22, 1957, Mrs. Cheasty pleaded that, with her husband away, she had to care not only for their five children (ages five to twelve) but for her mother, "a total invalid" who had "suffered two major heart attacks" in the past two

---

*Cheasty had been forced to retire from the navy and been classified as 80 percent disabled on account of a heart condition.[9]

†Williams had previously attempted to subpoena both Gasch and Attorney General Herbert Brownell—demanding a huge volume of files from each—but Judge Matthews had overruled him.[11]

months and had been released from the hospital that very day. Further-more, wrote Mrs. Cheasty, "I have absolutely no knowledge concerning the facts in the case presently before you."[13] Judge Matthews, swayed by Mrs. Cheasty's circumstances, quashed Williams's subpoena.[14]

Cheasty, the first witness called by prosecutor Troxell, spent more than three days under direct examination by Troxell, laying out the case against Hoffa. Late on the day of June 27, he was turned over to Williams for cross-examination.

Because he was the principal witness against Hoffa, Cheasty's back-ground had been investigated exhaustively by Robert Maheu and his agents, who had provided Williams with a "big dossier" on him. Iron-ically, during the campaign against Aristotle Onassis, Maheu had asked Cheasty, whom he knew as a veteran law-enforcement officer, to case Onassis's office in Manhattan and see who else had offices on the same floor. Cheasty immediately noticed three men waiting outside Onassis's building and suspected that they were part of Maheu's surveillance team. Cheasty says he called Maheu, asked if the men were his agents, and, when Maheu acknowledged that they were, told him, "'That smart Greek's gonna walk up and say "Good morning" to 'em.' You could spot 'em from a mile away." According to Cheasty, Maheu then changed the tail on Onassis so that it wasn't as obvious. Cheasty also reported to Maheu the identity of Onassis's neighbors in the office building. Now, three years later, Maheu was conducting a comprehensive investigation of Cheasty for Williams and Hoffa.

In preparation for cross-examining Cheasty, Williams also was allowed to examine all of Cheasty's statements to government investigators about Hoffa, thanks to a ruling by the U.S. Supreme Court shortly before the Hoffa trial opened.[15] Under the same decision, Williams also gained ac-cess to the very extensive notes Cheasty had made about the Hoffa case. He could then use any contradictions between Cheasty's numerous reports and his testimony in court to brand him either a liar or a bumbler.

Facing off against Cheasty before the jury, Williams immediately launched into an effort to embarrass him. At the beginning of his cross-examination, he asked Cheasty, "Have you taken any sedation or other drugs [during his testimony]?" The witness said he had been using nitro-glycerin for his heart ailment. Williams then asked, "Have you taken any form of narcotics?" Troxell objected at once: "This is an infraction which is disgraceful." "Objection sustained" was all Judge Matthews needed to say in order to show what she thought of Williams's line of questioning.[16]

Williams next brought up an associate of Cheasty's named Edward Jones. Cheasty had mentioned Jones as a "sidekick" with whom he had worked in the Secret Service more than twenty years earlier.[17] More re-cently, Jones had been an investigator for the McClellan Committee and had served as one of Cheasty's contacts before Cheasty himself went to work for the committee. Curiously, Williams had called Jones as a defense witness in the matter of alleged wiretapping of Hoffa during pretrial. But now he asked Cheasty,"Is this Jones . . . the wiretapper?" and was Jones the individual "who was convicted of bigamy in New York by the name of Joseph Leo Monaghan?" Troxell objected that what Williams was doing was "disgraceful. . . . Mr. Williams called Mr. Jones as his own witness the other day. . . . And now through this witness he is attempting to impeach his own witness, Mr. Jones." Judge Matthews sustained Troxell's objection.[18]

Focusing on Cheasty, Williams used some of the dirt Maheu had dredged up to ask if he had once attempted to bribe the police in Dade County (Miami) in order to set up a friend of Cheasty's, one Joe Basognio, in "a gambling joint or illicit still." Cheasty's answer was "Emphatically, no."[19]

Williams was now ready for big game. Disputing Cheasty's story that Hoffa had given him $1,000 at the February 13 conference, Williams asked, "And isn't it a fact, Mr. Cheasty, that on February 13, 1957, he [Hoffa] gave you $2,000?" An angry Cheasty retorted, "That is absolutely a lie." But Williams forced Cheasty to admit that he had spent nearly $100 of the initial $1,000 on himself and his family, even using some of it to buy Valentine's Day candy for his wife.[20] Thus, whether or not the jurors believed Cheasty had been given $1,000 or $2,000, Williams had given them cause to wonder about Cheasty's honesty.

The trial of Jimmy Hoffa was marked time and again by extralegal attempts to take advantage of the racial makeup of the jury (eight blacks and four whites).[21] The most controversial maneuver that could be attributed directly to Williams occurred when he questioned Cheasty about his use of an alias during the trip to Detroit for his first meeting with Hoffa. Williams asked,"Using a fictitious identity is not a rare thing with you in your investigative business, is it?" Cheasty acknowledged that he had "used fictitious names before."

At that point Williams dropped a bombshell: "Well, when you were employed by the City of Tallahassee to investigate the National Association for the Advancement of Colored People—" Troxell broke in with an objection, but before Judge Matthews could sustain it, Williams completed his thought: "—you used a fictitious identity didn't you?" Troxell then insisted that because "the question about the NAACP came out of this man's [Williams's] mouth," Cheasty should be allowed to "explain his answer carefully and without interruption."

Judge Matthews authorized the witness to tell the full story of his job in Tallahassee during the July 1956 bus boycott.

Cheasty delivered a fifteen-minute speech, taking credit for having "worked out this whole doggone bus strike there." Williams was certainly not scoring any points with the jury's black majority, and he tried to cut

Cheasty off, but the judge remained firm: "Mr. Williams, I have said this witness may answer. . . . Just quit interrupting. . . . Just quit interrupting then until he is finished." Cheasty wound up with a flourish:

> I recommended that they cut out the color line on the busses down there; that they let people come in and sit as they wanted to sit on a first-come-first-serve basis; and that they put colored drivers on certain runs and that they hire them and treat them the same as white drivers.

Not at all fazed, Williams next asked Cheasty about another job in Florida, as an investigator for the state legislature. Cheasty started to reply, "That takes a lot of explanation, but not the way you figure." Williams muttered, "It certainly does." Cheasty, apologizing to the judge, confessed, "I heard his aside there and I just couldn't help it if it stirred me up." "You heard an aside?" asked Judge Matthews, and, informed by Cheasty of Williams's remark, she directed, "The jury will disregard that remark if it was made."

Cheasty went on to describe how he had been called into a "very tense" situation regarding integration in Florida, had been hired to probe outbreaks of violence, and had dug up

> [f]ourteen cases of mob violence and one of them I had particularly written up was an eighteen year old woman who was pregnant at the time and she had been pistol-whipped by a deputy sheriff. She went and complained to the county attorney and he told her to come back and see the grand jury in the fall. She went to see the county judge and he told her to come back and see the grand jury in the fall.
>
> I had fourteen such incidents as that down there. Some of them involved killing. Some of them involved dynamite.

Cheasty's testimony was so explosive that both attorneys went up to the bench to discuss it with Judge Matthews. Troxell described Williams's original question about the NAACP as "highly inappropriate, prejudicial [and] improper," but added that "since the damage had been done by the question itself, obviously to influence the colored people on the jury," Cheasty should have been allowed to make "a complete and full answer."

Judge Matthews declared that she was "amazed" when "Mr. Williams went into that in the first place, but after he did it seemed to me, after he had mentioned it, then it was a matter that should be allowed."

Williams, however, was not at all ashamed of what he had wrought. He demanded a mistrial, based on "the inflammatory statement that came out of this witness' mouth."

Judge Matthews was shocked by Williams's nerve: "*You* have introduced this and now you are moving" for a mistrial? She went on to lecture him: "You could have avoided the whole thing by making no reference to [the NAACP]. . . . You introduced it yourself. . . . You had introduced the subject." She also took "judicial notice" that "the defendants exercised all their challenges [during jury selection] to challenge members of one race, to wit, the white race, while the Government exercised its challenges to challenge members of both races in equal proportion." After taking Williams to task, the judge rejected his motion for a mistrial.[22]

Nevertheless, Judge Matthews felt that the introduction of the racial issue might improperly sway the jury. She deemed it necessary to state to the jurors, "You are told that these matters are not related to this case and they have no place in this trial. You are instructed to disregard what was asked or said about such matters, and put it completely out of your minds."[23] But Williams was still bold enough to quote the Supreme Court as saying that "'[t]he naive assumption that prejudicial effects can be overcome by instructions to the jury, all practicing lawyers know to be unmitigated fiction.'"[24]

Before releasing Cheasty from his battering on the witness stand, Williams wanted to imprint on the minds of the jurors the point that Cheasty had deceived, even lied to, Hoffa.

> *Williams:* Were you working for both, for Mr. Hoffa and the Senate Committee?
>
> *Cheasty:* I was working for the Senate Committee. Mr. Hoffa believed I was also working for him.
>
> *Williams:* Were you working for him or were you not working for him?
>
> *Cheasty:* I was in his employ but I was working for the Senate Committee.
>
> *Williams:* In other words, you were working for both Mr. Hoffa and the Senate Committee, is that right?
>
> *Cheasty:* I don't think I was working for Mr. Hoffa.
>
> *Williams:* Then were you pretending that you were working for Mr. Hoffa?
>
> *Cheasty:* Yes, I was pretending that I was working for Mr. Hoffa.
>
> *Williams:* And you were not working for Mr. Hoffa?
>
> *Cheasty:* I was employed by him.
>
> *Williams:* To the extent that you were pretending to work for him, you were deceiving him, were you not?
>
> *Cheasty:* Yes, sir.
>
> *Williams:* And when you saw him on the 13th of March, you were pretending to be working for him, weren't you? . . .
>
> *Cheasty:* I did deceive him on the 12th and 13th of March, yes, sir.
>
> *Williams:* And on the 13th of February, when you pretended to take employment from him, to that extent you were deceiving him, were you not?
>
> *Cheasty:* Yes, sir.

Williams: So that from the month of February and the day of the 13th until the month of March and the day of the 13th, throughout that whole month, you were pretending to be something that you were not, were you?

Cheasty: I was, yes, sir.

Williams: And in that respect, you were deceiving Mr. Hoffa, were you not?

Cheasty: Yes, sir, I did deceive Mr. Hoffa.

Williams: And during that month of February 13 to March 13, you told him falsehoods, did you not?

Cheasty: I did, sir, I told him falsehoods.

Williams: And you told him many falsehoods, did you not?

Cheasty: Well, I told him several falsehoods. . . .

Williams: During this month, you told him, did you not, during your conversation with him, telephonically or person-to-person, lies?

Cheasty: There were a few lies in there, yes, sir.

Having got Cheasty to use the word *lies* to describe his own statements, Williams now sought to underscore Cheasty's admission, following up with:

"By your standard of morals, sir, is there ever a time when it is moral to lie?"

Troxell, unable to stand any more, objected; Williams said, "Very well, I withdraw it"; and Judge Matthews echoed Williams: "Very well."[25]

In other words, Williams had wound up his cross-examination of Cheasty by taking the very nature of Cheasty's role as an undercover agent and turning it against him. Obviously, every undercover agent lies to the people he is investigating; such investigations would be impossible without the use of deception. Williams, however, didn't give the jurors a chance to analyze the facts. Instead, employing Cheasty's own words to smear him, he branded the prosecution's star witness a liar, over and over and over.

After five and a half days of the most rigorous questioning by Williams, Cheasty was at last permitted to step down from the witness stand. Throughout his testimony, Hoffa had stared at him, hardly ever taking his eyes off his accuser.[26] Hoffa had been calm and expressionless for most of the time, appearing shaken only when the FBI photographs of his passing $2,000 to Cheasty at Dupont Circle were introduced into evidence. Then Hoffa had grown "morose," and had "drummed on the chair arms with his fingertips, and swallowed hard."[27]

According to Cheasty's tormentor, Williams, "Cheasty was pretty good. But I chinked so many holes in that fellow that there wasn't much left of him at the end when we picked up the pieces. It was invisible. There was nothing spectacular. I didn't all of a sudden hit him with a hammer and he fell apart. It was just a chink here, a chink there, every hour I was taking a piece out of the rock and pretty soon there was nothing left." Even prosecutor Edward Troxell admitted twenty-five years later that Williams was "an exceptionally able lawyer" and had conducted "a brilliant cross-examination." Cheasty himself went away thinking Williams had done a "tremendous job. I kind of admired the way he handled the thing. He was pretty damn smart."

Following Cheasty's testimony, the prosecution called into court a parade of witnesses, most of whom were FBI agents. But the Hoffa trial was for all intents and purposes a classic one-witness case: Cheasty's word against Hoffa's. When Williams reduced Cheasty to rubble, he left the prosecution's case in ruin as well. He pointed out to the jurors that Cheasty had admittedly lied to Hoffa many times; that he had spent some of Hoffa's money on himself and his family ("most damaging," in the opinion of Vincent Fuller, Williams's assistant in the courtroom); that Cheasty might actually have received $2,000 from Hoffa, not $1,000— and pocketed the extra $1,000; that Cheasty might be a racist; that he might have been fired from a job for padding his expense account; that he lurked around wearing sunglasses and hiding his face, even on snowy winter nights; that he might be on drugs; and even that one of his friends, Edward Jones, might be a bigamist. In the eyes of the jurors, John Cye Cheasty, and the prosecution's case, almost certainly had to be damaged goods.

Among the witnesses against Hoffa was McClellan Committee counsel Robert F. Kennedy. Williams forced his old friend to make a damaging admission: that Kennedy had habitually given information from committee files to the press. "Those files weren't like [confidential] files of a law enforcement agency, were they?" asked Williams of Kennedy. "No," acknowledged Kennedy. "No, they are not."

> *Williams:* There were occasions when you, as counsel to the committee, gave information to the press on the course of your investigation, isn't that so?
>
> *Kennedy:* Occasionally.
>
> *Williams:* As a matter of fact, you held press conferences in the regular course of your duty as chief counsel, didn't you?
>
> *Kennedy:* Yes.
>
> *Williams:* And there were occasions when you gave information to the press on what was unusual files, isn't that so?
>
> *Kennedy:* I suppose it would be, yes.

Williams then got Kennedy to admit that he had divulged information from the committee's files to more than half a dozen newsmen, starting with Clark Mollenhoff of Cowles Publications, who functioned as a *de facto* aide to Kennedy's staff, giving tips and leads, and who, Kennedy lamented, "unfortunately" was not working for the committee full-time. Williams also elicited from Kennedy that he had given access to the records of the committee to reporters from United Press, International News Service, the *New York Herald Tribune,* the *New York Times,* Scripps-Howard, the *Detroit Times,* and the *Washington Post.*[28]

Winding up his cross-examination of Kennedy, Williams also drew from Kennedy an admission that "[o]n those occasions when you showed files of the committee to members of the press . . . you [did not] get a majority vote of the committee before you did that in each case."[29] Williams's thrust was that the supposedly sacrosanct information Hoffa had allegedly bribed Cheasty to provide to him was readily obtainable from the daily newspapers. Prosecutor Troxell attempted to establish that the kind of data fed to Hoffa via Cheasty was sensitive and would not have been handed out to the press.[30] But Williams had knocked a few more "chinks" in the government's rapidly dissolving case.

The procession of government witnesses continued, but, as Hoffa pointed out to the press, the defense had not yet "'had our turn at bat.'"[31] When the defense's chance did arrive, Williams poked a few more holes in Cheasty's tale:

Max Lurie, a lawyer in practice with Hyman Fischbach in Miami, testified that Cheasty himself had instigated his employment by the Teamsters. Cheasty, according to Lurie, had called Fischbach and requested a job on the Teamsters case, because "'I need the work very badly.'"[32]

Frank Fitzsimmons, then vice-president of Local 299 in Detroit and later Hoffa's successor as international president of the Teamsters, stated that on the night of February 13 in Detroit, Hoffa had introduced him to Fischbach and Cheasty and told him, "'I have retained these lawyers . . . If they get in touch with you, you will know what to do.'"[33]

And at last Hoffa, clad in the same light brown suit, white socks, and light tie he had worn for most of the trial, "stepped briskly" past the jurors and up to the witness stand. He pushed aside the microphone used by the other witnesses, leaned his arms over the witness box, and began answering Williams's questions "with assurance, at times with indignation," but without ever losing his temper.[34]

Williams used Hoffa to make several points, among them:

- Fischbach "talked of him [Cheasty] as a lawyer who would go out and do the actual leg work, as he called it," to prepare Hoffa and his men for the McClellan Committee hearings.[35]
- Hoffa had planned on giving Cheasty a check—the usual method of paying a lawyer—that first night in Detroit. Cheasty, however, "said to me, 'Can you pay me in cash?'" As a result, Hoffa had paid Cheasty $2,000, or nine

hundred-dollar bills and twenty-two fifty-dollar bills. "How do you recall that fact?" asked Williams. "Because," Hoffa testified, "I counted it out, and when you count out that much money you don't generally forget it too quick." [36] *

- When Cheasty passed him an envelope containing information from committee files the night before his arrest (the exchange at Dupont Circle that was filmed by the FBI), Cheasty—Hoffa claimed under oath—"said he had got it from a newspaper man." Hoffa's testimony, of course, conveniently fit the pattern sketched when Kennedy acknowledged that he had often used committee records to brief the press.

Hoffa also testified under penalty of perjury that "I was never apprised that he [Cheasty] was working for the Committee until I was arrested and taken downtown, and downtown I was notified—I wasn't notified he was working for the Committee, but I saw his name on the warrant." [38]

How, then—assuming Hoffa was telling the truth while being questioned by his attorney—could he have intended to bribe an employee of the McClellan Committee? Answer: Hoffa couldn't have had any criminal intent, because he had no idea that Cheasty worked for the committee—if his testimony is to be believed.

Williams had done a remarkable job of knocking holes in the government's case. He would also receive a little help from some friends—the friends of Jimmy Hoffa. These friends would be responsible for a variety of extralegal tactics, such as bringing Joe Louis into the courtroom.

---

* It was not until over a year later, during an appearance before the McClellan Committee, that Hoffa admitted he had not entered the payment to Cheasty in the union books. [37] Had Edward Troxell thought to ask Hoffa this question during the trial, Hoffa's answer—if truthful—would have contradicted the impression that he had meant to pay Cheasty by check and thus retain a record of the transaction.

13

And in Jimmy Hoffa's Corner, Joe Louis

From the start of the Hoffa trial, attempts were made—nearly all by the Hoffa side—to influence the outcome by extralegal appeals to the predominantly black jury the defense had wanted and gotten by using all sixteen of its allotted challenges to dismiss whites from the jury panel.[1] Edward Bennett Williams maintains to this day that the defense did not purposely select blacks. "I think that we wanted as many people on the jury who were labor-oriented, who were members of unions," as possible. "It happened" that the people in those categories, "in this city, were black," and the defense exploited that circumstance to the maximum.

The circus began after the trial had been under way for about two weeks, when Martha Malone Jefferson, a black lawyer from Los Angeles, became the eighth member of the Hoffa defense team. The biweekly *Washington Afro-American* heralded the hiring of the "pert" and "widely-known" Jefferson to assist "that widely-known pro-labor barrister, Edward Bennett Williams, sometimes referred to as the Sir Galahad of the legal arena."[2]

Jefferson never actually entered an appearance in the trial record as an attorney for Hoffa, and Williams says that "she never had anything to do" with his presentation of the case, but the prosecution responded by bringing in a black lawyer of its own: Harry Alexander, then an assistant U.S. attorney and later a District of Columbia judge. Chief prosecutor Oliver Gasch now concedes that Alexander's presence in the courtroom "may have been tit for tat. They had Jefferson; we had Alexander."

Neither Jefferson nor Alexander played any role in the courtroom, other than to be present. But Martha Jefferson did have a very important part in the case. Several days after her arrival, she approached Williams "and asked me to have my picture taken with her" and Hoffa. "So I had my picture taken with her," says Williams. "She was a lawyer from somewhere out west, I didn't even know her name."

According to Williams, "The next thing, it was in the press." Sure enough, the July 6, 1957, edition of the *Washington Afro-American* carried a full-page advertisement identifying Hoffa as a "hard-hitting champion" for the "167,000 colored truck drivers in America" who belonged to the Teamsters Union.* Prominently displayed in the ad was a photograph of Hoffa, Williams, and Jefferson, along with the caption "JOINS DEFENSE—Mrs. Martha Malone Jefferson, famous West Coast lawyer, who joined the Hoffa case defense counsel, Tuesday, is shown with the defendant, James R. Hoffa (left) and Edward Bennett Williams, nationally known attorney."[4][†] The obvious implication of the photograph, as Senator Carl Curtis of the McClellan Committee observed, was that Jefferson was "conducting the defense," or at least "part of it."[7]

In the same issue of the *Afro-American* was a front-page story headlined, "L.A. WOMAN ATTORNEY IN HOFFA CASE." Another page-one story, announcing that "eight colored panelists" had been picked for the Hoffa jury, listed the names of the eight black jurors and the two black alternates.[8] The paper was delivered to the homes of all ten. Williams was "horrified" to see his photograph in the paper and described it as "the darkest day of my professional life."[9] Judge Burnita Shelton Matthews was equally displeased. She immediately decided to lock up the jurors for the remainder of the trial.[10]

With the jury under tight guard, appeals to the jurors via the press would no longer work. But Eddie Cheyfitz had an idea. Putting his imagination to work, Cheyfitz suggested that a black hero—someone like former heavyweight champion Joe Louis—be brought into the courtroom.[11]

---

*Interestingly enough, Hoffa reportedly said once that he "did not like over-the-road drivers of the colored race coming into Detroit; that if this were repeated, it might not be healthy for the drivers."[3]

†The ad was signed by "Frank Crowling, Director, Detroit Citizens Civic Committee."[5] Both "Crowling" and the "Civic Committee" were fictitious. There was, however, a John L. Cowling of Detroit, a leader of the National Negro Tavern Owners Association. The McClellan Committee discovered later that the Teamsters had given Cowling $260 shortly before Hoffa's trial started; the money apparently was used to pay for the advertisement.[6]

Hoffa claimed that he and Louis (who was also an acquaintance of Williams's) were friends. After consulting with Hoffa, Williams included Louis among some eight potential character witnesses, all of whom— including a labor leader, a member of Congress, at least two clergymen, a college professor, and the owner of a trucking company[12]—were in the courtroom and prepared to take the witness stand at a moment's notice. At the last minute, however, Williams decided to use none of them, "because I felt we would have opened up things that were going to be more harmful than beneficial," such as rumors about Hoffa's associations with gangsters. "So I excused them all."

Since Williams was aware all along of the pitfalls of calling character witnesses, it is hard to avoid speculating that the defense never had any intention of having Joe Louis and the others testify, and that Louis's role went exactly as had been planned from the start.

Williams maintains that he was "genuinely surprised" to notice the "Brown Bomber" sitting in the courtroom on July 15—the next court session after the lawyer had informed the character witnesses that their services would not be required. Precisely what then took place has been a matter of dispute for a quarter-century. Tradition has it that Louis greeted Hoffa, in full view of the jury and for the benefit of the black jurors. Williams himself gives apparently contradictory accounts of the incident on consecutive pages of his book, *One Man's Freedom,* published five years after the trial. "I very much doubt whether any juror ever saw him in that packed courtroom," Williams states on page 222. On the following page however, he says, "All of the jurors later attested that his appearance at the trial was meaningless insofar as the outcome was concerned." As William F. Buckley, Jr., observed, "How could it have been meaningless—or meaningful—if they had never seen him?"[13]

Williams declared recently that "that thing with Louis never happened. That never happened. He never greeted Hoffa in the courtroom. That was hokum. One hundred percent hokum. It's all mythology. It just didn't happen. It's just bullshit. They looked for twenty-nine reasons why they lost the case, and everyone that they could come up with, they came up with. They never wanted to concede that they lost it because they were incompetent." Practically shouting, Williams insisted, "That story is a hundred percent hokum, total fabrication, that he shook hands with Hoffa in the courtroom. Have you ever found anyone who said he saw that happen?"

The answer to Williams's question is yes. Prosecutor Edward Troxell recalls vividly that he watched from the counsel table as Hoffa walked to where Louis was sitting in the front of the courtroom and put his arm around the ex-champion, who remained seated. Troxell had "no doubt" that the embrace took place and that the jurors saw it. According to Troxell, this encounter occurred two or three times, with "Hoffa standing by Joe with his arm around him." He repeated this story during two separate interviews, several months apart, and his boss, Oliver Gasch, also said he saw Hoffa and Louis greet each other and was "sure" the jurors saw what happened. Gasch recalled that Hoffa and Louis embraced at the end of a recess, immediately before Judge Matthews returned to the courtroom, and he said the incident taught him a lesson that was useful after he was appointed a judge several years later. "Madame Matthews, wonderful old lady that she is, always believed that the judge should be the last person to come in," said Gasch. "So she didn't see it. I always remembered that, and since I became a judge, the jury is never brought in until I'm there. So nothing like that can happen. That's the thing that crystallized it in my mind."

The most detailed account of all was that of Clark Mollenhoff, who stated that at the afternoon recess he asked Louis why he was there, and Louis answered, "'I'm just here to see what they are doing to my old friend, Jimmy Hoffa,'" and Williams joked, "'We've got Joe down here to punch you in the nose.'" Louis and Williams went on into the courtroom and Mollenhoff and Hoffa stayed behind in the hall, chatting. "Suddenly" Hoffa broke off the conversation, scurried into the courtroom, and walked up to the aisle seat where Louis sat. Mollenhoff, watching "carefully," saw Hoffa place a hand on Louis's shoulder and thank him for coming. Louis, in return, "reached up and put his hand on Hoffa's arm, and the two engaged in conversation." Mollenhoff considered it "a strange scene, and a strange greeting, between two men I had seen talking together in the court corridor only a few minutes earlier." Furthermore, he said, the embrace "wasn't missed by some of the jurors. . . . One who didn't notice at first was elbowed by a neighbor, calling his attention to that touching scene between big Joe Louis and his little pal, Jimmy Hoffa, the defendant."[14]

Williams dismisses Mollenhoff as "not an objective reporter on this subject, as you know." True, Mollenhoff was a *de facto* member of Robert Kennedy's "Get Hoffa" team. Nevertheless, he was also a well-respected reporter and a Pulitzer Prize winner, and there is no reason to believe that his description of the Hoffa-Louis encounter was anything less than true. Even Vincent Fuller, who assisted Williams during the trial, said he saw Hoffa and Louis shake hands, although Fuller's recollection was that the jury was not present at that time.

The jurors themselves offered different versions of this event. One, identified only as "white" and a "Government Servant," said in a letter to the editor of the *Washington Star:* "There was only a passing comment [among the jurors] about Joe Louis's presence in the courtroom, just as there was to many prominent white spectators present during the trial." No mention was made of Hoffa and Louis greeting each other.[15] A black juror, Mrs. Conora Elliott, told the *Washington Afro-American* that "as far as she knew . . . Hoffa and Louis were never seen together by the jurors."[16]

A curious parallel was the experience of Monsignor George Higgins, a prominent Catholic priest in Washington. Higgins says that during the Hoffa trial he was approached by a former hoodlum named Barney Baker, one of Hoffa's principal hangers-on. "'You know our old friend James is in trouble,'" Higgins was told on the telephone by Baker, whom he knew slightly. "'James?'" asked Higgins. "'Jimmy Hoffa,'" was Baker's response. "'He needs a little spiritual consolation.'" Although Hoffa was not Catholic, Higgins promised Baker that "'if Jimmy wants to see me, I will see him any time that's convenient.'" But Baker had something specific in mind: "'I thought it would give him a lot of consolation if you could come sit down in the front row of the courtroom tomorrow.'" Father Higgins says he "laughed it off" and advised Baker, "'That's not the way we give spiritual consolation.'"

Whatever did happen in the courtroom on July 15 left Williams fuming. Back in his office at the end of the day, "Ed was so goddamned mad he couldn't see straight," according to Tom Wadden. "Ed was absolutely livid that they would pull this. He thought it was a cheap shot all the way around. He was ranting. If you've ever seen Ed mad, it's a terrifying subject; he runs around and rants like a small child. He was mad at Jimmy, he was mad at everybody."

Nevertheless, Williams, as one writer commented, was "Hoffa's lead lawyer in a criminal trial that highlighted many of the ethically questionable tactics that were used over the years by some Teamsters."[17] Joe Louis's visit to the courtroom was the most controversial of a series of borderline ploys that were used during the trial. The big question was: Did he or didn't he? That is, did Williams have anything to do with the incident or not?

Again, there is no proof that Williams was involved, and he could not be more emphatic in denying any role. Curiously, the prosecution team, while regarding the Louis appearance and the *Afro-American* advertisement as "dirty pool," in Oliver Gasch's words, claims not to hold Williams responsible for what happened; those who do believe that Williams had some connection with the Hoffa-Louis encounter tend to be Williams's friends and supporters. Rufus King, Jr., a Washington attorney who admires Williams (and who had Hoffa as a client years later), points out Williams's insistence on "total control" of a case: "I damn well have the impression he runs his courtroom," said King. "Having Joe Louis come into the courtroom and put his arm around Jimmy Hoffa, I think that was pretty damn close to the line. I know a little bit about what a tough, difficult client Hoffa could be. But I can't imagine Ed would let something like that happen if he didn't approve it. I'd be pleased and interested to know he didn't have anything to do with it."

Henry Ruth, now in private practice but during Watergate a prosecutor who had fairly extensive dealings with Williams, goes further. "I won't repeat what I've heard about it. I don't know myth from reality in that instance. I think people kind of characterize it as a cynical act to get a case decided aside from its merits." No less a friend of Williams's than Ben Bradlee declared, "Oh, shit, there's no doubt in my mind who brought him [Louis] in. Does he [Williams] deny bringing him in? Oh, bullshit. Does he really?"

In general, the most severe criticism of Williams's conduct of the Hoffa trial is that he failed to quit the case after all the extracurricular activities started. Edward Troxell says he has no reason to believe Williams was behind Louis's visit, "but he certainly didn't stop it." Warren Woods, who spoke warmly of Williams even though he opposed him on behalf of Drew Pearson and Jack Anderson, observed that Williams "probably didn't have anything to do with it. But as I remember, he took no steps to kick Joe Louis out of the courtroom."

The harshest statement came from Williams's archenemy, liberal attorney Joe Rauh, who conceded that Williams was probably not responsible for what happened, "but he should have resigned the minute it happened. If I had been in the courtroom, I would have found out who did it, and if Hoffa's people had done it, I would have said I have to withdraw. How can you possibly permit things like that, tricks like that, to go in for the jury? It's a little hard to believe that Williams would represent a person over whom he had so little control. *I* certainly wouldn't have. *I* would have just walked out in thirty seconds. I think an ethical person would have said, 'If you're doing those things, I can't go on.'"

Williams rejects the idea of dropping out of a case before it is over: "I'd never quit a case in the middle. You can't quit in the middle of a trial." He points out, however, that because of all the annoyances Hoffa and his crowd caused him, he declined to represent Hoffa personally (as opposed to the Teamsters Union) ever again.

The advertisement that was placed in the *Afro-American* and the importing of Joe Louis and Martha Jefferson were the two most conspicuous examples of unorthodox tactics during the trial.* In a similar move, Byrum Hurst, an attorney from Hot Springs, Arkansas, who was added to Hoffa's battery of lawyers at the defendant's insistence, turned out to be a

---

*Shortly after the Hoffa trial, Joe Louis split up with his wife. Two years later, Louis and Martha Jefferson—the principal figures in the two most blatant attempts to influence the jurors outside the normal scope of the trial—were wed. They remained married until the former champion died in 1981.

law partner of A. D. Shelton, brother of Judge Burnita Shelton Matthews.[18] *

Jimmy Hoffa and his entourage—including Joe Louis, Martha Jefferson, William Bufalino, Byrum Hurst, Frank Fitzsimmons, Barney Baker, and others—accumulated nearly $9,000 in bills at the Woodner Hotel in Washington during the trial. Those bills were footed by the truck drivers who paid their dues to the Teamster Union.[20] Their presence was not welcomed by the man they were ostensibly helping, Edward Bennett Williams, who says:

"Hoffa had an army of supporters. They just descended on the town like locusts. I divorced myself from them. They were just an army of second-guessers. They were constantly criticizing the way I was conducting the case. They asked repeatedly to have conferences with me. They wanted to make suggestions. I never took their suggestions. They were very offended by that, very hostile about that. Hoffa was unhappy about that.

"I didn't have the kind of control that I want in a case. I controlled Hoffa in the courtroom, but I didn't like the atmosphere. And I never represented Hoffa again in a courtroom."

Robert F. Kennedy took into account the sum total of the unusual methods employed by the defense: the racial aspect of jury selection; the appearance of Joe Louis; Martha Jefferson's presence; the advertisement in the *Afro-American* and its distribution to the black jurors; and Williams's questions to John Cye Cheasty about his investigation of the NAACP. "Such methods," Kennedy concluded, "seem extreme, and an insult to the court, to the judge, to the legal system, to the jury, and to the colored race." Kennedy wrote that "Ed Williams, one of the nation's top criminal attorneys, hardly needed this legal assistance."[21] But the implication was clear: Kennedy held Williams responsible for going beyond the bounds of fair play. The events that surrounded the Hoffa trial resulted in a decade-long break in the friendship of Edward Bennett Williams and Robert F. Kennedy.

---

*Another lawyer invited to sit in on the trial was one William Bufalino of Detroit, business representative of Teamsters Local 985, a union of jukebox employees, who had previously been tried on extortion charges and acquitted. Bufalino's role was to "consult with the other lawyers, and do whatever they thought was necessary," Hoffa testified during the McClellan Committee hearings. "You mean he was there in case Edward Bennett Williams needed some advice, and he would go to William Bufalino of the jukebox local?" Robert F. Kennedy inquired disbelievingly.[19]

14

Parachute Time

Jimmy Hoffa's bribery trial was a case of witness (Hoffa) against witness (John Cye Cheasty). It was a case of fact against fiction: The stories told by the two principals were so contradictory that one had to be a lie. The jurors, in their wisdom, disbelieved the tale told by the man who had no motive for lying—Cheasty—and accepted the word of the individual who had every reason for perjuring himself: Hoffa. For Hoffa, all the chips were riding on this trial. Acquittal, or even a hung jury, would mean that he would be the next leader of 1.5 million Teamsters, with his hands on the purse strings of tens of millions of dollars in pension funds, credit-union accounts, dues payments, and other receipts. Conviction would not only send him to prison but, much more important, deny him the presidency.

The trial was also a case of lawyer versus lawyer. Defense lawyer Edward Bennett Williams, thirty-seven, was establishing himself as perhaps the top trial lawyer in the country. Prosecutor Edward Troxell was, at forty-eight, the veteran of hundreds of trials as a private practitioner in Washington and as a government lawyer for the War Shipping Administration and the U.S. Attorney's Office. But he had never before conducted a trial of the magnitude of Hoffa's. The primary reason why U.S. Attorney Oliver Gasch picked Troxell to prosecute Hoffa was because he was available. Gasch explained that he initially considered trying the case himself, but decided not to leave his administrative duties and selected Troxell because "he was my first assistant. As first assistant he didn't have a big trial load. So when a big case came up he would be available for it." Within the U.S. Attorney's Office, the choice of Troxell was greeted with derision. Says one lawyer who worked there at the time: "Gasch and Troxell were close friends. Gasch was just one step ahead of Troxell himself. Everyone was critical of Troxell's assignment to the Hoffa case. It was almost a laughingstock in our office as to how that case was progressing. It was just pitiful."

Troxell stumbled in at least two crucial instances. The first involved the backgrounds of the jurors. Four of them were later found to have personal reasons for being "antagonistic to the aims of law enforcement in a criminal court," as Robert Kennedy pointed out. One had been arrested fourteen times, usually for drunkenness. A second had been convicted nine times, mostly for being drunk and disorderly—and several of these scrapes occurred during the Hoffa trial, before the jury was sequestered. The son of another juror was serving a jail term on a narcotics charge while the Hoffa trial was taking place. And a fourth juror had been dismissed from his government job for refusing to undergo a lie-detector test about whether he was a homosexual.[1] No prosecutor would have wanted any of these four to hear a criminal case, but Troxell was unaware of the skeletons in their closets. In 1981, he insisted that his office had had an inviolable rule in 1957: "You don't investigate jurors. Period!" But his opposite number, Williams, commented, "I can't imagine that the prosecutor would let people with arrest records on the jury." As it turned out, the jury that heard the Hoffa case was a defense counsel's dream.

Most glaring of Troxell's mistakes was his limiting his cross-examination of Hoffa to thirty-two minutes. Troxell thought the evidence against Hoffa was "so clearly inculpatory that it would be unwise to give Hoffa, who was an ingenious, brilliant guy, the opportunity to engage in false witness or whatever you want to call it." He says the rest of the prosecution team "concurred" in his decision to interrogate Hoffa so briefly.

Troxell's failure to probe in any detail the wide disparity between Hoffa's story and Cheasty's left one courtroom observer, Kennedy loyalist Clark Mollenhoff, feeling "shocked" and "sick" over the "pitiful mismatch."[2] Sitting next to Williams at the defense table, Vincent Fuller watched in "disbelief. It was as though they had capitulated." William Bittman, who questioned Hoffa for two days when he won a conviction against him for misuse of Teamster funds years later,* was incredulous

---

*Bittman prosecuted Hoffa in Chicago in 1964. Three years later, he prosecuted and convicted Bobby Baker, whom Williams defended (see chapter 20).

when he learned about the brevity of Troxell's cross-examination. "Thirty-two minutes?" he gasped. "That amazes me. Thirty-two minutes when they had pictures of Hoffa receiving the documents and giving the money, and they cross-examined him a total of thirty-two minutes? That seems a little bizarre. It's kind of difficult to justify."

As for Williams, he comments that "it's very hard to say whether Hoffa was an effective witness because the cross-examination was so incompetent or whether he was such a good witness that he was unassailable. I think it was that the cross-examination was so incompetent that he looked like a superb witness." A quarter-century later, the memory of his adversary caused Williams to laugh. "Troxell. Yeah. I always think of that case as being masterfully prepared [by the prosecution], like the Redcoats marching in step into the forest to fight the Indians. They're brilliantly prepared to march in and shoot down whatever forces are arrayed against them so long as they're on the ground marching toward then. But they're totally unprepared for a bunch of Indians in the trees shooting arrows right into their asses. Troxell was like a guy fighting in the gym—he's all right when he's punching a bag, but the moment somebody punches back, he collapses. The mere fact that in a major American case the defendant would be cross-examined for thirty-two minutes demonstrates that there was something wrong. He quit either because he was getting whipped by the witness or else he wasn't really prepared to cross-examine him." Others with the same view included Robert Kennedy;[3] his boss, Senator John L. McClellan;[4] and Kennedy's most trusted aide, Walter Sheridan.[5]

The differences between the spectacular Williams and the plodding Troxell were illustrated vividly in the closing arguments the two made to the jury. Williams, "pacing up and down in front of the jury, his voice pitched high with emotion and his arms flailing,"[6] mounted an all-out assault on Cheasty's credibility:

> What kind of man do you think it would be who would hear the indecent, illegal, criminal scheme [allegedly proposed by Hoffa] and the first moment spin from his lips a lie and begin a month's fabricated plan to bait a trap? Could anyone in whom there flickered a dying ember of decency and honor and integrity have spun from his lips without hesitation a lie and begun a pattern of deceit and falsehood and treachery?[7]

Noting that for "half a day from his lips came the admissions of falsehoods and deceits and fabrications," Williams reread to the jurors, word by word, Cheasty's admissions under cross-examination that he had lied to Hoffa repeatedly.[8] He also emphasized the gravity of Cheasty's confessed "lies":

> Now, from this man's lips we learn that he lies. From this man's lips we learn that he falsifies. From this man's lips we learn that he de-

ceives. What kind of a man is it who, while carrying a symbol of truth, honesty, beauty, a symbol of the faith some of us hold dear, the Rosary, can lie and deceive and falsify at the same time? You can search back through history from the beginning of time, when man first began to pay worship to a Supreme Being; you can look at every code of human behavior in the history of the world; you can look at every form of religion by which man paid his homage to his God, and you will find no religion, you will find no code of morals which condones a lie, deceit, falsehood, for any purpose. . . .

Mohammedanism, Buddhism, the Hebrew religion, Christianity, all universally without exception condemn the lie at all times.

When the Ten Commandments were passed to the world, the Fifth Commandment was not "Thou shalt not bear witness except for the Senate Select Committee." The Fifth Commandment was "Thou shalt not bear false witness, Thou shalt not deceive, falsify and lie."[9]

Williams also used the brief cross-examination of Hoffa as evidence of his innocence, citing a lawyer's axiom: "'You cannot cross-examine the truth.'. . . So the prosecutor backed off and quit after 32 minutes of questioning the key to this whole case."[10]

Winding up with the script that had stood him in such good stead over the years, Williams reminded the jurors that

[w]hat you do here I suppose will pass from [the minds of most of the people connected with the case] . . . and a year from now this whole thing will just be a memory, perhaps a vague one. But it won't be a memory to him [Hoffa], because what you do will be the most important thing that has ever taken place in his life. . . .

All the hopes and dreams and aspirations of this man are in your hands. All the hopes, dreams, and aspirations of his family, his wife and children, are in your hands. . . .

Ladies and gentlemen, Jimmy Hoffa has fought many battles for labor. He has fought for the people that he loves. He has fought with his head high. He has fought with a mind and heart without fear, and he has never betrayed a trust. . . . Now he is in a fight for his own life. . . . I ask you to send him back to the good fight.[11]

Troxell, trying to restore Cheasty's credibility, told the jury that if the investigator had turned down Hoffa's proposition, Hoffa "would have gotten another spy." Cheasty's course of action was "the only way you can root out spies and root out conspiracies. You have to have strength of character and courage to move in and do what Cheasty did in this instance."[12] In contrast to Williams, Troxell "talked quietly to the jury."[13] He seemed to speak with "no drama" and "no authority," and was "hardly . . . an advocate for conviction."[14]

Following the summations, the jurors retired. After they left the courtroom, Williams declared, "'I'll be satisfied with a hung jury.'"[15] The jurors began discussing the case at 11:00 A.M. on Friday, July 19. Ordinarily, a jury would spend at least a day or two reviewing the large volume of testimony, which ran to more than 3,000 pages. In this case, however, the jurors reached their verdict in less than five hours. They returned to Judge Matthews's courtroom at 3:45 the same afternoon. The verdict: Not guilty on all three counts.[16] Hoffa, crowing, "'I've hired lots of lawyers in my life, but Ed Williams is tops,'"[17] was a free man.

Jury foreman Roland Franklin, a Defense Department clerk, had this explanation: "The basic factor in the verdict . . . was the failure of the evidence to prove any conspiracy. That made the crux of the whole thing one man's word against another's—Hoffa's against Cheasty's. And the verdict shows who was believed."[18]

Two blocks from the courthouse, on Capitol Hill, Angela Novello, Robert F. Kennedy's secretary, received a phone call from Cye Cheasty telling her Hoffa had been acquitted. Novello wrote down the message and took it to Kennedy, who was questioning a witness at the McClellan Committee hearings. Novello's recollection is that Kennedy took the news in stride, but Kennedy himself wrote later, "I read the note with utter disbelief."[19] Before long, he had another message to consider—from Edward Bennett Williams, who sent his old friend a parachute to ease the trip from the Capitol dome. ("Quite justifiably," Kennedy commented.[20]) On the other hand, Frank Costello reportedly bet $1,000 at odds of 100 to 1 that Williams would pull off a mammoth upset in the Hoffa case.[21] If true, the wager netted Costello $100,000 to help him pay Williams's legal fees.

Williams, of course, drew rave reviews. *Time* said that thanks to "dazzling help from Washington's cleverest and busiest criminal lawyer," Hoffa had beaten the "airtight case against him."[22] To *U.S. News & World Report*, Williams was "Defender in Demand" (in boldface capitals).[23] The *Washington Post* praised "the superb quality of the defense presented by Edward Bennett Williams."[24] Even those who found the verdict hard to swallow had kind words for his skills: Drew Pearson said he "did a brilliant job,"[25] Robert F. Kennedy thought Williams had been "effective,"[26] and Clark Mollenhoff wrote that "the acquittal made it certain that Williams would be one of the most sought after defense lawyers in the nation."[27]

The gravest note of discord was sounded by *America,* the national Catholic weekly. Assessing the roles of the three Catholics who had been major figures in the case—Williams, Kennedy, and Cheasty—*America* editorialized, "In view of the nature of the defense conducted by Edward Bennett Williams, Hoffa's lawyer, our sympathy goes out to Mr. Kennedy."[28] The *Washington Post,* reconsidering its earlier stance, editorialized that "all the pains of the defense counsel, Mr. Williams," to use the question of race against Cheasty, combined with the visit by Joe Louis

and publication of the advertisement in the *Washington Afro-American,*
"certainly make an interesting series of coincidences."[29] Senator Irving
Ives of New York, senior Republican on the McClellan Committee, called
the verdict "'a miscarriage of justice,'" and another GOP member of the
committee, Williams's friend Barry Goldwater, remarked unhappily that
"'Joe Louis makes a pretty good defense attorney.'"[30]
Acquittal had an immediate and stunning effect on Jimmy Hoffa's
career. Within a week, "for all practical purposes," he had "moved into
command of the Teamsters."[31] After escaping "what looked to many as a
sure defeat in his month-long trial in Washington, he is more of a hero to
his friends, a more formidable foe to his enemies."[32] The "surprise acquittal" caused many Teamsters to "hop on the Hoffa bandwagon," which
"killed the Teamster reform movement. The leadership will change, almost inevitably, to Hoffa."[33]

Edward Bennett Williams won the battle on behalf of Jimmy Hoffa,
but in the process the country lost the war. Thanks to the triumph of
injustice, Hoffa graduated from being a totally corrupt individual on a
relatively minor scale, becoming one of the country's most powerful figures and a blight on the national landscape. As Dan Moldea, a journalist
and onetime trucker, said in the first sentence of his book about Hoffa
and the Teamsters, "Jimmy Hoffa's most valuable contribution to the
American labor movement came at the moment he stopped breathing on
July 30, 1975."[34]
As for the man who stood up against Hoffa, John Cye Cheasty, he did
not fare so well. "Not only did I not get anything out of that goddamned
situation, but for years afterwards I goddamned near starved to death,
just living on a pension and picking up a little case here and little case
there," says Cheasty. "I had no friends anywhere. None. I was stinko to
anybody who had any connection to a labor union or had to do any business with a labor union. I was a noisome smell in their nostrils. They
couldn't have me around them." Five or six years passed before Cheasty
lived down the Hoffa trial. Meanwhile, he raised five children somehow.
"We got along. The Cheastys are survivors," he laughs now. His marriage, however, broke up, in part because of the Hoffa case. In retrospect,
the subpoena that was served on his wife at the beginning of the trial
seems one of the most callous acts of all.
Cheasty at least retained the respect of Robert F. Kennedy, who wrote,
"The truth was and is that Cye Cheasty is an honest man—and Jimmy
Hoffa had failed to recognize that there is such a person."[35] Cheasty
returns the feeling, stating, "I admired the Kennedys. Because anybody in
the world would have told them it was damn poor politics to attack the
union, particularly if you're a Democrat and particularly if you have any
aspirations for high office. Here was Bob Kennedy and Jack Kennedy

doing precisely the thing they should not have done if they wanted to make the top. I kind of admired that."

In the last analysis, the judgment that Cye Cheasty had no motive for lying is inescapable. He was a sick man trying to eke out a living and he easily could have accepted the money Hoffa offered him—five times as much as Cheasty was paid by the McClellan Committee—unless he was telling the truth. If Troxell had been as skilled as Williams, he would have stated explicitly to the jury—over and over and over—that Cheasty had no motive for testifying falsely, and that unless the jurors could think of a motive, they had to believe Cheasty and convict Hoffa. Williams himself says,

"That was probably the argument they should have made."

The jury's verdict branded him a liar, but there is no question that if there was a hero in the Hoffa bribery trial, it was John Cye Cheasty.

15

Another Bribe
That Never Was

T he acquittal of Jimmy Hoffa in July 1957 on charges of trying to
bribe John Cye Cheasty removed the main obstacle from Hoffa's
drive for the Teamster presidency. True, there were still perjury
and wiretapping indictments pending against him in federal court in New
York, but neither of those cases would go to trial before the election to
choose Dave Beck's successor, scheduled for the fall of 1957.*

All that stood in Hoffa's way was a move by a group of Teamster
dissidents from New York and New Jersey to block his election. During
the late summer of 1957, Robert F. Kennedy worked closely with Godfrey
Schmidt, the attorney for the Teamsters opposed to Hoffa.[2] The joint
effort culminated on September 19, 1957, when the Teamster reform
group filed suit in U.S. District Court in Washington, seeking to prevent
the election of new officers at the union convention scheduled to start ten

---

*Hoffa was accused of hiring Bernard Spindel, a wiretap expert, to bug the phones of
Teamster business agents whom Hoffa distrusted. After one trial ended in a hung jury and a
juror in a second trial was removed following his disclosure that an illegal attempt had been
made to influence his vote, Hoffa was acquitted in the wiretap case. The perjury case was
dropped when the U.S. Supreme Court ruled that evidence had been gathered against Hoffa
illegally. Williams declined to represent Hoffa in either case.[1]

days later in Miami. About seventy disgruntled Teamsters were listed as plaintiffs, and the defendants included the Teamsters Union (represented by Edward Bennett Williams, along with Agnes Neill and Raymond Bergan from his office), Hoffa, and Beck.[3]*

The Teamster dissidents alleged that the forthcoming elections had been rigged to assure that Hoffa would be chosen president.† They asked for an injunction to prohibit the voting and to place the union in receivership. On September 28, 1957, the day before the convention was to open, Federal Judge F. Dickinson Letts issued a preliminary injunction that delayed the convention until the matter was resolved.[5] But the Hoffa side appealed, and Letts's ruling was overturned.[6] The convention proceeded, and Hoffa was elected by a margin of three to one. Addressing the 1,700 delegates, the new president vowed, "'I believe in good honest trade unionism.... This union will practice democracy in its fullest form, notwithstanding our enemies.'"[7]

Hoffa's opponents went back to Judge Letts, who handed down a new injunction, barring Hoffa and his cronies from taking office.[8] Again, the Hoffa faction appealed, but this time Letts's decision was upheld.[9] Meanwhile, the AFL-CIO suspended the Teamsters Union until it "'complies with the...directive to eliminate corrupt influences from positions of leadership.'"[10]

The case filed by the dissidents went to trial in November 1957. By then, Edward Bennett Williams had been appointed general counsel of the Teamsters Union, at a retainer of $50,000 a year.[11] Hoffa had not been able to take office, but he was calling the shots, and the choice of Williams for the highly paid part-time job was seen by such Williams critics as Robert Kennedy and Joe Rauh as a reward for Williams's successful defense of Hoffa in the bribery trial. States Rauh: "The general counsel's job was obviously a payoff of the debt for Williams's taking the bribery case. I think that was wrong. Edward Bennett Williams would not have known where the National Labor Relations Board's office was at the moment he became general counsel of the Teamsters."‡

The plaintiffs spent several weeks during November and December placing their case against Hoffa and the other Teamster leaders in the court record,[13] but before the defense started its presentation, Godfrey

---

*The case, known as Cunningham v. English, dragged on in various federal courts, including the Supreme Court, until 1963.

†Hoffa once said that a lawyer who suggested that the union choose its officers by secret ballot to guarantee free elections was "'out of his mind. In the Teamsters Union, every man stands up and has his vote counted and God help him if he votes the wrong way.'"[4]

‡A similar, although less harsh, view was offered by *Fortune* magazine, which reported in 1958: "Though Williams is one of the smartest criminal lawyers in the country, he is a novice in labor politics, so [Eddie] Cheyfitz will be Jimmy Hoffa's principal idea man and deal maker."[12]

Schmidt and Williams entered into secret discussions aimed at settling the suit.[14] Schmidt, lead attorney for the plaintiffs, had a background that overlapped Williams's in many ways. An active anti-Communist in New York, Schmidt was president of a group called "AWARE," which sought to deny work to entertainment figures believed to have Communist leanings;[15] Williams had fought organizations like AWARE on behalf of such clients as Howard Koch and Georgia Gibbs, who had been the targets of boycotts. On the other hand, Schmidt had been a leader of an outfit known as Ten Million Americans Mobilizing for Justice, which had tried to generate support for Joe McCarthy, and Schmidt had been a speaker at a pro-McCarthy rally at Madison Square Garden in November 1954, while Williams was defending McCarthy against censure charges in the Senate.[16] In the private negotiations between the two lawyers, each had a mutually contradictory bottom line: Williams's job was, at all costs, to win Hoffa his elected place as president of the Teamsters, while Schmidt declared, "'I shall not consent to any agreement under which Hoffa retains office.'"[17]

With the talks stalemated, a brainstorm was needed. As usual, Eddie Cheyfitz rose to the occasion. Cheyfitz proposed that Hoffa be allowed to take office and that a three-member board of monitors be appointed to oversee union affairs.[18]

Each side reluctantly accepted the concept of an impartial board to help administer the Teamsters Union. Godfrey Schmidt was eager to settle the lawsuit and limit Hoffa's power; Hoffa was "desperate" to take over the presidency, and was aware that failure to reach a compromise would mean a court fight that could delay him for months, if not years.[19] The board was to consist of three members—one chosen by the dissidents (Godfrey Schmidt), one nominated by the Hoffa side (Dallas attorney L. N. D. ["Nat"] Wells, who had often represented the Teamsters), and one selected jointly by both sides (retired federal judge Nathan Cayton, who was named chairman). The board was to "make recommendations" to and "counsel with" the executive board of the union, and was ultimately answerable to Judge Letts. Its key responsibilities were to make sure that the union conducted honest elections and handled its finances properly, and to see that Teamster officials had no conflict of interest between their personal business and union affairs.

The agreement was ratified by the signatures of Williams for the defendants and of Schmidt, Thomas Dodd,* and a third attorney for the plaintiffs.[20] Williams subsequently explained to the McClellan Committee that the Teamsters Union, by placing its operation under the control of a federal court for a period of one to five years (until the next Teamster elections), "voluntarily did unto itself what no union has done."[21]

---

* Later a U.S. Senator and a client of Williams's.

Hoffa became Teamster president in January 1958, and the board of monitors was formally constituted at the same time. The board operated well at first, but after four months Nathan Cayton resigned as chairman, and Judge Letts replaced him with Martin O'Donoghue, whose name had been on a list submitted by Williams. O'Donoghue, once one of Williams's law professors at Georgetown, had preceded Williams as Teamster general counsel. Williams says he "admired him [O'Donoghue] as a lawyer" and considered him "a friend" from law school days. But O'Donoghue immediately showed that, despite his past associations, he was impartial. He decreed that all communications between the union and the board be in writing, hired a full-time assistant and an investigator, and moved the board's offices out of Teamster headquarters.[22] One of the dissidents, a trucker named Pat Kennedy, was ecstatic: "'This O'Donoghue is the greatest. . . . This guy is a real lawyer. He makes the great Edward Bennett Williams look second rate.'"[23]

Williams was dismayed by the frequent clashes that developed between O'Donoghue and Hoffa. "I thought Martin O'Donoghue would do a superb job as a monitor," says Williams. "But I think he believed that the monitors were supposed to run the union," instead of being "purely advisory." On the other hand, Hoffa "was not a willing cohort. Hoffa resisted doing the things that I thought he should have done, and willingly and cheerfully and gladly done"—namely, clean up the union and oust the racketeers. "The monitors reacted to that by arrogating to themselves more power than it was ever dreamed they should have. The more power they took, the more Hoffa resisted, and the more Hoffa resisted, the more power they took, and the more hostile the relationship became until it was just a shambles."

From its inception, the board was surrounded by a series of unusual problems and circumstances:

- Robert F. Kennedy disclosed that John R. Cunningham, a New York truck driver who was the lead plaintiff in the 1957 court case against Teamster corruption, had apparently switched sides and been funneled money from Hoffa.[24]
- Kennedy also reported that Teamster funds were being used to pay both Cunningham and Williams, who had ostensibly been Cunningham's opponent in court.[25]
- Nat Wells quit, to be replaced by Daniel Maher, who had been the attorney for Hoffa's codefendant, Hyman Fischbach, in the 1957 bribery trial.[26]
- Godfrey Schmidt also resigned from the board after the U.S. Court of Appeals found a possible conflict of interest on his part because in his outside law practice he had some clients who did business with the Teamsters.[27]
- Williams, who had been trying for a year to oust Schmidt, was himself under scrutiny by the board of monitors, which was concerned that his representing both Hoffa and the Teamsters Union might constitute a conflict of interest.[28]

The machinations of Eddie Cheyfitz continued to affect Williams even after Cheyfitz's sudden death on May 24, 1959.[29] For it was Cheyfitz who had allegedly hatched a scheme to secure the resignation of Godfrey Schmidt from the board of monitors, in return for the payment of some $150,000 that Schmidt claimed the union owed him.[30]

Schmidt had been a thorn in Hoffa's side since mid-1957, when he had first taken on the Teamster dissidents as clients. He had especially rankled the Hoffa side by submitting the names of Robert F. Kennedy and Clark Mollenhoff as possible appointees to the board of monitors—a suggestion that reportedly sent Williams and Hoffa "'through the roof.'"[31] Williams's old chum, Robert Maheu, was then asked to investigate Schmidt with an eye toward digging up dirt that would result in his ouster.[32] But Maheu turned down the assignment. He explained in 1981 that "I was also doing some work for CIA. Bobby Kennedy was not favorable to CIA at the time, and I did not want to become involved" in the Hoffa campaign against Schmidt, for fear that Kennedy would try to harm the Agency in return.

Schmidt had been paid for his first six months on the board, but had received no money for his work after August 1, 1958. He claimed he was owed about $45,000 for his job as a monitor during the next year, plus approximately $105,000 for representing the Teamster dissidents against the Hoffa crowd in 1957 and 1958. (The Teamsters had been ordered to pay the dissenters' legal fees as part of the settlement that created the board of monitors.[33]) The union's refusal to pay Schmidt, the father of six children, had left him in dire straits: His creditors were harassing him, and even his electricity was cut off.[34]

To help him collect the money, Schmidt hired New York lawyer Bartley Crum, who had represented William Randolph Hearst (through whom he had come to know Clarence Darrow—Edward Bennett Williams's idol); had won a $1-million divorce settlement for Rita Hayworth from Prince Aly Khan; had helped draft the United Nations charter; had been an early advocate of the creation of the state of Israel; had served as a campaign manager for Wendell Willkie, Republican presidential candidate in 1940; and had been publisher of the New York tabloid *PM* from 1948 until the newspaper folded the next year.[35] Crum, then, was someone to be reckoned with.

Crum, called by Robert F. Kennedy as a witness before the McClellan Rackets Committee on July 13, 1959, unfolded a spellbinding tale that wound up with sensational charges against Edward Bennett Williams. According to Crum, he had been approached several times in the past year with proposals that Schmidt step down from the board of monitors, in return for which Schmidt's fees would be paid and Crum would be named to replace him. Crum listened to those proposals because "I thought it was my function to collect the fee owing to my client, if I could, legally." However, because he viewed as "improper" the suggestion that Schmidt would be paid only if he resigned, he informed Judge Letts, who instructed him to report these incidents to the FBI. Crum followed Letts's orders; meanwhile, Williams had been informed from the start that Crum was reporting all contacts to the FBI. In June 1959, Williams indicated to Crum that he agreed with a plan under which Schmidt would resign and be paid, with Crum replacing him on the board.

Finally, on July 9, 1959, four days before Crum was due to appear before the McClellan Committee, he had lunch with Williams at Duke Zeibert's, Williams's favorite wateringhole in Washington. Crum later testified under oath that Williams said at lunch "that Mr. Schmidt's fees as monitor would be paid by Friday [the next day] if I did not appear as a witness before this committee." Crum added that the impression he received "pretty clearly" from Williams's offer was "that if I told the truth before this committee, probably Schmidt would not get his fees until we went [all the way] up to the Supreme Court of the United States." And this, Crum continued, "was in my judgment an immoral exercise of power" intended "to frustrate Schmidt in his function as a monitor of the district court. . . . I think the approach was improper in intention . . . on the part of . . . Mr. Williams."[36]

Crum's were the most severe allegations ever made against Williams, and Committee Chairman John L. McClellan cautioned him that his claim that Williams indicated Schmidt's fees would be paid if Crum declined to be a witness "is a pretty serious charge."

"Well, it is the truth," declared Crum.

"I don't know. You are under oath. Mr. Williams is present here," McClellan reminded Crum.

"I am well aware I am under oath," Crum replied.

McClellan repeatedly impressed on Crum the gravity of his testimony, but Crum held firm:

> *McClellan:* I understand. It is a pretty serious charge you are making.
>
> *Crum:* I am sorry, that is precisely what was said to me.
>
> *McClellan:* OK. You know the full import of your testimony?
>
> *Crum:* Yes, I do.[37]

As Crum finished, Williams sat in the hearing room, "flushed with anger."[38] He demanded furiously that McClellan let him testify immediately in response. McClellan agreed, and asked Williams to identify himself for the record. Williams heatedly responded:

> My background is this: My name is Edward Bennett Williams. I am
> a lawyer who has practiced law in the District of Columbia for 15
> years.

I have a reputation. For whatever it is worth, I am not going to allow it to go without being defended against a false, vicious, and contrived smear that I have heard here this afternoon. That is my identification, sir.[39]

Williams then responded explicitly to Crum's charges:

The statement has been made here by Mr. Crum that on Thursday last at lunch that I said to him that I would recommend the payment of Mr. Godfrey Schmidt's fees as a monitor if Mr. Crum would not appear before this committee.

That statement, sir, is absolutely, completely, unequivocally, unqualifiedly false.

Williams said that upon reading in the *New York Herald Tribune* of an alleged attempt to bribe Schmidt in July 1958, he made an appointment with Judge Letts and asked for "a full and complete investigation" of the report. Both Crum and Martin O'Donoghue were notified in advance of this meeting. Letts "assured" Williams that the matter would be probed (by the FBI, Williams assumed). Williams continued:

Insofar as I know, no money, nothing of value, no remuneration, directly or indirectly, was paid to Mr. Schmidt to effect his resignation. I so told Mr. [Robert] Kennedy one night recently when he called me on the telephone at home, and told him that I had no information on anything being offered to Mr. Schmidt to resign, and that is the fact.[40]

As Williams went on, he became angrier and angrier at the brothers Kennedy. At one point, he snapped at Senator John F. Kennedy, "I hope you will let me finish." Kennedy answered, "I am trying to ask you questions," to which Williams rejoined, "I know you are trying to ask me questions before I finish my previous answer."[41] Again, when JFK observed that linking the payment of Schmidt's fees to his resignation was "highly improper," Williams shot back, "I understand what you think, Mr. Kennedy. I will be happy to have the opinion of the bar association's ethics committee on it, who, I believe are more qualified to pass upon it than you or I."[42] When Robert Kennedy said, regarding a point made by Williams, "I do not understand that, because I thought you just stated here—" Williams cut him off with "I am not surprised you don't understand it, Mr. Kennedy, but I hope the other members of the committee will."[43] *

Defending himself passionately after Senator Kennedy asked him disbelievingly if "you never saw anything improper or wrong in offering to

---

* No one appreciated Williams's contemptuous reply to Robert Kennedy more than Jimmy Hoffa, who commented in his own book fifteen years later, "It tickled the hell out of me. I thought Kennedy was going to crap in his drawers."[44]

pay Mr. Godfrey Schmidt's fee in full on one hand and on the other hand
his resigning as a monitor," Williams declared:

> I don't think it is improper now, Mr. Kennedy. I don't want you to
> think for one moment, for one moment, that I am suggesting to you
> that I or any associate connected with me was guilty of any impropri-
> ety. I don't consciously commit improprieties professionally. When I
> consciously do something, as I did in this case, I believe it to be right. I
> believe it to be morally right. I believe what we did in this case to be
> morally right. I am perfectly willing to submit it to the ethics associa-
> tion or committee of the American Bar Association and have them pass
> upon it. I believe that what we did was right. I believed it then, I believe
> it now, I believe that our efforts toward settlement were bona fide,
> valid, legitimate efforts toward settlement. I am appalled if Mr. Crum
> thinks differently. He has never said so prior to this morning, so far as I
> know. We were lawyers looking toward the settlement of a dispute, and
> an ugly dispute.[45]

Williams revealed, contrary to Crum's testimony, that there had been a
third person present at the crucial lunch, "thank God." Williams identified the third man as Harold Ungar, an attorney who was doing research
on the Teamster case and who happened to be in Williams's office when
Crum called and asked for a meeting. Williams asked McClellan to call
Ungar (who had been contacted at Williams's request when Crum made
his charges an hour or so earlier) as a witness. "I would like to have my
reputation on this matter either vindicated or destroyed this afternoon, so
that we can lay at rest what I say is apparently falsehood about that
conversation on Thursday. I say to you that I have had no conversation
with Mr. Ungar whatsoever."[46]

Ungar, sworn under oath, testified that during the lunch "[m]ostly we
exchanged anecdotes." He recalled that "Mr. Crum said, I suppose facetiously, that Mr. Schmidt was down to using candles for illumination, the
lights having been turned out, and needed some money." Ungar said repeatedly, under questioning by McClellan, Robert Kennedy and Sam Ervin, that there had been no mention of Schmidt being paid if Crum refused to testify or if Schmidt resigned. Ungar also answered affirmatively
a question from Ervin, "You went with Mr. Williams and left with Mr.
Williams?"—making it clear that Crum and Williams could not have had
a conversation outside of his presence.[47]

Following Ungar's testimony, Crum was recalled to the witness stand
and Chairman McClellan asked him, "Mr. Crum, have you got anything
to say?" Crum's response was "No, sir, except to repeat what I have
heretofore said to the committee." McClellan gave him one more chance
to recant his testimony in view of Williams's statements to the contrary:
"You have heard the testimony and you reassert your previously sworn
testimony?" Crum stood firm: "Yes, I do. That is true."

Something was obviously rotten on Capitol Hill, and McClellan declared, "The only thing the Chair can do is to make the observation that someone is certainly varying from the truth. . . . Such conduct should not be tolerated. . . . I do think that this record should go immediately, a copy of it to Judge Letts, a copy of it to the Monitors, and a copy of it to the Department of Justice" for an investigation leading to possible perjury charges.[48]

Before the committee adjourned for the day, though, Godfrey Schmidt was called as a witness. He substantiated Crum's story: "I want to say that everything that Mr. Crum said here under oath he had previously told me either orally or in letter form." Schmidt added that the proposed payment of his fees if he resigned was "improper" and fit "the very definition of a bribe." However, he did not offer testimony to any direct contacts with Williams; all Schmidt knew was that Crum had told him the same story he had just told the committee.[49]

(Schmidt now says that when he confirmed Crum's testimony in front of the McClellan Committee, he might have misunderstood what Crum had said and have thought that Crum was referring to bribe offers made by other people, not Williams. Although Schmidt said "I don't particularly like" Williams, he added, "I never regarded Edward Bennett Williams as willing to do anything like offer a bribe. I never in my life knew that Bartley Crum had charged Edward Bennett Williams with anything wrong like that. Never did I dream of suggesting that he would offer a bribe.")

The allegations by Crum were ten days old when Crum delivered still another bombshell: He recanted! On July 23, 1959, Crum went to Williams's office and, in an affidavit notarized by Geraldyne H. Wagner, Williams's personal secretary, swore as follows:

> An interpretation has been placed upon affiant's [Crum's] testimony that a "bribe" in effect was offered by Mr. Williams. Such inference is without any foundation whatsoever.
>
> My relations with Mr. Williams throughout the protracted litigation have been conducted on the highest professional level and in the best tradition of the legal profession.[50]

The *Washington Post* rushed to the defense of Williams, commenting in an editorial titled "About Face" that Crum's

> behavior has been, by any rational test, grossly irresponsible. Everyone who heard his testimony before the committee understood him to accuse Washington Attorney Edward Bennett Williams of having offered him a bribe. Mr. Williams himself so understood it and promptly, flatly and vehemently branded the testimony a "false, vicious and contrived smear." Now Mr. Crum asserts that the inference that a bribe was offered him by Mr. Williams is "without any foundation whatsoever."

... It is fair, we think, to ask whether the Committee exercised as much care as it should have before affording him a privileged sounding board for slander.[51]

Although Senator McClellan said that Crum's affidavit "re-emphasizes the necessity, if not the urgency, for the Justice Department to pursue this matter with the view toward determining if perjury was committed,"[52] Crum's allegations and retraction did not result in additional action.

Both Ungar and Williams offer similar explanations of the episode. Crum, according to Ungar, "was a little bit disturbed. He was no longer a fully responsible human being at that stage of his life." Williams went even further, declaring that Crum was "totally alcoholic. One hundred percent alcoholic. And he was suffering from severe mental problems. That's what my information was at the time. That he was totally irresponsible. He was a total rummy," and was "a very dissipated-looking man." Crum's alleged alcoholism, said Williams, is "the only thing that I can suggest to you that accounts for it. It gave me a period of anguish, I'll tell you that."

Williams reports that Crum gave his affidavit recanting his testimony immediately after Williams and Crum had been together at a conference on the Teamster case in the chambers of Supreme Court Justice Felix Frankfurter.* According to Williams, "When I saw Crum, which was the first time I had seen him from the time he had said these things in the Senate Caucus Room, I just blurted out, 'How could you have done this thing? How in the name of God could you have perjured yourself and slandered me in this way?' He responded in front of Frankfurter, 'I didn't mean it the way it came out.' Then Frankfurter said, 'Then you go correct it.'" Which Crum did. Williams says that although he was "anxious" to have Crum charged with perjury, he did not seek to have him prosecuted after he rescinded his story, because "he was sort of like a child" on account of his alleged alcoholism.

Less than five months after Bartley Crum dropped his successive lightning bolts, he was dead at the age of fifty-nine. He died in his sleep of a heart attack on December 9, 1959.[53] And something obviously was amiss in his personal affairs: He left no will and an estate of only $16,000,[54] strange circumstances for an attorney of his stature.

Crum's death occurred just three weeks before he and Godfrey Schmidt were to have opened a law partnership—and Schmidt states that he would neither have hired as an attorney nor became a partner of someone who had a drinking problem. Contrary to the versions of Williams and Ungar,

---

*Attorneys for Hoffa and the dissident Teamsters met in Frankfurter's chambers to discuss the board of monitors the same day Crum swore out his affidavit, according to an Associated Press story carried in the *New York Times* on July 24, 1959.

Schmidt says that although he occasionally had drinks with Crum, he never saw him drunk and never had reason to believe he was an alcoholic.

As for the other person involved in this mystery, Harold Ungar, he joined Williams's law firm soon after the scene before the McClellan Committee and the following year was listed as number three in the firm, behind only Williams and Tom Wadden, and ahead of Agnes Neill, Vincent Fuller, Raymond Bergan, Duke Guider, and Colman Stein.[55] Although the firm has grown from about a dozen lawyers in 1960 to some eighty currently, he has maintained that rank.

Eddie Cheyfitz's inspiration, the board of monitors, was an idea whose time had not yet come, and never would. The board was reduced to absurdity in May 1960, when William Bufalino—the Detroit jukebox lawyer who had once beaten an extortion rap—was named as a monitor in place of Daniel Maher, who had resigned.[56] Also in 1960, despite their differences, Williams and Godfrey Schmidt held secret discussions about abolishing the board of monitors,[57] and a year later, Judge Letts ordered the board dissolved.[58] In a vast understatement, Leonard B. Mandelbaum, a former board staffer who wrote a legal treatise on the monitors, concluded: "Most observers would agree that the Monitors and the Teamsters have not worked well together."[59] Even Edward Bennett Williams acknowledges that the board "didn't work."

It would take much more than three court-appointed supervisors to bring down Jimmy Hoffa. The plan conceived by Eddie Cheyfitz left Hoffa riding high, no doubt just as Cheyfitz had intended.

16

Choosing
Sides

An artist's sketch of Robert F. Kennedy, wearing a turtleneck sweater, ski goggles dangling from his neck, adorns a wall in Edward Bennett Williams's office. The inscription reads: "For Ed—who knew what it was to be both his challenger and advocate. Life for him was a challenge, perilous indeed, but men are not made for safe havens. With love from Ethel." The drawing, commissioned by Ethel Kennedy, was her gift to Williams at Christmas 1969, eighteen months after Robert Kennedy was murdered. During the intervening years, Ethel Kennedy has frequently been a guest in Williams's box at the Washington Redskins' home games in Robert F. Kennedy Memorial Stadium.

Williams and Kennedy became acquainted during the early 1950s, when Williams was Joe McCarthy's adviser and sometimes lawyer and Kennedy was an attorney on McCarthy's staff. The two had much in common. Both were devout Catholics and were starting to raise large families. Each had achieved prominence at a relatively early age: Kennedy was not yet thirty; Williams five years older. And each was driven in a way that the other could understand: Williams by a quest for wealth, fame, and influence; Kennedy by a father's ambition for his sons and by his own dream of righting the world's wrongs. In Williams's words, "I saw Bobby Kennedy all the time prior to the Hoffa case. We were very, very close friends," practically best friends.

On several occasions, according to Kennedy, Williams and Eddie Cheyfitz "spoke to me about leaving the Government and coming into their law firm. . . . I told them I thought I would stay in the Government a few years longer." And Kennedy said that it had been Williams and Cheyfitz who introduced him to Teamster leaders and familiarized him with their operations. Ironically, then, had it not been for Williams and Cheyfitz, Kennedy might never have grown interested enough in the Teamsters to launch the McClellan Rackets Committee probe of the union. In 1956, before that investigation started, Cheyfitz had invited Kennedy to tour the new Teamster offices near the Capitol and during the visit had suggested that Teamster president Dave Beck might like an autographed copy of John F. Kennedy's *Profiles in Courage,* which had just been published. Robert Kennedy did as Cheyfitz had asked,[1] but the following year Beck found himself destroyed, compliments of Robert F. Kennedy.

Once Eddie Cheyfitz's attempt to bring Kennedy and Hoffa together had failed, people in contact with both men were forced to choose sides; their mutual hatred bordered on obsession. Hoffa had discovered that after leaving the Capitol each night, Kennedy would drive past Hoffa's office to see if the lights were still on. If so, Kennedy would return to his office, feeling, "'If he's still at work, we ought to be.'" After Hoffa heard of Kennedy's interest in his work habits, according to Williams, he took to leaving his lights on after he had gone home as one way of disrupting Kennedy's life.[2]

The feud had a much more serious side, however; on at least one occasion, Hoffa allegedly threatened to assassinate Robert Kennedy.[3] Dan Moldea, a writer who has studied Hoffa in depth, is convinced that he was extensively involved in the assassination of John F. Kennedy. His motive, says Moldea, was to get the Kennedys off his back; he felt that if he removed only Robert Kennedy, the president would have found someone else to dog him.[4] Near the end of his life, Hoffa decided that his vendetta against the Kennedys had been one of the biggest mistakes of his life, and that the "blood feud" had been responsible for both John F. Kennedy's election as president* and his own eventual sentencing to federal prison.[6]

Robert Kennedy reciprocated Hoffa's animosity with at least equal fury. Commenting in 1958 on the proposed hookup of the Teamsters and

*Hoffa supported Hubert Humphrey against John F. Kennedy in the 1960 primaries. The Kennedys capitalized on Hoffa's backing of Humphrey, presenting him as Hoffa's candidate, which hurt Humphrey's cause and was a factor in his loss. With Humphrey out of the race, Hoffa switched to Lyndon Johnson, and when Kennedy defeated him, too, Hoffa changed horses again, this time to Richard Nixon, with the same results.[5]

the International Longshoremen's Association, Kennedy said:

> The worst elements of the American labor movement are creating an unholy alliance that could dominate the United States within three to five years. . . . Together, they would constitute a subversive force of unequaled power in this country. . . . The national economy could be paralyzed, so powerful is the one force that is instigating the alliance.
>
> That force is the Teamsters' union and its general president, James R. Hoffa. . . . Never in our history has such power been placed in the hands of a few men such as these. Next to the United States Government itself, they would be the most powerful group in the country. They could bring the activities of a city as large as New York to an absolute halt within a few days.[7]

Kennedy must have felt betrayed when Williams turned up at the Federal Courthouse as Hoffa's attorney in the bribery case. Kennedy "felt such tremendous antipathy toward Hoffa that he couldn't disassociate me from Hoffa when I was representing him," says Williams. Egged on by Hoffa, who baited Williams, telling him he expected the attorney would go easy on Kennedy because of their friendship, Williams "overcompensated" and was "especially tough" in cross-examining Kennedy when the latter was called as a prosecution witness in the bribery trial.[8] Ethel Kennedy, who was often in the audience at the trial, was disturbed by the harsh interrogation of her husband. "'They [meaning Williams] have no right to ask him those questions,'" she grumbled.[9]

After Hoffa was acquitted and the battleground shifted to the McClellan Committee hearings, another member of the Kennedy clan entered the fray. Williams gave a speech at the University of Virginia Law School, where Ted Kennedy was a student. The youngest Kennedy brother said that Williams had stated that the McClellan Committee, finding in closed session that a witness would plead the Fifth Amendment, had made a practice of then calling the same witness to a public hearing and forcing him to embarrass himself by openly taking the privilege against self-incrimination. Ted Kennedy challenged Williams on the point at the law school, and reported to his brother what Williams had said. RFK declared in a handwritten note to his files, "'As of yet we have not had a witness in Executive [session] who has taken 5th and whom we have had in open. Old McCarthy trick and it irritates me that he [Williams], now an officer of American Civil Liberties Union, should relate it to us.'"[10]

The McClellan Committee hearings were often the forum for snide remarks between Williams and Robert Kennedy. Williams repeatedly criticized Kennedy for making "reckless" charges against Hoffa;[11] for misquoting from documents,[12] and for being "discourteous" to Hoffa by "constantly quarreling" with him.[13] One hostile exchange had to do with Robert Scott, a former Hoffa crony who had turned against him and was called as a witness by Kennedy. Referring to Scott, Williams declared, "I understand that this is a wholly unreliable witness. . . . My information is that this man, Mr. Chairman, is a narcotic addict." Williams, however, offered no substantiation for his slur against Scott. Kennedy immediately said to Scott, "Mr. Edward Bennett Williams, the attorney for Mr. Hoffa, has made a statement here, without any proof, that you are a drug addict. Will you make any comment on that, please." Scott was emphatic: "No; I am not."[14]

Outside the hearing room, Clark Mollenhoff asked Williams what proof he had that Scott was an addict, and reminded him, "'You are the director of the American Civil Liberties Union, Mr. Williams. . . . You are the one who gives speeches on the abuses by unsupported charges—and the smears by Congressional committees.'"

Williams promised to provide evidence on Scott's drug habit in the future and, when pressed, named two Teamster officials from Michigan—one of whom had served a prison term for extortion.[15]

Kennedy also accused Williams of having committed "a fraud on the court" for having informed Judge Dickinson Letts, the overseer of the board of monitors, that two Teamster officials in Chattanooga who faced criminal charges had been suspended from their posts, when they not been suspended. Kennedy's allegation was made at a committee session in June 1959, and Williams, who was present, objected: "Just a minute. When you start flipping around the word 'fraud' I want to talk to you, Mr. Kennedy. There wasn't any fraud perpetrated on any court, and I am going to ask you to withdraw that statement." Williams insisted that Hoffa had suspended the officials, but that, without his knowledge, members of the Chattanooga local had ignored the suspension.

Although Chairman McClellan agreed with Kennedy that Williams's statement to Judge Letts "could constitute a fraud on the court," Senator Sam Ervin came to Williams's defense, commenting that "[t]here was, from his standpoint, evidence that, as far as he could ascertain, from the information he had, that they had been suspended." Ervin also said he had known Williams since the McCarthy censure hearings in 1954 and "I have a very high opinion of him, both from the standpoint of capacity and from the standpoint of character." Although Kennedy did not retract his charges of fraud, Ervin's support for Williams seemed to satisfy the other members of the committee and the matter was not pursued.[16]

Away from the committee hearings, Kennedy was getting in more licks, allegedly saying in private that Williams should be disbarred for permitting Teamster officials to invoke the Fifth Amendment a hundred times or more in front of the committee.[17]* And there was little doubt to whom

*Kennedy must not have appreciated it when Williams turned up at the Teamsters' 1961 convention in Miami Beach to praise the union leaders who he said had strengthened the Fifth Amendment by pleading it in their own cases.[18]

Kennedy was referring when he said publicly, "'The 200 lawyers who take their money from the Teamsters are legal prostitutes. . . . Most of them are criminal lawyers. They spend their time trying to keep Mr. Hoffa in office rather than representing the union membership.'"[19]

Gradually, Williams and Kennedy renewed their friendship. "I think the Hoffa phase just passed into history, and there was no reason for his distancing himself from me any longer," Williams comments. To some extent, touch-football games helped cement the reconciliation, as Williams returned to the games at Hickory Hill, Kennedy's home outside Washington. Huge, incorrigible dogs also figured in their revived association. Pet shows, with Art Buchwald as master of ceremonies awarding prizes for such distinctions as longest nose, were an annual tradition at Hickory Hill. The behavior of Kennedy's beloved Brumus resulted in a letter from Williams to Kennedy, dated August 7, 1967:

> I have been retained by Mr. Art Buchwald to represent him in the matter of the vicious and unprovoked attack made on him Wednesday, July 25, by the large, savage, man-eating coat-tearing black animal owned by you and responding to the name Broomass (phonetic).
>
> Mr. Buchwald has been ordered to take a complete rest by his physician until such time as he recovers from the traumatic neurosis from which he is suffering as a result of the attack. He will be in isolation at Vineyard Haven, Martha's Vineyard, Massachusetts for an indefinite period at a cost of $2,000 a month.
>
> He is concerned about the effect of exposing this ugly episode on your political future. . . . Since Broomass is black, the case is fraught with civil rights' undercurrents.[20]

Williams's own dog, a big red one of the setter persuasion, turned out to be Brumus's equal. The Williams setter, named Jason, "tried to hump every other dog in the ring" at the Hickory Hill dog show one year, according to the emcee, Art Buchwald. "So I ordered Jason out of the ring in disgrace. It was the first time that a dog had gone to that extreme." Jason's banishment, says Buchwald, led to "a pretty good exchange of correspondence" between him and his sometimes lawyer.

And RFK would have loved the telegram that was sent to EBW following an October 1973 burglary at Williams's home. A wire, ostensibly from the thief, complained about the slim pickings. The message turned out to have been sent by Mrs. Robert F. Kennedy.[21]

Although Williams says he and Kennedy were "never quite so close or quite so warm" friends as they had been before the Hoffa period, "we still had a good relationship at the end of his life." And four years after Kennedy's death, Williams hired Angela Novello, his friend's personal secretary, as his own confidential assistant.

Williams disclaims any responsibility for having had Washington's sports arena renamed for Robert F. Kennedy, but it seems appropriate that his football team should play in a stadium that memorializes Kennedy.

Ed Williams and Bob Kennedy had their problems, but their differences were overshadowed by a strong mutual affection. Kennedy and Jimmy Hoffa hated each other with a passion. Although Williams continued to represent the Teamsters until 1973, the personal relationship between him and Hoffa deteriorated steadily, until it was little better than that of Hoffa and Kennedy.

The big question with Williams and Hoffa was: Who would dump the other first? By the time the 1957 bribery case was nearly over, Williams was already fed up with his client. "'I've about had it,'" he said. "'I didn't know what I was getting into with Hoffa and his friends.'"[22] The memory of Hoffa's band of sycophants, like William Bufalino, whom Williams dismisses as "the jukebox man," and "their ridiculous suggestions" still rankles.

After Hoffa's acquittal, when the Teamster chieftain found himself facing a variety of other criminal charges in New York, Chattanooga, and Chicago, Williams was always the first lawyer he would ask to defend him. Williams, however, kept refusing. "I told him that there was a conflict of interest [with Williams's job as Teamster general counsel], because I didn't want to represent him and I didn't want to have him say that he'd obviate all the objectionable things that I'd found in the bribery case. Because I had no intention of representing him again whether there was a conflict or not, or whether he obviated the problems that I'd found in the first trial." Finally, "he stopped asking me.

"I don't regret having represented him in that case. It was an important case. But I just didn't want to have the experience again of having a client over whom I didn't have the requisite control and who had a battery of lawyers around second-guessing me all the time. I have to have total power. I'm a dictator, a one-hundred-percent dictator. If I'm going to make battlefield decisions, I have to have total power. You can't send me in there with a committee any more than you can send a general into battle and have him have to consult with four other people before he moves a division to the right. They'll get their asses blown off. That's what's going to happen to you if you tell me I can't make all the decisions. Unless you're willing to surrender absolutely, then I don't take the case. And that's why I never would represent him in another case in court. I didn't want to have another experience where I have a lot of lawyers swoop down from another city and sit and second-guess me and give counsel to the defendant, and have a defendant who was a willing recipient to that counsel."

Williams had been aware almost since the end of the bribery trial and Hoffa's hiring of him as union general counsel that "Hoffa would have liked to get rid of me. I think he just didn't feel comfortable and confident that he could do that. There's no doubt in my mind that he could have fired me if he had wanted to. But I don't feel he felt secure, that he could just ask the [Teamsters'] board to toss me out. He knew that I had good friends on the board. But my relationship with him was very cold."

Strangely enough, in view of the hostility between Williams and Hoffa, in 1959 the Teamster president listed Williams as one of the six or eight people closest to him.[23] Hoffa's identification of Williams as a friend is not only curious, it's a source of vast amusement to Williams. "It's like man is a dog's best friend, huh?" comments Williams, adding, "We were never friends. We had a professional relationship. He was the president of the union I represented. I *never* saw Hoffa socially."

Another noteworthy aspect of the Williams-Hoffa association is that, according to Robert F. Kennedy, the only personal check Hoffa had written in his entire life, as of 1960, was to Williams for his services in the bribery trial. Kennedy said that "Hoffa deals only in cash: he maintains no bank account; he has written only one personal check in his life that we are aware of (that was to Edward Bennett Williams); his records are apparently nonexistent; and his memory, when it comes to where he gets his money or where it goes, is terrible."[24]

By the mid-1960s, the relationship between Williams and Hoffa had dwindled from being "volatile" or "stormy," as Williams terms it, to being nonexistent. According to a story that circulates among lawyers who dealt with Hoffa, Williams and several other people were in Hoffa's office one day while he was opening mail and handing out assignments, and Hoffa "all of a sudden threw an envelope over and it hit the floor and he said, 'Williams, you take care of that.' And Ed just got up and walked out of the room." Williams says that tale is strictly legend, as is speculation that Hoffa once hit him and gave him a black eye. He does acknowledge that he got so angry during an argument with Hoffa that he burst a blood vessel under his eye, which left him with a shiner, but insists that Hoffa never struck him.

According to Williams, his relationship with Hoffa simply petered out, without any dramatic incident. His refusal to authorize the use of Teamster funds to defend Hoffa against criminal charges was a sore spot with Hoffa and must surely have eliminated any vestiges of cordiality between them. Also, Williams sat by while Hoffa went to prison in 1967 after convictions for jury-tampering and misuse of Teamster funds, cases in which Williams had refused to defend him. Williams did continue as general counsel for the Teamsters until 1973, when Frank Fitzsimmons yanked the account over Williams's persistence in investigating Watergate.

On the fate of Jimmy Hoffa, Williams remarks with no remorse whatsoever, "I think he was murdered. I think he coveted leadership in the

Teamsters. He wanted to return to leadership, and this was not desirable for some of the powerful people on the fringes of the Teamsters who were mob-connected."

Exit, Jimmy Hoffa. Continue onward and upward, Edward Bennett Williams.

Part
SIX

The
Superlawyer

17

Frank Costello: Try, and Try Again

By the time Edward Bennett Williams and Frank Costello entered each other's life in 1956, Costello—"The Prime Minister of the Underworld"[1]—was already in deep trouble. Then sixty-five, he had been New York's "boss of all bosses" since 1937, making him the most powerful Mob figure in the U.S.,[2] but in May 1956 he had been sent to the federal penitentiary in Atlanta to begin serving a five-year sentence for income-tax evasion.[3] In addition, the federal government had been trying since 1952 to revoke his citizenship and deport him to his native Italy.[4]

In view of Costello's dire predicament, George Wolf, his personal attorney for thirty years, felt a legal magician was needed. Even Wolf had concluded that his client had lied on his citizenship papers, filed in 1925; Costello, whose primary business at the time was bootlegging, had listed his occupation as realtor. Thus Wolf was dubious about Costello's prospects of beating the denaturalization rap,[5] and he consulted with Morris Ernst, one of New York's leading lawyers. In 1955, Ernst had rented his vacation home at Nantucket to Williams, and the two lawyers were good friends. Since Ernst did not try many cases in court, he suggested to both Williams and Costello that the latter retain Williams.

There was some initial reluctance on both sides. Costello noted that Williams was "'the guy who represented McCarthy,'" and objected to hiring him, Ernst reported to Williams. Meanwhile, Williams's associates were expressing their own reservations. According to Tom Wadden, who was then in Williams's office, "The four of us—Ed and I and Eddie Cheyfitz and Colman Stein—talked it over, and Cheyfitz didn't want us to take the case and Stein wasn't sure if it would be good for Ed. At that point, nobody really knew yet where Ed's star was going. He might have been a great corporate lawyer," and accepting the Costello case could hardly have enhanced his standing in the eyes of respectable business executives. "It's always true," says Williams, "that when you get a highly controversial case, some of your associates fear there will be some economic detriment that flows from the relationship. But it has never deterred us, I'm thankful to say, never deterred anybody from this office from taking a case."

Williams formally entered the Costello tax and denaturalization cases on June 27, 1956,[6] and his research soon indicated that Costello had been the subject of extensive wiretapping by various law-enforcement agencies. Williams then began a complex series of legal maneuvers aimed at overturning both the citizenship proceeding and the income-tax conviction on the ground that the government's evidence had been gathered illegally. His efforts succeeded at once when he secured Costello's release from prison on $25,000 bail in March 1957, pending a Supreme Court review of the income-tax case.[7] Costello regarded this success as "a miracle," and "hailed Williams as his knight in shining armor."[8] He gushed, "'I've had 40 lawyers. . . . But Ed's the champ. Ed's the champ. It's like playing dice. Man throws the six, he can't pay off. Ed makes the point. Ed makes the point.'"[9]

Williams's relationship with Costello was as warm as his and Jimmy Hoffa's had been cold. He regarded Costello as "a very pleasant fellow," one who "had his own strong moral code," although it may not have been "exactly your code or my code." Costello reciprocated Williams's affection, and his seal of approval made Williams a prince of the city. It entitled him to the best table at places like Toots Shor's, to tickets for Broadway smash hits that were impossible for common folk to obtain, to chauffeur service with Albert Anastasia's personal driver at the wheel. Once, before Costello was released on bail, Williams had arranged for him to be transferred to the West Street Federal Detention Center in New York, where attorney and client could meet more conveniently than in Atlanta. At the time, Williams had been trying unsuccessfully to get tickets to *My Fair Lady* for himself, his first wife, and her parents. During a jailhouse visit with Costello, Williams mentioned his disappointment. "He immediately said, 'You can't get any tickets? Let me see if I can't help you.' I was staying at the Ambassador Hotel. I went back and that afternoon some fellow knocked on the door and gave me four tickets. Frank just somehow made contact and got me the house seats." Tom Wadden recalls, "It was a heady time. Ed took New York by storm. Ed was thirty-five or so and I was a couple of years younger, and we had the world by the tail. I mean, hell, here are a couple of poor boys wandering around New York, Toots Shor's was our unofficial office, they're taking our phone calls, [Joe] Dimag[gio] was always around."

Albert Anastasia, a Costello henchman and the head of Murder, Incorporated, "took some strange liking to me," according to Williams, "and he always wanted to know when I was coming to New York so he could pick me up at the airport. He was always doing me favors"—favors that Williams had not sought. Early on in Williams's association with Costello and Anastasia, the latter "sent a sort of panel truck filled with toys" for the three Williams children to the lawyer's home outside of Washington. Williams was not there at the time, "and my wife was kind of frightened because these two fellows who didn't look too much as though they should be there were sitting out front in a truck. It turned out that Albert had sent all these toys to my kids. It was so incredible. They had just loads and loads of toys," which Williams sent to an orphanage. Everything Anastasia did "was in excess. He gave my wife a box of Joy perfume, the most expensive there was. And when I say a box, I mean one of those boxes," said Williams, extending his hands. "We used to make jokes about it." Such tokens of Anastasia's esteem for Williams did not continue for long. A year or so after Williams became Costello's attorney, Anastasia paid an ill-fated, and final, visit to his barber.

Several months before Anastasia was murdered, Williams's client was a victim of violence. On May 2, 1957, two months after Williams had obtained his release from Atlanta, Costello dined with his wife and friends at the Monsignore Restaurant on East Fifty-fifth Street near Madison Avenue.[10] About 10:45, he said he had to go home, where he was expecting "'a very important phone call'" from Williams. As he walked into the lobby of his apartment house at 115 Central Park West, a heavyset gunman approached him, said "'This is for you, Frank,'" and fired a shot at his head at point-blank range.[11] The hit man had a better way with words than with weapons; Costello suffered only a superficial head wound.[12] He was taken to Roosevelt Hospital, and while the injury was being treated, police removed some items from his jacket, which was hanging on a chair. Among them were $3,200 in cash—of which New York's finest returned all but $2,400[13]—and a slip of paper that bore the following figures: "Gross Casino Wins as of 4/26/57, $651,294; Casino Wins Less Markers, $434,695; Slot Wins, $62,844, Markers, $153,745; Mike, $150 per week; Jake, $100 per week; L, $30,000; H, $9,000." The police returned the paper, too, but not until after they had photocopied it.[14]

Costello told the police he hadn't seen his assailant, although one of his doctors said the path of the bullet along his scalp indicated that he must have been looking right at the gunman as he was shot. When Costello was called before a New York City grand jury investigating the attack, Al Scotti, chief assistant district attorney, realized he would follow the Mafia's code of silence and that any effort to learn from him who had shot him would be "'an exercise in futility.'" What Scotti did hope to learn, however, was any connection Costello might have had with the newly opened Tropicana Hotel and Casino in Las Vegas, where the gambling receipts matched the figures scrawled on the slip of paper found in Costello's jacket.

Costello refused to answer any questions about the matter, pleading the Fifth Amendment, despite being granted immunity from prosecution. Williams argued that the slip of paper had nothing to do with the attempt on Costello's life and was therefore irrelevant. But the judge found persuasive Scotti's claim that a fight over distribution of proceeds from the Tropicana could have caused the attack, and held that the paper was not seized illegally because Costello was not wearing the jacket when it was taken.[15]

At that point, Williams had no alternative but to inform Costello that he had to answer Scotti's questions. "I told him this in an empty courtroom where we had been permitted to go so that I could counsel with him. It was a very high, high-ceilinged courtroom in an old building. The ceilings were maybe three or four stories high. And he started to cry. He said, 'You've done so much for me. You've won my case for me. And now you have me released while the Supreme Court is considering my conviction. I want to do everything you tell me, but now you're asking me to do something I can't do any more than I could hit my head off that ceiling from a standing jump.' He couldn't bring himself ever to give evidence against anybody. It would have broken his code, and his code was part of his life."

Costello continued refusing to answer Scotti's questions, was found in contempt of court, just as Williams had told him he would be, and was sentenced to thirty days in jail. He served half the sentence, and was then released on $1,000 bail.[16] (He might have been freed four days earlier, but he insisted on waiting until Williams, who was tied up on another case, was able to return to court with him.[17])

A hood named Vincent Gigante, allegedly in the employ of Vito Genovese, who had hoped to replace Costello as Mafia boss in New York,[18] was subsequently tried for the attack on Costello. The victim hadn't even confided his assailant's identity to Williams; when Williams had asked, "'Frank, who the hell shot you?' he says, 'What do you think? McKinley knew who shot him?'" Naturally, then, he refused to finger Gigante, who was acquitted, even though the doorman who had been on duty at Costello's apartment house the night of the shooting identified Gigante as the gunman.[19]

In 1958, after Williams had exhausted Costello's appeals in the tax case, he was returned to Atlanta, where Genovese was also incarcerated. Because Costello had upheld the code of silence, the two patched up their differences and Genovese joined Costello in Williams's stable of clients.

In the income-tax-evasion case in which Costello had been indicted on March 11, 1953, he was charged with underpaying his federal taxes from 1946 through 1949. After a six-week trial in 1954, he had been acquitted as to his 1946 taxes, but convicted of evading about $51,000 in taxes for the years 1947, 1948, and 1949. On May 17, 1954, he was sentenced to five years in prison on each count, to run concurrently, and fined $10,000 for each of the three years he had underpaid his taxes.[20] In 1955, the U.S. Circuit Court of Appeals reversed his conviction for 1947, but let stand the guilty verdicts for 1948 and 1949, which reduced his fine but had no effect on his prison term.[21]

Before Williams entered the case, Costello's attorneys had already appealed the convictions to the U.S. Supreme Court, which had upheld the convictions for 1948 and 1949, rejecting Costello's argument that the original indictment against him had been based on inadmissible hearsay evidence.[22]

Following the loss of his first appeal, Costello, claiming that his age—sixty-five—and his poor health made his five-year sentence "tantamount to life imprisonment," offered to leave the country, which would have rendered unnecessary the government's efforts to deport him.[23] Prosecutors were in no mood for an after-the-fact bargain; to them, "Costello's name had become a household word for the successful tax evader who placed himself above the law," and his imprisonment "served notice to all taxpayers everywhere that no one was above the law."[24]

Costello's next ploy, just before Williams joined his team of lawyers in 1956, was an attempt to have his sentence overturned on the ground that it was excessive, an argument that was rejected by the U.S. District Court in Manhattan.[25] When Williams carried the appeal of this motion to the Supreme Court, it was on the question of the length of Costello's sentence that the High Court ordered him released on $25,000 bail on March 11, 1957. The Supreme Court held three months later that Costello had been sentenced properly,[26] but he remained free because in the meantime Williams had filed yet another motion for a new trial, this one based on the extensive wiretapping he said had been used to trap Costello.[27]

In support of this motion, Williams filed an affidavit in which he asserted that the New York District Attorney's Office had "continuously" tapped Costello's phones for at least eleven years, from May 1943 until Costello's conviction in the income tax case.[28] But Arthur Christy, the assistant U.S. attorney in charge of the Costello prosecution, maintained that while he had been aware that the New York D.A.'s Office had bugged Costello on occasion, he and his staff had not used information from the taps in assembling their case against Costello. "During the time I was assigned to the Costello case," declared Christy, "I never saw a transcript of any intercepted telephone conversation of Costello."[29]

During his research into the methods the D.A. had employed in the Costello probe, Williams obtained under subpoena transcriptions of 242 conversations involving Costello, his family and friends, and even innocent bystanders who had happened to place calls from pay phones Costello was known to use. These records disclosed that Costello had been the subject of wiretaps during six months in 1943, three months in 1946, and from September 1950 until April 15, 1952[30]—income-tax day. The extent of the taps enraged Williams, who reported that six policemen, working in teams of two, had listened in on Costello around the clock, monitoring "every conversation over Costello's telephone whether he was a participant or not," overhearing talks between the gangster and his wife, between Mrs. Costello and her family, and even between a Costello family maid and her husband, "baring the most confidential and intimate family secrets," and even eavesdropping on "the tender words of sweethearts" and others who used the pay phones in Costello's haunts.

"The most intimate details of the lives of these people became a matter of record in the files of the New York City Police Department," said Williams, adding that wiretapping is "like an atom bomb. You can't pick your victims. As many people can be killed by the fallout as by the hit."[31]

At one point, Williams tried to subpoena the entire wiretap file of the New York City Police Department,[32] perhaps because of the stiff resistance put up by the office of D.A. Frank Hogan. Williams stated that "I feel at this time . . . that maybe we are the world's leading authority on how much diligence it takes to get this information. . . . It has been acquisition of information by extraction and it has been . . . very, very difficult" to obtain.[33] In fact, Williams's efforts led him to subpoena Frank Hogan himself; New York Police Commissioner Stephen Kennedy; Charles Tenney, New York's commissioner of investigations; and the heads of the Manhattan offices of the U.S. Treasury Department, Immigration Service, Internal Revenue Service, and the tax unit of the federal Alcohol and Tobacco Agency.[34]

A hearing on the defense motion to overturn Costello's conviction because of the wiretaps opened in U.S. District Court in New York in June 1957. One of the first witnesses called by Williams was William J. Mellin, a retired special agent for the U.S. Treasury Department. Mellin, calling himself simply a technician whose specialty happened to be installing wiretaps, said that between 1934 and 1937 he had placed 9,800 bugs, or about ten a day,[35] several of which, at the direction of the IRS, were placed on telephones used by Costello. And, Mellin added, since his job was merely to install the wiretaps, not remove them, the Costello bugs, which he had installed in 1937, "might still be there" for all he knew.[36]

The hearing had been on for only two days when the crisis previously mentioned arose: Judge Burnita Shelton Matthews, who was presiding over the Hoffa bribery trial, demanded Williams's presence in her court-room in Washington. The Justice Department, which was involved in both cases, was so eager to proceed with the Hoffa trial that it allowed Costello to remain free on bail until the Hoffa matter was resolved. By the time Hoffa was acquitted in July, however, the federal courts in New York were in recess for the summer and the Costello hearing did not resume until October 7.

One week later, Williams called John Cye Cheasty to testify for Costel-lo. The wiretap records had disclosed that Cheasty had been one of the government agents who had listened in on Costello's conversations. Cheasty was, of course, the same man whose credibility Williams had destroyed three months earlier during the Hoffa trial. Giving his present occupation as assistant counsel for the McClellan Rackets Committee, Cheasty said that during the 1930s he had served as an intelligence agent for the IRS. In 1936 or 1937, "I assisted in the interception of some calls" involving Costello, said Cheasty, who enlivened the courtroom as he relat-ed how the surveillance turned into a circus: Mellin, intending to install a tap on the New Yorker Hotel room of Seymour Weiss, a Costello asso-ciate from New Orleans, instead set a bug on the phone of Harold G. Hoffman—who was then governor of New Jersey. As Cheasty admitted in a mild understatement, "That was a mistake.... We bridged the wrong ... [phone] there. Then we had to get hold of Mellin and change it." Asked by Williams whether he could have installed the tap himself, Cheasty replied, "Well, there are no qualifications. If you have a screw-driver and a pair of pliers, you can do it."

According to Cheasty, his job, in addition to monitoring the bug, was to "hang out there and hold on to"—meaning "to maintain a surveillance of"—"whoever it was that would seem to be moving, particularly Si Weiss." One day Costello, Weiss, and another man from New Orleans, Phil Kastel, ate lunch in the hotel's Manhattan Room. Who should be dining at the next table but J. Edgar Hoover and his best friend and most trusted aide, Clyde Tolson! While Cheasty watched, "those three fellows, Costello, Kastel and Weiss, hurriedly finished their meal and left there." In fact, Costello and his sidekicks not only left the Manhattan Room, they left town, tailed by Cheasty to Pennsylvania Station and then to Newark Airport.[37]

Williams contended that in addition to bugging Costello, the govern-ment had resorted to other illegal tactics, such as intercepting his mail and screening the tax returns of prospective jurors in the hope of picking a jury that would view favorably the evidence against Costello. The govern-ment's action, according to Williams, "deprived [Costello] of an impartial jury," and "should be condemned as a governmental intimidation of all prospective jurors."[38]

In a rather unusual tactic aimed at corroborating his claim that prospective jurors' tax returns had been scrutinized, Williams asked prosecutor Arthur Christy to testify—but got little out of him.[39] Christy recalls that he had been forewarned about Williams's courtroom skills, so nothing Williams did really shocked him. "He was a very able lawyer, certainly the best one that I had ever been up against," says Christy. "You had to watch him like a hawk." In contrast with other attorneys, "You couldn't let your mind wander at any time"—especially while being examined by Williams.

In spite of the various arguments that Williams propounded on Costello's behalf, Judge John F. X. McGohey denied his motion for a new trial "in all respects" in a ruling in December 1957.[40] Within a week Williams filed notice of an appeal.[41] The Second Circuit Court of Appeals not only upheld McGohey's decision but criticized the lawyers who had represented Costello at the original trial—before Williams's entry—because they had not "made any effort" to learn whether the evidence against Costello was the product of wiretaps. "Such inaction, in our opinion, constituted a lack of diligence which warranted denial of the motion" for a new trial.[42] Costello's last appeals were exhausted in June 1958 when the Supreme Court sustained the lower-court rulings,[43] and he returned to Atlanta—after an unusual eighteen-month interlude courtesy of Williams. With time off for good behavior, he was released in June 1961, having served forty-two months of his five-year term.[44]

What was Frank Costello's primary business in 1925? That was the central question in the federal government's action to strip him of his citizenship.

Costello, born Francesco Castiglia in Cosenza, Italy, on January 26, 1891, and brought to New York in 1895, married an American citizen in 1914 and applied for citizenship on May 1, 1925, listing his occupation as "'real estate.'" He became a naturalized U.S. citizen on September 10, 1925.[45]

The government opened its campaign to revoke his citizenship and deport him in October 1952, six months after he was convicted of refusing to answer questions as a witness during Senator Estes Kefauver's hearings on organized crime.[46] The case lay dormant while the government went ahead with its income-tax-evasion case and convicted him. After Costello went to prison in 1956, the citizenship proceedings were cranked up again and Williams was called into the case. At a September 1956 hearing before U.S. District Judge Edmund L. Palmieri in New York, Costello testified that during the five years before he was granted citizenship in 1925 he was in the ice-cream business, had sold Kewpie dolls, and was president of Koslo Real Estate Company in New York. Most of these answers were ordered by Judge Palmieri over Williams's objections that pertained to illegal wiretaps.[47]

The government offered an entirely different version of Costello's activities, calling a number of his former associates to show that at the time he had been granted citizenship and for several years before, his main source of income had been from bootlegging. One of his principal colleagues, Emanuel Kessler, testified that starting in 1920 he had owned a ship that carried liquor from Europe to the Long Island coast, where the contraband was landed at night in small boats and transported into New York in Costello's trucks. That partnership lasted until Kessler was sent to prison for bootlegging in 1923. Kessler also asserted that Costello had stolen 500 cases of whiskey from him during their alliance and that after he went to prison Costello took another 100 or 200 cases and refused to pay for them.

Albert Feldman, who had also been involved in the scheme, told the court Costello had agreed to store 1,000 cases of Kessler's liquor and then had claimed to have a customer for them in Buffalo; however, the booze disappeared en route and Costello never paid for it. Helen Sausser, daughter of another bootlegging associate of Costello's, said that her father and Costello were in the rum-running business together and that after her father's death in 1926 Costello had wired her mother "promising to forward money, but never did so." Several other witnesses gave similar testimony, identifying Costello as a bootlegger during the period immediately before he became an American citizen.

Costello's own earlier statements were also used against him. The government demonstrated that he had told an IRS agent in 1938 that he was a bootlegger from about 1923 until the early 1930s; had testified before a federal grand jury in 1939 that he "'did a little bootlegging,'" and that "'the last time was around 1926'"; had stated under oath before a New York State grand jury in 1943 that he earned money during Prohibition "'bringing a little whiskey in'"; and had told the same grand jury that he had reported total income of $305,000 on his state income-tax returns from 1919 to 1932, including $134,000 for the years 1927, 1929, and 1930, most of it from illegally transporting liquor.[48]

Williams reverted to the issue of wiretapping. He maintained that "it was common knowledge" that Costello's telephone had been tapped by law-enforcement officials in 1925, as a result of which Costello and many others had been indicted for violating the Prohibition Act. Later on, he said, the New York D.A.'s Office had tapped Costello's phone, then "exchanged these wire-taps around" with the U.S. attorney in Manhattan and the Kefauver Committee. The various incriminating statements made by Costello over the years, according to Williams, had been in response to questions based on facts gathered from the illegal bugging.[49]

Judge Palmieri ruled in favor of Costello, declaring that "Wiretaps were extensively used and ... there were innumerable wiretaps. ... The wiretapping was so extensive and of such a far-reaching nature that it is well nigh impossible for me to determine what may be admissible and untainted from that which is inadmissible and tainted." He ordered the case dismissed without prejudice, meaning that the government could file a new suit if it could prove that its evidence was not the product of illegal methods.[50]

Williams had won round one for Costello, but it would be more than six years before Costello was in the clear. The first setback occurred nearly a year after the initial victory, when the court of appeals reversed Judge Palmieri, holding that he should not have dismissed the case. The wiretap evidence, the court ruled, was admissible in federal court.[51] Williams quickly appealed that decision to the Supreme Court, which did indeed hold that the government had failed to file the proper documents in the Costello proceeding and that the complaint, therefore, should be dismissed.[52] But that win, too, was short-lived. The government at once filed a new suit to revoke Costello's citizenship.[53] This time, everything went in the government's favor. In the lower court, a different U.S. district judge, Archie Dawson, issued a scathing denunciation of Costello and his history:

> We have the situation, so far as the records indicate, that prior to the time that Costello had sworn that his occupation was "real estate" he personally had engaged in only one real estate transfer in his own name. ... During the same period, as the evidence shows and as Costello has admitted, he was actively engaged in bootlegging on a large scale and with very profitable results. If a man in that situation had been honest when asked what his occupation was, would he have answered "real estate?" If he had told the truth he probably would not have been naturalized, but this is no excuse for his using fraud and deceit to secure his naturalization.

Judge Dawson also rejected Williams's contention that when the naturalization form asked for Costello's occupation, it meant his legal occupation—as opposed to his illegal one. He took Costello to task for treating his application in cavalier form, as if he were seeking "to join the corner pinochle club," and ruled that he had "secured his naturalization by concealment of material facts and by willful misrepresentation."

As to the wiretapping aspect, Dawson stated that "not even Costello's ingeniously alert counsel" dared contend that the bugging of Costello's phones "gave him immunity for past illegal activities." He ruled that the government's case had not been based on information it had learned from the taps and that Costello's naturalization papers should be "revoked" and "cancelled."[54]

Once again Williams carried Costello's appeal to the top, but this time he lost, in both the Court of Appeals[55] and the Supreme Court. Speaking for the High Court, Justice William Brennan said, "We find no merit in any of these contentions" raised by Williams.[56] Costello's only consolation was a dissent by Justice William O. Douglas,* who reasoned that using bootlegging as a basis for denying citizenship in the 1920s "would be an act of hypocrisy unparalleled in American life," since "the 'bootlegger' in those days came into being because of the demand of the great bulk of people in our communities—including lawyers, prosecutors, and judges— for his products." Furthermore, said Douglas, the form Costello had filled out had merely asked for *an* occupation, not for his primary vocation, so Costello "answered truthfully when he listed 'real estate' as his 'occupation.'"[58]

Costello regarded Douglas's dissent as "one of the great legal opinions of our time," since it embraced his own explanation for his involvement in bootlegging: "This was a public demand, and he merely filled the demand."[59] But unless Williams could pull another rabbit out of his hat, Costello would soon find himself in another country.

On May 23, 1961, three months after the Supreme Court ruling, Costello was called to a hearing inside the Atlanta Federal Penitentiary "to determine whether or not you should be deported from the United States."[60] At the hearing, conducted by a special federal officer and attended by an agent of the Immigration and Naturalization Service, Williams, who was allowed to be present, refused to permit Costello to answer any questions of substance. His position was that Costello "does not have to give evidence against himself in this hearing," and he prevented Costello from responding even to the question "Mr. Costello, are you here in this institution, United States Penitentiary, Atlanta, Georgia, serving a five-year term of imprisonment imposed upon your conviction on May 17, 1954 [for tax evasion]?"[61]

To the hearing examiner's final question—"Mr. Costello, this is a question asked of all respondents in deportation hearings. In the event you are deported, to which country do you prefer to go?"—Williams answered for Costello: "The respondent, Mr. Examiner, wants to decline most respectfully to name a preference."[62]

Williams still chuckles over the memory of the government's invitation. "We had an obligation under the McCarran Act; once you're denaturalized and they want to deport you, the act made it mandatory that you try to get some country to take you. So we used to write these letters to various countries, and we'd make full disclosure of Costello's *curriculum vitae*"—including his various arrests, convictions, imprisonments, and

---

*The decision was by a vote of 6–2, with Justice Hugo Black joining in Douglas's dissent and Justice John M. Harlan—who, as an assistant U.S. attorney in New York, had at one time been in charge of the Costello investigation—abstaining.[57]

aliases, along with pointed references to his past occupations as bootlegger and gambler. In each letter, Costello would say, "'I'd very much like to come and live in your country.'" Strangely enough, says Williams, every letter would "come back and they'd say, no, he can't come. But we complied with the law. We applied to all these countries, but they wouldn't take him."

But Williams did tell the examiner that, in view of the decisions revoking Costello's citizenship,. "He is not now and never was a citizen. . . . So that there is no mystery . . . it is our legal position that he is now a citizen of nowhere."[63]

Even though Costello was for all intents and purposes a man without a country, the hearing officer ruled that he should be deported because he had been convicted of two crimes involving moral turpitude: purposely evading his federal income taxes for both 1948 and 1949. The officer noted that Costello was "given the opportunity to specify the country to which he would prefer to go if deported, and he declined to do so."[64]

Williams sought to overturn the decision before the Board of Immigration Appeals, but, predictably, the Board ruled against Costello and, on January 2, 1962, ordered him deported.[65] Nine days later, INS notified Costello and Williams that Costello was being deported to Italy.[66] This did not sit well with them or with the Italian government. A spokesman for the Italian foreign ministry declared:

> "Italy should not be expected to carry the burden of a man who was born in Italy, lived here only a short time, and then spent most of his life in the United States. . . . It's not blood that makes a man a criminal; it's society, and we definitely do not want to pay for such men."[67]

As a last slim hope, Williams filed a petition with the Second Circuit Court of Appeals, asking for yet another review of Costello's case.[68] Most lawyers familiar with the proceedings thought he "was skating on very thin ice," and his moves were viewed as "merely delaying tactics."[69] The experts seemed to be right when the circuit court turned down the appeal.[70] But there was room for one last appeal to the Supreme Court, which did agree to review the deportation on one point raised by Williams: whether the INS had correctly applied to Costello's situation the section of the Immigration Act that provided for the deporting of aliens convicted of two or more crimes. Williams argued that the provision did not apply to Costello because he was a naturalized citizen, and not an alien, at the time of his convictions.[71]

Williams and Costello won the only decision that counted—the last one—when the High Court ruled in their favor. On February 17, 1964, in another 6–2 verdict, the Court held that the law under which the INS had sought to deport Costello applied only to aliens, not to naturalized citizens. In an opinion delivered by Justice Potter Stewart, the Court majority decreed, "The reality is that the petitioner's convictions occurred when he was a naturalized citizen, as he had been for almost 30 years"—even though the government had since revoked his citizenship. Therefore, the section of the law that the INS had relied on did not cover the case.[72] Justice Byron White, in an angry dissent joined by Justice Tom Clark, pointed out that Costello's "fraud" in obtaining his citizenship "becomes his ready and effective shield." According to White, Costello "was not a citizen in 1954 [when he was convicted of tax evasion] because he did not become a citizen [legally] in 1924." For that reason, Costello had always been "actually an alien under the law," but the Court's present decision enabled him to use "a certificate of citizenship, obtained by his own fraud," as a means "to continue the masquerade and to claim the protections of citizenship."[73]

Both White's logic and his words were strong. But, as a veteran gambler like Costello knew very well, any bettor who cashes six out of eight tickets is on Easy Street.

Frank Costello died on February 18, 1973, at the age of eighty-two, after suffering a heart attack at his home at 115 Central Park West. Thanks to the campaign mounted by Williams, he spent his last years puttering around the garden of his home on Long Island,[74] and he is generally believed to have been Mario Puzo's model for *The Godfather*. Costello and Williams remained friendly until the end.

The talents Williams displayed on behalf of Costello earned him not only the affection of his client but also the praise of an expert observer, Supreme Court Justice William O. Douglas. Douglas singled out Williams's conduct of the Costello immigration case as substantiation for his statement that

> Edward Bennett Williams, best known perhaps as a criminal lawyer, could certainly be in any list of the top appellate advocates who appeared [before the Court] in my time [1939 to 1975]. He argued both civil and criminal cases and had the rare capacity of being able to reduce a complicated record to a few simple capsules that marked the heart of the case.[75]

18

Bernard Goldfine:
Jack Anderson's Close Call

T he greatest morass of concealment, dissemblance and demonstrable perjury to which I have ever been exposed in a courtroom"[1]—thus Edward Bennett Williams described the testimony of Jack Anderson, then Drew Pearson's top reporter, and Baron Shacklette, a congressional investigator, in a case involving Williams's client, Bernard Goldfine. Williams had summoned Anderson and Shacklette into court to have them explain why they and a recording device had been discovered in a Washington hotel room next door to that of Goldfine, a New England industrialist and influence-seeker whose machinations helped bring down Sherman Adams, top aide to President Eisenhower.

Williams was attempting to prove that Goldfine had been unfairly indicted for contempt of Congress because the questions Goldfine had refused to answer at a congressional hearing were based on information obtained illegally by Anderson and Shacklette. Assistant U.S. Attorney William Hitz, Goldfine's prosecutor, was on the opposite side from Williams in the Goldfine contempt-of-Congress case, but he felt the same way about the veracity of the testimony by Anderson and Shacklette. Hitz argued to his superior, Oliver Gasch, U.S. attorney for the District of Columbia, that a federal grand jury should be convened to review Anderson's statements under oath, as a first step toward prosecuting Anderson for perjury. But Gasch swiveled around in his chair, "gazed out the window and was silent." Gasch never mentioned Anderson's situation again, and in the absence of any authorization from the chief prosecutor, Hitz did not pursue the matter.

Bernard Goldfine had immigrated from Europe to East Boston in 1897 when he was seven and a half. Twelve years later, he had scraped together $1,200, which he used to start his own business. During the next half-century, he amassed a half-dozen New England textile mills, as well as extensive real-estate holdings. He had a policy of "always supporting my friends as I could within my means," and those friends included New Hampshire's two GOP senators—Norris Cotton (a partner in one of Goldfine's ventures) and Styles Bridges; Senator Frederick Payne (R-Maine); Governor Foster Furcolo of Massachusetts (one of the few Democrats among Goldfine's "friends"); and, most important of all, Sherman Adams, a former governor of New Hampshire who had become Eisenhower's chief of staff. Along the way, Goldfine had also acquired so much legal talent that it was said, "'He doesn't have a lawyer, he's got a bar association.'"[2]

In 1958, when Goldfine was first under scrutiny for his alleged efforts to buy powerful politicians by distributing vicuna coats and other goodies, he had hired Edward Bennett Williams on the advice of Payne and Cotton. When Sherman Adams pointed out that Williams had represented Joe McCarthy* and Jimmy Hoffa, so perhaps Goldfine should consider another lawyer, he did call Williams, said he had decided to change attorneys, but "requested that Williams send him a big bill. Williams replied that he had been fired before and there would be no charge."[3]

Hearings before the House of Representatives Subcommittee on Legislative Oversight in June 1958 disclosed that Goldfine had purchased a vicuna coat and two suits for Adams and paid $3,000 worth of Adams's hotel bills, and that Adams had made phone calls to the Federal Trade Commission and the Securities and Exchange Commission, which were studying Goldfine's affairs.[4] Adams, who had previously asserted executive privilege when refusing to testify before congressional committees, broke precedent and agreed to appear at a hearing of the Legislative Oversight Subcommittee. At the time, the White House issued a statement that the president "knows of no individual in or out of Government that he has more confidence in than Sherman Adams."[5] As the evidence mounted up, however, Eisenhower conceded that his most prized assistant

---

*Unlike Vice President Nixon, who was friendly with McCarthy and had tried to ease him out of his difficulties in the Senate, Eisenhower had been a behind-the-scenes advocate of the Senate's disciplining McCarthy.

had been "'imprudent'" in making contacts on behalf of Goldfine,[6] and Adams, described by former president Truman as the man who was "'running'" the government under Eisenhower,[7] was finally forced to resign from the White House staff in September 1958 as a result of his dealings with Goldfine.[8]

During the course of the subcommittee's investigations, Goldfine himself was called as a witness. He showed up with several attorneys, led by Roger Robb of Washington, later a federal appellate judge. Testifying voluntarily, Goldfine admitted that he had given Christmas checks to thirty-three past and current White House and congressional employees, but he declined to answer several dozen other questions about his personal finances. Williams was not yet his attorney, but on the advice of Robb and his other lawyers, he said repeatedly that questions posed by members of the subcommittee were "'not pertinent to the committee's inquiry'"[9]—the same line Williams had used successfully in defending Aldo Icardi. He was then placed under subpoena, the same questions were posed to him again, and he was ordered by Subcommittee Chairman Oren Harris (D-Ark.) to answer them.[10] But Goldfine persisted in his refusal to respond and the House of Representatives voted almost unanimously to cite him for contempt.[11]

Several months later, on December 9, 1958, Goldfine was indicted on eighteen counts of contempt of Congress, each count based on a question he had declined to answer. He faced a year in prison and a fine of $1,000 on each count.[12] But Williams, whom Goldfine had recently rehired to defend him against the contempt charges, had reason to believe he could have the indictment quashed.

Unknown to Roger Robb, the shoes he could see near a door between Bernard Goldfine's hotel suite and the adjacent room were filled by the feet of Jack Anderson. Robb made this discovery late on Sunday evening, July 6, 1958, while he and Jack Lotto, one of Goldfine's publicists, awaited the arrival of reporters who had been promised a press release. The Goldfine crew was staying at Washington's Sheraton Carlton Hotel while the financier was appearing before the House subcommittee. Robb observed "a bar of light" shining under the door from the next room. Robb later testified that, lying down flat on his belly,

> I saw within about 2 or 3 inches of the door on the other side the toes of a man's shoes. I remember they were tan shoes. They were pointing toward the door and my first thought was that somebody had put his shoes down and then they moved and I knew there was a man in the shoes and he was obviously standing facing the door in close proximity to it, in a position that one would occupy if he were eavesdropping.[13]

Another Goldfine aide had a look and reported to Robb, "'I saw the man's hand on the floor down there. He is apparently on the floor.'" Robb went to the lobby to use a pay phone and called Lloyd Furr, a private detective and former policeman. Furr arrived before long and, according to Robb, used "some electronic device" to determine that there was "a microphone next door." Furr then looked under the door, saw the microphone, and asked Robb, "'Do you want me to get it?'" Robb said, "'Sure.' So [Furr] took a coat hanger out of the closet, a wire coat hanger, and bent a hook in the end of it and inserted the hook under the door and with a very quick movement sneaked out the microphone and about 8 or 10 feet of wire."[14]

Panic prevailed on the other side of that door. The occupants of the room adjoining Goldfine's suite were Baron Shacklette, an investigator for the Legislative Oversight Subcommittee, and Jack Anderson. Shacklette testified later that he was resting on the bed and Anderson was "lying on the floor beside the bed." Suddenly, "Mr. Anderson grabbed hold of my arm and said, 'I think they found the mike.' I was pretty much asleep but I jumped up and . . . grabbed the wire and pulled and somebody pulled on the other side and the wire broke."[15]

Anderson had registered in the hotel as "Elliott Brooks of Salt Lake City,"[16] and an assistant manager of the hotel, summoned by Goldfine's people, called into the room, "'Mr. Brooks, will you please come to the door?'" The hotel man also used a passkey to unlock the door, but Anderson and Shacklette refused to remove the chain.[17] Meanwhile, according to Anderson, a woman from the Goldfine suite telephoned the "Brooks" room "and shouted a couple of obscenities into the phone."

Anderson and Shacklette, who understandably "were quite startled at getting caught, and very disturbed over it," attempted "to recoup our forces. . . . We talked it over for a bit."[18] But after a half-hour, an impatient newsman climbed on a chair in the hall, peaked over the transom into the "Brooks" room, and exclaimed, "'Well, I saw who is in there, it is Jack Anderson.'"[19] Anderson and Shacklette finally opened the door, whereupon Lloyd Furr administered the ultimate insult to a rival investigator, handing the sheepish Shacklette his card and saying, "'I am a private detective. The next time you want any investigating work done, call me.'"[20] Shacklette then spotted Roger Robb and said, "'You stole my microphone,' to which I smiled," Robb said.[21]

Shortly after breakfast the next morning, Goldfine and his entourage moved with great fanfare to the Statler Hotel across the street, as Goldfine's press agent, Lotto, announced, "'We're leaving the bughouse.'"[22] And Baron Shacklette called Oren Harris, chairman of the Legislative Oversight Subcommittee, and told him, "'I got caught, boss, I am sorry.'"[23] Harris promptly called his panel into emergency session, during which Shacklette described what had happened and "resigned."[24] Jack Anderson also notified his boss, Drew Pearson, of the catastrophe. Some of Pearson's advisers suggested that he suspend Anderson over this "very embarrassing situation," but Pearson instead issued a statement paraphrasing Eisenhower's initial defense of Sherman Adams: "'Jack Anderson, of course, has been imprudent. But I need him.'"[25]

In fact, there was a suspicion that Anderson and Shacklette were up to other tricks beside eavesdropping. At the hearing on Williams's motion to quash the indictment of Goldfine, Tom LaVenia, a private detective who had done work for Williams and was friendly with Shacklette, testified that Shacklette had invited him to the "Elliott Brooks" hotel room, showed him a large closet, and said, "'I can stand here,' and he did say . . . 'Jack went to the door, I could not be seen from the door by Jack's contact. Jack brought in the material, handed it to me in the closet, and I photostated it. The contact came back twice to find out if we were finished, and I could hear Jack talking to him at the door. When he came back the second time, Jack turned the papers over to him.'"[26]

In this connection, while Anderson was on the witness stand, Williams charged that "documents belonging to Mr. Goldfine . . . which were in Miss Paperman's room [Mildred Paperman was Goldfine's secretary] bore your fingerprints."[27] A police fingerprint expert testified that twenty-one points of an Anderson print—nine more than were necessary for a "very safe" identification—had been found on an envelope marked "personal" that was in Paperman's room at the hotel.[28] A police detective, asked by Williams why Anderson had not been charged with illegal entry, testified that the decision not to arrest Anderson was "based on my belief that Anderson, himself, did not go into the room, but it was my belief that he had seen the papers."[29] Anderson, while admitting that he felt "a little sheepish" about eavesdropping on what turned out to be a press conference at the time he was caught,[30] stated emphatically, "I had nothing to do, directly, indirectly, at any time or any place, in any hotel, from anybody's room, with any theft of any documents."[31]

But Anderson's most serious scrape was the result of his refusal to disclose who had provided him with a tape recorder he took to Goldfine's hotel.* He did testify that "right after church" on Sunday, June 29, 1958, he had driven to a home in Chevy Chase, Maryland, several blocks from the line between Maryland and Washington, where he picked up the recorder. He insisted, however, that he couldn't recall the identity of the person who had given it to him, or the man's address.[33] In fact, he was so secretive about the arrangement that he even withheld the name from Shacklette.[34]

It now appears that the audio equipment was provided by a top official

---

* After all the trouble Anderson went to to obtain the instrument and protect the identity of its owner, the tape recorder did not work properly and had to be replaced with one that Tom LaVenia provided.[32]

of the FBI, perhaps with the Bureau's knowledge and consent. An unimpeachable source says that Warren Woods, the attorney for Anderson and Drew Pearson, called prosecutor William Hitz at his home in Bethesda, Maryland, right after Anderson testified, and requested an urgent meeting. At Woods's suggestion, the two men met in Hitz's garden, where they could talk "privately," without fear of being overheard, and Woods told Hitz that "Jack Anderson had committed perjury when he stated on the stand that he did not know from whom he had obtained the tape recorder. In actuality," the same source states, "he got it from an assistant director of the FBI. Anderson and this assistant director had been very good friends, and of course he knew where the man lived, although he said that he did not under oath." Woods is further reported to have said that he "hoped" Hitz would "not get him [Anderson] indicted for perjury," because he was only protecting his source.

But Hitz refused to make any promises. He pursued the matter and then asked Oliver Gasch for permission to present the case to the grand jury. Gasch took no action. In 1981, Woods admitted several times that he was "surprised" that Anderson had not been prosecuted over the Goldfine case. Yet Anderson still maintains that he doesn't know who gave him the recorder. Ironically, in view of the furor over Anderson's actions, Williams is said to have approached Pearson and Anderson and suggested a deal: He would keep the columnists informed of "any inside news" about Sherman Adams if they would help Goldfine by giving evidence about the bugging that would result in the dismissal of the contempt case against him.[35] Williams dismisses that story as "preposterous," and insists, "I never asked Drew Pearson for help" in the Goldfine case or any other.

The hearing on Williams's motion to have the Goldfine case dropped began in late April 1959, but was interrupted after only a few days. Williams's wife, who had long suffered from respiratory ailments and other health problems, had rushed one of their children to a doctor during a downpour. She had not bothered to put up the top of the convertible she was driving, got soaked, soon became seriously ill, and was admitted to Georgetown University Hospital, where she died on May 10, 1959, at the age of thirty-four.[36] Williams says he had known for several years that "it was inevitable that she was going to die before long. There was just no reversing the process, and there was no cure."

In a 1957 will, Dorothy Williams left her entire estate to her husband.* Williams inherited property worth about $180,000, consisting mainly of a

---

* Dorothy Williams's will was witnessed by Tom Wadden; Agnes Neill (whom Williams married in 1960); and Geraldyne H. Wagner, Williams's secretary, who notarized the 1959 statement in which Bartley Crum retracted his accusation that Williams had offered him a bribe.[37]

minority share in the Hill Building and an interest in a trust fund set up
for his wife by the Guider family. In addition, he received outright various
assets that he and his wife had owned jointly, including stocks and other
personal property worth more than $60,000 and seven valuable lots in the
exclusive Tulip Hill subdivision of Bethesda,[38] where the couple lived.
(Williams says these assets were bought with money furnished by him,
and that his wife "didn't have any money. She had an expectation to
receive money" from her family.) Two weeks after his wife died, while
Williams was still trying to cope with her death and with the burden of
caring for three small children (the eldest of whom was five), he received
another blow when a heart attack killed Eddie Cheyfitz, who was only
forty-five.[39]

Dorothy Williams's final illness had a direct bearing on the Goldfine
case. When the hearing resumed after several weeks, Tom LaVenia testified that Williams had badgered him while he was in the hospital and
Mrs. Williams was a patient down the hall. According to LaVenia, Williams

> visited me several times at the hospital. . . . I didn't know it then, but I
> do now, that Mrs. Williams was down the hall from me, and while he
> was there, he was apparently impelled to relax and continue the conver-
> sation into the areas of this case, and at that time I told him: I said, "I
> am sorry, Ed, this is not the place to do it, and I don't want to get into it
> now." I will say this, he was pretty strong on that visit . . . and was
> pecking away at the hospital, pecking away on the phone and pecking
> away at his home.[40]

Prosecutor William Hitz then asked LaVenia whether "on that occasion . . . for any reason" he'd had "to terminate the conference and put
them [Williams and his associate, Tom Wadden, who was also present]
out of the room." LaVenia denied that, but Hitz persisted, asking, "Didn't
you tell Mr. Shacklette the very night such a thing happened that it did
happen and you were terribly distressed about it?" LaVenia acknowledged, "I told Mr. Shacklette that I was distressed by Mr. Williams' visit
and his pressing me for a variety of answers while I was in the hospital.
Yes, I did." Hitz then raised the question, "Did you not tell him [Shack-
lette] some of the attendants had to cause that conference to terminate
and that Mr. Williams and Mr. Wadden were told to leave?" LaVenia's
answer was, "Absolutely, no. . . . My memory is as clear as my name is
Tom LaVenia, I never told him that."[41]

It should be pointed out that LaVenia, who has since died, had a motive
for trying to retain Williams's goodwill and phrase his answers accordingly: LaVenia, by his own testimony, did investigative work for Williams,
and, in fact, "was just finishing up" a case for Williams when he was
hospitalized.[42] Naturally, LaVenia hoped to be paid for the work he had

done and to receive additional assignments from Williams. Furthermore, at that same time, LaVenia was also asking Williams for help in securing payment for work he had done during the Hoffa bribery trial two years earlier and for which he was still owed almost $1,400.[43]

Williams's alleged harassment of LaVenia in the hospital was just one of several complaints against him during the Goldfine case. Jack Anderson accused him of attempting to threaten Baron Shacklette via Anderson. According to Anderson, he went to Williams's office about three weeks before the hearing, at Pearson's request, to prepare for the trial, and Williams

> said that he wasn't interested in going after me, but . . . he asked me to pass on a message to Mr. Shacklette. He asked me to tell Mr. Shacklette that Mr. Williams knew that a Mr. Walters* had stolen some documents and delivered them to Mr. Shacklette. And he told me to tell Mr. Shacklette that he had better testify to that. That if he didn't, he would be found guilty of perjury and that if he did testify to it, that Mr. Williams could assure him that there would be no prosecution, because Mr. Williams said prosecution would be impossible without a complaint. And Mr. Williams said that he—that Mr. Goldfine would not bring a complaint . . . for being implicated in an alleged housebreaking. . . . He just wanted the testimony. . . . [Furthermore], he said that Mr. Shacklette might prefer to take the Fifth Amendment.[45]

Williams also ran the risk of being cited for contempt of court over his refusal to reveal where he had obtained a confidential police report about the alleged break-in of Mildred Paperman's room. While Williams was asking Baron Shacklette questions that were apparently based on the report, Hitz protested that Williams must have in his possession "a confidential report, I presume, of the Police Department, and Mr. Williams has no business whatever reading it." Hitz asked U.S. District Judge James W. Morris if he "would care to ask Mr. Williams how he obtained that police report." The judge inquired, "Can you inform us of that, Mr. Williams?" But Williams demurred:

> I will say this to you, Your Honor, I don't believe it is material, but if Your Honor should rule it was material, I would most respectfully have to refuse to give that information on the ground that I gave my word that I would not . . . and I must live with that commitment and take the consequences.

Hitz labeled Williams's remark "the most amazing statement I have heard from an attorney at this bar in over 20 years, to attempt to justify

---

* William Jackson Walters, a cashier at the Sheraton Carlton, who allegedly contacted Anderson and offered him the chance to take the room next to Goldfine's. Anderson accepted Walters's offer and invited Shacklette to join him.[44]

the possession of a confidential police report that he has no business to have." He requested that the judge "require Mr. Williams to state where he got that report, whom he got it from, and when he got it."

Judge Morris replied, "Mr. Hitz, I somewhat sympathize with your asking, but I fail to see wherein that matter that you just raised, while it may be material to some wrongful possession of some police record, I don't see how it can possibly affect the merits of the matter that is before me now.... You will just have to assume that Mr. Williams, in some fashion, which is not conventionally proper ... came in possession of that information." [46]

Hitz continues to believe that Williams was "unwise" to display the report in the courtroom. Williams "made no effort at all to hide it or conceal it," says Hitz. "I thought he was unwise to do it in the fashion that he did, because if he had done it more carefully, I probably never would have known about it." Hitz also thinks that Judge Morris caved in to Williams, who was able to "bamboozle" the judge because of his "prominence" as a lawyer. "I think had it been another lawyer, Judge Morris might have pursued the matter."

In a more humorous vein, Williams threatened several times to ask that Warren Woods be cited for contempt. Woods had been a court reporter before he became a lawyer, was proficient in shorthand, and was taking down the testimony "verbatim," then reading it to his client, Jack Anderson, who was not permitted to listen to other witnesses until he had given his own testimony. According to Woods, "Williams caught me doing this. I wasn't trying to disguise it. He told me he was going to have to complain to the judge if I didn't stop it, that I was coaching my own witness. I said, 'I'm representing this witness. I'm his counsel and I'll conduct my investigation any way I want to to help guide him.' He kept needling me about this and threatened several times to rise and ask to hold me in contempt of court. But he never did. I think he was probably uncertain of his rights to restrain me from taking notes."

But all the fireworks went for naught. Judge Morris ruled against Williams's bid to have Goldfine's indictment dismissed, although the judge did express his sympathy for Goldfine as the victim of Anderson's and Shacklette's maneuvers: "It is certainly understandable that the defendant should complain of and be indignant at the intrusion upon his conversations with his counsel in the manner revealed at the hearing." He indicated that he might consider those tactics "in mitigation of any punishment which would be visited upon ... [Goldfine] if convicted of the charges in the indictment." Nevertheless, Morris held, there was "credible evidence" that the subcommittee members received no information from Shacklette and that the subcommittee questions Goldfine refused to answer had been asked of him legitimately. [47]

On July 24, 1959, over Hitz's objections, Judge Morris—again mentioning "mitigating circumstances"—allowed Goldfine to plead *nolo contendere* to the contempt charges. Morris handed him a suspended sentence of one year in jail, fined him $1,000, and directed him to answer the subcommittee's questions if he was recalled as a witness.[48] In the end, Goldfine returned as a witness before the Harris Subcommittee and answered all questions except one, on which he invoked the Fifth Amendment. His second appearance seemed to satisfy all parties.[49]

Goldfine later hired Williams to defend him in a tax-evasion case in Boston when the financier was accused of failing to pay nearly $800,000 in federal income taxes between 1953 and 1957—the biggest tax-evasion case in history, until that time.[50] But when Williams examined Goldfine's records, he found that his client had not filed a tax return for any of those years, and he was forced to give Goldfine the bad news: "'I'm sorry, you just don't have any defense.'" Goldfine "greeted this observation with stony silence, and he looked at me with steely blue eyes." When Williams stepped outside, Goldfine turned to another lawyer and said, "'Who does that smart alec think he is, telling me I have no defense? If I had a defense, I'd have Ralph Slobotkin try the case.'" Slobotkin, a Boston attorney, was one of Goldfine's gofers.

Williams later appropriated the Slobotkin story for his own use on the banquet circuit. He liked to say that when he hired Otto Graham as head coach of the Redskins in 1966, Graham complained, "'Ed, we don't have any running backs, we don't have any defensive linemen, and we need a second quarterback.'" Williams's response supposedly was "'Look, Otto, if we had running backs, and a second quarterback, and defensive linemen, we'd have Ralph Slobotkin coaching.'"[51]

As the tax case progressed, it was reported in the press that Goldfine owed as much as $9 million in back taxes. Williams fired off a telegram to Elliot Richardson, then the U.S. attorney in Boston, demanding that a federal grand jury investigate alleged leaks by IRS officials in order to determine who was "'criminally responsible for the divulgence of this information.'"[52]

In October 1960, just as the tax-evasion case was coming to court, Goldfine was found mentally unfit to stand trial and was committed to St. Elizabeth's Hospital in Washington for psychiatric treatment.[53] That Christmas Eve, U.S. District Judge George Hart ordered him transferred to Boston for further care; U.S. Attorney Oliver Gasch then requested that Goldfine be sent to Boston in the custody of federal marshals. Gasch still remembers an informal hearing on the matter that was held in Hart's chambers. Christmas carols were being broadcast on the radio, and "Ed put on one of his stellar performances, playing hearts and flowers." Hart decreed that Gasch's plan "would not be in the Christmas spirit," and Goldfine was allowed to travel without supervision.

A few weeks later, the Kennedy administration took office, placing the new attorney general, Robert F. Kennedy, in charge of the Goldfine case. Justice Department lawyer Bill Hundley, Goldfine's prosecutor, accompanied Kennedy to a meeting at Williams's office in the Hill Building. "I would say that they didn't have a very warm or cordial relationship at that time," recalls Hundley, although "they were on speaking terms." Kennedy emerged from the elevator on the tenth and top floor of the building, where Williams then had his office, glanced around at the "rather elaborate and comfortable" furnishings, and said to Williams—who had come out to the elevator to greet his visitors—"'Am I responsible for all of this?'"

According to Hundley, Goldfine was "sending out signals"—via Williams—"that he wanted to cooperate" and give evidence against Sherman Adams, who, like Jimmy Hoffa, "was very dear to Bobby Kennedy's heart." But "this guy Goldfine was some piece of work," and "it was like Lucy holding the football for Charlie Brown—every time he said he was ready to talk, he would pull the ball back." Williams, Hundley, and Goldfine "set up meeting after meeting. Goldfine would always say he was ready to talk. We'd attend the meeting and he wouldn't be ready." Finally, Goldfine said, "'The only one I'm going down the list [of politicians he had bribed] with is Number One,' which meant Bobby Kennedy. I was Number Two," said Hundley, "which wasn't good enough.

"So Kennedy comes all the way back from Chicago, I'll never forget it, he meets with Ed and Goldfine up in his office on the fifth floor" of the Justice Department. "And Goldfine pulled the football away again. He said, 'I'll tell your brother, but not you.' Williams was absolutely beside himself. He dumped Goldfine in a cab and that was the end" of attempts to work out a plea bargain in exchange for Goldfine's turning government witness. Williams says that both he and Kennedy were "very upset" over Godfine's ultimate refusal to talk. "I never could figure out why" he wouldn't give evidence.

Goldfine was left with no choice but to plead guilty to all the tax-evasion charges, and on May 15, 1961, he entered a plea of guilty to evading $791,745 in taxes. During his appearance in federal court in Boston, he said he was pleading guilty on the advice of Williams.[54] He was sentenced to a year and a day in prison, fined $110,000, and placed on probation for five years.[55]

During the Goldfine tax case, Williams and Hundley had become close friends. Hundley still enjoys the memory of what happened when his first son was born during the Goldfine case; the infant was named William G. and often called "BG." "So Williams gets ahold of Goldfine and he says, 'Look, you don't have anything to worry about. Hundley thinks so much of you he calls his first kid BG just like everybody calls you.' So whenever I'd get with that son of a bitch Goldfine, he'd say, 'How's little BG?' He said, 'If everything works out okay, a little trust fund for BG.' So I said to Williams, 'Don't ever do that to me again, will you?' We never called him BG again after that."

Bernard Goldfine would not set up trust funds for BG Hundley or anyone else, ever again. He was declared insolvent[56] as the IRS filed tax liens totaling $8 million against him and his companies,[57] and he wound up petitioning a court in Boston to allot him $200 a week for living expenses.[58]

19
Adam Clayton Powell: The Cutest Trick

Morton Robson thought he had Adam Clayton Powell, Jr., nailed. The tax case against the Harlem congressman seemed that strong. The star witness for prosecutor Robson was Hattie Freeman Dodson, a Powell aide who was going to testify that the incriminating data on Powell's tax returns had originated with Powell himself. Then, about a week before the case went to trial in March 1960, Hattie Dodson visited Robson's office for her final preparation. This time she was accompanied by her new attorney: Edward Bennett Williams—the same Edward Bennett Williams who was defending Powell. From then on, Hattie Dodson seemed to have difficulty remembering even her own name. An infuriated Morton Robson watched helplessly as his airtight case vanished, along with Hattie Dodson's memory.

Adam Clayton Powell almost certainly would not have been indicted but for the vendetta waged against him by William F. Buckley, Jr., and his magazine, the *National Review*—a vendetta that was instigated by Thomas A. Bolan, a disgruntled former assistant U.S. attorney in New York.

The Powell matter went back to July 3, 1956, when the U.S. Attorney's

Office announced a probe into Powell's taxes. It was an election year, and on October 11—exactly five days after he had told his Harlem congregation that no black person could in good conscience campaign for either President Eisenhower or his Democratic opponent, Adlai Stevenson—Democrat Powell visited the White House, called a press conference, and urged all blacks to vote for Eisenhower's reelection. This was at a time when Eisenhower's Justice Department was examining Powell's tax returns.[1] Nevertheless, a month after Eisenhower was reelected, a federal grand jury in Manhattan began hearing evidence on Powell's taxes. Prosecutor Thomas Bolan presented his case to the jury at twenty different sessions between December 1956 and February 1957, but nothing happened. Seven months later, with the jurors still having taken no action, Bolan resigned in disgust, claiming that a "political deal" had been struck, in consequence of which the Powell case was being killed in exchange for the black leader's support of Eisenhower in 1956. Bolan, by then a private citizen, started leaking the information he had gathered to Buckley.[2]

The immediate result was an article entitled "Death of an Investigation: The Wheels of Justice Stop for Adam Clayton Powell, Jr.," in the December 14, 1957, issue of the *National Review,* which was mailed to each of the grand jurors. Starting with the February 22, 1958, edition of the *National Review,* eleven consecutive issues carried stories and comments about Powell, culminating in an editorial entitled "The Jig Is Up for Adam Clayton Powell, Jr.," on May 3.[3] And each issue carried "pointed reminders" that the term of the Powell grand jury would expire on June 4, and that unless the jury acted before then, the Powell case would die.[4]

The Powell grand jury began holding rump sessions in April 1958, fourteen months after it had last considered the case. These meetings were held at the Commodore Hotel instead of at the U.S. Courthouse, and the panel was now a full-fledged runaway jury. Arthur Christy, who had replaced Bolan as prosecutor, was asked to appear before the jurors and explain why they should not take the unusual step of firing the U.S. Attorney's Office and hiring Bolan to prosecute the case. He spoke for about fifteen minutes, then Bolan addressed the jurors for an hour, and finally the jury voted by a narrow margin to stick with Christy and the U.S. Attorney's Office.

Although Bolan lost his bid to replace Christy, a three-count indictment was finally handed down against Powell on May 8, 1958, just a few weeks before the jury would have been forced to go out of business. The congressman was charged with being the moving force behind the filing of a false and fraudulent 1951 tax return for his wife, pianist Hazel Scott; with trying to evade some $1,400 in his wife's taxes for that same year; and with attempting to evade nearly $1,700 in taxes on the joint return he and his spouse filed for 1952.[5]

Five days after Powell was indicted, Buckley was called before another grand jury, which was considering whether he and Bolan should be prosecuted for tampering in the Powell case. Buckley stated publicly, "The grand jury now has before it information on the basis of which it can decide whether to indict me, or whether to investigate and hand up a presentment against the office of the U.S. Attorney, for negligence in the performance of its duties."[6] Arthur Christy—who had roomed with Buckley's brother, James, at law school—declined to take part in any move to charge Buckley, reasoning that "it was a silly thing to do to call Buckley before a grand jury. You'd just wind up with egg all over your face."

In the end, no charges were filed against Buckley and Bolan, but Williams attempted to overturn Powell's indictment because of the "highly inflammatory articles" Buckley had published. The defense attorney maintained that Bolan had "breached his oath of secrecy by revealing to the *National Review* what had transpired in the grand jury room," and claimed that the indictment against Powell "would never have been returned but for the activities of the *National Review* and . . . Bolan."[7] (Williams is still grousing that Buckley "was wholly responsible for the prosecution" of Powell.) Buckley himself bragged, "It is now established beyond reasonable doubt that only the combined actions of Mr. Thomas A. Bolan, of individual members of the grand jury, and of *National Review,* forced . . . [the U.S. attorney] to do his duty as regards Representative Powell."[8]

After hearing Williams's presentation, Federal Judge William Herlands, who presided over the early stages of the trial, ruled that in spite of "the extraordinary conduct of Bolan and Buckley," the indictment of Powell "was returned in accordance with law." He did, however, take Buckley to task, saying he was "assuming without deciding that Bolan and Buckley committed crimes," and concluding that while Buckley was entitled to write his "editorial comments, suggestive questions and adroit insinuations," his sending the *National Review* stories to the grand jurors may have been "criminally improper."[9]

Buckley waited four years, and then, following publication of Williams's *One Man's Freedom,* he sought to even the score. Noting that Williams had devoted a portion of his book to the Powell case (Williams wrote that "without the external pressures . . . Adam Powell would never have been indicted"),[10] Buckley commented that Williams's charge for appearing in court was "one thousand dollars a day, which is a highish fee, but rendered less painful by the knowledge that your case may be a chapter in a future book by Ed Williams." In Buckley's opinion, "If Mr. Williams' treatment of the Powell case is typical of either his capacity for the truth or of his access to it, then his book should be dismissed for what it seems to me to be: a venture in cynicism, or a venture in helpless confusion."[11] Buckley also savaged Williams on a number of other grounds, including his relationship with Joe McCarthy and his alleged role in inducing Joe Louis to pay a friendly courtroom visit to Jimmy Hoffa while Williams was defending Hoffa before a mostly black jury in 1957.

By 1968, Buckley had decided that his onetime adversary had rehabilitated himself; at least, Buckley asked Williams to represent Edgar Smith, a convicted murderer and death-row inmate in New Jersey in whose case Buckley had become interested.[12] And in 1979, after Buckley ran afoul of the SEC over the operation of Starr Broadcasting, a company in which he owned a large interest, he again retained Williams's firm. A settlement was reached under which Buckley forfeited stock worth between $600,000 and $1.4 million and agreed not to serve as an officer or director of a public company for at least five years.[13] Buckley said in 1981, "I had a disagreement with Williams 25 years ago which I have no appetite whatever to recall as we have been friends now (though I do not see him frequently) for over 15 years."[14] Williams affirms that since "Buckley called me and asked if I would take on" the Edgar Smith case for him, "we've had a cordial relationship."

On the eve of his trial, Adam Clayton Powell felt—perhaps with good cause—that he was the victim of a vendetta on the part of the government, the press, and some powerful individuals. His view was that "[n]ot a single newspaper in the United States of America said one word about fair play, except the Negro press and the *Washington Evening Star*." He also claimed to have reason to believe that Senator James Eastland, (D-Miss.), head of the Senate Judiciary Committee and one of the most powerful politicians in the country, was out to get him.[15]

Powell further cited Eleanor Roosevelt, who was then writing a newspaper column, as one of his harshest critics.[16] During the Powell trial, Williams was invited by his friend John Roosevelt to meet Roosevelt's mother, and wound up dining with Eleanor Roosevelt, John Roosevelt, and the latter's wife. Williams recalls, "During the course of the evening, I asked her how in the name of reason she possibly could lead so active a life. She was an elderly woman and she was leading a full, full life with a schedule that would be backbreaking for a young person. And she said to me, 'When I was a young woman at the age of twenty-six I did a long, thoughtful analysis of my life and I realized for the first time how much time I was wasting on indecision and regret. And I decided right then and there that I should never again leave room in my life for either of those two thieves.'" According to Williams, "It was one of the most significant statements anyone ever made to me." At the end of the evening, Mrs. Roosevelt said to Williams, "'Oh, it's been so nice meeting you. I just wish you weren't representing that rogue [Powell]. I wish that there were some way you could win the case and he could go to jail.'"

Like Powell, Williams thought the Harlem congressman had been singled out for prosecution, when others might not have been. Even Arthur Christy, Powell's prosecutor for a time, now says the case was "not very strong," and that any violations by Powell were "more technical" than substantive.

During its investigation, the Justice Department had written to virtually every black newspaper and college in the country, asking if Powell had been paid for any articles or speeches, and revealing that a tax case against him was being considered. This tactic was "wrong" and "indecent," Williams later told Powell's jury, because "if these letters were designed to elicit information helpful to the tax investigation, they would have been sent to other than Negro papers and other than Negro schools." Instead, said Williams, "They [the prosecutors] told every Negro university and every Negro paper . . . they told everybody among his people . . . that a grand jury was sitting on him."[17] Presiding Judge Frederick van-Pelt Bryan noted that the Justice Department had not received a single reply to its blanket mailing, leading to the inference that the government attorneys were more interested in sending news out than in obtaining evidence for use in making their case.[18]

Hattie Freeman Dodson, whom the courtroom prosecutor of Powell, Morton Robson, described in a recent interview as "my main witness," had been secretary and business manager for some thirty years at Harlem's Abyssinian Baptist Church, where Powell, and his father before him, had served as pastor. From 1945 to 1956, Dodson had also been Powell's congressional secretary, until she was replaced by her husband, Howard T. Dodson, who still held the congressional job at the time of Powell's trial and was also minister of music at Powell's church.[19] In 1956, Mrs. Dodson stood trial in federal court on nine counts of tax evasion and making false statements on her tax return. Evidence at her trial showed that from 1948 to 1952 she had filed two tax returns each year—one for her congressional salary under her maiden name, Hattie Freeman, and one joint return with her husband, in which the Dodsons listed their earnings from the church. Mrs. Dodson explained that her reason for filing two returns each year was that she was kicking back her congressional pay to Powell.[20] But the congressman, testifying at her trial, denied receiving such kickbacks,[21] and Mrs. Dodson was found guilty of trying to evade taxes, both by filing two returns for each year and by claiming nonexistent children as dependents.[22] Protesting her innocence, she was sentenced to seven months in prison and fined $1,000.[23]

The government's interest in investigating Powell was apparently aroused both by the Dodson case and by Powell's life-style—he owned two homes and three cars (a Jaguar, a Cadillac, and a Chrysler), employed two servants, and yet had paid only $1,700 in federal taxes on income of $160,000 for 1951 and 1952.[24]

Prosecutor Robson expected Mrs. Dodson to testify that she had copied figures given her by Powell onto a work sheet, which the congressman's tax attorney had then used to prepare his returns. She was to have made it clear that Powell was the source of the information, and that any inaccuracies were his fault. "Had she testified that way, there's no question in my mind that we would have convicted him," Robson says. "She cooperated with us fully and indicated her willingness to testify, until a week before the trial when I called her down for final preparation, at which time she showed up with her new attorney—Edward Bennett Williams. From there on, she was hopeless. She refused to recall anything and was a hopeless witness."

When Williams "just showed up with her," his explanation was "simply . . . that he had been retained to represent her." Robson thought it was "outrageous" for Williams to serve as lawyer for both the defendant and the key witness for the prosecution. "I didn't see how he could in good conscience come in, and his response in substance was, 'She has a constitutional right to choose anybody she wants as her attorney, and she's chosen me. You go ahead and ask her anything you want.' Of course, I couldn't question her in his presence. There was no way I could prepare her without revealing to him my whole case.

"I objected strenuously to his representing her, did a lot of research on our ability to stop him, but there was nothing I could do about it. It was a very cute stunt on his part"—one that Robson had never before seen pulled, nor has he since. "Williams is a very clever guy and over the years has come up with some very cute stunts.

"She was the one who could testify as to the source of the information that went onto" Powell's work sheet, Robson added. "When she refused to recall how any of the information got there, we were forced to rely on" inferences and what Powell should have known. But the government couldn't prove any direct knowledge on Powell's part without Dodson's testimony.

Informed of Robson's comments, Williams retorted, "It was the most natural thing in the world" to take on Dodson as a client. "When you're representing someone, you represent everyone" who works for them. "It was the most normal thing in the world for me to go with her" to see Robson. "Everyone," he added, "has their reasons for why they lost a case. It's not because I was able or talented or worked hard. Defeat is a bastard" that no one wants to claim as his own. "No one ever says, 'I lost because I should have lost.'" He characterized Dodson as "a nice woman, kind of a simple woman, who really screwed up the tax returns quite badly."

Just as Robson had feared, Mrs. Dodson during her testimony had trouble recalling damaging information that would link Powell directly with the faulty data.[25] And Robson grew so frustrated that he complained to Judge Bryan, "With respect to 90 per cent of her testimony, her recollection has lapsed very badly in the last two or three weeks. She recalled almost everything that I asked her on the witness stand without hesitation in my office three weeks ago." [26]

Having neutralized the prosecution's star witness, Williams turned his attention to IRS agent Morris Emanuel, the government's expert on the finances of Adam Clayton Powell, Jr., and, except for Hattie Dodson, the person whose testimony was potentially most threatening to the defendant. Early on in his cross-examination of Emanuel, Williams won an admission that when the IRS agent had testified before the grand jury about Powell, he had been aware of the fact that the congressman and his wife had overstated their 1951 income by $6,000, but later Emanuel had discovered that the overstatement amounted to $11,000—which was even more favorable to Powell. [27] Williams next forced Emanuel to concede that he had accused Powell of failing to report nearly $1,200 in income for 1951, even though Emanuel had known that Powell had reported the money in question on his 1950 return. "I was not investigating 1950," was Emanuel's lame explanation. "But at the time you testified here before this jury, you knew that he had reported this income in 1950 . . . didn't you?" asked Williams. Emanuel could only agree. [28]

"Then," Williams continued, "the full extent of the duplications known to the Government in April, 1959, would have completely wiped out the understatement of income charged in the indictment?" Emanuel again answered, "Yes, sir." [29]

Williams, however, knowing that Robson would try to restore Emanuel's credibility on redirect examination, had saved his best for later re-cross. In the meantime, he had suggested to judge and jury that Emanuel was avoiding answers to some questions and volunteering too much information on others.

The next day, Friday, April 1, 1960, following Robson's redirect questioning of Emanuel, Williams returned to the attack.

> *Williams:* What you told the grand jury . . . was inaccurate?
>
> *Emanuel:* As of today; not as of 1958. . . . [At the time] we felt it was proper. We have found subsequently that we were wrong in some areas and right in other ones, and we have adjusted it.
>
> *Williams:* Do you mean the facts themselves were different in 1958 than they are now, or that you were mistaken about the facts then?
>
> *Emanuel:* No, I mean and you know and I know that the facts were the same. . . .
>
> *Williams:* Then the grand jury did not have the benefit of a complete and accurate investigation from you. Is that right?
>
> *Emanuel:* You make that sound a little difficult, Mr. Williams. The—

At that point Judge Bryan interrupted Emanuel and instructed him, "All right, that is a question and it requires an answer, Mr. Emanuel. Did it [the grand jury] or did it not [have all the facts before it]?" Emanuel did the best he could, still declining to give a yes or no answer and replying, "It received whatever information our investigation had developed up to that point."

But Williams had the perfect question for Emanuel: "And you now know, do you not, Mr. Emanuel, on April Fool's Day 1960, that that was not accurate information?" Emanuel was left with nothing to say except "That's correct." [30]

The judge had previously decided to give the jury Friday afternoon off, and Williams wanted to leave the jurors with three days to contemplate Emanuel's admissions. As *New York Post* columnist Murray Kempton said, "Williams looked at the clock, the way Ray Robinson* used to." With time running out on the court session and on the government's case, "Williams looked at the clock; he had hit it on the nose." [32] He forced Emanuel to admit that Powell had omitted $7,000 in deductions he could have claimed, more than wiping out an alleged $6,700 deficiency in reporting income. [33] And having gotten what he wanted, he "shouted, with an air of satisfaction," [34] "I have no further questions." [35] Just as he had planned, the trial ended for the day and for the week, leaving the weekend for the jurors to think about the points he had made.

Kempton also wrote that "[t]he case of the United States against Adam Clayton Powell today is a drip castle of damp black sand. It has taken six years to build," but in just a few days "Edward Bennett Williams, Powell's counsel, had crumbled its towers and overrun its outerworks." [36] Kempton also credited Williams with taking some elaborate charts about Powell's income that Emanuel had brought into court with him and, "without intention of course . . . rendering what had been merely confusing entirely incomprehensible." [37] All the while, as Williams forced Emanuel into damaging admissions and into conceding time and again that if Powell had cheated anyone it had been himself, Powell watched in delight. He commented, "'They better adjourn this case. I'm making more money every day.'" [38]

Williams ranks his cross-examination of Emanuel as one of his best. "He just came apart," says Williams. "I timed it so that he'd come apart just as the judge recessed. I waited until it got to be one minute" before the hour the judge had set as the end of the session. "When the gong was hitting the hour, Emanuel came apart. And he collapsed on the stand. And the judge gave him a withering look such as I have never seen a judge give a witness, and the jury went home to think about it all weekend."

---

*Both Sugar Ray, a friend and client of Williams's, and Toots Shor were part of an overflow crowd that watched Williams try the Powell case. [31]

Vincent Fuller, who assisted Williams in the Powell trial, considers the Emanuel cross-examination Williams's best. "It was most dramatic in the sense that he got admissions of gross errors, the grossest errors." Murray Kempton wrote that "Williams is one of the few Americans left who work at a trade. Lawyers come to look at him as the children stop to look at glassblowers in Venice."[39] Milton Lewis, who covered the trial for the *New York Herald Tribune,* offered a similar assessment: "In court circles, Mr. Williams is known as the legal Miracle Worker. Watching the master at work is an ever-changing, fascinated clutch of lawyers who have had their own clients' cases adjourned to attend a miracle in the making. This happens whenever he is trying a case these days."[40]

Even Morton Robson acknowledged that Williams had conducted a "very, very good cross-examination," although he added that Judge Bryan "was very favorably inclined" toward the defense, "which rankled then and rankles today." Nevertheless, Williams's reference to April Fool's Day near the end of the Emanuel Destruction Derby still drew praise from Robson more than two decades later. The ultimate accolade, however, came from a most unexpected source: John Cye Cheasty, who watched Williams's interrogation of Emanuel. Cheasty says, "I thought that was a hell of a performance." After Williams was through with Emanuel, Cheasty recalls, "I went up to him at the bar and I said, 'That's a pretty good cross-examination.' And he turned around and said, 'Oh, one of the alumni, huh?'"

In his closing argument to the jury, Williams fell back on his old standby:

> Five years from now this case will have faded into the dimmest recesses of your minds. It will be a blurred memory. It will be just a paragraph in one chapter of your lives. His Honor will have gone on and tried scores of other cases, and so, too, will the prosecutor. But for this defendant what you do—and this is true of any defendant—what you do is the most important thing in his life, and it has been a full life.
>
> I say to you that all of the dreams and the hopes and the aspirations of over a half century hang on your verdict.[41]

Williams also charged during his summation that Powell was "the victim of the worst political vendetta engineered by an agency of the government in modern history." Robson was on his feet quickly, protesting that Williams's allegations "reflect on me and every member of my staff. I may say that they are lies."[42]

Williams ignored Robson for the moment, concluding his oration by telling the jurors that Powell had been singled out for "political liquidation," and imploring:

> By your verdict you should give thundering notice, a thundering notice that will reverberate through the corridors of this courthouse that

there is no room for political trials in this land, and that the indictment is no substitute for the ballot, and that every man, whoever he may be, whatever his cause, whatever his beliefs, whatever his heritage, whatever his color, is entitled under our system to equal justice under law.

I ask no more for this man.[43]

The next day, in the judge's robing room, as Bryan, Williams, and Robson were preparing to enter court for Robson's final argument, Williams made a move that was calculated to throw the prosecutor off stride, asking for a mistrial on the ground that Robson "has accused me of lying. In fact, he called me a liar before this jury without any basis whatsoever," which "lethally prejudiced" the jurors. Bryan asked Robson for comment, and the prosecutor said he hesitated to reply, "because I may find it difficult to control myself." He charged that Williams had "played fast and loose" and had "turned this case from an income tax case into a trial of the government for political persecution, or attempted to do that, in any event."[44]

Judge Bryan denied Williams's motion for a mistrial,[45] but Williams was just getting warmed up. As the lawyers started to go from the robing room into court, Williams, according to Robson, "asked me if I would waive my privilege and allow him to sue me for defamation. I was furious at that point. I said, 'I would, except I wouldn't trust you.'" Williams "did me one of the biggest favors of my career," says Robson. "I walked into the courtroom with my adrenaline pounding through my system. I was so exhausted by that time, I had been up until about four o'clock in the morning preparing for my summation after eight weeks, seven days a week, of trial. I was really wiped out. I was wondering how I was going to get through the summation. He got me going to such a point that I talked for four hours without ever looking at my notes."

In his closing argument, Robson criticized Williams for having devoted "three-quarters of his time in his summation yesterday" to "an attack on the motivations of the prosecution," which Robson said was "a shabby stunt" often used by defense counsel "confronted with incriminating facts which cannot be easily explained away." Robson said Powell and Williams were seeking to shift blame for Powell's crimes from the congressman to "poor, unfortunate" Hattie Dodson, who was "completely dependent upon this defendant for her livelihood and for her husband's livelihood, and she has been for many, many years," and he asked the jurors to bear in mind that during his questioning of Dodson, "the only answer she was capable of was, 'I am not sure,' 'I don't recall,' and 'I don't remember.' But do you remember how her recollection brightened when Mr. Williams stepped up for cross-examination?"[46] Robson also asserted that Powell, whom Williams had called as a witness in his own defense, had "perjured himself" several times.[47]

By the time the case went to the jury, Judge Bryan had dismissed the counts charging that Powell had tried to evade taxes in 1951 and 1952, leaving the jurors to decide only whether he had attempted to file a fraudulent return for 1951.[48] The jury apparently never had much hope of reaching a unanimous verdict. After deliberating for nine hours on the first day, they sent Bryan a note at 10:15 P.M. saying they had been deadlocked since three o'clock. Judge Bryan sent them to a hotel overnight and asked them to resume their deliberations the next day, but the situation grew worse. Early in the afternoon of April 22, a second message was sent, informing the judge that the jury was hopelessly deadlocked, and that the more the jurors talked, the farther apart they became. Williams asked that the jury be discharged without a verdict, but Robson argued that the jurors should be given at least one more chance to reach a verdict, and the judge agreed and ordered the jurors to try once more. Right after the jurors filed out of the courtroom, Williams pointed out to Judge Bryan that one female juror "was in open tears. She was trembling from weeping" and "continued to cry throughout the time you talked to the jury," which Williams said was "terribly disturbing" to him. Judge Bryan said the juror may have been "upset," but she wasn't in as bad shape as Williams thought.[49]

Williams says, "I just wanted to leave. I was defending. For a defense lawyer, a hung jury's a victory."

Judge Bryan gave Williams his wish; after letting the jurors deliberate for two more hours, he discharged them.[50] Although they disclosed later that they were split 10–2 in favor of acquittal, Williams, according to Powell, was still "a little crestfallen" that he had not won a complete vindication for his client.[51]

Despite the split decision, kudos for Williams poured in from many sides, as often happened after his important cases. In a story in the *New York Times* Sunday magazine a few months later, Gay Talese called Williams "the nation's 'hottest' lawyer," and reported an incident during the Powell trial when Robson had objected that a question Williams asked a witness during cross-examination had not been covered during Robson's direct examination and therefore was not a proper subject for cross-examination. Judge Bryan initially sided with Robson, but then "Williams, without referring to the record or even to his notes, called out the date on which the prosecution had covered the subject and the exact page of the 4,000-page transcript on which it had appeared. The judge checked, flinched, and said, 'You're right, Mr. Williams; proceed with your question.'"[52]

No one was more effusive than Powell. He declared that Williams was "a thing of beauty to watch in a courtroom, where he stands like a Jesuit priest ticking off the facts, propagating the faith, and trying to convert all within earshot. He is a number-one fighter for civil liberties . . . the reincarnation of Clarence Darrow. This was the man I needed."[53] Powell also mentioned Williams's dedication to the case, telling how one night when he, Williams, and Vincent Fuller were going over the trial at Williams's New York apartment, he saw Williams "suddenly collapse and turn gray in the face" from overwork. Powell said he put Williams to bed and insisted he get a good night's sleep, but "in ten minutes he was up, charging out the door, yelling, 'What are you guys talking about?' He had slept all of seven or eight minutes." Powell said, "Suddenly it dawned on me that here I was standing the trial of my life, and I was taking care of" Williams and Fuller. He added, "My defense attorney, Edward Bennett Williams, performed a dedicated and masterful service for which I shall ever be grateful."[54] As a token of his debt, Powell had Williams named "Harlem Man of the Year"; the citation, dated June 25, 1960, two months after the trial ended, still hangs on Williams's office wall.

Because the jury had been unable to reach a verdict, the one count that Judge Bryan had not dismissed was still pending against Powell, but a year later Robson ordered the case dismissed—primarily because of Hattie Dodson's abrupt loss of memory. In a statement filed in court on April 11, 1961, Robson declared that the evidence against Powell "consisted principally of the testimony of Hattie Dodson, the defendant's secretary." However, said Robson, Dodson was

> an extremely uncooperative and hostile witness. Her trial testimony differed markedly from previous statements she had made, some of them as recently as three weeks before the trial. Moreover, she professed to be unable to recall many important facts of which she had a clear recollection three weeks earlier. As a result, it is believed that at a new trial more than one year later, her testimony would be virtually worthless.[55]

Hattie Dodson's faulty memory had gotten Adam Clayton Powell off the hook—for good.

20

Bobby Baker:
The Biggest Defeat

N ovember 22, 1963. Like so many others, Bobby Baker still recalls
vividly what he was doing when the news came in from Dallas. He
was in an office at the firm of his lawyer, Abe Fortas, preparing to
defend himself against charges of political corruption. When Baker heard
from the mailman that President Kennedy had been shot, "I immediately
rushed into Abe's office and told him." After the news came that the
president had died, Baker told Fortas, "'My country is more important
than who my attorney is. President Johnson is going to need you and your
advice.'" Baker, until recently Johnson's protégé, knew that Johnson
would want Fortas by his side and that the tar from the Baker case would
smear him.

When Baker insisted that he was going to hire another attorney, Fortas
recommended Joseph ("Jiggs") Donohue, formerly a powerful District of
Columbia politician. But Baker wanted Edward Bennett Williams, who
had impressed him during the McCarthy hearings, even though Williams
had been on the opposite side from Lyndon Johnson. And Baker did go
with Williams. Lately, however, Baker has concluded that Fortas was
right. A conviction on seven counts of financial misdeeds and nearly a
year and a half in federal prison concentrated Baker's mind wonderfully.

Although he is grateful for Williams's work on his behalf and considers him "a pro's pro" as a lawyer, Bobby Baker is now of the opinion that "if I had my life to live over, I would never have hired Ed Williams." That decision was "the biggest mistake of my life," because, he explains, retaining Williams was like waving a red flag in front of the jury and admitting that he was in deep trouble.

Like Edward Bennett Williams, Robert Gene Baker knew how it was to scratch his way up from the bottom. The son of a mailman in Pickens, South Carolina, fourteen-year-old Bobby Baker arrived in Washington in 1943—just about the same time as Williams—to become a Senate page.[1] Only eleven years later, his meteoric rise was certified when Senate Majority Leader Lyndon B. Johnson appointed him secretary of the Senate Democrats. Johnson described Baker as "'my strong right arm. The last man I see at night, the first I see in the morning.'" And in 1960, Baker was cited to freshman Capitol pages as a "'powerful demonstration of just how far intelligence combined with a gracious personality can take a man.'"[2]

Two decades after he reached the nation's capital with $60 in his pocket, Baker's net worth was estimated at $2 million.[3] He led a life filled with wine, women, and song; and thanks to his access to Johnson and to Senate Finance Chairman Robert Kerr, he was one of the most powerful people in the country. His clout was such that Milton Young, Quentin Burdick, and Ralph Yarborough believed it was he who had kept them from seats on the Senate Judiciary Committee,[4] and Senator Clinton Anderson felt that Baker had played a key role in defeating the 1962 Medicare bill.[5]

In his personal life, Baker was also in the big time. He was the guiding spirit behind the Quorum Club on Capitol Hill, where political figures made both deals and friends. When President Kennedy appointed Luther Hodges his secretary of Commerce in 1961, Hodges sold his one-third interest in a Howard Johnson Motor Lodge in Charlotte, North Carolina, to his partners—Baker and another man.[6] Baker was also one of the founders of the Carousel Motel in Ocean City, Maryland, which became a gathering place for vacationing politicians (and also helped cause Baker's eventual downfall). His financial interests extended overseas to such places as Curaçao[7] and the Dominican Republic, where he and his associates tried to establish casinos.[8] In another transaction, he was paid handsomely for acting as middleman between the oil-rich Murchisons of Texas and Jose Bonitez, Democratic leader of Puerto Rico, in a plan to have Haitian meat licensed for import into Puerto Rico and the United States.[9] Back in the States, Baker also helped Clint Murchison obtain the Dallas Cowboy franchise in the National Football League.[10]

Even after the tide started to turn against Baker, his standing was such that Attorney General Robert F. Kennedy supposedly telephoned to encourage him: "'Bobby, my brother is fond of you and remembers your many kindnesses. I want you to know that we have nothing of any consequence about you in our files. . . . My brother and I extend our sympathies to you. I know that you'll come through this.'"[11] A few weeks after that phone call, President Kennedy spent part of what would be his final press conference trying to put distance between his administration and the growing Baker scandal,[12] although, according to Baker, JFK had arranged for his personal tax lawyer to represent the central figure in the controversy.

Baker's downfall started in October 1963, when Ralph Hill, president and part owner of Capitol Vending Company, filed a $300,000 suit charging that Baker had accepted monthly payments in return for guaranteeing that Hill's firm could operate vending machines at a Washington area defense plant, Melpar, Inc. According to Hill, Baker had instead turned around and forced out Capitol Vending in favor of the Serv-U Corporation, owned by the Senate aide and his cronies.[13] Three days after Hill initiated his suit, Baker resigned his post as secretary to the Senate Democrats.[14] And the following week, the Senate voted to have its Rules Committee investigate whether any present or former Senate employees had been involved in "conflict of interest or other improprieties" that warranted new legislation.[15]

Two months later, following the assassination of President Kennedy and after Baker had replaced Abe Fortas with Williams, Baker was subpoenaed to testify before the Senate Rules Committee. On February 17, 1964, two days before Baker was due to appear, Williams wrote to Committee Chairman Everett Jordan that "I have now advised Mr. Baker not to produce" the records demanded by the committee. He offered several reasons:

- "You are conducting a trial of Mr. Baker" and "we do not recognize that your committee or any other committee of the Senate has the right to conduct a legislative trial."
- Baker was also being investigated by the FBI and the IRS, so any evidence he might offer the committee could be incriminating and could give the government an unfair advantage if Baker were to be prosecuted.
- FBI agents had tapped the phones of Edward Levinson, owner of the Fremont Hotel in Las Vegas and and associate of Baker's in Serv-U and other enterprises (as well as a client of Williams's); "numerous" conversations between Levinson and Baker had been recorded, which amounted to "an unconscionable and unlawful invasion" of Baker's privacy.[16]

Baker appeared before the committee in closed session on February 19 as ordered. Williams had told him he would be "'a *complete* Mongolian idiot to do anything other than take the fifth amendment,'"[17] and, citing Williams's letter of February 17, he invoked the First, Fourth, Fifth, and

Sixth amendments, "specifically . . . the privilege against self-incrimination," and refused to provide his records or answer any questions.[18] Committee Chairman Jordan directed Baker to return for further questioning
in public, even though Williams, who had accompanied his client, told the
senators, "I can save some time by telling you . . . we will not change our
position. . . . I don't think there are any questions that the committee can
propound that he will answer." He added, "It will not be an exercise of
bona fide legislative purpose to recall him in open session," because Baker
would answer no questions, so "the calling in open session can only be for
the purpose of degrading the witness."[19]

Baker nonetheless returned for the public session on February 25, and
Williams at once objected that the public hearing was being "held solely
for the purpose of holding Mr. Baker up to public obloquy on television
cameras." Thereupon Republican Senator Hugh Scott charged that Williams's statement was "an unfair attack upon the committee" and was
"thoroughly and totally unwarranted," and another Republican, Carl
Curtis, declared that Williams was "entirely out of line" and should be
cited for contempt of the Senate, which generated applause. Chairman
Jordan finally agreed to remove television and still-camera crews from the
hearing room,[20] but Baker still had to face and refuse to answer a series of
embarrassing questions from Senators Curtis and Scott:

- Had Baker arranged the gift of a stereo set "costing something over $500" to
"one Lyndon Johnson" in order to buy Johnson's influence while he was still
a senator?
- Had Carole Tyler (Baker's secretary and girlfriend) joined him on business
trips while she was on the federal payroll?
- Had Baker used government telephones to place bets with "one Snags Lewis,
a . . . well known . . . bookie," or with another "bigtime bookmaker" named
Mike Shapiro?
- Had Baker not filed papers in connection with the purchase of a town house
stating that Carole Tyler was his "cousin"?
- Was Joseph Fabianich, then serving time at Leavenworth Prison on "white
slavery charges," a Baker associate?
- "How many people" had Baker "referred to a Puerto Rican doctor for the
performance of abortions?"
- Had Baker provided "party girls" to contractors who did business with the
government?
- What was Baker's relationship with Ellen Rometsch?[21] (Baker described her
as "a lady about town" whom he had introduced to President Kennedy at
JFK's request, after which Attorney General Robert F. Kennedy "had her
rush-deported to Germany."[22])

Through all these questions, Baker could only "bite my tongue"; every
time "I appeared to be on the verge of blurting out an answer, Ed Williams gave me looks that said *Watch your ass. Only you can protect it.*"[23]

Having remained silent from beginning to end, Baker was finally released by the committee for the time being, but the embarrassment of the scandal was spreading to the entire Democratic party. No less an expert than Richard Nixon warned that unless LBJ "'breaks silence on the Bobby Baker case and unless he disassociates himself from this kind of hanky-panky . . . this country could be in for four more years of wheeling and dealing and influence-peddling unprecedented in this country.'"[24]

After Barry Goldwater won the 1964 Republican presidential nomination, his speeches concentrated on the Baker case, and Williams—who had recently switched from Republican to Democrat—was asked to try to keep Baker out of the headlines. Two of Johnson's most trusted advisers, Abe Fortas and Walter Jenkins, had urged Williams to negotiate a settlement in the suit brought by Ralph Hill, but Williams had been unable to. He could only stall for so long, and on October 5, 1964, just a month before the election, David Carliner, Hill's attorney, scheduled the taking of Baker's deposition. Carliner also subpoenaed Bobby Kennedy, Walter Jenkins, Luther Hodges, and Acting Attorney General Nicholas Katzenbach in the case, which promised to be damaging to Johnson and other Democrats.

Hordes of reporters assembled to see Carliner question Baker, but just before Baker was to testify, Carliner left the room and motioned Williams to follow. The two went to the men's room, where Carliner offered to settle the $300,000 suit for $100,000. Williams bargained him down to $30,000 and sold the settlement to an initially reluctant Baker on the ground that going to trial would cost more than that, win or lose. Baker agreed—on condition that word of the accord not leak out until after the elections. The deposition-taking was postponed, the press went away disappointed, and the settlement did remain a secret until Ben Bradlee broke the story in the first issue of *Newsweek* after the election.[25] *

Williams had taken care of the Hill suit, but Baker's troubles continued to mount. In December 1964, he was recalled before the Senate Rules Committee, which was then probing alleged irregularities in the awarding of contracts for construction of Washington's new stadium—the home of Williams's Washington Redskins since 1961. Once again, with Williams beside him, Baker declined to answer the committee's questions, among them whether ex-president Truman and Baker had met with an insurance man seeking to carry a performance bond on construction of the stadium, and whether Ellen Rometsch had mentioned during her travels with Bak-

---

* Baker immediately told UPI that the *Newsweek* story was "'absolutely not true'" and that he had "'never heard of'" a settlement.[26] However, in 1978, in his own book, Baker confirmed every detail in Bradlee's story, right down to the men's room negotiations between Williams and Carliner. He even added that $10,000 of the $30,000 he paid Hill was "sneaked to me" by an executive of Melpar, the firm with which both Hill and Baker had sought to do business.[27]

er that she worked for the Communist East German government. The proceedings ended after Williams pointedly told the committee that Baker wouldn't even answer a question about the Brink's robbery, because he might then waive his privilege against self-incrimination and be forced to respond to more relevant inquiries.[28]

By then, however, Baker was in greater difficulty: A grand jury had started examining his case. On January 5, 1966, after a fifteen-month probe during which 170 witnesses had given 10,000 pages of testimony,[29] a nine-count indictment was returned against him. He was charged with two counts of tax evasion; five counts of defrauding some California savings and loan executives of a total of $100,000; one count of assisting his close friend Wayne Bromley in preparing a false tax return; and one count of conspiring with Bromley and Cliff Jones, former lieutenant governor of Nevada, to file false tax returns.[30] If convicted on all counts, Baker faced up to fifty-seven years in prison and fines of $47,000.[31]

Baker received more bad news when Federal Judge Oliver Gasch was assigned by lot to preside over his trial. Gasch (who had been appointed a judge by President Johnson on the recommendation of Abe Fortas) had, of course, crossed swords with Williams many times in the past, although he and Agnes Neill—by now Williams's second wife—were old family friends. In fact, Gasch, as U.S. attorney for the District of Columbia in the late 1950s, had tried to hire Neill away from Williams's office (before she and Williams were married). "To Ed Williams's credit," says Baker, "when Judge Gasch was selected to be my judge, he demanded that I release him as my counsel. He said, 'This man hates my guts. He is the worst judge in America for you. He will rule against you on every motion I make.' And he did." Baker adds that he kept Williams "because I thought he was so good he would win the case anyway."[32] Williams himself comments, "It was an extraordinarily bad break for the defense to have gotten Gasch to be the judge," because he "came out of the Hoffa trial very hostile toward me." Yet Williams did not attempt to have Gasch disqualified from the case, because "I never try to disqualify a judge. I think in order to get a disqualification, you have to show that the judge is prejudiced against the defendant, not the lawyer."

Williams and Baker were also troubled by the choice of prosecutor, Justice Department lawyer William O. Bittman. Baker disparages Bittman as "the kind of guy who'd cite you for going fifty-seven miles an hour" in a fifty-five-mile zone, and adds that Bittman "looked like he'd just come off the farm" and was nothing but "a Midwest shitkicker." Bittman had indeed kicked up a storm only a few years earlier in Chicago, where he had won a conviction against Jimmy Hoffa for misuse of Teamster funds. Despite Baker's low opinion of him, Bittman was a heavyweight, and Williams against Bittman would prove to be a no-holds-barred, anything-goes fight to the finish, the kind where it's almost a shame to have a referee halt the bloodshed.

Before the case actually went to trial, Williams attempted to have the indictment dismissed, claiming that "unusual and intensive publicity" had helped convince the grand jury to charge Baker. To this end, he presented a collection of nearly 200 articles and editorials from Washington media, which he said were "universally unfavorable" to Baker and "must have biased the grand jurors."[33] But Judge Gasch denied the motion, pointing out that the grand jury, having heard 10,000 pages of testimony, had had ample evidence to justify the indictment.[34] Williams did not ask for a change of venue to counteract the media blitz, because he and Baker wished to avoid the expense of hotel rooms and the like that holding the trial in another city would have involved.

Williams's major procedural effort—before, throughout, and after the trial—was to have the Baker case dropped because some of Baker's conversations had been overheard and recorded by federal agents. Although the prosecution denied vigorously that taps had ever been placed on phones in Baker's home or offices,[35] the phones of all three his partners in Serv-U (Edward Levinson of Las Vegas, Benjamin Sigelbaum of Miami, and Fred Black of Washington) had been tapped, and several of Baker's conversations had been picked up.[36] Most sensitive of all, Baker had been taped while talking by phone with Oscar Genera, the finance minister of the Dominican Republic, that country's embassy in Washington having been bugged by U.S. agents. Secretary of State Dean Rusk himself asked Gasch to suppress any references to the embassy bugging, and Gasch went along—on national-security grounds—over "the vehement protest" of Williams, who argued to Gasch, "'You are tying my client's hands behind him. . . . He loves his country and wants to help it, but this issue goes to the heart of our defense. You and the secretary of state are effectively leaving us powerless.'"[37]

Williams continued to protest the "widespread criminal activities engaged in" by the Justice Department while investigating Baker,[38] and claimed that the government's tactics and "the utter disregard for law exhibited by the agents . . . almost defy belief."[39] He was especially upset when an FBI agent, after testifying that "the informant advised that Edward Levinson received an incoming telephone call from Robert Baker," admitted that "the informant" was not a person at all, but a "microphone,"[40]* and he went so far as to try to subpoena J. Edgar Hoover to

---

*Williams also represented Levinson, who was charged with failing to pay taxes on money he had allegedly skimmed from profits at his Fremont casino in Las Vegas; Levinson in turn sued the FBI and the phone company in Las Vegas for $4.5 million for invasion of privacy. The *Washington Post* described the Levinson bugging as "one of the most embarrassing chapters in recent law enforcement history." In the end, Williams and Tom Wadden worked out a settlement under which Levinson dropped his suit and was allowed to plead *nolo contendere* and fined a minimal $5,000 on the tax charge.[41]

testify about the bugging of Baker's friends. (Gasch quashed the subpoena and was upheld by the U.S. Court of Appeals.[42]) Prosecutor Bittman admitted that Baker's constitutional right to privacy had been invaded when his conversations with Black, Levinson, and Sigelbaum were monitored,[43] but both Gasch[44] and the Court of Appeals agreed that the bugging had not tainted the government's investigation.[45]

Another use of bugging, of even greater concern to Williams, involved Wayne Bromley, whom Bittman described as "the Government's key witness."[46] Bromley, insisting that Baker was "my closest friend," described how he and the defendant had become friendly when both were Capitol pages in 1944. They had attended American University Law School together and been fraternity brothers. Also, Bromley said, Baker had once obtained a job for him in the Senate library.[47] But part of the case against Baker was based on his alleged plotting with Bromley and with Clifford Jones—owner of the Thunderbird Hotel in Las Vegas, an officer and director of First Western Financial Corporation in that city, and former lieutenant governor of Nevada, and a client of Baker's—to funnel money from Jones to Baker via Bromley. Baker desired this arrangement because Bromley was in a lower tax bracket than he,[48] and because, as Baker testified, his boss—then Senate Majority Leader Lyndon Johnson—had said that "in his judgment I had a fulltime job" and should not be doing outside work. Nevertheless, Baker acknowledged, he continued to represent Jones and other businessmen: "I was in essence moonlighting or sundowning or what you want to call it, but I was doing it contrary to the instructions of my boss."[49]

According to Bromley, he, Baker, and Jones had met in April 1963 at the Thunderbird and Jones had proposed paying Bromley the fees for Baker's services. Bromley would then turn over the money to Baker in secret. "I looked at Mr. Baker and he nodded," Bromley said, "so I told Mr. Jones if that was what everybody wanted, it was o.k. with me."[50]

When Bromley and Jones were called before the grand jury investigating Baker, Bromley testified first, in October 1964. Four months later, he was notified that the prosecutors considered some of his previous testimony false, and he was subpoenaed to appear again. He then hired a lawyer, Mark Sandground, who met with Bittman and his staff and learned that his client now faced perjury and tax charges of his own, but that any "cooperation" would be "appreciated." No promises were made, but Sandground "got the message," and Bromley became a most cooperative witness for the government. When he testified before the grand jury for the second time, on February 23, 1965, he spoke what the prosecution regarded as "the truth," stating that Jones had known that Bromley was merely a conduit for money actually meant for Baker.

Jones denied this when he in turn testified on March 17, claiming instead that Bromley was being paid for lobbying on behalf of First Western.[51] He was apparently unaware that Bromley had already talked to the grand jury once, let alone twice. In fact, he telephoned Bromley on March 22 and reported his testimony. Describing that telephone call on the witness stand, Bromley testified that Jones had insisted that he "tell the Grand Jury that he knew nothing" about a scheme to cover up payments to Baker. "Otherwise, he [Jones] would be in the soup." Bromley also quoted Jones as saying that the three of them had to "get our stories together," or else Jones "was going to be in trouble for perjury."[52]

Immediately after Jones's telephone call, Bromley had reported it to his lawyer, Sandground, who relayed the news to Bittman. That same night, Sandground, Bittman, and Donald Page Moore, an attorney assisting Bittman, went to Bromley's home, along with a court reporter. After Bromley gave his written consent, a listening device was installed on one of his phones. Bromley then called Jones in Las Vegas, on the pretext that he had had guests and had not been able to talk freely during their earlier conversation. With the court reporter transcribing the entire exchange, Bromley told Jones he would like to meet with him and Baker so that the three could coordinate their versions of their April 1963 conference. Then, again giving his written consent, he allowed Bittman's agents to hook up a tape recorder to his phone and made a series of calls to Baker and Jones, setting up a three-way meeting for March 26 in Los Angeles.

Having obtained authorization from the attorney general, Bittman arranged for Bromley to wear a transmitter strapped to his abdomen for his appointment with Baker and Jones. Nearby agents were to receive transmissions of the talks,* but the equipment malfunctioned and the assembled multitude, consisting of about ten narcotics agents and assistant U.S. attorneys, could hear little of what was said.[54]† In the end, Bromley and Jones were listed as unindicted co-conspirators in the Baker case and Jones was charged in a separate perjury suit.[56]

On top of broadcasting his conversations with Baker and Jones to government agents, Bromley paid a visit to Williams's law office on June 2, 1965, more than three months after he had signed on with the Bittman team. Dropping in without an appointment, he asked for Williams and was told he was unavailable. Bromley then met with Vincent Fuller, who

---

*After J. Edgar Hoover refused to allow the FBI to participate, agents of the Treasury Department's Narcotics Bureau, "all too eager to experiment with a new electronic gadget," as one federal judge put it, monitored the meeting[53]—even though the Baker case had nothing to do with drugs.

† Baker believes that Bromley cut off the transmitter and told his disappointed audience it hadn't worked because his "conscience began to hurt him." After the three men had their talk, Baker took Bromley to a party attended by Marlon Brando, Anita Ekberg, and other stars, and fixed up his longtime friend with "a date with a cute starlet." Baker's help in the dating game may have made Bromley feel even guiltier, and he later confessed that he had permitted himself to be turned into "'a walking microphone'" as part of the government's campaign against Baker.[55]

says that Bromley "told me a long story [about his dealings with Baker], after which I told him, 'You have a conflict of interest with this law firm, but you should not go back before the grand jury without counsel.'" Williams later talked to Bromley by phone and gave him the same advice.

Bromley's motive for going to Williams's office is in dispute. He himself testified that Baker had asked him to go, "to inform Mr. Baker's attorneys as to the general areas of which I had been asked questions by different investigative groups," and he acknowledged that he had not called on Williams "to seek legal advice as such."[57] Williams tried yet again to have the Baker indictment dismissed, or at least to have Bromley's testimony excluded from the record, claiming that his "invasion" of Baker's lawyer's office in "the guise of a *bona fide* client" had deprived Baker of his constitutionally protected privilege against self-incrimination and rights to due process of law and to counsel.[58] Every motion that Williams filed, however, was rejected by both Gasch and the court of appeals.[59]*

As a result of his contacts—although limited—with Bromley, Williams refrained from questioning him during the trial. Williams was present at the defense table while other lawyers for Baker interrogated Bromley, and, like a baseball manager who has been kicked out of the game and continues to give orders from the clubhouse, he was still able to suggest what questions to ask. And Bromley was forced by other defense lawyers to admit that he had lied on at least five different occasions during the Baker probe: to the FBI; to Senate investigators; to an intelligence agent from the Treasury Department; to an investigator from the office of the Comptroller of Currency; and to the Baker grand jury.[62] Nevertheless, the Baker trial was unique among Williams's major cases because it was the only one in which he did not cross-examine a key prosecution witness.

The foundation of the other charges against Baker was that several California savings and loan executives had given him nearly $100,000 in cash, which he was to pass on to Senator Robert Kerr, who, in turn, was to distribute the money to the reelection campaigns of politicians he favored. In exchange, Kerr would allegedly see to it that the Senate Finance Committee he chaired acted in the best interests of the savings and loan industry. However, the prosecution claimed Baker had pocketed the money.

---

* In the Clifford Jones perjury case, though, a federal judge ruled that Bromley had been coerced into cooperating with the government under strong threat of being prosecuted himself, and that Bromley's actions "bordered on entrapment." His testimony was ordered suppressed at Jones's trial,[60] but the court of appeals reversed, holding that Bromley "was not an illiterate or unworldly," but was accustomed to "moving in very sophisticated circles indeed," and, rather than being forced to go along with the government, had acted voluntarily.[61]

A procession of government witnesses offered testimony to bolster the charge that Baker had kept the $100,000. One of them, Kenneth Childs, president of Home Savings and Loan of Los Angeles, the nation's largest such financial institution, testified as follows:

> Mr. Baker told me that he felt the savings and loan industry had been very backward and far behind other businesses in recognizing the necessity of becoming politically active; that it was important for a business to get out and work politically, to make friends and to make contacts, so that when legislation came along that affected that business, there would be an open door and an attentive ear.... Mr. Baker told me of two instances in which candidates who had publicly stated they were in favor of the oil depletion law had received substantial campaign help the following day, from major oil companies. He mentioned that he was the secretary, I believe it is, of the majority, that he also was collector ... of campaign funds for the Senate Campaign Committee.... I believe Mr. Baker had suggested that it would be very impressive if the California savings and loan industry made campaign contributions in the amount of $100,000 and that would certainly start them along the line that we had been talking about.[63]

Other savings and loan officials described a series of meetings with Baker in which they turned over to him $100,000,* which he said would be used to aid the campaigns of Senators Everett Dirksen (Republican leader in the Senate), Carl Hayden, Thruston Morton, Wallace Bennett, Frank Carlson, William Fulbright, and George Smathers and Congressman Wilbur Mills.[65] The government then called as witnesses the seven senators and Congressman Mills. After Mills and Fulbright testified that Kerr had never given them any money from the savings and loan executives (Mills, in fact, said he was unopposed in his next race), Williams, recognizing that the parade of respected politicians was hurting Baker, stipulated to the testimony of the other six, who did not take the witness stand.[66]

The defense was now in a very tough position. The savings and loan officers had testified they had given Baker money that was to be used in political campaigns. The politicians for whom the funds had supposedly been intended had denied receiving them. *Something* had happened to the $100,000, and the obvious inference was that Baker had enriched himself by that amount. There was, however, another possible explanation: What if Kerr, not Baker, had taken the money? What if Kerr had viewed the $100,000 as a reward for his watching over the savings and loan interests

---

*Of that money, $10,000 was provided by Joseph L. Allbritton, then the relatively obscure owner of a Houston financial institution.[64] Allbritton later became a newspaper, television, and banking magnate in Washington, and, in 1982, attempted to purchase the *New York Daily News.*

in the Senate? Since Kerr had died on New Year's Day, 1963, it would be Baker's word against a dead man's, and a dead man tells no tales. Williams advised Baker that although it was both "'risky'" and "'not popular'" to "'badmouth the dead,'" Baker had "'no choice'" but to point the finger at Kerr.[67] Williams says emphatically that the defense was "not concocted"; it was simply a matter of "putting the best face on the facts." This strategy seems more than simply "risky." Not only had Kerr, along with Lyndon Johnson, served as Baker's surrogate father, but Kerr was also a fabulously wealthy oilman; a jury might have trouble believing that so rich a man could be bribed, even for $100,000. But, as Michael Tigar, a young lawyer who assisted Williams in the case, explains, "When we began to pull apart the elements, it became clear that since there was no question that Baker got the money, what other defense was there?"

Williams and Baker decided to take the desperate gamble. Making his opening argument at the conclusion of the prosecution's case, Williams characterized Kerr as Baker's "second closest friend among the Senators," and a man with whom Baker had "an almost father-son relationship." Kerr had converted the savings and loan donation to his own use and then had loaned part of it to Baker, according to Williams. The point was that instead of stealing the $100,000, his client "did with the money that was turned over to him precisely what he was expected to do with that money"—he gave it to Kerr.[68] As Williams delivered his fifty-five minute speech to a "rapt" jury without referring to notes, the packed courtroom "was as silent as a church."[69] This was what those in the audience had been waiting for: Williams at his fabled best, in his first major trial in Washington since the Hoffa case in 1957.

Calling Baker as the first defense witness, Williams led him through a point-by-point denial of the prosecution's case. As to the Kerr money, Baker testified that he had gotten into "very, very serious financial difficulty" after his Carousel Motel in Ocean City was severely damaged in a 1962 storm and his partner in the venture died at the same time. Then, Baker said, "I went to the best friend that I ever had around the Capitol. I went to see the then Vice President [Johnson] and told him that I had a serious problem . . . and asked his advice. He picked up the phone and called his friend and my friend, Senator Kerr, and he then advised me to go immediately to Senator Kerr's office; which I did." Kerr arranged a $250,000 loan for Baker from an Oklahoma City bank and promised to lend him another $50,000 himself from the $100,000 savings and loan money, which, Baker said, Kerr subsequently did. And Baker went on to tell of Kerr's telephone call from a hospital at Christmas 1962, just a week before the senator died.

> [He] said he wanted to call me to let me know that he loved me and my family, and he said that—he said, "Bob, I hope this is the best Christmas that you ever had." . . . And he said, "The reason that I

wanted to talk to you was I wanted to . . . sort of wipe your slate clean
of the money that I have loaned to you. . . . Just put down that you got
a legal fee, or a fee from me for the many wonderful things that you
have done for me." And I asked him not to talk to me about it. But he
said, "No, this is what I want to do." And I never talked to him again. I
went to his funeral [a week later].

An emotional Baker concluded by telling the jurors that Kerr's death
was "probably the biggest personal loss I ever suffered."[70]

Williams called Fred Black, Baker's friend and business partner, to
back up his story, and Black testified that, about a month before Kerr's
death, the senator had asked him if he thought Baker would be able to
repay the loan, which Kerr said he had advanced Baker "out of what he
called campaign funds and that he would have to replenish out of his own
pocket if he couldn't pay it." Black reported telling Kerr that he doubted
that Baker would be able to repay it.[71]

Black apparently was not a very credible witness, at least in the opinion
of Bittman—who said during a bench conference, "Fred Black, in my
opinion, will say anything Bobby Baker wants him to say. . . . He has done
it before and he will do it again"[72]—and Gasch, who agreed, "I don't
know who would believe Black. I have some reservations about believing
Black myself."[73] Williams did offer partial substantiation from another
witness, who testified that Black had once quoted Kerr as having said,
"'As long as I have a Bobby Baker here, I don't need my sons.'"[74] But
Bittman had a rebuttal witness who was perhaps more persuasive: Robert
Kerr, Jr., who said he had heard his father mention Baker only two or
three times, and that Kerr Sr. was in the habit of keeping records of loans
as small as $15 to members of his family. The only record of a loan his
father had made to Baker was one of $500 in 1951, which, according to
the elder Kerr's meticulous records, had been repaid.[75]

Part of the risk in having Baker testify in his own defense was that it
gave Bittman an opportunity to cross-examine him, but Williams felt his
client would have little chance of being acquitted unless he took the witness stand. In the judgment of one reporter at the trial, Bittman treated
Baker "with all the compassion of a mortally wounded rhinoceros."[76] But
Baker compounded the difficulty by responding to Bittman's questions
with long, rambling answers that may have made him appear evasive. In
one instance, Bittman asked if Baker had gone to Kerr's home to deliver
part of the savings and loan money, and Baker launched into a lengthy
monologue about Kerr's various residences in the Washington area and a
ranch house the senator was building in Oklahoma. Bittman finally cut
off the defendant: "Mr. Baker, please."[77] Baker also may have had trouble hiding his hostility toward Bittman; he later wrote that when Bittman

inquired if there were any witnesses to his turning money over to Kerr, he was tempted to reply, "'You don't hand over bribes in a crowd,'" but Williams had warned him against "getting into a pissing contest with Bittman."[78]

Williams's plan to offer character witnesses was nullified by Bittman's threats—both veiled and blatant—to expose Baker's sex life. During one conference at the bench, Bittman said he had refrained from disclosing to the jury that Baker had often traveled with Carole Tyler instead of his wife. Williams exploded. "You have made this reckless allegation about ten times in this case, both to me and to the Judge, His Honor, that it wasn't Mrs. Baker" who accompanied Baker. Bittman explained that he had learned from phone records that while Baker was at hotels with a woman, he was placing long-distance calls to his wife in Washington.[79] When Bittman ultimately asked Williams if he planned to put on character witnesses, and when Williams said he did, Bittman told him he had "'hotel and motel records from all over the country'" documenting Baker's infidelity to his wife, but "'we won't introduce those records provided you don't call character witnesses.'"

Baker wanted to call the witnesses to the stand anyway, but Williams persuaded him otherwise.[80] In Williams's words, "It was my habitual routine to put character witnesses on," but in the Baker case, "I feared the cross-examination" of them "would get in rumors and innuendo of things that hadn't been before the jury. When you cross-examine a character witness as to the reputation of the defendant, anything goes. They can ask you about any rumor. Baker had a girlfriend—it was notorious that he had a girlfriend that he was keeping. There were all kinds of things like that in his life that just would not have been profitable to lay open in front of that jury."

As a result, a jury that had been handpicked for its responsiveness to Baker's character witnesses—not for its ability to comprehend a very complex case—never heard from those witnesses what a fine fellow Baker was.

The exchanges between Williams and Bittman over Baker's love life were among many of that nature between the two lawyers, leading Williams to observe that with Bittman "I had the most unpleasant relationship that I ever had" with a lawyer during a trial. "I found him thoroughly obnoxious. I just didn't like the way he conducted himself in that case." Bittman himself praises Williams's skills as a lawyer, but limits his comments about Williams as a person, in accordance with the "If you can't say anything nice . . . " school of thought. He does say that "there are cases where you can sit down with the other lawyer and have a drink with him or go out to lunch with him, but I would not have done that with Williams." But at least one observer enjoyed the battle. Judge Oliver

Gasch says, "That was a good matchup. They were punching each other all around the courtroom. But it was a well-prepared, well-tried case. I've never seen a better one."

As the trial wore on, tempers became more frayed. During one discussion in chambers, Bittman denied (as he had before) that he had been responsible for intercepting Baker's calls, and Williams muttered something. Gasch said innocently, "I didn't hear your comment, Ed," and Williams apologized, "I said it and I shouldn't have. It was an extemporaneous ejaculation for which I am sorry."[81]

The dispute that might have had the greatest impact on the jurors took place while Fred Black was testifying. As Bittman cross-examined Black about statements he had given IRS agents in 1964, Williams objected that he did not have a copy of Black's comments. Bittman declared, "That is right, you don't. Otherwise, he probably—well—."[82]

The most logical interpretation of Bittman's remark was that if Williams had known what Black had said three years earlier, he might have advised Black to testify differently at the trial; in other words, that Williams would have suborned perjury. That was exactly the impression that Williams received. Rushing to the bench, he complained to Gasch that "Mr. Bittman has just suggested to the jury something I think is grossly improper. He has suggested by what he has just directed at me that there was some subornation on the part of this witness. That was the clear implication left with this jury and I ask for" a mistrial. "I think it was grossly improper of him. It was a foul blow; it was a low blow; I resent it bitterly."

Gasch denied Williams's motion for a mistrial, but, noting that Bittman had said to Williams, "That is right, you don't," he lectured Bittman. "I have warned counsel from the outset that there was to be no colloquy between counsel and I want that rule adhered to . . . by both of you and particularly you," he said, addressing Bittman.[83]

As the time arrived for closing arguments, Williams attempted to throw Bittman off stride, just as he had done with Morton Robson in the Adam Clayton Powell trial. Bittman was about to go into the courtroom when Williams initiated a fifteen-minute argument in Gasch's chambers over the charts Bittman planned to use in his speech.[84] His objections, of course, were to no avail.

Hardly anyone could have been disappointed over the closing performances of Williams and Bittman. Speaking first and last, as is customary, Bittman told the jury in the opening part of his statement that Baker "stole" the $100,000, "as simple as that." He reminded the jurors of a witness who had said she went into Baker's office in the Capitol and saw "piles of money on the defendant's desk," which, Bittman said sarcastically, would be "the scene of a typical Government office." Noting that the witness in question, the widow of Baker's partner in the Carousel

Motel, had testified that Baker had given her $18,300 in cash, after which Carole Tyler put the rest of the money in a safe, Bittman observed: "Normally, people deal in cash when they are trying to conceal something, normally."

Speaking of Baker's business interests, Bittman declared, "We know of probably 30 outside activities . . . and I submit to you, if he will be deceitful to the Majority Leader, he will be deceitful to you." He also pointed out "the flaw" in Baker's "incredible story": Baker "left the Senate on October 7, 1963" so for most of the period in question he had no need to try to conceal his sources of income from the Senate majority leader. Nonetheless, he was trying to hide the fact that he had stolen the $100,000 and conspired with Bromley and Jones to evade his taxes. And the prosecutor was most eloquent in telling the jurors what kind of person Baker was:

> His desires and his motivations are based on one great defect in his character. The Old Testament describes it best, "The love of money is the root of all evil," and he loved it in cash. The feel of it. The power of it. Through his office and through his hands there constantly flowed huge amounts of cash. Why? Because Robert Baker consciously chose to trade on his position of trust for his own pecuniary profit. . . . Motivated by greed and spurred on by an insatiable lust for power and money, he built a financial empire so huge that he had to steal to save it from destruction. And was himself destroyed in the process. That is why he is here today.[85]

In his own closing speech to the jury, Williams bore in on the missing $100,000, where it had come from, and where it had gone. Never once using the word *bribe,* he declared that the prosecution was

> asking you to believe that six of the leading executives in the savings and loan industry in the state of California, six financial tycoons put together $100,000 and turned it over for the benefit of some Senators, whose names they didn't remember until thirty days ago, about whose politics they asked nothing, from whom they expected no acknowledgment. . . .
>
> Whom did it [the government] call in here to support that story? It didn't call in a group of gullible farmers. It didn't call in six slack-jawed bumpkins. It called in six flinty-eyed bankers . . . these marble-hearted bankers. . . .
>
> Why, you would have a better chance to walk out of the Louvre Museum with the Venus de Milo under your arm than to get $100,000 from those bankers unless they knew where it was going, why it was going there, whether it got there, and when it got there. However, the Government says to you? "They wanted some friends in Washington." They paid $100,000 for eight friends and they forgot to find out the names of the friends. . . . I say, members of the jury, that that story was

a gratuitous insult to our intelligence. I say further to you that it is the greatest hoax that has ever been served up to a jury.

Williams also referred with indignation to Bittman's alleged criticism of Baker's lawyers:

Now, the suggestion has been made that we tailored this defense. That we concocted it. I don't resent it for myself. I have been here in front of you for three weeks, and you either think by this time that I would be a party to that kind of thing or you don't. And I am not going to make any defense of my integrity to you, but I resent bitterly that accusation leveled against the young lawyers sitting with me in this room, and against Mr. [Boris] Kostelanetz [another of Baker's attorneys], and I say to you that I hope the lust for victory never pulses through my veins so fast and so hard that I would make a vicious, rotten attack like that for the sake of winning any case.

The bottom line, though, was that "Senator Kerr got the money . . . it went to him as it was intended to go to him." Furthermore, Williams asked the jury, "Have you ever heard of a larceny case . . . when the victim did not make a complaint? Didn't murmur one word that there had been a theft? None of the savings and loan men ever said one word about it."[86]

Bittman, in his rebuttal, turned folksy: "Ladies and gentlemen, there is an old adage among lawyers, particularly trial lawyers, particularly criminal trial lawyers, and that is when you are weak on the facts, you argue the law, and when you are weak on the law, you argue the facts, and when you are weak on the facts and the law, you attack the prosecution. That thumbnail sketch is what Mr. Williams has done today."

His final words cast the prosecution as the protector of an innocent dead man's reputation:

He [Williams] never comes out and says it, but the inference is this was a bribe to Senator Kerr. Let's call it. Let's bring it out in front. Let's talk about it. That's what he says. He tried to get cute . . . but that is what he is saying. His whole defense . . . [is] predicated on Senator Kerr accepted a $100,000 bribe to fix the legislation. . . . When the man is dead and enjoyed an exemplary reputation all his life. And then four years after he is dead, he accepted a $100,000 bribe because it is convenient for my defense.

Bittman hammered it across one last time: "Whatever wrongs Robert Baker . . . has committed in his life, they are small compared to what he has attempted to do to his former deceased friend, Senator Kerr. And I submit to you, that Senator Kerr has testified, has spoken in this case, through his books and records, which reflect the meticulous way [in] which he maintained his life." Concluded Bittman, "Ladies and gentlemen, I believe that you can go a long way in vindicating a great man in his memory to many people."[87]

Washington Post reporter Richard Harwood thought highly of both summations, saying Williams had been "masterful," but so had Bittman, "whose indignation at Baker and his associates was apparent throughout the trial."[88]

After the closing arguments and Judge Gasch's instructions to the jury, the panel retired to its deliberations on January 28, 1967. The next day, a Sunday, Baker was convicted on seven of the nine counts—the most on which the jury could have found him guilty, because two of the seven counts were alternates to two others.[89] One juror said of Baker's testimony, "'We caught him in lies. He was fabricating,'"[90] while another said, "'Baker had nothing to go on other than he had a good lawyer.'"[91]

As for that lawyer, he "appeared to have been hit with a brick," according to his client. A little while later, the defense group gathered at Baker's home, where Williams wept. "He did not cry a silent, gentlemanly stream of tears; his thick body shook and jerked almost convulsively as he sobbed," said Baker. "Mucus ran from his nose. I wiped it off, mixed him a stiff drink, and tried to comfort him." Baker told his attorney, "'Ed, I could not have been better represented. You worked your ass off,'" but "Williams was inconsolable."[92] *

Reasons for the loss offered by those involved range from Baker's performance as a witness to the makeup of the jury to the smear on Senator Kerr. Judge Gasch feels that Baker "wasn't too good a witness in his own behalf," an opinion shared by Bittman, who thinks the substantiation provided for Baker by Fred Black was even less credible. (To Bittman's surprise, Black asked Bittman to defend him in a tax case of his own when Bittman entered private practice after the Baker trial; Bittman replied that he did "not think it would be appropriate.") Michael Tigar also says Baker was a poor witness, and Baker himself says that Williams subjected him to "I guess the worst tongue-lashing I've ever had in my life" because Bittman "made a monkey out of me. Williams said, 'You're the worst witness that ever appeared on a witness stand.'"

Gasch says that the accusations against Kerr and Baker's admission of deceiving Lyndon Johnson about his moonlighting "were both gifts" to the prosecution; the Kerr theory in particular "was a killer"to the defense case. And Bittman agrees, considering the Kerr bribe "just too convenient a story. I think it's very dangerous when your defense is based on someone who can't speak for himself."

Baker himself thinks the defense story was "too complicated. Those

---

* Baker says his vivid description upset Williams; the defense attorney now asserts that Baker's account is completely inaccurate.

people on that jury had an average of a tenth-grade education, if that."
Michael Tigar substantiates that view, recalling that after a witness had
referred to capital gains, "the marshal [assigned to care for the jurors]
reported the next morning that one juror turned to another and said,
'Who's that Captain Gains that they were talking about today?' And the
other one said, 'Oh, he's going to testify tomorrow.'" Says Tigar, "A lot
of this was just beyond their reach. A jury in the District of Columbia is
just not your best forum" for such a convoluted case as the defense offered.

Judge Oliver Gasch sentenced Bobby Baker to a term of one to three
years in prison. No fine was imposed.[93] Baker remained free for almost
four years while Williams argued appeals based on wiretapping, the
makeup of the jury, and the contention that several different charges had
improperly been combined into a single case. The process was exhausted
just before Christmas 1970, when the Supreme Court refused to review an
appeals-court decision that sustained Gasch's rulings,[94] and Baker became
Williams's only client in a major trial to serve time in prison. He entered
the minimum-security federal facility at Allenwood, Pennsylvania, in January 1971 and was released for good behavior after sixteen months.[95] A
decade later, he was still trying to overturn his conviction, but Williams,
who feels "he won't get anywhere," was no longer his lawyer.

To the chagrin of Edward Bennett Williams, William O. Bittman
joined the firm of Hogan & Hartson immediately after the Baker trial.
Although Williams would not have given Bittman a recommendation, he
maintains, "I had no interest where he went to practice law." Bittman,
however, says, "I had heard—I don't know if it's true—that Ed wasn't too
happy" about his becoming a partner at the firm that had played such an
important part in Williams's own life.

Williams can scarcely restrain his glee over the circumstances surrounding Bittman's departure from the Hogan firm in 1974, after seven
years there. What had happened was that Bittman represented E. Howard Hunt during Watergate, and, by his own admission, had received
about $40,000 in cash on his client's account, which Bittman turned over
to Hogan & Hartson. Nixon bagman Tony Ulasewicz left the currency
for Bittman in his mailbox at home during the night, or in a phone booth
in his office building in daytime. Many people familiar with the events
believe that Bittman was encouraged to leave Hogan & Hartson, and that
he came close to being indicted himself over Watergate. Bittman insists,
"I was not asked to leave Hogan and Hartson. There were a number of
factors. I think Watergate was one of them. There was a lot of publicity,
not all of it laudatory." His attitude at the time was "If there are people
around here who don't appreciate my efforts for the firm, I'll take my
clients and go elsewhere. Which, I might add, I did. I had a lot of clients.

They were clients that had come to me, not to Hogan and Hartson. Practically every client I represented went with me."

John Sirica, the Watergate judge, recalls that Bittman apparently withheld evidence from Watergate investigators, after which Sirica, formerly of Hogan & Hartson, had to call in "other partners from my old firm to be questioned about" the case. "The whole incident was unpleasant for me," Sirica said. He also mentioned the cash payments to Bittman and commented, "Most lawyers I know refuse large cash payments and insist on bank checks, for their records and for their own protection."[96] Williams adds, "*I* don't receive payments in cash in a telephone booth." It is one of life's little ironies that Bittman, who castigated Baker because "he loved it in cash," later got in trouble for accepting cash payments himself.

For the past ten years, Ed Williams and Bill Bittman have been neighbors. Their paths cross frequently, for they both belong to the same country club, worship in the same parish, and sometimes wind up at the same parties, although not at each other's houses. Furthermore, their offices in downtown Washington, fifteen miles from their homes, are three blocks apart.

Several years ago, they fought side by side to keep a garbage dump from being opened near their homes. Bittman was chairman of a neighborhood committee dedicated to killing the project, and he says that "Ed and I worked very closely together." Williams even attended a meeting on the subject at Bittman's office, but if he saw the sketches on Bittman's wall showing the prosecutor in action during the Baker trial, he gave no indication.

In spite of the similarities in their lives, Ed Williams and Bill Bittman have as little to do with each other as they can.

21

John Connally:
Back in the Winner's Circle

Like Bobby Baker, John Connally was the defendant in a political corruption case in which the primary witness was an informer. Like Bobby Baker, John Connally is a white southerner who was tried in a District of Columbia courtroom by a predominantly black jury. Like Bobby Baker, John Connally was prosecuted by a young government lawyer (Frank Tuerkheimer) who, in the words of Michael Tigar, Edward Bennett Williams's courtroom assistant in both cases, "sought to win his spurs by knocking off Ed." Unlike Bobby Baker, John Connally was acquitted.

The root of John Connally's troubles was Richard Nixon's White House taping system. Connally served as secretary of the Treasury for most of 1971 and the first half of 1972 (resigning just before the ill-fated Watergate break-in), and Nixon's tapes disclosed snatches of a conversation between the president and Connally that took place on March 23, 1971. According to the tape, Connally seemed to say to Nixon that if the administration would allow federal milk-price supports to rise, "it's on my honor to make sure that, that, there there's a very substantial allocation of oil in Texas that you, that that will be at your, at your discretion." Nixon

320

answered, "Fine."* The conversation continued:

> *Nixon:* This is a, this is a cold—
>
> *Connally:* Oh—
>
> *Nixon:* —political deal. They're very—
>
> *Connally:* [Unintelligible]
>
> *Nixon:* tough political operators.
>
> *Connally:* And they've, they've got it.
>
> *Nixon:* They've got it. . . .
>
> *Connally:* If this is done, I'm going to expect to call on you for one [unintelligible].
>
> *Nixon:* [laughs] Okay, I'll catch up, thank you.[1]

After members of the Watergate Special Prosecutor's Office listened to this tape, they reconstructed the following version of what had happened: Connally had promised Nixon that if milk prices rose, the dairy industry would give Nixon "a very substantial allocation of oil in Texas," where Connally had once been governor. Milk prices did in fact go up several days later, after which, the government claimed, Jake Jacobsen,[†] a lawyer for Associated Milk Producers, Inc., a dairy industry group, gave Connally two payments of $5,000 each as a "thank you."[2‡]

Both Connally and Jacobsen were called before a federal grand jury in Washington that was investigating Watergate-related matters. When Connally found out in late 1973 or early 1974 that he was a target of the probe, he asked Williams to defend him, even though Williams at the time was number one on the White House enemies list, and Connally was still close to Nixon. Williams and Connally got along famously, just as their mutual friend, Democratic honcho Robert Strauss, had predicted, and Williams agreed to take the case. Several months later, on July 29, 1974, Connally was charged with two counts of receiving $5,000 in illegal gratuities from Jacobsen on May 14, 1971, and again on September 24, 1971;

---

*Much of the tape was inaudible or subject to differing interpretations—Williams says that where Connally supposedly said "Texas" he might just as easily have said "taxes," and adds that the tape does not prove that the discussion was about milk prices. Furthermore, both Nixon and Connally were remarkably inarticulate, as if each was afraid to say anything specific that might come back to haunt him.

†Connally and Jacobsen had been close friends for many years through Texas politics. Jacobsen had once been an assistant to Governor Price Daniel, and both Jacobsen and Connally had been allies of Lyndon Johnson.

‡Although Connally was commonly thought to have been accused of taking a bribe, he was actually indicted for accepting an illegal gratuity. The difference is that there is no *quid pro quo* in a gratuity case; Connally was said to have lobbied for the milk-price increase and later been paid $10,000 for his help, rather than having been promised the money in exchange for his influence.

one count of conspiring with Jacobsen to obstruct justice by testifying falsely about the payoff; and two counts of perjury before the grand jury. Jacobsen was charged with giving Connally the money illegally; he pleaded guilty and promised to testify against Connally in return for having other charges against him dismissed.[3]

Among several attempts by Williams to have the charges against Connally dropped or reduced, or to have evidence excluded from the trial, the most notable was his effort to have Nixon called into court to authenticate the White House tape. Had Nixon appeared, it could only have been humiliating to him; but if he declined, some potentially convincing evidence against Connally would have to be tossed out. The likelihood was that Nixon would not testify voluntarily, both to avoid embarrassment and to help Connally by invalidating the tapes—as Williams well knew. Williams argued that "where one undertakes to offer a transcript of a conversation which has been recorded with the consent of one of the parties . . . it is necessary to have one of the parties identify that conversation as having been accurately reflected by the transcript." The prosecution could not offer the tape "unless and until someone who was a party to that conversation takes the witness stand." Since there were only two people involved, and one of them (Connally) certainly was not going to help the government prosecute him, that left only Nixon to back up the tape. "We are standing on this point . . . which requires one of the participants to come and identify the conversation," Williams insisted.

Grasping his point, Federal District Judge George L. Hart, Jr., who was hearing the case, observed, "Which in this case would be Nixon."

Williams affirmed, "In this case it would be the other participant, Mr. Nixon."

Hart, as might be expected, refused to order Nixon into court, but he ruled that the tape could be admitted.[4] However, Williams actually gained his objective, because Hart ordered the jurors to listen to the tape without a written transcript to help them follow it. And the tape was of such poor quality that "none of them appeared to make out what was being said—thus effectively eliminating the alleged payoff offer from the prosecution's case."[5]

Williams also tried to find out the substance of another Connally conversation when he learned that the defendant had once been overheard "during the course of electronic surveillance conducted by the federal government."[6] But Attorney General William Saxbe swore in an affidavit that Connally had been talking with someone who was the subject of a "national security electronic surveillance" that had been "authorized by the President of the United States." The attorney general urged Judge Hart to study the tape by himself and not reveal its contents to the defense or anyone else.[7] Hart went along, despite Williams's argument that "invoking the 'national security,' the Government claims that this surveillance was lawful, though never authorized by a judicial officer and that the fruits of this surveillance need not be turned over to the defendant. Both these claims are not only wrong, but—if sustained—would be subversive of constitutional liberty."[8]

Williams also moved for a change of venue from Washington to some other federal district—preferably San Antonio, near Connally's 9,000-acre cattle ranch—claiming that extensive publicity had rendered impossible "a fair and impartial trial" in Washington.[9] And he asked that the case be severed, so that Connally would stand separate trials on the two counts of accepting gratuities and on the three other counts of perjury and conspiracy.[10]

Hart denied the motion for a site change, but granted Williams's request for a severance,[11] in what many observers regard as the most important ruling in the entire case. One source incomparably familiar with the case says, "That probably meant the difference between conviction and acquittal." Noting that Hart had been chairman of the Republican party in the District of Columbia before he was appointed to the bench by President Eisenhower, and that Connally had switched to the GOP in 1973 and been an insider in the Nixon administration even before that, the same source commented, "Judge Hart definitely, very definitely, was trying to hold an umbrella over John Connally. He was trying to help him in every way he could." And Henry Ruth, who supervised the Connally case within the Special Prosecutor's Office, says, "In particular cases, there are prosecutors' judges and defense judges. In this case, I think the defense got most of what they asked for. . . . It was not improper" for Hart to have granted the severance, but "most judges probably would not have." According to Chip Yablonski, an outspoken critic of Williams, "The rumor around the courthouse was that John Connally was acquitted in chambers"—a reference to Williams's alleged influence over Hart.

Williams, of course, believes that the splitting of the charges was fair, as it prevented evidence that was relevant to only some counts from prejudicing Connally's chances on other counts. He also is of the opinion that Judge Oliver Gasch should have made a similar ruling in Bobby Baker's case, and he thinks it would have resulted in Baker's acquittal.

Connally went to trial on April 1, 1975. He was to be tried first on the two gratuities counts (he faced a sentence of two years in prison and a $10,000 fine on each); the perjury and conspiracy counts were held over for a later date.

As the trial opened, Williams—a civil-rights activist who had been a leader in integrating the D.C. Bar—renewed his motion for a change of venue, this time because of the the racial makeup of the jury. During a hearing that for obvious reasons was held in the privacy of Judge art's chambers, Williams noted that out of forty-four remaining members of the jury pool, thirty-eight were black. Therefore, he said, the prosecution could use its six peremptory challenges to remove the six whites and thus compel Connally to face a jury that would be 100 percent black. (Williams also noted that only one of the forty-four potential jurors was a registered Republican, like the defendant.) Williams declared, "I believe in affirmative action programs very deeply." However, "I think if ever there was an affirmative action program, it's needed for whites on the juries in the District of Columbia so that we can have representative juries, and I don't think we have a representative jury here." He asked that his comments on the race issue be sealed by Hart, "for fear they are misunderstood." *

Frank Tuerkheimer of the Watergate Special Prosecutor's Office, who was conducting the Connally case for the government, also touched on the race issue when he opposed Williams's motion to relocate the trial:

> Mr. Williams knows that in this case once we get past Mr. Jacobsen's testimony, that our evidence is basically circumstantial, that to . . . whatever extent there is substantial corroboration, the evidence I have, I would submit, depends in large part on having a jury that is intelligent, without for a moment suggesting there is a correlation between race and intelligence. If he thinks that we are trying to get a jury that is less than intelligent, that is not in conformity with our interest as I see it.

Hart replied that each side could challenge whichever jurors it chose, but "if we end up with an all-black jury, while I feel you will still get a fair trial, I think that the repercussions throughout the country may be very adverse on the system of justice, which, of course, I would deplore." He asked both sides to "give serious consideration not to striking any white people except for very good cause," and ordered the trial to proceed in Washington.[12]

Having to try the case before a mostly black jury in the District of Columbia continued to be of great concern to Williams, especially after he ran into Spiro T. Agnew, who is said to have told him, "'I think you're going to lose. That's not saying anything about your client. I was innocent too. But I couldn't go to trial before a bunch of black people. They wouldn't have understood.'" And so, Agnew said, he decided to plead *nolo contendere* in his tax-evasion case.

As it turned out, three whites were seated on the Connally jury, which consisted originally of seven women and five men,[†] almost all people with low or moderate incomes (also in marked contrast to the defendant); among the twelve who finally delivered a verdict, three were unemployed,

---

* Hart lifted the seal after the trial was over.

† During the trial, one of the original jurors, a white male, was replaced by a black female from among the six alternates.

two worked as clerks, one was a maid, one a cook, and two were retired from blue-collar jobs.[13]

Edward Bennett Williams probably never confronted a more vulnerable witness than Jake Jacobsen, Connally's accuser. Jacobsen, as Williams informed the jury over and over, from his opening argument on, had entered into a plea bargain to avoid prosecution on seven counts of perjury and bank fraud in Texas, as well as one count of perjury in Washington. He had decided to testify against Connally "in consideration for the prosecution's agreement to drop those charges against him, [which could have resulted in] possible imprisonment of 40 years, and allow him to plead to a one-count indictment for which his possible imprisonment is two years," Williams told the jury. Furthermore, Jacobsen had not only pocketed the $10,000 of dairy industry money he claimed to have given to Connally, but had obtained another $5,000 from the milk lobby, which he didn't even pretend to have given to Connally, "confident that Connally would not accept it." (The defense acknowledged that Jacobsen had offered $10,000 to Connally, but maintained that Connally had turned it down; the third $5,000 Jacobsen simply "converted . . . to his own use: . . . he embezzled the money," Williams said.) In fact, according to Williams, Jacobsen had admitted on six different occasions that Connally had never accepted any money from him—twice to the Senate Watergate Committee, twice to a Watergate grand jury in Washington, once to a grand jury in Texas, and once to an attorney for the dairy lobby. That, said Williams, was what "the evidence will show . . . on Jake Jacobsen."[14]

When Jacobsen was called to the stand by prosecutor Frank Tuerkheimer, he testified as follows:

The Nixon administration's decision to raise milk prices was announced in March 1971. About a month later, during a talk between Jacobsen and Connally in the defendant's office at the Treasury Department, Connally "told me how helpful he had been on the price support matter and said in effect that the dairy people raised a lot of money for a lot of people and why didn't I get them to raise a little money for him?" Jacobsen said he would see what he could do, and on May 14, 1971, he visited Connally's office and handed him an envelope containing $5,000 in cash from the dairy lobby. "He said thank you very much, and he took the envelope and went into the bathroom which was adjoining his office and when he came out I didn't see the money anymore." Jacobsen said the two staged a repeat performance on September 24, 1971.[15]

In October 1973, Jacobsen learned that federal authorities were probing the alleged payoff to Connally. He discussed the situation with Connally, who said, "'Well, these investigating committees are really after me. Every time something comes up they . . . want to see what John Connally had to do with it.'" Jacobsen volunteered to tell investigators, "'I never gave you any money,'" but that left unaccounted for at least $10,000 he had supposedly obtained from the milk industry for Connally.

Soon after, when Jacobsen was subpoenaed by the Watergate Prosecutor's Office to testify in front of a grand jury, he immediately reported to Connally that "something had happened that would kind of speed up the matter" they had discussed, "and something had to be done about getting that matter straightened out . . . that it had to be done quickly because I wanted it to be a fact when I appeared before the grand jury." Connally then agreed to give Jacobsen $10,000 in cash; Jacobsen would put it in his safe-deposit box and testify that it had been there all along.

The two met, and Connally had "a cigar box that was filled with money, [which he handled] with either a rubber glove or gloves and threw them in the wastebasket and handed me the box with money in it." Unfortunately, it turned out that some of the bills Connally delivered to Jacobsen were too new to have been in circulation when Jacobsen allegedly received the first $10,000 from the dairy interests. Another meeting was arranged, and Connally gave Jacobsen another $10,000, this time in older bills that were in "a package wrapped in newspapers." After that, they went on with their respective appearances before the Watergate grand jury, and each denied that Jacobsen had paid Connally for influencing the milk-price hike.[16]

Jacobsen told his whole story in one hour and twenty minutes of direct examination by Tuerkheimer. According to one report, Tuerkheimer "seemed at times a bit ashamed of his key witness, rushing through his questioning" as a result.[17] He must have realized that Williams would bring out Jacobsen's six statements that he had not paid Connally, and so he decided to develop the contradictions during his own examination of his principal witness.[18]

When Williams's turn came, he wasted little time before going after Jacobsen, starting off with questions about his bank-fraud case in Texas,[19] and then portraying him as disloyal to his onetime boss, Lyndon Johnson. "Didn't you offer, Mr. Jacobsen," he said, "to give evidence against former President Lyndon Johnson . . ." Tuerkheimer tried to object, but Williams finished his question anyway: ". . . if you could plea bargain your way out of these charges?"

Hart denied Tuerkheimer's objection, and Jacobsen answered, "No, sir."

Williams repeated his charge: "You did not?"

"No, sir."

"Do you deny that, Mr. Jacobsen?"

"Yes, sir."

"You deny you offered to give evidence to the Department of Justice against the former President of the United States whom you had worked for?"

"Yes, sir, I deny that."[20]

Several days later, during a conference in chambers, Williams told Hart, "I had three sources for the question" about Jacobsen's supposed betrayal of Johnson. "I did not blindside the man or ask him blindly; I had three sources and disclosed them to Mr. Tuerkheimer when I asked the question. It came as a great surprise to me that he denied it." Nevertheless, Tuerkheimer protested that Williams had really "planted the idea in the jury's mind that this happened with one purpose"—to make Jacobsen look like a turncoat against his benefactor. Williams still insisted that both former attorney general John Mitchell and former assistant attorney general Henry Petersen had heard about the offer by Jacobsen and would so testify if called.

Judge Hart declared it would be best for both sides to refrain from mentioning the Johnson matter again; however, if Tuerkheimer were to refer to it in his closing argument, Hart would feel obliged to let Williams present both Mitchell and Petersen as witnesses. Tuerkheimer, who had hoped to tell the jurors that Williams had not proved any basis for his questions about Johnson and that they should therefore ignore them, decided to play safe; he did not bring the matter up again, and Mitchell and Petersen were not brought in to rebut Jacobsen.[21]

In his subsequent devastating cross-examination of Jacobsen, Williams concentrated on a discrepancy about the number of gloves Jacobsen said Connally had used to handle money:

Williams: You told us . . . that Mr. Connally and you had a meeting in his office alone, that he excused himself, left his office for ten minutes and came back with a cigar box and a rubber glove or rubber gloves on top of a pile of money in the cigar box, is that right?

Jacobsen: Well, it was something like that.

Williams: No, tell me what it was, Mr. Jacobsen, not whether it was something like that or not. . . . You tell us exactly how it was, Mr. Jacobsen.

Jacobsen: I believe the rubber glove was on the side of the money in the cigar box. The rubber glove or gloves was on the side of the money.

Williams: I'm sorry?

Jacobsen: I say the rubber glove or gloves was on the side of the money, not on top of the money.

Williams: Now, when you told Mr. Tuerkheimer in your interview with him back last year about this episode, you told him it was *a* rubber glove, did you not?

Jacobsen: Yes.

Williams: And when you testified before the grand jury on March 23rd you told the grand jury it was *a* rubber glove, did you not?

Jacobsen: Yes, sir.

Williams: But when you testified on Thursday here in this courtroom before His Honor and this jury, you said it was a rubber glove or gloves; is that correct?

Jacobsen: Yes, sir.

Williams: When did you decide it might have been a glove or gloves?

Jacobsen: Between the time I testified before the grand jury and the time I testified here.

Williams: What was it that changed your recollection from it being a glove to it being a glove or gloves?

Jacobsen: Just the logic of it being gloves instead of glove.

Williams: It was the logic of it, is that right?

Jacobsen: Yes.

Williams: Was that because, Mr. Jacobsen, the prosecutors pointed out to you that nobody could count money with one glove on one hand and a big pile?

Jacobsen: No, sir.

Williams: Well, what was the logic of it that changed your mind . . . and caused you to testify on Thursday that it was a glove or gloves?

Jacobsen: Well, the fact that you couldn't hardly handle money with one glove.

Williams: Well, that was what I just asked you, Mr. Jacobsen.[22]

Williams had taken an apparently minor point and shown the jurors that Jacobsen would tailor his testimony to "logic" or—presumably—to anything. He followed up by pressing Jacobsen about the color of the gloves. Jacobsen said, "I'm not sure about the color. It was either that light beige or yellow, one or the other, I'm not sure." Williams kept hammering away:

Williams: It was either beige or yellow but you are not sure?

Jacobsen: I'm not sure.

Williams: Could it have been black?

Jacobsen: I don't believe so.

Williams: Or white?

Jacobsen: It could have been. It was a light color.[23]

Near the end of his cross-examination, Williams said, "I now want to ask you, Mr. Jacobsen, when you were negotiating with the Prosecutor with respect to your testimony and the disposition of the pending criminal cases against you, you asked the Prosecutor, did you not, whether they would dispose of the other cases in which you were being investigated in Texas, did you not?"

Jacobsen answered in the affirmative, but added that he couldn't recall "what cases I was talking about." That answer gave Williams just the opening he needed:

"Well, did you mean the Robert Taft case, the Harold Hill case, the Patchett Bus and Transportation case . . ." Tuerkheimer objected at that point, but Williams continued as if he hadn't heard the prosecutor: ". . . and the Las Lomas case and the Sharpstown loan case?" Tuerkheimer again protested that Williams's question was "improper and assumes important facts," but Hart directed Jacobsen to answer, and Jacobsen said, "I don't remember what I was referring to."[24]

Williams had thus succeeded in reminding the jury that Jacobsen was being investigated in at least five different potentially criminal matters. The cross-examination lasted for a day and a half and ended only after Williams "got everything out of him he wanted," as one interested observer in the packed courtroom, Bill Hundley, put it.

When the time came for the defense to present its case, Williams paraded before the jury a star-studded cast of character witnesses for his client, including Lady Bird Johnson; the Reverend Billy Graham; Texas Congresswoman Barbara Jordan; former secretary of state Dean Rusk; World Bank head and former secretary of defense Robert McNamara; and Robert Strauss, chairman of the Democratic National Committee and a classmate of Connally's at the University of Texas Law School.[25] Hubert Humphrey also would have been part of the array, but he reneged; according to Williams, Humphrey originally told Connally he would testify for the defense, but when Williams went to prepare Humphrey for his appearance, he said he had changed his mind. With the 1976 presidential primaries less than a year away, attesting to the character of a Democrat recently turned Republican may have bothered him.

In view of the fact that the jury included seven black women, probably the most effective character witness was Barbara Jordan. Robert Strauss believes that she was "highly essential," although at first "she was very reluctant" to speak up for Connally. Jordan did not particularly like the defendant, but after Strauss pointed out to her, "'Barbara, they're not asking you to testify to anything except what John Connally's reputation is for truth and veracity,'" and suggested soothingly, "'Why don't I get Ed Williams to call you?'" she came around. Another testimonial that made an impact on the jury was that of Billy Graham. After Williams asked him, "What is your profession?" and Graham replied, "I teach the gospel of Jesus Christ across the face of the earth," an "Amen," sounded from the jury box. Williams later told the press, "'I thought that that was a good sign.'"[26]

From the jury box, the procession of upstanding citizens on behalf of Connally seemed "very effective," according to jury foreman Dennis O'Toole. Williams "knew his jury very well," says O'Toole. "The parade of character witnesses was to my mind carefully contrived but nonetheless effective—he had something for everyone." O'Toole, a historian who was then with the Smithsonian, added, "Even for someone like myself—least likely to be awed—nevertheless, I was impressed with people like Billy Graham and Barbara Jordan. I had to think, 'Now, why on earth would Barbara Jordan testify for John Connally?'" And O'Toole could only conclude that "she genuinely respected" him, "as a politician and as a man." An outside observer, Williams's friend Eugene McCarthy, says he likes to tell Williams, "'You ought to put that crowd on the road, you wouldn't lose a case.'"

After the character witnesses, the defendant took the stand. Positioning himself so that Connally would have to look directly across the jury box at him,[27] Williams led Connally through a series of emphatic denials of Jacobsen's allegations. Had Connally "ever ask[ed] Mr. Jacobsen for any money or anything of value?" The answer: "I did not. . . . No such conversation ever took place. . . . Not in the Treasury, not anywhere, no such conversation ever took place. I never asked him for anything at any time."[28] Similarly, Williams would summarize each point made by Jacobsen and ask, "Did such a thing ever happen?" triggering a long string of "It did not"; "No, sir"; and "That is absolutely false."[29] Was Jacobsen in doubt about the color of the glove or gloves he remembered Connally putting on? The color was irrelevant, because, under questioning by Williams, Connally firmly rejected the notion that he had ever owned a pair of rubber gloves, much less used them to handle ill-gotten money in the office of the secretary of the Treasury of the United States of America.[30]

As several people, including at least one reporter, observed, Connally was "a marked contrast to his accuser, a crumpled-looking man." The defendant "held his head high, smiled occasionally and testified in a strong expressive voice, fixing his gaze on his questioner or the jury."[31] Williams regards Connally as "a very strong" witness in his own behalf; "He obviously didn't have to carry the burden of hundreds of inconsistent statements that he'd made, as Jacobsen did." Michael Tigar, a horseman, compares Connally the witness to Connally the rider: "When John Connally rides a horse, he sits very tall and straight. Certainly there is no better natural horseman in a western saddle that I've ever seen. He had that same posture throughout the case, even though you knew his gut was just roiling." Even Henry Ruth concedes that "Connally was an attractive, tall, smooth, actorlike witness. Jacobsen had long silver fingernails. He looked down at the floor. From a courtroom sense, somebody could say John Connally was a ten times more attractive witness than Jake Jacobsen."

In his closing argument, Williams spared little detail in denigrating the witness on whom the prosecution's case rested almost entirely. He declared that the government's case had been offered through the lips of a man whom they have characterized in an indictment as a fraud and a swindler, whom they have characterized on two occasions . . . as a swindler. . . .

Have we reached that point in our society where scoundrels can escape their punishment if only they inculpate others? If so, we should mark it well, that although today it is John Connally, tomorrow it may be you or me.

Noting that "only a year ago" the government had within two weeks twice indicted Jacobsen for perjury, Williams continued:

Now, what is perjury? Perjury is lying under oath. The words "lie" and "liar" do not flow easily from my lips, and I think they flow very uneasily from the lips of most people. They are words at which most of us recoil. We don't like those ugly words, and, so, we use softer words all the time when we can. We say falsehood, and untruth and prevaricator, we say perjury, when we mean liar under oath. I think perjury may be one of the most heinous forms of crime in the whole United States Criminal Code. . . .

In short, members of the jury, the man who was brought here upon whom the prosecution asks you to predicate a verdict of guilty in this case, beyond all reasonable doubt, it is a man whom they have charged with swindling and fraud, a man whom they have charged with perjury, a self-confessed habitual liar and I suggest to you a proven embezzler. . . .

They [the prosecutors] put him on the stand. He takes the same oath that he says he has defiled a hundred times. And they asked of you, the jury, to bring in a verdict of guilty beyond a reasonable doubt on the testimony of Jacobsen.[32]

Winding up with his familiar theme, Williams implored the jury "at long last . . . to lift the pain and anguish, the humiliation, the ostracism and the suffering from false accusation and innuendo, vilification and slander from John Connally and his family."[33]

Jury foreman O'Toole was impressed by the way Williams "made contact with everyone on that jury. He was close to you. Physically close. He made sure that he spoke to everyone on that jury." His summation "wasn't theatrical, it wasn't arm-waving, but it was well conceived and presented. It didn't make a mediocre case suddenly seem gilt-edged. It was a fine conclusion for a strong case. It was a match for the case that he had built during the days of the trial."

A newspaper profile of Williams said approvingly: "In a nation where the criminal trial is a native form of drama, Edward Bennett Williams may be the consummate leading man. He moves about a courtroom as though he had designed it. He does not raise his voice; he aims it. He does not so much address a jury as woo it."[34]

Whereas Williams's voice had "boomed off the pale-paneled courtroom walls," prosecutor Tuerkheimer had to rely on a microphone "to amplify his soft voice."[35] Acknowledging the mismatch, he was reduced to pleading with the jurors to

> understand that this is not a contest among lawyers. It is your job to determine the facts of the case, not to decide whether Edward Bennett Williams or any of us is the better lawyer. I don't think there would be much contest on that point. I hope that you don't hold any inadequacies on our part against the government or the prosecution in this case.[36]

Just in case any of the jurors retained a shred of belief in Jacobsen's tale, Judge Hart instructed them that when considering evidence offered by an "informer" such as Jacobsen, who had been allowed to plead guilty to a lesser offense, they "should receive such testimony with suspicion and act upon such testimony with caution."[37]

On April 17, 1975, after deliberating for less than six hours, the jurors acquitted Connally on both counts. Williams was surprised the jury took even that long; he thought the case was so strong. Bill Hundley regards the victory as "unbelievable" in a Watergate-related case before a Washington jury. (This was the only defeat in court for the Watergate Special Prosecutor's Office.) Aside from such intangible rewards, Williams was said to have been paid $500,000 for defending Connally.[38] However, he refuses to discuss his fee in that or any other case.

The triumph was of great consolation to the man who had named Connally to the cabinet—Richard Nixon. The former president, who had been Williams's friend in the 1950s, his implacable enemy during Watergate, and, in a dramatic turnabout, a would-be client, phoned to congratulate both Connally and Williams. Several days later, he phoned Williams again to rehash the case and told Williams "how pleased he was, how he wished that he'd had me for a lawyer, how it was too bad that I represented the *Washington Post* [during Watergate], that kind of thing. I think he did wish that he'd had me as his lawyer."

Impressive as Connally's acquittal was, the victory does not rank with Williams's destruction of the "airtight" case against Jimmy Hoffa—simply because of the weakness of the case against Connally. One source within the Prosecutor's Office still believes that Connally "never should have been indicted," because "unquestionably, what happened is that Jacobsen had pocketed that money himself and didn't want to admit it." The person who was sworn by oath to be impartial—Judge George Hart—feels exactly the same. He declares, "I think they made a mistake in bringing the case. . . . It was my opinion that in any normal time Connally would not have been indicted. Although this was not strictly a Watergate case, it came up in a Watergate atmosphere." Another unbiased observer, jury foreman Dennis O'Toole, comments, "I think Edward Ben-

nett Williams couldn't have made the government's case for them if he
had been on the other side. He probably would have been smart enough
not to have taken a case that depended upon the testimony of Jake Jacobsen."

The day after Connally was acquitted, Tuerkheimer moved to dismiss
the remaining three counts against him, because they were based on substantially the same evidence—the testimony of Jacobsen. Judge Hart
granted the motion.[39] During his abortive try for the presidency in 1980,
Connally told those who asked about his indictment that he was the only
candidate who had been "'certified innocent by a jury'"—although as
Connally, an attorney for some forty years, certainly knows, there is no
such thing as a "verdict" of innocence. Williams chuckled when asked
about Connally's "certified innocent" boast. "He had to have some response. For certain, he was going to be asked that question." And although Williams, a Democrat, did not support Connally, he believes "he
would have made a hell of a president. I thought he was the brightest man
I had ever met who aspired to the presidency. And I met almost everybody who has seriously aspired to the presidency from the 1960s on."

Jake Jacobsen also returned to Judge Hart's court, and escaped with a
slap on the wrist. Hart sentenced Jacobsen to two years in prison and
fined him $10,000, but then suspended the prison term and remitted the
fine, placing him on two years' probation.[40] And while Connally has lived
a high-profile existence that included his run for president, Jacobsen
"dropped out of sight" after the trial and hasn't been heard from since,
according to Robert Strauss, who was once a close friend of Jacobsen's as
he has long been of Connally's.

22
Echoes of
Damon Runyon

C harles E. Nelson was just the sort of client who had driven Nicholas Chase, Edward Bennett Williams's first law partner, up the wall—and then out of the Hill Building. Nelson lived the life of a gentleman farmer, breeding fine cattle and racehorses at Ritchie, Maryland, outside Washington. When it turned out that his life-style was supported by a $6-million-a-year numbers racket, Nelson and fifteen of his associates were indicted in October 1951 on charges of participating in a lottery and conspiring to operate a lottery. Others named in the suit were Nelson's wife, Virginia Madge, referred to as the "brains" of the business; the couple's daughter and son-in-law, Bertha N. and William K. McWilliams; and three high-ranking law-enforcement officers: Inspector Albert I. Bullock and homicide detective Sergeant Robert G. Kirby, both of Washington's police force, and James E. Lowry, a deputy U.S. marshal and former Washington police detective.[1] In a related case, Nelson was also indicted on five counts of perjury after he denied to the Kefauver Rackets Committee that he was involved in the numbers business.[2]

At first, Williams represented the McWilliams couple, and another lawyer from his office conducted the defense of several others charged in the case. Charles Nelson and his wife were themselves defended by Leo

Rover,[3] a onetime U.S. attorney whose son had been Williams's friend at law school. The numbers case went to trial in January 1952, with Assistant U.S. Attorneys Tom Wadden and Alfred Hantman as prosecutors. It had, in fact, been Wadden and Hantman who uncovered the evidence that resulted in the indictments, "making almost nightly forays into underworld haunts" because no other investigators were available.[4] After a two-week trial, the Nelsons, the McWilliamses, and most of the others were found guilty.[5] Williams recalls vividly that U.S. District Judge James Kirkland, who heard the case, "believed with a passion that, on verdict, everybody should go to jail. Even if he was going to put them on probation, he thought everybody should have a taste of jail." Several of the defendants were women, and "when the verdict came in, he remanded them all to jail. When he said 'All the defendants will be remanded to jail,' all the women fainted in unison. They all went out" cold.

Wadden and Hantman had won their case, but, even so, Wadden had been extremely impressed by one lawyer on the other side: "The defense had some of the leading criminal lawyers in town, but they weren't bothering us. It was this young guy who kept kicking us in the ass because he knew a little law. That's how I got to know Ed. Every time I turned around in the courtroom, I was getting kicked in the ass by Williams. He was just on top of everything. Every time we would make a little maneuver on our side that maybe was going to gain a little ground, Williams would turn around and kick us in the ass. And he had that boyish baloney in those days. It was quite frustrating because we were the same age. And I admired him. In the courtroom, you always admire a guy who knows what he's doing."

The convictions were overturned when the U.S. Court of Appeals ruled that records Nelson had reluctantly surrendered to the Senate committee headed by Estes Kefauver had been passed on improperly to the U.S. Attorney's Office.[6] The case was retried in 1954, this time with Williams defending both the Nelsons and the McWilliamses. During the second trial, the charges against the McWilliams couple were thrown out and ultimately Nelson and one of his associates brought the trial to an end by pleading guilty to operating a lottery—as part of a plea bargain that saw several other defendants set free and the perjury case dropped as well.[7] Nelson, declaring his "'love [for] America'" and stating that he wanted "'to apologize to the American people'" for his crimes,[8] was sentenced to one to three years in prison and fined $1,000.[9]

By the time of the second Nelson trial, Tom Wadden had left the government and set up shop in the Hill Building with another ex-prosecutor, Roy Kelly, a neighbor of Williams's in Bethesda. Wadden quickly became friendly with Williams and others in his office, and went into practice with him in early 1955.

Several years later, Williams took on the case of three Washington bookmakers, including Robert L. Martin, who has gone on to be "the most respected handicapper in the country."[10] In 1958, Martin and two partners, Julius ("Crippled Julius") Silverman and Meyer ("Nutsy") Schwartz, were charged with operating a huge gambling ring.[11] Williams might have turned down the case as nothing more than a run-of-the-mill betting bust of a type he had long outgrown, but the three bookies showed him evidence that the government had illegally eavesdropped on them, and he agreed to defend them.[12]

This was the background: Silverman, Martin, and Schwartz ran a betting shop in a row house in Washington's Foggy Bottom, near the U.S. State Department and the present site of the Watergate compound. Suspecting the nature of their business, police got permission from the owners of the adjoining row house, which was vacant, to install in it their electronic surveillance equipment.[13] A microphone on a foot-long baton (known in the trade as a "spike mike") was inserted into the common wall between the two houses until it struck a radiator on the suspects' side and turned it into what one judge called "a giant microphone," enabling the police to overhear everything that was said next door.[14] On April 30, 1958, police and IRS intelligence agents swooped down on the three gamblers, put them under arrest, and spent several hours gathering evidence from their quarters. (During the whole time the police were there, the three phone lines rang "continuously," and officers who answered the phones gave callers odds on various sporting events.) Investigators collected slips showing that in part of just one day $37,950 had been wagered (most of it on baseball games) and the "house" had won $27,928. The U.S. Court of Appeals described Martin and his partners as "'big time' gamblers" who conducted a "major gambling operation,"[15] while the press called the betting ring "one of the largest encountered by police here in the last 10 years."[16]

Before the three went to trial in March 1959, Williams moved to suppress the evidence produced by the spike mike, but the judge ruled that the Fourth Amendment prohibition on illegal searches and seizures "does not ban eavesdropping," and was "confined to physical invasion and to the seizure of physical objects."[17] After a week-long trial, Silverman, Martin, and Schwartz were convicted on three out of five counts of unlawful gambling,[18] and were sentenced to up to five years in prison and fined $1,000 apiece.[19]

When Williams carried the case to the U.S. Court of Appeals, the court sustained the lower court by a vote of 2–1, the majority holding that even though the spike mike might have trespassed into the defendants' office by five-sixteenths of an inch, "[w]e are unwilling to believe that the respective rights are to be measured in fractions of inches."[20] Both the lower court[21] and the appeals court rejected Williams's motion to toss out the data obtained from the bugging because the Supreme Court was likely to suppress such evidence. As the appeals-court majority declared, "It is not our duty to speculate as to what the Supreme Court will say in the future; it is our duty to follow the Court's past rulings as we understand them."[22]

Williams kept on. He argued the case before the Supreme Court on December 5, 1960.[23] Among those on hand were Bob Martin, one of his clients, and Duke Zeibert, a pal of both Martin and Williams and the owner of a restaurant-saloon that was Washington's version of Toots Shor's. Martin and Zeibert repaired there after the Supreme Court hearing, and Zeibert egged Martin on: "'You're always making a line on something, what do you make the odds on your case in the Supreme Court?'" Martin replied, "'I make the Supreme Court a 10–1 favorite,'" whereupon Zeibert bet $100 on the defendants. Three months later, Martin called Zeibert to break the news, "'We win, nine-love.'"[24] Martin was out $1,000 to Zeibert, but the three gamblers were off the hook.

Persuaded by Williams of the terrors of that "frightening paraphernalia which the vaunted marvels of an electronic age may visit upon human society," the Court, in a unanimous opinion, declined to affirm the right of the police to "go beyond" previous limits restricting entry into private premises, "by even a fraction of an inch." According to the nine justices, "A fair reading of the record in this case shows that the eavesdropping was accomplished by means of an unauthorized physical penetration into the premises occupied by" Silverman, Martin, and Schwartz.[25]

In 1962, the government again brought a case against the three bookies on the basis of evidence prosecutors considered untainted. In a bargain negotiated by Williams and Tom Wadden, the trio pleaded guilty to one gambling-related count apiece, and each was fined $5,000.[26] Martin, who subsequently moved to Las Vegas, where he became oddsmaker (strictly legitimate) at the Union Plaza Hotel,[27] is today so respected that he is known in gambling circles as "The Head Linesman"—the experts' expert who sets the betting lines on sporting events that are followed by bettors all over the country. He and Williams are still on friendly terms (Silverman and Schwartz are dead), and Williams regards his ex-client as "an extraordinarily bright man who probably is the best handicapper of sports events in the country today." As owner of the Baltimore Orioles and president of the Washington Redskins, Williams says he "never" bets on baseball or football games, so he himself does not profit from Martin's expertise. Nevertheless, he gained from the Martin-Silverman-Schwartz case the satisfaction of establishing an important legal precedent: that law-enforcement officers may not physically intrude into a suspect's home or office "by even a fraction of an inch."

Justices of the Supreme Court were so impressed by Williams's conduct of the Martin case that they appointed him to handle the appeal of two San Francisco men who had been convicted of transporting heroin, James Wah Toy and Wong Sun (alias "Sea Dog"). Following several arguments by Williams during 1962, the Court, in another precedent-setting deci-

sion, voted 5–4 to overturn the convictions on the grounds that evidence
seized after an illegal arrest was inadmissible and that without additional
corroborating evidence, the statement of someone who had been arrested
improperly could not be used to incriminate anyone else.[28]

Ray Ryan, a wildcat oil driller, was supposedly "one of the biggest
gamblers in the country." He is said to have described as "'his pigeon'"
billionaire H. L. Hunt, who Ryan said "'bets close to a million dollars a
week during the football season.'"[29] * Ryan and the legendary high roller
Nick the Greek[†] engaged in a week-long card game in Las Vegas during
the early 1960s that ended with the Greek down about $1 million. But the
loser learned that Ryan had had an accomplice spying from a two-way
mirror in the ceiling and tipping off Ryan to his opponent's cards via a
device that sent electric impulses to Ryan's leg. The Greek was not
amused. Not at all. He hired Charles ("Chuckie") Del Monico, a small-
time thug, and another man of the same ilk to impress upon Ryan the
error of his ways. Del Monico and his colleague applied their persuasive-
ness to Ryan, who called in the FBI, and Del Monico wound up being
indicted in Los Angeles for extortion.

Ryan was from Evansville, Indiana, and the papers there played up the
story, complete with pictures of Del Monico. No sooner did John Stinson,
vice-president of the First Federal Savings and Loan Association in Evansville, gaze upon Del Monico's mug than he was struck with the likeness between Nick the Greek's enforcer and the man who had walked into
his office on October 8, 1962, said he was from the Better Business Bureau, and then pulled a gun, herded Stinson, eight other employees, and a
customer into the vault, and walked off with $22,500. Stinson and nine
others identified Del Monico as the robber. Meanwhile, Del Monico had
been convicted of trying to extort money from Ryan, sentenced to five
years in prison, and freed pending appeal. Realizing that he was in deep
trouble, Del Monico visited Williams—in the company of his father, one
Charlie ("The Blade") Tourine[31][‡]—and asked Williams to defend him in
the robbery case.

* Hunt's son Lamar owns the Kansas City Chiefs of the National Football League.

† The Greek, real name Nicholas Andrea Dandolos, claimed to have won and lost $500
million and to have swung between wealth and poverty seventy-three times.[30]

‡ Tourine has been described as "Washington's absentee Godfather . . . a New York–
based impresario of dope, pornography, numbers and backroom gambling." Tourine, a reputed "enforcer" in the 1950s for Meyer Lansky and "Trigger Mike" Coppola, was himself
charged over the years with murder, robbery, kidnapping, gambling, tax evasion, and threats
against government witnesses. He is said to have owned large interests in casinos in pre-
Castro Cuba, where Chuckie Del Monico was a casino manager. In 1963, several days after
Tourine opened a lounge in Maryland near Washington, police raided the establishment and
arrested a number of people on gambling charges, including Tourine (who suffered a mild
heart attack when he was taken into custody) and Williams's chum, restaurateur Duke
Zeibert.[32]

Del Monico told Williams a long tale, the gist of which was that "he'd never even been to Evansville. I had grave doubts about his story," says Williams. "I asked him to take a polygraph test. I had no confidence in polygraph tests, but I wanted to see if he would be willing to do it. He surprised me by saying he would do it. So I made arrangements for him to be hospitalized so he could take no sedatives and no tranquilizers, no drugs of any kind to help him with the test."

To administer the test, Williams hired Robert Eichelberger—"the man that I believed was the foremost polygraph man in America." Del Monico continued to amaze his lawyer by passing the test with flying colors, after which Williams called Attorney General Nicholas Katzenbach, and "I told him he had a mistake on his hands; that notwithstanding that he had all those eyewitnesses, that he was wrong. And I offered Katzenbach, to his dismay, the opportunity to give a polygraph test to Del Monico." Williams told Katzenbach to select an expert, and before long the attorney general called back and said he had his man: Robert Eichelberger. "Naturally, I was tempted to let him do it again, but I said to him, 'I've already used him.'" Katzenbach picked two other experts who tested Del Monico, and again he passed.

"So now Katzenbach was upset. So he picked the foremost narcoanalyst in America" to question Del Monico while the accused was given drugs commonly known as "truth serum." "Chuckie recited a litany of offenses that he'd committed throughout his life," but "again he denied he'd ever been in Indiana," much less Evansville.

On February 1, 1965, just before he was to have stood trial, the government announced it was dropping the case (Williams still praises Katzenbach for his courage), leaving the eyewitnesses "boiling." The main witness, John Stinson, fumed, "'It stinks,'" but Richard Stein, the U.S. attorney in Indiana, commented, "'We were afraid of a miscarriage of justice.'" He said that if the case had gone to trial, Del Monico most likely would have been convicted, even though he was apparently innocent.[33] Williams agrees: "It was just a cold case of mistaken identity. He'd done a million other bad things, but he hadn't stuck up that bank. But it was an absolute certainty that he would have been convicted." According to *Newsweek,* the government, at Williams's instigation, had "set an out-of-court legal landmark—and clearly hastened the time that narcoanalysis and lie-detector tests may be accepted as respectable courtroom evidence."[34] Williams was proved correct when another man was later convicted of holding up the savings and loan.

The Baltimore Colts marched down the field and the New York Giants tried desperately to halt them, in what many purists regard as the best football game of all time. It was late on a dying winter's day at Yankee Stadium, and the Colts of John Unitas, Alan Ameche, Lenny Moore, and Gino Marchetti were playing for the world championship against the

Giants, led by Frank Gifford, Kyle Rote, and Sam Huff. After four quarters, the two teams had played to a 17–17 tie, and for the first time in
history the title would be determined in sudden-death overtime. Also on
the line was a fortune that supposedly had been bet on the outcome by
Colts' owner Carroll Rosenbloom and his sidekick, Lou Chesler. The two
men watched in anguish as the Colts moved steadily toward the Giants'
goal line, instead of scoring a touchdown in one long-distance strike. The
logical move would have been for the Colts to kick a field goal as soon as
they were in range, passing up the chance for a touchdown, which would
have meant running more plays and risking a fumble or interception that
might cost them the game. But a field goal would result in a three-point
win, and the point spread had the Colts favored by three and a half points.
So Rosenbloom and Chesler stood to see the Colts win the game and cost
them a bundle.

Contrary to normal strategy, the Colts never attempted a field goal.
They carried the ball into the end zone, making the final score 23–17,
Baltimore. Everybody went back to Chesapeake Bay happy. Most ecstatic
of all were Rosenbloom and Chesler. Many people would never forget
December 28, 1958, not so much for the outcome as for the margin of
victory.[35] And Lou Chesler and some of his associates turned out to be
among Edward Bennett Williams's most fascinating clients.

Lou Chesler, weighing in at 256 pounds, and the son of a Lithuanian
who had migrated to Canada,[36] impressed one acquaintance as "the most
outstanding real estate salesman he had ever come across." A "flamboy-
ant" individual, he was also a "compulsive gambler."[37] He figured prominently in an inquiry into the operation of casinos in the Bahamas that was
made in 1967 by a commission appointed by Queen Elizabeth II. Chesler
(represented by Williams) was one of fifty-four witnesses who was called
before the commission during its six-week study.[38] He had "appeared on
the [Bahamas gambling] scene" just as plans to build casinos were being
launched in 1961.[39] One source identified him as "the man who fronted"
in the Bahamas for Meyer Lansky, the reputed Mafia financial genius
with whom Chesler had previously been involved in Canadian mining
deals.[40] After two years of laying the groundwork, Chesler saw his efforts
pay off in the spring of 1963. On March 20, the Bahamas Amusements
Company was incorporated, with Chesler owning 498 of the 500 Class A
shares, and Mrs. Georgette Groves taking title to 498 of the 500 Class B
shares.[41] Mrs. Groves, like Chesler a native of Canada, was the wife of
Wallace Groves, a Wall Street financier who was the "architect" of development in the Bahamas, according to the commission.[42] Less than two
weeks after Bahamas Amusements Ltd. was set up, on April 1, 1963,
Bahamas governor Sir Robert Stapledon—acting with what the commission called "unusual expedition"—gave Bahamas Amusements the exclusive right to operate casinos on Grand Bahama Island for ten years, beginning in 1964.[43]

To run the first gaming house in the Bahamas, the Monte Carlo Casino at the Lucayan Beach Hotel in Freeport, Chesler turned to his bookies —Frank Ritter (alias Frank Reid); Max Courtney (a.k.a. Morris Schmerzler); and Charles Brudner (alias Charles Brud).[44] Known in some circles as "the three mongrels,"[45] they had been large-scale bookmakers in New York and Montreal[46]—at least until Ritter and Courtney were run out of Canada.[47] One expert, Dan Sullivan, director of the Miami Crime Commission, described Courtney and Ritter in 1964 as "'the two biggest layoff operators and the two biggest and heaviest bookmakers and sports bookmakers in the country.'"[48] And Ritter had been "prominent" in Mafia "infiltration" of the casinos at the Nacionale and Riviera Hotels in Havana in the late 1950s, before Fidel Castro ousted Fulgencio Batista from power, according to the Bahamas Commission of Inquiry.[49] *

Chesler placed "the three mongrels" in "absolute control"[51] of the Monte Carlo Casino, with Ritter having the title of general manager, Courtney that of "craps supervisor," and Brudner the office of "floor manager."[52] † The selection of the three men for those jobs was curious, as they had no background of managing casinos, except for Ritter's experience in Cuba. Chesler knew them primarily as his personal bookmakers, and he knew them well in this capacity—he was "a loser" in "a big way," wagering on "horses, football, base-ball, jai alai—almost anything"—according to the Commission of Inquiry.[55]

What Ritter, Courtney, and Brudner did have to offer, aside from their history of handling Chesler's wagers, was expertise in the form of a system of credit ratings for the "big time gamblers" who were flown in from the States to lose their money at the casino's tables. "The three mongrels" kept their data ("often supplied by the individual's bank") in a card index at the casino. The gamblers' credit ratings were registered in a group of code numbers—which only Ritter, Courtney, and Brudner could interpret—and to the astonishment of the Bahamas Commission, some of the highest rollers were good for as much as "several million!" in credit.[56] ‡ (The credit records are referred to by some observers as "lists of suckers"[58] and "pigeon lists."[59]) The credit information was considered so valuable that Ritter, Courtney, and Brudner were each paid $36,500 a year in salaries, plus 30 percent of the casino's annual profits to divide

---

* In 1958, the year of their betting coup on the Colts-Giants title game, Rosenbloom and Chesler reportedly put up the money for another gambler, Mike McLaney, to buy the Nacionale in Havana. The investment must have been a poor one; that December, while the Colts were running toward the Giants' goal line, Castro was running Batista out of Cuba and the casinos out of business.[50]

† Ritter and Courtney started work when the casino opened in January 1964, but Brudner, who was ill (and, like the other two, well into his sixties),[53] did not come aboard until October 1964.[54]

‡ One of the names on the sucker list was that of Art Modell, owner of the Cleveland Browns.[57] Williams identifies Modell as one of his closest friends among NFL owners, along with members of the Mara family to whom the New York Giants belong.

among themselves. The commission found that in three years each member of the trio earned at least $400,000 in bonuses, plus $110,000 in salaries and free room and board. And, said the commissioners, "The one thing we are sure of is that the figures we have quoted represent the minimum. . . . To say that these figures staggered the Commission would be to understate our reactions."[60]

The Commission of Inquiry decided that Ritter, Courtney, and Brudner were paid these huge amounts for the credit ratings they owned, not for their operational skills. Their official titles, the commission said, were "a travesty of their true function. . . . Their solitary professional advantage lay in their personal acquaintance with the credit rating of the high players in North America." The three men "did not have, nor did they need, experience of casinos."[61]

Having fulfilled his tasks of setting up the casino and recruiting his three friends, Lou Chesler was eased out of the scene in 1964.[62] Chesler and Rosenbloom later were partners in several enterprises, including the Baltimore-based American Totalizer Company, which owned and leased to racetracks the machines that tabulated odds and winnings on races.[63] One losing venture for Chesler was the purchase of 150,000 shares of IT&T—on the advice of Edward Bennett Williams. After Chesler bought the stock, the Justice Department barred IT&T's proposed merger with ABC, and the value of the shares declined sharply.[64] Chesler also operated resorts elsewhere in the Caribbean, where Williams was said to be a "frequent" guest. And Chesler entertained Williams's quarterback, Sonny Jurgensen, and other football types, including New York Jets' owner Sonny Werblin and quarterback Joe Namath.[65] *

Meanwhile, back in the Bahamas, "the three mongrels" were seeing their warm welcome wear out. They were mentioned extensively in a Pulitzer Prize–winning series in the *Wall Street Journal* in October 1966 that exposed links between organized crime and Bahamian politicians.† Bahamian authorities learned that in 1964 Ritter, Courtney, and Brudner had been indicted in New York for violating federal gambling laws.

---

*Chesler's choice of football friends is intriguing. Both the Redskins and the Jets of the mid- to late 1960s lacked strong defenses and running attacks, so each team literally relied on a pass and a prayer. In other words, the quarterback on each team was in a unique position to determine the outcome of games. Gamblers are notoriously superstitious, and Chesler may well have felt that by associating with Jurgensen and Namath, he could generate good luck vibrations that would help the teams he bet on to win games. He must have had mixed emotions when Namath guided the Jets to a shocking upset of Rosenbloom's Colts in the 1969 Super Bowl, one of the biggest surprises in sports history.

†Much of the information for the *Journal's* stories was provided by PR man Tex McCrary, who, like Williams, had once worked for Bernard Goldfine. While acknowledging that McCrary had been "instrumental" in uncovering the ties between criminals and politicos, the Bahamas Commission of Inquiry nevertheless characterized McCrary as "irresponsible and meddlesome," and recommended that "further dealings with him at Government level would bode the Bahamas no good."[66]

(Their attorney in that case was Williams.) In January 1967, as a result of "adverse publicity," the trio resigned from the Monte Carlo Casino.[67]

Ritter, Courtney, and Brudner did not leave empty-handed, however. In return for their agreement to quietly fade from the scene, the three arranged to "lease" their credit files to the casino. As payment, each was to receive the modest sum of $70,000 for the next ten years—a total of $2.1 million for the pigeon lists.* The severance contract between Bahamas Amusements Ltd. (identified as the "Lessee") and Ritter, Courtney, and Brudner (referred to as "Lessors") was witnessed by Tom Wadden, Williams's law associate.[69] According to Wadden, "Ed's the one that handled the overall negotiations," and Wadden was involved only because the contract was finalized in the Bahamas on that country's election day, January 10, 1967, just as the Bobby Baker trial was opening in Washington.

The Bahamas Gambling Commission was not necessarily impressed with the terms of the agreement, which the members viewed as simply a means of providing blood money to insure that casino employees hired by Ritter, et al., would not think the three men had been "unfairly treated"—leading to the possibility of "a mass walk-out" by the "junior casino staff." The commission pointed out that although the index of 18,000 to 20,000 high rollers might have belonged to Ritter and the other two when they joined the casino in 1964, "credit ratings are bound to fluctuate with the passage of time." Therefore, the most up-to-date information should have belonged to the casino, not to the trio. Furthermore, the $2.1 million seemed "exorbitant" to the commission, and the whole pact was "another example" of how Ritter, Courtney, and Brudner—"the real masters" of the casino—had "called the tune to which the [Bahamas Amusements] Company danced."[70]

But if the commissioners did not like the outcome, they were awestruck by the skills used in drafting the severance contract. Among its provisions were a requirement that the three men at once be given promissory notes for the entire $2.1 million, and language entitling the trio to "immediate" payment of the balance owed if the casino ever missed a payment or if the casino's license was transferred at any time during the next ten years.[71] The agreement, said the commission, "must be one of the tightest contracts ever drawn"—quite a testimonial to Williams's abilities. "For this reason it is set out in full" in the Appendix to the commission's report,[72] perhaps in hopes that the Bahamas government could sell copies of the document to contracts classes at law schools around the world.

Regardless of the cost, the Commission of Inquiry was glad to have the casino rid of the three men, who the commissioners felt may have been subject to "the influence of sinister masters across the water." Ritter was seen as having close links to Meyer Lansky,[73] whom the commissioners did not hold in high esteem. In fact, the commission noted that Ben Novack,

* Meyer Lansky was said to have taken a 25-percent cut of the $2.1 million.[68]

the owner of Miami's Fontainebleu Hotel—whose own connections to Frank Costello and Sam Giancana were outlined[74]—said that Lansky "was a man of notoriously undesirable reputation whom he would prefer not to see" at the Fontainebleu. Weighing all the evidence, including the testimony of Ritter, Courtney, Chesler, and Novack, the commission concluded that Ritter, Courtney, and Brudner "were not suitable persons to have been employed in the Bahamas venture."[75] And in large part because of the unsavory backgrounds of the trio, the commission recommended that in the future neither "citizens" nor "former residents" (to cover all the bases) of the U.S. should be permitted to work in the casinos.[76]

Although Ritter, Brudner, and Courtney were wearing out their welcome in the Bahamas, or at least in the casinos, they might have had a hard time leaving the country, since their American passports had been impounded on orders of the U.S. consul general in the Bahamas; they were, after all, fugitives from justice in New York. But when Courtney wanted to go to England in 1965 to inspect a school for croupiers, he simply used his connections to obtain a Bahamas Certificate of Identity, which allowed him to travel as he pleased.[77] Finally, in July 1967, Bahamian Prime Minister Lynden O. Pindling announced that the trio's permits to reside in the Bahamas would not be renewed when they expired in January 1968. Brudner, sixty-six and ill, surrendered himself in New York and was released on $100,000 bail in his U.S. gambling case; while Ritter and Courtney fled to Israel, where they awaited the outcome of efforts by Williams (whom the three had paid $50,000) to bargain with U.S. Attorney Robert M. Morgenthau in Manhattan.[78] Williams was eventually able to work out a settlement under which none of the three went to trial or to prison.*

---

* In 1966, Bill Hundley, who had befriended Williams during the Goldfine case, resigned from the Justice Department. According to Hundley, he needed a job that would sanitize his years as a prosecutor and enable him to represent defendants in criminal cases without subjecting him to conflict-of-interest problems. Williams arranged with NFL commissioner Pete Rozelle for the league to hire Hundley as director of security, a job that gave Hundley responsibility for separating football personnel from gamblers and for screening prospective owners of franchises. A year later, he went into private law practice. He and Williams had often discussed Hundley's joining Williams's firm, but both felt that Hundley could enter only as a very senior partner, which might upset some attorneys who had been in the firm for years. Instead, Hundley set up shop elsewhere in the Hill Building; Williams was his landlord for several years until Williams needed the space to expand his own firm, and Hundley moved to other quarters. Nevertheless, Williams has referred many cases to Hundley, and the two often share clients. When Hundley was in the Hill Building, his first partner was another alumnus of the Justice Department, Robert Peloquin. Although Hundley devoted himself primarily to his law business, he and Peloquin organized an investigative agency known as Intertel, which was affiliated with Resorts International, the gambling conglomerate. Most of Peloquin's time was spent on Intertel's affairs, and one of his first customers was a Bahamas casino managed by Eddie Cellini,[79] brother of Dino Cellini, who had worked for Ritter, Courtney, and Brudner at the Monte Carlo. Dino Cellini was listed as a person who was "not . . . in the best interests of the Colony to be employed in the casino."[80] Peloquin ultimately went full-time with Intertel, while Hundley continued to practice law.

When Robert Sunshine mishandled money belonging to Ruby Kolod and Willie Alderman, he made a very serious blunder. Back in 1959, Sunshine, a Denver oilman, had induced Kolod, an officer and part owner of the Desert Inn in Las Vegas, and Alderman to invest $78,000 in oil leases. Not only were no oil royalties forthcoming, but Sunshine invaded the escrow account he had set up for the funds of Kolod and Alderman. Within a year, all the money was gone, and Kolod and Alderman called on Sunshine in Denver "to express their displeasure with the transaction." By 1961, Kolod and Alderman were still out most of their money, and they warned Sunshine that he would soon be visited by "'a Chicago lawyer' who would not be coming for the purpose of suing." Sunshine understood these remarks to mean that he would be killed if he did not repay the money in full.

On July 6, 1961 Sunshine was called on by a man who, if not a lawyer, was at least from Chicago: Felix Antonio Alderisio, who was accompanied by one Americo Di Pietto.[81] Alderisio, known as "Milwaukee Phil," even though his normal stomping grounds were in Chicago, is referred to by Edward Bennett Williams as "a collector"; others describe him as a "notorious Capone syndicate hoodlum"[82] and a "reputed 'enforcer' for a Chicago crime syndicate."[83] Alderisio entered Sunshine's office, introduced himself, sat down, and declared matter-of-factly, "'Ruby sent us. We came here to kill you.'" The only thing Mr. Americo Di Pietto had to say was that he was "'Pete.'" Alderisio finally told Sunshine that "only Kolod could save him," and at Alderisio's suggestion, Sunshine phoned Kolod and Alderman at the Concord Hotel near Monticello, New York, where they were vacationing, and vowed to repay their money.

Prodded by Kolod's and Alderman's constant references to a second and final meeting Sunshine would have with Alderisio unless he made good, Sunshine continued to send payments until late 1962, when he was reduced to such dire straits that he attempted to borrow money from Kolod, of all people. Kolod refused, Sunshine was soon indicted for embezzling money from another man, and "all of his contacts with . . . Kolod, Alderman and Alderisio were terminated." Sunshine then complained to federal authorities that he had been the victim of extortion; and Kolod, Alderman, and Alderisio were charged, tried in federal court in Colorado, and convicted of conspiring to transmit via interstate communications threats to injure and murder Sunshine. All three received long prison terms. (The trio, along with Di Pietto, were also tried for attempted extortion of Sunshine and acquitted.)

Kolod, Alderman, and Alderisio hired Williams to carry their appeals to the Supreme Court. Although the court of appeals ruled against him, the Supreme Court overturned the convictions because the defendants had not been allowed to inspect the records of federal agents who had eavesdropped on conversations at the executive offices in the Desert Inn where Kolod worked[84] (the proceedings were rendered moot as to Kolod, who died while the case was making its way through the courts), and at Alderisio's place of business in Chicago.[85]

Also affected by the Supreme Court's March 1969 ruling were the consolidated cases of two Soviet citizens convicted of stealing national defense secrets—I. A. Ivanov (who was also represented by Williams before the high court) and J. W. Butenko.[86] In its decision, the Supreme Court relied heavily on two of Williams's earlier cases—those of Julius Silverman, et al., and Wong Sun. The court cited *Silverman* as having established the right of "conversational privacy . . . in one's own home," and extended that holding to prohibit electronic "surveillance which penetrates a private area without a technical trespass," as well as "surveillance which is carried out by means of a physical entry." "The existing doctrine, recognized at least since *Silverman*," the Court said, is "that conversations as well as property are excludable from the criminal trial when they are found to be the fruits of an illegal invasion of the home." The *Wong Sun* case was cited as precedent for ruling that a defendant's words "when the police illegally entered his house were not usable against him because they were the fruits of a physical invasion of his premises which violated the Fourth Amendment."[87]

In the three cases—*Silverman, Wong Sun,* and *Kolod*—Williams made great strides in advancing the right of an accused to be protected from law-enforcement officers who use state-of-the-art technology to overhear private conversations virtually anyplace and anytime.

23

The EBW
Law Machine

W hen somebody gets in trouble, there's one name they know. They say, 'I'm going to get the best. I'm going to get Ed Williams.'"

Thus former Watergate prosecutor Henry Ruth characterizes Edward Bennett Williams's law practice for the last thirty years—from the defense of Joseph McCarthy in the early 1950s to the representation of major corporations in the 1980s. For many years lawyers as renowned as Louis Nizer and Clark Clifford have referred clients in need of the best criminal attorney to him.

By 1957, Williams was so much in demand that a profile of him in the *New York Daily News* observed: "Lawyer Edward Bennett Williams . . . faced the dilemma similar to that of a doctor with four patients ready for the operating table—three of them in another city." The story went on to report that "the tall, baby-faced, 36-year-old Williams is now the most sought-after criminal attorney on the Eastern seaboard. . . . Williams is to Washington what Jerry Giesler is to Hollywood. Anyone who claims to be victimized by courts or Congressional committees now automatically cries: 'Get Ed Williams!'"[1] The *News* noted that the clients seeking Williams's services at the same time were Dave Beck, Jimmy Hoffa, Frank Costello and a Washington woman charged in a sensational murder case, Edith Louise Hough.

Hough, forty-one, was variously described as "stylish,"[2] "honey blonde,"[3] "attractive brunette,"[4] "trim,"[5] and a "smart" dresser.[6] She came from a patrician background: her ancestors had been among the first settlers of Virginia's Shenandoah Valley; George Washington had been a guest of her great-great-grandfather, John Hough, Sr.; and her father, Dr. William Hite Hough, a neurologist, had been president of the District of Columbia Medical Society. Edith Louise had been educated at Washington's National Cathedral School for Girls and at Radcliffe. After graduation from college in 1938, she had lived in Europe, served in the OSS, and written a book on medieval Sicily.[7] Her victim, Zurab Abdusheli, forty-four, had fled from the Soviet Union about 1950 and moved to Washington, where he wrote broadcasts that the Voice of America beamed to his former homeland.[8]

Hough and Abdusheli had been lovers for several years when they were neighbors at the Woodner Apartments.* Abdusheli was said to have repeatedly forced his attentions upon Hough; beaten her up; and failed to repay money he borrowed from her.[10] Hough broke off with him in 1956, but he continued to pester her to the point where, in order to avoid him, she answered her phone only by prearrangement.[11] In May 1957, Abdusheli married another woman, but during the next few weeks he nevertheless kept on badgering Hough whenever he could get through to her. He even told her he would divorce his bride and marry Hough if she would have him.[12]

On May 26, 1957, Hough's father died. An only child, she took his death hard,[13] and forgetting the precautions she habitually used to avoid her former lover, she resumed answering her telephone. On the morning of May 30, 1957, Abdusheli reached her and insisted that he must visit her to express his sympathy in person. She agreed, but, as she later told a police officer, her former lover started "pawing" her, "and she didn't want him pawing at her, so she then got the gun and shot him."[14] Using a .25-caliber Colt automatic, Hough shot Abdusheli from behind as he gazed out her eleventh-floor window at the spectacular view of Rock Creek Park. As he turned to face her, she continued to blaze away, hitting him repeatedly in the chest, arm, and head.[15] During her trial, the prosecutor described her actions as "an extremely brutal murder. The defendant shot the deceased five times and as he lay wounded placed a gun to his head and deliberately shot him through the brain, killing him."[16]

In a later era, Williams might have been able to employ a battered-

---

*The Woodner Hotel-Apartments seems permanently linked to Williams. Not only was it the headquarters for Jimmy Hoffa and his entourage during his bribery trial, but Williams also defended its builder, Ian Woodner, who was charged with lying to the Federal Housing Administration in order to obtain several million dollars' worth of mortgage insurance. After a three-week trial in 1957, a jury took only two hours to find Woodner innocent.[9]

lover defense, but in the late 1950s there was no alternative to arguing that Hough had been insane when she killed Abdusheli. Since even the prosecution acknowledged that Hough had been seriously ill for many years with paranoid schizophrenia,[17] she was allowed to plead not guilty by reason of insanity; her plea was accepted by the court, and she was sent to St. Elizabeth's Hospital in Washington, where she was confined for three years.[18]

The Hough case was one of a handful of suits involving violent crimes that Williams has taken in the last thirty years. It was also one of the first in which Vincent Fuller, a newcomer to Williams's firm, assisted his senior partner in the courtroom. A quarter-century later, Fuller would put the lessons from the Hough suit to use when he defended presidential assailant John Hinckley; in both the Hough and Hinckley cases, there was no doubt that the defendant had committed the crime, and the sole question was whether the accused was sane at the time. Like Hough, Hinckley was acquitted on grounds of insanity (by a jury, not a judge) and committed to St. Elizabeth's.

In 1957, Williams was elected to the board of directors of the American Civil Liberties Union, and during the mid- and late 1950s he was in the forefront of efforts to integrate the District of Columbia Bar Association. Several times, members of the bar voted by substantial majorities to admit blacks but did not achieve the two-thirds vote required.[19] Once, when there were enough votes in favor, six members of the bar sued the association to nullify the outcome, and a judge ruled in the dissidents' favor on procedural grounds.[20] Nevertheless, Williams and two other attorneys were given a citation by the Bar Association for defending the case without charge,[21] and Williams was appointed chairman of the Bar Association's Committee on Civil Rights. The bar group finally was integrated after Williams's nineteen-member committee (one of its members was Abe Fortas) recommended in May 1958 that "the word 'white' be eliminated from the By-Laws of our Association." The committee had pointed out that blacks and whites belonged to the same bar associations even in many Deep South states; that in Washington, professional societies of doctors, dentists, nurses, accountants, teachers, journalists and many others were integrated; and that the Bar Association was "virtually the only professional organization in the District of Columbia which still excludes professionally qualified persons solely because of their race." Furthermore, the American Bar Association had started admitting blacks a few years earlier, and the exclusion of blacks in Washington was hampering moves to discipline several nonwhite lawyers who refused to comply with the edicts of a segregated group.[22]

In a sense, the case of Bob Martin, Julius Silverman and Meyer

Schwartz served as a reunion: Tom Wadden and Agnes Neill assisted Williams, and Oliver Gasch was on the prosecution team. In June 1960, however, while the case was moving from the court of appeals to the Supreme Court, the defense lost one of its attorneys and Williams's law office had its ranks reduced from ten to nine: he and Agnes Neill were married, and she immediately gave up the practice of law. Wadden still remembers how abrupt her departure from the firm was. After the couple returned from their elopement, he dropped in on the newly married pair to wish them well and to talk business. "I went into the living room and we sat down and I said, 'Agnes, we've got a problem in this case, we've got a problem in that case.' She sat there and smiled and said, 'We don't have a problem anymore. Because I'm not concerned with those cases.' I thought she was kidding me. I said, 'Come on, Nembus [her nickname].' I remember there was one pressing case. And she said, 'Look, I don't practice law anymore. I'm now Ed's wife.' And I'll tell you, I never saw Agnes down at the office again except socially. She just like that walked out of the office."

According to Williams, "It was her decision" to quit. Even so, "I wasn't sorry to see her stop practicing. I wanted her to go home and be a mother to my children," who were then five, three, and one. But Williams speaks proudly of his wife as "an absolutely dazzling lawyer" who was offered a clerkship by Supreme Court Justice Stanley Reed. "I always say she was one of the three best lawyers I ever met, and I don't say who the other two were." He likes to tell her that "if she hadn't been so dumb as to get married, she would have been my senior partner now. I tell her she could have been one of the highest-paid women in America now. I'd love to see her come back here, but she won't do it." Agnes Neill Williams now confines her legal talents to working as a volunteer lawyer for the Children's Defense Fund. She has also had extensive experience raising children—the four she bore Williams and the three he and his first wife adopted.

By the mid-1960s, Williams could have his pick of dozens of bright young lawyers who sought to join his firm. One who approached him about a job was Henry Ruth, who was leaving the Justice Department, although he would return to the prosecution side in the wake of Watergate and oversee the government's case against John Connally. But about 1965 or 1966, Henry Ruth had a job interview of sorts with Williams—not that Ruth specifically asked for a job, and not that Williams offered him one. "I think he thought I was too naïve," says Ruth. "I don't think Ed thought I was quite ready for the Frank Costellos of the world." Bill Hundley, a friend of both Williams and Ruth, recalls hearing from one of them that Ruth said he would particularly want to represent a client who had been unjustly accused and was in fact innocent. Williams's response was, "'Look, kid, if anybody like that walks in here, I'm taking him.' Which is to say, 'We don't get many like that.'" Adds Hundley, "Ed doesn't take his clients all that seriously. He is well aware of their weak points."

If Henry Ruth wasn't quite hard-nosed enough for Williams's taste, Michael Tigar was. Tigar arrived in Washington in the summer of 1966, fresh from Berkeley, where he had been at the top of his class and editor in chief of the law review at the University of California's law school there. He had been promised a clerkship by Supreme Court Justice William Brennan, but Tigar's left-wing activism upset many conservatives, and Brennan started to feel the heat. In the end, Brennan "fired" Tigar one week before Tigar was to have started work at the Court, which Justice William O. Douglas termed a "'scandalous'" and "'shocking cave-in.'"[23] Brennan called Williams and "strongly recommended" Tigar, whom Williams invited in for a talk. Tigar, who had previously written to Williams about working for him, told Williams exactly why Brennan had withdrawn his job offer, after which, Tigar reports, the following dialogue ensued:

> *Williams:* I don't believe that. Bill Brennan's one of my best friends.*
>
> *Tigar:* Why don't you call him?
>
> *Williams:* What do you want to do?
>
> *Tigar:* I wrote you a letter last year.
>
> *Williams:* Oh, yeah? Did you? [To his secretary]: Did he write us a letter? Well, if he did, then find it. Oh, yeah, you did. Well, what do you want to do?
>
> *Tigar:* I'm really interested in criminal litigation, sir.
>
> *Williams:* Well, I wasn't thinking of hiring anybody.
>
> *Tigar:* Well, then don't. I mean, I'm not the United Way or the Community Chest. If you have a job and it pays what lawyers are paying around town, then I wish you'd consider me for it.
>
> *Williams:* Well, let me think about it.

All this time, says Tigar, who switches back and forth from his own voice to a perfect imitation of Williams, the latter was "sitting there in his chair looking out at Farragut Square [the park across the street]." That's how a job interview with Edward Bennett William goes. And if Williams likes the applicant, as he did Tigar, the would-be employee no sooner arrives home than the phone rings and there's "that soft voice. 'This is Ed Williams. If you want a job with us, you can have it.'"

---

*In 1956, when President Eisenhower nominated Brennan to the High Court, the only vote against the appointment was cast by Williams's client, Senator Joseph McCarthy, who sought to annoy Ike.[24]

Between 1966 and 1978, Tigar would assist Williams on his two biggest cases of the last twenty years—Bobby Baker and John Connally—and Tigar and Williams would form a mutual admiration society, even though Tigar would quit once, return to the firm, and then leave for good. His participation in the Baker and Connally trials gave Tigar as much insight as anyone has ever had into the way Williams works.

"There would be these long, loud, book-throwing, people-scattering sessions in the library. Someone would cite Ed a case and he'd shout, 'That's a bunch of shit. They're never going to believe that.' 'But, Ed, Wigmore said that.' 'Wigmore, my butt. What circuit is Wigmore on? You are so full of shit.'" But if Williams liked the argument, his reaction would be "'I want two Xeroxes of this right away.' There's that process that everyone gets involved in and that's the fun part, that's the genius part of Ed Williams, who worries over every question and who asks himself the hard questions.

"After a particularly loud argument one Friday, I went home. Sunday morning the phone rang and it was Ed. He said, 'You know, I didn't want to wait until Monday; I thought a lot about this and I think you're right and that we would make a terrible mistake that we would regret if we did this, and I'm going to tell the client that.' The client got the best legal advice that any law firm in the world could produce, because, in my view, Ed Williams brooks interference, brooks arguments about what ought to be done."

Tigar also speaks of an instance during the Connally trial when Williams was asking a witness questions from a list Tigar had prepared. Dissatisfied with the way the interrogation was going, Williams strode over to the defense table and, pretending to ask Tigar about something, muttered, "'You fucked up again. You are fucking me up.' He says, "I'm dying out there. What am I supposed to do?' I said, "Ed, just ask the questions.'" Williams did, and both he and Tigar were satisfied with the results.

After Tigar left the firm for several years to teach law and to practice in Paris, Williams welcomed him back like a prodigal son, and also protected him from criticism within the firm over some of Tigar's clients and causes. In 1978, Tigar resigned for a second time, this time to set up his own practice a few blocks away, where he continues to represent some clients referred to him by his mentor. Williams was sorry to lose Tigar, but, having quit Hogan & Hartson thirty years earlier to go out on his own, he understood, saying, "'You'll feel better if you do it yourself, and you'll probably do better if you do it yourself.'"

One reason Tigar decided to move on was that Williams's firm had grown to forty lawyers by the time he left, and despite Williams's best efforts, it was becoming an institution. One eager-beaver computer expert set up an area in the firm's offices which he called "The Control Module" until Williams put a stop to it. The name was changed to "Executive Services," but that was scrapped after Tigar discovered "that there was a massage parlor on 'K' Street that had the same name."

Tigar opened an office with eight other lawyers, who devote one-third of their time to *pro bono* work. "Give Ed a few drinks," says Tigar, "and he'll say he wants to come practice with us." Once, at dinner not so long ago, Williams complained to Tigar, "'Jesus Christ, that's not a law firm. That's a prison.'" Such is the price he has to pay for having an economic base that provides for his continued financial success. "He really does have something to leave to his kids," according to Tigar.

After Nicholas Chase and Williams split up in 1951, Williams's firm, which included a growing number of lawyers, was known as the law offices of Edward Bennett Williams. In 1962, the firm became Williams & (Colman) Stein, and the next year it was Williams, Wadden & Stein. Stein resigned in 1966 to move on to a less hectic life in Florida, and the firm was called Williams & Wadden. Two years later, the office was transformed, with the addition of Paul Connolly and the subtraction of Tom Wadden.

Connolly had been one of Williams's students at Georgetown Law School; and after Connolly graduated in 1948, it was partly on the strength of Williams's recommendation that he was offered a job at Hogan & Hartson. Two decades later, Williams and Connolly decided to join forces. Connolly's specialty was civil litigation, and his entry into the firm meant that, for the first time, criminal and civil practice would be on a relatively equal footing within the office. Tom Wadden's name was dropped as the firm evolved into Williams & Connolly, although Wadden stayed on for several months before departing.* The end of the road for Williams & Wadden was in part due to Wadden taking on as a client Fred Black (who had given testimony to back up Bobby Baker's story about Robert Kerr at Baker's trial) over Williams's objections. "I didn't know this at the time, but Ed had been asked to represent Fred and had absolutely refused," says Wadden. "Ed never cottoned to" the witness he called to testify for Baker. Because Wadden did choose to represent Black, "Ed wasn't at all happy with me, and I wasn't happy with him."

In the end, Wadden was shunted aside in favor of Connolly. "I don't think I was actually consulted to the point where I would have had much to say about it one way or the other," comments Wadden. "I can't answer that [why his name was dropped from the firm]. That's something you'll

---

* In 1981, a quarter-century after Jimmy Hoffa was elected Teamster president while he faced criminal charges and Williams was his attorney, Roy Williams (no relation to Edward Bennett) became president of the union. Roy Williams was under indictment at the time for conspiring to bribe Senator Howard Cannon (D-Nev). Roy Williams was convicted at a 1982 trial; his defense lawyer was Tom Wadden.

have to fathom for yourself. I'm not going to give you an answer to that."

Williams has even less to say about the parting, but one measure of his attitude toward Wadden is revealed when remarks by Wadden or anec-dotes reported by Wadden are related to him. Williams dismisses those as "Wadden fantasizing again." If, on the other hand, the source is Bill Hundley, the response is, "I don't remember that, but if Bill says so, it must have happened."

On the last day of the 1960s, there occurred an "act of vengeance" that one of Williams's most outspoken critics, Washington lawyer and liberal activist Joe Rauh, would seize upon to make a no-holds-barred attack on Williams. Shortly after midnight on December 31, 1969, three gunmen broke into the Pennsylvania home of United Mine Workers dissident Jo-seph A. ("Jock") Yablonski and murdered him, his wife, and daughter. Yablonski had long been a thorn in the side of UMW head A. W. ("Tony") Boyle, whom Yablonski had opposed in a union election just three weeks earlier. Boyle had defeated Yablonski by a vote of 74,000 to 41,000, but Yablonski was challenging the results, claiming the election had been rigged.[25] Yablonski, with Rauh as his lawyer, had previously filed several suits against UMW officials, including Boyle, alleging mis-management of the union and misuse of UMW funds.[26] The UMW had several in-house attorneys of its own, but in August 1969, Williams's law firm was hired to represent the union, Boyle, and the other officers. As Yablonski's son, Joseph A. ("Chip") Yablonski, Jr., described the situa-tion during testimony before a Senate subcommittee that studied the elec-tion in which his father had run against Boyle:

> Tony Boyle apparently discovered that his people weren't good enough to come up against a guy like Joe Rauh, so they shot for bigger fish. They brought in Edward Bennett Williams' firm. In one suit it was almost comical. There in the U.S. district court sat eight lawyers. Gen-eral Motors would have been proud to have that many at the counsel table. They were defending Tony Boyle. At the other counsel table was Joe Rauh. He won.[27]*

---

*Unaware that Bill Hundley was one of Williams's best friends, Rauh had approached him about serving as Senate counsel in the probe of the UMW election. Hundley said he would have to check with Williams. Hundley then turned Rauh down, but told him there wasn't much to be investigated because, as Rauh remembers it, "'Ed said his FBI infor-mants said the union wasn't connected'" with the Yablonski murders. Rauh labels the claim Hundley attributed to Williams "a deliberate lie" and "a pile of crap by Williams," stating that "at that very time" the FBI was learning that Boyle and other UMW officials had ordered the slayings. A year or so after Rauh asked Hundley to head the UMW investiga-tion, Hundley's law partner, Plato Cacheris (giving his address as the Hill Building), turned up as defense counsel for Boyle and other UMW executives accused of embezzling money from the union. Boyle was found guilty on all thirteen counts against him.[28]

The bad blood between Rauh and Williams dated back more than ten years. Once again Jimmy Hoffa was the flash point. Both lawyers had been friendly with Harold Gibbons, the Teamster leader from St. Louis who was also one of the top people in Americans for Democratic Action, the liberal group that Rauh had founded. Ironically, both Williams and Rauh had viewed Gibbons as the man to take over the Teamster presidency from Hoffa and clean up the union. Over a lunch in 1958, Rauh persuaded Gibbons to "go to Bobby [Kennedy]" and turn over records that would incriminate Hoffa and lead to his ouster. The two shook hands on the agreement, and Rauh felt good about it because they were "old comrades-in-arms. We'd been in so many things together, Harold and I," says Rauh.

Gibbons and Rauh shared a taxi from the restaurant where they had dined to the Hill Building, where Williams's office is located (one block from Rauh's). Gibbons left the cab, walked into the building and, comments Rauh, "I've never seen him since that moment. All I know is he went in that building and he never did what he promised me he was going to do. Williams said he didn't tell him not to do it. I don't believe that." Williams retorts, "Never. Never happened. I don't know anything about [a friendship between] Rauh and Gibbons [who has been a client of Williams's]. I didn't even know that Gibbons ever even knew Rauh." Gibbons himself denies that he ever had lunch with Rauh in his life, much less that the incident reported by Rauh occurred.

Given the background of unpleasantness between Williams and Rauh, having the two attorneys on opposite sides of the UMW dispute could only have resulted in fireworks. The first salvo came from Rauh in May 1970, when he filed a motion in one of the suits brought against the UMW, Boyle, and other union leaders by Jock Yablonski shortly before his death; Rauh asked the U.S. District Court in Washington to disqualify Williams's firm from representing both the union and the individual officers at the same time, arguing that such an arrangement constituted a conflict of interest.[29] Several days later, Williams called Rauh and suggested they get together. At a lunch meeting, Williams told Rauh that he was unfamiliar with the details of the Yablonski-Boyle feud and pointed out that Paul Connolly and other lawyers from his firm were the ones handling the case. But, Williams said, he would recommend to Boyle that he step aside as president and allow the union to hold another election.

Although Williams and Rauh talked once more about the case a few days later, no further mention was made of Boyle giving up his office. Williams's firm continued to represent Boyle and other officers individually, as well as the union itself, and this situation was upheld by U.S. District Court Judge Howard F. Corcoran.[30] However, Rauh pressed on with his argument that Williams's firm should not have both the union and its officers as clients, and ultimately the U.S. Court of Appeals sided with him. Noting that "some of the issues raised by the regular UMWA counsel [Williams's firm] would seem to be of more interest to the position of the officers than to the union,"[31] the appeals court disqualified Williams & Connolly from serving as the union's counsel. Commenting that "even if we assume . . . that there is no visible conflict of interest, yet we cannot be sure that such will not arise in the future,"[32] the court softened its ruling a little by declaring, "Our ruling herein do[es] not imply any censure of counsel's action during this period of joint representation."[33]*

The Williams firm did stay on as counsel for Boyle and other top UMW officials. In one of the most controversial aspects of the dispute, the firm advised Boyle and Secretary-Treasurer John Owens that "the union may continue to pay Mr. [Albert] Pass his salary for a reasonable period of time pending resolution of the charges against him." "The charges" against UMW Executive Board member Pass were for complicity in the murder of Jock Yablonski and his family. (Subsequently, Pass was convicted of three counts of murder in the first degree.)[35] The letter authorizing the payments to Pass, on the stationery of Williams's firm and dated May 25, 1972, was signed by Jeremiah C. Collins, one of several lawyers assisting Paul Connolly in the case. In the letter (which was hand-delivered to UMW officials), Collins, then the seventh-ranking member of the firm, declared, "We see nothing in the union's Constitution or in any legal authorities which would require the president to suspend or remove a union official merely because unproved criminal charges have been leveled against him." Pass, after all, was entitled to a "presumption of innocence" that "fully justifies the union" to continue paying him his salary, said Collins. Rauh considered the payments to Pass nothing less than hush money and backed up his allegation with a sworn statement of UMW official William Turnblazer, who told of attending a meeting with Boyle and other union executives on May 25, 1972, the date Collins's letter was delivered. According to Turnblazer:

> Tony Boyle took me aside . . . and showed me a letter that he had received from the law firm of Williams and Connolly, Washington, D.C., stating that it was their legal opinion that the UMWA was justified in keeping . . . Pass on the payroll, although . . . [he was] in custody of the authorities on a murder charge. Tony Boyle commented to me that this

---

*One year later, the same jurist who had approved Williams & Connolly's continuing as counsel for both the UMW and its officers, District Judge Howard F. Corcoran, found a "potential conflict of interest" in the firm's representing both the Teamsters Union and its president, Frank Fitzsimmons, along with former president Jimmy Hoffa and several other officers. The union and its current officers were accused of illegally paying retirement and severance benefits to Hoffa and with breach of fiduciary duties. Corcoran ordered Williams's firm disqualified from representing the individual officers.[34]

action should please Pass . . . and suggested that I get this information
[to him]. I . . . sent word [to Pass] . . . concerning this information.[36]

Rauh also points out that Boyle solicited the opinion of the Williams
firm only after UMWA staff counsel Harrison Combs (a friend of Williams's first partner, Nicholas Chase) told the UMW president it would
be wrong to continue paying Pass. Rauh adds that shortly after Collins
gave his opinion, a federal judge directed that the UMW's generosity to
Pass be halted.

With the help of a friendly congressman, Joe Rauh was able to insert
into the *Congressional Record* a scathing (and privileged) attack on Williams. In 1974, the Antioch School of Law honored Williams for helping
make the practice of criminal law respectable and for championing individual rights. Arnold Miller, a Yablonski ally who had succeeded convicted murderer Tony Boyle as president of the UMW, was also designated
for an award by Antioch. But on September 12, 1974, Miller angrily
refused to accept the honor, writing to Paul A. Porter, the law school's
general chairman:

> Bluntly put, I cannot accept an award on the same platform with
> Edward Bennett Williams because of his unethical and improper con-
> duct in the representation of Tony Boyle against the reform elements in
> the union and because of his appropriation of hundreds of thousands of
> dollars out of the dues of coal miners as payment for his efforts to keep
> them in Tony Boyle's bondage. The fact that the Bar has done nothing
> about this wrongful conduct is no excuse for my demeaning the memory
> of the martyred Yablonski family and betraying the trust of the coal
> miners by pretending that all this never happened. . . .
>
> What Williams & Connolly did as Boyle's lawyers . . . was unethical
> and improper, including their pretense that they were representing the
> union and its membership when, in fact, every act they took was in
> direct contravention of the interests of the union and its membership.
> From the beginning, Williams & Connolly represented Boyle's interest
> and not that of the union and its membership who were paying them.

Miller concluded by saying, "You will understand the depth of my feelings if you will only think of the additional length of time that Tony
Boyle, a murderer, was kept as President of the union through the tactics
of Williams & Connolly, and of the three Yablonski graves on a hillside
near a coal village in Pennsylvania."[37]

Miller's letter was placed in the *Congressional Record* by Congressman
Ken Hechler (D-W. Va.) on October 15, 1974. Taking note of the Watergate scandal, which had just culminated in President Nixon's resignation,
Hechler declared that Miller "has exhibited a new and higher morality
which is refreshing in this city, by refusing to accept this award on the
same platform with Edward Bennett Williams, whose conduct during the

infamous and murderous regime of Tony Boyle was an insult to every coal miner."[38]

Although Miller signed the letter, Rauh admits that he, not Miller, wrote most of it. Rauh was also able to give information to a sympathetic columnist, John Herling of the *Washington Daily News*, that produced commentary by Herling such as: "Understandably considerations of conflict of interest are—consciously or not—often subdued by the irresistible attraction of lush fees."[39] Herling also took Williams to task for "looking down his nose at the lesser breed within the law," and complaining about lawyers who defended indigent clients and expected to be paid out of public funds. Pointing out that "Mr. Williams' acquired distaste for Hoffa has been made palatable by fees from the Teamsters Union," Herling went on to say that Williams "is like the mouse who cried, 'I've had enough cheese, let me out of the trap.' Out of that trap nobody can spring Ed Williams, but Ed Williams. But why should he be so uncharitable to the other mice?"[40]

Rauh continued his barrage against Williams in a 1979 address at the University of Minnesota Law School, speaking of "the prestigious Washington firm" that "simply gave Boyle the opinion he was asking for—that it was legal to pay salaries to these officials in jail under indictment for first degree murder when such payments could have no conceivable purpose other than to keep these officials from talking and implicating Boyle."[41] Rauh also touched on one of Williams's favorite stances, that "'everybody is entitled to a lawyer,'" which he said is actually a "euphemistic way of stating the 'hired gun' theory," espoused by an attorney who "is . . . really . . . selling himself in the manner of the ladies of the evening."[42]

Rauh elaborated on his "hired gun" reference in a recent interview, declaring, "If Jock Yablonski and his wife and his daughter had not been murdered, I might not feel this deeply about it. I'm perfectly willing to admit that my mind is affected by the death of my client."

Yablonski's son, Chip, is also bitter. Acknowledging that he has never even met Williams and that Williams was never an attorney of record in the Mine Workers cases, Chip Yablonski even so states, "My gut churned" over the tactics of Williams's firm, for which he blames Williams. He is still upset that several days after the bodies of his family were found, lawyers from Williams & Connolly moved to have Jock Yablonski's suits dismissed on the grounds he was dead. What it amounts to, says Chip Yablonski, is that someone can try to win a lawsuit by murdering the opposition. He believes Tony Boyle was "emboldened" by having Williams as his lawyer, although there is no evidence that Williams was personally involved in the case. "Just to have Williams representing you in this town" means a great deal, remarks Chip Yablonski, a Washington lawyer himself, who, as of 1982, was one of several attorneys for the

National Football League Players Association—on the opposite side from
the owners, such as Williams.

Williams is emphatic on the subject of Tony Boyle and the UMW: "I
never had one frigging thing to do with that case." He concedes, "That
does not remove me from responsibility, because I'm the head of this law
firm," but insists, "That case was run entirely by other lawyers." Adds
Williams, "I never represented Tony Boyle in my life. That's one of the
goddam outrageous misstatements that Rauh keeps making. I had no
more to do with the United Mine Workers case than you had. I was never
in any way involved in the case. We have thousands of cases. I do not
know everything that happens in every case." As for Rauh, Williams
states, "Maybe he's hoping that someday I'll take action against him."

In fact, Rauh once said for publication that Williams has "'all the
ethics of a pigsty,'" and challenged, "'Let him sue me.'"[43]

"I'm not going to take action against poor Rauh," answers Williams.
"Poor Rauh has less influence in America today than anyone I know. You
just don't pay any attention to him."

For many years Joe Rauh has lived two doors from Robert Schulman,
now the number two partner in Williams's firm. Schulman also worked
closely with Williams in operating the Redskins during the mid- and late
1970s. And Rauh and Schulman are not only close friends, they are related by marriage. The Schulmans frequently have parties for people from
the worlds of the law and sports, but, as Joe Rauh puts it, "Much as the
Schulmans and the Rauhs love each other, the Schulmans don't invite me
when Williams is there." That arrangement suits both Rauh and Williams perfectly.

In 1971, during the UMW battle, Joseph Califano joined Williams's
office, which had two dozen lawyers and was renamed Williams, Connolly
& Califano. Califano, forty, had served as President Johnson's chief adviser on domestic affairs in the late 1960s, before entering law practice in
Washington. After Califano left the White House, he and Williams, fellow alumni of Holy Cross, took to having lunch together frequently over a
two-year period. Williams proposed that they become partners as a means
of "adding a State Department to the War Department," in Califano's
words. "I clearly added a third leg to the stool that they needed," with
Williams specializing in criminal work, Paul Connolly in charge of civil
litigation and Califano responsible for supervising contacts with government agencies and overseeing the administration of the firm.

Califano's move was a blow to former Supreme Court Justice Abe
Fortas, and ended once and for all the longtime friendship between Fortas
and Williams. In May 1969, Fortas had resigned from the Supreme Court
(the first justice to do so after being accused of misconduct) in the wake
of disclosures that he had arranged in 1965, when Johnson appointed him

to the Court, to receive $20,000 a year for life from the family foundation of Louis E. Wolfson. Wolfson had gone to prison after being convicted of stock manipulation[44] and was a client of Williams's.*

Following his resignation, Fortas sought to rejoin his old firm, Arnold & Porter (formerly Arnold, Porter & Fortas), but was not invited back. According to informed sources, he approached Williams about moving into his office. Williams was fairly receptive, but quickly discovered that a job offer to Fortas would cause a revolt by some of his Young Turks, because of the power Fortas would presumably be able to wield, combined with his reputation for being a domineering boss. Williams had to turn down Fortas, and Williams took the heat. Fortas was embittered by the rejection, and two years later, when Califano moved from his firm— Arnold & Porter—into Williams's office, the breach was complete and final.

Califano's appointment as secretary of Health, Education and Welfare in 1977 offered a rare glimpse into Williams's finances. Like all cabinet appointees of Jimmy Carter, Califano was required to disclose his income for 1976, and his cut of the Williams, Connolly & Califano pie turned out to be a whopping $555,000—more, as the *Washington Post* pointed out, than even the president of General Motors had earned. Williams criticized the Carter administration for "'publishing past earnings,'" but said there was "'no windfall explanation'" for Califano's income; "'The facts are the facts.'"[46]

Although Williams consistently declined to discuss his personal finances, he did say in 1981 that as the senior partner he "obviously" earned more than any other member of the firm each and every year. He also explained how he bills clients for the work he does himself. "I don't have a charge for my own time. Because I sometimes am able to do things in a half an hour as a result of thirty-seven years' experience that might take six months for someone else to do. I don't want to work on a clock. I want to work with other factors weighed in—the result, the experience I've had. I keep a record of how much time I put in, but we don't bill for my time." After a job is completed, Williams decides how much it should be worth to his client, depending primarily on the outcome and only secondarily on how long he spent on the case.

Williams's work was temporarily disrupted when he underwent surgery in the summer of 1977 for cancer of the stomach. Until then, his most serious ailment had been chronic hoarseness, which forced him to stop teaching law in the 1950s and also caused a delay of several weeks in one

---

*In 1972, Wolfson, in a deal arranged by Williams, pleaded no contest to filing a false corporate financial statement and was fined $10,000. The plea avoided a fourth trial on charges of corporate misconduct and perjury. Wolfson had been convicted in 1968, had the verdict reversed in 1970,[45] and then had two more trials, with Williams as his attorney, in which the juries were hung, 11–1 and 10–2 for acquittal.

of his trials in 1956.[47] Ben Bradlee, who talked to Williams's surgeon, learned that the malignancy apparently was "encapsulated" and the doctors felt they removed all of it. Williams says each of his parents had a similar operation and lived to be well over eighty. In 1982, a second operation removed a malignant tumor from his liver, but after several weeks he was once again going full speed.

A year after Williams's first operation, his partner, Paul Connolly, succumbed to a heart attack at the age of fifty-six. His death compounded the loss of Califano and made the latter's possible return, after Carter fired him in 1979, even more desirable to Williams. After great deliberation, Califano elected to start his own law firm, in what he calls "the second hardest personal decision in my life," behind only separating from his wife. "The partnership was a phenomenal financial and professional success," says Califano, adding that there was no problem that prevented his return; Williams would have agreed to almost anything in order to get him back. But, like Williams, Michael Tigar, and others, Califano felt he had to go out on his own, in spite of initial financial sacrifices. Flying to Washington for a few hours from Cape Cod, where he was writing his memoir of the Carter administration, Califano informed Williams of his decision over a dinner that Califano calls "the most emotional meal of my life." His refusal to return did not affect the friendship, but it left Williams with the unwelcome burden of having to administer a firm that now included about sixty lawyers.

By 1982, that number had increased to about eighty, and each year nearly 1,500 candidates were applying for six openings for young lawyers. Williams takes pride in the fact that most of his new associates are graduates of top law schools like Harvard and Yale and have held judicial clerkships, often with Supreme Court justices. He seems almost to have forgotten that his own career proves that one need not attend the most prestigious law school or clerk for a judge in order to be an outstanding lawyer.

Some of the would-be clients Williams has rejected have been as interesting as the ones he has taken on. During the Vietnam War, Dr. Benjamin Spock asked Williams to defend him against charges stemming from peace demonstrations in Boston, but Williams turned him down. "It was quite clear that I would never get the kind of control over that case that I insist upon," he declares. Spock and his codefendants "wanted to use the case as a vehicle for articulating their antiwar feelings," instead of merely trying to defend themselves against the charges, which is what Williams considers the purpose of any trial. He confided in a friend, "'Those fuckers don't need a lawyer, they need a toastmaster.'"

He was also approached on behalf of fugitive heiress Patty Hearst, following her arrest on bank-robbery charges in September 1975, a year and a half after she had been kidnapped by the Symbionese Liberation Army. "The difficulty," according to Williams was that he was not contacted directly by Patty Hearst, but by her father, newspaper publisher Randolph Hearst. "Patty Hearst, I assumed, could speak for herself and she could select her own lawyer. It was quite apparent to me after a conversation with him that she had some hostility to her mother and that if I went in there as the choice of mother and father, then I wouldn't have the kind of relationship that I needed to have with her in order to be effective. So I suggested that he have her communicate with me, which she could have done, but she never did."

After Williams declined the case, the Hearsts hired F. Lee Bailey. Patty Hearst was convicted and spent two years in prison before President Carter commuted her sentence. Meanwhile, she fired Bailey and retained San Francisco attorney George Martinez to appeal her conviction on five grounds, alleging among them that Bailey had been guilty of "incompetence" and—because he had contracted to write a book about the case— conflict of interest. The U.S. Court of Appeals for the Ninth Circuit ordered a lower court to grant Ms. Hearst a hearing on her allegations. The Court of Appeals said that while "Bailey acted well within the scope of 'reasonably competent and effective representation,'" Bailey's "conflict of interest is virtually admitted," adding, "Bailey's decision to enter into a book contract during the course of the trial was most unfortunate . . . to an even greater degree when the case is a *cause célèbre* and the attorney has the reputation of being an outstanding lawyer." The court also said that if Hearst's allegations were proved, they might show that Bailey "misled" the Hearsts by withholding details of his book contract and again, if proved, might have violated a rule of the American Bar Association that prohibits lawyers from engaging in "conduct involving dishonesty, fraud, deceit, or misrepresentation." The Appeals Court also suggested that the lower court might find it advisable to direct Bailey to show cause why he should not be disciplined.[48] Before the lower court could hold a hearing, Ms. Hearst dropped her appeal. According to Bailey's replacement, George Martinez, she decided she didn't want to undergo "another circus" in court. "It was not an easy suit for me to have to withdraw," Martinez added.

Williams believes that Bailey made the mistake of becoming too concerned about press reaction to the case, and therefore spent too much time playing to the press instead of to the jury. Louis Nizer, who was asked to handle Patty Hearst's appeal, but who also refused, expresses with a very eloquent "no comment" his analysis of Bailey's trial tactics. Martinez says "it's too bad" that Williams would not defend Hearst, who might have escaped both conviction and imprisonment if she had called Williams herself.

Williams (or his office) went on to represent other notorious clients, such as John Hinckley, which has continued to raise eyebrows. One "very dear friend" of Williams complained of his allowing Vincent Fuller to defend President Reagan's assailant: "'Well, I understand the right to counsel, but does he have a right to the best?'" Williams told the woman he thought Hinckley did have that right, just as he would to the best doctor if he needed one. Meanwhile, syndicated columnist Andy Rooney was writing that "Williams is so good as a criminal defense lawyer that we'll have to be careful he doesn't end up convincing us that Reagan shot Hinckley. He's that good."[49]

By 1982, however, most of Williams's clients were business-oriented, such as International Harvester, Boeing Aircraft and the Motion Picture Association of America. About the time Hinckley shot Reagan, for instance, Williams was winding up negotiations for a friend, Denver oilman Marvin Davis, to purchase Twentieth Century-Fox Film Corporation. Just before the agreement was to have been consummated, Davis announced that he was pulling out, but several days later it was on again. Williams, who did most of the bargaining for Davis, had gone to Miami for what he hoped would be a week at the Baltimore Orioles' training camp. After two days, he left to shuttle back and forth from Denver to Los Angeles to New York to Washington to Denver to New York, before "some very, very big egos were brought into submission" and Davis proceeded with the acquisition.

Several months later, Davis named Williams to Twentieth Century's board of directors (along with Gerald Ford and Henry Kissinger), which seemed fitting for someone whose clients have included not only the Hollywood writers of the HUAC era but such entertainment personalities as Frank Sinatra, Burt Lancaster, Georgia Gibbs, Faye Emerson (whom he represented in contract negotiations and a divorce case), and Angie Dickinson (Williams dealt with her domestic problems and with a publisher that Dickinson believed had defamed her). Williams and the reclusive Davis, one of America's richest men, had been friendly since 1977 or 1978, when Davis asked Williams to handle all his legal affairs. Judging from the amount of money Davis paid for Twentieth Century-Fox—about $750 million, according to Williams—Williams was becoming a go-between and a dealmaker on a scale Eddie Cheyfitz never dreamed of.

Five men have been identified by name over the years as Williams's partners: Nick Chase, Colman Stein, Tom Wadden, Paul Connolly, and Joe Califano. One died; two (Stein and Califano) left on friendly terms; the departure of Wadden was with mixed feelings on both sides; and the split-up with Chase was markedly hostile. Starting in three rooms in the Hill Building, the firm outgrew the whole building during the next three decades, leaving Williams to wish that interest rates would come down so he could erect a much larger building to house them all. After losing

Connolly and Califano, he was also looking for someone to whom he could delegate much of the work of running the office. Still known in 1982 as Williams & Connolly, the firm was actually what it had been after the dissolution of the short-lived partnership between Chase and Williams: Law Offices of Edward Bennett Williams.

Even his worst enemies would not deny that Ed Williams is a brilliant individual who is gifted with a phenomenal memory and an almost incomparable courtroom presence. Perhaps his most valuable asset, though, is his uncanny ability to read people and understand what makes them tick. Jury selection undoubtedly is of greater importance to Williams than to most trial lawyers. While questioning prospective jurors, Williams is able to grasp intuitively how to appeal to each one of them, and then, as Dennis O'Toole, the foreman in the John Connally trial, observed, he is able to provide something for everybody. If Williams has an Achilles' heel, it is that in spite of his astonishing skills at analyzing character, he tends to underestimate many people he deals with one-to-one over a long period of time (as opposed to the relationship between attorney and jury during the relatively brief span of a trial), and to treat them with disrespect. He is also an extraordinarily moody individual; his associates know better than to approach him without first ascertaining whether he's in good spirits. They call his secretary, who has a kind of mood meter, and ask, "What's the number today?" If she says it's a two or something that low on a scale of one to ten, the caller responds, "Never mind, I'll get in touch with him some other time."

Williams's critics gnash their teeth over some of his tactics. Who else, for instance, has turned up as attorney for both defendant and main prosecution witness, as Williams did during the Adam Clayton Powell trial? Prosecutor Morton Robson was unhappy but he couldn't find any rule to prohibit Williams's move. That is usually what happens. Williams does not pretend to be a saint, and his clients do not hire him to lead them into the kingdom of heaven. They retain him to keep their cases from going to trial if possible—and if not, to win in court. And generally Williams is successful. He is a practical man with practical goals. In the "contest living" he loves so well, the bottom line is winning, and the lawyer who reaps the glory is the one who wins, not the one who says, "I could have won, but I wouldn't do this or that." Williams exploits the rules to the hilt, but he always knows exactly how far he can go. In nearly forty years of trying the most controversial cases, he has never been disciplined by any court or by any lawyers' group. Proceedings of attorneys' organizations that do not result in disciplinary action are confidential, but, so far as is known, no complaints have ever been brought against him. Joe Rauh says he considered filing a grievance over the Tony Boyle–Jock Yablonski matter, but it is very doubtful that such a complaint would have accomplished anything, since Williams was not directly involved in that case.

Ed Williams knows that in baseball or football or tennis, the ball that is most difficult to defend against is the one right on the line. Blindfolded, in the middle of the night and ailing, Ed Williams can kick up chalk, time after time after time. That is very frustrating to some lawyers. But Ed Williams believes in winning. And Ed Williams wins. Every time, he goes right to the line, but never quite seems to step into foul territory. Ed Williams wins.

Williams is often compared to other famous trial lawyers, such as Melvin Belli and F. Lee Bailey. Mentioning Belli and Bailey in the same sentence as Williams is ludicrous; the difference is like night and day. Five days after an Air Florida plane crashed into the Potomac River in 1982, killing seventy-eight people, Belli placed a tasteless advertisement in the *Washington Post* seeking clients whose cases involved "SERIOUS PERSONAL INJURY AND WRONGFUL DEATH"—in boldface caps.[50] That same week, Mr. Bailey starred in a full-page ad for Smirnoff Vodka that ran in *Newsweek*. ("Everyone admitted to the bar at my house, [sic] always gets Smirnoff. And no one ever raises an objection."[51]) Ed Williams has never advertised for business, and never will. Ed Williams has never endorsed liquor or other products, and never will. Also unlike Bailey, Belli and, for that matter, Louis Nizer, Williams has never written a book the primary message of which appears to be self-glorification. Edward Bennett Williams is the real McCoy.

Appendix

Overview of the Career of Edward Bennett Williams

1920   Born, Hartford.

1941   Graduates from Holy Cross College.

1944   Graduates from Georgetown Law School, admitted to District of Columbia Bar, joins law firm of Hogan & Hartson.

1949   Leaves Hogan & Hartson to establish own law practice.

1951   Represents Jon M. Jonkel, who testifies in Senate probe of 1950 Maryland Senate election, pleads guilty to violating Maryland election law.

1951   Defends Senator Joseph McCarthy in suit filed against him by Drew Pearson. Suit settled out of court in 1956.

1951–1953   Represents conservative-targeted entertainment figures Martin Berkeley, Sidney Buchman, Harold Hecht, Max Benoff, Robert Rossen, Howard Koch, Georgia Gibbs.

1951   Charles Nelson gambling case begins. Ends with Nelson pleading guilty, 1954.

1952   Represents Joe McCarthy in libel suit against Senator William Benton (D-Conn.) McCarthy drops suit in 1954.

1953   Wins $50,000 from Drew Pearson for libeling Norman Littell. This is only libel judgment ever won against Pearson, who settles suit for $40,000.

1953   Acquittal of Robert W. Dudley on perjury charge leads to friendship between Williams and Richard Nixon.

1953–1955   Defends Congressman Ernest Bramblett, (R-Calif.), indicted on eighteen counts in connection with scheme to receive kickbacks from his office employees. Case becomes part of feud within California GOP between Nixon-led supporters of Bramblett and Earl Warren forces.[1] At trial in 1954, Bramblett convicted on seven counts after eleven counts dismissed.[2] Williams puts on no defense because "I didn't have any defense." Case is appealed to Supreme Court, oral arguments scheduled for February 7, 1955. Williams fails to appear and several justices are "whispering louder and louder: 'Where's the other attorney?' 'Where's the other attorney?'" Williams arrives an hour late, "apologizing profusely."[3] It turns out that Williams had been given wrong date by alcoholic court clerk. Williams accepts blame instead of pointing finger at clerk, but Chief Justice Warren learns what happened and he and Williams become friends. Supreme Court rules against Bramblett 6–0 (with Warren and two others abstaining).[4] Before long, Williams runs into Justice Felix Frankfurter, who tells him, "'You made a brilliant argument.' I said, 'I wish you'd write a letter to my client and tell him that, because we lost.' He said, 'Oh, you were clearly right, you know.' I said, 'Why did you vote against me if you thought I was clearly right?' He said, 'Don't you know about substantial justice?' He wasn't going to let this guy slip the noose just because the government had made a mistake."

1954   Joseph McCarthy censured.

1954–1955   Surplus-ship cases involving Aristotle Onassis, Robert W. Dudley, Joseph Casey, et al.

1954–1956   Files defamation suit against Onassis on behalf of Spyridon Catapodis, who drops case eighteen months later.

1955   IRS investigates McCarthy taxes; McCarthy winds up receiving refund.

1955   Defends Rea Van Fosson, retired air force intelligence officer accused of stealing secret FBI report on Jay Lovestone, former leader of Communist party who had become an official of American Federation of Labor, and giving it to House Un-American Activities Committee. Works out bargain under which Van Fosson pleads guilty to one of eight counts and gets six-month suspended sentence.[5]

1955–1956   Represents *Confidential* magazine, overturns Post Office ban.

1956   Aldo Icardi acquitted of perjury on Williams's motion to judge.

1956   Sidney Brennan, Gerald Connelly, et al., found guilty of Taft-Hartley violations in Minneapolis.

1956–1964 Handles Frank Costello tax-evasion and denaturalization cases, culminating in Supreme Court holding that Costello cannot be deported.

1957 Ian Woodner acquitted of filing false statements with FHA.

1957 Elected to American Civil Liberties Union board of directors.

1957 Accompanies Teamster president Dave Beck to Senate Rackets Committee hearings.

1957 Jimmy Hoffa acquitted of bribery.

1957–1973 Teamster general counsel.

1957–1958 Leads successful move to integrate D.C. Bar.

1958 Edith Louise Hough pleads not guilty to murder by reason of insanity; is committed to St. Elizabeth's Hospital.

c. 1958 Represents Robert Stroud (Birdman of Alcatraz), gets him removed from Alcatraz to federal prison hospital.

1958–1962 Gambling case of Julius Silverman, Meyer Schwartz, and Robert Martin ends with Supreme Court holding "spike mike" evidence illegal.

1959 Bernard Goldfine plea-bargains on contempt-of-Congress charges.

1959 Bartley Crum, attorney for Teamster monitor Godfrey Schmidt, makes charge before Senate Rackets Committee that Williams offered bribe if Schmidt would resign. Crum recants a few days later, dies several months after that.

1960 Admitted to American College of Trial Lawyers.

1960 Adam Clayton Powell tax case results in hung jury; case later dropped on motion of prosecution.

1960–1961 Goldfine tax case, biggest in history, ends in guilty plea.

1960–1961 Defends Igor Melekh, Russian diplomat at U.N. accused of espionage. Williams proposes that case, in precedent-setting move, be assigned to International Court of Justice, but at last minute Kennedy administration decides to drop charges (and expel Melekh), in hopes of winning better treatment for Francis Gary Powers and other American prisoners in Russia.[6]

1961 Featured in thirty-minute film, *Defending the Unpopular Client,* produced by National Council on Legal Clinics.[7]

1962 Buys 5-percent interest in Washington Redskins.

1962 *One Man's Freedom* published.

1962–1963 Supreme Court overturns convictions of James Wah Toy and Wong Sun.

1963 Drafts two wills for *Washington Post* publisher Philip Graham, who commits suicide several months later. Wills declared invalid after Williams tells court Graham was insane at the time they were drafted.

1963 Defends former congressman Frank W. Boykin (D-Ala.), charged along with former congressman Thomas F. Johnson (D-Md.) and two other men in Maryland savings and loan scandal. After Johnson's attorney, George Cochran Doub, makes mistake of introducing defense evidence before prosecution finishes presenting evidence—thereby jeopardizing defense's right to move for directed verdict of acquittal at end of government case—Williams stalks out of courtroom to underline his scorn for Doub.[8] All four defendants convicted on all eight counts,[9] and Williams's client, Boykin, fined $40,000 and placed on six months' probation, then pardoned by President Johnson because of age (eighty) and ill health.[10] Mass convictions helped advance career of chief prosecutor, Joseph Tydings, U.S. attorney for Maryland, who was elected to U.S. Senate the next year.

1964   Accompanies Bobby Baker to Senate Rules Committee hearings.

1964   Switches political affiliation from Republican to Democratic.

1965   Chuckie Del Monico freed of charges of robbing Evansville, Indiana, savings and loan.

1965   Represents Sam Giancana during federal grand jury probe of organized crime in Chicago. Giancana does not take Williams's advice to testify after grant of immunity, is sent to jail for contempt.

1965   Becomes managing partner of Washington Redskins.

1965   Wins court fight over control of Paramount Pictures. Opposed by Louis Nizer in what press called clash of "two of America's most spectacular trial lawyers . . . acknowledged rivals for national top courtroom billing."[11]

1966   Succeeds in having death sentence reduced to life imprisonment on behalf of William C. Coleman, convicted of murdering Washington policeman after liquor store robbery. Williams had been appointed by courts to conduct Coleman's appeal after his conviction.[12]

1966   Named lawyer of the year by District of Columbia Bar.

1966   Arranges settlement between Edward Levinson, owner of Fremont Casino in Las Vegas, and government. Levinson, accused of tax evasion after skimming profits, had sued government for invasion of privacy, charging he had been wiretapped.[13]

1966-1967   Negotiates "airtight" contract transferring ownership of "pigeon lists" from Frank Ritter, Max Courtney, and Charles Brudner to Bahamas Amusements Ltd. (casino operators) for $2.1 million to be paid over ten-year period.

1967   Bobby Baker tried and convicted. Williams also handles Baker appeals, which are exhausted in 1970, and Baker goes to prison.

1967   Turns down LBJ offer to appoint him Washington mayor.

1967-1968   Defends James L. Marcus, New York's commissioner of water supply, gas and electricity, and insider to Mayor John Lindsay. Marcus pleads guilty to taking bribe, draws fifteen-month sentence.[14]

1968   Hired by William F. Buckley to represent convicted murderer Edgar Smith.

1968-1970   Defendants in Colonial Pipeline case found guilty of accepting bribes to permit construction of cross-country oil line through Woodbridge Township, New Jersey. Among those convicted were Williams's client, former Woodbridge Mayor Walter Zirpolo; and his son-in-law, former town council president Robert Jacks.[15]

1969   Supreme Court overturns convictions of "Milwaukee Phil" Alderisio, Willie Alderman, and Ruby Kolod for making threats via interstate communications.

1969   U.S. Army decides to drop prosecution of several Green Berets—including Williams's client, Colonel Robert B. Rheault, former commander of the Green Berets in Vietnam—who were accused of summarily executing a Vietnamese suspected of being a double agent. Decision based on CIA's refusal to permit any of its operatives to give evidence for the prosecution.[16]

1969   Attorney General John Mitchell advises Williams, as lawyer for Senator Thomas Dodd (D-Conn.), that two-year probe of Dodd's finances had not turned up enough evidence to warrant prosecution of Dodd for tax evasion. In 1967, Dodd was censured by his fellow senators for converting to his own use over $100,000 in political donations, leading to IRS investigation.[17]

1969ff   United Mine Worker dispute between union president A. W. ("Tony") Boyle, represented by Williams's law firm, and reform element, led by "Jock" Yablonski, whose cause was carried on by Joe Rauh following murder of Yablonski, his wife, and daughter.

1970   Calls for abolition of death penalty in Washington while arguing appeal of Bernard J. Heinlein, a drifter sentenced to die for participating in rape-murder of skid row woman.[18]

1970   Folksinger Peter Yarrow sentenced to only three months in jail for sexual misconduct with fourteen-year-old groupie during trip to Washington to give concert. Williams was asked to argue for light sentence after Yarrow had already pleaded guilty.[19]

1971   Arranges for Heidi Fletcher to plead guilty to first-degree murder, armed robbery, and other charges and be sentenced leniently under federal Youth Corrections Act just six days before she would have been too old for act to apply. Fletcher, daughter of former HUD and Washington city official, was charged with involvement in murder of D.C. policeman after bank robbery. She was sentenced to maximum of nine years in prison and released after several years.[20]

1972   Otto Kerner, U.S. Appeals Court judge and ex-governor of Illinois, accused of taking bribe, perjury, tax evasion, and other crimes. Found guilty after trial in which Williams's partner, Paul Connolly, defended him.[21]

1972   Cartoonist Al Capp, a client of Williams's, pleads guilty to attempted adultery and is fined $500 after being accused of more serious sex crimes with a Wisconsin college coed one-third his age.[22]

1972   Three months after the Watergate arrests, President Nixon, in Oval Office chat with aides H. R. Haldeman and John Dean, vows to "fix the son of a bitch" in reaction to Williams's investigation of the case on behalf of his clients, the Democratic National Committee and the *Washington Post.*

1972   Legal odyssey of financier Louis Wolfson ends with plea bargain worked out by Williams: Wolfson doesn't contest charge of filing false corporate financial statement, is fined $10,000.

1973ff   Represents fugitive financier Robert Vesco, accused of illegal donations to Nixon campaign.

1973   Wins acquittal in conspiracy and bank-fraud case of Walter H. Jones, former New Jersey state senator and Bergen County GOP leader, and his codefendant, Peter Moraites, former Speaker of the New Jersey Assembly.[23]

1974   Named treasurer of Democratic National Committee.

1974   Declines to represent President Nixon, who is forced to resign.

1974   Defends New York Yankee owner George Steinbrenner in court and in front of baseball commissioner Bowie Kuhn, after Steinbrenner is accused of making illegal donations to Nixon fund.

1974   Wins case for Minneapolis businessman Dwayne Andreas, accused of making illegal gift of $100,000 to Hubert Humphrey's 1968 presidential campaign.

1974   Testifies in New Jersey state court that he had advised Mafia leader Gerardo V. Catena to testify before state Commission of Investigation after he was granted immunity from prosecution. Catena refuses to answer questions, spends four years in prison on contempt citation.[24]

1975   John Connally acquitted of accepting illegal gratuities.

1975   Williams, as friend of Earl Warren, invited to eulogize the late chief justice in ceremonies at Supreme Court.[25]

1975   Former senator Daniel Brewster (D-Md.) pleads guilty to accepting illegal gratuity, is fined $10,000, but not sent to prison.[26]

1975   Turns down offer of President Ford to appoint him head of CIA.

1975   Along with Louis Nizer, defends Dr. Armand Hammer, chairman of Occidental Petrolem, against charges of making illegal contributions to Nixon campaign. Quits case after Hammer, over his objections, refuses to admit guilt as part of plea bargain.

1975   Refuses to represent Patty Hearst in ex-fugitive's bank robbery case.

1975   Serves as attorney for Playboy emperor Hugh Hefner, target of federal probe in Chicago. Investigation ends without any action being taken against Hefner or his company.[27]

1976   Considers running for U.S. Senate from Maryland, decides not to.

1976   Named by President Ford to his Foreign Intelligence Advisory Board.

1976   Declines to defend Maryland governor Marvin Mandel in political corruption case.

1976   Retained as Washington counsel for Coca-Cola; Charles Kirbo, confidant of Democratic presidential nominee Jimmy Carter, is company's lawyer in Atlanta.

1976-1977   Attorney for Patrick J. Cunningham, New York State Democratic chairman, accused of selling judgeships, fixing a criminal case, and accepting bribes.[28] Succeeds in having all charges dropped.

1977   Hired by Russian exile Aleksandr Solzhenitsyn to defend fellow writer Aleksandr Ginzburg, imprisoned in Soviet Union for expressing dissent. Applies for visa to go to Russia and argue Ginzburg's case, but is lectured over telephone by Soviet Ambassador Anatoly Dobrynin that his request is "'unprecedented, presumptuous and arrogant.'"[29] Thereafter continues to use public forums to advocate Ginzburg's release.[30]

1977   Resigns as Democratic party treasurer.

1977   Operated on for removal of malignant tumor from stomach.

1977   Negotiates plea bargain for former CIA director Richard Helms, accused of testifying falsely before Senate committee.

1977   Argues to Supreme Court that record companies and networks should be allowed to disseminate Nixon Watergate tapes; Court holds for Nixon.

1978   Succeeds in having case against former FBI official John J. Kearney (accused of illegal surveillance of Weather Underground sympathizers) dropped.

1978–1979   Washington parking-lot magnate Dominic Antonelli (whom Williams defends) and former city official Joseph Yeldell convicted in bribery/conspiracy case. Verdict overturned following disclosure one of jurors may have been prejudiced against defendants; case transferred to Philadelphia and retried; Antonelli and Yeldell acquitted.[31]

1979   William F. Buckley, Jr., retains Williams firm to work out settlement of SEC case against him re Starr Broadcasting Company.

1979   Hired by Henry Ford II and William Clay Ford to fight family battle against their nephew, Benson Ford, Jr. (represented by Roy Cohn).[32]

1979   Purchases Baltimore Orioles; relinquishes control of Washington Redskins.

1980   Named chairman of Committee to Continue an Open (Democratic) Convention, but move to deny Jimmy Carter renomination fails.

1980   Carter goes down to landslide defeat and Ronald Reagan names Williams to his transition team.

1981   President Reagan reappoints Williams to Foreign Intelligence Advisory Board, which Carter had abolished.

1981   Arrives at plea bargain with prosecution in case of Warner Communications chief executive Jay Emmett, charged with taking bribes of $70,000 and "'corruptly siphoning'" another $150,000 from Westchester Premier Theater as part of "'pattern of racketeering activity.'" Emmett resigns and pleads guilty to lesser charges, while his codefendant, Leonard Horwitz, quits and admits evading taxes.[33] Settlement of case seen as "ostensibly serious setback" for probe into "crime-ridden, drug-oriented" Warner firm, as trial might have provided proof of company's links to organized-crime figures, such as alleged "key connecting link between the underworld and the upper crust of America's political and corporate leadership"—California lawyer Sidney Korshak. Korshak, reportedly "'one of the half-dozen most powerful men at the very top of the national crime syndicate,'" said to have associated with Al Capone, Meyer Lansky, and Sam Giancana.[34]

1981   Negotiates sale of Twentieth Century-Fox Film Corporation to Marvin Davis for $750 million; named to firm's board of directors, along with Gerald Ford and Henry Kissinger.

1981–1982   Vincent Fuller, Williams's longtime partner, defends John Hinckley, who shot and wounded President Reagan.

1981–1982   Clients include International Harvester, Motion Picture Association of America, *National Enquirer,* boxing promoter Don King, National Consumer Cooperative Bank.

1982   After Reagan crony Justin Dart calls Gerald Ford "'a dumb bastard'" in newspaper interview, Ford retains Williams to seek satisfaction from Dart.

1982   Operated on for removal of malignant tumor from liver.

Acknowledgments

Although Edward Bennett Williams said repeatedly that he would prefer not to have a book written about him, and although he knew from the start that my intent was to produce a balanced book that would contain parts he would not like, he cooperated by granting me numerous interviews and answering most of the questions I asked him. For this he has my utmost gratitude and respect. My thanks also to his secretaries, Julie Allen and Lenore Mannes.

Without slighting any of those who shared their time and thoughts with me, I would like to single out some people who were exceptionally helpful. They are Bobby Baker, Bill Bittman, Ben Bradlee (to whom I am also grateful for permitting me to use the library of the *Washington Post*, which, of course, was invaluable), Howard Boyd, Joe Califano, Nicholas Chase, John Cye Cheasty, Jack Kent Cooke, William Hitz, Bill Hundley, Aldo Icardi, the late Leon Jaworski, Robert Maheu, Joe Rauh, David Rosen, John ("Bud") Ryan, Judge John Sirica, Michael Tigar, Tom Wadden, and the late Warren Woods.

My thanks also to everyone else who agreed to talk to me, including Jack Anderson, Bobby Beathard, Mark Belanger, Brent Bozell, Art Buchwald, Al Bumbry, Maxine Cheshire, Arthur Christy, Clark Clifford, Julia

Cheyfitz Cohen, Sidney Cohn, Harrison Combs, Doug DeCinces, Robert Dudley, Senator Sam Ervin, Dorothea Fricke, Vincent Fuller, Judge Oliver Gasch, Harold Gibbons, Fred Graham, Judge George Hart, Richard Helms, Monsignor George Higgins, Jerold Hoffberger, Ed Hookstratten, Jane Dargan Humphries, Al Philip Kane, Paul Kaplan, Judge Richmond B. Keech, Roy Kelly, Bill Kilmer, Rufus King, Jr., Larry Leamer, Norman Littell, the late Marie Lombardi, Senator Eugene McCarthy, Robert McChesney, Murdaugh Madden, Morton Mintz, Charles P. Muldoon, Senator Edward Muskie, Louis Nizer, Angela Novello, Dennis O'Toole, Jim Palmer, Jack Pardee, Kenneth Wells Parkinson, Hank Peters, Bill Ragan, Geraldine Kenney Ray, Father William Richardson, Judge Charles R. Richey, Judge Roger Robb, Morton Robson, Edward Ross, Father Tom Rover, Pete Rozelle, Henry Ruth, Godfrey Schmidt, Ken Singleton, Dave Slattery, Colman Stein, Robert Strauss, Edward Troxell, Harold Ungar, Mike Wallace, Muriel Waterhouse, Earl Weaver, Les Whitten, Joseph A. ("Chip") Yablonski, Jr., and several others who spoke on a not-for-attribution basis.

Two writers familiar with the subject matter, Dan Moldea and Jim Hougan, served as sounding boards during the time I was researching this book. My wife, Jane, and several colleagues—Bill Mead, Jack Limpert, Mary Ann Seawell, John Sansing, Dick Victory, and Dave Burgin—read all or part of the manuscript and offered helpful advice.

My thanks also to Selma Rubin of the Montgomery County Public Library in Bethesda, Maryland; Sandy Davis of the *Washington Post* library; Steve Tilley of the National Archives; Jim Davey, Bob Line, and the records staff at the U.S. District Courthouse in Washington; Mitch Lustgarten, who made worthwhile several seemingly unending trips from Manhattan to the Federal Record Center in Bayonne, New Jersey, and the staff of the main reading room, law library, and newspaper and reading rooms at the Library of Congress. I also appreciate the help of Tom Simonton of *U.S. News & World Report*, Vince Mele of Wide World Photos, and Ken Feil of the *Washington Post* in locating pictures. Thanks also to Gerry Gabrys of the Washington Redskins and Bob Brown, John Blake and Helen Conklin of the Baltimore Orioles.

Finally, I greatly appreciate the help of Coral Tysliava, Diana Perez, Mark Hammer, Linda Rawson and Frances Lindley of Harper & Row and the encouragement of my agent, Mel Berger, and my former editor, Ned Chase, who believed in this project from day one.

Bibliography*

Criminal Cases†

U.S. v. *Dominic F. Antonelli, Jr.,* CR 78-175-1, and U.S. v. Joseph P. Yeldell, CR 78-175-2, U.S. District Court for the District of Columbia.

U.S. v. *Robert G. Baker,* CR 39-66, U.S. District Court for the District of Columbia, 262 F. Supp. 657 (1966), 266 F. Supp. 456 (1967), 266 F. Supp. 461 (1967), 301 F. Supp. 973 (1969), 301 F. Supp. 977 (1969); case nos. 21, 154, and 23,327, U.S. Court of Appeals, District of Columbia Circuit, 401 F.2d 958 (1968), 430 F.2d 499 (1970); 400 US 965 (1970, certiorari denied).

U.S. v. W. A. Boyle, John Owens, and James Kinetz, CR 346-71 and 1741-71, U.S. District Court for the District of Columbia.

U.S. v. *Ernest K. Bramblett,* CR 971-53, U.S. District Court for the District of Columbia.

U.S. v. *Sidney L. Brennan,* Eugene J. Williams, Jack J. Jorgensen, and Gerald P. Connelly, CR 15,557-560, U.S. District Court, District of Min-

---

*This is a general bibliography. For more detail, see chapter notes and sources.

†Edward Bennett Williams's client in italics for all court cases.

nesota (1956), 137 F. Supp. 888 (1956), 240 F.2d 253 (U.S. Court of Appeals, 8th Cir. 1957), 353 U.S. 931 (1957, certiorari denied).

U.S. v. *Daniel Brewster,* CR 1872-69, U.S. District Court for the District of Columbia.

U.S. v. *Sidney Buchman,* CR 469-52, U.S. District Court for the District of Columbia.

U.S. v. *William C. Coleman,* CR 163-60, U.S. District Court for the District of Columbia.

U.S. v. *John B. Connally,* CR 74-440, U.S. District Court for the District of Columbia.

U.S. v. *Frank Costello,* Crim. no. C-141-9, U.S. District Court for the Southern District of New York (1953), 146 F. Supp. 63 (1956), 157 F. Supp. 461 (1957); case no. 24,997, U.S. Court of Appeals, 2d Cir., 255 F.2d 876 (1958); 353 US 978 (1957), 357 US 937 (1958).

U.S. v. *Robert Whittier Dudley,* CR 1724-51, U.S. District Court for the District of Columbia.

U.S. v. *Heidi A. Fletcher,* et al., CR 1421-71, U.S. District Court for the District of Columbia.

U.S. v. *Bernard Goldfine,* CR 1158-58, U.S. District Court for the District of Columbia.

U.S. v. *Armand Hammer,* CR 75-668, U.S. District Court for the District of Columbia.

U.S. v. *Bernard J. Heinlein,* CR 1138-68, U.S. District Court for the District of Columbia.

U.S. v. *Richard M. Helms,* CR 77-650, U.S. District Court for the District of Columbia.

U.S. v. *James Riddle Hoffa* and Hyman I. Fischbach, CR 294-57, U.S. District Court for the District of Columbia.

U.S. v. *Edith Louise Hough,* CR 566-57, U.S. District Court for the District of Columbia.

U.S. v. *Aldo Lorenzo Icardi,* CR 821-55, U.S. District Court for the District of Columbia.

U.S. v. *Roy B. Kelly,* 384 US 947 (1966, certiorari denied).

U.S. v. *Ruby Kolod, Willie Israel Alderman,* and *Felix Antonio Alderisio,* 371 F.2d 983 (1967); 390 US 136 (1968), 392 US 919 (1968), 394 US 165 (1969).

U.S. v. *Manuel Kulukundis,* et al., CR 2027-53, 2-54 and 3-54, U.S. District Court for the District of Columbia.

U.S. v. *Charles E. Nelson,* et al., CR 1469-51, U.S. District Court for the District of Columbia.

U.S. v. Stavros Niarchos, *Joseph E. Casey, E. Stanley Klein, Julius C. Holmes,* et al., CR 685-53, U.S. District Court for the District of Columbia, 125 F. Supp. 214 (1954).

U.S. v. Aristoteles S. Onassis, Robert L. Berenson, Nicolas Cokkinis, *Joseph E. Casey, Joseph H. Rosenbaum, Robert W. Dudley,* et al., CR 1647-53, U.S. District Court for the District of Columbia, 125 F. Supp. 190 (1954).

U.S. v. *Adam Clayton Powell, Jr.,* CR 156-15, U.S. District Court for the Southern District of New York.

U.S. v. Charles E. Shaver, et al., CR 944-52, 945-52 and 946-52, U.S. District Court for the District of Columbia.

U.S. v. *Julius Silverman, Robert L. Martin,* and *Meyer Schwartz,* CR 730-58, 1135-58 and 455-62, U.S. District Court for the District of Columbia, 166 F. Supp. 838 (1958); 275 F.2d 173 (1960); 365 US 505 (1961).

U.S. v. *Rea S. Van Fosson,* CR 756-55, U.S. District Court for the District of Columbia.

U.S. v. *Ian Woodner,* CR 335-56, U.S. District Court for the District of Columbia.

U.S. v. *Peter Yarrow,* CR 528-70, U.S. District Court for the District of Columbia.

Wong Sun, et al. v. U.S., 371 US 471 (1963).

Civil Cases

Spyridon Catapodis v. Aristotle Socrates Onassis, CA 5126-54, U.S. District Court for the District of Columbia.

Confidential, Inc. v. Arthur J. Summerfield, CA 3982-55, U.S. District Court for the District of Columbia.

Cunningham, et al. v. *English,* et al., CA 2361-57, U.S. District Court for the District of Columbia, 269 F.2d 517 (1958), 361 US 897 and 361 US 905 (1959).

Democratic National Committee, Lawrence F. O'Brien, et al. v. Committee for the Re-election of the President, James W. McCord, et al., CA 1233-72, U.S. District Court for the District of Columbia.

In re Estate of Philip L. Graham, Administration no. 109,223, U.S. District Court for the District of Columbia, Holding Probate Court (1963).

Freeman A. Grant and Corinne H. Grant v. Edward Bennett Williams, CA 4838-54, U.S. District Court for the District of Columbia.

Dayton M. Harrington, et al. v. *Bar Association of the District of Columbia,* CA 2393-56, U.S. District Court for the District of Columbia.

Milton King and Edward Bennett Williams v. George Preston Marshall, Jr., Catherine M. Price, et al., CA 136-72, U.S. District Court for the District of Columbia.

Norman M. Littell v. Drew Pearson, CA 2959-49 and 2505-50, U.S. District Court for the District of Columbia.

Joseph R. McCarthy v. William Benton, CA 1335-52, U.S. District Court for the District of Columbia.

In re Appointment of a Conservator for George Preston Marshall, CA 2979-63, U.S. District Court for the District of Columbia; U.S. Court of Appeals, District of Columbia Circuit, case no. 20,655, 393 F.2d 348 (1968).

In re Estate of George P. Marshall, Administration No. 1741-69, U.S. District Court for the District of Columbia, Holding Probate Court.

George Preston Marshall by Catherine Marshall Price, his next friend, v. C. Leo DeOrsey, CA 492-64, U.S. District Court for the District of Columbia.

Richard M. Nixon v. *Warner Communications, Inc.*, et al., 435 US 589 (1978).

Drew Pearson v. *Joseph R. McCarthy*, Fulton Lewis, Jr., Washington Times Herald, Inc., *Don Surine*, Westbrook Pegler, et al., CA 897-51, U.S. District Court for the District of Columbia.

U.S. v. *Frank Costello*, Civil no. 79-309, U.S. District Court for the Southern District of New York (1952), 144 F. Supp. 779 (1956), 145 F. Supp. 892 (1956), 171 F. Supp. 10 (1959); case nos. 24,470, 25,690, and 27,597, U.S. Court of Appeals, 2d Cir., 247 F.2d 384 (1957), 275 F.2d 355 (1960), 311 F.2d 343 (1962); 356 US 256 (1958), 365 US 265 (1961), 372 US 975 (1963), 376 US 120 (1964).

Estate of Dorothy Adair Williams, case no. 11,641, in the Orphans' Court for Montgomery County, Maryland.

Joseph A. Yablonski v. United Mine Workers of America, W. A. Boyle, and Justin McCarthy, CA 2413-69, U.S. District Court for the District of Columbia.

Joseph A. Yablonski v. United Mine Workers of America, W. A. Boyle, John Owens, and George J. Titler, CA 3061-69, U.S. District Court for the District of Columbia, 448 F.2d 1175 (1971).

Congressional Proceedings

U.S. Congress, House, Committee on Un-American Activities, *Communist Infiltration of Hollywood Motion Picture Industry*, 82d Cong., 1st sess., 1951; *Communist Activities in the Los Angeles Area*, 83d Cong., 1st sess., 1953; *Communist Activities in the New York Area*, 83d Cong., 1st sess., 1953.

U.S. Congress, House, Congressman Ken Hechler, "A Breath of Fresh Air," introducing letter of Arnold Miller to Paul A. Porter, *Congressional Record,* 93d Cong., 2d sess., 15 October 1974, 120, pt. 26: 35,658.

U.S. Congress, Senate, Floor debate on resolution to censure Senator McCarthy, *Congressional Record,* 83d Cong., 2d sess., 8 Nov–2 December 1954, 100, pt. 12.

U.S. Congress, Senate, Committee on Government Operations, Permanent Subcommittee on Investigations, *Hearings on the Sale of Government-Owned Surplus Tanker Vessels,* 82d Cong., 2d sess., 1952.

U.S. Congress, Senate, Committee on Labor and Public Work, Subcommittee on Labor, *Investigation of Mine Workers' Election,* 91st Cong., 2d sess., 1970.

U.S. Congress, Senate, Committee on Rules and Administration, *Construction of District of Columbia Stadium,* 88th Cong., 2d sess., 1964.

U.S. Congress, Senate, Committee on Rules and Administration, *Financial or Business Interests of Officers or Employees of the Senate,* 88th Cong., 2d sess., 1964.

U.S. Congress, Senate, Committee on Rules and Administration, Subcommittee on Privileges and Elections, *Hearings on Maryland Senatorial Race of 1950,* 82d Cong., 1st sess., 1951.

U.S. Congress, Senate, Select Committee to Study Governmental Operations with Respect to Intelligence Activities, *Alleged Assassination Plots Involving Foreign Leaders* (an interim report), 94th Cong., 1st sess., 1975.

U.S. Congress, Senate, Select Committee on *Improper Activities in the Labor or Management Field,* 85th and 86th Cong., 1957–1959.

U.S. Congress, Senate, Select Committee *to Study Censure Charges Pursuant to the Order of Senate Resolution 301 and Amendments—A Resolution to censure the Senator from Wisconsin, Mr. McCarthy* (hearings and report), 83d Cong., 2d sess., 1954.

Foreign Government Report

Bahama Islands. *Report of the Commission of Inquiry into the Operation of the Business of Casinos in Freeport and in Nassau.* London: Her Majesty's Stationery Office, 1967.

Books

Abell, Tyler. *Drew Pearson Diaries, 1949–1959.* New York: Holt, Rinehart & Winston, 1974.

Anderson, Jack, with Boyd, James. *Confessions of a Muckraker.* New York: Random House, 1979.

Armbrister, Trevor. *Act of Vengeance.* New York: Saturday Review Press/E. P. Dutton, 1975.

Baker, Bobby, with King, Larry L. *Wheeling and Dealing.* New York: W. W. Norton, 1978.

Bernstein, Carl, and Woodward, Bob. *All the President's Men.* New York: Simon & Schuster, 1974.

Brill, Steven. *The Teamsters.* New York: Simon & Schuster, 1978.

Cheyfitz, Edward T. *Constructive Collective Bargaining.* New York: McGraw-Hill, 1947.

Cohn, Roy. *McCarthy.* New York: Lancer Books, 1968.

Davis, Deborah. *Katharine the Great.* New York: Harcourt Brace Jovanovich, 1979.

Douglas, William O. *The Court Years, 1939–1975.* New York: Random House, 1980.

Fraser, Nicholas: Jacobson, Philip; Ottaway, Mark; and Chester, Lewis. *Aristotle Onassis.* New York: Lippincott, 1977.

Frischauer, Willi. *Onassis.* New York: Meredith Press, 1968.

Goulden, Joseph C. *The Superlawyers.* New York: Weybright & Talley, 1972.

Halberstam, David. *The Powers That Be.* New York: Alfred A. Knopf, 1979.

Hoffa, James R., as told to Fraley, Oscar. *Hoffa: The Real Story.* Briarcliff Manor, N.Y.: Stein & Day, 1975.

Hougan, Jim. *Spooks.* New York: Bantam Books, 1979.

Icardi, Aldo. *American Master Spy.* New York: University Books, 1956.

Joesten, Joachim. *Onassis.* New York: Abelard-Schuman, 1963.

Katz, Leonard. *Uncle Frank: The Biography of Frank Costello.* New York: Drake Publishers, 1973.

Kennedy, Robert F. *The Enemy Within.* New York: Harper & Brothers, 1960.

Koch, Howard. *As Times Goes By.* New York: Harcourt Brace Jovanovich, 1979.

Leamer, Laurence. *Playing for Keeps in Washington.* New York: Dial Press, 1977.

Liddy, G. Gordon. *Will.* New York: St. Martin's Press, 1980.

Love, Albert, and Childers, James Saxon, eds. *Listen to Leaders in Law* (contains chapter by Edward Bennett Williams, "You in Trial Law"). New York: Holt, Rinehart & Winston, 1963.

McClellan, John L. *Crime Without Punishment.* New York: Duell, Sloan & Pearce, 1962.

Messick, Hank. *John Edgar Hoover*. New York: David McKay, 1972.

———. *Lanksy*. New York: G.P. Putnam's Sons, 1971.

———. *Syndicate Abroad*. New York: Macmillan, 1969.

Moldea, Dan E. *The Hoffa Wars*. New York: Paddington Press, 1978.

Mollenhoff, Clark R. *Tentacles of Power*. Cleveland: World Publishing, 1965.

Navasky, Victor S. *Naming Names*. New York: Viking Press, 1980.

Nizer, Louis. *Reflections Without Mirrors*. Garden City, N.Y.: Doubleday, 1978.

Parrish, Bernie. *They Call It a Game*. New York: Dial Press, 1971.

Pilat, Oliver. *Drew Pearson, An Unauthorized Biography*. New York: Harper's Magazine Press, 1973.

Potter, Charles E. *Days of Shame*. New York: Coward-McCann, 1965.

Powell, Adam Clayton, Jr. *Adam by Adam*. New York: Dial Press, 1971.

Powers, Thomas. *The Man Who Kept the Secrets: Richard Helms and the CIA*. New York: Alfred A. Knopf, 1979.

Reid, Ed. *The Grim Reapers*. Chicago: Henry Regnery, 1969.

Roberts, Chalmers M. *The Washington Post: The First 100 Years*. Boston: Houghton Mifflin, 1977.

Rovere, Richard H. *Senator Joe McCarthy*. Cleveland: World Publishing, 1959.

Schlesinger, Arthur M., Jr. *Robert Kennedy and His Times*. Boston: Houghton Mifflin, 1978.

Sheresky, Norman. *On Trial: Masters of the Courtroom*. New York: Viking Press, 1977.

Sheridan, Walter. *The Fall and Rise of Jimmy Hoffa*. New York: Saturday Review Press, 1972.

Stern, Michael. *An American in Rome*. New York: Bernard Geis, 1964.

———. *No Innocence Abroad*. New York: Random House, 1953.

Sussman, Barry. *The Great Coverup: Nixon and the Scandal of Watergate*. New York: Thomas Y. Crowell, 1974.

Veeck, Bill, with Linn, Ed. *Veeck as in Wreck*. New York: G. Putnam's Sons, 1962.

Watkins, Arthur V. *Enough Rope*. New York: Prentice-Hall, 1969.

Williams, Edward Bennett. *One Man's Freedom*. New York: Atheneum, 1962.

Wolf, George, with Di Mona, Joseph. *Frank Costello: Prime Minister of the Underworld*. New York: William Morrow, 1974.

Law Journals

Dalton, Donald H., "William E. Leahy, a Great Lawyer," *Journal of the Bar Association of the District of Columbia* 23 (1956).

Jacobs, Paul, "Extracurricular Activities of the McClellan Committee," *California Law Review* 51 (1963).

Mandelbaum, Leonard B., "The Teamster Monitorship: A Lesson for the Future," *Federal Bar Journal* 20 (1960).

"Report of the Committee on Civil Rights," *Journal of the Bar Association of the District of Columbia* 25 (1958).

Williams, Edward Bennett, Address at the 91st annual banquet, Connecticut Bar Association, *Connecticut Bar Journal* 40 (1966).

———, "Crime, Punishment, Violence: The Crisis in Law Enforcement," *Judicature* 54 (1971).

———, "Criminal Justice and the Challenge of Change," *New York County Lawyers' Association Bar Bulletin* 23 (1965–1966).

———, "A Defense Counsel's View" (on Wiretapping). *Minnesota Law Review* 44 (1960).

———, "In Memoriam, Earl Warren, Chief Justice of the United States," *California Law Review* 64 (1976).

———, "OPA, Small Business and the 'Due Process' Clause—A Study in Relations," *The Georgetown Law Journal* 32 (1943–1944).

———, "The Problems of Long Criminal Trials," 34 *Federal Rules Decisions* 155 (1963).

———, "Some Goals for the Trial Bar in the New Decade," *New York State Bar Bulletin* 32 (1960).

———, "The Trial of a Criminal Case," *New York State Bar Bulletin* 29 (1957).

———, "Edward Bennett Williams Speaks," *New York County Lawyers' Association Bar Bulletin* 18 (1960–1961).

Magazines

Anson, Robert Sam, "Why Fast Eddie Williams Keeps on Running," *American Lawyer,* May 1979.

Boyle, Robert, H., "A Legal Eagle and His Boy Scout," *Sports Illustrated,* July 25, 1966.

Bradlee, Ben, "Bobby Baker: The Deal," *Newsweek,* November 16, 1964.

Buchwald, Art, "An Absolutely Surefire Guaranteed Way to Lose Weight," *Saturday Evening Post,* January/February 1974.

Buckley, William F., Jr., "The Unexamined Side of Edward Bennett Williams," *National Review,* July 31, 1962.

"Defender in Demand," *U.S. News & World Report,* August 2, 1957.

Dowling, Tom, "Saint Ed and the Dragon," *Washingtonian,* June 1978.

Graham, Fred, "The Secret Trial of John Connally," *New Republic,* June 21, 1975.

"If You're in a Jam," *Newsweek,* January 5, 1959.

Jacobs, Paul, "Edward Bennett Williams, Courtroom Virtuoso," *Coronet,* December 1957.

Kelly, Tom, "The Chief," *Washingtonian,* July 1967.

King, Larry L, "Williams for the Defense: The Trial of John Connally," *Atlantic,* July 1975.

Nocera, Joseph, "The Screwing of the Average Fan: Edward Bennett Williams and the Washington Redskins," *Washington Monthy,* June 1978.

O'Neil, Paul, "Star Attorney for the Defense," *Life,* June 22, 1959.

"Pen as Camera," *Life,* May 7, 1956.

Smith, C. Fraser, "Buy, Buy Birdie," *Real Estate Washington,* November/December 1979.

Williams, Edward Bennett, "The High Cost of Television's Courtroom," *Television Quarterly,* Fall 1964.

———, "There Has Been a Terrible Breakdown in Criminal Justice," (Interview on WMAL-TV, Washington, February 15, 1970), *U.S. News & World Report,* March 16, 1970.

———, "What's Needed to Speed up Justice," (Interview), *U.S. News & World Report,* September 21, 1970.

"The Winning Loser," *Time,* February 10, 1967.

Newspapers

"Capital Circus," *New York Daily News,* June 13, 1957.

Carmody, John, "Ed Williams Looks at his Redskins," *Washington Post* magazine, September 29, 1968.

"Counsel for Marcus: Edward Bennett Williams," *New York Times,* December 23, 1967.

"A Criminal Trial Lawyer of Classic Mold: Edward Bennett Williams." *New York Times,* April 8, 1975.

"Crum Charges Hoffa Tried to Pack Monitors' Board." *New York Times,* July 14, 1959.

"Crum Repudiates Bribe Inference." *New York Times,* July 24, 1959.

"Crum Swears Inference of 'Bribe' Was Wrong." *Washington Post,* July 24, 1959.

"Ed Williams Plagued by 'Guilt by Client.'" *Washington Post,* May 19, 1957.

"Edward Bennett Williams: Superstar-Alumnus-Lawyer." *Evening Gazette* (Worcester, Mass.), May 26, 1981.

Fuller, Jack. "Words for Hire Add a Disturbing Note to the Helms Case." *Chicago Tribune,* November 13, 1977.

Herling, John. "Cry to the Bank." *Washington Daily News,* June 15, 1972.

———. "The Sensitive Bar." *Washington Daily News,* July 29, 1971.

Hickey, Neil. "For the Defense." *American Weekly—New York Journal-American,* July 17, 1960.

"Hoffa, Attorney Said at Odds on Union Funds." *Washington Post* (Associated Press), April 26, 1964.

"Inquiry Is Jolted by Lawyer's Charge." *Washington Post,* July 14, 1959.

Kempton, Murray. "The Cross." *New York Post,* March 30, 1960.

———. "On the Beach." *New York Post,* April 1, 1960.

"Legal Stars Shine in M'Carthy Case." *New York Times* (Associated Press), August 23, 1954.

"Man to Watch: Is Lawyer Williams Another Darrow?" *New York Herald Tribune,* November 27, 1957.

Pett, Saul (Associated Press). "A Dreadnought of the Bar." *Washington Post,* April 20, 1980.

Rooney, Andy. "He Could Convince You That Reagan Shot Hinckley." *Baltimore News-American,* April 6, 1981.

Shapiro, Leonard, and Scannell, Nancy. "The Final Plays." *Washington Post* magazine, April 16, 1978.

"6th Amendment Lawyer, Edward Bennett Williams." *New York Times,* April 20, 1956.

Smith, Red. "Ice Cold, Red Hot." *New York Times,* August 12, 1979.

Talese, Gay. "Counsel (Extraordinary) for the Defense." *New York Times* magazine, September 25, 1960.

Wallace, William N. "Williams and the Seats of Power." *New York Times,* August 9, 1979.

Wechsler, James A. "Advice of Counsel." *New York Post,* May 27, 1975.

"When in Trouble Get Ed Williams." *New York Post* magazine, March 24, 1957.

Williams, Edward Bennett. "Debasing Hokum About the Redskins." *Washington Post,* February 18, 1973.

———. "In Defense of St. Clair's Role as Counsel." *New York Times,* March 22, 1974.

"Williams Firm Disqualified." *Washington Post,* July 12, 1972.

"Williams—Legal Miracle Worker." *New York Herald Tribune,* April 26, 1960.

Miscellaneous

CBS, "Face the Nation," April 30, 1967.

———, August 3, 1980.

Rauh, Joseph L., Jr. "A Public Interest Standard of Ethics for Lawyers." Law Day Lecture, University of Minnesota Law School, May 1, 1979.

Notes and Sources

1. WHITE HOUSE ENEMY NUMBER ONE

Sources*

Interviews
Information from interviews with Edward Bennett Williams appears in every chapter. Remarks not designated by a note number (and often in the present tense) are from these interviews with Williams and with others, who, in this chapter, include Ben Bradlee, Joe Califano, Sam Ervin, Leon Jaworski, Louis Nizer, Kenneth Wells Parkinson, Judge Charles Richey, Henry Ruth, and Judge John Sirica.

Court Cases
Democratic National Committee, Lawrence F. O'Brien, et al. v. Committee for the Re-election of the President, James W. McCord, et al., CA 1233–(19)72, U.S. District Court for the District of Columbia.
U.S. v. Armand Hammer, CR (19)75–668, U.S. District Court for the District of Columbia.

---

*Material singled out is only that which provides new or extensive information about Williams, and does not include everything cited in footnotes.

Richard M. Nixon v. Warner Communications, Inc., et al., 435 US 589 (1978).

Books

Carl Bernstein and Bob Woodward, *All the President's Men* (New York: Simon & Schuster, 1974).

G. Gordon Liddy, *Will* (New York: St. Martin's Press, 1980).

Jeb Stuart Magruder, *An American Life* (New York: Atheneum, 1974).

Louis Nizer, *Reflections Without Mirrors* (New York: Doubleday, 1978).

John Sirica, *To Set the Record Straight* (New York: W. W. Norton, 1979).

Staff of the New York Times, *The End of a Presidency* (New York: Bantam Books, 1974).

Barry Sussman, *The Great Coverup* (New York: Thomas Y. Crowell, 1974).

Newspapers

Stuart Auerbach, "Corrupt Politics Spawns a New Kind of Lawyer," *Washington Post,* March 16, 1977.

Tad Szulc, "Expensive Line-up of Legal Talent Enters Case of Raid on Democratic Office," *New York Times,* July 10, 1972.

James A. Wechsler, "Advice of Counsel," *New York Post,* May 27, 1975.

Edward Bennett Williams, "In Defense of St. Clair's Role as Counsel," *New York Times,* March 22, 1974.

Notes

1. *New York Times,* July 10, 1972.
2. Complaint, dated June 20, 1972, in Democratic National Committee, Lawrence F. O'Brien, et al. v. Committee for the Re-election of the President, James W. McCord, et al., CA 1233–(19)72, U.S. District Court for the District of Columbia.
3. *New York Times,* July 10, 1972.
4. Complaint in DNC v. McCord, op. cit.
5. DNC v. McCord, op. cit., transcript of hearing on June 26, 1972, pp. 26–32.
6. Ibid., p. 32.
7. *Washington Post,* June 27, 1972. (The story appeared on the front page of the paper's local section.)
8. DNC v. McCord, op. cit., Parkinson addressing Richey during hearing on September 2, 1972, transcript, p. 23.
9. Ibid., hearing on August 22, 1972, transcript, p. 25.
10. G. Gordon Liddy, *Will* (New York: St. Martin's Press, 1980), p. 273.
11. DNC v. McCord, op. cit., Liddy deposition, August 24, 1972, transcript, p. 67.

12. Ibid., deposition of Maurice Stans, August 28, 1972, transcript, p. 49.
13. *New York Times,* July 13, 1974.
14. Stans deposition, op. cit., pp. 30–32.
15. Ibid., p. 12.
16. Ibid., p. 19.
17. Ibid., pp. 54–55.
18. DNC v. McCord, op cit., E. Howard Hunt deposition, August 29, 1972, transcript, p. 10.
19. Ibid., pp. 10–12.
20. Ibid., p. 60.
21. For links between Hunt and Barker involving the Bay of Pigs, see Bernstein and Woodward, op. cit., pp. 22 and 24; *New York Times,* August 30, 1972; Ibid., July 10, 1972.
22. Hunt deposition, op. cit., p. 4.
23. Ibid., p. 21.
24. Ibid., p. 16.
25. Ibid., pp. 29–30.
26. Ibid., pp. 35–37.
27. Ibid., pp. 61–62.
28. *New York Times,* August 30, 1972.
29. DNC v. McCord, op. cit., deposition of Charles Colson, August 30, 1972, transcript, pp. 14–15.
30. Ibid., pp. 16–17.
31. DNC v. McCord, op. cit., deposition of John Mitchell, September 1, 1972, transcript, pp. 17–19.
32. DNC v. McCord, op. cit., court record of hearing on September 2, 1972.
33. DNC v. McCord, op. cit., deposition of John Mitchell, September 5, 1972, transcript, p. 6.
34. Ibid., pp. 55–56.
35. Ibid., pp. 15–16.
36. DNC v. McCord, op. cit., court records, September 21, 1972.
37. Barry Sussman, *The Great Coverup* (New York: Thomas Y. Crowell, 1974), pp. 4–9.
38. Bernstein and Woodward, op. cit., pp. 108–10.
39. See, for instance, Laurence Leamer, *Playing for Keeps in Washington* (New York: Dial Press, 1977), p. 270, and an Associated Press profile of Williams, "A Dreadnought of the Bar," by Saul Pett, published in the *Washington Post,* April 20, 1980.
40. *Washington Post,* June 13, 1963.
41. Quotations from a meeting among President Nixon, H. R. Haldeman, and John Dean in the Oval Office, September 15, 1972, 5:27 to 6:17 P.M. Entered as government's exhibit 4A in U.S. v. Harry R. Haldeman, John D. Ehrlichman, Robert C. Mardian, and John N.

Mitchell, CR (19) 74–110, U.S. Appeals Court record, tape transcripts, vol. I, pp. 7–8.
42. Ibid., p. 10.
43. Ibid., pp. 14–16.
44. Ibid., pp. 17–18.
45. Ibid., pp. 24–25.
46. Docket entry in DNC v. McCord, op. cit., September 12, 1972.
47. DNC v. McCord, op. cit., hearing on September 13, 1972, transcript, p. 3.
48. Ibid., hearing record.
49. Nixon-Haldeman-Dean Oval Office tape, op. cit., pp. 14–15.
50. Staff of the New York Times, *The End of a Presidency* (New York: Bantam Books, 1974), pp. 151–152.
51. DNC v. McCord, op. cit., amended complaint offered for filing by Williams on September 11, 1972, accepted by Judge Richey on September 20, 1972, according to docket entries.
52. Maurice Stans and Frances L. Dale v. Lawrence F. O'Brien, CA 1847–(19)72, U.S. District Court of the District of Columbia.
53. Maurice Stans v. Lawrence F. O'Brien, CA 1854–(19)72, U.S. District Court for the District of Columbia.
54. Nixon-Haldeman-Dean Oval Office tape, op. cit., p. 9.
55. Ibid., p. 15.
56. Bernstein and Woodward, op. cit., pp. 103–5.
57. Jim Hougan, *Spooks* (New York: Bantam Books, 1979), p. 265.
58. Tom Dowling, "Saint Ed and the Dragon," *Washingtonian,* June 1978, p. 60.
59. The Baldwin interview appeared in the *Los Angeles Times* on October 5, 1972.
60. Bernstein and Woodward, op. cit., pp. 222–25.
61. John Sirica, *To Set the Record Straight* (New York: W. W. Norton, 1979), p. 55.
62. Liddy, op. cit., p. 282.
63. Bernstein and Woodward, op. cit., pp. 225–27.
64. Ibid., p. 210.
65. Leamer, op. cit., pp. 41–42.
66. Edward Bennett Williams, "In Defense of St. Clair's Role as Counsel," *New York Times,* March 22, 1974.
67. James A. Wechsler, "Advice of Counsel," *New York Post,* May 27, 1975.
68. Leamer, op. cit., p. 270.
69. Bernstein and Woodward, op. cit., pp. 286–87.
70. *New York Times,* April 6, 1974.
71. Ibid., August 31, 1974.
72. Ibid., March 1, 1976.

73. Ibid., July 25, 1978.
74. Louis Nizer, *Reflections Without Mirrors* (New York: Doubleday, 1978), pp. 438–39.
75. Ibid., pp. 431–45, for background of Hammer case.
76. *Washington Post,* November 9, 1977.
77. Richard M. Nixon v. Warner Communications, Inc., et al., 435 US 589.

2. THE INSIDER'S INSIDER

Sources

Interviews
Ben Bradlee, Art Buchwald, Clark Clifford, Richard Helms, Eugene McCarthy, Edmund Muskie, Robert Strauss.

Court Cases
U.S. v. Richard M. Helms, CR (19)77–650, U.S. District Court for the District of Columbia.

Book
Thomas Powers, *The Man Who Kept the Secrets: Richard Helms and the CIA* (New York: Alfred A. Knopf, 1979).

Magazines
Art Buchwald, "An Absolutely Surefire Guaranteed Way to Lose Weight," *Saturday Evening Post,* January/February 1974.

Newspapers
"Fighting that Losing Battle," *Washington Post,* November 23, 1972.
Jack Fuller, "Words for hire add a disturbing note to the Helms case," *Chicago Tribune,* November 13, 1977.
Allen Weinstein, "Some Candidates for F.B.I. Leader," *New York Times,* January 18, 1978.

Other
CBS, "Face the Nation," August 3, 1980, Edward Bennett Williams as guest.

Notes

1. *Washington Post,* March 5, 1970.
2. *New York Times,* October 6, 1960.
3. Bobby Baker with Larry L. King, *Wheeling and Dealing* (New York: W. W. Norton, 1978), p. 274.
4. *Washington Post,* March 31, 1972.
5. *New York Times,* July 13, 1976.

6. White House press release, March 11, 1976.
7. *Los Angeles Times,* February 6 and 12, 1982.
8. Background on break-in at photo studio from the *Washington Post,* February 20, 1976.
9. *New York Times,* January 13, 1976.
10. February 20, 1976.
11. Indictment, dated October 31, 1977, in U.S. V. Richard M. Helms, CR 77–650, U.S. District Court for the District of Columbia.
12. *New York Times,* January 15, 1977.
13. Thomas Powers, *The Man Who Kept the Secrets: Richard Helms and the CIA* (New York: Alfred A. Knopf, 1979), p. 52.
14. *New York Times* (Associated Press story), September 22, 1977.
15. Robert Sam Anson, "Why Fast Eddie Keeps on Running," *American Lawyer,* May 1979, p. 28.
16. *Washington Post,* November 13, 1977.
17. Ibid., January 27, 1978.
18. Powers, op. cit., p. 299.
19. Ibid., pp. 302–3.
20. U.S. v. Helms, op. cit., indictment.
21. U.S. Code Service, Lawyers Edition, Titles 1 to 4 (1980 edition), p. 520.
22. Powers, op. cit., p. 304.
23. U.S. v. Helms. op. cit., transcript of hearing at which Helms entered plea, October 31, 1977, p. 21.
24. U.S. v. Helms, op. cit., transcript of sentencing, November 4, 1977, pp. 3–5.
25. Ibid., p. 9.
26. Ibid., pp. 11–12.
27. Ibid., p. 17.
28. Ibid., p. 19.
29. Jack Fuller, "Words for hire add a disturbing note to the Helms case," *Chicago Tribune,* November 13, 1977.
30. Ibid.
31. *New York Times,* January 18, 1978.
32. Information distributed by the Committee to Continue the Open Convention (1980).
33. Ibid.
34. *Washington Post,* August 1, 1980.
35. CBS, "Face the Nation," August 3, 1980, transcript, p. 5.
36. Ibid., p. 10.
37. *Washington Post,* November 22, 1980.
38. Art Buchwald, "An Absolutely Surefire Guaranteed Way to Lose Weight," *Saturday Evening Post,* January/February 1974, p. 16, and *Washington Post,* November 23, 1972.

3. THE CHAMPEEN OF THE FREE PRESS

Sources

Interviews
Jack Anderson, Ben Bradlee, Fred Graham, Paul Kaplan, Laurence Leamer, Norman Littell, Morton Mintz, Mike Wallace, Les Whitten, Warren Woods.

Court Cases
Norman M. Littell v. Drew Pearson, CA 2959–(19)49 and CA 2505–(19)50 (consolidated into one case), U.S. District Court for the District of Columbia.

Drew Pearson v. Joseph R. McCarthy, Fulton Lewis, Jr., Washington Times Herald, Inc., Don Surine, Westbrook Pegler, et al., CA 897–(19)51, U.S. District Court for the District of Columbia.

Confidential, Inc. v. Arthur J. Summerfield, CA 3982–(19)55, U.S. District Court for the District of Columbia.

In re Estate of Philip L. Graham, Administration no. 109,223, U.S. District Court for the District of Columbia, Holding Probate Court (1963).

Books
Tyler Abell, ed., *Drew Pearson Diaries, 1949–1959* (New York: Holt, Rinehart & Winston, 1974).

Douglas A. Anderson, *A "Washington Merry-Go-Round" of Libel Actions* (Chicago: Nelson-Hall, 1980).

Jack Anderson with James Boyd, *Confessions of a Muckraker* (New York: Random House, 1979).

David Halberstam, *The Powers That Be* (New York: Alfred A. Knopf, 1979).

Oliver Pilat, *Drew Pearson, An Unauthorized Biography* (New York: Harper's Magazine Press, 1973).

Chalmers M. Roberts, *The Washington Post: The First 100 Years* (Boston: Houghton Mifflin, 1977).

Notes

1. U.S. v. John B. Connally, CR (19)74–440, U.S. District Court for the District of Columbia, discussion in chambers, March 31, 1975, transcript, pp. 12–13.
2. Norman M. Littell v. Drew Pearson, CA 2959–49, U.S. District Court for the District of Columbia, complaint, filed July 12, 1949.
3. Ibid., Littell testimony, May 15, 1953, transcript, p. 272.
4. Ibid., Littell complaint.

5. Ibid., Pearson deposition, March 9, 1950, transcript, pp. 22–23.
6. Ibid., docket entry.
7. Pearson's broadcast, quoted in Littell complaint filed June 9, 1950, in case no. CA 2505–50.
8. Description of Eisler from opening statement of Pearson's attorney, H. Graham Morison, at the trial, April 27, 1953, transcript p. 15–16.
9. Pearson broadcast, op. cit.
10. Littell complaint in case no. CA 2505–50, op. cit.
11. Jack Anderson with James Boyd, *Confessions of a Muckraker* (New York: Random House, 1979), p. 213.
12. Drew Pearson v. McCarthy, et al., CA 897–51, complaint filed March 2, 1951, p. 4.
13. Oliver Pilat, *Drew Pearson, An Unauthorized Biography* (New York: Harper's Magazine Press, 1973), p. 27.
14. *Newsweek,* December 25, 1950.
15. Anderson, *Muckraker,* op. cit., p. 214.
16. *Time,* December 25, 1950.
17. Pilat, op. cit., p. 26.
18. Pearson v. McCarthy, op. cit., script of Fulton Lewis radio show of December 13, 1950, in Pearson brief.
19. Ibid., Lewis script from December 14, 1950.
20. Ibid., McCarthy speech excerpts from Pearson complaint, filed March 2, 1951, pp. 6–7.
21. Ibid., Lewis script for December 15, 1950.
22. Pearson complaint in case no. CA 897–51, op. cit.
23. William F. Buckley, Jr., "The Unexamined Side of Edward Bennett Williams," *National Review,* July 31, 1962, p. 60.
24. Pearson deposition taken by Williams in Littell v. Pearson, op. cit., April 8, 1953, transcript, pp. 60–61.
25. Ibid., Pearson affidavit, dated April 18, 1951.
26. Abell, op. cit., pp. 159–60.
27. Ibid., pp. 267–68.
28. Ibid., p. 270.
29. Littell v. Pearson, op. cit., Pearson brief seeking to overturn verdict, May 25, 1953, p. 5 and pp. 15–16.
30. Pilat, op. cit., p. 255.
31. Littell v. Pearson, op. cit.; Bell Syndicate was dismissed as defendant on November 24, 1952, according to entry on docket sheet.
32. Ibid., docket entries for May 15, 1953.
33. Anderson, op. cit., p. 21.
34. Abell, op. cit., pp. 270–71.
35. Undated memorandum in files of Pearson's attorneys.
36. Memorandum from one of Pearson's lawyers, W. A. Roberts, to another, Warren Woods, September 18, 1953, and undated Woods memorandum to Roberts.

37. Interview with Warren Woods, March 20, 1981.
38. W. A. Roberts memorandum, June 22, 1953.
39. Littell v. Pearson, op. cit., docket entries for September 30 and October 1, 1953.
40. Memorandum in files of Pearson's attorneys, May 15, 1953.
41. Woods affidavit filed in Pearson v. McCarthy, op. cit., September 4, 1951.
42. Ibid., W. A. Roberts brief asking to vacate notice by McCarthy to take Pearson's deposition, dated September 12, 1951.
43. Ibid. W. A. Roberts read part of McCarthy's deposition into hearing record on May 26, 1952, before U.S. District Judge Walter M. Bastian, transcript, pp. 40–41.
44. Ibid., pp. 41–42.
45. Ibid., excerpts from Surine deposition read into record, pp. 32–33.
46. Ibid., docket entry for October 29, 1955.
47. Ibid., docket entry for December 19, 1955.
48. Ibid., docket entry for February 13, 1956.
49. Abell, op. cit., p. 379.
50. Confidential, Inc. v. Arthur J. Summerfield, CA 3982–55, U.S. District Court for the District of Columbia, affidavit of Robert Harrison, September 8, 1955.
51. Ibid., background of case outlined by Williams at hearing on January 4, 1956, transcript, pp. 3–4.
52. Ibid., Williams's brief, dated September 30, 1955, p. 2 and p. 18, and Williams's argument at hearing on October 7, 1955, transcript, pp. 4–13 and pp. 30–31.
53. Ibid., Youngdahl ruling of October 7, 1955.
54. Ibid., hearing on January 4, 1956, transcript, pp. 4–5.
55. Ibid., *Confidential* cover and table of contents from court record.
56. Ibid., *Confidential,* January 1956, p. 35 and p. 38 (entered into court record).
57. Ibid., affidavit of William C. O'Brien, December 16, 1955.
58. Ibid., *Confidential,* March 1956, p. 9 (from court record).
59. Ibid., O'Brien affidavit.
60. Ibid., Williams's argument at January 4, 1956, hearing, transcript, pp. 16–18 and p. 31.
61. Ibid., pp. 43–46.
62. Ibid., pp. 46–47.
63. Ibid., pp. 48–49.
64. Ibid., p. 6.
65. Ibid., docket entry for September 9, 1956.
66. Abell, op. cit., pp. 469–70.
67. Records of Estate of Philip L. Graham, Administration no. 109,223, U.S. District Court for the District of Columbia, Holding Probate Court (1963).

68. Chalmers M. Roberts, *The Washington Post: The First 100 Years* (Boston: Houghton Mifflin, 1977), pp. 192–95 and 134–35.

69. Ibid., p. 257–58.

70. David Halberstam, *The Powers That Be* (New York: Alfred A. Knopf, 1979), pp. 312–15.

71. For details on Phil Graham's mental illness, see Roberts, op. cit., pp. 331–32 and 360–63; Halberstam, op. cit., pp. 376–83.

72. Graham Estate, op. cit., report and recommendation of guardian ad litem, October 18, 1963, p. 6.

73. Deborah Davis, *Katharine the Great* (New York: Harcourt Brace Jovanovich, 1979), p. 162.

74. Graham Estate, op. cit., petition of guardian ad litem to compromise threatened caveat, October 18, 1963, pp. 1–2.

75. Ibid.; guardian's report and recommendations of October 18, 1963, p. 6, said Graham left two-thirds of estate to his children in will of February 18, 1963; Williams confirmed in an interview that the remaining one-third was given to Robin Webb.

76. Guardian's report and recommendations of October 18, 1963, op. cit., p. 6, and guardian's petition of same date, op. cit., p. 3, said that Graham left one-third of estate to his children; Williams confirmed in an interview that the other two-thirds were left to Webb.

77. Roberts, op. cit., pp. 362–63.

78. Guardian's report and recommendations, op. cit., p. 6.

79. Guardian's petition, op. cit., p. 3.

80. Guardian's report and recommendations, op. cit., p. 6.

81. Ibid.

82. Guardian's petition, op. cit., pp. 1–4.

83. Ibid., p. 4.

84. Guardian's report and recommendations, op. cit., p. 7.

85. Guardian's petition, op. cit., p. 4.

86. Ibid., pp. 5–6.

87. Graham Estate, Cogswell recommendation to Judge McGarraghy, October 17, 1963.

88. Graham Estate records.

89. Halberstam, op. cit., p. 520 and p. 381.

90. For details on "Pentagon Papers," ibid., pp. 565–78.

91. Walter Sheridan, *The Fall and Rise of Jimmy Hoffa* (New York: Saturday Review Press, 1972), pp. 443–44.

92. *Washington Post,* January 22, 1973.

93. Edward Bennett Williams, *One Man's Freedom* (New York: Atheneum, 1962), p. 12.

94. Leamer, op. cit., p. 280.

95. *Washington Post,* November 2, 1977.

96. Ibid., March 10, 1974.

4. THE SPORTSMAN

Sources

Interviews
Bobby Beathard, Mark Belanger, Al Bumbry, Jack Kent Cooke, Doug DeCinces, Jerold Hoffberger, Ed Hookstratten, Bill Kilmer, Marie Lombardi, Jim Palmer, Jack Pardee, Hank Peters, Pete Rozelle, Ken Singleton, Dave Slattery, Earl Weaver.

Court Cases
In re Appointment of a Conservator for George Preston Marshall, CA 2979-(19)63, U.S. District Court for the District of Columbia; U.S. Court of Appeals, District of Columbia Circuit, case no. 20,655; 393 F.2d 348 (1968).
George Preston Marshall by Catherine Marshall Price, his next friend, v. C. Leo DeOrsey, CA 492-(19)64, U.S. District Court for the District of Columbia.
In re Estate of George P. Marshall, Administration no. 1741-(19)69, U.S. District Court for the District of Columbia, Holding Probate Court.
Milton King and Edward Bennett Williams v. George Preston Marshall, Jr., Catherine M. Price, et al., CA 136-(19)72, U.S. District Court for the District of Columbia.

Books
Corinne Griffith, *My Life with the Redskins* (New York: A. S. Barnes, 1947).
Bill Veeck with Ed Linn, *Veeck as in Wreck* (New York: G. Putnam's Sons, 1962).

Magazines
Robert H. Boyle, "A Legal Eagle and His Boy Scout," *Sports Illustrated,* July 25, 1966.
Tom Dowling, "Saint Ed and the Dragon," *Washingtonian,* June 1978.
Joseph Nocera, "The Screwing of the Average Fan: Edward Bennett Williams and the Washington Redskins," *Washington Monthly,* June 1978.
John Sansing, "And Let the Boys Club Eat Cake," *Washingtonian,* August 1976.
C. Fraser Smith, "Buy, Buy, Birdie," *Real Estate Washington,* November/December 1979.

Newspapers (a sampling)
"Redskins Hear from Ed Williams," *Washington Post,* October 20, 1965.
"George Marshall Still Center of Controversy," *Washington Post,* January 28, 1968.

John Carmody, "Ed Williams Looks at His Redskins," *Washington Post* magazine, September 29, 1968.

"Redskins Hire Allen in $1 Million Deal," *Washington Star,* January 7, 1971.

"Allen Receives All-Pro Defense," *Washington Post*, May 31, 1972.

"Redskin Boss Lets Allen Run the Show," *Los Angeles Times* (UPI), January 8, 1973.

Edward Bennett Williams, "Debasing Hokum About the Redskins," Letter to the Editor, *Washington Post,* February 18, 1973.

"Cooke, Partners Buying up Redskin Foundation Stock," *Washington Post,* February 9, 1974.

David D. Slattery, "So Long, Washington, And You, Too, George Allen: Key West, Here I Come," *Washington Post* magazine, March 20, 1977.

"Allen Signs New Redskin Pact," *Washington Post,* July 14, 1977.

"Firing of Allen Not Based on Wins, Losses," *Washington Post,* January 19, 1978.

"How Williams Decided He'd Had Enough," *Washington Star,* January 19, 1978.

"Bitter Allen Tells His Side of the Story, *Washington Star,* January 19, 1978.

"Ex-Coach Hits 'Meddling,'" *Washington Post,* January 20, 1978.

"Allen Excised for Arrogance," *Washington Post,* January 20, 1978.

"Allen: 'Stabbed in Back'; Williams: No Deception," *Washington Post,* January 20, 1978.

Leonard Shapiro and Nancy Scannell, "The Final Plays," *Washington Post* magazine, April 16, 1978.

"Redskin Boss Williams Out to Buy Orioles," *Washington Post,* June 8, 1979.

"Hoffberger Sells Orioles to Williams," *Washington Post,* August 3, 1979.

Williams Prepares to Battle Rozelle," *Washington Post,* August 3, 1979.

William N. Wallace, "Williams and the Seats of Power," *New York Times,* August 9, 1979.

"Listening to Williams at Each End of the Parkway," *Washington Post,* August 10, 1979.

Red Smith, "Ice Cold, Red Hot," *New York Times,* August 12, 1979.

"Williams Group Stirred Kuhn, Spurred Settlement," *Washington Post,* May 24, 1980.

"Williams: Big Bird Plans, Another Warning for Fans," *Washington Post,* August 6, 1980.

"Oriole Fans Rap Williams," *Washington Post,* August 9, 1980.

"Ed Williams May Be Next to Take a Walk," *Washington Star,* January 6, 1981.

"Ed Williams: The Owner is Learning," *Washington Star,* March 16, 1981.

"Back from the Brink: How Season Was Saved," *Washington Post,* August 2, 1981.

"Edward Bennett Williams and the Orioles," *Washington Post,* October 3, 1981.

Notes

1. *Washington Star,* January 19, 1978.
2. Corinne Griffith, *My Life with the Redskins* (New York: A. S. Barnes, 1947), pp. 37–39.
3. Ibid., p. 61.
4. In re Appointment of a Conservator for George Preston Marshall, CA 2979-63, U.S. District Court for the District of Columbia, Report of guardian ad litem John J. Carmody, January 6, 1964, pp. 9–10.
5. Ibid., p. 11.
6. Ibid., brief by Bernard Nordlinger, March 16, 1967, p. 8.
7. Ibid., petition for temporary conservatorship by Milton King, C. Leo DeOrsey, and Edward Bennett Williams, December 12, 1963.
8. Ibid. (See also guardian's report of January 6, 1964, p. 16.)
9. Ibid., order of Judge Alexander Holtzoff, December 13, 1963.
10. Ibid., guardian's report of January 6, 1964, pp. 17–18.
11. Ibid., p. 19.
12. Ibid., guardian's affidavit, May 18, 1964, pp. 4–6.
13. Ibid., court order of August 13, 1964.
14. Ibid., court record. (DeOrsey died April 30, 1965, in Miami.)
15. Ibid., guardian's statement seeking fee, March 16, 1969, pp. 12–18.
16. Ibid., brief by George C. Summers opposing appointment of King, DeOrsey, and Williams as conservators, January 24, 1964, Appendix, p. 5.
17. Ibid., brief by Francis X. McLaughlin, March 29, 1966.
18. Ibid., motion by McLaughlin to remove conservators for cause, June 13, 1966, pp. 3–4.
19. Ibid., McLaughlin brief, September 21, 1966, p. 3.
20. Ibid., McLaughlin brief, June 23, 1966, p. 2.
21. Ibid., McLaughlin brief, September 29, 1966, p. 2.
22. Ibid., brief by Paul Connolly and Bernard Nordlinger, August 1, 1968, p. 3, and Nordlinger brief, February 13, 1964, pp. 2–3.
23. Ibid., Nordlinger brief, February 13, 1964, pp. 2–3.
24. Ibid., affidavit of Dr. Stephen N. Jones, October 13, 1966.
25. Ibid., Nordlinger brief, September 26, 1966.
26. In re Estate of George P. Marshall, Administration no. 1741-69,

U.S. District Court for the District of Columbia, Holding Probate Court, George Preston Marshall will of July 25, 1958, with codicils of July 16, 1959, and February 2, 1963.

27. Ibid., Marshall will of July 25, 1958, and codicil of July 16, 1959.
28. Appointment of Marshall conservator, op. cit., Nordlinger brief, June 15, 1966, pp. 1–2.
29. Ibid., sworn statement of Juanita Y. Belanger, May 23, 1966.
30. Ibid., motion by Nordlinger to enjoin Marshall children from interfering with affairs of George Preston Marshall, June 14, 1966; affidavit of George Preston Marshall, Jr., October 14, 1966; affidavit of George Preston Marshall, Jr., June 20, 1966.
31. Ibid., Marshall, Jr., affidavit of October 14, 1966.
32. Ibid., Marshall, Jr., affidavit of June 12, 1966.
33. Ibid., Nordlinger brief, June 15, 1966.
34. Ibid., Marshall, Jr., affidavit of June 20, 1966.
35. Ibid., guardian's affidavit, June 21, 1966, and guardian's answer to motion to dismiss him, June 27, 1966.
36. Ibid., affidavit of Williams and King, July 6, 1966.
37. George P. Marshall Estate, op. cit., "will" of July 2, 1966.
38. Appointment of Marshall conservator, op. cit., motion by conservators to hold Marshall children in contempt of court, July 7, 1966.
39. Ibid., motion by conservators to order document turned over to them, July 11, 1966.
40. Ibid., order of Judge Alexander Holtzoff that document be given to conservators within 10 days, October 13, 1966; order of Holtzoff citing Marshall, Junior for contempt of court and ordering him jailed, January 6, 1967.
41. *Washington Star,* January 12, 1967.
42. *Washington Post,* January 13, 1967.
43. Appointment of Marshall conservator, op. cit.; docket entries say that Marshall, Jr., was transferred to D.C. General Hospital on February 3, 1967, and Judge Holtzoff ordered him released on motion by conservators, February 16, 1967.
44. Ibid., June 25, 1968, report of Preston C. King, Jr., court-appointed master.
45. Ibid., master's report; deposition of Catherine Marshall Price, January 8, 1968; letter of November 28, 1967, from Dr. James H. Ryan of New York to Paul R. Connolly, re George Marshall Price.
46. *Washington Star,* January 27, 1969.
47. Appointment of Marshall conservator, op. cit., McLaughlin brief, May 6, 1969, p. 2.
48. Ibid., Connolly brief, May 22, 1969, pp. 5–6.
49. George P. Marshall Estate, op. cit., Marshall will of July 25, 1958, and codicil of July 16, 1959.

50. Ibid. On September 28, 1971, Standard Research Consultants of New York, hired to appraise assets in Marshall estate, set fair market value of Redskins as of August 31, 1971, at $10,250,000, and valued George Preston Marshall's 520 shares at $11,141 per share, for total of $5,793,320.

51. Ibid. Terms of settlement approved by Judge John H. Pratt, January 21, 1972.

52. Marshall, Jr., expressed his objections to the sale according to an entry dated March 28, 1974 in the case of Milton King and Edward Bennett Williams v. George Preston Marshall, Jr., Catherine M. Price, et al., CA 136-72, U.S. District Court for the District of Columbia.

53. *Washington Post,* February 9, 1974.

54. 1981 interviews with Williams and Jack Kent Cooke.

55. *Washington Post,* September 8, 1980.

56. Ibid., March 4, 1973.

57. Ibid., August 26, 1975.

58. Ibid., September 23, 1976.

59. Ibid., September 23, 1976 and March 4, 1973.

60. Joseph Nocera, "The Screwing of the Average Fan: Edward Bennett Williams and the Washington Redskins," *Washington Monthly,* June 1978, p. 37.

61. Ibid., pp. 35–41.

62. Ibid., p. 40.

63. Robert Sam Anson, "Why Fast Eddie Keeps on Running," *American Lawyer,* May 1979, p. 27.

64. Appointment of Marshall conservator, op. cit., statement of guardian at May 20, 1966, hearing before Judge William B. Jones, transcript, p. 30.

65. Ibid., statement by Holtzoff at hearing on October 11, 1966, transcript, pp. 68–71.

66. Ibid., statement by Hart at hearing on February 1, 1968, transcript, p. 5.

67. Ibid., ruling by U.S. Court of Appeals, District of Columbia Circuit, case no. 20,655, 393 F.2d 348, at pp. 350–51 (1968).

68. Ibid., statement by U.S. District Judge Alexander Holtzoff at hearing on October 11, 1966, transcript, pp. 35–36.

69. Ibid., Hart statement at January 30, 1968, hearing, transcript, p. 35.

70. Ibid., affidavit of Dr. Stephen N. Jones, October 13, 1966.

71. Letter from Dr. Stephen N. Jones to U.S. District Judge Bolitha Laws, entered into record in U.S. v. Ian Woodner, CR 335-(19)56, U.S. District Court for the District of Columbia.

72. Appointment of Marshall conservator, op. cit., Dr. Jones affidavit, October 13, 1966.

73. *Washington Post,* July 26, 1965.
74. Robert H. Boyle, "A Legal Eagle and His Boy Scout," *Sports Illustrated,* July 25, 1966, p. 55.
75. *Washington Post,* November 9, 1965.
76. Boyle, op. cit., p. 56 and p. 60.
77. Ibid., p. 60.
78. John Carmody, "Ed Williams Looks at his Redskins," *Washington Post* magazine, September 29, 1968, p. 13 and p. 16. (Note: The author of this story, a reporter for the *Post,* is not to be confused with the John J. Carmody who was the court-appointed guardian ad litem during the Marshall conservatorship.)
79. *Washington Post,* October 30, 1967, and *New York Times,* August 9, 1979.
80. Boyle, op. cit., p. 60.
81. For instance, the *Washington Star* reported on January 7, 1971, that Allen gave his age then as 48.
82. Leonard Shapiro and Nancy Scannell, "The Final Plays," *Washington Post* magazine, April 16, 1978, p. 20.
83. Washington Redskin Press Guide, 1977, p. 9.
84. *Washington Star,* January 7, 1971.
85. *Washington Post,* September 23, 1976.
86. *Washington Star,* January 7, 1971.
87. Shapiro and Scannell, op. cit., p. 22.
88. *Washington Post,* June 17, 1978.
89. Tom Dowling, "Saint Ed and the Dragon," *Washingtonian,* June 1978, p. 56 and pp. 59–60.
90. Shapiro and Scannell, op. cit., p. 20.
91. *Washington Post,* May 31, 1972.
92. Ibid.
93. Ibid., March 4, 1973.
94. Washington Redskin Press Guide, 1975, p. 73.
95. Ibid., 1981, p. 24.
96. *Ring* magazine, June 1981, p. 30.
97. *Washington Post,* July 15, 1977.
98. Shapiro and Scannell, op. cit., p. 18.
99. Ibid.
100. *Washington Post,* November 1, 1977.
101. David D. Slattery, "So Long, Washington, And You, Too, George Allen: Key West, Here I Come," *Washington Post* magazine, March 20, 1977, p. 15.
102. *Washington Post,* January 19, 1978.
103. *Washington Star,* January 19, 1978.
104. Shapiro and Scannell, op. cit., p. 31.
105. *Washington Post,* January 19, 1978.
106. *Washington Star,* January 19, 1978.

107. Ibid.
108. Ibid.
109. *Washington Post,* January 20, 1978.
110. *Washington Star,* January 22, 1978.
111. *Washington Post,* February 20, 1982.
112. *Washington Star,* January 22, 1978.
113. Shapiro and Scannell, op. cit., p. 41.
114. *Washington Post,* January 25, 1978.
115. Ibid., June 17, 1978.
116. Shapiro and Scannell, op. cit., p. 20 and p. 22.
117. Ibid., p. 30.
118. Dowling, op. cit., p. 60 and p. 67.
119. *Washington Post,* July 19, 1978.
120. Background on award of expansion franchise from interviews with Williams; Bill Veeck with Ed Linn, *Veeck as in Wreck* (New York: G. Putnam's Sons, 1962), pp. 353–63, and Boyle, op. cit., p. 58.
121. Carmody, op. cit., p. 13.
122. *Washington Post,* August 3, 1979.
123. Ibid., December 11, 1980.
124. Ibid., June 22, 1967.
125. Ibid., September 9, 1973.
126. Ibid., June 3, 1976.
127. Ibid., June 21, 1981.
128. Ibid., August 2, 1981.
129. Ibid., August 3, 1979.
130. Ibid., August 8, 1979.
131. Ibid., August 9, 1979.
132. Ibid., August 6, 1980.
133. *Baltimore Sun* editorial quoted in the *Washington Post,* August 9, 1980.
134. *Washington Post,* November 14, 1980.
135. *Spot Television Rates and Data,* November 15, 1981, p. 14.
136. *1981 Editor and Publisher Market Guide,* p. 180.
137. Baltimore Orioles 1981 Information Guide, p. 14.
138. Ibid., p. 2.
139. Veeck, op. cit., p. 354.

5. FROM HARTFORD TO GEORGETOWN

Sources

Interviews

Dorothea Fricke, Jane Dargan Humphries, Robert Maheu, Bill Ragan, Geraldine Kenney Ray, William Richardson, David Rosen, Thomas Rover, John ("Bud") Ryan, Muriel Waterhouse.

Law Reviews
Edward B. Williams, "OPA, Small Business and the 'Due Process' Clause: A Study in Relations," *Georgetown Law Journal* 32 (1943–44): 75–87.

Newspapers
The Torch, Bulkeley High School, Hartford, 1935–37.
"Edward Bennett Williams: Superstar-Alumnus-Lawyer," *Evening Gazette* (Worcester, Mass.), May 26, 1981.

Notes

1. Background on Gerald Chapman is from the *New York Times,* April 6, 1926; April 5, 1925; March 5, 1926; and April 1, 1925.
2. *New York Times,* April 5, 1925.
3. U.S. Commerce Department, *Statistical Abstract of the United States,* 1960.
4. Background on Williams's family was provided by Dorothea Fricke, his first cousin on the Williams side; and Geraldine Kenney Ray, his first cousin on the Bennett side.
5. Information about Williams's parents from interviews with Williams, Geraldine Kenney Ray, and David Rosen.
6. Gay Talese, "Counsel (Extraordinary) for the Defense," *New York Times* magazine, September 25, 1960, p. 56.
7. Boyle, op. cit., p. 57.
8. *Torch,* May 14, 1937.
9. Ibid., April 5, 1935.
10. Ibid., January 17, 1936.
11. Ibid., December 18, 1936.
12. Ibid., April 2, 1937.
13. Edward B. Williams, "OPA, Small Business and the 'Due Process' Clause: A Study in Relations," *Georgetown Law Journal* 32 (1943–44): pp. 79–80.

6. THE YOUNG LAWYER

Sources

Interviews
Howard Boyd, Nicholas Chase, Al Philip Kane, Robert McChesney, Bill Ragan, Judge John Sirica, Tom Wadden.

Court Case
U.S. v. *Charles E. Shaver,* et al., CR 944-(19)52, 945-52, and 946-52, U.S. District Court for the District of Columbia.

Law Reviews

Donald H. Dalton, "William E. Leahy, a Great Lawyer," *Journal of the Bar Association of the District of Columbia* 23 (1956): pp. 436–38.

91st annual banquet, Connecticut Bar Association, Hartford, October 18, 1966, reported in *Connecticut Bar Journal* 40 (1966): pp. 738–39.

Notes

1. 91st annual banquet, Connecticut Bar Association, Hartford, October 18, 1966, reported in *Connecticut Bar Journal* 40 (1966): pp. 738–39.
2. Tom Kelly, "The Chief," *Washingtonian,* July 1967, p. 33.
3. Donald H. Dalton, "William E. Leahy, a Great Lawyer," *Journal of the Bar Association of the District of Columbia* 23 (1956): pp. 436–38.
4. Ibid., p. 436.
5. Ibid., p. 437.
6. U.S. v. James M. Curley, et al., case no. 73,085, U.S. District Court for the District of Columbia (1944).
7. *New York Times,* April 15, 1950.
8. *Martindale-Hubbell Law Directory* (Summit, N.J.: Martindale-Hubbell, 1951), vol. 1, p. 424.
9. Information on Shaver from U.S. v. Charles E. Shaver, et al., CR 944-52, 945-52, and 946-52, U.S. District Court for the District of Columbia, and from the *Washington Post,* October 22, 1951; October 28, 1951; November 18, 1951; November 16, 1951; November 9, 1951; and October 27, 1951.

7. HOLLYWOOD WRITERS AND HUAC

Sources

Interviews
Sidney Cohn, William Hitz.

Court Cases
U.S. v. Sidney Buchman, CR 469-(19)52, U.S. District Court for the District of Columbia.

Congressional Hearings
U.S. Congress, House, Committee on Un-American Activities, *Communist Infiltration of Hollywood Motion Picture Industry*, 82d Cong., 1st sess., 1951; *Communist Activities in the Los Angeles Area,* 83d Cong., 1st sess., 1953; *Communist Activities in the New York Area,* 83d Cong., 1st sess., 1953.

Books

Howard Koch, *As Time Goes By* (New York: Harcourt Brace Jovano-vich, 1979).

Victor S. Navasky, *Naming Names* (New York: Viking Press, 1980).

Edward Bennett Williams, *One Man's Freedom* (New York: Atheneum, 1962).

Notes

1. U.S. Congress, House, Committee on Un-American Activities, *Communist Infiltration of Hollywood Motion Picture Industry,* 82d Cong., 1st sess., September 19, 1951, p. 1,577. (Referred to hereafter as HUAC-Hollywood.)
2. Ibid.
3. Ibid., pp. 1,576–77.
4. Ibid., p. 1,576.
5. Ibid., pp. 1,576–77.
6. Ibid., pp. 1,577–1,612.
7. Ibid., pp. 1,577–1,601.
8. Ibid., p. 1,599.
9. Ibid., pp. 1,608–12.
10. Ibid., p. 1,612.
11. Edward Bennett Williams, *One Man's Freedom* (New York: Atheneum, 1962), p. 135.
12. Victor S. Navasky, *Naming Names* (New York: Viking Press, 1980), p. 285.
13. Ibid., pp. 229–30.
14. Ibid., pp. 317–18.
15. Ibid., p. 85.
16. Leslie Halliwell, *The Filmgoer's Companion* (New York: Hill & Wang, 1977), p. 111.
17. HUAC-Hollywood, op. cit., September 25, 1951, pp. 1,856–80.
18. Williams, *One Man's Freedom,* op. cit., p. 139.
19. Ibid.
20. U.S. v. Sidney Buchman, CR 469-52, U.S. District Court for the District of Columbia.
21. U.S. Congress, House, Committee on Un-American Activities, *Communist Activities in the Los Angeles Area*, 83d Cong., 1st sess., March 23, 1953, p. 293. (Referred to hereafter as HUAC–Los Angeles.)
22. Ibid., p. 311.
23. Ibid., p. 294 and p. 315.
24. Ibid., pp. 312–13.
25. HUAC-Hollywood, op. cit., pp. 1,595–96.

26. HUAC–Los Angeles, op. cit., March 24, 1953, pp. 355–61.
27. Ibid., 23 November 1953, pp. 3,503–7.
28. U.S. Congress, House, Committee on Un-American Activities, *Communist Activities in the New York Area*, 83d Cong., 1st sess., May 7, 1953, pp. 1,456–57. (Referred to hereafter as HUAC–New York.)
29. HUAC-Hollywood, op. cit., June 25, 1951, pp. 671–718.
30. Navasky, op. cit., p. 303.
31. HUAC–New York, op. cit., 1,454–99.
32. Ibid., p. 1,456.
33. Navasky, op. cit., p. 361.
34. Howard Koch, *As Time Goes By* (New York: Harcourt Brace Jovanovich, 1979), pp. 210–11.
35. Williams, *One Man's Freedom,* op. cit., p. 201.
36. Ibid., pp. 201-2.
37. Ibid., p. 22.
38. *New York Times,* April 12, 1954.
39. Ibid., May 3, 1957.
40. Ibid., April 12, 1954.

8. JOE McCARTHY

Sources

Interviews
Brent Bozell, Sam Ervin, Judge John Sirica, Warren Woods.

Court Cases
Joseph R. McCarthy v. William Benton, CA 1335-(19)52, U.S. District Court for the District of Columbia.

Congressional Hearings and Reports
U.S. Congress, Senate, Committee on Rules and Administration, Subcommittee on Privileges and Elections, *hearings on Maryland senatorial race of 1950*, 82d Cong., 1st sess., 1951.
U.S. Congress, Senate, *hearings before a Select Committee to Study Censure Charges pursuant to the order of Senate Resolution 301 and amendments: A Resolution to censure the Senator from Wisconsin, Mr. McCarthy,* 83d Cong., 2d sess., 1954.
U.S. Congress, Senate, *report of the Senate Select Committee to study censure charges pursuant to the order of Senate Resolution 301 and amendments: A Resolution to censure the Senator from Wisconsin, Mr. McCarthy*, 83d Cong., 2d sess., September 27, 1954.
U.S. Congress, Senate, *Congressional Record,* 83d Cong., 2d sess. (Floor debate on resolution to censure Senator McCarthy), November 8–December 2, 1954; Vol. 100, pt. 12.

Books

Roy Cohn, *McCarthy* (New York: Lancer Books, 1968).

Richard H. Rovere, *Senator Joe McCarthy* (New York: World Publishing, 1959).

Edward Bennett Williams, *One Man's Freedom* (New York: Atheneum, 1962).

Newspapers

"Legal Stars Shine in M'Carthy Case," *New York Times* (AP), August 23, 1954.

James Reston, "Point of Order Becomes Out of Order," *New York Times,* September 1, 1954.

"M'Carthy to Open 'A Vigorous Fight,'" *New York Times,* September 28, 1954.

Notes

1. *New York Times,* May 3, 1957.
2. Ibid., August 1, 1954.
3. U.S. Congress, Senate, Committee on Rules and Administration, Subcommittee on Privileges and Elections, *hearings on Maryland senatorial race of 1950,* 82d Cong., 1st sess., 1951, pp. 1,190–91. (Referred to hereafter as Maryland senatorial race.)
4. Ibid., p. 1,180.
5. Ibid., pp. 184–85, 190, 197, 213, 220–23, 252–67, 783–91, and 1,180.
6. *Washington Star,* June 4, 1951.
7. Maryland senatorial race, op. cit., p. 190.
8. *Washington Post,* June 5, 1951.
9. Maryland senatorial race, op. cit., pp. 222–23.
10. Joseph R. McCarthy v. William Benton, CA 1335-52, U.S. District Court for the District of Columbia, complaint, March 26, 1952, p. 3.
11. *New York Times,* August 7, 1951.
12. McCarthy v. Benton, op. cit., complaint, p. 3.
13. Ibid., p. 1.
14. Ibid., p. 2.
15. Ibid., pp. 4–5.
16. Ibid., Benton deposition, June 4, 1952, p. 167.
17. Ibid., pp. 50–51 and 55.
18. *New York Times,* August 20, 1952.
19. Ibid., January 18, 1953.
20. Lately Thomas, *When Even Angels Wept* (New York: William Morrow, 1973), p. 477.

21. Roy Cohn, *McCarthy* (New York: Lancer Books, 1968), p. 209.
22. William F. Buckley, Jr., "The Unexamined Side of Edward Bennett Williams," *National Review,* July 31, 1962, p. 60.
23. *Washington Post,* September 19, 1954.
24. Roy Cohn, op. cit., p. 183.
25. Williams, *One Man's Freedom,* op. cit., p. 61.
26. *New York Times,* August 8, 1954.
27. Ibid.
28. Ibid., August 1, 1954.
29. Williams, *One Man's Freedom,* op. cit., p. 62.
30. Leamer, op. cit., p. 249.
31. Williams, *One Man's Freedom,* op. cit., pp. 62-3.
32. Ibid.
33. Charles E. Potter, *Days of Shame* (New York: Coward-McCann, 1965), p. 286.
34. U.S. Congress, Senate, *report of the Senate Select Committee to study censure charges pursuant to the order of Senate Resolution 301 and amendments: A Resolution to censure the Senator from Wisconsin, Mr. McCarthy,* 83d Cong., 2d sess., September 27, 1954, pp. 5–47. (Referred to hereafter as Watkins Committee Report.)
35. Arthur V. Watkins, *Enough Rope* (Englewood Cliffs, N.J.: Prentice-Hall, 1969), p. 36.
36. U.S. Congress, Senate, *hearings before a Select Committee to Study Censure Charges pursuant to the order of Senate Resolution 301 and amendments: A Resolution to censure the Senator from Wisconsin, Mr. McCarthy,* 83d Cong., 2d sess., 1954, pp. 15–16. (Referred to hereafter as Watkins Committee Hearings.)
37. Ibid., pp. 23–24.
38. Ibid., p. 44.
39. Ibid., pp. 64–65.
40. Ibid., p. 388.
41. Ibid., pp. 145–54.
42. Ibid., pp. 155–62.
43. Ibid., p. 151.
44. Ibid., p. 179.
45. *New York Times,* September 9, 1954.
46. Watkins Committee Hearings, op. cit., p. 472.
47. Ibid., p. 488.
48. Ibid., p. 502.
49. Ibid., p. 501.
50. Ibid., p. 469.
51. Ibid., p. 505.
52. *New York Times,* September 9, 1954.

53. Watkins Committee Hearings, op. cit., p. 337.

54. Ibid., pp. 202–4.

55. Ibid., p. 186.

56. Ibid., p. 265.

57. Ibid., pp. 274–75.

58. Ibid., pp. 271–72.

59. *New York Times,* September 10, 1954.

60. Watkins Committee Hearings, op. cit., pp. 272–75.

61. Ibid., pp. 526–31.

62. *Denver Post* story was quoted in the *New York Times,* August 31, 1954.

63. Watkins Committee Hearings, op. cit., pp. 36–37.

64. *New York Times,* September 1, 1954.

65. Watkins Committee Hearings, op. cit., p. 38.

66. *New York Times,* September 1, 1954.

67. Ibid., September 3, 1954.

68. Watkins Committee Report, op. cit., pp. 30–31.

69. Ibid., pp. 60–61.

70. Ibid., pp. 38–39.

71. Ibid., pp. 44–45.

72. Ibid., pp. 45–46.

73. *New York Times,* September 28, 1954.

74. Ibid.

75. Ibid.

76. Ibid., September 25, 1954.

77. Ibid., November 5, 1954.

78. Ibid., November 9, 1954.

79. U.S. Congress, Senate, *Congressional Record,* 83d Cong., 2d sess. (Floor debate on resolution to censure Senator McCarthy), November 8, 1954, Vol. 100, pt. 12, p. 15,851.

80. Ibid., November 10, 1954, p. 15,953.

81. Ibid., November 16, 1954, p. 16,058.

82. Ibid., November 15, 1954, pp. 16,020–21.

83. Ibid., p. 16,018.

84. Ibid., p. 16,022.

85. Ibid., November 16, 1954, pp. 16,058–61.

86. Ibid., p. 16,071.

87. Ibid., November 11, 1954, pp. 15,959–62.

88. Ibid., November 29, 1954, p. 16,154.

89. Ibid., p. 16,150.

90. *New York Times,* December 5, 1954.

91. *Congressional Record,* op. cit., December 1, 1954, pp. 16,292–93.

92. *New York Times,* December 5, 1954.

93. Ibid., December 2, 1954.

94. *Congressional Record,* op. cit., December 2, 1954, p. 16,373.
95. Ibid., p. 16,392.
96. Watkins Committee Report, op. cit., p. 61.
97. Williams, *One Man's Freedom,* op. cit., p. 68.
98. Ibid., pp. 68-71.
99. Watkins Committee Hearings, op. cit., p. 521.
100. Ibid., p. 562.
101. *New York Times,* December 3, 1954.
102. Roy Cohn, op. cit., pp. 240-1.
103. *New York Times,* April 20, 1955.

9. THE ONASSIS SHIP DEALS

Sources

Interviews
Robert Whittier Dudley, Robert Maheu, Edward J. Ross.

Court Cases
U.S. v. Robert Whittier Dudley, CR 1724-(19)51, U.S. District Court for the District of Columbia.
U.S. v. Stavros Niarchos, Joseph E. Casey, E. Stanley Klein, Julius C. Holmes, et al., CR 685-(19)53, U.S. District Court for the District of Columbia, 125 F. Supp. 214 (1954).
U.S. v. Aristoteles S. Onassis, Robert L. Berenson, Nicolas Cokkinis. Joseph E. Casey, Joseph H. Rosenbaum, Robert W. Dudley, et al., CR 1647-(19)53, U.S. District Court for the District of Columbia, 125 F. Supp. 190 (1954).
U.S. v. Manuel Kulukundis, et al., CR 2027-(19)53, 2–54, 3–54, U.S. District Court for the District of Columbia.
Spyridon Catapodis v. Aristotle Socrates Onassis, CA 5126-(19)54, U.S. District Court for the District of Columbia.

Congressional Hearings and Reports
U.S. Congress, Senate, Government Operations Committee, Permanent Subcommittee on Investigations, *hearings on the Sale of Government-Owned Surplus Tanker Vessels,* 82d Cong., 2d sess., 1952.
U.S. Congress, Senate, a Select Committee to study governmental operations with Respect to Intelligence Activities, *An Interim Report on Alleged Assassination Plots Involving Foreign Leaders,* 94th Cong., 1st sess., 1975.

Books
Nicholas Fraser, Philip Jacobson, Mark Ottaway, and Lewis Chester, *Aristotle Onassis* (New York: Lippincott, 1977).

Willi Frischauer, *Onassis* (New York: Meredith Press, 1968).
Jim Hougan, *Spooks* (New York: Bantam Books, 1979).
Joachim Joesten, *Onassis* (New York: Abelard-Schuman, 1963).

Magazines
"Trouble for Onassis?" *Time,* November 22, 1954.
"Moment for Socrates," *Newsweek,* November 29, 1954.

Newspapers
"Agent Accuses Onassis of Fraud in Tanker Deal," *New York Herald Tribune,* November 20, 1954.
"Onassis Accused of Defrauding His Agent on Arabian Oil Deal," *New York Times,* November 20, 1954.

Notes

1. U.S. v. Robert Whittier Dudley, CR 1724-51, U.S. District Court for the District of Columbia, prosecutor's opening statement, June 3, 1953, transcript, pp. 3–4.
2. Ibid., indictment, December 19, 1951, p. 2.
3. Ibid., Williams's opening argument, June 3, 1953, transcript, pp. 21–27.
4. Ibid., Williams's brief on motion to dismiss the case, December 23, 1952, p. 11.
5. *Washington Star,* June 6, 1953. (Court records for the last two days of the three-day trial are missing, so it was necessary to rely on newspaper accounts.)
6. *Washington Post,* June 6, 1953.
7. Ibid.
8. *Washington Star,* June 6, 1953.
9. U.S. v. Aristoteles S. Onassis, et al., CR 1647-53, U.S. District Court for the District of Columbia, indictment, October 13, 1953.
10. U.S. v. Stavros Niarchos, et al., CR 685-53, U.S. District Court for the District of Columbia, indictment, April 23, 1953. (The indictments of both Onassis and Niarchos were kept under seal until February 1954 to await the return of the defendants to the U.S.)
11. U.S. Congress, Senate, Government Operations Committee, Permanent Subcommittee on Investigations, *hearings on the Sale of Government-Owned Surplus Tanker Vessels,* 82d Cong., 2d sess., 1952, pp. 269–70. (Referred to hereafter as Surplus Ship Hearings.)
12. Ibid., p. 279.
13. Joachim Joesten, *Onassis* (New York: Abelard-Schuman, 1963), p. 48.
14. Nicholas Fraser, Philip Jacobson, Mark Ottaway, and Lewis Chester, *Aristotle Onassis* (New York: Lippincott, 1977), pp. 104–5.

15. Joesten, op. cit., p. 47 and pp. 53–54.
16. Surplus Ship Hearings, op. cit., p. 278.
17. Docket entries, U.S. v. Onassis, et al., op. cit., and U.S. v. Niarchos, et al., op. cit.
18. Joesten, op. cit., p. 55.
19. U.S. v. Onassis, et al., op. cit., 125 F. Supp. 190, at pp. 203–5 (1954).
20. *New York Times,* November 19, 1954.
21. Joesten, op. cit., pp. 58–59.
22. U.S. v. Manuel Kulukundis, et al., CR 2027-53, 2–54, and 3–54, U.S. District Court for the District of Columbia.
23. *Parade* magazine, April 26, 1981.
24. Joesten, op. cit., p. 60.
25. Willi Frischauer, *Onassis* (New York: Meredith Press, 1968), p. 155.
26. Joesten, op. cit., p. 54.
27. Fraser, et al., op. cit., p. 114.
28. Joesten, op. cit., p. 140.
29. CIA report of July 1, 1954, quoted by Fraser, et al., op. cit., p. 143.
30. Joesten, op. cit., p. 141.
31. Ibid., pp. 145–46.
32. Jim Hougan, *Spooks* (New York: Bantam Books, 1979), p. 290.
33. Joesten, op. cit., pp. 113–15.
34. Ibid., pp. 115–16, quoting Catapodis's affidavit.
35. Frischauer, op. cit., p. 153.
36. Joesten, op. cit., pp. 113–27.
37. Spyridon Catapodis v. Aristotle Socrates Onassis, CA 5126-54, U.S. District Court for the District of Columbia; Catapodis's affidavit quoted in defendant's answer to complaint, September 30, 1955, p. 11.
38. Joesten, op. cit., p. 127.
39. Ibid.
40. Ibid., pp. 128–29.
41. Ibid., pp. 133–35.
42. Hougan, op. cit., pp. 290–91.
43. Frischauer, op. cit., p. 164.
44. Joesten, op. cit., p. 135.
45. U.S. Congress, Senate, a Select Committee to Study Governmental Operations with Respect to Intelligence Activities, *An Interim Report on Alleged Assassination Plots Involving Foreign Leaders,* 94th Cong., 1st sess., 1954, p. 74. (Referred to hereafter as Assassination Report.)
46. Joesten, op. cit., pp. 135–37.
47. Fraser, et al., op. cit., pp. 133–38.
48. Joesten, op. cit., p. 130.
49. Hougan, op. cit., p. 287.

50. Assassination Report, op. cit., p. 74.
51. Catapodis v. Onassis, op. cit., defendant's answer to complaint, September 30, 1955, pp. 5–6.
52. Ibid., pp. 6–7.
53. Ibid., complaint filed by Williams, December 3, 1954, pp. 1–2.
54. Ibid., pp. 1–7.
55. Ibid., defendant's answer to complaint, September 30, 1955, pp. 12–13.
56. Ibid., plaintiff's deposition notices, April 26, 1956.
57. Ibid., docket entry.
58. *New York Times,* April 5, 1956.
59. Ibid.
60. Fraser, et al., op. cit., p. 151.
61. Joesten, op. cit., p. 151.
62. Ibid.
63. Ibid., p. 150.
64. Fraser, et al., op. cit., p. 152.
65. Ibid., p. 149.
66. Assassination Report, op. cit., pp. 74–75.
67. See, for instance, Ed Reid, *The Grim Reapers* (Chicago: Henry Regnery, 1969), pp. 294–95.
68. Assassination Report, op. cit., pp. 74–83.
69. *New York Times,* August 9, 1976.

10. ALDO ICARDI: ESPIONAGE AND MURDER

Sources

Interviews
Aldo Icardi, Judge Richmond B. Keech, Robert Maheu.

Court Cases
U.S. v. Aldo Lorenzo Icardi, CR 821-(19)55, U.S. District Court for the District of Columbia, 140 F. Supp. 383 (1956).

Books
Aldo Icardi, *American Master Spy* (New York: University Books, 1956).
Michael Stern, *No Innocence Abroad* (New York: Random House, 1953).
———, *An American in Rome* (New York: Bernard Geis Associates, 1964).
Edward Bennett Williams, *One Man's Freedom* (New York: Atheneum, 1962).

Magazines
Michael Stern, "The Man Who Killed Major Holohan," *True,* March 1954.

———, "The Case Against Aldo Icardi, Murderer," *True,* May 1956.
"Pen as Camera," *Life,* May 7, 1956 (sketches of Williams in action at Icardi trial).

Newspaper
"6th Amendment Lawyer, Edward Bennett Williams," *New York Times,* April 20, 1956.

Notes

1. Williams, *One Man's Freedom* (New York: Atheneum, 1962).
2. Michael Stern, "The Case Against Aldo Icardi, Murderer," *True,* May 1956, pp. 50-51. (Referred to hereafter as Stern, Case.)
3. Michael Stern, *No Innocence Abroad* (New York: Random House, 1953), p. 280. (Referred to hereafter as Stern, Innocence.)
4. Michael Stern, *An American in Rome* (New York: Bernard Geis Associates, 1964), p. 245. (Referred to hereafter as Stern, American.)
5. Stern, Innocence, op. cit., pp. 300–303.
6. Ibid., p. 278.
7. Michael Stern, "The Man Who Killed Major Holohan," *True,* March 1954, p. 26 and p. 64. (Referred to hereafter as Stern, Man.)
8. Stern, Case, op. cit., p. 50.
9. Stern, Innocence, op. cit., pp. 307–308.
10. *Pittsburgh Press,* April 22, 1956.
11. Stern, Case, op. cit., p. 102.
12. Ibid.
13. Stern, Man, op. cit., p. 66.
14. Stern, American, op. cit., p. 257.
15. Williams, op. cit., p. 33.
16. Stern, Man, op. cit., pp. 67–68.
17. Ibid., p. 22 and p. 68.
18. U.S. v. Aldo Lorenzo Icardi, CR 821-55, U.S. District Court for the District of Columbia, indictment, August 29, 1955.
19. Williams, op. cit., pp. 34–35.
20. U.S. v. Icardi, op. cit., affidavit by Williams, March 27, 1956, p. 1.
21. Stern, Innocence, op. cit., p. 300.
22. Williams, op. cit., p. 43.
23. Aldo Icardi, *American Master Spy* (New York: University Books, 1956).
24. "Pen as Camera," *Life,* May 7, 1956, pp. 20–21.
25. U.S. v. Icardi, op. cit., trial transcript, pp. 3–7.
26. Stern, Case, op. cit., pp. 50–51.
27. Ibid., p. 106.
28. U.S. v. Icardi, op. cit., trial transcript, pp. 13–14.
29. Ibid., pp. 142–150.

30. Ibid., pp. 200–201.
31. Ibid., pp. 209–10.
32. Ibid., p. 219.
33. Ibid., p. 224.
34. Ibid., pp. 210–11, 216–17.
35. Ibid., pp. 215–16.
36. Williams, op. cit., p. 52.
37. U.S. v. Icardi, op. cit., trial transcript, pp. 236–39.
38. Ibid., pp. 240–41.
39. Ibid., pp. 276–78.
40. Ibid., p. 308.
41. Ibid., p. 350.
42. Ibid., p. 352.
43. Ibid., 140 F. Supp. 383, at p. 385 (1956).
44. Ibid., at pp. 387–88.
45. Ibid., at p. 389.
46. *Pittsburgh Press,* April 19, 1956.
47. *Pittsburgh Post Gazette,* April 20, 1956.
48. *New York Times,* April 20, 1956.
49. Stern, Innocence, op. cit., p. 278.
50. Stern, American, op. cit., p. 277.
51. Ibid., pp. 277–78.
52. Ibid., p. 264.

PART V: JIMMY HOFFA AND THE TEAMSTERS

Sources

Interviews

John Cye Cheasty, Julia Cheyfitz Cohen, Judge Oliver Gasch, Harold Gibbons, Monsignor George Higgins, Bill Hundley, Rufus King, Jr., Angela Novello, Godfrey Schmidt, Edward P. Troxell, Tom Wadden.

Court Cases

U.S. v. Sidney L. Brennan, Eugene J. Williams, Jack J. Jorgensen, and Gerald P. Connelly, CR 15,557-560, U.S. District Court, District of Minnesota (1956), 137 F. Supp. 888 (1956), 240 F.2d 253 (U.S. Court of Appeals, 8th Cir. 1957), 353 US 931 (1957)—certiorari denied.

U.S. v. James Riddle Hoffa and Hyman I. Fischbach, CR 294-(19)57, U.S. District Court for the District of Columbia.

Cunningham, et al. v. English, et al., CA 2361-(19)57, U.S. District Court for the District of Columbia, 269 F.2d 517 (1958), 361 US 897 and 361 US 905 (1959).

Congressional Hearing
U.S. Congress, Senate, Select Committee on *Improper Activities in the Labor or Management Field,* 85th and 86th Cong., 1957–59.

Books
Steven Brill, *The Teamsters* (New York: Simon & Schuster, 1978).
Edward T. Cheyfitz, *Constructive Collective Bargaining* (New York: McGraw-Hill, 1947).
James R. Hoffa as told to Oscar Fraley, *Hoffa: The Real Story* (Briarcliff Manor, N.Y.: Stein & Day, 1975).
Robert F. Kennedy, *The Enemy Within* (New York: Harper & Brothers, 1960).
Dan E. Moldea, *The Hoffa Wars* (New York: Paddington Press, 1978).
Clark R. Mollenhoff, *Tentacles of Power* (Cleveland: World Publishing, 1965).
Arthur M. Schlesinger, Jr., *Robert Kennedy and His Times* (Boston: Houghton Mifflin, 1978).
Walter Sheridan, *The Fall and Rise of Jimmy Hoffa* (New York: Saturday Review Press, 1972).

Law Reviews
Paul Jacobs, "Extracurricular Activities of the McClellan Committee," *California Law Review* 51 (1963): 296.
Leonard B. Mandelbaum, "The Teamster Monitorship: A Lesson for the Future," *Federal Bar Journal* 20 (1960): 125.

Magazines (a sampling, in chronological order)
"Into the Trap," *Time,* March 25, 1957.
"Whose Goose?" *Time,* April 1, 1957.
"How the FBI Caught Jimmy Hoffa," *Parade,* May 5, 1957.
"I Was to Be a Spy," *U.S. News & World Report,* July 5, 1957.
"Our Turn at Bat," *Newsweek,* July 8, 1957.
"Hoffa: Free to Follow Ambitions," *Business Week,* July 27, 1957.
"One Man's Word," *Newsweek,* July 29, 1957.
"Out of the Trap," *Time,* July 29, 1957.
"Defender in Demand," *U.S. News & World Report,* August 2, 1957.
"With Eight Negroes on the Jury," *U.S. News & World Report,* August 2, 1957.
"Hoffa Acquittal" (editorial), *America,* August 3, 1957.
"Hoffa at the Crest of the Wave," *Business Week,* August 3, 1957.
"Background of Hoffa Case: Was Race Issue a Factor?" *U.S. News & World Report,* August 16, 1957.
"Hoffa Ascendant" (editorial), *America,* September 7, 1957.
"Hoffa's Deal Maker," *Fortune,* April 1958.

Robert F. Kennedy, "Hoffa's Unholy Alliance," *Look,* September 2, 1958.

"If You're in a Jam," *Newsweek,* January 5, 1959.

John Bartlow Martin, "The Struggle to Get Hoffa," *Saturday Evening Post,* June 27, 1959 ff.

Newspapers (a sampling, in chronological order)

"When in Trouble Get Ed Williams," *New York Post* magazine, March 24, 1957.

"Hoffa Counsel Says 'Hysteria' Prejudiced Case," *Washington Star,* May 10, 1957.

"Ed Williams Plagued by 'Guilt by Client,'" *Washington Post,* May 19, 1957.

"Capital Circus" (Williams profile), *New York Daily News,* June 13, 1957.

"Backstage: Hoffa's Bribery Trial," *Washington Afro-American,* July 6, 1957.

"The Facts Behind the Hoffa Trial: 'Cloak & Dagger' Tactics Charged" (advertisement), *Washington Afro-American,* July 6, 1957.

"L.A. Woman Attorney in Hoffa case," *Washington Afro-American,* July 6, 1957.

"The Hoffa Case: Where Does the Truth Lie?" (editorial), *Washington Afro-American,* July 13, 1957.

"Mr. Hoffa's Acquittal" (editorial), *Washington Post,* July 22, 1957.

"Epilogue to the Hoffa Trial" (editorial), *Washington Post,* August 6, 1957.

"Crum Charges Hoffa Tried to Pack Monitors' Board," *New York Times,* July 14, 1959.

"Inquiry Is Jolted by Lawyer's Charge," *Washington Post,* July 14, 1959.

"Crum Repudiates Bribe Inference," *New York Times,* July 24, 1959.

"Crum Swears Inference of 'Bribe' Was Wrong," *Washington Post,* July 24, 1959.

"About Face" (editorial), *Washington Post,* July 25, 1959.

"Hoffa, Attorney Said at Odds on Union Funds," *Washington Post* (AP), April 26, 1964.

"Williams Firm Disqualified," *Washington Post,* July 12, 1972.

11. THE TEAMSTERS' MEN IN WASHINGTON

Notes

1. Profile of Eddie Cheyfitz, sent out over Associated Press wire on December 27, 1958.
2. Clark R. Mollenhoff, *Tentacles of Power* (Cleveland: World Publishing, 1965), p. 186.

3. For Communist links of Mine, Mill and Smelter Workers union, see, for example, John L. McClellan, *Crime Without Punishment* (New York: Duell, Sloan & Pearce, 1962), pp. 62–64.
4. Cheyfitz background drawn from AP profile of him, op. cit., and *Martindale-Hubbell Law Directory* (Summit, N.J.: Martindale-Hubbell, 1956), vol. 1, p. 841.
5. Edward T. Cheyfitz, *Constructive Collective Bargaining* (New York: McGraw-Hill, 1947), pp. 150–55.
6. AP profile of Cheyfitz, op. cit.
7. Cheyfitz, op. cit., p. vii.
8. Ibid., p. 121.
9. Additional background on Cheyfitz from AP profile, op. cit., Martindale-Hubbell, op. cit.; and "Hoffa's Deal Maker," *Fortune,* April 1958, p. 216.
10. Mollenhoff, op. cit., pp. 186–87.
11. "Hoffa's Deal Maker," op. cit.
12. U.S. v. Sidney L. Brennan, Eugene J. Williams, Jack J. Jorgensen, Gerald P. Connelly, et al., U.S. District Court, District of Minnesota, 137 F. Supp. 888 (1956).
13. Sidney Brennan, et al. v. U.S., 353 US 931 (1957)—certiorari denied.
14. *Minnesota Tribune,* March 21, 1956.
15. Ibid.
16. U.S. Congress, Senate, Select Committee on *Improper Activities in the Labor or Management Field,* 85th Cong., 1st sess., 1957, pp. 5,382–85. (Referred to hereafter as McClellan Committee.)
17. Ibid.
18. Robert F. Kennedy, "Hoffa's Unholy Alliance," *Look,* September 2, 1958, p. 32.
19. *Washington Daily News,* May 21, 1957.
20. "Hoffa's Deal Maker," op cit.
21. Robert F. Kennedy, *The Enemy Within* (New York: Harper & Brothers, 1960), p. 22.
22. McClellan Committee, op. cit., pp. 1,511–77 and 1,654–84.
23. *New York Times,* May 3, 1957.
24. Williams, *One Man's Freedom,* op. cit., p. 3.
25. McClellan Committee, op. cit., p. 2046.
26. Ibid., p. 2,375 and pp. 2038–39.
27. Ibid., p. 2,375.
28. Ibid., p. 2,383.
29. Ibid., pp. 2,383–85.
30. Ibid., pp. 2,403–4.
31. Ibid., p. 2,404.
32. Ibid., p. 5,272.

33. *New York Times,* May 21, 1957.
34. Ibid., May 26, 1957.
35. Ibid., August 29, 1957.
36. Ibid., October 4, 1957.
37. Ibid., December 15, 1957.
38. Ibid., December 11, 1964.
39. U.S. v. James Riddle Hoffa and Hyman I. Fischbach, CR 294-57, U.S. District Court for the District of Columbia, testimony by John Cye Cheasty, trial transcript, pp. 418–20.
40. See, for instance, Hank Messick, *John Edgar Hoover* (New York: David McKay, 1972), p. 182.
41. U.S. v. Hoffa, op. cit. (Cheasty testimony), p. 420.
42. Ibid., pp. 418–28.
43. Ibid., p. 455.
44. Ibid. (closing argument by prosecutor Edward P. Troxell), p. 3,304.
45. Ibid. (Cheasty testimony), pp. 457–58.
46. Ibid., p. 480.
47. Ibid. (Cheasty's notes read into record by Troxell), pp. 400–401.
48. *Washington Daily News,* May 21, 1957.
49. U.S. v. Hoffa, op. cit. (Cheasty testimony), p. 480.
50. Ibid., pp. 484–85.
51. Ibid., testimony by Robert F. Kennedy, p. 1,987.
52. Ibid. (Cheasty testimony), pp. 466–68.
53. Ibid., pp. 492–505.
54. Ibid., pp. 515–17.
55. Ibid.
56. Ibid., transcript of closed session of McClellan Committee on February 15, 1957, entered into trial record.
57. Ibid., Kennedy cross-examined by Williams, p. 2,217–18 and Williams's summation, p. 3,243.
58. Ibid., transcript of McClellan Committee closed session.
59. McClellan, *Crime Without Punishment,* op. cit., p. 22.
60. *Time,* March 25, 1957.
61. U.S. v. Hoffa, op. cit. (Kennedy testimony), pp. 2,205–6.
62. Ibid. (Cheasty testimony), p. 559.
63. Ibid., pp. 567–73.
64. Kennedy, *The Enemy Within,* op. cit., pp. 40–43.
65. U.S. v. Hoffa, op. cit., Hoffa, under direct examination by Williams, p. 2,959.
66. James R. Hoffa as told to Oscar Fraley, *Hoffa: The Real Story* (Briarcliff Manor, N.Y.: Stein & Day, 1975), p. 95.
67. U.S. v. Hoffa, op. cit., Kennedy questioned by Troxell, p. 1,962.
68. Kennedy, *The Enemy Within,* op cit., pp. 42–43.

69. Abell, *Drew Pearson Diaries,* op. cit., pp. 377–78.
70. U.S. v. Hoffa, op. cit. (Kennedy testimony), p. 1,964.
71. Ibid., indictment, pp. 5–7.
72. Ibid. (Williams's summation), p. 3,290.
73. Ibid. (Cheasty testimony), pp. 776–86A.
74. Ibid., government exhibits.
75. Ibid., indictment, p. 7.
76. Ibid. (Kennedy cross-examined by Williams), pp. 2,211–16.
77. Ibid. (Cheasty testimony), pp. 883–86.
78. Ibid., Hoffa affidavit, filed April 22, 1957.
79. *Washington Star,* March 24, 1957.
80. Abell, op. cit., p. 378.
81. U.S. v. Hoffa, op. cit., Williams statement at hearing on May 10, 1957, transcript, p. 5.
82. *Newsweek,* March 25, 1957.
83. "When in Trouble Get Ed Williams," *New York Post* magazine, March 24, 1957.
84. U.S. v. Hoffa, op. cit., Hoffa affidavit, April 22, 1957.
85. Mollenhoff, op. cit., p. 188.
86. U.S. v. Hoffa, op. cit., Williams statement at hearing on May 10, 1957, transcript, p. 5.
87. John Bartlow Martin, "The Struggle to Get Hoffa," *Saturday Evening Post,* June 27, 1959, p. 94.
88. *Time,* March 25, 1957.
89. Kennedy, *The Enemy Within,* op cit., p. 56.
90. U.S. v. Hoffa, op. cit., Williams statement at hearing on May 10, 1957, transcript, pp. 5–7.
91. Ibid., Williams's brief on his motion for dismissal of case, a continuance, or a change of venue, filed April 22, 1957, pp. 11–12.
92. Ibid., p. 12.
93. Ibid., Williams statement at hearing on May 10, 1957, transcript, pp. 60–61.
94. Ibid., indictment.
95. See, for instance, the *Washington Post,* May 19, 1957; the *New York Daily News,* June 13, 1957.
96. Kennedy, *The Enemy Within,* op. cit., p. 56.
97. U.S. v. Hoffa, op. cit., Williams's brief on his motion for dismissal of case, a continuance, or a change of venue, filed April 22, 1957, Exhibit A, p. 3.
98. Ibid. (Cheasty cross-examined by Williams), trial transcript, pp. 1,419–24.
99. Mollenhoff, op. cit., p. 194.

12. THE BEST DEFENSE IS A GOOD OFFENSE

Notes

1. U.S. v. Hoffa, op. cit., Williams's brief, April 22, 1957, pp. 11–12.
2. Ibid., affidavit by Robert A. Maheu, May 9, 1957.
3. Ibid., May 10, 1957 hearing, transcript, pp. 31–32.
4. Ibid., pp. 116–17.
5. Ibid., June 14, 1957 hearing, transcript, pp. 9–11.
6. Ibid., pp. 13–16.
7. Ibid., pp. 40–42.
8. Ibid., June 15, 1957 hearing, transcript, pp. 53–88.
9. Ibid. (Cheasty testimony), trial transcript, p. 1,397.
10. Mollenhoff, op. cit., p. 197.
11. U.S. v. Hoffa, op. cit., court records, June 18 and 19, 1957.
12. Ibid., prosecution motion to quash subpoena of Mrs. Cheasty, June 24, 1957.
13. Ibid., Mrs. Virginia Cheasty's letter, entered into court record on June 22, 1957.
14. Ibid., court record, June 24, 1957.
15. Jencks v. U.S., 353 US 657 (1957).
16. U.S. v. Hoffa, op. cit., trial transcript, pp. 937–39.
17. Ibid., p. 459.
18. Ibid., pp. 955–58.
19. Ibid., p. 1,895 and pp. 1,011–12.
20. Ibid., pp. 1,162–67.
21. Ibid., p. 1,018.
22. Ibid., pp. 1,000–38 and pp. 1,485–86.
23. Ibid., p. 1,348.
24. Opinion of Justice Robert Jackson in U.S. v. Krulewitch, 336 US 440 (1948), at p. 453, quoted by Williams at p. 1,828 of trial transcript in U.S. v. Hoffa, ibid.
25. Ibid., pp. 1,880–87.
26. *Business Week,* July 27, 1957.
27. *Newsweek,* July 8, 1957.
28. U.S. v. Hoffa, op. cit., pp. 2,219–25.
29. Ibid., p. 2,240.
30. Ibid., pp. 2,238–40.
31. *Newsweek,* July 8, 1957.
32. U.S. v. Hoffa, op. cit., p. 2,406.
33. Ibid., pp. 2,435–40.
34. *Business Week,* July 27, 1957.
35. U.S. v. Hoffa, op. cit., p. 2,518.

36. Ibid., pp. 2,524–27.
37. McClellan Committee, op. cit., pp. 15,026–27 (September 15, 1958).
38. U.S. v. Hoffa, op. cit., pp. 3,008–23.

13. AND IN JIMMY HOFFA'S CORNER, JOE LOUIS

Notes

1. U.S. v. Hoffa, op. cit., trial transcript, pp. 332–42.
2. *Washington Afro-American,* July 6, 1957.
3. Hoffa's remark was made to George S. Maxwell, according to Maxwell's testimony before the McClellan Committee, quoted in McClellan, *Crime Without Punishment,* op. cit., p. 56.
4. *Washington Afro-American,* July 6, 1957.
5. Ibid.
6. McClellan Committee, op cit., pp. 5086–87.
7. Ibid., p. 5,139.
8. *Washington Afro-American,* July 6, 1957.
9. Williams, *One Man's Freedom,* op. cit., pp. 220–21.
10. U.S. v. Hoffa, op. cit., trial transcript, pp. 1,618–25.
11. *Washington Post,* August 1, 1957 (Drew Pearson's column).
12. Williams, *One Man's Freedom,* op. cit., pp. 221–22.
13. William F. Buckley, Jr., "The Unexamined Side of Edward Bennett Williams," *National Review,* July 31, 1962, p. 62.
14. Mollenhoff, op. cit., pp. 205–7.
15. *Washington Star,* August 6, 1957.
16. *Washington Afro-American,* August 6, 1957.
17. Steven Brill, *The Teamsters* (New York: Simon & Schuster, 1978), p. 36.
18. McClellan Committee, op. cit., pp. 5,140–42.
19. Ibid., pp. 5,132–35.
20. Ibid., pp. 5,088–90.
21. Kennedy, *The Enemy Within,* op. cit., p. 57.

14. PARACHUTE TIME

Notes

1. Kennedy, *The Enemy Within,* op. cit., pp. 59–60.
2. Mollenhoff, op. cit., p. 208.
3. Kennedy, *The Enemy Within,* op. cit., p. 58.
4. McClellan, *Crime Without Punishment,* op. cit., p. 23.
5. Walter Sheridan, *The Fall and Rise of Jimmy Hoffa* (New York:

Saturday Review Press, 1972), p. 33.
6. *Business Week,* July 27, 1957.
7. U.S. v. Hoffa, op. cit., trial transcript, p. 3,232.
8. Ibid., pp. 3,234–38.
9. Ibid., pp. 3,238–40.
10. Ibid., p. 3,284.
11. Ibid., pp. 3,294–95.
12. Ibid., p. 3,299.
13. *Business Week,* July 27, 1957.
14. Mollenhoff, op. cit., p. 210.
15. Ibid., p. 211.
16. U.S. v. Hoffa, op. cit., trial transcript, pp. 3,359–62.
17. Paul Jacobs, "Edward Bennett Williams, Courtroom Virtuoso," *Coronet,* December 1957.
18. *Newsweek,* July 29, 1957.
19. Kennedy, *The Enemy Within,* op. cit., p. 60.
20. Ibid., p. 56.
21. *Coronet,* December 1957.
22. *Time,* July 29, 1957.
23. *U.S. News & World Report,* August 2, 1957.
24. *Washington Post,* July 22, 1957 (editorial).
25. Ibid., August 1, 1957.
26. Kennedy, *The Enemy Within,* op. cit., p. 58.
27. Mollenhoff, op. cit., p. 213.
28. *America,* August 3, 1957.
29. *Washington Post,* August 6, 1957.
30. *U.S. News & World Report,* August 2, 1957.
31. *Newsweek,* August 5, 1957.
32. *Business Week,* July 27, 1957.
33. Ibid., August 3, 1957.
34. Dan E. Moldea, *The Hoffa Wars* (New York: Paddington Press, 1978), p. 3.
35. Kennedy, *The Enemy Within,* op. cit., p. 40.

15. ANOTHER BRIBE THAT NEVER WAS

Notes

1. Moldea, op. cit., pp. 75–76.
2. *New York Times,* January 10, 1958 (UP).
3. Court record, Cunningham, et al. v. English, et al., CA 2361-57, U.S. District Court for the District of Columbia.
4. McClellan Committee, op. cit., pp. 19,629–31.

5. Leonard B. Mandelbaum, "The Teamster Monitorship: A Lesson for the Future," *Federal Bar Journal* 20 (1960): 126.

6. Paul Jacobs, "Extracurricular Activities of the McClellan Committee," *California Law Review* 51 (1963): 301.

7. Moldea, op. cit., pp. 81–82.

8. Mandelbaum, op. cit., p. 126.

9. Jacobs, op. cit., p. 301.

10. Mandelbaum, op. cit., p. 126.

11. Cunningham v. English, op. cit., docket entry, November 19, 1957, and *New York Times,* November 7, 1957.

12. *Fortune,* April 1958.

13. Cunningham v. English, op. cit., court records.

14. Jacobs, op. cit., p. 302.

15. Ibid., p. 300.

16. *New York Times,* November 29, 1954.

17. Jacobs, op. cit., p. 302, quoting Godfrey Schmidt's letter of December 16, 1957, to George Meany.

18. *Fortune,* April 1958, and Mollenhoff, op. cit., p. 267.

19. Jacobs, op. cit., pp. 302–3.

20. Cunningham v. English, op. cit., consent order, January 31, 1958.

21. McClellan Committee, op. cit., p. 13,278.

22. Mandelbaum, op. cit., pp. 127–28.

23. Mollenhoff, op. cit., pp. 297–98.

24. McClellan Committee, op. cit., pp. 16,140–47.

25. Ibid., p. 16,146.

26. Cunningham v. English, op. cit., court records, March 18, 1959.

27. Jacobs, op. cit., p. 306.

28. *Washington Post,* June 29, 1959.

29. Estate of Edward Theodore Cheyfitz, case no. 11,654, in the Orphans' Court for Montgomery County, Maryland.

30. McClellan Committee, op. cit., p. 19,649.

31. Mollenhoff, op. cit., p. 295.

32. McClellan Committee, op. cit., testimony by Hoffa, pp. 15,247–49.

33. Ibid., testimony by Bartley Crum, p. 19,649.

34. Ibid., pp. 19,644–45 and 19,636.

35. *New York Times,* December 11, 1959.

36. McClellan Committee, op. cit., testimony by Bartley Crum, pp. 19,616–18, 19,626, 19,635, and 19,639–49.

37. Ibid., Crum-McClellan exchange at pp. 19,641–42.

38. *Washington Post,* July 14, 1959.

39. McClellan Committee, op. cit., p. 19,661.

40. Ibid., pp. 19,662–67.

41. Ibid., p. 19,670.

42. Ibid., p. 19,674.

43. Ibid., p. 19, 675.
44. Hoffa, *Hoffa: The Real Story,* op. cit., p. 110.
45. McClellan Committee, op. cit., p. 19,674.
46. Ibid., p. 19,662 and 19,676.
47. Ibid., pp. 19,677–82.
48. Ibid., p. 19,683.
49. Ibid., pp. 19,685–90.
50. Crum affidavit quoted in the *New York Times,* July 24, 1959.
51. *Washington Post,* July 25, 1959.
52. Ibid., July 24, 1959.
53. *New York Times,* December 11, 1959.
54. Ibid., December 24, 1959.
55. *Martindale-Hubbell Law Directory,* op. cit. (1960), vol. 1, p. 1,016.
56. Cunningham v. English, op. cit., court record.
57. Jacobs, op. cit., p. 308.
58. Cunningham v. English, op. cit., court record.
59. Mandelbaum, op. cit., p. 139.

16. CHOOSING SIDES

Notes

1. Kennedy, *The Enemy Within,* op. cit., pp. 4–5.
2. Arthur M. Schlesinger, Jr., *Robert Kennedy and His Times* (Boston: Houghton Mifflin, 1978), p. 161.
3. *New York Times,* April 12, 1964.
4. Dan E. Moldea, seminar on Jimmy Hoffa and organized crime, Institute for Policy Studies, Washington, D.C., July 30, 1981.
5. Mollenhoff, op. cit., p. 337.
6. Hoffa, *Hoffa: The Real Story,* op. cit., p. 13.
7. Kennedy, "Hoffa's Unholy Alliance," *Look,* op. cit., p. 31.
8. Schlesinger, op. cit., pp. 154–55.
9. Martin, "The Struggle to Get Hoffa," *Saturday Evening Post,* June 27, 1959, p. 92.
10. Robert F. Kennedy memo of November 2, 1957, quoted in Schlesinger, op. cit., pp. 188–89.
11. McClellan Committee, op. cit., p. 13,502.
12. Ibid., pp. 13,656–57 and 13,949–50.
13. Ibid., pp. 13,949–50.
14. Ibid., pp. 13,667–73.
15. Mollenhoff, op. cit., pp. 314–15.
16. McClellan Committee, op. cit., pp. 18,911–42.

17. Joseph C. Goulden, *The Superlawyers* (New York: Weybright & Talley, 1972), p. 61.
18. *New York Times,* July 6, 1961.
19. Neil Hickey, "For the Defense," *American Weekly (New York Journal-American),* July 17, 1960.
20. Schlesinger, op. cit., p. 810.
21. *Washington Post,* November 1, 1973.
22. Mollenhoff, op. cit., p. 211.
23. Martin, op. cit., *Saturday Evening Post,* September 8, 1959, pp. 61–62.
24. Kennedy, *The Enemy Within,* op. cit., p. 99.

17. FRANK COSTELLO: TRY, AND TRY AGAIN

Sources

Interviews
John Cye Cheasty, Arthur Christy, Vincent Fuller, Tom Wadden.

Court Cases
U.S. v. Frank Costello (tax-evasion case), Crim. no. C-141-9, U.S. District Court for the Southern District of New York (1953), 146 F. Supp. 63 (1956), 157 F. Supp. 461 (1957); case no. 24,997, U.S. Court of Appeals, 2d Cir., 255 F.2d 876 (1958), 353 US 978 (1957), 357 US 937 (1958).
U.S. v. Frank Costello (denaturalization case), Civil no. 79-309, U.S. District Court for the Southern District of New York (1952), 144 F. Supp. 779 (1956), 145 F. Supp. 892 (1956), 171 F. Supp. 10 (1959); case nos. 24,470, 25,690, and 27,597, U.S. Court of Appeals, 2d Cir., 247 F.2d 384 (1957), 275 F.2d 355 (1960), 311 F.2d 343 (1962); 356 US 256 (1958), 365 US 265 (1961), 372 US 975 (1963), 376 US 120 (1964).

Books
Leonard Katz, *Uncle Frank: The Biography of Frank Costello* (New York: Drake Publishers, 1973).
George Wolf with Joseph Di Mona, *Frank Costello: Prime Minister of the Underworld* (New York: William Morrow, 1974).

Newspapers
"Costello's Case Delayed By U.S.: His Attorney Is Also Hoffa's, Whose Trial Is Put First?" *New York Times,* June 15, 1957.
"Man To Watch: Is Lawyer Wiliams Another Darrow?" *New York Herald Tribune,* November 27, 1957.

Notes

1. *New York Times,* February 19, 1973.
2. Ed Reid, *The Grim Reapers* (Chicago: Henry Regnery, 1969), p. 28.
3. U.S. v. Frank Costello (denaturalization case), case no. 27,597, U.S. Court of Appeals, 2d Cir., hearing before Abraham Gold, special federal inquiry officer, Federal Penitentiary, Atlanta, May 23, 1961, transcript, p. 10.
4. U.S. v. Frank Costello (denaturalization case), Civil no. 79-309, U.S. District Court for the Southern District of New York (1952).
5. George Wolf with Joseph Di Mona, *Frank Costello: Prime Minister of the Underworld* (New York: William Morrow, 1974), p. 249.
6. U.S. v. Frank Costello, op. cit., court records.
7. U.S. v. Frank Costello (tax case), Crim. no. C-141-9, U.S. District Court for the Southern District of New York (1953), court records.
8. Leonard Katz, *Uncle Frank: The Biography of Frank Costello* (New York: Drake Publishers, 1973), p. 200.
9. *Life,* June 22, 1959.
10. *New York Times,* May 3, 1957.
11. Katz, op. cit., p. 29.
12. *New York Times,* May 3, 1957.
13. Katz, op. cit., pp. 205–10.
14. Williams, *One Man's Freedom,* op. cit., pp. 141–42.
15. Katz, op. cit., pp. 208–11.
16. *New York Times,* May 22, 1957.
17. *New York Herald Tribune,* November 27, 1957.
18. Katz, op. cit., p. 141, pp. 200–1.
19. Ibid., p. 211.
20. Docket entry, Costello tax case, op. cit.
21. 221 F.2d 668.
22. 350 US 359 (1956).
23. Costello affidavit, dated May 1, 1956, filed in tax case, op. cit.
24. Ibid., affidavit of U.S. Attorney Whitney North Seymour, Jr., May 7, 1956, pp. 3–6.
25. 146 F. Supp. 63 (1956).
26. 353 US 978 (1957).
27. Williams's motion, filed November 28, 1956, in Costello tax case, op. cit.
28. Williams's affidavit, November 27, 1956, Costello tax-case appeal, case no. 24,997, U.S. Court of Appeals, 2d Cir., pp. 19a–22a of court record.
29. Christy affidavit, May 7, 1957, Costello tax case, Crim. no. C-141-9, U.S. District Court for the Southern District of New York.

30. U.S. v. Costello, 157 F. Supp. 461 (1957), at p. 466.

31. Williams, *One Man's Freedom,* op. cit., pp. 107–9.

32. 157 F. Supp. 461, op. cit., at p. 466.

33. Williams's statement during hearing on June 13, 1957, before U.S. District Judge John F. X. McGohey, reported at p. 36a in U.S. Appeals Court record, case no. 24,997, op. cit.

34. Ibid., Christy statement at same hearing, pp. 42a–43a.

35. Mellin statement at same hearing, reported at pp. 122–27 of court record.

36. Ibid., pp. 35–37.

37. Cheasty testimony at hearing on October 15, 1957, reported at pp. 665a–678a in U.S. Appeals Court record, case no. 24,997, op. cit.

38. Ibid., Williams's amended motion for new trial, pp. 25a–26a (October 9, 1957).

39. Ibid., Christy testimony, pp. 702a–709a.

40. 157 F. Supp. 461, at p. 473.

41. Appeal filed December 23, 1957, appellate record, pp. 803a–804a.

42. 255 F.2d 876 (1958), at p. 880.

43. 357 US 938 (1958).

44. Katz, op. cit., p. 201.

45. Costello's background from his hearing before Abraham Gold, special federal inquiry officer, Federal Penitentiary, Atlanta, May 23, 1961, transcript, pp. 10 and 21, reported in appellate record, case no. 27,597; 247 F.2d 384 (1957), at p. 385, and 365 US 265 (1961), at pp. 266–67.

46. Hearing before Abraham Gold, op. cit., p. 16, and court records in U.S. v. Costello, Civil no. 79-309, U.S. District Court for the Southern District of New York.

47. Hearing before Judge Palmieri reported at pp. 72a–84a, appellate record, case no. 24,470, U.S. Court of Appeals, 2d Cir.

48. From statement of the case, Costello brief, June 25, 1959, pp. 6–10, case no. 25,690, U.S. Court of Appeals, 2d Cir.

49. Hearing before Judge Palmieri, pp. 73a–94a, case no. 24,470, U.S. Court of Appeals, 2d Cir.

50. Ibid., pp. 102a–103a.

51. 247 F.2d 384 (1957).

52. 356 US 256 (1958).

53. U.S. v. Costello, Civil no. 133-28 (1958), U.S. District Court for the Southern District of New York.

54. 171 F. Supp. 10 (1959), at pp. 18–26.

55. 275 F.2d 355 (1960).

56. 365 US 265 (1961), at p. 268.

57. Ibid., p. 288.

58. Ibid., pp. 288–89.

59. Katz, op. cit., p. 202.
60. Hearing before Abraham Gold, op. cit., p. 10.
61. Ibid., p. 18.
62. Ibid., p. 41.
63. Ibid., pp. 25–28.
64. Gold's ruling, June 21, 1961, pp. 60–62, reported in case no. 27,597, U.S. Court of Appeals, 2d Cir.
65. Board of Immigration Appeals ruling, reported in case no. 27,597, U.S. Court of Appeals, 2d Cir., pp. 65–66.
66. INS notification, reported at p. 91, ibid.
67. Katz, op. cit., p. 202.
68. Williams's petition, filed August 2, 1962, reported at pp. 92–95, case no. 27,597, U.S. Court of Appeals, 2d Cir.
69. Katz, op. cit., p. 202.
70. 311 F.2d 343 (1962).
71. 372 US 975 (1963).
72. 376 US 120 (1964), at pp. 131–32.
73. Ibid., pp. 135, 140, 147.
74. *New York Times,* February 19, 1973.
75. William O. Douglas, *The Court Years, 1939–1975* (New York: Random House, 1980), p. 186.

18. BERNARD GOLDFINE: JACK ANDERSON'S CLOSE CALL

Sources

Interviews
Jack Anderson, Judge Oliver Gasch, William Hitz, Bill Hundley, Judge Roger Robb, Warren Woods.

Court Cases
U.S. v. Bernard Goldfine, CR 1158-(19)58, U.S. District Court for the District of Columbia, 174 F. Supp. 255 (1959).
Estate of Dorothy Adair Williams, case no. 11,641, in the Orphans' Court for Montgomery County, Maryland

Notes

1. U.S. v. Bernard Goldfine, CR 1158-58, U.S. District Court for the District of Columbia, trial transcript, p. 1,158.
2. "Up from East Boston: The Man Who Was Friend to Politicians," *Time,* June 23, 1958.
3. *Washington Post,* June 23, 1958.
4. *New York Times,* December 10, 1958.

5. Ibid., June 17, 1958.

6. Ibid., July 3, 1958.

7. Ibid., July 10, 1958.

8. Ibid., December 10, 1958.

9. Ibid., July 4, 1958.

10. Ibid., July 12, 1958.

11. Ibid., August 14, 1958.

12. U.S. v. Goldfine, op. cit., indictment.

13. Ibid., Roger Robb examined by Williams, trial transcript, pp. 139–40.

14. Ibid., pp. 140–41.

15. Ibid., testimony of Baron Shacklette, p. 676.

16. Ibid., testimony of Jack Anderson, pp. 252–65.

17. Ibid., testimony of Roger Robb, p. 141.

18. Ibid., testimony of Jack Anderson, pp. 293–96.

19. Ibid., testimony of Roger Robb, p. 141.

20. Ibid., testimony of Baron Shacklette, p. 685.

21. Ibid., testimony of Roger Robb, p. 142.

22. *New York Times,* July 10, 1958.

23. U.S. v. Goldfine, op. cit., testimony of Oren Harris, p. 1,061.

24. Ibid., p. 1,072.

25. Abell, op. cit., pp. 462–63.

26. U.S. v. Goldfine, op. cit., testimony of Tom LaVenia, pp. 961–62.

27. Ibid., Williams's examination of Jack Anderson, p. 422.

28. Ibid., testimony of Lt. Joseph B. Bohannan, Metropolitan (Washington) Police Dept., p. 757.

29. Ibid., testimony of Sgt. Schuyler F. Cox, Metropolitan Police Dept., pp. 843–44.

30. Ibid., testimony of Jack Anderson, p. 333.

31. Ibid., p. 324.

32. Ibid., testimony of Jack Anderson, p. 271, and Baron Shacklette, pp. 464–65.

33. Ibid., testimony of Jack Anderson, p. 256ff.

34. Ibid., testimony of Baron Shacklette, p. 472.

35. Abell, op. cit., p. 510.

36. Details on Dorothy Williams's death from interviews with Williams and from records in Estate of Dorothy Adair Williams, case no. 11,641, in the Orphans' Court for Montgomery County, Maryland.

37. Will of Dorothy Adair Williams, dated February 4, 1957, included in records of her estate, op. cit.

38. Inventory of assets in Dorothy Adair Williams estate, op. cit.

39. Estate of Edward Theodore Cheyfitz, case no. 11,654, in the Orphans' Court for Montgomery County, Maryland.

40. U.S. v. Goldfine, op. cit., testimony of Tom LaVenia, pp. 980–84.

41. Ibid., pp. 984–85.
42. Ibid., p. 981.
43. Ibid., pp. 990–92, pp. 1,012–20.
44. Ibid., Williams's argument at hearing on his motion to suppress evidence, April 10, 1959, transcript, p. 5.
45. Ibid., testimony of Jack Anderson, trial transcript, pp. 356–57.
46. Ibid., discussion among Judge Morris, Williams, and Hitz, pp. 587–95.
47. U.S. v. Goldfine, 174 F. Supp. 255 (1959), at pp. 258–59.
48. U.S. v. Goldfine, op. cit., transcript of sentencing.
49. *Washington Post,* July 19, 1959.
50. Neil Hickey, "For the Defense," *American Weekly (New York Journal-American),* July 17, 1960.
51. 91st annual banquet, Connecticut Bar Association, Hartford, October 18, 1966, reported in *Connecticut Bar Journal* 40 (1966): pp. 740–1.
52. *Washington Post,* December 19, 1959.
53. *New York Times,* October 18, 1960.
54. Ibid., May 16, 1961.
55. Ibid., June 6, 1961.
56. Ibid., April 7, 1962.
57. Ibid., May 17, 1962.
58. Ibid., August 3, 1962.

19. ADAM CLAYTON POWELL: THE CUTEST TRICK

Sources

Interviews
Arthur Christy, Morton Robson, Vincent Fuller.

Court Case
U.S. v. Adam Clayton Powell, Jr., CR 156-15, U.S. District Court for the Southern District of New York (1958).

Book
Adam Clayton Powell, Jr., *Adam by Adam* (New York: Dial Press, 1971).

Magazine
William F. Buckley, Jr., "The Unexamined Side of Edward Bennett Williams," *National Review,* July 31, 1962.

Newspapers
Murray Kempton, "The Cross," *New York Post,* March 30, 1960.
Murray Kempton, "On the Beach," *New York Post,* April 1, 1960.

"Williams: Legal Miracle Worker," *New York Herald Tribune,* April 26, 1960.

Gay Talese, "Counsel (Extraordinary) for the Defense," *New York Times* magazine, September 25, 1960.

Notes

1. William F. Buckley, Jr., "The Unexamined Side of Edward Bennett Williams," *National Review,* July 31, 1962, p. 59.
2. U.S. v. Adam Clayton Powell, Jr., CR 156-15, U.S. District Court for the Southern District of New York, opinion of Judge William Herlands, July 22, 1958, p. 3–9.
3. Ibid., Williams's brief on his motion to dismiss indictment, June 16, 1958, p. 1.
4. Ibid., Herlands opinion, p. 6.
5. Ibid., indictment, May 8, 1958.
6. Ibid., Buckley statement (entered into court records), May 13, 1958, p. 1.
7. Ibid., Williams's brief on motion to dismiss, p. 1.
8. Ibid., Buckley statement, p. 2.
9. Ibid., Herlands opinion, pp. 6, 10–11, 18, and 22.
10. Williams, *One Man's Freedom,* op. cit., p. 214.
11. Buckley, op. cit., pp. 57–58.
12. *New York Times,* April 26, 1968.
13. Ibid., February 8, 1979.
14. Letter from William F. Buckley, Jr., to author, July 21, 1981.
15. Adam Clayton Powell, Jr., *Adam by Adam* (New York: Dial Press, 1971), pp. 162–63.
16. Ibid., p. 162.
17. U.S. v. Powell, op. cit., Williams's closing argument, trial transcript, pp. 3,378–80.
18. Ibid., Bryan comment at p. 3,269.
19. Ibid., testimony of Hattie Freeman Dodson, pp. 716–20.
20. *New York Times,* May 8, 1956.
21. Ibid., May 15, 1956.
22. Ibid., May 19, 1956.
23. Ibid., June 5, 1956.
24. Ibid., March 10, 1960.
25. U.S. v. Powell, op. cit., Dodson testimony, pp. 716–950.
26. Ibid., Robson statement, pp. 904–5.
27. Ibid., Emanuel cross-examination by Williams, pp. 2,028–31.
28. Ibid., pp. 2,144–45.
29. Ibid., p. 2,224.
30. Ibid., (Emanuel re-cross-examination), pp. 2,298–2,300.

31. *New York Daily News,* April 20, 1960.
32. Murray Kempton, "On the Beach," *New York Post,* April 1, 1960.
33. U.S. v. Powell, op. cit. (Emanuel re-cross-examination), p. 2,307.
34. *New York Post,* April 1, 1960 (regular news story about Powell trial).
35. U.S. v. Powell, op. cit. (Emanuel re-cross-examination), p. 2,307.
36. Kempton, op. cit.
37. Murray Kempton, "The Cross," *New York Post,* March 30, 1960.
38. *New York Herald Tribune,* April 26, 1960.
39. Kempton, "On the Beach," op. cit.
40. *New York Herald Tribune,* April 26, 1960.
41. Powell, *Adam by Adam* (quoting Williams's summation), op. cit., p. 180.
42. U.S. v. Powell, op. cit., Robson protest, p. 3,379.
43. Powell, *Adam by Adam,* op. cit., p. 180.
44. U.S. v. Powell, op. cit., transcript, pp. 3,384–87.
45. Ibid., p. 3,387.
46. Ibid., pp. 3,395–3,404.
47. Ibid., p. 3,462.
48. Ibid., court records.
49. Ibid., transcript, pp. 3,584–97.
50. Ibid., p. 3,598.
51. Powell, *Adam by Adam,* op. cit., p. 181.
52. Gay Talese, "Counsel (Extraordinary) for the Defense," *New York Times* magazine, September 25, 1960.
53. Powell, *Adam by Adam,* op. cit., pp. 159–61.
54. Ibid., pp. 174–75.
55. U.S. v. Powell, op. cit., Robson statement, April 11, 1961, p. 3.

20. BOBBY BAKER: THE BIGGEST DEFEAT

Sources

Interviews
Bobby Baker, Bill Bittman, Vincent Fuller, Judge Oliver Gasch, Michael Tigar.

Court Cases
U.S. v. Robert G. Baker, CR 39-(19)66, U.S. District Court for the District of Columbia, 262, F. Supp. 657 (1966), 266 F. Supp. 456 (1967), 266 F. Supp. 461 (1967), 301 F. Supp. 973 (1969), 301 F. Supp. 977 (1969); case nos. 21,154 and 23,327, U.S. Court of Appeals, District of Columbia Circuit, 401 F.2d 958 (1968), 430 F.2d 499 (1970); 400 US 965 (1970, certiorari denied).
U.S. v. Clifford A. Jones, CR 40-(19)66, U.S. District Court for the

District of Columbia, 292 F. Supp. 1001 (1968); case no. 22,529, U.S. Court of Appeals, District of Columbia Circuit, 433 F.2d 1176 (1970).

Congressional Hearings

U.S. Congress, Senate, Committee on Rules and Administration, *Construction of District of Columbia Stadium,* 88th Cong., 2d sess., 1964.

U.S. Congress, Senate, Committee on Rules and Administration, *Financial or Business Interests of Officers or Employees of the Senate,* 88th Cong., 2d sess., 1964.

Book

Bobby Baker with Larry L. King, *Wheeling and Dealing* (New York: W. W. Norton, 1978).

Magazines

Ben Bradlee, "Bobby Baker: The Deal," *Newsweek,* November 16, 1964.
"The Winning Loser," *Time,* February 10, 1967.

Notes

1. Bobby Baker with Larry L. King, *Wheeling and Dealing* (New York: Norton, 1978), pp. 21–28.
2. *New York Times,* December 27, 1970.
3. Ibid.
4. Ibid., November 15, 1963, and November 21, 1963.
5. Ibid., November 15, 1963.
6. U.S. v. Robert G. Baker, CR 39-66, U.S. District Court for the District of Columbia, testimony of Luther Hodges, trial transcript, pp. 1,270E–F.
7. Ibid., testimony of John Gates, pp. 1,548–52.
8. Baker, *Wheeling and Dealing,* op. cit., p. 211.
9. Ibid., p. 169.
10. Ibid., pp. 49–50.
11. Ibid., p. 183.
12. *New York Times,* November 15, 1963.
13. *Newsweek,* November 16, 1964.
14. U.S. Congress, Senate, Committe on Rules and Administration, hearings on *Financial or Business Interests of Officers or Employees of the Senate,* 88th Cong., 2d sess., 1964, p. 1,337 (Baker testimony). (Referred to hereafter as Senate-Employees.)
15. Ibid., p. 1,322 (from statement by Senator Everett Jordan).
16. Ibid., Williams's letter of February 17, 1964, entered into hearing record at pp. 1,304–6.
17. Baker, *Wheeling and Dealing,* op. cit., p. 187.
18. Senate-Employees, op. cit., pp. 1,311–17 (Baker testimony).
19. Ibid., Williams's remarks at pp. 1,322–5.
20. Ibid., Williams's exchange with Scott and Curtis at pp. 1,328–33.

21. Ibid., questions asked of Baker at pp. 1,344–56.
22. Baker, *Wheeling and Dealing,* op. cit., pp. 79–80.
23. Ibid., pp. 190–91.
24. *New York Times,* March 12, 1964.
25. Ben Bradlee, "Bobby Baker: The Deal," *Newsweek,* November 16, 1964.
26. *Washington Post* (UPI), November 9, 1964.
27. Baker, *Wheeling and Dealing,* op. cit., pp. 204–5.
28. U.S. Congress, Senate, Committee on Rules and Administration, hearings on *Construction of District of Columbia Stadium,* 88th Cong., 2d sess., 1964, pp. 251–67.
29. U.S. v. Baker, 262 F. Supp. 657 (1966), at pp. 668–69.
30. U.S. v. Baker, op. cit., indictment.
31. Baker, *Wheeling and Dealing,* op. cit., p. 205.
32. Ibid., p. 206, and 1981 interview with Baker.
33. U.S. v. Baker, op. cit., Williams motion to dismiss, April 25, 1966.
34. 262 F. Supp. 657 (1966), at p. 668.
35. U.S. v. Baker, op. cit., prosecution answer to defense motion to suppress evidence, June 24, 1966.
36. 262 F. Supp. 657 (1966), at pp. 664–66.
37. Baker, *Wheeling and Dealing,* op. cit., pp. 210–11; Baker v. U.S., 401 F.2d 958 (1968), at p. 968.
38. U.S. v. Baker, op. cit., statement by Williams at hearing on defense motion to suppress evidence, October 21, 1966, transcript, p. 32.
39. Ibid., Williams's brief on motion to suppress evidence, April 25, 1966, p. 3.
40. Ibid., testimony of FBI agent John Shedd at hearing on wiretap evidence, November 16, 1966, transcript, pp. 234–35.
41. *Washington Post,* March 29, 1968.
42. Baker v. U.S., 401 F.2d 958 (1968), at p. 981.
43. U.S. v. Baker op. cit., hearing on wiretap evidence, November 17, 1966, transcript, pp. 323–24.
44. 262 F. Supp. 657 (1966), at pp. 666–67.
45. Baker v. U.S., 430 F.2d 499 (1970), at p. 502.
46. U.S. v. Baker, op. cit., trial transcript, p. 1,107.
47. Ibid., pp. 1,123–24 and 1,424–25.
48. Ibid., testimony by Bromley, p. 1,267.
49. Ibid., testimony by Baker, p. 2,113.
50. Ibid., testimony by Bromley, pp. 1,267–68.
51. For best account of Bromley-Baker-Jones dealings, see U.S. v. Clifford A. Jones, 292 F. Supp. 1001 (1968), at pp. 1003–6.
52. U.S. v. Baker, op. cit., testimony by Bromley, trial transcript, pp. 1,385–88 and 1,417–22.
53. U.S. v. Jones, op. cit., 292 F. Supp. 1001, at pp. 1,004–9.

54. Ibid., p. 1,006.
55. Baker, *Wheeling and Dealing,* op. cit., p. 199.
56. U.S. v. Baker, op. cit., and U.S. v. Clifford A. Jones, CR 40-66, U.S. District Court for the District of Columbia.
57. U.S. v. Baker, op. cit., trial transcript, p. 1,152.
58. Ibid., Williams's brief on motion to dismiss, January 11, 1967, p. 2; Williams's affidavit, January 11, 1967, p. 2; U.S. v. Baker, 266 F. Supp. 456 (1967), at p. 457.
59. Gasch's adverse rulings at 266 F. Supp. 456 (1967) and 301 F. Supp. 977 (1969); U.S. Court of Appeals decision at 430 F.2d 499 (1970).
60. U.S. v. Jones, op. cit., 292 F. Supp. 1001.
61. U.S. v. Jones, 433 F.2d 1176 (1970).
62. U.S. v. Baker, op. cit., trial transcript, pp. 1,501–15.
63. Ibid., pp. 676–77.
64. Ibid., testimony of William H. Ahmanson, pp. 817–18.
65. Ibid., testimony of Ahmanson and others, pp. 817–35.
66. Ibid., testimony of Mills and Fulbright, pp. 899–912.
67. Baker, *Wheeling and Dealing,* op. cit., pp. 212–13.
68. U.S. v. Baker, op. cit., trial transcript, pp. 1,869–91.
69. *Washington Post,* January 20, 1967.
70. U.S. v. Baker, op. cit., trial transcript, pp, 1,982–2,063.
71. Ibid., pp. 2,708–9.
72. Ibid., pp. 2,451A–B.
73. Ibid., p. 2,696.
74. Ibid., testimony of IRS agent Joseph R. Rosetti, rebuttal witness for the government, on cross-examination by Williams, p. 2,763.
75. Ibid., testimony of Robert Kerr, Jr., pp. 2,791–93.
76. *Washington Daily News,* January 24, 1967.
77. U.S. v. Baker, op. cit., trial transcript, p. 2,167.
78. Baker, *Wheeling and Dealing,* op. cit., p. 217.
79. U.S. v. Baker, op. cit., trial transcript, p. 2,823.
80. Baker, *Wheeling and Dealing,* op. cit., pp. 209–10.
81. U.S. v. Baker, op. cit., trial transcript, p. 2,356.
82. Ibid., pp. 2,717–19.
83. Ibid.
84. Ibid., pp. 3,105–3,116A.
85. Ibid., pp. 3,131–90.
86. Ibid., pp. 3,219–64.
87. Ibid., pp. 3,281–95.
88. *Washington Post,* January 30, 1967.
89. U.S. v. Baker, op. cit., court records.
90. *New York Times,* January 30, 1967.
91. Ibid., April 8, 1975.
92. Baker, *Wheeling and Dealing,* op. cit., pp. 219–20.

93. U.S. v. Baker, op. cit., court record, April 7, 1967.
94. 400 US 965.
95. U.S. v. Baker, op. cit., court records.
96. Sirica, op. cit., pp. 290–91.

21. JOHN CONNALLY: BACK IN THE WINNER'S CIRCLE

Sources

Interviews
Judge George Hart, Dennis O'Toole, Henry Ruth, Robert Strauss, Michael Tigar.

Court Case
U.S. v. John B. Connally, CR (19)74-440, U.S. District Court for the District of Columbia.

Magazine
Fred Graham, "The Secret Trial of John Connally," *New Republic,* June 21, 1975.

Newspapers
"A Criminal Trial Lawyer of Classic Mold: Edward Bennett Williams," *New York Times,* April 8, 1975.
Saul Pett, "A Dreadnought of the Bar," *Washington Post* (AP), April 20, 1980.

Notes

1. Transcript of March 23, 1971 meeting between Nixon and Connally (version of the Watergate Special Prosecutor's Office), pp. 39–40, included in records of U.S. v. John B. Connally, CR 74-440, U.S. District Court for the District of Columbia.
2. Ibid., indictment, July 29, 1974.
3. Ibid.
4. Ibid., trial transcript, pp. 6–15.
5. Fred Graham, "The Secret Trial of John Connally," *New Republic,* June 21, 1975.
6. U.S. v. Connally, op. cit., Williams's brief on motion for disclosure of material gathered from electronic surveillance, November 18, 1974.
7. Ibid., Saxbe affidavit, November 5, 1974.
8. Ibid., Williams's brief of November 18, 1974.
9. Ibid., Williams's brief on change of venue and other points, September 23, 1974.
10. Ibid.

11. Ibid., court records, November 25, 1974.
12. Ibid., trial transcript, pp. 46A–N.
13. Ibid., juror roll (unsealed June 23, 1980).
14. Ibid., trial transcript, pp. 107–32.
15. Ibid., pp. 231–47.
16. Ibid., pp. 253–72.
17. *Wall Street Journal,* April 18, 1975.
18. U.S. v. Connally, op. cit., trial transcript, pp. 265–80.
19. Ibid., pp. 307–21.
20. Ibid., pp. 324–25.
21. Ibid., pp. 1,005A–E.
22. Ibid., pp. 471–73.
23. Ibid., p. 485.
24. Ibid., pp. 513–14.
25. Ibid., transcript for April 14, 1975.
26. *Washington Post* (AP), April 20, 1980.
27. *New York Times,* April 15, 1975; *Wall Street Journal,* April 15, 1975.
28. U.S. v. Connally, op. cit., trial transcript, pp. 981–82.
29. Ibid., pp. 982–1,030.
30. Ibid., p. 1,016.
31. *Wall Street Journal,* April 15, 1975.
32. U.S. v. Connally, op. cit., trial transcript, pp. 1,222–34.
33. Ibid., pp. 1,273–74.
34. "A Criminal Lawyer in the Classical Mold: Edward Bennett Williams," *New York Times,* April 8, 1975.
35. *New York Times,* April 17, 1975.
36. U.S. v. Connally, op. cit., trial transcript, p. 1,146.
37. Ibid., p. 1,295.
38. *Washington Post,* October 16, 1977.
39. U.S. v. Connally, op. cit., court record, April 18, 1975.
40. Ibid., August 20, 1976.

22. ECHOES OF DAMON RUNYON

Sources

Interviews
Bill Hundley, Tom Wadden

Court Cases
U.S. v. Charles E. Nelson, et al., CR 1469-(19)51, U.S. District Court for the District of Columbia.
U.S. v. Julius Silverman, Robert L. Martin, and Meyer Schwartz, CR

730-(19)58, CR 1135-58, CR 455-62, U.S. District Court for the District of Columbia, 166 F. Supp. 838 (1958); 275 F.2d 173 (1960); 365 US 505 (1961).

Wong Sun, et al. v. U.S., 371 US 471 (1963).

U.S. v. Ruby Kolod, Willie Israel Alderman, and Felix Antonio Alderisio, 371 F.2d 983 (1967); 390 US 136 (1968), 392 US 919 (1968), 394 US 165 (1969).

Government Report

Bahama Islands, *Report of the Commission of Inquiry into Operation of the Business of Casinos in Freeport and in Nassau* (London: Her Majesty's Stationery Office, 1967).

Magazine

"Needlepoint Justice," *Newsweek,* February 22, 1965.

Notes

1. U.S. v. Charles E. Nelson, et al., CR 1469-51, U.S. District Court for the District of Columbia (gambling case); *Washington Post,* October 11, 1951 and October 23, 1951.
2. U.S. v. Charles E. Nelson, CR 1441-51, U.S. District Court for the District of Columbia (perjury case).
3. U.S. v. Nelson (gambling case), op. cit., court records.
4. *Washington Post,* October 23, 1951.
5. U.S. v. Nelson (gambling case), op. cit., court records, February 1, 1952.
6. Ibid., court records, October 21, 1953.
7. Ibid., court records, March 30, 1954, and April 5, 1954; U.S. v. Nelson (perjury case), op. cit., court records, April 30, 1954.
8. *Washington Post,* May 1, 1954.
9. U.S. v. Nelson (gambling case), op. cit., court records, April 30, 1954.
10. *Washington Post,* September 15, 1981.
11. U.S. v. Julius Silverman, Robert L. Martin, and Meyer Schwartz, CR 730-58, U.S. District Court for the District of Columbia, indictment, July 30, 1958.
12. Williams, *One Man's Freedom,* op. cit., pp. 92–93.
13. Silverman, et al. v. U.S., 275 F.2d 173 (1960), at pp. 175–78.
14. Ibid., pp. 179–80 (dissenting opinion of Judge George T. Washington).
15. Ibid., pp. 175–77 (majority opinion).
16. *Washington Post,* February 5, 1960.
17. U.S. v. Silverman, et al., 166 F. Sup. 838 (1958), at p. 840.
18. U.S. v. Silverman, et al., CR 730-58 and 1135-58, U.S. District Court for the District of Columbia, court records, March 24, 1959.
19. Ibid., May 29, 1959.

20. Silverman, et al. v. U.S., 275 F.2d 173 (1960), at p. 178.
21. U.S. v. Silverman, et al., 166 F. Supp. 838 (1958), at p. 840.
22. Silverman, et al. v. U.S., 275 F.2d 173 (1960), at p. 178.
23. 365 US 505.
24. *Washington Star,* May 1, 1980.
25. 365 US 505, at pp. 508–12.
26. U.S. v. Silverman, Martin, and Schwartz, CR 455-62 (the three defendants were charged and pleaded guilty on May 25, 1962, and were sentenced on June 15, 1962, according to court records).
27. *Washington Post,* September 15, 1981.
28. Wong Sun, et al. v. U.S., 371 US 471 (1963).
29. Bernie Parrish, *They Call It a Game* (New York: Dial Press, 1971), pp. 208–9.
30. *New York Times,* December 27, 1966.
31. "Needlepoint Justice," *Newsweek,* February 22, 1965.
32. Frank Browning, "Organized Crime in Washington," *Washingtonian,* April 1976, pp. 93 and 96.
33. *Newsweek,* February 22, 1965.
34. Ibid.
35. Parrish, op. cit., p. 198.
36. Ed Reid, *The Grim Reapers* (Chicago: Henry Regnery, 1969), p. 105.
37. Bahama Islands, *Report of the Commission of Inquiry into the Operation of the Business of Casinos in Freeport and in Nassau* (London: Her Majesty's Stationery Office, 1967), p. 15. (Referred to hereafter as Bahamas Gambling Report.)
38. Ibid., pp. xi and 112, and interviews with Williams.
39. Bahamas Gambling Report, op. cit., p. 15.
40. Hank Messick, *Lansky* (New York: G. P. Putnam's Sons, 1971), pp. 247 and 228.
41. Bahamas Gambling Report, op. cit., p. 23.
42. Ibid., p. 13.
43. Ibid., pp. 23–26.
44. Ibid., p. 154.
45. Hank Messick, *Syndicate Abroad* (New York: Macmillan, 1969), p. 216.
46. Bahamas Gambling Report, op. cit., p. 54.
47. Reid, op cit., p. 111.
48. Parrish, op. cit., p. 196; Reid, op. cit., p. 112.
49. Bahamas Gambling Report, op. cit., p. 17.
50. Parrish, op. cit., p. 199.
51. Bahamas Gambling Report, op. cit., p. 54.
52. Ibid., p. 86.
53. *New York Times,* July 17, 1967.

54. Bahamas Gambling Report, op. cit., p. 62.
55. Ibid., p. 54.
56. Ibid., p. 55.
57. Parrish, op. cit., p. 209.
58. Messick, *Syndicate Abroad,* op. cit., p. 217.
59. Hougan, *Spooks,* op. cit., p. 221.
60. Bahamas Gambling Report, op. cit., pp. 61–62.
61. Ibid., p. 86.
62. Messick, *Lansky,* op. cit., p. 232.
63. Reid, op. cit., p. 107.
64. Parrish, op. cit., p. 196.
65. Ibid., pp. 196 and 208.
66. Bahamas Gambling Report, op. cit., p. 95.
67. Ibid., pp. 61 and 57.
68. Messick, *Syndicate Abroad,* op. cit., p. 218.
69. Bahamas Gambling Report, op. cit., pp. 136–39.
70. Ibid., p. 63.
71. Ibid., pp. 137–38.
72. Ibid., p. 63.
73. Ibid., pp. 86–87.
74. Ibid., p. 68.
75. Ibid., pp. 86–87.
76. Ibid., p. 111.
77. Ibid., pp. 99–100.
78. *New York Times,* July 17, 1967, and September 16, 1967.
79. Messick, *Lansky,* op. cit., p. 233.
80. Bahamas Gambling Report, op. cit., p. 57.
81. Background of case summarized in Ruby Kolod, Willie Israel Alderman, and Felix Antonio Alderisio v. U.S., 371 F.2d 983 (1967), at pp. 985–86.
82. Reid, op. cit., p. 264.
83. *Washington Post,* May 3, 1968.
84. Additional background in case from Kolod, et al. v. U.S., 371 F.2d 983, op. cit., at pp. 985–90.
85. Kolod, et al., v. U.S., 390 US 136 (1968), at pp. 136–37.
86. Alderman, et al. v. U.S. 394 US 165 (1969).
87. Ibid., pp. 178–80.

23. THE EBW LAW MACHINE

Sources

Interviews

Joe Califano, Harold Gibbons, Bill Hundley, Roy Kelly, Murdaugh Madden, Charles P. Muldoon, Louis Nizer, Joe Rauh, Henry Ruth, Colman Stein, Michael Tigar, Tom Wadden and Joseph A. ("Chip") Yablonski, Jr.

Court Cases
Dayton M. Harrington, et al. v. Bar Association of the District of Columbia, CA 2393-(19)56, U.S. District Court for the District of Columbia.
U.S. v. Edith Louise Hough, CR 566-(19)57, U.S. District Court for the District of Columbia.
Joseph A. Yablonski v. United Mine Workers of America, W. A. Boyle, and Justin McCarthy, CA 2413-(19)69, U.S. District Court for the District of Columbia.
Joseph A. Yablonski v. United Mine Workers of America, W. A. Boyle, John Owens, and George J. Titler, CA 3061-(19)69, U.S. District Court for the District of Columbia, 448 F.2d 1175 (1971).
U.S. v. W. A. Boyle, John Owens, and James Kinetz, CR 346-(19)71 and 1741-71, U.S. District Court for the District of Columbia.

Congressional proceedings
U.S. Congress, Senate, Committee on Labor and Public Works, Subcommittee on Labor, *Investigation of Mine Workers' Election,* 91st Cong., 2d sess., 1970.
U.S. Congress, House, *Congressional Record,* 93rd Cong., 2d sess., Speech by Congressman Ken Hechler, "A Breath of Fresh Air" (15 October 1974), introducing letter of Arnold Miller to Paul A. Porter of 12 September 1974, Vol. 120, pt. 26: 35,658.

Law Journal
"Report of the Committee on Civil Rights," *The Journal of the Bar Association of the District of Columbia* 25 (August 1958): 416.

Speech
Joseph L. Rauh, Jr., "A Public Interest Standard of Ethics for Lawyers," Law Day Lecture, University of Minnesota Law School, May 1, 1979.

Book
Trevor Armbrister, *Act of Vengeance* (New York: Saturday Review Press/E. P. Dutton, 1975).

Newspapers
"Capital Circus" (profile of Williams), *New York Daily News,* June 13, 1957.
John Herling, "The Sensitive Bar," *Washington Daily News,* July 29, 1971.
John Herling, "Cry to the Bank," *Washington Daily News,* June 15, 1972.
Andy Rooney, "He could convince you that Reagan shot Hinckley," *Baltimore News-American,* April 6, 1981.

Notes

1. "Capital Circus" (profile of Williams), *New York Daily News,* June 13, 1957.
2. *Washington Post,* May 31, 1957.
3. *New York Daily News,* June 13, 1957.
4. *Washington Star,* May 30, 1957.
5. Ibid., May 31, 1957.
6. Ibid.
7. Details on Hough background from affidavit of Louise S. Hough (defendant's mother), March 4, 1960; Dr. Manfred S. Guttmacher (defendant's psychiatrist), April 4, 1960, filed in U.S. v. Edith Louise Hough, CR 566-57, U.S. District Court for the District of Columbia, and from the *Washington Post,* May 31, 1957.
8. *Washington Star,* May 30, 1957.
9. U.S. v. Ian Woodner, CR 335-(19)56, U.S. District Court for the District of Columbia.
10. U.S. v. Hough, op. cit., testimony of Dr. David Warren Harris (defendant's psychiatrist at St. Elizabeth's Hospital in Washington), Apirl 29, 1960, transcript, p. 66.
11. *Washington Post,* May 31, 1957.
12. U.S. v. Hough, op. cit., Dr. Harris testimony, p. 66.
13. Ibid., Louise Hough affidavit, March 4, 1960.
14. Ibid., testimony of Pvt. Augustine Joseph Anastasi, Metropolitan Police Department, hearing on July 10, 1958, p. 11.
15. Ibid., testimony of Dr. Christopher Murphy (who performed autopsy), at hearing on July 10, 1958, pp. 19–21.
16. Ibid., brief by Asst. U.S. Atty. Thomas A. Flannery, June 21, 1961, p. 2.
17. Ibid.
18. Ibid. The plea was entered and accepted and the defendant committed to St. Elizabeth's Hospital by U.S. District Judge Edward A. Tamm on July 10, 1958.
19. "Report of the Committee on Civil Rights," *Journal of the Bar Association of the District of Columbia* 25 (August 1958): 416.
20. Dayton M. Harrington, et al. v. Bar Association of the District of Columbia, CA 2393-56, U.S. District Court for the District of Columbia.
21. Citation to Williams for D.C. Bar Association, September 6, 1957.
22. Report of the D.C. Bar's Committee on Civil Rights, op. cit., pp. 416–19.
23. Justice Douglas's assessment of Justice Brennan's actions from Bob Woodward and Scott Armstrong, *The Brethren* (New York: Simon & Schuster, 1979), p. 77.

24. *New York Times,* May 3, 1957.
25. Trevor Armbrister, *Act of Vengeance* (New York: Saturday Review Press/E. P. Dutton, 1975), especially p. 150 for background on UMW election and pp. 29–32 for background on Yablonski murders.
26. For instance, Joseph A. Yablonski v. United Mine Workers of America, W. A. Boyle, and Justin McCarthy, CA 2413-69, and Joseph A. Yablonski v. United Mine Workers of America, W. A. Boyle, John Owens, and George J. Titler, CA 3061-69, both in U.S. District Court for the District of Columbia.
27. U.S. Congress, Senate, Committee on Labor and Public Works, Subcommittee on Labor, Investigation of *Mine Workers' Election,* 91st Cong., 2d sess., 1970, p. 26.
28. U.S. v. W. A. Boyle, John Owens, and James Kinetz, CR 346-71 and 1741-71, U.S. District Court for the District of Columbia.
29. Yablonski v. UMW, Boyle, et al., 448 F.2d 1175 (1971).
30. Ibid., pp. 1175–76.
31. Ibid., p. 1181.
32. Ibid., p. 1179.
33. Ibid., p. 1177.
34. *Washington Post,* July 12, 1972.
35. Armbrister, op. cit., p. 313.
36. U.S. Congress, House, *Congressional Record,* 93rd Cong., 2d sess., letter from Arnold Miller to Paul A. Porter of 12 September 1974 (15 October 1974), 120, pt. 26: 35,659–60.
37. Ibid.
38. Ibid., Congressman Ken Hechler, "A Breath of Fresh Air" (15 October 1974), pp. 35,658–59.
39. John Herling, "The Sensitive Bar," *Washington Daily News,* July 29, 1971.
40. John Herling, "Cry to the Bank," *Washington Daily News,* June 15, 1972.
41. Joseph L. Rauh, Jr., "A Public Interest Standard of Ethics for Lawyers," Law Day Lecture, University of Minnesota Law School, May 1, 1979, p. 3.
42. Ibid., pp. 14–15.
43. Robert Sam Anson, "Why Fast Eddie Williams Keeps on Running," *American Lawyer,* May 1979, p. 26.
44. *New York Times,* May 16, 1969.
45. Ibid., December 1, 1972.
46. *Washington Post,* March 2, 1977.
47. U.S. v. Ian Woodner, op. cit., letter of December 3, 1956, from Dr. Stephen N. Jones to U.S. District Judge Bolitha Laws.
48. U.S. v. Patricia Campbell Hearst, 638 F.2d 1190 (1980).
49. Andy Rooney, "He could convince you that Reagan shot Hinckley,"

Baltimore News-American, April 6, 1981.
50. *Washington Post,* January 18, 1982.
51. *Newsweek,* January 25, 1982.

APPENDIX

Notes

1. Abell, *Drew Pearson Diaries,* op. cit., p. 258.
2. U.S. v. Ernest K. Bramblett, CR 971-(19)53, U.S. District Court for the District of Columbia, court records.
3. *Washington Post,* February 8, 1955.
4. U.S. v. Bramblett, 348 US 503 (1955), at pp. 509–10.
5. U.S. v. Rea S. Van Fosson, CR 756-(19)55, U.S. District Court for the District of Columbia.
6. Williams, *One Man's Freedom,* op. cit., pp. 310–12 and 319–22.
7. *Washington Post,* October 18, 1961.
8. Ibid., April 10, 1963.
9. Ibid., June 14, 1963.
10. Ibid., October 10, 1967.
11. Ibid., October 9, 1965.
12. U.S. v. William C. Coleman, CR 163-(19)60, U.S. District Court for the District of Columbia.
13. *Washington Post,* March 29, 1968.
14. *New York Times,* September 10, 1968.
15. Ibid., November 19, 1968; January 24, 1969; and May 16, 1970.
16. Ibid., September 30, 1969.
17. Ibid., December 24, 1969.
18. U.S. v. Bernard J. Heinlein, CR 1138-(19)68, U.S. District Court for the District of Columbia.
19. U.S. v. Peter Yarrow, CR 528-(19)70, U.S. District Court for the District of Columbia.
20. U.S. v. Heidi A. Fletcher, et al., CR 1421-(19)71, U.S. District Court for the District of Columbia.
21. *New York Times,* February 20, 1973.
22. Ibid., May 8, 1971 and February 12, 1972.
23. Ibid., February 4, 1974.
24. Ibid., December 3, 1974.
25. "In Memoriam, Earl Warren, Chief Justice of the United States," Address by Edward Bennett Williams, U.S. Supreme Court, May 27, 1975, reported in *California Law Review* 64 (January 1976): 5.
26. U.S. v. Daniel Brewster, CR 1872-(19)69, U.S. District Court for the District of Columbia.

27. *New York Times,* December 30, 1975.
28. Ibid., January 11, 1976.
29. *Washington Post,* June 2, 1977.
30. Ibid., June 4, 1977.
31. U.S. v. Dominic F. Antonelli, Jr., CR (19)78-175-1, and U.S. v. Joseph P. Yeldell, CR 78-175-2, U.S. District Court for the District of Columbia.
32. *Wall Street Journal,* April 25, 1979.
33. *New York Times,* February 11, 1981.
34. *Spotlight,* February 23, 1981.

Index

451